*Welcome to*

**Reading Statistics**
**and Research,**
**Fifth Edition**

**with Research Navigator™**

This text contains some special features designed to aid you in the research process and writing research papers. As you read this textbook, you will see special Research Navigator™ (RN) icons cueing you to visit the Research Navigator™ website to research important concepts of the text.

To gain access to Research Navigator™, go to **www.researchnavigator.com** and login using the passcode you'll find on the inside front cover of your text.

Research Navigator™ includes three databases of dependable source material to get your research process started:

**EBSCO's ContentSelect Academic Journal Database.** EBSCO's ContentSelect Academic Journal Database contains scholarly, peer-reviewed journals. These published articles provide you with a specialized knowledge and information about your research topic. Academic journal articles adhere to strict scientific guidelines for methodology and theoretical grounding. The information obtained in these individual articles is more scientific than information you would find in a popular magazine, newspaper article, or on a web page.

**The New York Times *Search by Subject Archive*.** Newspapers are considered periodicals because they are issued in regular installments (e.g., daily, weekly, or monthly) and provide contemporary information. Information in periodicals—journals, magazines, and newspapers—may be useful, or even critical, for finding up-to-date material or information to support specific aspects of your topic. Re-search Navigator™ gives you access to a one-year, "search by subject" archive of articles from one of the world's leading newspapers—the *New York Times*.

**"Best of the Web" Link Library.** Link Library, the third database included on Research Navigator™, is a collection of web links, organized by academic subject and key terms. Searching on your key terms will provide you a list of five to seven editorially reviewed websites that offer educationally relevant and reliable content. The web links in Link Library are monitored and updated each week, reducing your incidence of finding "dead" links.

In addition, Research Navigator™ includes extensive online content detailing the steps in the research process including:

- Starting the Research Process
- Finding and Evaluating Sources
- Citing Sources
- Internet Research
- Using Your Library
- Starting to Write

For more information on how to use Research Navigator go to
**www.ablongman.com/aboutrn**

FIFTH EDITION

# Reading Statistics
# and Research

**Schuyler W. Huck**
*University of Tennessee,
Knoxville*

PEARSON

Boston   New York   San Francisco
Mexico City   Montreal   Toronto   London   Madrid   Munich   Paris
Hong Kong   Singapore   Tokyo   Cape Town   Sydney

**Senior Editor:** *Arnis E. Burvikovs*
**Editorial Assistant:** *Erin Reilly*
**Marketing Manager:** *Erica DeLuca*
**Editorial Production Service:** *Omegatype Typography, Inc.*
**Composition Buyer:** *Linda Cox*
**Manufacturing Buyer:** *Linda Morris*
**Electronic Composition:** *Omegatype Typography, Inc.*
**Cover Administrator:** *Kristina Mose-Libon*

For related titles and support materials, visit our online catalog at www.ablongman.com.

Between the time website information is gathered and then published, it is not unusual for
some sites to have closed. Also, the transcription of URLs can result in typographical
errors. The publisher would appreciate notification where these errors occur so that they
may be corrected in subsequent editions.

ISBN-10: 0-205-51067-1
ISBN-13: 978-0-205-51067-2

**Library of Congress Cataloging-in-Publication Data**

Huck, Schuyler W.
　Reading statistics and research. — 5th ed. / Schuyler W. Huck.
　　　p.　cm.
　Includes bibliographical references and index.
　ISBN 0-205-51067-1 (pbk.)
　1.　Statistics. 2.　Research. 3.　Experimental design. I.　Title.
　QA276.H788 2008
　001.4'22—dc22

　　　　　　　　　　　　　　　　　　2006052494

Printed in the United States of America

10　9　8　7　6　5　4　　　　　　RRD-VA　　　11　10

*This book is dedicated to two groups: those consumers of research reports who work at developing the skills needed to critically evaluate (and sometimes reject!) the claims made by researchers, and those researchers whose claims ought to be believed (and acted upon!) because they take the time to carefully analyze the data gleaned from thoughtfully designed studies that address worthy questions.*

# About the Author

**Schuyler (Sky) Huck** (Ph.D., Northwestern) is Distinguished Professor and Chancellor's Teaching Scholar at the University of Tennessee, Knoxville. His concerns for improving statistical instruction and helping consumers decipher and critique research reports show up in his books, journal articles, and convention presentations, and on his website (www.readingstats.com). In addition, Sky's applied/theoretical work has been cited by scholars in 337 different academic journals. Despite these achievements and other honors that have come his way, Sky takes his greatest pride in (1) the fact that two of his students have won Outstanding Dissertation Awards in stiff national competitions and (2) comments from his students that say, in essence, "You helped me learn!" Sky's hobbies include photography, puzzles, and poetry. In addition, he regularly helps prepare and serve hot meals for the homeless and makes deliveries of nonperishable groceries to those in need.

# Brief Contents

# Contents

## 14   *Analyses of Variance with Repeated Measures*     **346**

## 15   *The Analysis of Covariance*     **379**

# Preface

This preface is devoted to three topics of likely concern to anyone who may be considering reading or adopting this book. These topics concern my assessment of people's need to critically evaluate research claims; the book's main objectives; and differences between the fourth and fifth editions of this book. The material contained in the following paragraphs contains the answers to three legitimate questions that might be directed my way:

1. For whom is this book intended?
2. In what ways will this book benefit its readers?
3. Is this simply a cosmetic revision of the fourth edition, and, if not, how does this new edition differ in significant ways from its predecessor?

## *People's Need to Critically Evaluate Research Claims*

In the first edition of this book, I claimed that humanity could be divided into three groups: (1) those who conduct their own research studies, (2) those who do not formally engage in the research process but nonetheless encounter the results of others' investigations, and (3) those who are neither "makers" nor "consumers" of research claims. Now, nearly 35 years since I made that statement, I *still* believe that every person on the face of the earth can be classified into one of those three groups. However, it is clear to me that the relative sizes and the needs of the three groups are different now than they were in 1974 (when the first edition of this book was published) or even in 2004 (when the fourth edition appeared).

Regarding the size of the three groups mentioned above, the first group (the "doers" of research) has grown slightly larger, while the second group (the "consumers" of research) has expanded geometrically over the past few years. The odds are extremely high that any randomly selected person belongs to one of these two groups. The first would be populated with lots of professors, any graduate student preparing to write a master's thesis or doctoral dissertation, most employees of the many research units located in both public and private organizations, and a handful of independent researchers. Whoever isn't a member of the first group most likely is a member of the second group. That's because it is virtually impossible to avoid coming into contact with research findings.

In one way or another, almost everyone encounters the findings of empirical investigations. First of all, formal and full-length research reports are presented each year in thousands of technical journals and at meetings of countless international, national, regional, and local professional associations. Summaries of such studies make their way into newspaper and magazine stories, television and radio news programs, and informal conversations among coworkers, family members, and friends. Computer availability and the staggering increase in Internet websites make it possible for growing numbers of people to have access to the research "evidence" that stands behind online advice from "experts" regarding everything from arthritis to Zen Buddhism. And then there are the innumerable advertisements and commercials that bombard us on a daily basis and contain the results of so-called scientific studies that supposedly demonstrate the worth of the products or services being hawked.

Everyone in the huge second group needs to become a more discerning consumer of research findings and research claims. Such individuals, located on the receiving end of research summaries, cannot be *competent* consumers of what they read or hear unless they can both understand and evaluate the investigations being discussed. Such skills are needed because (1) trustworthy research conclusions come only from those studies characterized by a sound design and a careful analysis of the collected data, and (2) the screening process—if there is one in place—that supposedly prevents poor studies from being disseminated is only partially successful in achieving its objective. For these reasons, consumers must acquire the skills needed to protect themselves from overzealous or improperly trained researchers whose work leads to exaggeration, false "discoveries," and unjustified claims of "significance."

Individuals who conduct research investigations—the doers of research—also should be able to critically evaluate others' research reports. Almost every research project is built on a foundation of knowledge gleaned from previous studies. Clearly, if a current researcher cannot differentiate legitimate from unjustified research conclusions, his or her own investigation may well be doomed from the outset because it is pointed in the wrong direction or grounded in a research base made of sand. If applied researchers could more adequately critique the studies cited within their own literature reviews, they also would be able to apply such knowledge to their own investigations. The result would be better designed studies containing more appropriate statistical analyses leading to more justifiable conclusions and claims.

This edition of *Reading Statistics and Research* is targeted at two groups: those who conduct their own research investigations and those who are the recipients of research-based claims. I have tried to keep both groups in mind while working on this revision project. I hope members of *both* groups will benefit from this edition's textual discussion of statistics and research design, the many excerpts taken from published research reports, and the review questions for each chapter.

## This Book's Objectives

The seven specific objectives of this edition are basically the same as those of the previous four editions. These goals include helping readers increase their ability to (1) make sense out of statistical jargon, (2) understand statistical tables and figures, (3) know what specific research question(s) can be answered by each of a variety of statistical procedures, (4) remain aware of what can and cannot be accomplished when someone sets up and tests one or more null hypotheses, (5) detect the misuse of statistics, (6) distinguish between good and poor research designs, and (7) feel confident when working with research reports.

The seven objectives just listed can be synthesized nicely into two words: *decipher* and *critique*. This book is designed to help people *decipher* what researchers are trying to communicate in the written or oral summaries of their investigations. Here, the goal is simply to distill meaning from the words, symbols, tables, and figures included in the research report. (To be competent in this arena, one must be able not only to decipher what's presented but also to "fill in the holes"; this is the case because researchers typically assume that those receiving the research report are familiar with unmentioned details of the research process and the statistical treatment of data.) Beyond being able to decipher what is presented, I very much want readers of this book to improve their ability to *critique* such research reports. This is important because research claims are sometimes completely unjustified due to problems associated with the way studies are planned or implemented or because of problems in the way data are collected, analyzed, summarized, or interpreted.

## Differences between the Fourth and Fifth Editions

In an effort to assist readers to better decipher and critique research reports, I have done my best to update, expand, and in other ways improve this edition and make it superior to the previous edition. Several of these changes are quite minor and need not be discussed. There are, however, five important ways in which this edition is different from the one published in 2004. These changes *are* worth discussing.

### Excerpts

It is not an exaggeration to say that the boxed excerpts constitute the "lifeblood" of this book. I have included these tables, figures, and passages of text from published research reports to illustrate both good and not-so-good practices, to instruct via the words of others, and to demonstrate that contemporary researchers do, in fact, use the statistical procedures discussed in this text.

A total of 519 excerpts appear in this edition. Of these, precisely 501 (96 percent) are new, with only 18 carried forward from the fourth edition. These numbers can be used to back up the claim that this book contains an *extensive* array of material that illustrates what contemporary researchers put into their research reports.

It should be noted that the 519 excerpts included here were not chosen indiscriminately. They were not identified by students in the courses I teach, nor were they plucked from the research literature by graduate assistants. In every instance, I personally selected the excerpt because I believed it could help others understand a concept or practice. Moreover, I worked hard to select excerpts from a variety of disciplines. This was done to increase the reader's ability to cross disciplinary lines when reviewing research reports. This final point deserves a bit of explanation.

In contrast to those books that focus on a single discipline (such as education or nursing), the manifest purpose here is to help readers feel more at ease when confronted by research claims that emanate from disciplines other than their own. Unless people have the ability to decipher and critique research in a multidisciplinary fashion, they become easy targets for those who inadvertently or purposefully present research "evidence" that comes from studies characterized by ill-conceived questions, poor methodology, and sloppy statistical analysis. Unfortunately, some researchers begin their studies with a strong bias as to what they would like the results to show, and the results of such biased investigations are summarized on a near daily basis in the popular press. Clearly, a person is more likely to detect such bias if he or she can decipher and critique research *across disciplines,* recognizing, for example, that the purpose of and issues related to a one-way ANOVA are the same regardless of whether the data come from psychology, ecology, or epidemiology.

## *A New Chapter on Mixed Methods Research*

During the past few years, the practice of combining quantitative and qualitative methodologies has gained enormous appeal in a wide variety of disciplines. In a sense, the longstanding "war" between qualitative and quantitative researchers has ended, and we hear only infrequent claims these days that one of these approaches to research is superior to the other. Instead, there is a growing chorus of voices arguing that important insights can be gained by applying statistics to numerical data *and* by using qualitative methodologies to collect and/or analyze data that involve words, pictures, artifacts, maps, and other nonnumerical traces of people's thoughts and behavior. Investigations that have this two-pronged format are referred to as mixed methods studies.

This fifth edition includes a new chapter on mixed methods research. In this chapter, I make no attempt to show how the qualitative component of a mixed methods study should be conducted or reported, I do not try to illustrate how qualitative and quantitative methodologies can be "merged" within a single investigation, and I say nothing whatsoever that's negative about qualitative research. Instead, my focus in this new chapter is entirely on the quantitative portion of mixed methods studies. Using excerpts from such studies as my evidence, I argue that competent mixed methods researchers follow the principles of good research discussed in other chapters of this book. Moreover, I take the position that the readers of mixed methods studies should apply the same high standards to the statistical parts of mixed methods research reports as they should to the statistical parts of research reports that come from studies that are fully quantitative in nature.

Initially, I considered putting this new chapter into this edition as Chapter 1. However, I decided that its proper place was at the end, not the beginning. This final positioning does not reflect a view on my part that mixed methods studies are of less importance than "pure" quantitative investigations. Rather, I felt strongly that the high-quality content of the excerpts in the new mixed methods chapter could not be understood until *after* a person had first gained an understanding of things such as the Bonferroni adjustment procedure, eta squared, a priori power analyses, and the assumption of homoscedasticity. For most readers, the new chapter's excerpts (and the discussion of them) would have been gobbledygook if the mixed methods chapter had been positioned early rather than late in the book.

## *Content*

Several content changes were made as the fourth edition was transformed into this fifth edition. The biggest content change concerns the addition of a new chapter on mixed methods studies. In addition to that major addition, the following items are new to this fifth edition:

- $\eta_p^2$, $V$, and $r$ as effect size indices
- The use of interactions as independent variables in multiple regression
- An overview of meta analysis
- The "percent-agreement" procedure for assessing interrater reliability
- Determining what the criterion variable is in concurrent/predictive validity
- Electronic collection of data

- Tamhane's post hoc test
- Holm's sequential Bonferroni adjustment procedure
- Nonrandom groups in ANCOVA
- Sample size determination in survey research
- The distinction between cluster samples and stratified random samples

I have made a slew of other small and large changes for the purposes of increasing clarity, updating material, emphasizing critical concepts, and improving review questions.

## Electronic Resources

The book's companion website (www.ablongman.com/huck5e) has been updated and expanded. This website remains easy to navigate, it continues to offer different kinds of information for users with different kinds of needs, and it has been field-tested and modified on the basis of student feedback. The website and the book function to complement each other, with neither one able to successfully do alone what both can do together.

In addition, I capitalized on the information and technology available in Research Navigator™ by connecting the fifth edition to full-text e-articles published since 2000. As a result, the book's statistical/research terms and tools "come alive" for the reader within settings where they are actually used.

## Emphasis

As in earlier editions, I have made a concerted effort to point out what kinds of questions can legitimately be answered by the statistical analyses considered in this book. In this edition, however, I try even harder to show that there is often a difference—and sometimes a giant difference—between what researchers are entitled to say following their data analyses and what they actually do say. My concern about this shows up throughout the many chapters concerned with inferential techniques.

Of this book's 19 chapters, 13 deal with statistical procedures that bring forth claims of "significance" or "significant differences." Such procedures inherently involve sample-to-population inferences, null hypotheses, underlying assumptions, the possibility of inferential error, and "significance" that may exist in a statistical sense but not in any practical manner. I have purposely emphasized these facets of statistical analysis more here than in the previous edition, for it is my growing observation that applied researchers often forget about inference and instead reify their sample statistics into population parameters.

The difference between practical significance is emphasized far more in this fifth edition than in any previous edition. The effect size indices referred to as partial eta squared, $V$, and $r$ are new to this edition, as are tables designed to help readers understand the criteria used by researchers to label an effect size as small, medium, or large. You will also find that the umbrella terms *effect size measure* and *strength of association index* used in the fourth edition have been combined and are referred to here simply as *effect size*. This change was made because many applied researchers refer to eta squared, partial eta squared, omega squared, partial omega squared, $V$, and $r$ as measures or estimates of effect size.

## Four Important Similarities in the Fourth and Fifth Editions

During the past four years, several individuals have contacted me with comments about this book. Most of those comments have been positive, and they have prompted me to maintain (as much as possible) two features of the fourth edition as I revised this book. First, I kept the format the same, with excerpts from recent journal articles serving as the book's core structure. Second, I tried to keep the text material outside those excerpts as straightforward, clear, and helpful as people have said it has been in earlier editions of the book.

I have worked to maintain two other features of the previous edition. First, I try at every opportunity to point out that complex statistics do not have the magical power to create a silk purse out of a sow's ear. Unless the research questions being addressed are worthy, a study is doomed from the start. Accordingly, there is continued emphasis on critically evaluating research questions and null hypotheses as the first step in assessing the potential value of any investigation.

The second feature I have tried to maintain concerns the excerpts. As before, I have been very, very careful in selecting the 519 excerpts that appear in this edition. Many of these excerpts came from studies that dealt with important questions, that were designed thoughtfully, and that produced findings that may impact the way you think or act. Many other excerpts came from studies focused on topics that were undoubtedly fun for the researchers to research. By considering the research questions and methodology associated with these studies, perhaps more than a few readers will adopt the view that research can be both fun and relevant to our daily lives.

## Supplements to This Text

### Research Navigator™

The **Research Navigator**™ link provides students with quick access to a voluminous online library of scholarly journals, searchable by topic or key term. Students can find the latest information about teaching practice and learning. Research Navigator™ is integrated with the book via two features that facilitate student learning and increase motivation to learn:

- Fun end-of-chapter exercises that entice readers to examine carefully selected e-articles
- Icons in the margin next to important terms used in the e-articles of several disciplines

Although both of these features encourage use of the ContentSelect portion of Research Navigator™, it is the end-of-chapter exercises that will capture the interest of both students and instructor. Each such exercise contains (1) a brief summary of an *interesting* research investigation; (2) a question from me that asks the reader to make a "guess" about the study; and (3) directions as to which database of ContentSelect to enter, what article to examine, and where to look in the article to find out whether one's guess is correct. To illustrate, one exercise involves a study focused on college students' reported cheating behavior on tests and papers. After summarizing this investigation, the reader is asked to guess whether this study's results showed statistically significant differences between the reported cheating of male versus female and of older versus younger college students. I then indicate precisely where to look in the article to see the evidence (from a two-way ANOVA) that answers these gender and age questions.

### Companion Website

Found at www.ablongman.com/huck5e, this website contains over 400 viewable pages, plus links to more than 150 carefully selected pages on other sites. The content of these pages is designed to help students learn.

The largest and most important part of the website involves information, exercises, and links carefully organized in a chapter-by-chapter format. The following items are available for each chapter:

- Chapter outlines, interactive quizzes with immediate feedback, and online resources
- Jokes, quotations, and poetry about statistics
- Statistical misconceptions
- Biographies of significant people in the field
- Email messages to my students that address pertinent topics
- Best passages from each chapter

It should be noted that certain features of this book's companion website provide a form of instruction that is literally impossible to duplicate either by an instructor or a book. For example, the links to other sites bring the learner into contact with interactive exercises that actually *show* statistical concepts in operation, thereby permitting a kind of presentation that no instructor or book could ever accomplish.

## Acknowledgments

As with most large projects, the revision of this book was made possible because of the hard work on the part of many talented people. I wish now to express my sincere appreciation to these individuals. They are not responsible, of course, for any mistakes that may have inadvertently crept into this work. They *are* responsible, however, for initiating this project, for moving it along, and for making the finished product far superior to what it would have been had they not been involved.

First and foremost, I want to thank two individuals at Allyn & Bacon who have supported and protected this project from beginning to end. Arnis Burvikovs and Erin Reilly have been enormously helpful to me over the past two years, and I truly feel as if each one functioned, at different times, as my handler, my mentor, and my guide. Though the three of us were separated by hundreds of miles, we kept in constant communication via telephone, email, fax, and "snail mail." Without exception, the many questions I posed were answered promptly and clearly by Arnie and Erin. They also raised important questions I never would have considered, passed along a variety of relevant questions from others, and (most importantly) they offered wise counsel and moral support.

During the past few years, several students identified passages in the previous editions that were ambiguous, contradictory, or unnecessarily repetitious. Many professors at other universities and a handful of independent researchers also contacted me with questions, comments, and suggestions. None of these individuals probably realizes how much I value their important roles in this revision project. Nevertheless, I am indebted to each of them for their contributions. In addition, I would like to thank the following reviewers of this edition's manuscript: Judith W. Alexander, University of South Carolina; John G. Caras, Georgia State University; Bob Ives, University of Nevada, Reno; Daniel Kmitta, University of Idaho; and Marilyn Korostoff, California State University, Long Beach.

Several graduate students were involved in this revision project, and I want to thank them for their assistance. Extensive library research was conducted by Kathy Goodcook. Internet searches were conducted by Allison Runner, Gary Cattman, Jordan Hoops, and Jared Checker. Draft copies of excerpts were reviewed by Andrew Ironwood, Emily Deacon, Turner Wiggle, and Elle Kategirl. The many pages of new text were typed by David Bigheart and Nancy Reeder. Page proofs were carefully read by Alex Dunwork, Patricia Gardener, Jason Frisco, Jennifer Hyatt, and Josh Tenderbar. The permission file was overseen by Candace Westerly, Todd Laffalot, and Keith Chessman.

Shannon Foreman and the team at Omegatype Typography, Inc., took charge of the revision project as it moved through its production phase. I am extremely grateful to Shannon and the Omegatype team for their work on this project.

My heartfelt appreciation is extended to Ammar Safar and John Wesley Taylor, who created the companion website for this book. This website (www.ReadingStats.com) contains extensive information and interactive exercises not contained here, and it is far more than simply a book supplement. In several respects, this companion website is equivalent in importance to the book. Having such a website would not have been possible had it not been for Ammar's and Wesley's generous contributions of their time and talent. I want to thank them for those contributions.

Finally, I want to thank my family for being supportive of my efforts to complete this revision project. At every step along the way, members of my nuclear and extended family encouraged me to consider this project to be the second highest priority (behind my students) among my many professional obligations. Had they not encouraged me to hole up in my little home office and to keep my nose to the grindstone, this revision project would have been delayed for months, if not years!

Schuyler W. Huck
Knoxville, 2007

# Using Research Navigator

This edition of *Reading Statistics and Research* is designed to integrate the content of the book with the following resources of Research Navigator™, a collection of research databases and instructional and contemporary publications available to you online at www.researchnavigator.com.

- **EBSCO's ContentSelect Academic Journal Database.** This database, organized by subject, contains leading academic journals for each discipline.
- **The *New York Times* Search by Subject Archive.** The *New York Times* is one of the most highly regarded publications of today's news. Users can view the full text of articles from the previous year.
- **Link Library.** This database connects users to thousands of websites based on discipline-specific key terms.
- **Research Review and Preparation.** A special section called "Understanding the Research Process" helps users work through the research process.

## Connecting the Book with RN

As you read the book, you'll see special Research Navigator™ (RN) icons cueing you to visit the Research Navigator™ website to expand upon the concepts of the text and to further explore the work being done in the field of Statistics and Research. RN learning aids include:

**Research Navigator.c⊕m**

Mixed methods

1. **Marginal keyword search terms.** Appearing in the margins of the text, these already tested terms will guide your search on topics relevant to the course content and will yield an abundance of sources from a variety of perspectives that will broaden your exposure to key topics.
2. **Applied research activities and projects.** These suggestions provide more practice using the databases in Research Navigator™, and move you beyond the book to library and field research.

## Your "Key" to Research Navigator™

It's now time to enter Research Navigator™. Purchase of this book provides you free access to this exclusive pool of information and data. You can find your personal access code to Research Navigator™ just inside the front cover of this book. The following walk-through provides a series of screen captures that illustrate, step-by-step, the various ways this valuable resource can make your research process more interesting and successful. Enjoy your entry into Research Navigator™!

## Registration

In order to begin using Research Navigator™, you must first register using the personal access code found on the inside of the front cover of your book. Follow these easy steps:

1. Click Register under New Users on the left side of the home page screen.

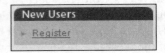

2. Enter the access code exactly as it appears on the inside front cover of your book or on your access card. (Note: Access codes can only be used once to complete one registration. If you purchased a used text, the access code may not work.)

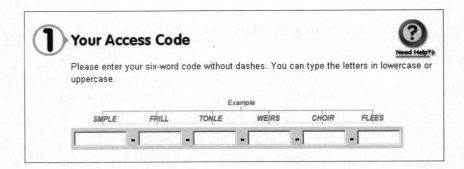

3. Follow the instructions on screen to complete your registration. You may click the Help button at any time if you are unsure how to respond.
4. Once you have successfully completed registration, write down the Login Name and Password you just created and keep them in a safe place. You will

need to enter them each time you want to revisit Research Navigator™.

5. Once you register, you have access to all the resources in Research Navigator™ for six months. Each time you enter Research Navigator™, log in by simply going to the Returning Users section on the left side of the home page and type in your Login Name and Password.

## Getting Started

You're now official! The options available to you on Research Navigator™ are plenty. From Research Navigator's™ home page, you have easy access to all of the site's main features, including a quick route to the three exclusive databases of source content. If you are new to the research process, you may want to start by browsing "Understanding the Research Process."

This section of the site can be helpful even for those with some research experience but who might be interested in some helpful tips. Here you will find extensive help on all aspects of the research process, including:

- Introduction to the research paper
- Gathering data
- Searching the Internet
- Evaluating sources
- Organizing ideas
- Writing notes
- Drafting the paper
- Academic citation styles (MLA, APA, CME, and more)
- Blending reference material into your writing
- Practicing academic integrity
- Revising
- Proofreading
- Editing the final draft

## Completing Research

The first step in completing a research assignment or research paper is to select a topic. (In some cases, your instructor may assign you a topic, or you may find suggested topics in the margins or at the ends of chapters throughout this book.) Once you have selected and narrowed your research topic, you are now ready to *gather data.* Research Navigator™ simplifies your research efforts by giving you a convenient launching pad for gathering data. The site has aggregated three distinct types of source material commonly used in research assignments: academic journals (ContentSelect), newspaper articles (the *New York Times*), and websites (Link Library).

## 1) *EBSCO's ContentSelect*

The first database you'll find on Research Navigator™ is the EBSCO Academic Journal and Abstract Database containing scholarly, peer-reviewed journals (such as *Journal of Education Policy* and *Assessment and Evaluation in Higher Education*). The information obtained in these individual articles is more scientific than information you would find in a popular magazine, in a newspaper article, or on a web page. Searching for articles in ContentSelect is easy!

Within the ContentSelect Research Database section, you will see a list of disciplines and a space to type keywords. You can search within a single discipline or multiple disciplines. Choose one or more subject databases, and then enter a keyword you wish to search. Click on Go.

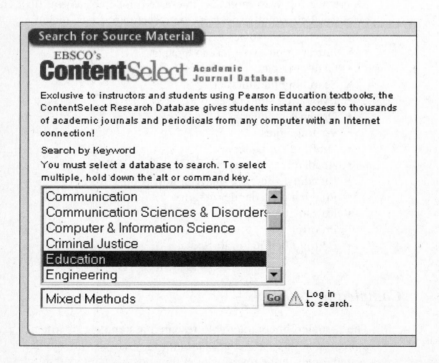

The next thing you'll see is a list of articles that match your search. From this page you can examine either the full text or the abstract of each of the articles and determine which will best help with your research. Print out the articles or save them in your Folder for later reference. From this page you can also complete more focused searches by using the Basic Search or Advanced Search options in the navigator bar.

### 2) *The New York Times*

Searching the *New York Times* gives you access to articles from one of the world's leading newspapers. The first step in using the search-by-subject archive is to indicate the subject area you wish to search. You have the option of searching one specific subject at a time by highlighting the subject area or searching all subjects by highlighting All. Click on Go for a complete listing of articles in your chosen subject area that have appeared in the *New York Times* over the last year, sorted by most recent article first. For a more focused search, type a word, or multiple words separated by commas, into the search box and click Go for a list of articles. Articles can be printed or saved for later use in your research assignment.

### 3) *"Best of the Web" Link Library*

The third database of content included on Research Navigator™ is a collection of web links, organized by academic subject and key terms. To use this database, simply select a subject from the drop-down list and find the key term for the topic you are searching. Click on the key term to see a list of editorially reviewed websites that offer educationally relevant and credible content. The web links in Link Library are monitored and updated each week, reducing your incidence of finding dead links.

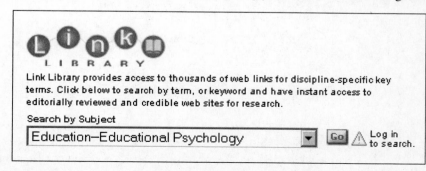

## *Using Your Library*

Although Research Navigator™ does contain a vast amount of information to assist you with your research, it does not try to replace the library. After you have selected your topic and gathered source material from the three databases of content, you may need to go to your school library to complete your research. Finding information at the library, however, can seem overwhelming. Research Navigator™ provides some assistance in this area as well, serving as a bridge to the library by helping you understand how to use library resources effectively and efficiently.

In addition, when you are ready to use the library to complete a research assignment or research paper, Research Navigator™ includes 31 discipline-specific library guides for you to use as roadmaps. Each guide includes an overview of the discipline's major subject databases, online journals, and key associations and newsgroups. Feel free to print them out and take them with you to the library!

**CAUTION!** Please note that the Research Navigator™ site undergoes frequent changes as new and exciting options are added to assist with research endeavors. For the latest information on the options available to you on Research Navigator™, visit www.ablongman.com/researchnavigator.

1

# The Typical Format
# of a Journal Article

Almost all journal articles dealing with research studies are divided into different sections by means of headings and subheadings. Although there is variation among journals with respect to the terms used as the headings and the order in which different sections are arranged, there does appear to be a relatively standard format for published articles. Readers of the professional literature will find that they can get the most mileage out of the time they invest if they are familiar with the typical format of journal articles and the kind of information normally included in each section of the article.

We are now going to look at a particular journal article that does an excellent job of illustrating the basic format that many authors use as a guide when they are writing their articles. The different sections of our model article could be arranged in outline form as follows:

1. Abstract
2. Introduction
   a. Background
   b. Statement of purpose
   c. Hypotheses
3. Method
   a. Participants
   b. Materials
   c. Procedure
   d. Statistical procedures
4. Results
5. Discussion
6. References

Let us now examine each of these items.

# *Abstract*

An **abstract,** or *précis,* summarizes the entire research study and appears at the beginning of the article. Although it normally contains fewer than 150 words, the abstract usually provides the following information: (1) a statement of the purpose or objective of the investigation, (2) a description of the individuals who served as participants, (3) a brief explanation of what the participants did during the study, and (4) a summary of the important findings.

Excerpt 1.1 is the abstract from our model journal article. As in most articles, it was positioned immediately after the title and authors' names. This abstract was easy to distinguish from the rest of the article because it was indented and printed in a small font size. In some journals, the abstract will be italicized to make it stand out from the beginning paragraphs of the article.

## EXCERPT 1.1 • *Abstract*

This study investigated the hypothesized relationship between internal locus of control and academic achievement among a sample of 187 students in Grades 8 through 12 using the Nowicki-Strickland Locus of Control Scale for Children. Analysis indicated that students in the higher GPA group reported higher scores on internal locus of control.

*Source:* Shepherd, S., Fitch, T. J., Owen, D., and Marshall, J. L. (2006). Locus of control and academic achievement in high school students. *Psychological Reports, 98*(1), p. 318.

The sole purpose of the abstract is to provide readers with a brief overview of the study's purpose, methods, and findings. Thus, most abstracts indicate *why* the study was conducted, *how* the researcher went about trying to answer the questions of interest, and *what* was discovered after the study's data were analyzed. Even though the abstract in Excerpt 1.1 is extremely brief, it addresses these why, how, and what issues.

In some articles, the abstracts will mention the statistical techniques that were used to analyze the study's data. Most abstracts, however, are like the one in Excerpt 1.1 in that they include no statistical jargon. Because of this, the abstract in the typical research article is quite "readable," even to those who do not have the same level of research expertise as the individual(s) who conducted the study.

On the basis of abstracts such as the one shown in Excerpt 1.1, you can decide that the article in front of you is a veritable gold mine, that it *may* be what you have been looking for, or that it is not at all related to your interests. Regardless of how you react to this brief synopsis of the full article, the abstract serves a useful purpose. Note, however, it's dangerous to think you've found a gold mine after reading nothing more than an article's abstract. I will elaborate on this important point near the end of the chapter.

## Introduction

*Incudes!*

The **introduction** of an article usually contains two items: a description of the study's **background** and a **statement of purpose.** Sometimes, as in our model journal article, a third portion of the introduction will contain a presentation of the researcher's **hypotheses.** These components of a journal article are critically important. Take the time to read them slowly and carefully.

### Background

Most authors begin their articles by explaining what caused them to conduct their empirical investigations. Perhaps the author developed a researchable idea from discussions with colleagues or students. Maybe a previous study yielded unexpected results, thus prompting the current researcher to conduct a new study to see if those earlier results could be replicated. Or, maybe the author wanted to see which of two competing theories would be supported more by having the collected data conform to its hypotheses. By reading the introductory paragraph(s) of the article, you will learn why the author conducted the study.

*Review of literature*

In describing the background of their studies, authors typically highlight the connection between their studies and others' previously published work. Whether this review of literature is short or long, its purpose is to show that the current author's work has been informed by, or can be thought of as an extension of, previous knowledge. Such discussions are a hallmark of scholarly work. Occasionally, a researcher will conduct a study that is based on an idea that is not connected to anything anyone has investigated or written about; such studies, however, are rare.

Excerpt 1.2 comes from our model article. Though only two paragraphs in length, this portion of the introduction sets the stage for a discussion of the authors' investigation. If you read these two paragraphs, I think you will understand everything with the possible exception of one technical research term.

In the second of the two paragraphs of Excerpt 1.2, the researchers use the term *meta-analytic review*. Simply stated, a **meta analysis** is a researcher's attempt to assess the strength of a relationship or the worth of an intervention by reviewing other studies and by combining the findings of those earlier studies to come up with a "finding" based on multiple studies rather than just one. A meta analysis is analogous to asking several people what they think of a popular new movie that you have not yet seen. By pooling together the opinions of several people, you're probably in a better position to decide whether to go see the movie than if you sought an opinion from just one person.

In this book, we will not consider the statistical procedures used by researchers when they conduct meta-analytic investigations. Instead, the focus here is on the individual studies that might serve as the ingredients for a meta analysis. There are two reasons for doing this. First, you are more likely to come across the summaries of individual research studies than summaries of meta analyses. Second, it's important to know what's going on in individual studies before their findings

## EXCERPT 1.2 • *Background*

Locus of control (Rotter, 1954) is one of the most researched constructs in the field of personality psychology (Leone & Burns, 2000). Locus of control is defined as the tendency of people to ascribe achievements and failures either to internal factors (effort, ability, motivation) or external factors (chance, luck, others' actions) (Rotter, 1966). Prior research indicated the construct of locus of control is associated with students' attitudes toward participation and achievement in school (Nunn, Montgomery, & Nunn, 1986).

Recent research (Skaalvik & Skaalvik, 2004) has reiterated the connection between self-efficacy and grades for high school students. Specifically, higher achievement has been related to a more internal locus of control. Kalechstein and Nowicki (1997) conducted a meta-analytic review and restated the association, but they highlighted the lack of diverse samples. Past studies have outlined a general connection between academic achievement and locus of control and provide a foundation for the present study in which samples not previously studied were tested.

*Source:* Shepherd, S., Fitch, T. J., Owen, D., and Marshall, J. L. (2006). Locus of control and academic achievement in high school students. *Psychological Reports, 98*(1), p. 318.

are combined within a meta analysis. For obvious reasons, a meta analysis cannot be any better than "the sum of its parts." As you will see from our consideration here of many individuals' studies, the limitations of some investigations—in terms of the samples selected, the measurement instruments used, and the statistical procedures employed (or *not* employed)—make them inappropriate for inclusion in a meta analysis. An old saying applies to meta analyses as well as computers that analyze data: "garbage in, garbage out."

## Statement of Purpose

After discussing the study's background, an author usually states the specific purpose or goal of the investigation. This statement of purpose is one of the most important parts of a journal article since, in a sense, it explains what the author's "destination" was. It would be impossible for us to evaluate whether the trip was successful—in terms of research findings and conclusions—unless we know where the author was headed.

The statement of purpose can be as short as a single sentence or as long as a full paragraph. It is often positioned just before the first main heading of the article, but it can appear anywhere in the introduction. Regardless of its length or where it is located, you will have no trouble finding the statement of purpose if the researcher begins a sentence with the words, "The purpose of this study was to . . ." or "This investigation was conducted in order to compare. . . ." In Excerpt 1.3, we see the statement of purpose from our model journal article.

## EXCERPT 1.3 • *Statement of Purpose*

No recent studies were found in which all grades of high school were tested along with a representative sample of African-American students, all of whom were drawn from multiple schools. The current study met these three criteria. The purpose then was to compare students in a higher GPA group with those in a lower GPA group on locus of control scores for a sample from multiple schools and grades.

*Source:* Shepherd, S., Fitch, T. J., Owen, D., and Marshall, J. L. (2006). Locus of control and academic achievement in high school students. *Psychological Reports, 98*(1), p. 318.

## Hypotheses

After articulating the study's intended purpose, some authors disclose the hypotheses they had at the beginning of the investigation. Other authors do not do this, either because they didn't have any firm expectations or because they consider it unscientific for the researcher to hold hunches that might bias the collection or interpretation of the data. Although there are cases (as you will see in Chapter 7) in which a researcher can conduct a good study without having any hypotheses as to how things will turn out, and although it is important for researchers to be unbiased, there is a clear benefit in knowing what the researcher's hypotheses were. Simply stated, outcomes compared against hypotheses usually are more informative than are results that stand in a vacuum. Accordingly, I applaud those researchers who disclose in the introduction any a priori hypotheses they had.

Excerpt 1.4 comes from our model journal article, and it contains the different hypotheses the researchers stated in their study of locus of control and grades. In light of the research findings cited in the article's first two paragraphs, it is not surprising that the hypothesis in this study was that students with high GPAs would have more of an "internal" orientation than students with low GPAs. Regarding ethnicity and gender, the researchers simply share their hypothesis that these factors have a weak (or perhaps a nonexistent) connection to locus of control compared with GPA.

## EXCERPT 1.4 • *Hypotheses*

The High GPA Group were hypothesized to have a more internal locus of control. Ethnic and sex differences in locus of control were hypothesized to be less evident than academic achievement.

*Source:* Shepherd, S., Fitch, T. J., Owen, D., and Marshall, J. L. (2006). Locus of control and academic achievement in high school students. *Psychological Reports, 98*(1), p. 318.

In most articles, the background, the statement of purpose, and hypotheses are not identified by separate headings, nor are they found under a common heading. If a common heading were to be used, though, the word *introduction* would probably be most appropriate because these three items set the stage for the substance of the article—an explanation of what was done and what the results were.

# Method

In the **method** section of a journal article, an author will explain in detail how the study was conducted. Ideally, such an explanation should contain enough information to enable a reader to replicate (i.e., duplicate) the study. To accomplish this goal, the author will address three questions: (1) Who participated in the study? (2) What kinds of measuring instruments were used to collect the data? and (3) What were the participants required to do? The answer to each of these questions is generally found under an appropriately titled subheading in the method section.

## Participants

Each of the individuals (or animals) who supplies data in a research study is considered to be a **participant** or a **subject.** (In some journals, the abbreviations *S* and *S*s are used, respectively, to designate one subject or a group of subjects.) Within this section of a journal article, an author usually indicates how many participants or subjects were used, who the participants were, and how they were selected.

A full description of the participants is needed because the results of a study will often vary according to the nature of the participants who are used. This means that the conclusions of a study, in most cases, are valid only for individuals (or animals) who are similar to the ones used by the researcher. For example, if two different types of counseling techniques are compared and found to differ in terms of how effective they are in helping clients clarify their goals, it is imperative that the investigator indicate whether the participants were high school students, adults, patients in a mental hospital, or whatever. What works for a counselor in a mental hospital may not work at all for a counselor in a high school (and vice versa).

It is also important for the author to indicate how the participants were obtained. Were they volunteers? Were they randomly selected from a larger pool of potential participants? Were any particular standards of selection used? Did the researcher simply use all members of a certain high school or college class? As you shall see in Chapter 5, certain procedures for selecting samples allow results to be generalized far beyond the specific individuals (or animals) included in the study, while other procedures for selecting samples limit the valid range of generalization.

Excerpt 1.5 comes from our model journal article. Labeled "Participants," it was the first portion of the article's method section.

## EXCERPT 1.5 • *Participants*

The participants were 187 secondary school students from public schools in Kentucky. Data were collected in seven schools in three different cities. The students ranged in age from 14 to 19 years and were enrolled in Grades 8 through 12. There were 81 girls (43.3%) and 106 boys (56.7%). The sample included 125 Caucasian (66.8%), 49 African-American (26.2%), 4 Native-American (2.1%), and 2 Hispanic and Asian students (1.1%). Distribution by Grades 9, 10, 11, and 12 was 57, 72, 32, and 19. Seven were below Grade 9. The mean age was 16 yr.

*Source:* Shepherd, S., Fitch, T. J., Owen, D., and Marshall, J. L. (2006). Locus of control and academic achievement in high school students. *Psychological Reports, 98*(1), p. 319.

## Materials

This section of a journal article is normally labeled in one of five ways: **materials, equipment, apparatus, instruments,** or **scales.** Regardless of its label, this part of the article contains a description of the things (other than the participants) used in the study. The goal here, as in other sections that fall under the method heading, is to describe what was done with sufficient clarity that others could replicate the investigation to see if the results remain the same.

Suppose, for example, that a researcher conducts a study to see if males differ from females in the way they evaluate various styles of clothing. To make it possible for others to replicate this study, the researcher would need to indicate whether the subjects saw actual articles of clothing or pictures of clothing (and if pictures, whether they were prints or slides, what size they were, and whether they were in color), whether the clothing articles were being worn when observed by participants (and if so, who modeled the clothes), what specific clothing styles were involved, how many articles of clothing were evaluated, who manufactured the clothes, and all other relevant details. If the researcher does not provide this information, it would be impossible for anyone to replicate the study.

Often, the only material involved is the measuring device used to collect data. Such measuring devices—whether of a mechanical variety (e.g., a stopwatch) or of a paper-and-pencil variety (e.g., a questionnaire)—ought to be described very carefully. If the measuring device is a new instrument designed specifically for the study described in the article, the researcher will typically report evidence concerning the instrument's technical psychometric properties. Generally, the author accomplishes this task by discussing the reliability and validity of the scores generated by using the new instrument.[1] Even if an existing and reputable measuring instrument has been used, the researcher ought to tell us specifically what instrument was used (by indicating form, model number, publication date, etc.). One would need to know

[1]Later, in Chapter 4, we will talk more about the kinds of evidence researchers normally offer to document their instruments' technical merit.

such information, of course, before a full replication of the study could be attempted. In addition, the researcher ought to pass along reliability and validity evidence cited by those who developed the instrument. Ideally, the authors ought to provide their *own* evidence as to the reliability and validity of scores used in their study, even if an existing instrument is used.

Excerpt 1.6 contains the materials section from our model article. The materials were called "scales" because the data for this study were gathered by administering two paper-and-pencil measuring instruments to the study's participants.

## EXCERPT 1.6 • *Materials*

Students were given the Nowicki-Strickland Locus of Control Scale for Children (Nowicki & Strickland, 1973), a paper-and-pencil measure of 40 dichotomous questions. The scale was chosen because it is written for children and adolescents, published validities and reliabilities are satisfactory, and it has been used extensively in past research. The items are based upon the definitions of internal-external control as set forth previously by Rotter (1954). Items are given 1 point per reply that would correspond to the more external response; the higher the score, the more externally oriented the respondent. Conversely, responses corresponding to internally oriented ratings are scored as zero. Test-retest reliability was reported with a 6-wk. interval at .75 for a group of 12- to 15-yr.-old children (n = 54). Also, a test-retest reliability of .71 was found for a sample in Grade 10. A Spearman-Brown split-half reliability of .74 was found for Grades 9 through 11 in the normative sample. Construct validity based on correlations with scores on scales, such as the Bialer-Cromwell Scale, have yielded fair estimates. Concurrent validity as associations with other constructs has been adequate. A sample question is "Are you often blamed for things that just aren't your fault?"

*Source:* Shepherd, S., Fitch, T. J., Owen, D., and Marshall, J. L. (2006). Locus of control and academic achievement in high school students. *Psychological Reports, 98*(1), p. 319.

This section of the research report contains several important statistical terms and numbers. To be more specific, there are 5 technical terms contained in Excerpt 1.6 (test-retest reliability, Spearman-Brown split-half reliability, construct validity, concurrent validity, and "associations with") and three numbers (.75, .71, and .74). In Chapter 4, we will focus our attention on these and other measurement-related concepts and numerical summaries.

In most empirical studies, the **dependent variable** is closely connected to the measuring instrument used to collect data. In fact, many researchers operationally define the dependent variable as being equivalent to the scores earned by people when they are measured with the study's instrument. Though this practice is widespread (especially among statistical consultants), it is *not* wise to think that dependent variables and data are one and the same.

Although there are different ways to conceptualize what a dependent variable is, a simple definition is useful in most situations. According to this definition, a dependent variable is simply a characteristic of the participants that (1) is of interest to the researcher; (2) is not possessed to an equal degree, or in the same way, by all participants; and (3) serves as the target of the researcher's data-collection efforts. Thus, in a study conducted to compare the intelligence of males and females, the dependent variable would be intelligence.

In the study associated with our model article, there were several variables of concern to the researchers. These were GPA, locus of control, grade in school, age, and ethnicity. In one sense, all five of these variables were dependent variables. As you will learn in other chapters of this book, sometimes a particular statistical analysis causes a given dependent variable to assume the role of an "independent" variable when data are analyzed. For example, GPA was considered an independent variable in our model study when the researchers analyzed their data so as to assess their main hypothesis (about the connection between GPA and locus of control). For now, don't worry about this "role-reversal" when dependent variables become independent variables. I assure you that this potentially confusing labeling of variables will become fully clear in later chapters.

## Procedure

How the study was conducted is explained in the **procedure** section of the journal article. Here, the researcher explains what the participants did—or what was done to them—during the investigation. Sometimes an author will even include a verbatim account of instructions given to the participants.

Remember that the method section is included so as to permit a reader to replicate a study. To accomplish this desirable goal, the author must outline clearly the procedures that were followed, providing answers to questions such as these: Where was the study conducted? Who conducted the study? In what sequence did events take place? Did any of the subjects drop out prior to the study's completion? (In Chapter 5, we will see that subject dropout can cause the results to be distorted.)

Excerpt 1.7 is the procedure section from our model article. Even though this section is extremely brief, it provides information regarding who collected the data,

### EXCERPT 1.7 • *Procedure*

Three high school teachers in different schools assisted in data collection. After permission from children and parents was obtained by the principal, the classroom teachers in the three schools were given research packets including an informed consent statement, a demographic form, and the Nowicki-Strickland Locus of Control Scale. Students who agreed to participate completed the form and survey in class and returned them in an envelope to the teacher. Students reported their grade point average on a form provided. All students in the sampled classrooms participated.

*Source:* Shepherd, S., Fitch, T. J., Owen, D., and Marshall, J. L. (2006). Locus of control and academic achievement in high school students. *Psychological Reports, 98*(1), p. 319.

when this took place, and where this was done. In addition, the researcher points out that permission was granted to collect the data.

### Statistical Procedures

In most research reports, researchers will indicate which statistical procedures were used to analyze their data. In some reports, this information will be presented near the end of the method section; in other reports, a listing of the researcher's statistical tools is positioned at the beginning of the report's results section. Excerpt 1.8 comes from the final portion of our model article's method section, and it was called **analyses.**

### EXCERPT 1.8 • *Analyses*

For the purposes of this study, a self-reported grade point average above 3.0 on a 4-point scale, A or B grades were used to construct a higher grade point average group; those below formed a lower achieving group. Measures on locus of control orientation for the two groups were compared by *t* test. Correlations were also examined.

*Source:* Shepherd, S., Fitch, T. J., Owen, D., and Marshall, J. L. (2006). Locus of control and academic achievement in high school students. *Psychological Reports, 98*(1), pp. 319–320.

In Excerpt 1.8, we learn that students were put into two groups based on their self-reported GPAs. The authors then indicate that they used a *t*-test to compare these two groups regarding the students' locus of control scores. (We will consider *t*-tests in Chapter 10.) The researchers also report that "correlations were examined." (In Chapter 3, we will spend quite a bit of time looking at the topic of correlation.)

## Results

There are three ways in which the results of an empirical investigation will be reported. First, the results can be presented within the text of the article—that is, with only words. Second, they can be summarized in one or more tables. Third, the findings can be displayed by means of a graph (which is technically called a **figure**). Not infrequently, a combination of these mechanisms for reporting results is used to help readers gain a more complete understanding of how the study turned out. In Excerpt 1.9, we see that the authors of our model article presented their results by means of two paragraphs of text and three tables.

Excerpt 1.9 contains a slew of statistical terms, abbreviations, and numerical results. If you find yourself unable, as this point, to make much sense out of the material presented in Excerpt 1.9, do not panic or think that this statistical presentation is

## EXCERPT 1.9 • *Results*

A higher score on the Nowicki-Strickland Locus of Control Scale (1973) represents a more external locus of control. The mean score was 14.5 ($SD = 4.6$) for boys and 14.2 ($SD = 4.5$) for girls. Obtained mean scores for African-American and Caucasian students were 14.0 ($SD = 4.6$) and 14.4 ($SD = 4.6$), respectively; see Table 1.

**TABLE 1   *Locus of Control Means and Standard Deviations by Self-Reported Grade Point Average***

| GPA | n | M | SD |
|-----|-----|------|-----|
| A | 48 | 12.7 | 3.8 |
| B | 68 | 13.7 | 5.0 |
| C | 58 | 15.7 | 4.3 |
| D | 12 | 15.6 | 5.0 |
| F | 2 | 19.5 | 4.5 |

A *t* test for students grouped by grade point average showed a significant mean difference on locus of control scores and self-reported grade point averages among the Higher GPA group ($M = 13.3$, $SD = 4.5$) and the Lower GPA group ($M = 15.8$, $SD = 4.7$; $t_{185} = 3.55$, $p < .0005$). The effect size of .25 was small (Cohen, 1988) and the power was computed, using GPower (Erdfelder, Faul, & Buchner, 1996) at .56. No significant differences were found by ethnic groups on locus of control; see Table 2.

**TABLE 2   *Locus of Control Means by Ethnic Group and Grade Point Average Means, Standard Deviations, and Correlations***

| Ethnicity | n | M | SD | r |
|-----------|-----|------|-----|------|
| African-American | 49 | 14.0 | 4.6 | −.37 |
| Caucasian | 125 | 14.2 | 4.8 | −.26 |

*Note.* No other ethnic group included more than 5 cases. As the higher the locus of control scores the more external the locus of control, a negative correlation reflects a positive relationship.

For ratings of both African-American and Caucasian students negative Pearson correlations for scores on locus of control with self-reported grade average were obtained. Regardless of ethnicity, those scoring as more external locus of control had lower grade point averages. Correlations by ethnicity, grade, age, and self-reported grade average in Table 3 are low values; only the correlation for self-reported grade point average was statistically significant.

*(continued)*

**EXCERPT 1.9 • *(continued)***

---

TABLE 3    *Pearson Product-Moment Correlations for Locus of Control with Independent Variables*

| Variable | Coefficient | *p* |
|---|---|---|
| Grade Point Average | −.27 | <.0005 |
| Grade | .07 | .35 |
| Sex | −.02 | .81 |
| Age | .01 | .17 |

*Source:* Shepherd, S., Fitch, T. J., Owen, D., and Marshall, J. L. (2006). Locus of control and academic achievement in high school students. *Psychological Reports, 98*(1), pp. 320–321.

---

beyond your reach. Everything in this excerpt will be considered in Chapters 2, 3, and 5 through 10. By the time you finish reading those chapters, you will be able to look again at Excerpt 1.9 and experience no difficulty deciphering the statistically based results of this investigation.

Although the **results** section of a journal article contains some of the most crucial information about the study (if not *the* most crucial information), readers of the professional literature often disregard it. They do this because the typical results section is loaded with statistical terms and notation not used in everyday communication. Accordingly, many readers of technical research reports simply skip the results section because it seems as if it came from another planet.

If you are to function as a discerning "consumer" of journal articles, you must develop the ability to read, understand, and evaluate the results provided by authors. Those who choose not to do this are forced into the unfortunate position of uncritical acceptance of the printed word. Researchers are human, however, and they make mistakes. Unfortunately, the reviewers who serve on editorial boards do not catch all of these errors. As a consequence, there sometimes will be an inconsistency between the results discussed in the text of the article and the results presented in the tables. At times, a researcher will use an inappropriate statistical test. More often than you would suspect, the conclusions drawn from the statistical results will extend far beyond the realistic limits of the actual data that were collected.

You do not have to be a sophisticated mathematician in order to understand and evaluate the results sections of most journal articles. However, you must become familiar with the terminology, symbols, and logic used by researchers. This text was written to help you do just that.

Look at Excerpt 1.9 once again. The text material included in this excerpt is literally packed with information intended to help you. Unfortunately, many readers miss out on the opportunity to receive this information because they lack the skills needed to decode what is being communicated or are intimidated by statistical presentations. One of my goals in this book is to help readers acquire (or refine) their decoding skills. In doing this, I hope to show that there is no reason for anyone to be intimidated by what is included in technical research reports.

## Discussion

The results section of a journal article contains a technical report of how the statistical analyses turned out, while the **discussion** section is usually devoted to a nontechnical interpretation of the results. In other words, the author will normally use the discussion section to explain what the results mean in regard to the central purpose of the study. The statement of purpose, which appears near the beginning of the article, usually contains an underlying or obvious research question; the discussion section ought to provide a direct answer to that question.

In addition to telling us what the results mean, many authors use this section of the article to explain *why* they think the results turned out the way they did. Although such a discussion will occasionally be found in articles where the data support the researchers' hunches, authors are much more inclined to point out possible reasons for the obtained results when those results are inconsistent with their expectations. If one or more of the scores turn out to be highly different from the rest, the researcher may talk about such serendipitous findings in the discussion section.

Sometimes an author will use the discussion section to suggest ideas for further research studies. Even if the results do not turn out the way the researcher had hoped they would, the study may be quite worthwhile in that it might stimulate the researcher (and others) to identify new types of studies that need to be conducted. Although this form of discussion is more typically associated with unpublished master's theses and doctoral dissertations, you will occasionally encounter it in a journal article.

It should be noted that some authors use the term **conclusion** rather than discussion to label this part of the journal article. These two terms are used interchangeably. It is unusual, therefore, to find an article that contains both a discussion section and a conclusion section.

Excerpt 1.10 contains the discussion section that appeared in our model journal article. Notice how the authors used the first paragraph to argue that their main hypothesis was supported by the empirical evidence of the study. In the second paragraph, the authors point out that their study was important because it filled a hole in the research literature that was identified by previous investigators.

In the third paragraph of the research report's discussion section, the authors point out some of the limitations of their study. These researchers deserve high praise for pointing out potential problems associated with their study because the data came from self-report measures, on the one hand, nor was there any control

**EXCERPT 1.10 • *Discussion***

The significant relationship between locus of control and academic achievement in this sample of high school students supported prior findings (e.g., Skaalvik & Skaalvik, 2004). Higher academic achievement was correlated with locus of control scores, indicating a more internal control orientation. According to Janssen and Carton's research (1999) with college students, those who are classified by external locus of control tend to procrastinate on tasks and are more likely to be affected by task difficulty both of which would lower achievement. Among the variables considered, one showing the relation of locus of control with academic achievement was statistically significant. Correlations of control were found by grade, ethnic group, and sex.

Kalechstein and Nowicki (1997) concluded that further studies of locus of control and academic achievement would be warranted because prior samples were mostly all Caucasian. The current study included a replication of findings with a larger sample of African-American students and was based on a sample from multiple schools.

Several limitations of this study are evident. Locus of control and students' achievement were obtained through self-reports which are subject to personal bias. Also, possible confounding variables such as socioeconomic status and community support could explain the mean differences. It seems likely these variables may be part of a related cluster of factors which influence students' achievement.

*Source:* Shepherd, S., Fitch, T. J., Owen, D., and Marshall, J. L. (2006). Locus of control and academic achievement in high school students. *Psychological Reports, 98*(1), p. 321.

over possible confounding variables. Unfortunately, many researchers fail to discuss the potential shortcomings of their investigations. That's why *you* need to hone your skills at being able to both decipher *and* critique statistically based research reports.

# References

A journal article normally concludes with a list of the books, journal articles, and other source material referred to by the author. Most of these items were probably mentioned by the author in the review of the literature positioned near the beginning of the article. Excerpt 1.11 is the **references** section of our model article.

The references can be very helpful to you if you want to know more about the particular study you are reading. Journal articles and convention presentations are usually designed to cover one particular study or a narrowly defined area of a subject. Unlike more extended writings (e.g., monographs and books), they include only a portion of the background information and only partial descriptions of

## EXCERPT 1.11 • *References*

Cohen, J. (1988) *Statistical power analysis for the behavioral sciences.* (2nd ed.). Hillsdale, NJ: Erlbaum.

Erdfelder, E., Paul, F., & Buchner, A. (1996) GPOWER: a general power analysis program. *Behavior Research Methods, Instruments, & Computers,* 28, 1–11.

Janssen, T., & Carton, J. (1999) The effects of locus of control and task difficulty on procrastination. *Journal of Genetic Psychology,* 160, 436–443.

Kaleschstein, A. D., & Nowicki, S., Jr. (1957) A meta-analytic examination of the relationship between control expectancies and academic achievement. *Genetic, Social, and General Psychology Monographs,* 123, 29–37.

Leone, C., & Burns, J. (2000) The measurement of locus of control: Assessing more than meets the eye? *The Journal of Psychology,* 134, 63–76.

Nowicki, S., & Strickland, B. R. (1973) Locus of control scale for children. *Journal of Counseling & Clinical Psychology,* 40, 148–154.

Nunn, G. D., Mongomery, J. D., & Nunn, S. J. (1986) Criterion-related validity of the Nowicki-Strickland Locus of Control Scale with academic achievement. *Psychology: A Quarterly Journal of Human Behavior,* 23, 9–11.

Rotter, J. B. (1954) *Social learning and clinical psychology,* New York: Prentice-Hall.

Rotter, J. B. (1966) Generalized expectancies for internal Versus external control of reinforcement. *Journal of Educational Research,* 74, 185–190.

Skaalvik, E. M., & Skaalvik, S. (2004) Self-concept and self-efficacy: A test of the internal/external frame of reference model and predictions of subsequent motivation and achievement. *Psychological Reports,* 95, 187–202.

*Source:* Shepherd, S., Fitch, T. J., Owen, D., and Marshall, J. L. (2006). Locus of control and academic achievement in high school students. *Psychological Reports, 98*(1), pp. 321–322.

related studies that would aid the reader's comprehension of the study. Reading books and articles listed in the references section will provide you with some of this information and probably give you a clearer understanding as to why and how the author conducted the particular study you have just read. Before hunting down any particular reference item, it is a good idea to look back into the article to reread the sentence or paragraph containing the original citation. This will give you an idea of what is in each reference item.

## Notes

Near the beginning or end of their research reports, authors sometimes present one or more **notes.** In general, such notes are used by authors for three reasons: (1) to thank others who helped them with their study or with the preparation of the technical report, (2) to clarify something that was discussed earlier in the journal article, and (3) to indicate how an interested reader can contact them to discuss this particular study or other research that might be conducted in the future. In our model journal article, there was a single note. This note contained the second author's postal address and email address.

## *Two Final Comments*

As we come to the end of this chapter, I would like to make two final points. One concerns the interconnectedness among the different components of the research summary. The other concerns the very first of those components: the abstract.

In this chapter, we have dissected a journal article that summarizes a research study focused on GPA and locus of control scores among eighth- through twelfth-graders. In looking at this particular article section by section, you may have gotten the impression that each of the various parts of a research article can be interpreted and evaluated separately from the other sections that go together to form the full article. You should not leave this chapter with that thought, because the various parts of a well-prepared research report are tied together so as to create an integrated whole.

In our model journal article, the researchers had one principal hypothesis. That hypothesis appears in Excerpt 1.4. That same hypothesis is the focus of the first paragraph in the research report's Results section (see Excerpt 1.9), the first paragraph of the Discussion section (see Excerpt 1.10), and the second sentence of the abstract (see Excerpt 1.1). The authors who prepared this journal article deserve high marks for keeping focused on the study's central hypothesis and for showing a clear connection between that hypothesis and their findings. Unfortunately, many journal articles display very loose (and sometimes undetectable) connections between the component parts of their articles.

My final comment takes the form of a warning. Simply stated, do not read an abstract and then think that you understand the study well enough to forgo reading the entire article. As was stated earlier, an abstract gives you a thumbnail sketch of a study, thus allowing you to decide whether the article fits into your area of interest. If it does not, then you rightfully can move on. On the other hand, if an abstract makes it appear that the study is, in fact, consistent with your interests, you need to then read the entire article for two reasons. First, the results summarized in the abstract may not coincide with the information that appears in the results section of the full article. Second, you cannot properly evaluate the quality of the results—even if they are consistently presented in the abstract, results, and discussion sections of the article—without coming to understand who or what was measured, how measurements were taken, and what kinds of statistical procedures were applied.

If you read an abstract (but nothing else in the article) and then utilize the abstract's information to bolster your existing knowledge or guide your own research projects, you potentially harm rather than help yourself. That is the case because the findings reported in many abstracts are simply not true. To be able to tell whether or not an abstract can be trusted, you will need to read the full article. The rest of this book has been written to help make that important task easier for you.

## Review Terms

| | |
|---|---|
| Abstract | Method |
| Analyses | Notes |
| Dependent variable | Participants |
| Discussion | Procedure |
| Figure | References |
| Hypotheses | Results |
| Materials | Subject |

## The Best Items in the Companion Website

1. An important email message sent by the author at the beginning of the semester to students enrolled in his statistics and research course.
2. An interactive online quiz (with immediate feedback provided) covering Chapter 1.
3. Gary Gildner's wonderful poem entitled "Statistics."
4. Five misconceptions about the content of Chapter 1.

To access chapter objectives, practice tests, weblinks, and flashcards, visit the companion website at www.ablongman.com/huck5e.

Research
Navigator.c☺m

## Fun Exercises inside Research Navigator

### 1. What kind of "no-suicide" contract do college students prefer?

In this study, each of 112 college students evaluated three different "no-suicide" contracts on how well each one might help prevent suicides on college campuses. The three contracts differed in length and complexity. One contained a single sentence; one was made up of two sentences; one had nine sentences covering six points. Each research participant rated each contract on several criteria (e.g., effectiveness in stopping suicidal thoughts, potential for lessening depression). Which of the three contracts do you think was evaluated as being the best? Do you think the subgroups of participants who had or had not contemplated suicide felt the same way about which contract was best? To find out the research-based answers to these questions, locate the PDF version of the research report in the Helping Professions database of ContentSelect and read (on page 588) the first paragraph of the section entitled "Discussion." In addition, take a look at *all* of the article's sections and headings. This will give you a feel for the way most research articles are organized.

G. Buelow & L. M. Range. No-suicide contracts among college students. *Death Studies.* Located in the HELPING PROFESSIONS database of ContentSelect.

## 2. Do college students get anxious about aging when taking a course on aging?

In this investigation, 256 college students were measured as to their knowledge about aging, their attitudes toward elderly people, and their anxiety about becoming old. Half were seniors who had just completed a course on aging; the other half were freshmen who had never taken such a course. The researchers compared the seniors with the freshmen on each of the study's three dependent variables: knowledge, attitude, and anxiety. As expected, the seniors did better on the knowledge-of-aging measure. But what about the other two measures? Do you think the seniors differed from the freshmen on either the attitude measure or the anxiety measure? To find out, locate the PDF version of the research report in the Nursing, Health, and Medicine database of ContentSelect and read (on page 664) the first two paragraphs of the "Discussion." Also, skim through the entire article, noting the different sections and headings. Most articles are set up like this one.

L. A. Harris & S. Dollinger. Participation in a course on aging: Knowledge, attitudes, and anxiety about aging in oneself and others. *Educational Gerontology*. Located in the NURSING, HEALTH, AND MEDICINE database of ContentSelect.

**Review Questions and Answers begin on page 513.**

# 2

# Descriptive Statistics

## *The Univariate Case*

In this chapter we will consider descriptive techniques designed to summarize data on a single dependent variable. These techniques are often said to be **univariate** in nature because only one variable is involved. (In Chapter 3, we will look at several techniques designed for the **bivariate** case—that is, for situations where data have been collected on two dependent variables.)

We begin this chapter by looking at several ways data can be summarized using pictures. These so-called picture techniques include frequency distributions, stem-and-leaf displays, histograms, and bar graphs. Next, the topic of distributional shape is considered; here, you will learn what it means when a data set is said to be normal, skewed, bimodal, or rectangular. After that, we examine the concept of central tendency and various methods used to represent a data set's average score. We then turn our attention to how researchers usually summarize the variability, or spread, within their data sets; these techniques include four different kinds of range, the standard deviation, and the variance. Finally, we consider two kinds of standard scores: *z* and *T*.

## Picture Techniques

In this section, we consider some techniques for summarizing data that produce a picture of the data. I use the term *picture* somewhat loosely, since the first technique really leads to a table of numbers. In any event, our discussion of descriptive statistics begins with a consideration of three kinds of frequency distributions.

### Frequency Distributions

A **frequency distribution** shows how many people (or animals or objects) were similar in the sense that, measured on the dependent variable, they ended up in the same category or had the same score. Three kinds of frequency distributions are often seen in published journal articles: simple (or ungrouped), grouped, and cumulative.

In Excerpt 2.1, we see an example of a **simple frequency distribution,** also called an **ungrouped frequency distribution.** The numbers in the left-hand column are the scores that could be earned on a personality inventory that focused on people's sensation-seeking thoughts. The numbers in the middle column indicate how many of the study's participants got each possible score. (Thus, there were four people who ended up with a score of 0, four others who got a score of 1, and so on.) The numbers in the right column indicate the percent of the full group that ended up with each possible score.

*also called ungrouped*

## EXCERPT 2.1 • *Simple Frequency Distribution*

**TABLE 2**  *The Distribution of the Participants' Sensation-Seeking Scores (TAS)*   *AKA: Number ORf*   *cumulative*

| TAS | Frequency | Percent |
|-----|-----------|---------|
| 0 | 4 | 5.1 |
| 1 | 4 | 5.1 |
| 2 | 3 | 3.8 |
| 3 | 7 | 9.0 |
| 4 | 7 | 9.0 |
| 5 | 6 | 7.7 |
| 6 | 17 | 21.8 |
| 7 | 6 | 7.7 |
| 8 | 7 | 9.0 |
| 9 | 6 | 7.7 |
| 10 | 11 | 14.1 |
| Total | N = 78 | 100.0 |

*scores that can be earned*   *How many got each score*   *Percent of the full group that ended up c̄ that score*

*Source:* Rosenbloom, T. (2006). Sensation seeking and pedestrian crossing compliance. *Social Behavior and Personality, 34*(2), p. 116.

*Simple*
*2.1 ungrouped*
*2.2 (grouped)*
*categorical*
*qualatative*

*f = frequency or number*

Two features of Excerpt 2.1 are worth noting. First, the authors used the word *frequency* to label the middle column of numbers. Sometimes you will see the word *number* or the abbreviation *f* used instead. Second, the number at the bottom of the middle column is sometimes labeled *N,* to represent the number of individuals in the group.

Excerpt 2.2 shows how a frequency distribution can help us understand the characteristics of a group relative to some categorical (rather than numerical) variable of interest. In the study associated with this excerpt, the researchers compared two groups of people—abstinent drug abusers and nonuser controls—in terms of a variety of measures while people in the two groups performed several different tasks. The frequency distribution shown here was included in the research report to show the "drug history" of the individuals in the abstinent group.

**EXCERPT 2.2** • *Simple Frequency Distribution for a Qualitative Variable*

**TABLE 2**   *History of Substance Abuse*

| | Drug Abusers | |
|---|---|---|
| **Abused Substance** | *No.* | *%* |
| Marijuana | 6 | 29.0 |
| Cocaine only | 1 | 4.8 |
| Marijuana/cocaine only | 4 | 24.0 |
| Multiple drugs, not including heroin | 3 | 15.0 |
| Multiple drugs, including heroin | 6 | 29.0 |

*Source:* Fishbein, D., Eldreth, D., Matochik, J., Isenberg, N., Hyde, C., London, E. D., Ernst, M., and Steckley, S. (2005). Cognitive performance and autonomic reactivity in abstinent drug abusers and nonusers. *Experimental and Clinical Psychopharmacology, 13*(1), p. 28.

In Excerpt 2.3, we see an example of a **grouped frequency distribution.** This frequency distribution deals with the complaints that college students had when they used a web-based triage system. There were 1,290 contacts over a four-month time period, with records kept as to the chief complaint of each contact. (The most frequent chief complaint was a sore throat.) The information in Excerpt 2.3 was included in the research report to show how long the college students said they had lived with their problems before using the web-based triage system.

The table in Excerpt 2.3 is a *grouped* frequency distribution because the far left-hand column has, on each row, a group of possible durations. This grouping of the chief complaints into the duration period—into what are technically called *class intervals*—allows the data to be summarized in a more compact fashion. If the data in this excerpt had been presented in an ungrouped frequency distribution with

**EXCERPT 2.3** • *Grouped Frequency Distribution*

**TABLE 3**   *Duration of Chief Complaint*

| *Duration* | *f* | *%* |
|---|---|---|
| <1 d | 184 | 14.3 |
| 1–3 d | 413 | 32.0 |
| 4.7 d | 209 | 16.2 |
| >1 w | 484 | 37.5 |
| Total | 1290 | 100.0 |

*Source:* Sole, M. L., Stuart, P. L., and Deichen, M. (2005). Web-based triage in a college health setting. *Journal of American College Health, 54*(5), p. 292.

the duration column set up to reflect single 24-hour periods, at least 9 rows would have been needed, and probably many more than that. (I'm guessing that some of the college students waited well over a week before making contact.)

In addition to simple and grouped frequency distributions, **cumulative frequency distributions** sometimes appear in journal articles. With this kind of summarizing technique, a researcher tells us, through an additional column of numbers labeled *cumulative frequency* or *cumulative percentage,* how many measured objects ended up with any given score and all other lower scores (or how many scores ended up in a given score interval and all other lower intervals). This kind of frequency distribution is shown in Excerpt 2.4. Notice how the cumulative percentage of 55.1 can be obtained by (1) adding together 1, 2, 14, and 42, (2) dividing that sum by the sum of the frequencies, 107, and (3) multiplying by 100. Or, you can obtain the same cumulative percentage by adding together the top four numbers in the percent column.

**EXCERPT 2.4 • *Cumulative Frequency Distribution***

**TABLE 1**   *Frequency Distribution of SMOG Scores*

| SMOG Score | Frequency | % | Cumulative % |
|------------|-----------|------|--------------|
| 7th grade  | 1         | 0.9  | 0.9          |
| 8th grade  | 2         | 1.9  | 2.8          |
| 9th grade  | 14        | 13.1 | 15.9         |
| 10th grade | 42        | 39.3 | 55.1         |
| 11th grade | 39        | 36.4 | 91.6         |
| 12th grade | 9         | 8.4  | 100.0        |

*Source:* Wegner, M. V., and Girasek, D. (2003). How readable are child safety seat installation instructions? *Pediatrics, 111*(3), p. 589.

## Stem-and-Leaf Displays

Although a grouped frequency distribution provides information about the scores in a data set, it carries with it the limitation of "loss of information." The frequencies tell us how many data points fell into each interval of the score continuum but they do not indicate, within any interval, how large or small the scores were. Hence, when researchers summarize their data by moving from a set of raw scores to a grouped frequency distribution, the precision of the original scores is lost.

A **stem-and-leaf display** is like a grouped frequency distribution that contains no loss of information. To achieve this objective, the researcher first sets up score intervals on the left side of an imaginary vertical line. These intervals, collectively called the *stem,* are presented in a coded fashion by showing the lowest score of each interval. Then, to the right of the vertical line, the final digit is given for each observed score that fell into the interval being focused on. An example of a stem-and-leaf display is presented in Excerpt 2.5.

**EXCERPT 2.5 • *Stem-and-Leaf Display***

**TABLE 2**   *Stem-and-Leaf Display of Compliance on a Per-Participant Basis for Study 1*

| Stem | Leaf |
|------|------|
| 100 | 000000000000 |
| 90 | 888888776666655541 1000 |
| 80 | 8764 |
| 70 | |
| 60 | 8 |
| 50 | |
| 40 | 0 |
| 30 | |
| 20 | 40 |

*Note.* Leaf values correspond to the units digit of each participant's compliance score for the given stem (e.g., there were 6 individuals with a compliance score of 98%).

*Source:* Green, A. S., Rafaeli, E., Bolger, N., Shrout, P. E., and Reis, H. T. (2006). Paper or plastic? Data equivalence in paper and electronic diaries. *Psychological Methods, 11*(1), p. 90.

In the fifth row of this stem-and-leaf display, there is a 60 on the left (stem) side and an 8 on the right (leaf) side. This indicates that there was one score, a 68, within the interval represented by this row of the display (60–69 percent). The third row has four digits on the leaf side, and this indicates that four scores fell into this row's interval (80–89 percent). Using both stem and leaf from this row, we see that those four scores were 88, 87, 86, and 84. All other rows of this stem-and-leaf display are interpreted in the same way.

Notice that the 42 actual compliance scores in Excerpt 2.5 show up in the stem-and-leaf display. There is, therefore, no loss of information. Take another look at Excerpt 2.3, where a grouped frequency distribution was presented. Because of the loss of information associated with grouped frequency distributions, you cannot tell what the highest and lowest earned scores were, what specific scores fell into any interval, or whether gaps exist inside any intervals (as was the case in Excerpt 2.5 because no compliance scores fell between 70–79 percent, for instance).

## *Histograms and Bar Graphs*

In a **histogram,** vertical columns (or thin lines) are used to indicate how many times any given score appears in the data set. With this picture technique, the baseline (that is, the horizontal axis) is labeled to correspond with observed scores on the dependent variable while the vertical axis is labeled with frequencies.[1] Then,

[1]Technically speaking, the horizontal and vertical axes of any graph are called the **abscissa** and **ordinate,** respectively.

columns (or lines) are positioned above each baseline value to indicate how often each of these scores was observed. Whereas a tall bar indicates a high frequency of occurrence, a short bar indicates that the baseline score turned up infrequently.

A **bar graph** is almost identical to a histogram in both form and purpose. The only difference between these two techniques for summarizing data concerns the nature of the dependent variable that defines the baseline. In a histogram, the horizontal axis is labeled with numerical values that represent a quantitative variable. In contrast, the horizontal axis of a bar graph represents different categories of a qualitative variable. In a bar graph, the ordering of the columns is quite arbitrary, whereas the ordering of the columns in a histogram must be numerically logical.

In Excerpt 2.6, we see an example of a histogram. Notice how this graph allows us to quickly discern the Rotter scores for the individuals included in the researchers' sample. Also notice that the columns had to be arranged as they were because the variable on the baseline was clearly quantitative in nature.

## EXCERPT 2.6 • *Histogram*

A histogram shows the distribution of Rotter scale scores within the final sample (Figure 1). Recall that lower scores are associated with an internal orientation and higher scores are indicative of external orientation. The sample distribution of scores was roughly bell shaped but with a fatter lower tail and a relatively thinner upper tail, suggesting that the majority of students lay somewhere in between the two extremes and that internally oriented students were represented slightly more in the sample relative to their externally oriented cohorts.

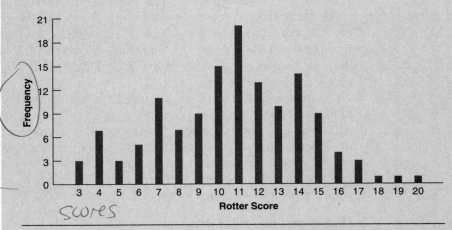

**FIGURE 1**   *Histogram of Rotter scores for final sample (N = 136).*

*Source:* Grimes, P. W., Millea, M. J., and Woodruff, T. W. (2004). Grades—Who's to blame? Student evaluation of teaching and locus of control. *Journal of Economic Education, 35*(2), pp. 135, 137.

**EXCERPT 2.7 • *Bar Graph***

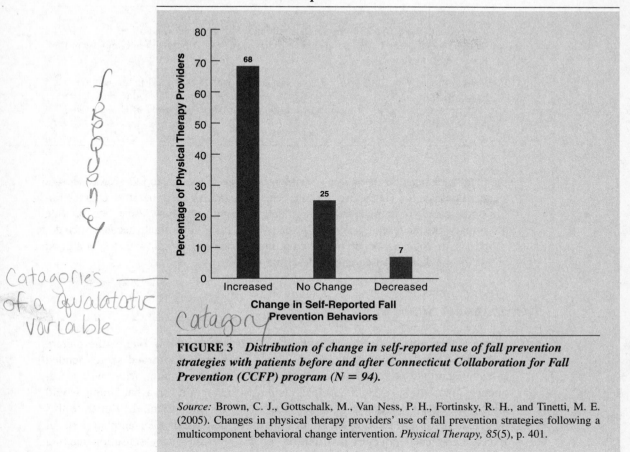

*Frequency*

*Catagories of a Qualatative Variable*

*Catagory*

**FIGURE 3**   *Distribution of change in self-reported use of fall prevention strategies with patients before and after Connecticut Collaboration for Fall Prevention (CCFP) program (N = 94).*

*Source:* Brown, C. J., Gottschalk, M., Van Ness, P. H., Fortinsky, R. H., and Tinetti, M. E. (2005). Changes in physical therapy providers' use of fall prevention strategies following a multicomponent behavioral change intervention. *Physical Therapy, 85*(5), p. 401.

An example of a bar graph is presented in Excerpt 2.7. Here, the order of the bars is completely arbitrary. The short bars could have been positioned on the left with the taller bars positioned on the right. Or, the bars could have been arranged alphabetically based on the labels beneath the bars.

### *Frequency Distributions in Words*

Researchers sometimes present the information of a frequency distribution in words rather than in a picture. Excerpt 2.8 illustrates how this can be done for a grouped frequency distribution.

In describing the age of their patients or research participants, many researchers summarize their data in one of three ways: (1) by reporting the range, (2) by reporting

**EXCERPT 2.8** • *A Frequency Distribution in Words*

> The patients were 36 to 67 years old: 1 patient was between 30 and 39 years old, 10 were between 40 and 49 years old, 6 were between 50 and 59 years old, and 3 were between 60 and 69 years old.
>
> *Source:* Blissitt, P. A., Mitchell, P. H., Newael, D. W., Woods, S. L., and Belza, B. (2006). Cerebrovascular dynamics with head-of-bed elevation in patients with mild or moderate vasospasm after aneurysmal subarachnoid hemorrhage. *American Journal of Critical Care, 15*(2), p. 210.

the mean and standard deviation, or (3) by reporting the range and the mean and the standard deviation.[2] That's also the case when researchers describe other characteristics of the people or animals from whom data were gathered. Few researchers provide a summary like the researchers did in Excerpt 2.8. This is unfortunate because such descriptions, as you can see, do not take up much space and yet allow us to get a good "feel" for the data the researcher is describing.

## Distributional Shape

If researchers always summarized their quantitative data using one of the picture techniques just covered, then you could *see* whether the observed scores tended to congregate at one (or more) point along the score continuum. Moreover, a frequency distribution, a stem-and-leaf display, a histogram, or a bar graph would allow you to tell whether a researcher's data were symmetrical. To illustrate this nice feature of the picture techniques we have discussed, take another look at Excerpt 2.1. The frequency distribution for the 78 pedestrians' sensation-seeking scores shows nicely that (1) the TAS scores were spread out along the full range of the score continuum, and (2) the most frequently earned score was a 6.

Unfortunately, pictures of data sets do not appear in journal articles very often because they are costly to prepare and because they take up lots of space. By using some verbal descriptors, however, researchers can tell their readers what their data sets look like. To decipher such messages, you must understand the meaning of a few terms that researchers use to describe the **distributional shape** of their data.

If the scores in a data set approximate the shape of a **normal distribution,** most of the scores will be clustered near the middle of the continuum of observed scores, and there will be a gradual and symmetrical decrease in frequency in both directions away from the middle area of scores. Data sets that are normally

---

[2]We will consider the *mean* and the *standard deviation* later in this chapter.

distributed are said to resemble a bell-shaped curve, since a side drawing of a bell will start out low on either side and then bulge upward in the center. In Excerpt 2.6, we saw a histogram that resembles a normal distribution.

In **skewed distributions,** most of the scores end up being high (or low), with a small percentage of scores strung out in one direction away from the majority. Skewed distributions, consequently, are not symmetrical. If the tail of the distribution (formed by the small percentage of scores that is strung out in one direction) points toward the upper end of the score continuum, the distribution is said to be **positively skewed;** if the tail points toward the lower end of the score continuum, the term **negatively skewed** applies. In Excerpt 2.9, we see an example of a positively skewed distribution.

Research
Navigator.com

Positively skewed
Negatively
skewed

⊕ tail to
the ℝ
⊖ tail to
the left

## EXCERPT 2.9 • *A Positively Skewed Distribution*

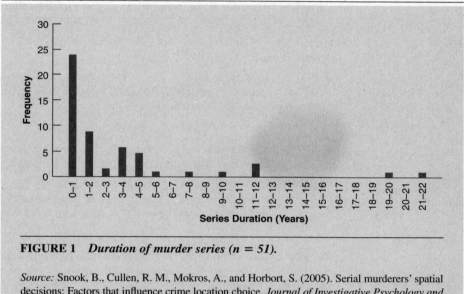

**FIGURE 1** *Duration of murder series (n = 51).*

*Source:* Snook, B., Cullen, R. M., Mokros, A., and Horbort, S. (2005). Serial murderers' spatial decisions: Factors that influence crime location choice. *Journal of Investigative Psychology and Offender Profiling, 2,* p. 153.

modality

If the scores tend to congregate around more than one point along the score continuum, the distribution is said to be **multimodal** in nature. If there are two such places where scores are grouped together, we could be more specific and say that the data are distributed in a **bimodal** fashion. If scores are congregated at three distinct points, the term **trimodal** would come into play.[3]

---

[3]Distributions having just one "hump" are said to be **unimodal** in nature.

If scores are fairly evenly distributed along the score continuum without any clustering at all, the data set is said to be **rectangular.** Such a distributional shape would probably show up if someone (1) asked each person in a large group to indicate his or her birth month, and (2) created a histogram with 12 bars, beginning with January, arranged on the baseline. The bars making up this histogram would probably be approximately the same height. Looked at collectively, the bars making up this histogram would resemble a rectangle.

In Excerpts 2.10 through 2.12, we see a few examples of how researchers will sometimes go out of their way to describe the distributional shape of their data sets. Such researchers should be commended for indicating what their data sets looked like because these descriptions help others to understand the nature of the data that have been collected.

**EXCERPTS 2.10–2.12 • *References to Different Distributional Shapes***

Scores on the internalizing difficulties scales were normally distributed at both 2 and 4 years of age.

*Source:* Bayer, Jordana K., Sanson, Ann V., Hemphill, Sheryl A. (2006). Children's moods, fears, and worries: Development of an early childhood parent questionnaire. *Journal of Emotional & Behavioral Disorders, 14*(1), p. 45.

The FNQ data for proportion of met need in the outpatient group were found to be positively skewed (as many participants reported low proportions of met need).

*Source:* Smith, M. J., Vaugban, F. L., Cox, L. J., McConville, H., Roberts, M., Stoddart, S., and Lew, A. R. (2006). The impact of community rehabilitation for acquired brain injury on carer burden: An exploratory study. *Journal of Head Trauma Rehabilitation, 21*(1), p. 80.

The total months of co-op per student ranged from three to 27; this distribution was bimodal, with 23 [of the 85] students completing nine months and 28 of the students completing 21 months of co-op.

*Source:* Hoffart, N., Diani, J. A., Connors, M., and Moynihan, P. (2006). Outcomes of cooperative education in a baccalaureate program IN NURSING. *Nursing Education Perspectives, 27*(3), p. 140.

Kurtosis

As we have seen, two features of distributional shape are modality and skewness. A third feature is related to the concept of **kurtosis.** This third way of looking at distributional shape deals with the possibility that a set of scores can be nonnormal even though there is only one mode and even though there is no skewness in the data. This is possible because there may be an unusually large number of scores at the center of the distribution, thus causing the distribution to be overly peaked. Or, the hump in the middle of the distribution may be smaller than is the case in normal distributions, with both tails being thicker than in the famous bell-shaped curve.

When the concept of kurtosis is discussed in research reports, you may encounter the terms **leptokurtic** and **platykurtic.** These terms denote distributional shapes that are more peaked and less peaked (as compared with the normal distribution), respectively. The term **mesokurtic** signifies a distributional shape that is neither overly peaked nor overly flat.

As illustrated in Excerpts 2.9 through 2.12, researchers can communicate information about distributional shape via a picture or a label. They can also compute numerical indices that assess the degree of skewness and kurtosis present in their data. In Excerpt 2.13, we see a case in which a group of researchers presented such indices in an effort to help their readers understand what kind of distributional shape was created by each set of scores that had been gathered.

### EXCERPT 2.13 • *Quantifying Skewness and Kurtosis*

To test whether the distribution of the PPVT–III scores within the African American sample deviated from normal, and to determine whether there was a floor effect, skewness and kurtosis values were examined. The skewness value of −.07 . . . and kurtosis value of −.14 . . . indicated a relatively normal distribution.

*Source:* Huaqing Qi, C., Kaiser, A. P., Milan, S., and Hancock, T. (2006). Language performance of low-income African American and European American preschool children on the PPVT-III. *Language, Speech, & Hearing Services in Schools, 37*(1), p. 9.

To properly interpret coefficients of skewness and kurtosis, keep in mind three things. First, both indices will turn out equal to zero for a normal distribution.[4] Second, a skewness value lower than zero indicates that a distribution is negatively skewed, whereas a value larger than zero indicates that a distribution is positively skewed; a kurtosis value less than zero indicates that a distribution is platykurtic, whereas a value greater than zero indicates that the distribution is leptokurtic. Finally, although there are no clear-cut guidelines for interpreting measures of skewness and kurtosis (mainly because there are different ways to compute such indices), most researchers consider data to be approximately normal in shape if the skewness and kurtosis values turn out to be anywhere from −1.0 to +1.0.

Depending on the objectives of the data analysis, a researcher should examine coefficients of skewness and kurtosis before deciding how to further analyze the

---

[4]Some formulas for computing skewness and kurtosis indices yield a value of +3 for a perfectly normal distribution. Most researchers, however, use the formulas that give values of zero for both skewness and kurtosis.

data. If a data set is found to be grossly nonnormal, the researcher may opt to do further analysis of the data using statistical procedures created for the nonnormal case. Or, the data can be "normalized" by means of a formula that revises the value of each score such that the revised data set represents a closer approximation to the normal.

## Measures of Central Tendency

To help readers get a feel for the data that have been collected, researchers almost always say something about the typical or representative score in the group. They do this by computing and reporting one or more **measures of central tendency.** There are three such measures that are frequently seen in the published literature, each of which provides a numerical index of the **average** score in the distribution.

### The Mode, Median, and Mean

The **mode** is simply the most frequently occurring score. For example, given the nine scores 6, 2, 5, 1, 2, 9, 3, 6, and 2, the mode is equal to 2. The **median** is the number that lies at the midpoint of the distribution of earned scores; it divides the distribution into two equally large parts. For the set of nine scores just presented, the median is equal to 3. Four of the nine scores are smaller than 3; four are larger.[5] The **mean** is the point that minimizes the collective distances of scores from that point. It is found by dividing the sum of the scores by the number of scores in the data set. Thus for the group of nine scores presented here, the mean is equal to 4.

In journal articles, authors sometimes use abbreviations or symbols when referring to their measure(s) of central tendency. The abbreviations *Mo* and *Mdn,* of course, correspond to the mode and median, respectively. The letter *M* always stands for the mean, even though all three measures of central tendency begin with this letter. The mean is also symbolized by $\overline{X}$ and $\mu$.

In many research reports, the numerical value of only one measure of central tendency is provided. (That was the case with the model journal article presented in Chapter 1; take a look at Excerpt 1.9 to see which one was used.) Because it is not unusual for a real data set to be like our sample set of nine scores in that the mode, median, and mean assume different numerical values, researchers sometimes compute and report two measures of central tendency, or all three, so as to help readers better understand the data being summarized.

---

[5]When there is an even number of scores, the median is a number halfway between the two middle scores (once the scores are ordered from low to high). For example, if 9 is omitted from our sample set of scores, the median for the remaining eight scores would be 2.5—that is, the number halfway between 2 and 3.

In Excerpt 2.14, we see a case where two measures of central tendency were reported for the same data set. Excerpt 2.15 contains an example where all three averages—the mode, the median, and the mean—were provided.

**EXCERPTS 2.14–2.15 • *Reporting Multiple Measures of Central Tendency***

The participating [nursing home] facilities varied in size from 7 to 164 beds, with a mean of 42 and a median of 30 beds.

*Source:* Charach, A., Hongmei, C., Schachar, R., and To, T. (2006). Correlates of methylphenidate use in Canadian children: A cross-sectional study. *Canadian Journal of Psychiatry, 51*(1), p. 21.

----------------------------------------------------------------

The number of PT visits varied among the 66 patients (mean = 11.4, median = 9, mode = 6).

*Source:* Harp, S. S. (2004). The measurement of performance in a physical therapy clinical program: A ROI approach. *Health Care Manager, 23*(2), p. 117.

## The Relative Position of the Mode, Median, and Mean

In a true normal distribution (or in any unimodal distribution that is perfectly symmetrical), the values of the mode, median, and mean will be identical. Such distributions are rarely seen, however. In the data sets typically found in applied research studies, these three measures of central tendency assume different values. As a reader of research reports, you should know not only that this happens but also how the distributional shape of the data affects the relative position of the mode, median, and mean.

In a positively skewed distribution, a few scores are strung out toward the high end of the score continuum, thus forming a tail that points to the right. In this kind of distribution, the modal score ends up being the lowest (that is, positioned farthest to the left along the horizontal axis) while the mean ends up assuming the highest value (that is, positioned farthest to the right). In negatively skewed distributions, just the opposite happens; the mode ends up being located farthest to the right along the baseline while the mean assumes the lowest value. In Figure 2.1, we see a picture showing where these three measures of central tendency are positioned in skewed distributions.

After you examine Figure 2.1, return to Excerpt 2.6 and look at the histogram that summarizes the data. Because the distribution is not skewed very much, we should expect the mean, the median, and the mode to end up being similar. The actual values for these three measures of central tendency are 10.7, 10.8, and 11.0, respectively.

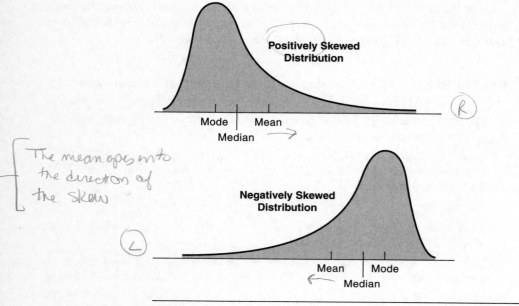

The mean goes into the direction of the skew

FIGURE 2.1   *Location of the Mean, Median, and Mode in Skewed Distributions*

To see a case where the computed measures of central tendency turned out to be quite dissimilar, thus implying skewed data, consider Excerpt 2.16. With the median and mean equal to 2 and 9.5, respectively, and with the lowest possible value being 0, we should have been able to guess that the distribution was skewed even if the researchers had not mentioned this. To see if you can determine the nature of skewness from reported values of central tendency, take another look at Excerpt 2.15. For the 66 men in that study, were the number of visits to physical therapy positively skewed or negatively skewed?

### EXCERPT 2.16 • *The Mean and Median in a Skewed Distribution*

At subsequent assessments, youths were asked about the number of individuals to whom the youth had disclosed during the past six months (i.e., since the last assessment). The number of individuals reported was used as the indicator of self-disclosure to others [and] the follow-up data were positively skewed [as] most youths reported very few new disclosures in the past 6 months; for example, median = 2.0, M = 9.5. . . .

*Source:* Rosario, M., Schrimshaw, E. W., Hunter, J., and Braun, L. (2006). Sexual identity development among lesbian, gay, and bisexual youths: Consistency and change over time. *Journal of Sex Research, 43*(1), p. 50.

In a bimodal distribution, there will be two points along the score continuum where scores tend to "pile up." If the distribution is symmetrical, the mean and median will be located halfway between the two modes. In a symmetrical trimodal distribution, the median and mean will assume a value equal to the middle of the three modes. Real data sets, however, rarely produce symmetrical bimodal or trimodal distributions. Any asymmetry (that is, skewness) will cause the median to be pulled off center toward the side of the distribution that has the longer tail—and the mean will be pulled even farther in that direction.

With full-fledged rectangular distributions, the mean and median will assume a value halfway between the high and low data points. In such distributions, there is no mode because all earned scores occur with equal frequency. If the distribution turns out to be only roughly rectangular, the median and mean will be located close together (and close to the halfway point between the high and low scores), but the mode could end up anywhere.

### Other Measures of Central Tendency

Although the mode, median, and mean are the most popular measures of central tendency, there are other techniques for summarizing the average score in a data set. (Examples include the geometric mean and the harmonic mean.) Because these indices are rarely seen in research reports, they will not be discussed here. If you take an advanced course in statistics, however, you will encounter these alternative methods for computing an average score.

## Measures of Variability

Descriptions of a data set's distributional shape and reports as to the central tendency value(s) help us to better understand the nature of data collected by a researcher. Although terms (e.g., *roughly normal*) and numbers (e.g., $M = 67.1$) help, they are not sufficient. To get a true feel for the data that have been collected, we also need to be told something about the variability among the scores. Let us consider now the standard ways that researchers summarize this aspect of their data sets.

### The Meaning of Variability

Most groups of scores possess some degree of variability. That is, at least some of the scores differ (vary) from one another. A **measure of variability** simply indicates the degree of this **dispersion** among the scores. If the scores are very similar, there is little dispersion and little variability. If the scores are very dissimilar, there is a high degree of dispersion (variability). In short, a measure of variability does nothing more than indicate how spread out the scores are.

The term *variability* can also be used to pinpoint where a group of scores might fall on an imaginary homogeneous–heterogeneous continuum. If the scores are similar, they are **homogeneous** (and have low variability). If the scores are dissimilar, they are **heterogeneous** (and have high variability).

Even though a measure of central tendency provides a numerical index of the average score in a group, we need to know the variability of the scores to better understand the entire group of scores. For example, consider the following two groups of IQ scores:

| Group I | Group II |
|---------|----------|
| 102 | 128 |
| 99 | 78 |
| 103 | 93 |
| 96 | 101 |

In both groups the mean IQ is equal to 100. Although the two groups have the same mean score, their variability is obviously different. While the scores in the first group are very homogeneous (low variability), the scores in the second group are far more heterogeneous (high variability).

The specific measures of variability that we will now consider are similar in that the numerical index will be zero if all of the scores in the data set are identical, a small positive number if the scores vary to a small degree, or a large positive number if there is a great deal of dispersion among the scores. (No measure of variability, no matter how computed, can ever turn out equal to a negative value.)

### The Range, Interquartile Range, Semi-Interquartile Range, and Box Plot

The **range** is the simplest measure of variability. It is the difference between the lowest and highest scores. For example, in Group I of the example just considered, the range is equal to 103–96, or 7. The range is usually reported by citing the extreme scores, but sometimes it is reported as the difference between the high and low scores. When providing information about the range to their readers, authors normally will write out the word *range*. Occasionally, however, this first measure of variability is abbreviated as *R*.

To see how the range can be helpful when we try to understand a researcher's data, consider Excerpts 2.17 and 2.18. Notice in Excerpt 2.17 how information concerning the range allows us to sense that the patients in this study were quite heterogeneous in terms of age. In contrast, the presentation of just the mean in Excerpt 2.18 puts us in the position of not knowing anything about how much variability existed among the patients' ages. Perhaps it was a very homogeneous group, with everyone in their early 60s. Or maybe the group was bimodal, with half the patients in their 50s and half in their 70s. Unless the range (or some other measure of variability) is provided, we are completely in the dark as to how similar or different the patients were in terms of their age.

*[handwritten notes in left margin:]*
1
2
4      $Q_1 = 3$
5
5
6      $Q_3 = 6.5$
7
9

Interquartile
Range = $Q_3 - Q_1$

IQR ③.5

SIQR (3.5/2) = 1.75

## EXCERPTS 2.17–2.18 • *Summarizing Data with and without the Range*

The mean age of the sample was 48.65 years (range = 23–64 years).

*Source:* Hacker, E. D., Ferrans, C., Verlen, E., Ravandi, F., van Besien, K., Gelms, J., and Dieterle, N. (2006). Fatigue and physical activity in patients undergoing hematopoietic stem cell transplant. *Oncology Nursing Forum, 33*(3), p. 618.

---

Patients had a mean age of 62.5 years.

*Source:* Gates, R., Cookson, T., Ito, M., Marcus, D., Gifford, A., Le, T. N., and Canh-Nhut, N. (2006). Therapeutic conversion from fosinopril to benazepril at a Veterans Affairs medical center. *American Journal of Health-System Pharmacy, 63*(11), p. 1067.

**Research Navigator.com**

Interquartile range

*[handwritten notes in left margin:]*
interquartile
range = spread
in middle 50%
of scores
(middle half)

$Q_3$ = upper quartile

$Q_1$ = lower quartile

$Q_2$ = median

middle 50%
of a
distribution
25th      75th
$Q_1$      $Q_3$

$Q_2$
mean

Whereas the range provides an index of dispersion among the full group of scores, the **interquartile range** indicates how much spread exists among the middle 50 percent of the scores. Like the range, the interquartile range is defined as the distance between a low score and a high score; these two indices of dispersion differ, however, in that the former is based on the high and low scores within the full group of data points whereas the latter is based on only *half* of the data—the middle half.

In any group of scores, the numerical value that separates the top 25 percent scores from the bottom 75 percent scores is the **upper quartile** (symbolized by $Q_3$). Conversely, the numerical value that separates the bottom 25 percent scores from the top 75 percent scores is the **lower quartile** ($Q_1$).[6] The interquartile range is simply the distance between $Q_3$ and $Q_1$. Stated differently, the interquartile range is the distance between the 75th and 25th percentile points.

In Excerpts 2.19 and 2.20, we see two cases in which the upper and lower quartiles were presented. In both of these excerpts, the values of $Q_1$ and $Q_3$ give us

## EXCERPTS 2.19–2.20 • *Quartiles and the Interquartile Range*

The range of [scores] was 0.00 to 92.30, with a mean of 47.20. Scores of 24 and 64 were at the first and third quartiles of the sample, respectively.

*Source:* Kimonis, E. R., Frick, P. J., and Barry, C. T. (2004). Callous-unemotional traits and delinquent peer affiliation. *Journal of Consulting and Clinical Psychology, 72*(6), p. 958.

---

Interquartile range (IQR) = $34,140–$67,506.

*Source:* Boudreaux, E. D., Kim, S., Hohrmann, J. L., Clark, S., and Camargo, C. A. (2005). Interest in smoking cessation among emergency department patients. *Health Psychology, 24*(2), p. 222.

---

[6]The middle quartile, $Q_2$, divides any group of scores into upper and lower halves. Accordingly, $Q_2$ is always equal to the median.

information as to the dispersion among the middle 50 percent of the scores. In Excerpt 2.19, for example, the scores for the middle half of the tested individuals extended from 24 to 64, with the top one-fourth of the study's participants having scores between 64 and 92.30, and the bottom fourth of the participants having scores between 0 and 24. In Excerpt 2.20, the interquartile range regarding family income—used as a measure of socioeconomic status—helps us understand the children who were the focus of this investigation.

Sometimes, a researcher will compute the **semi-interquartile range** to index the amount of dispersion among a group of scores. As you would guess on the basis of its name, this measure of variability is simply equal to one-half the size of the interquartile range. In other words, the semi-interquartile range is nothing more than $(Q_3 - Q_1)/2$.

With a **box-and-whisker plot,** the degree of variability within a data set is summarized with a picture. To accomplish this objective, a rectangle (box) is drawn to the right of a vertical line labeled so as to correspond with scores on the dependent variable. The positions of the top and bottom sides of the rectangle are determined by $Q_3$ and $Q_1$, the upper and lower quartile points. On the outside of the rectangle, two vertical lines—called the *whiskers*—are drawn. Researchers use different rules for drawing the whiskers. Sometimes the whiskers extend up to the highest observed score and down to the lowest observed score. Other researchers use a rule that says that neither whisker should be longer than 1.5 times the height of the rectangle. If any scores are further out than this, they are considered to be outliers, and their positions are indicated by small circles or asterisks. Other researchers draw the whiskers so they extend out to points that represent the 5th and 95th percentiles.

In Excerpt 2.21, we see a case in which box-and-whisker plots were used to show how different sets of data compared with each other in a fully descriptive sense. Note the differences in the heights of the boxes and the length of the whiskers.

Although box-and-whisker plots are designed to communicate information about variability, they also reveal things about central tendency and distributional shape. Within the rectangle, a horizontal line is positioned so as to correspond to $Q_2$, the median. If this median line appears in the center of the box and if the whiskers are of equal lengths, then we can infer that the distribution of scores is probably symmetrical. On the other hand, the median will end up off-center and the whiskers will be of unequal lengths in skewed distributions. (If the median is on the lower side of the box while the top whisker is longer, the distribution is positively skewed; conversely, negatively skewed distributions cause the median line to be on the upper side of the box and the bottom whisker to be longer.)

### Standard Deviation and Variance

Two additional indices of dispersion, the **standard deviation** and the **variance,** are usually better indices of dispersion than are the first three measures of variability

**EXCERPT 2.21 • *Box-and-Whisker Plot***

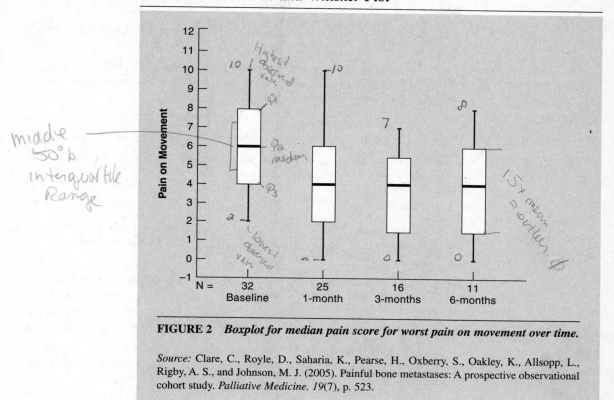

**FIGURE 2**    *Boxplot for median pain score for worst pain on movement over time.*

*Source:* Clare, C., Royle, D., Saharia, K., Pearse, H., Oxberry, S., Oakley, K., Allsopp, L., Rigby, A. S., and Johnson, M. J. (2005). Painful bone metastases: A prospective observational cohort study. *Palliative Medicine, 19*(7), p. 523.

that we have considered. This is due to the fact that the standard deviation and variance are each based on all of the scores in a group (and not just the high and low scores or the upper and lower quartile points). The standard deviation is determined by (1) figuring how much each score deviates from the mean and (2) putting these deviation scores into a computational formula. The variance is found by squaring the value of the standard deviation.

In reporting their standard deviations, authors may employ the abbreviation *SD,* utilize the symbol $s$ or $\sigma$, or simply write out the word **sigma**. Occasionally, authors will report the standard deviation using a plus-and-minus format—for example, $14.83 \pm 2.51$, where the first number (14.83) stands for the mean and the second number (2.51) stands for the standard deviation. The variance, being the square of the standard deviation, is symbolized as $s^2$ or $\sigma^2$.

Excerpts 2.22 through 2.25 illustrate four of the ways researchers indicate the numerical value of the standard deviation. In the first of these, the abbreviation *SD* was used. In the second, the "plus-and-minus" format was employed. In the third

## EXCERPTS 2.22–2.25 • *Reporting on the Standard Deviation*

The age of the mothers ranged from 28 to 55 years old, with an average age of 40.56 years ($SD = 5.05$).

*Source:* Villar, P., Luengo, M. Á., Gómez-Fraguela, J. A., and Romero, E. (2006). Assessment of the validity of parenting constructs using the multitrait-multimethod model. *European Journal of Psychological Assessment, 22*(1), p. 61.

---

The mean age ($\pm SD$) of participants was $51.8 \pm 13.4$ years, and 63.5% were men.

*Source:* Sadri, H., MacKeigan, L. D., Leiter, L. A., and Einarson, T. R. (2005). Willingness to pay for inhaled insulin: A contingent valuation approach. *PharmacoEconomics, 23*(12), p. 1220.

---

The participants were 30 university students and 30 community-dwelling older adults. The mean age of the young adults was 19.7 (2.2) years while the older adults was 70.6 (4.7) years.

*Source:* Gilmore, G. C., Spinks, R. A., and Thomas, C. W. (2006). Age effects in coding tasks: Componential analysis and test of the sensory deficit hypothesis. *Psychology and Aging, 21*(1), p. 9.

---

Lucid dream recall frequency was found to increase from a mean of .33, ($s = .55$) dreams per week before the program started to a mean of .74, ($s = 1.09$) after the program terminated. . . .

*Source:* Paulsson, T., and Parker, A. (2006). The effects of a two-week reflection-intention training program on lucid dream recall. *Dreaming, 16*(1), p. 25.

excerpt, the researchers put values for the standard deviation in parentheses after each mean, without a $\pm$ symbol. And in the last of these four excerpts, we see the single letter $s$ used to represent the standard deviation.

Excerpt 2.26 shows how information on the standard deviation can be included in a table. In this excerpt, each row of numbers corresponds to a different measuring instrument used within the researchers' study. The data in the first four rows came from scoring and then summarizing tests that were administered to the study's 79 children. The information in the fifth and sixth rows of the excerpt came from summarizing data collected from the children's parents on two social competence measures.

Although the standard deviation appears in research reports far more often than does any other measure of variability, a few researchers choose to describe the dispersion in their data sets by reporting the variance. Excerpt 2.27 is a case in

## EXCERPT 2.26 • *Reporting the Standard Deviation in a Table*

**TABLE 1**   *Descriptive Statistics for the Measure of Cognitive Ability and Social Competence*

| Measures | M | SD | Range |
|---|---|---|---|
| Reading Span | 2.84 | 0.80 | 2–5 |
| Digit Span | 5.80 | 1.98 | 2–11 |
| Inhibition | 50.94 | 6.95 | 33–76 |
| Verbal Ability | 109.46 | 12.86 | 65–134 |
| MCB | 1.71 | 0.21 | 1.02–1.95 |
| SSRS | 1.46 | 0.27 | 0.71–1.89 |

*Note:* MCB = My Child's Behavior social competence rating scale; SSRS = Social Skills Rating System.

*Source:* Tsethlikai, M., and Greenhoot, A. F. (2006). The influence of another's perspective on children's recall of previously misconstrued events. *Developmental Psychology, 42*(4), p. 737.

## EXCERPT 2.27 • *Using the Variance to Measure Dispersion*

In addition, the ε4+ group had a larger variance ($\sigma^2 = .32$) relative to the ε4− group ($\sigma^2 = .12$).

*Source:* Jacobson, M. W., Delis, D. C., Lansing, A., Houston, W., Olsen, R., Wetter, S., Bondi, M. W., and Salmon, D. P. (2005). Asymmetries in global-local processing ability in elderly people with the Apolipoprotein E-ε4 Allele. *Neuropsychology, 19*(6), p. 825.

point. Note that the researchers associated with this excerpt used the symbol $\sigma^2$ to represent this measure of variability.

Before concluding our discussion of the standard deviation and variance, I would like to offer a helpful hint concerning how to make sense out of these two indices of variability. Simply stated, I suggest using an article's reported standard deviation (or variance) to estimate what the range of scores probably was. Because the range is such a simple concept, the standard deviation or variance can be demystified by converting it into an estimated range.

To make a standard deviation interpretable, just multiply the reported value of this measure of variability by about 4 to obtain your guess as to what the range of the scores most likely was. Using 4 as the multiplier, this rule of thumb would tell you to guess that the range is equal to 20 for a set of scores in which the standard deviation is equal to 5. (If the research report were to indicate that the variance is equal to 9, you would first take the square root of 9 to get the standard deviation, and then you would multiply by 4 to arrive at a guess that the range was equal to 12.)

When giving you this rule of thumb, I have said that you should multiply the standard deviation by "about 4." To guess more accurately what the range most likely was in a researcher's data set, your multiplier will sometimes need to be a bit smaller or larger than 4. That's because the multiplier number needs to be adjusted on the basis of the number of scores on which the standard deviation is based. If there are 25 or so scores, use 4. If $N$ is near 100, multiply the standard deviation by 5. And if $N$ is gigantic, multiply by 6. With small $N$s, use a multiplier that is smaller than 4. With 10–20 scores in the group, multiplying by 3 works fairly well; when $N$ is smaller than 10, setting the multiplier equal to 2 usually produces a good guess as to range.

It may strike you as somewhat silly to be guessing the range based on the standard deviation. If researchers regularly included the values of the standard deviation and the range when summarizing their data (as was done in Excerpt 2.26), there would be no need to make a guess as to the size of $R$. Unfortunately, most researchers present only the standard deviation—and by itself, a standard deviation provides little insight into the degree of variability within a set of scores.

One final comment is in order regarding this technique of using $SD$ to guess $R$. What you will get is nothing more than a rough approximation, and you should not expect your guess of $R$ to "hit the nail on the head." Using the standard deviation and range presented in Excerpt 2.26 (and using a multiplier of 5 because the $n$ was 79), we see that our guess of $R$ is never perfect for any of the six rows of table in the excerpt. But each of our six guesses turns out to approximate well the actual range, and it would help us understand how much spread was in the data if only the standard deviation is presented.

## Other Measures of Variability

Of the five measures of variability discussed so far, you will encounter the range and the standard deviation most often when reading researcher-based journal articles. Occasionally, you will come across examples of the interquartile range, the semi-interquartile range, and the variance. And once in a great while, you will encounter some other measure of variability.

In Excerpt 2.28, we see a case where the *coefficient of variation* was used. As indicated within this excerpt, this measure of dispersion is nothing more than the standard deviation divided by the mean.

The coefficient of variation is useful when comparing the variability in two groups of scores where the means are known to be different. For example, suppose we wanted to determine which of two workers has the more consistent commuting time driving to work in the morning. If one of these workers lives five miles from work whereas the second lives 25 miles from work, a direct comparison of their

**EXCERPT 2.28 • *Coefficient of Variation***

Variability was measured using a coefficient of variation (standard deviation/mean) to remove the effect of the magnitude of the data from the description of error. . . . As expected, the variability of articulator movement and of VOT, as measured by the coefficient of variation, was greater in the children as compared with the adults.

*Source:* Grigos, M. I., Saxman, J. H., and Gordon, A. M. (2005). Speech motor development during acquisition of the voicing contrast. *Journal of Speech, Language & Hearing Research, 48*(4), p. 743.

standard deviations (each based on 100 days of commuting to work) would not yield a fair comparison because the worker with the longer commute would be expected to have more variability. What *would* be fair would be to divide each commuter's standard deviation by his or her mean. Such a measure of variability is called the coefficient of variation.

## Standard Scores

All of the techniques covered thus far in this chapter describe features of the entire data set. In other words, the focus of attention is on all $N$ scores whenever a researcher summarizes a group of numbers by using one of the available picture techniques, a word or number that reveals the distributional shape, a numerical index of central tendency, or a quantification of the amount of dispersion that exists among the scores. Sometimes, however, researchers want to focus their attention on a single score within the group rather than on the full data set. When they do this, they usually convert the raw score being examined into a **standard score.**

Although many different kinds of standard scores have been developed over the years, the ones used most frequently in research studies are called *z*-**scores** and *T*-**scores.** These two standard scores are identical in that each one indicates how many standard deviations a particular raw score lies above or below the group mean. In other words, the numerical value of the standard deviation is first looked upon as defining the length of an imaginary yardstick, with that yardstick then used to measure the distance between the group mean and the individual score being considered. For example, if you and several other people took a test that produced scores having a mean of 40 and a standard deviation of 8, and if your score on this test happened to be 52, you would be one and one-half yardsticks above the mean.

The two standard scores used most by researchers—*z*-scores and *T*-scores—perform exactly the same function. The only difference between them concerns the arbitrary values given to the new mean score and the length of the yardstick within the revised data set following conversion of one or more raw scores into standard scores. With *z*-scores, the mean is fixed at zero and the yardstick's length is set equal

Research
Navigator.com

*z*-scores
*T*-scores

to 1. As a consequence, a *z*-score directly provides an answer to the question, "How many *SD*s is a given score above or below the mean?" Thus a *z*-score of $+2.0$ indicates that the person being focused on was 2 standard deviations above the group mean. Likewise, a *z*-score of $-1.2$ for someone else indicates that this person scored 1.2 standard deviations below the mean. A *z*-score close to 0, of course, would indicate that the original raw score was near the group mean.

With *T*-scores, the original raw score mean and standard deviation are converted to 50 and 10, respectively. Thus a person whose raw score positioned him or her two standard deviations above the mean would receive a *T*-score of 70. Someone else positioned 1.2 standard deviations below the mean would end up with a *T*-score of 38. And someone whose raw score was near the group mean would have a *T*-score near 50.

Although researchers typically apply their statistical procedures to the raw scores that have been collected, they occasionally will convert the original scores into *z*-scores or *T*-scores. Excerpts 2.29 and 2.30 provide evidence that these two standard scores are sometimes referred to in research summaries.

### EXCERPTS 2.29–2.30 • *Standard Scores (z and T)*

Scores for each scale were transformed to *z* scores to facilitate comparison and analyses.

*Source:* Reynolds, S. J. (2006). Moral awareness and ethical predispositions: Investigating the role of individual differences in the recognition of moral issues. *Journal of Applied Psychology*, *91*(1), p. 236.

------------------------------------------------------------------------

Child behavior problems were assessed using the Child Behavior Checklist (CBCL), a 113-item, caregiver-report measure of child behavior problems [that] generates *T* scores ($M = 50$; $SD = 10$) for 3 summary scales (including total, internalizing, and externalizing behavioral problems) and 8 subscales (including attention problems, anxiety/depression, and withdrawal).

*Source:* Wade, S. L., Michaud, L., and Brown, T. M. (2006). Putting the pieces together: Preliminary efficacy of a family problem-solving intervention for children with traumatic brain injury. *Journal of Head Trauma Rehabilitation*, *21*(1), p. 61.

## A Few Cautions

Before concluding this chapter, I want to alert you to the fact that two of the terms discussed earlier are occasionally used by researchers who define them differently than I have. These two terms are *skewed* and *quartile*. I want to prepare you for the alternative meanings associated with these two concepts.

Regarding the term *skewed,* a few researchers use this word to describe a complete data set that is out of the ordinary. Used in this way, the term has nothing to do with the notion of distributional shape but instead is synonymous to the term *atypical.* In Excerpt 2.31, we see an example of how the word *skewed* was used in this fashion.

## EXCERPT 2.31 • *Use of the Term Skewed to Mean Unusual or Atypical*

This study is not without limitations. The low response rate and hence small sample size of adolescents with AS significantly limits the ability to make generalizations. Sample selection was another limitation. The AS group was informed about the nature of the study, which might have skewed the sample toward adolescents already suspected of having anxiety.

*Source:* Farrugia, S., and Hudson, J. (2006). Anxiety in adolescents with Asperger Syndrome: Negative thoughts, behavior problems, and life interference. *Focus on Autism and Other Developmental Disabilities, 21*(1), p. 33.

The formal, statistical definition of *quartile* is "one of three points that divide a group of scores into four subgroups, each of which contains 25 percent of the full group." Certain researchers use the term *quartile* to designate the subgroups themselves. In this usage there are four quartiles (not three), with scores falling in the quartiles. Excerpt 2.32 provides an example of *quartile* being used in this fashion.

## EXCERPT 2.32 • *Use of the Term Quartile to Designate Four Subgroups*

For the principal analyses reported here, we compared participants in the lowest quartile of frequency of exercise (<3 times/week) with those in the top 3 quartiles.

*Source:* Larson, E. B., Li, W., Bowen, J. D., McCormick, W. C., Teri, L., Crane, P., and Kukull, W. (2006). Exercise is associated with reduced risk for incident dementia among persons 65 years of age and older. *Annals of Internal Medicine, 144*(2), p. 76.

My second warning concerns the use of the term *average.* In elementary school, students are taught that (1) the average score is the mean score and (2) the median and the mode are *not* conceptually the same as the average. Unfortunately, you will have to undo your earlier learning if you're still under the impression that the words *average* and *mean* are synonymous.

In statistics, the term *average* is synonymous with the phrase "measure of central tendency," and either is nothing more than a generic label for *any* of several techniques that attempt to describe the typical or center score in a data set. Hence, if a researcher gives us information as to the "average score," we cannot be absolutely sure which average is being presented. It might be the mode, it might be the median, or it might be any of the many other kinds of average that can be computed. Nevertheless, you won't be wrong very often when you see the word "average" if you guess that reference is being made to the arithmetic mean. In Excerpt 2.33, for example, the average score is most likely a mean.

### EXCERPT 2.33 • *Use of the Term Average*

Participants were 1,400 North American women, with an average age of 19.5 ($SD = 5.87$).

*Source:* Williams, M. T., and Bonner, L. (2006). Sex education attitudes and outcomes among North American women. *Adolescence, 41*(161), p. 3.

Research
Navigator.com

Outliers

My final comment of the chapter concerns scores in a data set that lie far away from the rest of the scores. Such scores are called **outliers,** and they can come about because someone doesn't try when taking a test, doesn't understand the instructions, or consciously attempts to sabotage the researcher's investigation. Accordingly, researchers should (1) inspect their data sets to see if any outliers are present and (2) either discard such data points before performing any statistical analyses or perform analyses in two ways: with the outlier(s) included and with the outlier(s) excluded. In Excerpts 2.34 and 2.35, we see two cases in which data were examined for possible outliers. Notice how the researchers associated with these excerpts explained the rules they used to determine how deviant a score needed to be before it was tagged as an outlier. Also notice how these rules differed.

### EXCERPTS 2.34–2.35 • *Dealing with Outliers*

Of returned surveys, three were deleted due to being outliers—the mean of their total scores was at least three standard deviations above or below the mean; two were upper outliers and one was a lower outlier.

*Source:* Johnson, H. L., and Fullwood, H. L. (2006). Disturbing behaviors in the secondary classroom: How do general educators perceive problem behaviors? *Journal of Instructional Psychology, 33*(1), p. 23.

------------------------------------------------------------------------

Boxplots were used to identify outliers, defined as values >1.5 times the interquartile range away from the median. Identified outliers were removed from the data before statistical analysis of the differences between groups.

*Source:* Milner, C. E., Ferber, R., Pollard, C. D., Hamill, J., and Davis, I. S. (2006). Biomechanical factors associated with tibial stress fracture in female runners. *Medicine and Science in Sports and Exercise, 38*(2), p. 326.

If allowed to remain in a data set, outliers can create skewness and in other ways create problems for the researcher. Accordingly, the researchers who conducted the studies that appear in Excerpts 2.34 and 2.35 deserve credit for taking extra time to look for outliers before conducting any additional data analyses.

I should point out, however, that outliers potentially can be of legitimate interest in and of themselves. Instead of quickly tossing aside any outliers, researchers would be well advised to investigate any "weird cases" within their data sets. Even if the identified outliers have come about because of poorly understood directions, erratic measuring devices, low motivation, or effort to disrupt the study, researchers in these situations might ask the simple question, "Why did this occur?" More importantly, outliers that exist for other reasons have the potential, if considered thoughtfully, to provide insights into the genetic, psychological, and/or environmental factors that stand behind extremely high or low scores.

### One Final Excerpt

As we finish this chapter, I want you to look at one final excerpt. Although it is quite short and despite the fact that it contains no tables or pictures, I think this excerpt stands as a good example of how researchers should describe their data. Judge for yourself. Read Excerpt 2.36 and then ask yourself this simple question: Can you imagine what the data looked like?

### EXCERPT 2.36 • *A Good Descriptive Summary*

Mean scores were 23.5 ($SD = 6.6$) and 23.1 ($SD = 6.6$) on the MLQ Presence (MLQ–P) and Search (MLQ–S) subscales, respectively. Scores were slightly above but close to the midpoint of the scale (20). The shape of the distributions approximated normality, and scores were variable, as demonstrated by their standard deviations.

*Source:* Steger, M. F., Frazier, P., Oishi, S., and Kaler, M. (2006). The Meaning in Life Questionnaire: Assessing the presence of and search for meaning in life. *Journal of Counseling Psychology, 53*(1), p. 84.

### Review Terms

| | |
|---|---|
| Average | Distributional shape |
| Bar graph | Grouped frequency distribution |
| Bimodal | Heterogeneous |
| Bivariate | Histogram |
| Box-and-whisker plot | Homogeneous |
| Cumulative frequency distribution | Interquartile range |
| Dispersion | Kurtosis |

| | |
|---|---|
| Leptokurtic | Rectangular |
| Mean | Semi-interquartile range |
| Measure of central tendency | Sigma |
| Measure of variability | Simple frequency distribution |
| Median | Skewed distribution |
| Mesokurtic | Standard deviation |
| Mode | Standard score |
| Multimodal | Stem-and-leaf display |
| Negatively skewed | *T*-score |
| Normal distribution | Trimodal |
| Outlier | Ungrouped frequency distribution |
| Platykurtic | Univariate |
| Positively skewed | Variance |
| Quartile | *z*-score |
| Range | |

## *The Best Items in the Companion Website*

1. An email message from the author to his students explaining what a standard deviation really is (and what it is not).
2. An interactive online quiz (with immediate feedback provided) covering Chapter 2.
3. A challenging puzzle question created by the author for use with an interactive online resource called "Fun with Histograms."
4. Twelve misconceptions about the content of Chapter 2.
5. What the author considers to be the best passage from Chapter 2.

To access chapter objectives, practice tests, weblinks, and flashcards, visit the companion website at www.ablongman.com/huck5e.

## *Fun Exercises inside Research Navigator*

### 1. Do college men and women perceive "male sexual self-control" the same way?

In this study, 523 college students (193 male, 330 female) read 15 different vignettes describing a dating situation. In each vignette, things evolve to the point where a man attempts to have intercourse with his date, she resists, and then he considers various strategies to reduce her resistance. After reading each short vignette, the research participants were asked to rate the man's ability to stop himself. The rating scale extended from 0 to 100. After being averaged over the 15 vignettes, the participants' mean ratings were summarized (separately for each gender group) via (1) a grouped frequency distribution and (2) the three most popular measures of central tendency (the mean, median, and mode). How do you think the ratings provided by the 193 males compared to the ratings provided by the 330 females? To find out, locate the PDF version of the research report in the Helping Professions database of ContentSelect. Once you have this article in front of you, examine Table 1 on page 306.

M. Shively. Male self-control and sexual aggression. *Deviant Behavior*. Located in the HELPING PROFESSIONS database of ContentSelect.

## 2. What do police officers say when asked why they drink?

In this study, 749 state police officers from Australia responded to a survey that asked, among other things, what the officers considered to be the major reasons for drinking in the workplace. This was not an open-ended question; instead, 10 reasons for drinking (gleaned from the literature and focus groups) were listed. Four of these 10 reasons were: "To cope with stress," "To be a part of the team," "To wind down after shift," and "To celebrate special occasion." The survey respondents rated each of the 10 reasons on a 10-point scale. One of the four sample items presented above received the highest mean rating, the highest median rating, and the largest percentage of high ratings. None of the other three reasons for drinking came close to being the top choice. Which one do you think came in first place? To find out, locate the PDF version of the research report in the Helping Professions database of ContentSelect. Once you have this article in front of you, examine Table 2 on page 146.

J. D. Davey, P. L. Obst, & M. C. Sheehan. It goes with the job: Officers' insights into the impact of stress and culture on alcohol consumption within the police occupation. *Drugs: Education, Prevention and Policy*. Located in the HELPING PROFESSIONS database of ContentSelect.

**Review Questions and Answers begin on page 513.**

# Bivariate Correlation

In Chapter 2, we looked at the various statistical procedures that researchers use when they want to describe single-variable data sets. We saw examples where data on two or more variables were summarized, but in each of those cases the data were summarized one variable at a time. Although there are occasions when these univariate techniques permit researchers to describe their data sets, most empirical investigations involve questions that call for descriptive techniques that simultaneously summarize data on more than one variable.

In this chapter, we will consider situations in which data on two variables have been collected and summarized, with interest residing in the relationship between the two variables. Not surprisingly, the statistical procedures that we will examine here are considered to be **bivariate** in nature. In a later chapter, we will consider techniques designed for situations wherein the researcher wishes to simultaneously summarize the relationships among three or more variables.

Three preliminary points are worth mentioning as I begin my effort to help you refine your skills at deciphering statistical summaries of bivariate data sets. First, the focus in this chapter will be on techniques that simply summarize the data. In other words, we are still dealing with statistical techniques that are fully descriptive in nature. Second, this chapter is similar to Chapter 2 in that we consider ways to summarize data that involve both picture and numerical indices. Finally, the material covered in the next chapter, Reliability and Validity, draws *heavily* on the information presented here. With these introductory points now behind us, let us turn to the central concept of this chapter, correlation.

## The Key Concept behind Correlation: Relationship

Imagine that a researcher measures each of nine families with respect to two variables: average daily phone use (measured in minutes) and the number of teenagers within each family. The data for this imaginary group of families might turn out as follows:

| Family | Average Daily Phone Use (Minutes) | Number of Teenagers |
|---|---|---|
| Abbott | 75 | 2 |
| Donatelli | 100 | 3 |
| Edwards | 60 | 1 |
| Franks | 20 | 0 |
| Kawasaki | 70 | 2 |
| Jones | 120 | 4 |
| Lopez | 40 | 1 |
| Meng | 65 | 2 |
| Smith | 80 | 3 |

While it would be possible to look at each variable separately and say something about the central tendency, variability, and distributional shape of the nine scores (first for phone use, then for number of teenagers), the key concept of correlation requires that we look at the data on our two variables *simultaneously*. In doing this, we are trying to see (1) whether there is a **relationship** between the two sets of scores and (2) how strong or weak that relationship is, presuming that a relationship does in fact exist.

On a simple level, the basic question being dealt with by **correlation** can be answered in one of three possible ways. Within any bivariate data set, it *may* be the case that the high scores on the first variable tend to be paired with the high scores on the second variable (implying, of course, that low scores on the first variable tend to be paired with low scores on the second variable). I refer to this first possibility as the *high-high, low-low* case. The second possible answer to the basic correlational question represents the inverse of our first case. In other words, it *may* be the case that high scores on the first variable tend to be paired with low scores on the second variable (implying, of course, that low scores on the first variable tend to be paired with high scores on the second variable). My shorthand summary phrase for this second possibility is *high-low, low-high*. Finally, it is possible that little systematic tendency exists in the data at all. In other words, it *may* be the case that some of the high and low scores on the first variable are paired with high scores on the second variable while other high and low scores on the first variable are paired with low scores on the second variable. I refer to this third possibility simply by the three-word phrase *little systematic tendency*.

As a check on whether I have been clear in the previous paragraph, take another look at the hypothetical data presented earlier on the number of teenagers and amount of phone use within each of nine families. More specifically, indicate how that bivariate relationship should be labeled. Does it deserve the label *high-high, low-low*? Or the label *high-low, low-high*? Or the label *little systematic tendency*? If you haven't done so already, look again at the data presented and formulate your answer to this question.

To discern the nature of the relationship between phone use and number of teenagers, one must first identify each variable's high and low scores. The top three values for the phone use variable are 120, 100, and 80, while the lowest three values in this same column are 60, 40, and 20. Within the second column, the top three values are 4, 3, and 3; the three lowest values are 1, 1, and 0. After identifying each variable's high and low scores, the next (and final) step is to look at both columns of data simultaneously and see which of the three answers to the basic correlational question fits the data. For our hypothetical data set, we clearly have a *high-high, low-low* situation, with the three largest phone-use values being paired with the three largest number-of-teenagers values and the three lowest values in either column being paired with the low values in the other column.

The method I have used to find out what kind of relationship describes our hypothetical data set is instructive, I hope, for anyone not familiar with the core concept of correlation. That strategy, however, is not very sophisticated. Moreover, you won't have a chance to use it very often because researchers will almost always summarize their bivariate data sets by means of pictures, a single numerical index, a descriptive phrase, or some combination of these three reporting techniques. Let us now turn our attention to these three methods for summarizing the nature and strength of bivariate relationships.

## Scatter Diagrams

*method for summarizing the nature & strength of bivariate relationships*

Like histograms and bar graphs, a **scatter diagram** has a horizontal axis and a vertical axis. These axes are labeled to correspond to the two variables involved in the correlational analysis. The abscissa is marked off numerically so as to accommodate the obtained scores collected by the researcher on the variable represented by the horizontal axis; in a similar fashion, the **ordinate** is labeled so as to accommodate the obtained scores on the other variable. (With correlation, the decision as to which variable is put on which axis is fully arbitrary; the nature of the relationship between the two variables will be revealed regardless of how the two axes are labeled.) After the axes are set up, the next step involves placing a dot into the scatter diagram for each object that was measured, with the horizontal and vertical positioning of each dot dictated by the scores earned by that object on the two variables involved in the study.

In Excerpt 3.1, we see the raw data and a scatter diagram associated with a recent election in North Carolina. For each of the 28 counties in the First Congressional District, the researchers found out two things: (1) the percentage of black voters who were registered and (2) the percentage of votes cast for black candidates. Those data are presented as numbers in Table 3 and then as dots within Figure 1. The dot in the scatter diagram that is furthest to the right came from

**EXCERPT 3.1** • *Raw Data and a Scatter Diagram*

**TABLE 3** *North Carolina First Congressional District Democratic Primary*

| County | % of Black Voters Registered | % of Votes Cast for Black Candidates | County | % of Black Voters Registered | % of Votes Cast for Black Candidates |
|---|---|---|---|---|---|
| Wayne | 8.4 | 11.7 | Nash | 49.7 | 60.9 |
| Beaufort | 22.6 | 34.2 | Northampton | 53.4 | 49.7 |
| Columbus | 29.4 | 71.3 | Warren | 55.1 | 70.0 |
| Chowan | 31.0 | 36.4 | Vance | 55.3 | 66.2 |
| Perquimans | 33.4 | 37.8 | Pender | 55.4 | 68.3 |
| Bladen | 35.8 | 58.7 | Hertford | 55.4 | 49.6 |
| Greene | 36.0 | 21.8 | Pasquotank | 55.7 | 63.8 |
| Martin | 39.5 | 31.1 | Bertie | 55.7 | 56.2 |
| Pitt | 42.1 | 33.5 | Halifax | 61.0 | 65.8 |
| Washington | 42.2 | 41.7 | Lenoir | 61.1 | 51.7 |
| Duplin | 43.3 | 51.5 | Wilson | 61.3 | 72.5 |
| Craven | 45.2 | 46.7 | New Hanover | 61.8 | 88.8 |
| Gates | 45.2 | 37.2 | Cumberland | 67.4 | 80.6 |
| Jones | 48.5 | 56.2 | Edgecombe | 72.4 | 79.0 |

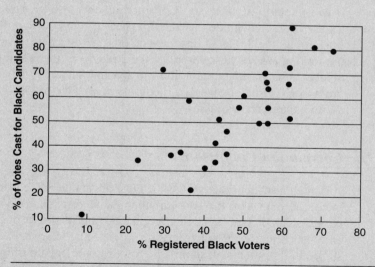

**FIGURE 1** *Black Voting in North Carolina First Congressional District*

*Source:* Clayton, D. M., and Stallings, A. M. (2000). Black women in Congress: Striking the balance. *Journal of Black Studies, 30*(4), pp. 593–594.

Edgecombe County where the two percentages were 72.4 and 79.0. Due to the way the axes were set up, that county's dot was positioned so as to correspond with 72.4 on the abscissa and 79.0 on the ordinate. All other dots in this scatter diagram were positioned in a similar fashion.

A scatter diagram reveals the relationship between two variables through the pattern that is formed by the full set of dots. To discern what pattern exists, I use a simple (though not completely foolproof) two-step method. First, I draw an imaginary perimeter line, or "fence" around the full set of data points—and in so doing, I try to achieve a tight fit. Second, I look at the shape produced by this perimeter line and examine its tilt and its thickness. Depending on these two characteristics of the data set's scatter, I arrive at an answer to the basic correlational question concerning the nature and strength of the relationship between the two variables.

Consider once again the scatter diagram shown in Excerpt 3.1. Our perimeter line produces a rough oval that is tilted from lower-left to upper-right. Tilts going in this direction imply a *high-high, low-low* relationship, whereas tilts going in the opposite direction, from upper-left to lower-right, imply a *high-low, low-high* relationship. (In cases where there is no discernible tilt to the shape produced by the perimeter line, there is little systematic tendency one way or the other.)

After establishing the tilt of the oval produced by our perimeter line, I then turn to the issue of the oval's thickness. If the oval is elongated and thin, then I conclude that there is a *strong* relationship between the two variables. On the other hand, if the oval is not too much longer than it is wide, then I conclude that a *weak* relationship exists. Considering one last time the scatter diagram in Excerpt 3.1, I conclude that the thickness of the oval produced by the perimeter line around the 34 dots falls between these two extremes; accordingly, I feel that the term *moderate* best describes the strength of the relationship that is visually displayed. Combining the notions of tilt and thickness, I feel that the scatter diagram in Excerpt 3.1 reveals a moderate *high-high, low-low* relationship between the two measured variables.

## The Correlation Coefficient

Although a scatter diagram has the clear advantage of showing the scores for each measured object on the two variables of interest, many journals are reluctant to publish such pictures because they take up large amounts of space. For that reason, and also because the interpretation of a scatter diagram involves an element of subjectivity, numerical summaries of bivariate relationships appear in research reports far more frequently than do pictorial summaries. The numerical summary is called a **correlation coefficient.**

Symbolized as *r*, a correlation coefficient is normally reported as a decimal number somewhere between −1.00 and +1.00. In Excerpts 3.2 and 3.3, we see examples of correlation coefficients.

## EXCERPTS 3.2–3.3 • *Correlation Coefficients*

The total knowledge score was significantly correlated with the use of self-regulation skills ($r = .54$), but not with the other SCT variables.

*Source:* Suminski, R. R., and Petosa, R. (2006). Web-assisted instruction for changing social cognitive variables related to physical activity. *Journal of American College Health, 54*(4), p. 221.

However, time since injury was negatively associated ($r = -0.68$) with reaching one's initial goals.

*Source:* Wade, S. L., Michaud, L., and Brown, T. M. (2006). Putting the pieces together: Preliminary efficacy of a family problem-solving intervention for children with traumatic brain injury. *Journal of Head Trauma Rehabilitation, 21*(1), p. 63.

To help you learn how to interpret correlation coefficients, I have drawn a straight horizontal line to represent the continuum of possible values that will result from researchers putting data into a correlational formula:

$$-1.00 \qquad 0.00 \qquad +1.00$$

This correlational continuum will help you pin down the meaning of several adjectives that researchers use when talking about correlation coefficients and/or relationships: direct, high, indirect, inverse, low, moderate, negative, perfect, positive, strong, and weak.

First, consider the two halves of the correlational continuum. Any *r* that falls on the right side represents a **positive correlation;** this indicates a **direct relationship** between the two measured variables. (Earlier, I referred to such cases by the term *high-high, low-low.*) On the other hand, any result that ends up on the left side is a **negative correlation,** and this indicates an **indirect,** or **inverse, relationship** (i.e., *high-low, low-high*). If *r* were to land on either end of our correlation continuum, the term **perfect** could be used to describe the obtained correlation. The term **high** comes into play when *r* assumes a value close to either end (thus implying a **strong** relationship); conversely, the term **low** is used when *r* lands close to the middle of the continuum (thus implying a **weak** relationship). Not surprisingly, any *r* that ends up in the middle area of the left or right sides of our continuum will be called **moderate.**

In Excerpts 3.4 through 3.6, we see cases where researchers used adjectives to label their *r*s. In the first two of these excerpts, we see the concepts of weak and moderate being used to describe correlation coefficients. In the third excerpt, we see the concept of strong being used. Excerpt 3.6 is especially instructive because it shows that both positive and negative correlations are considered to be strong if they are far away from zero.

Before concluding our discussion of how to interpret correlation coefficients, I feel obligated to reiterate the point that when the issue of relationship is addressed,

### EXCERPTS 3.4–3.6 • *Use of Modifying Adjectives for the Term Correlation*

When the patients' scores on ASASFA were compared with their scores on the ADAS, the correlation ($r = 0.18$) was weak.

*Source:* McAdam, J. L., Stotts, N. A., Padilla, G., and Puntillo, A. (2005). Attitudes of critically ill Filipino patients and their families toward advance directives. *American Journal of Critical Care, 14*(1), p. 22.

---

The internalizing problem scale and the externalizing problem scale intercorrelated moderately ($r = .37$).

*Source:* Rönnlund, M., and Karlsson, E. (2006). The relation between dimensions of attachment and internalizing or externalizing problems during adolescence. *Journal of Genetic Psychology, 167*(1), p. 53.

---

Correlations between plasma caffeine and changes in performance were inconclusive, with the exception of a strong positive correlation with tackle sprint speed ($r = 0.63$) and a strong negative correlation with Drive 1 power ($r = -0.80$).

*Source:* Stuart, G. R., Hopkins, W. G., Cook, C., and Cairns, S. P. (2005). Multiple effects of caffeine on simulated high-intensity team-sport performance. *Medicine and Science in Sports and Exercise, 37*(11), p. 2001.

the central question being answered by $r$ is: "To what extent are the high scores of one variable paired with the high scores of the other variable?" The term *high* in this question is considered separately for each variable. Hence, a strong positive correlation can exist even though the mean of the scores of one variable is substantially different from the mean of the scores on the other variable. As proof of this claim, consider again the data presented earlier on nine families who had varying numbers of teenagers and also varying amounts of phone use; the correlation between the two sets of scores turns out equal to $+.96$ despite the fact that the two means are quite different (2 versus 70). This example makes clear, I hope, the fact that a correlation does *not* deal with the question of whether two means are similar or different.[1]

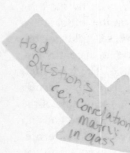

Had question re: Correlation matrix in class

## The Correlation Matrix

When interest resides in the bivariate relationship between just two variables or among a small number of variables, researchers will typically present their $r$s within the text of their article. (This reporting strategy was used in Excerpts 3.2 through 3.6.)

[1]In many research studies, the focus is on the difference between means. Later, our discussion of $t$-test and $F$-tests will show how researchers compare means.

Research Navigator.c⊛m

Correlation matrix

When interest centers on the bivariate relationships among many variables, however, the resulting *r*s will often be summarized within a special table called a **correlation matrix.**

It should be noted that *several* bivariate correlations can be computed among a set of variables, even for relatively *small* sets of variables. With six variables, for example, 15 separate bivariate *r*s can be computed. With 10 variables, there will be 45 *r*s. In general, the number of bivariate correlations is equal to $k(k-1)/2$, where *k* indicates the number of variables.

In Excerpt 3.7, we see a correlation matrix that summarizes the measured bivariate relationships among five variables. In the study associated with this excerpt, 344 college students in Taiwan responded to an inventory focused on the way people respond to stressful events. The inventory produced five scores, or factors, for each of the college students, with each of these scores corresponding to a mechanism used by people in the face of traumatic events. As you can see, this correlation matrix contains *r*s arranged in a triangle. Each *r* indicates the correlation between the two variables that label that *r*'s row and column. For example, the value of .37 is the correlation between Family Support and Religious/Spirituality.

### EXCERPT 3.7 • *A Standard Correlation Matrix*

**TABLE 2**   *Intercorrelations among Factors of the CCS*

| Factor | 1 | 2 | 3 | 4 | 5 |
|---|---|---|---|---|---|
| 1. Acceptance, Reframing, and Striving | — | | | | |
| 2. Family Support | .33 | — | | | |
| 3. Religious/Spirituality | .13 | .37 | — | | |
| 4. Avoidance and Detachment | .15 | .02 | .05 | — | |
| 5. Private Emotional Outlets | .28 | .34 | .34 | .29 | — |

*Note:* CSS = Collectivist Coping Styles

*Source:* Heppner, P. P., Heppner, M. J., Lee, D., Wang, Y., Park, H., and Wang, L. (2006). Development and validation of a collectivist coping styles inventory. *Journal of Counseling Psychology,* 53(1), p. 113.

Two things are noteworthy about the correlation matrix shown in Excerpt 3.7. First, when a row and a column refer to the same variable (as is the case with the top row and the left column, the second row and the second column, etc.), there is no correlation positioned at the intersection of that row and column. Instead, a dash has been put in each of those spots. This simply indicates that no one cares about the correlation of a variable with itself. (Such correlations, if they were computed, would be guaranteed to be equal to 1.00.)

− 1.0 invrse
+ 1.0 direct
0 weak

The second thing to notice about the correlation matrix in Excerpt 3.7 is that there are no correlation coefficients above the diagonal formed by the dashes. If correlations did appear there, they would be a mirror image of the *r*s positioned below the diagonal. The value .33 would appear on the top row in the second column, .13 would appear on the top row in the third column, and so on. Such *r*s, if they were put into the correlation matrix, would be fully redundant with the *r*s that already are present; accordingly, they would add nothing.

In Excerpt 3.7, the correlation matrix was set up with the 10 bivariate correlation coefficients positioned below the diagonal of the dashes. At times, you will come across a correlation matrix in which (1) the values of the correlation coefficients are positioned above rather than below the diagonal or (2) each diagonal element has either 1.00 or nothing at all. Such alternative presentations should not cause you any difficulty, for they still will contain all possible bivariate correlations which are interpreted in the same way that we interpreted the *r*s in Excerpt 3.7.

Now consider the correlation matrix in Excerpt 3.8. On first glance, this one seems just like the one in Excerpt 3.7 because each of these correlation matrices has five rows and five columns of correlation coefficients. However, if you look closely at Excerpt 3.8, you will notice two things. First, the variable names used to label the rows are not exactly the same as those used to label the columns. The variable called Math, which labels the top row, does not appear as a label for any of the columns. Similarly, the variable called Spelling, which labels the right column, does not appear as a label for any of the rows. Second, the diagonal is filled with correlation coefficients.

If the correlation matrix in Excerpt 3.8 had been set up with a bottom row called Spelling and a left column called Math, it would have resembled the first correlation matrix we considered, except this one would have nothing at all in the

**EXCERPT 3.8 • *A Correlation Matrix with One Row and One Column Deleted***

**TABLE 3**   *Correlations among Self-Perception Items*

|  | Science | Social Studies | Reading | English | Spelling |
|---|---|---|---|---|---|
| Math | .306 | .297 | .217 | .318 | .265 |
| Science |  | .429 | .252 | .337 | .241 |
| Social Studies |  |  | .331 | .386 | .299 |
| Reading |  |  |  | .483 | .369 |
| English |  |  |  |  | .429 |

*Source:* Swiatek, M. A. (2005). Gifted students' self-perceptions of ability in specific subject domains: Factor structure and relationship with above 3-level test scores. *Roeper Review,* 27(2), p. 106.

diagonal. However, nothing would be gained by the addition of those new rows and columns. That's because neither the new bottom row nor the new left column would have any entries. (If you look again at Excerpt 3.7, you will discover that one row and one column did not contain any correlation coefficients of interest.)

Occasionally, researchers will set up their correlation matrices like the one in Excerpt 3.8. By deleting one empty row and one column, a little space is saved. Knowing that this is sometimes done, you must be careful when trying to figure out how many variables were involved; simply counting the number of rows (or columns) may cause you to end up one variable short.

Excerpt 3.9 illustrates how two correlation matrices can be combined into one table. In the study associated with this table, a personality inventory that yields five main scores (for emotional stability, extroversion, openness, agreeableness, and conscientiousness) was administered to a group of 162 undergraduates twice, once in a paper-and-pencil format and once over the Internet. After collecting the data, the researchers computed bivariate correlation coefficients among the personality dimensions. They did this twice, once using the data from the paper-and-pencil version and then again using data from the online version. Using the note beneath the correlation matrix as a guide, we can look to see if the bivariate correlation between any two dimensions was influenced very much by the way the personality inventory was administered. For example, the correlation between openness and extroversion was .54 in the Internet version compared to .51 in the paper-and-pencil version.

**EXCERPT 3.9 • *Two Correlation Matrices Combined into One Table***

**TABLE 2** *Intercorrelations among the Big Five Personality Dimensions in the Paper-and-Pencil and Internet-Based Versions*

| | *ES* | *EX* | *OP* | *AG* | *CO* |
|---|---|---|---|---|---|
| ES | — | .32 | .15 | .17 | −.08 |
| EX | .27 | — | .54 | .00 | .03 |
| OP | .11 | .51 | — | .00 | .08 |
| AG | .20 | −.06 | −.08 | — | −.08 |
| CO | −.13 | .01 | .12 | −.10 | — |

*Note:* Correlations below the diagonal correspond to the paper-and-pencil version and the correlations above the diagonal correspond to the Internet-based version. $N = 162$.

*Source:* Salgado, J. F., and Moscoso, S. (2003). Internet-based personality testing: Equivalence of measures and assessees' perceptions and reactions. *International Journal of Selection & Assessment, 11*(2/3), p. 199.

Now consider Excerpt 3.10. This correlation matrix is different in two ways from the others we have examined. First, the mean and standard deviation are

## EXCERPT 3.10 • *A Correlation Matrix with Means and Standard Deviations*

**TABLE 3** *Descriptive Statistics and Intercorrelations for Study Variables*

| Variable | M | SD | 1 | 2 | 3 | 4 | 5 |
|---|---|---|---|---|---|---|---|
| 1. Injuries | 13.91 | 4.25 | — | | | | |
| 2. Safety Events | 22.83 | 7.33 | .68 | — | | | |
| 3. Safety Climate | 34.00 | 5.74 | −.42 | −.47 | — | | |
| 4. Safety Consciousness | 3.96 | 0.69 | −.26 | −.29 | .63 | — | |
| 5. Passive Leadership | 2.19 | 0.99 | .33 | .41 | −.57 | −.45 | — |
| 6. Transformational Leadership | 3.08 | 0.90 | −.24 | −.22 | .56 | .41 | −.48 |

*Source:* Kelloway, E. K., Mullen, J., and Francis, L. (2006). Divergent effects of transformational and passive leadership on employee safety. *Journal of Occupational Health Psychology, 11*(1), p. 8.

presented for each of the six study variables. Second, there are six rows but only five columns in the correlation matrix part of the table. All bivariate *r*s are presented, however. The researchers did not deprive us of anything by failing to include a sixth column (labeled 6) in the correlation matrix. Had they included it, the only thing in it would have been a dash.

# Different Kinds of Correlational Procedures

In this section, we take a brief look at several different correlational procedures that have been developed. As you will see, all of these techniques are similar in that they are designed for the case in which data have been collected on two variables.[2] These bivariate correlational techniques differ, however, in the nature of the two variables. In light of this important difference, you need to learn a few things about how variables differ.

The first important distinction that needs to be made in our discussion of variables is between quantitative and qualitative characteristics. With a **quantitative variable,** the targets of the measuring process vary as to how much of the characteristic is possessed. In contrast, a **qualitative variable** comes into play when the things being measured vary from one another in terms of the categorical group to

[2]Some authors use the term **zero-order correlation** when referring to bivariate correlations. They do this to distinguish this simplest kind of correlation—that involves data on just two variables—from other kinds of correlations that involve data on three or more variables (such as partial correlations, multiple correlations, and canonical correlations).

which they belong relative to the characteristic of interest. Thus if we focus our attention on people's heights, we have a quantitative variable (because some people possess more "tallness" than others). If, on the other hand, we focus our attention on people's favorite national park, we would be dealing with a qualitative variable (because people simply fall into categories based on which park they like best).

From the standpoint of correlation, quantitative variables can manifest themselves in one of two ways in the data a researcher collects. Possibly, the only thing the researcher will want to do is order individuals (or animals, or objects, or whatever) from the one possessing the greatest amount of the relevant characteristic to the one possessing the least. The numbers used to indicate ordered position normally are assigned such that 1 goes to the person with the greatest amount of the characteristic, 2 goes to the person with the second greatest amount, and so on. Such numbers are called **ranks** and are said to represent an **ordinal** scale of measurement. A researcher's data would also be ordinal in nature if each person or thing being measured is put into one of several ordered categories, with everyone who falls into the same category given the same score. (For example, the numbers 1, 2, 3, and 4 could be used to represent freshmen, sophomores, juniors, and seniors.)

With a second kind of quantitative variable, measurements are more precise. Here, the score associated with each person supposedly reveals how much of the characteristic of interest is possessed by that individual—and it does this without regard for the standing of any other measured person. Whereas ranks constitute data that provide relative comparisons, this second (and more precise) way of dealing with quantitative variables provide absolute comparisons. In this book, we will use the term **raw score** to refer to any piece of data that provides an absolute (rather than relative) assessment of one's standing on a quantitative variable.[3]

Qualitative variables come in two main varieties. If the subgroups into which people are classified truly have no quantitative connection with each other, then the variable corresponding to those subgroups is said to be **nominal** in nature. Your favorite academic subject, the brand of jelly you most recently used, and your state of residence exemplify this kind of variable. If there are only two categories associated with the qualitative variable, then the variable of interest is said to be **dichotomous** in nature. A dichotomous variable actually can be viewed as a special case of the nominal situation, with examples being "course outcome" in courses where the only grades are pass and fail (or credit and no credit), gender, party affiliation during primary elections, and graduation status following four years of college.

In Excerpts 3.11 through 3.14, we see examples of different kinds of variables. The first two of these excerpts illustrate the two kinds of quantitative variables we have discussed: ranks and raw scores. The last two of these excerpts

---

[3]Whereas most statisticians draw a distinction between interval and ratio measurement scales and between discrete and continuous variables, readers of journal articles do not need to understand the technical differences between these terms in order to decipher research reports.

## EXCERPTS 3.11–3.14 • *Different Kinds of Data*

The third step of the interview asked participants to rank, from best to worst, a set of randomly presented cards representing four health states: (a) your health, (b) mild stuttering, (c) moderate stuttering, and (d) severe stuttering.

*Source:* Bramlett, R. E., Bothe, A. K., and Franic, D. M. (2006). Using preference-based measures to assess quality of life in stuttering. *Journal of Speech, Language, and Hearing Research, 49*(2) p. 386.

-----------------------------------------------------------------------------------

We obtained sleep data by using Actiwatch (Mini Mitter, Bend, Oregon) activity monitors, which detected each participant's movement. . . . Reported as a percentage, sleep efficiency is defined as the total sleep time divided by the total time in bed multiplied by 100.

*Source:* Arora, V., Dunphy, C., Chang, V. Y., Ahmad, F., Humphrey, H. J., and Meltzer, D. (2006). The effects of on-duty napping on intern sleep time and fatigue. *Annals of Internal Medicine, 144*(11), p. 793.

-----------------------------------------------------------------------------------

The predictor variable race was a polytomous variable with four levels, as defined by the RSA in the national database (White, Black, American Indian or Alaskan Native, and Asian or Pacific Islander).

*Source:* Rogers, J. B., Bishop, M., and Crystal, R. M. (2005). Predicting rehabilitation outcome for supplemental security income and social security disability income recipients: Implications for consideration with the ticket to work program. *Journal of Rehabilitation, 71*(3), p. 8.

-----------------------------------------------------------------------------------

The type of school each student attended (public or parochial) was assessed, and a dichotomous score for school type was created, with 1 representing public schools.

*Source:* Nichols, T. R., Graber, J. A., Brooks-Gunn, J., and Botvin, G. J. (2006). Ways to say no: Refusal skill strategies among urban adolescents. *American Journal of Health Behavior, 30*(3), p. 230.

exemplify qualitative variables (the first being a four-category nominal variable, the second being a dichotomous variable).

Researchers frequently will derive a raw score for each individual being studied by combining that individual's responses to the separate questions in a test or survey. As Excerpts 3.15 and 3.16 show, the separate items can each be ordinal or even dichotomous in nature, and yet the sum of those item scores is looked upon as being what I have called a raw score. Although theoretical statistical authorities argue back and forth as to whether it is prudent to generate raw scores by combining ordinal or dichotomous data, doing so is an extremely common practice among applied researchers.

### EXCERPTS 3.15–3.16 • *Combining Ordinal or Dichotomous Data to Get Raw Scores*

The resultant 31-item SES was scored on a 1- to 4-point Likert scale (1 = *never,* 2 = *seldom,* 3 = *fairly often,* 4 = *frequently*). A student's total score was determined by summing the responses on the 31 items, for a scale range of 31 to 124.

*Source:* Phillips, K. A., and Barrow, L. H. (2006). Investigating high school students' science experiences and mechanics understanding. *School Science & Mathematics, 106*(4), p. 204.

---

The VR-based pre-test and VR-based post-test that were employed in this study were computer based. Each test consisted of 15 questions and aimed to assess the learners' understanding of traffic rules and traffic signs. . . . For each question, participants received a score of either 1 (correct answer) or 0 (incorrect answer), and a total score ranging from 0 to 15.

*Source:* Chwen, J. C., Seong, C. T., and Wan Moh, F. W. I. (2005). Are learning styles relevant to virtual reality? *Journal of Research on Technology in Education, 38*(2), p. 128.

One final kind of variable needs to be briefly mentioned. Sometimes a researcher will begin with a quantitative variable but then classify individuals into two categories on the basis of how much of the characteristic of interest is possessed. For example, a researcher conceivably could measure people in terms of the quantitative variable of height, place each individual into a tall or short category, and then disregard the initial measurements of height (that took the form of ranks or raw scores). Whenever this is done, the researcher transforms quantitative data into a two-category qualitative state. The term **artificial dichotomy** is used to describe the final data set. An example of this kind of data conversion appears in Excerpt 3.17.

### EXCERPT 3.17 • *Creating an Artificial Dichotomy*

Maternal reports of annual household income were used as a marker for socioeconomic disadvantage. Respondents were given a list of income ranges (e.g., $21,000–$23,999) from "no income" to "$150,000 and over" and were asked to choose the range in which their annual household income fell. Annual household income was made into a dichotomous variable for model-fitting analyses, using $24,000 as a cut point. This created a "high" income group ($24,000 and over) and a "low" income group ($0–$23,999).

*Source:* Cronk, N. J., Slutske, W. S., Madden, P. A. F., Bucholz, K. K., and Heath, A. C. (2004). Risk for separation anxiety disorder among girls: Paternal absence, socioeconomic disadvantage, and genetic vulnerability. *Journal of Abnormal Psychology, 113*(2), p. 240.

Research
Navigator.c⊕m

Pearson's
product-moment
correlation

## Pearson's Product-Moment Correlation

The most frequently used bivariate correlational procedure is called **Pearson's product-moment correlation.** It is designed for the situation in which (1) each of the two variables is quantitative in nature and (2) each variable is measured so as to produce raw scores. The scatter diagram presented earlier in Excerpt 3.1 provides a good example of the kind of bivariate situation that is dealt with by means of Pearson's technique.

Excerpts 3.18, 3.19, and 3.20 illustrate the use of this extremely popular bivariate correlational technique. Note, in the second of these excerpts, that the label "Pearson" is used by itself without the follow-up phrase "product-moment." In the third excerpt, note that only the symbol $r$ is presented, and there is no adjective such as Pearson's, Pearson's product-moment, or product-moment. (In cases like this, where the symbol $r$ stands by itself without a clarifying label, it's a good bet you're looking at a Pearson product-moment correlation coefficient.)

### EXCERPTS 3.18–3.20 • *Pearson's Product-Moment Correlation*

The Pearson product-moment correlation coefficients of the participants' MTEBI and STEBI scores and math anxiety scores were calculated to explain the possible relationships between these variables.

*Source:* Bursal, M., and Paznokas, L. (2006). Mathematics anxiety and preservice elementary teachers' confidence to teach mathematics and science. *School Science & Mathematics, 106*(4), p. 175.

-----

First, Pearson correlation coefficients were calculated for the physical performance measures (SMW, TUG, and STR) and all of the psychosocial and mechanical variables.

*Source:* Maly, M. R., Costigan, P. A., and Olney, S. J. (2005). Contribution of psychosocial and mechanical variables to physical performance measures in knee osteoarthritis. *Physical Therapy, 85*(12), p. 1323.

-----

BD [body dissatisfaction] and DT [drive for thinness] scores correlated ($r = .72$ in females and $r = .65$ in males).

*Source:* Keski-Rahkonen, A., Bulik, C. M., Neale, B. M., Rose, R. J., Rissanen, A., and Kaprio, J. (2005). Body dissatisfaction and drive for thinness in young adult twins. *International Journal of Eating Disorders, 37*(3), p. 191.

## Spearman's Rho and Kendall's Tau

The second most popular bivariate correlational technique is called **Spearman's rho.** This kind of correlation is similar to the one we just discussed (Pearson's) in that it is appropriate for the situation in which both variables are quantitative in

nature. With Spearman's technique, however, each of the two variables is measured in such a way as to produce ranks. This correlational technique often goes by the name **rank-order correlation** (instead of Spearman's rho). The resulting correlation coefficient, if symbolized, is usually referred to as $r_s$ or $\rho$.

In Excerpt 3.21, we see two sets of ranks. This table comes from an article in which the researchers wanted to see what kinds of medical problems plagued psychiatry patients who had been seen in emergency departments of hospitals. There were two groups of psychiatric patients: (1) those whose primary problem was psychiatric in nature and (2) those whose primary problem was nonpsychiatric. What the researchers ranked within each of these two groups was the co-occurrence of various medical problems. If we correlate the two sets of ranks in Excerpt 3.21, using Spearman's rho, it turns out that $r_s = .89$. (If you scan the two sets of ranks in the excerpt, you should be able to see a *high-high, low-low* relationship.)

## EXCERPT 3.21 • *Two Sets of Ranks*

**TABLE 2**  *Percentage of Patients in Each Medical Category with Either a Primary or Secondary Psychiatric Diagnosis*

| Medical category | Patients with a psychiatric diagnosis as primary | | | Patients with a psychiatric diagnosis as secondary | | |
|---|---|---|---|---|---|---|
| | Rank | $\%^a$ | n | Rank | $\%^b$ | n |
| Circulatory | 1 | 12.61 | 104 | 1.5 | 13.71 | 71 |
| Endocrine | 2 | 7.64 | 63 | 3 | 9.65 | 50 |
| Respiratory | 3 | 3.27 | 27 | 4 | 9.46 | 49 |
| Digestive | 4.5 | 2.42 | 20 | 1.5 | 13.71 | 71 |
| Musculoskeletal | 4.5 | 2.42 | 20 | 5 | 7.92 | 41 |
| Nervous system | 6 | 1.58 | 13 | 7.5 | 4.63 | 24 |
| Infections | 7 | 1.33 | 11 | 6 | 6.18 | 32 |
| Blood | 8 | 1.09 | 9 | 10.5 | 2.12 | 11 |
| Genitourinary | 9.5 | 0.49 | 4 | 9 | 4.05 | 21 |
| Skin | 9.5 | 0.49 | 4 | 10.5 | 2.12 | 11 |
| Congenital | 11.5 | 0.12 | 1 | 7.5 | 4.63 | 24 |
| Neoplasms | 11.5 | 0.12 | 1 | 13 | 0.39 | 2 |
| Pregnancy | 13 | 0.00 | 0 | 12 | 1.35 | 7 |

[a]Percentage of patients with a primary psychiatric diagnosis and no secondary psychiatric diagnosis.
[b]Percentage of patients with a secondary psychiatric diagnosis and no primary psychiatric diagnosis.

*Source:* Kunen, S., Niederhauser, R., Smoth, P. O., Morris, J. A., and Marx, B. D. (2005). Race disparities in psychiatric rates in emergency departments. *Journal of Consulting and Clinical Psychology, 73*(1), p. 121. (Modified slightly for presentation here.)

Only rarely will a researcher display the actual ranks utilized to compute Spearman's rho. Most of the time, the only information you will be given will be (1) the specification of the two variables being correlated and (2) the resulting correlation coefficient. Excerpts 3.22 and 3.23, therefore, are more typical of what you will see in published journal articles than is the material in Excerpt 3.21.

### EXCERPTS 3.22–3.23 • *Spearman's Rank-Order Correlation*

Spearman's rank correlation coefficients were used to determine the correlation between the clinic-based gait velocity over 10 m and the overall time it took to complete the community walking course.

*Source:* Taylor, D., Stretton, C. M., Mudge, S., and Garrett, N. (2006). Does clinic-measured gait speed differ from gait speed measured in the community in people with stroke? *Clinical Rehabilitation, 20*(5), p. 440.

-----------------------------------------------------------------------------

Spearman's correlation coefficient ($r_s$) between the change in CPH42 Profile score with the change in pain intensity at week 3 after the beginning of physiotherapy was 0.45.

*Source:* Chiu, T. T. W., Tai-Hing, L., and Hedley, A. J. (2005). Psychometric properties of a generic health measure in patients with neck pain. *Clinical Rehabilitation, 19*(5), p. 508.

Research
Navigator.c⊛m

Kendall's tau

**Kendall's tau** is very similar to Spearman's rho in that both of these bivariate correlational techniques are designed for the case in which each of two quantitative variables is measured in such a way as to produce data in the form of ranks. The difference between rho and tau is related to the issue of ties. To illustrate what we mean, suppose six students took a short exam and earned these scores: 10, 9, 7, 7, 5, and 3. These raw scores, when converted to ranks, become 1, 2, 3.5, 3.5, 5, and 6, where the top score of 10 receives a rank of 1, the next-best score (9) receives a rank of 2, and so on. The third- and fourth-best scores tied with a score of 7, and the rank given to each of these individuals is equal to the mean of the separate ranks that they would have received if they had not tied. (If the two 7s had been 8 and 6, the separate ranks would have been 3 and 4, respectively; the mean of 3 and 4 is 3.5, and this rank is given to each of the persons who actually earned a 7.)

Kendall's tau is simply a bivariate correlational procedure that does a better job of dealing with tied ranks than does Spearman's rho. For the two sets of ranks shown in Excerpt 3.21, Kendall's tau turns out equal to .75, which is smaller than the Spearman rho value of .89 derived from the same set of ranks. Because there were tied ranks for some of the medical categories within each set of patients, many statisticians would consider tau to be the more accurate of these two correlation coefficients. In Excerpt 3.24, we see a case where Kendall's tau was used.

## EXCERPT 3.24 • *Kendall's Tau*

The anaesthetists' VAS scores for elderly patients' correlated well with their anxiety for anaesthesia and surgery (Kendall's $\tau = 0.647$ and $0.524$) and the surgeons made moderate estimation of patients' surgery-related anxiety on those undergoing major surgery (Kendall's $\tau = 0.480$).

*Source:* Fekrat, F., Sahin, A., Yazici, K. M., and Aypar, U. (2006). Anaesthetists' and surgeons' estimation of preoperative anxiety by patients submitted for elective surgery in a university hospital. *European Journal of Anaesthesiology, 23*(3), p. 230.

### Point Biserial and Biserial Correlations

Research
Navigator.com

Point biserial

Sometimes a researcher will correlate two variables that are measured so as to produce a set of raw scores for one variable and a set of 0s and 1s for the other (dichotomous) variable. For example, a researcher might want to see if a relationship exists between the height of basketball players and whether they score any points in a game. For this kind of bivariate situation, a correlational technique called **point biserial** has been designed. The resulting correlation coefficient is usually symbolized as $r_{pb}$.

If a researcher has data on two variables where one variable's data are in the form of raw scores while the other variable's data represent an artificial dichotomy, then the relationship between the two variables will be assessed by means of a technique called **biserial correlation.** Returning to our basketball example, suppose a researcher wanted to correlate height with scoring productivity, with the second of these variables dealt with by checking to see whether each player's average is less than 10 points or some value in the double digits. Here, scoring productivity is measured by imposing an artificial dichotomy on a set of raw scores. Accordingly, the biserial techniques would be used to assess the nature and strength of the relationship between the two variables. This kind of bivariate correlation is usually symbolized by $r_{bis}$.

In Excerpt 3.25, we see a case where the point-biserial correlation was used in a published research article. In this study, the researchers collected data to see if

## EXCERPT 3.25 • *Point Biserial Correlation*

Treating the household as the unit of analysis and employing the age of the household head to identify the household's position in the life cycle, we indeed find home-ownership to increase with age. . . . Stated more formally, the point-biserial correlation coefficient—used to estimate the degree of relationship between a binary and a continuous variable—between home-ownership and age is positive with a value of 0.29.

*Source:* Başlevent, C., and Dayioglu, M. (2005). The effect of squatter housing on income distribution in urban Turkey. *Urban Studies, 42*(1), p. 39.

home ownership and age were correlated. As indicated in this excerpt, the variable of home ownership was binary (i.e., dichotomous) in nature because each household head either did or didn't own the home. Because the second variable, age, was a raw score variable, a point-biserial correlation was utilized to assess the relationship between the two variables.

### Phi and Tetrachoric Correlations

If both of a researcher's variables are dichotomous in nature, then the relationship between the two variables will be assessed by means of a correlational technique called **phi** (if each variable represents a true dichotomy) or a technique called **tetrachoric correlation** (if both variables represent artificial dichotomies). An example calling for the first of these situations would involve, among high school students, the variables of gender and car ownership; since each variable represents a true dichotomy, the correlation between gender (male/female) and car ownership (yes/no) would be accomplished using phi. For an example of a place where tetrachoric correlation would be appropriate, imagine that we measure each of several persons in terms of height (with people classified as tall or short depending on whether or not they measure over 5'8") and weight (with people classified as "OK" or "not OK" depending on whether or not they are within 10 pounds of their ideal weight). Here, both height and weight are forced into being dichotomies.

Excerpt 3.26 illustrates the use of phi. This excerpt shows nicely how the two variables involved in a correlation can each represent a true dichotomy.

### EXCERPT 3.26 • Phi

We computed a phi coefficient to estimate the degree of relationship between the intervention score and posttest score. [The first of these scores was a 1 or 0 depending on whether the single intervention question was answered correctly or incorrectly; likewise, the second of these scores was a 1 or 0 depending on whether the single posttest question was answered correctly or incorrectly.]

*Source:* Fernandez-Berrocal, P., and Santamaria, C. (2006). Mental models in social interaction. *Journal of Experimental Education, 74*(3), p. 235.

### Cramer's V

If a researcher has collected bivariate data on two variables where each variable is nominal in nature, the relationship between the two variables can be measured by means of a correlational technique called **Cramer's V.** In Excerpt 3.27, we see a case where Cramer's *V* was used. In this study focused on a group of teenagers, two of the variables of interest were abstinence and parental marital status. As indicated in the excerpt, Cramer's *V* measured the strength of the relationship between these variables. This correlational technique yields coefficients that must lie somewhere between 0 and 1.

**EXCERPT 3.27 • *Cramer's V***

More of sexually abstinent teens (50.3%) reported that their parents are married, compared to 32.4% of their sexually active peers (Cramer's $V = .18$).

*Source:* Vélez-Pastrana, M. C., Gonzádez-Rodríguez, R. A., and Borges-Hernández, A. (2005). Family functioning and early onset of sexual intercourse in Latino adolescents. *Adolescence, 40*(160), p. 787.

## Warnings about Correlation

At this point, you may be tempted to consider yourself a semiexpert when it comes to deciphering discussions about correlation. You now know what a scatter diagram is, you have looked at the correlational continuum (and know that correlation coefficients extend from $-1.00$ to $+1.00$), you understand what a correlation matrix is, and you have considered several different kinds of bivariate correlation. Before you assume that you know everything there is to know about measuring the relationship between two variables, I'd like to provide you with six warnings. These warnings deal with the issue of cause, the coefficient of determination, the possibility of outliers, the assumption of linearity, the notion of independence, and criteria for claims of high and low correlations.

### Correlation and Cause

It is important for you to know that a correlation coefficient does not speak to the issue of **cause and effect.** In other words, whether a particular variable has a causal impact on a different variable cannot be determined by measuring the two variables simultaneously and then correlating the two sets of data. Many recipients of research reports (and even a few researchers) make the mistake of thinking that a high correlation implies that one variable has a causal influence on the other variable. To prevent yourself from making this mistake, we suggest that you memorize this simple statement: correlation $\neq$ cause.

Consider Excerpt 3.28. In this excerpt, the researchers point out that their correlational findings should *not* be interpreted to mean that clear-cut cause-and-effect connections have been identified. Whereas these researchers set a good example of how researchers should talk about their correlational results, it is unfortunately the case that not all researchers follow their lead. Stated more forcefully, you need to be on guard for the many instances where researchers wrongfully impute "cause" into their correlational findings.

Later in this book, you will learn how researchers often collect data in such a way as to address the issue of cause. In such situations, however, researchers typically use data-gathering strategies that help them assess the possibility that one variable actually has a determining influence on a second variable. Those strategies

## EXCERPT 3.28 • *Correlation and Cause*

Finally, it should be noted that correlation does not imply causation. The cross-sectional design of our study does not allow definitive causal inferences concerning the role of disturbed attachment patterns in the development of BPD.

*Source:* Fossati, A., Feeney, J. A., Carretta, I., Grazioli, F., Milesi, R., Leonardi, B., and Maffei, C. (2005). Modeling the relationship between adult attachment patterns and borderline personality disorder: The role of impulsivity and aggressiveness. *Journal of Social & Clinical Psychology, 24*(4), pp. 531–532.

require a consideration of issues that cannot be discussed here; in time, however, I am confident that you will come to understand the extra demands that are placed on researchers who want to investigate causal connections between variables. For now, all I can do is ask that you believe me when I say that correlational data alone cannot be used to establish a cause-and-effect situation.

### Coefficient of Determination

Research
Navigator.com

Coefficient of
determination

To get a better feel for the strength of the relationship between two variables, many researchers will square the value of the correlation coefficient. For example, if $r$ turns out equal to .80, the researcher will square .80 and obtain .64. When $r$ is squared like this, the resulting value is called the **coefficient of determination.** In Excerpts 3.29 and 3.30, we see two research reports in which $r^2$ is presented. In the first of these excerpts, we see $r^2$ defined as the coefficient of determination. In Excerpt 3.30, we

## EXCERPTS 3.29–3.30 • *The Coefficient of Determination*

Pearson product-moment correlation coefficient ($r$) was employed for correlational analysis. The coefficient of determination ($r^2$) was used to measure the meaningfulness of the relationship.

*Source:* Smitz, L. L., and Woods, A. B. (2005). Prevalence, severity, and correlates of depressive symptoms on admission to inpatient hospice. *Journal of Hospice & Palliative Nursing, 8*(2), p. 88.

- - - - - - - - - - - - - - - - - - - - - - - - - - - - - - - - - - - - - - - - - - - - - - - - - - - - - - - - - - - - - - - - - - - - -

[Results indicated that] participants who scored high on adherence were significantly more likely to have controlled blood pressure than were participants who scored low on adherence ($r = .58$). The coefficient of determination ($r^2$), indicating strength of the relationship between the Medication Adherence Scale and blood pressure control, was .33.

*Source:* Hill-Briggs, F., Gary, T. L., Bone, L. R., Hill, M. N., Levine, D. M., and Brancati, F. L. (2005). Medication adherence and diabetes control in urban African Americans with Type 2 diabetes. *Health Psychology, 24*(4), pp. 350, 351.

see that an *r* of .58 was "downsized" to .33 (by converting it into a coefficient of determination) in the sentence that discusses the "strength of the relationship."

The coefficient of determination indicates the proportion of variability in one variable that is associated with (or explained by) variability in the other variable. The value of $r^2$ will lie somewhere between 0 and $+1.00$, and researchers usually multiply by 100 so they can talk about the *percentage* of explained variability. In Excerpt 3.31, we see an example of where $r^2$ was converted into a percentage. As this excerpt indicates, researchers sometimes refer to this percentage as the amount of variance in one variable that's "accounted for" by the other variable, or they sometimes say that this percentage indicates the amount of "shared variance."

### EXCERPT 3.31 • $r^2$ *and Explained Variation*

The Wheelchair User's Shoulder Pain Index (WUSPI) . . . measures how shoulder pain has interfered with different daily activities, such as transferring, wheeling, and self-care. . . . The Brief Pain inventory (BPI) (Short Form) was used to assess the subject's general experience of overall body pain, not isolated to the shoulder joint. . . . A modest correlation existed between WUSPI and BPI ($r = 0.35$) for all subjects, collectively. This translates to shoulder pain accounting for 12 percent of the variance of average whole body pain.

*Source:* Sawatzky, B. J., Slobogean, G. P., Reilly, C. W., Chambers, C. T., and Hol, A. T. (2005). Prevalence of shoulder pain in adult- versus childhood-onset wheelchair users: A pilot study. *Journal of Rehabilitation Research & Development, 42,* p. 4.

As suggested by the material in Excerpt 3.31, the value of $r^2$ indicates how much (proportionately speaking) variability in either variable is explained by the other variable. The implication of this is that the raw correlation coefficient (that is, the value of *r* when not squared) exaggerates how strong the relationship really is between two variables. Note that *r* must be stronger than .70 in order for there to be at least 50 percent explained variability. Or, consider the case where $r = .50$; here, only one-fourth of the variability is explained.

### Outliers

My third warning concerns the effect of one or more data points that are located away from the bulk of the scores. Such data points are called **outliers,** and they can cause the size of a correlation coefficient to understate or exaggerate the strength of the relationship between two variables. Excerpt 3.32 very nicely illustrates this point.

In contrast to the good example provided in Excerpt 3.32, most researchers fail to check to see if one or more outliers serve to distort the statistical summary of the bivariate relationships they study. You won't see many scatter diagrams in journal articles, and thus you will not be able to examine the data yourself to see if

### EXCERPT 3.32 • *Outliers*

This [calculated *r* of .433] suggests a positive relationship between the frequency of a product advertisement and the number of requests for that product. However, this may be a spurious relationship as two outliers, Barbie and Action Man products, appear to be responsible for the strength of this relationship. If these two products are excluded from the calculation, then the Pearson correlation changes completely [to *r* = .065, suggesting] no relationship between the two variables. . . .

*Source:* Pine, K. J., and Nash, A. (2002). Dear Santa: The effects of television advertising on young children. *International Journal of Behavioral Development, 26*(6), p. 536.

*Remember this*

outliers were present. Almost always, you will be given just the correlation coefficient. Give the researcher some extra credit, however, whenever you see a statement to the effect that the correlation coefficient was computed after an examination of a scatter diagram revealed no outliers (or revealed an outlier that was removed prior to computing the correlation coefficient).

## Linearity

The most popular technique for assessing the strength of a bivariate relationship is Pearson's product-moment correlation. This correlational procedure works nicely if the two variables have a linear relationship. Pearson's technique does not work well, however, if a curvilinear relationship exists between the two variables.

A **linear** relationship does *not* require that all data points (in a scatter diagram) lie on a straight line. Instead, what *is* required is that the *path* of the data points be straight. The path itself can be very narrow, with most data points falling near an imaginary straight line, or the path can be very wide—so long as the path is straight. (Regardless of how narrow or wide the path is, the path to which we refer can be tilted at any angle.)

If a **curvilinear** relationship exists between two variables, Pearson's correlation will underestimate the strength of the relationship that is present in the data. Accordingly, you can place more confidence in any correlation coefficient you see when the researcher who presents it indicates that a scatter diagram was inspected to see whether the relationship was linear before Pearson's *r* was used to summarize the nature and strength of the relationship. Conversely, add a few grains of salt to the *r*s that are thrown your way without statements concerning the linearity of the data.

In Excerpts 3.33 and 3.34, we see two examples where researchers checked to see if their bivariate data sets were linear. The first of these excerpts illustrates how scatter diagrams can be used to accomplish this task. In Excerpt 3.34, we see that an inspection of a scatter diagram can provide a "red flag" that a relationship is not linear. The researchers associated with these two excerpts deserve high praise for taking the time to check out the linearity assumption before computing Pearson's *r*. Unfortunately, however, most researchers collect their data and compute correlation coefficients without ever thinking about linearity.

**EXCERPTS 3.33–3.34** • *Linearity and Curvilinearity*

Pearson's product-moment correlations were used to examine the nature of the relationships between the subscales . . . and linearity between variables was assessed by inspection of bivariate scatter plots.

*Source:* Jurkovic, D., and Walker, G. A. (2006). Examining masculine gender-role conflict and stress in relation to religious orientation and spiritual well-being in Australian men. *Journal of Men's Studies, 14*(1), pp. 34, 35.

----

Inspection of scatter plots of outcome and treatment duration showed a curvilinear relationship.

*Source:* Lorentzen, S., and Høglend, P. (2005). Predictors of change after long-term analytic group psychotherapy. *Journal of Clinical Psychology, 61*(12), p. 1547.

## Correlation and Independence

In many empirical studies, the researcher will either build or use different tests in an effort to assess different skills, traits, or characteristics of the people, animals, or objects from whom measurements are taken. Obviously, time and money will be wasted if two or more of these tests are redundant. Stated differently, it is desirable (in many studies) for each measuring instrument to accomplish something unique compared to the other measuring instruments being used. Two instruments that do this are said to be **independent.**

The technique of correlation often helps researchers assess the extent to which their measuring instruments are independent. Independence exists to the extent that $r$ turns out to be close to zero. In other words, low correlations imply independence whereas high positive or negative correlations signal lack of independence.

Excerpt 3.35 illustrates how authors will sometimes use the term *independent* in their research reports. Note that it is *low* values of $r$ that signal independence. Also note that it is the variables (and not the correlations themselves) that are considered to be independent; a low $r$ is simply the "signpost" that suggests the presence of independence.

### EXCERPT 3.35 • *Independence*

Parent and adolescent reports of parental monitoring correlated only .26 [thereby] indicating that the two measures are largely independent ($r^2 = .07$).

*Source:* Donenberg, G. R., Wilson, H. W., Emerson, E., and Bryant, F. B. (2002). Holding the line with a watchful eye: The impact of perceived parental permissiveness and parental monitoring on risky sexual behavior among adolescents in psychiatric care. *AIDS Education and Prevention, 14*(20), p. 153.

## Relationship Strength

My final warning concerns the labels that researchers attach to their correlation coefficients. There are no hard and fast rules that dictate when labels such as "strong" or "moderate" or "weak" should be used. In other words, there is subjectivity involved in deciding whether a given *r* is "high" or "low." Not surprisingly, researchers are sometimes biased (by how they *wanted* their results to turn out) when they select an adjective to describe their obtained *r*s. Being aware that this happens, you need to realize that you have the full right to look at a researcher's *r* and label it however you wish, even if your label is different from the researcher's.

Consider Excerpt 3.36. In this passage, the researchers assert that two of the obtained *r*s indicate "a strong correlation." Knowing now about how the coefficient of determination is computed and interpreted, you ought to be a bit hesitant to swallow the researchers' assertion that .396 and .310 are strong correlations. If squared and then turned into percentages, these *r*s indicate that (1) less than 16 percent of the variability in TV watching time was associated with BMI (body mass index) and (2) less than 10 percent was associated with triceps skinfold thickness.

### EXCERPT 3.36 • *Questionable Labels Used to Describe Relationships*

Pearson's correlation analysis was used to correlate television watching and body composition. . . . When the correlation was investigated between TV watching time and weight, BMI, skinfold thickness, waist to hip ratio and %BF, it was seen that there was a strong correlation between TV watching time and BMI [$r = 0.396$] and triceps skinfolds [$r = 0.310$].

*Source:* Özdirenç, M., Özcan, A., Akin, F., and Gelecek, N. (2005). Physical fitness in rural children compared with urban children in Turkey. *Pediatrics International, 47*(1), pp. 28, 29.

### Review Terms

| | |
|---|---|
| Abscissa | High |
| Biserial correlation | Independent |
| Bivariate | Indirect relationship |
| Cause and effect | Inverse relationship |
| Coefficient of determination | Kendall's tau |
| Correlation coefficient | Linear |
| Correlation matrix | Low |
| Cramer's *V* | Moderate |
| Curvilinear | Negative correlation |
| Dichotomous variable | Nominal |
| Direct relationship | Ordinal |

Ordinate                                      Scatter diagram
Outlier                                       Spearman's rho
Pearson's product-moment correlation          Strong
Perfect                                       Tetrachoric correlation
Phi                                           Weak
Point biserial correlation                    $r$
Positive correlation                          $r_s$
Qualitative variable                          $r^2$
Quantitative variable                         $r_{pb}$
Rank-order correlation                        $r_{bis}$
Ranks                                         $V$
Raw score                                     $\rho$
Relationship

## The Best Items in the Companion Website

1. An interactive online quiz (with immediate feedback provided) covering Chapter 3.
2. Ten misconceptions about the content of Chapter 3.
3. The author's poem "True Experimental Design."
4. An email message from the author to his students in which he asks an honest question about Pearson's $r$ and Spearman's rho.
5. Two jokes about statistics, the first of which concerns a student in a statistics course.

To access chapter objectives, practice tests, weblinks, and flashcards, visit the companion website at www.ablongman.com/huck5e.

Research
Navigator.com

## Fun Exercises inside Research Navigator

### 1. Is IQ correlated with reaction time?

The 81 adult participants in this study were measured on two kinds of reaction time: how fast they could respond to auditory stimuli and how fast they could respond to visual stimuli. They were also measured on several other variables, one of which was IQ. The correlation between the two kinds of reaction time turned out as most people would expect—it was moderate and positive, with Pearson's $r = .69$. But what about the correlation between IQ and each of the two kinds of reaction time? These two $r$s were about the same size and they had the same sign. But what was that sign? In other words, do you think this study revealed a direct relationship or an indirect relationship between IQ and reaction time? After you make your guess, refer to the PDF version of the research report in the Communication database of Content-Select and look at the correlation matrix at the bottom of page 46.

R. Stringer & K. E. Stanovich. The connection between reaction time and variation in reading ability: Unraveling covariance relationships with cognitive ability and phonological sensitivity. *Scientific Studies of Reading.* Located in the COMMUNICATION database of ContentSelect.

## 2. How does emotional intelligence correlate with general intelligence?

In this study, 107 undergraduate students, graduate students, and college graduates were measured in terms of their general intelligence. In addition, the research participants completed the *Multifactorial Emotional Intelligence Scale.* This instrument provided four scores per participant, three based on its subscales (Emotional Knowledge, Emotional Perception, and Emotional Regulation) and one composite score. The correlation matrix included in the research report contained 21 bivariate correlation coefficients, four of which showed the relationship between the study's measures of general intelligence and the four scores on emotional intelligence. These four *r*s turned out equal to .40, .23, .04, and −.03. Which emotional intelligence score do you think correlated most highly with general intelligence? After making a guess, locate the PDF version of the research report in the Psychology database of Content-Select and look at Table 1 at the bottom of page 188.

J. Pellitteri. The relationship between emotional intelligence and ego defense mechanisms. *Journal of Psychology.* Located in the PSYCHOLOGY database of ContentSelect.

**Review Questions and Answers begin on page 513.**

# Reliability and Validity

Empirical research articles focus on data that have been collected, summarized, and analyzed. The conclusions drawn and the recommendations made in such studies can be no better than the data on which they are based. As a consequence, most researchers describe the quality of the instruments used to collect their data. These descriptions of instrument quality normally appear in the method section of the article, either in the portion that focuses on materials or in the description of the dependent variables.

Regardless of where it appears, the description of instrument quality typically deals with two measurement-related concepts—reliability and validity. In this chapter, I will discuss the meaning of these two concepts, various techniques employed by researchers to assess the reliability and validity of their measuring instruments, and numerical indices of instrument quality that are reported. My overall objective here is to help you refine your skills at deciphering and evaluating reports of reliability and validity.

## Reliability

This discussion of reliability is divided into three sections. We begin by looking at the core meaning of the term *reliability*. Next, we examine a variety of techniques that researchers use to quantify the degree to which their data are reliable. Finally, I will provide five cautionary comments concerning reports of reliability that will help you as you read technical research reports.

### The Meaning of Reliability and the Reliability Coefficient

The basic idea of **reliability** is summed up by the word *consistency.* Researchers can and do evaluate the reliability of their instruments from different perspectives, but the basic question that cuts across these various perspectives (and techniques) is always the same: "To what extent can we say that the data are consistent?"

As you will see, the way in which reliability is conceptualized by researchers can take one of three basic forms. In some studies, researchers ask, "To what degree does a person's measured performance remain consistent across repeated testings?" In other studies, the question of interest takes a slightly different form: "To what extent do the individual items that go together to make up a test or inventory consistently measure the same underlying characteristic?" In still other studies, the concern over reliability is expressed in the question "How much consistency exists among the ratings provided by a group of raters?" Despite the differences among these three questions, the notion of consistency is at the heart of the matter in each case.

Different statistical procedures have been developed to assess the degree to which a researcher's data are reliable, and we will consider some of the more frequently used procedures in a moment. Before doing that, however, I want to point out how the different procedures are similar. Besides dealing, in one way or another, with the concept of consistency, each of the reliability techniques leads to a single numerical index. Called a **reliability coefficient,** this descriptive summary of the data's consistency normally assumes a value somewhere between 0.00 and +1.00, with these two "end points" representing situations where consistency is either totally absent or totally present.

## Different Approaches to Reliability

*Test-Retest Reliability.*    In many studies, a researcher will measure a single group of subjects twice with the same measuring instrument, with the two testings separated by a period of time. The interval of time may be as short as one day or it can be as long as a year or more. Regardless of the length of time between the two testings, the researcher will simply correlate the two sets of scores to find out how much consistency is in the data. The resulting correlation coefficient is simply renamed the **test-retest reliability coefficient.**[1]

With a test-retest approach to reliability, the resulting coefficient addresses the issue of consistency, or stability, over time. For this reason, the test-retest reliability coefficient is frequently referred to as the **coefficient of stability.** As with other forms of reliability, coefficients of stability reflect high reliability to the extent that they are close to 1.00.

In Excerpts 4.1 through 4.3, we see three examples of test-retest reliability. In the first two of these excerpts, there is no indication of the statistical procedure used to compute the reliability coefficient. In cases like these, you'll probably be right if you guess that the stability coefficient came from Pearson's correlation. (This is a safe bet because test-retest reliability is typically estimated via *r*.) As shown in Excerpt 4.3, another technique used to estimate test-retest reliability is called the

---

[1]As you recall from Chapter 3, correlation coefficients can assume values anywhere between −1.00 and +1.00. Reliability, however, cannot logically turn out to be negative. Therefore, if the test-retest correlation coefficient turns out to be negative, it will be changed to 0.00 when relabeled as a *reliability coefficient*.

## EXCERPTS 4.1–4.3 • *Test-Retest Reliability*

Test–retest reliability over a 9-week period was .59, as assessed for a sample of 95 health education participants.

*Source:* Kenny, M. E., Blustein, D. L., Haase, R. F., Jackson, J., and Perry, J. C. (2006). Setting the stage: Career development and the student engagement process. *Journal of Counseling Psychology, 53*(2), p. 274.

- - - - - - - - - - - - - - - - - - - - - - - - - - - - - - - - - - - - - - - - - - - - - - - - - - - - - -

Test-retest stability was measured to determine the reliability of scores over time. A group of approximately 100 K–6 teachers completed the survey, once in January and once in April. The scores from each were correlated and the coefficient of stability was calculated to be 0.92.

*Source:* Marlow, L., Inman, D., and Shwery, C. (2005). To what extent are literacy initiatives being supported: Important questions for administrators. *Reading Improvement, 42*(3), p. 181.

- - - - - - - - - - - - - - - - - - - - - - - - - - - - - - - - - - - - - - - - - - - - - - - - - - - - - -

The final instrument consisted of 15 questions. Seven questions assessed perceived barriers to exercise, 5 assessed activity level, and 3 were demographic questions (age, gender, and race/ethnicity). . . . In order to examine test-retest reliability, the test was administered to 35 female students in a physical education class of mixed ethnicities, on 2 occasions, 2 weeks apart. The intraclass correlation coefficient was .82 for barriers and .89 for activity level.

*Source:* Fahlman, M. M., Hall, H. L., and Lock, R. (2006). Ethnic and socioeconomic comparisons of fitness, activity levels, and barriers to exercise in high school females. *The Journal of School Health, 76*(1), p. 13.

*intraclass correlation.* The intraclass correlation procedure is quite versatile, and it can be used for a variety of purposes (e.g., to see if ratings from raters are reliable). In the case of a test-retest situation, all you need to know is that the intraclass correlation yields the same estimate of reliability as does Pearson's correlation.

With most characteristics, the degree of stability that exists decreases as the interval between test and retest increases. For this reason, high coefficients of stability are more impressive when the time interval is longer. If a researcher does not indicate the length of time between the two testings, then the claims made about stability must be taken with a grain of salt. Stability is not very convincing if a trait remains stable for only an hour.

 ***Equivalent-Forms Reliability.***[2]     Instead of assessing stability over time, researchers sometimes measure people with two forms of the same instrument. The two forms are similar in that they supposedly focus on the same characteristic (e.g.,

[2]The terms *parallel-forms reliability* and *alternate-forms reliability* are synonymous (as used by most applied researchers) with the term *equivalent-forms reliability.*

intelligence) of the people being measured, but they differ with respect to the precise questions included within each form. If the two forms do in fact measure the same thing (and if they are used in close temporal proximity), we would expect a high degree of consistency between the scores obtained for any examinee across the two testings. With **equivalent-forms reliability,** a researcher is simply determining the degree to which this is the case.

To quantify the degree of equivalent-forms reliability that exists, the researcher will administer two forms of the same instrument to a single group of individuals with a short time interval between the two testings.[3] After a score becomes available for each person on each form, the two sets of data are correlated. The resulting correlation coefficient is interpreted directly as the equivalent-forms reliability coefficient.[4] Many researchers refer to this two-digit value as the **coefficient of equivalence.**

To see an example where this form of reliability was used, consider Excerpt 4.4. Notice how these researchers point out that their equivalent-forms reliability coefficient (that turned out equal to .96) was found by simply correlating the participants' scores on the two forms, A and B, of the test. Most likely, this correlation was a Pearson's *r*. As I hope you remember from our discussion in the previous chapter, a correlation coefficient does not assess the equality of means. For this reason, the researchers reported not just the correlation but also the two means. Together, the two nearly identical means and the extremely high correlation of .96 provide strong evidence that List A was equivalent to List B.

### EXCERPT 4.4 • *Equivalent-Forms Reliability*

The experimental design called for the 250 test stimuli to be divided into two lists (A and B), each consisting of 125 representative items and 12 foils. . . . For the quiet listening condition, the mean score of all 53 participants on List A was 121.6 (*SD* = 23.4) and the mean score on List B was 122.0 (*SD* = 20.7). Equivalent forms reliability (correlation between scores on Lists A and B) was .96.

*Source:* Bochner, J. H., Garrison, W. M., Sussman, J. E., and Burkard, R. F. (2003). Development of materials for the clinical assessment of speech recognition: The Speech Sound Pattern Discrimination Test. *Journal of Speech, Language, and Hearing Research, 46*(4), pp. 893, 895.

***Internal Consistency Reliability.***   Instead of focusing on stability across time or on equivalence across forms, researchers sometimes assess the degree to which their measuring instruments possess internal consistency. When this perspective

---

[3]The two forms will probably be administered in a *counterbalanced* order, meaning that each instrument is administered first to one-half of the examinees.

[4]As is the case with test-retest reliability, any negative correlation would be changed to 0. Reliability by definition has a lower limit of 0.

is taken, reliability is defined as consistency across the parts of a measuring instrument, with the "parts" being individual questions or subsets of questions. To the extent that these parts "hang together" and measure the same thing, the full instrument is said to possess high **internal consistency reliability.**

To assess internal consistency, a researcher need only administer a test (or questionnaire) a single time to a single group of individuals. After all responses have been scored, one of several statistical procedures is then applied to the data, with the result being a number between 0.00 and +1.00. As with test-retest and equivalent-forms procedures, the instrument is considered to be better to the extent that the resulting coefficient is close to the upper limit of this continuum of possible results.

One of the procedures that can be used to obtain the internal consistency reliability coefficient involves splitting each examinee's performance into two halves, usually by determining how the examinee did on the odd-numbered items grouped together (i.e., one half of the test) and the even-numbered items grouped together (i.e., the other half). After each person's total score on each half of the instrument is computed, these two sets of scores are correlated. Once obtained, the *r* is inserted into a special formula (called **Spearman-Brown**) that makes a "correction" based on the length of the full instrument. The final numerical result is called the **split-half reliability coefficient.**

Use of this first procedure for assessing internal consistency can be seen in Excerpts 4.5 and 4.6. In the first of these excerpts, we see split-half reliability coefficients for two subtests of an instrument designed to assess children's reading skills. In Excerpt 4.6, the researchers report that they computed the split-half reliability estimate "using the Spearman-Brown correction formula." Though not

**EXCERPTS 4.5–4.6 • *Split-Half Reliability***

The WI and WA subtests of the WRMT-R were used to measure children's word reading skills. . . . The split-half reliability is 0.97 and 0.87 for the WRMT-R WI and WA subtests, respectively.

*Source:* Nelson, J. R., Stage, S. A., and Epstein, M. H. (2005). Effects of a prereading intervention on the literacy and social skills of children. *Exceptional Children, 72*(1), p. 36.

-----------------------------------------------------------------------------------------------

Responses to the 12 short-answer comprehension questions were assigned scores from 0 (no answer or completely wrong answer) to 1 (complete, correct answer), with partial credit given when a response contained some but not all of the correct information. . . . The split-half reliability for the comprehension questions using the Spearman-Brown correction formula was .80.

*Source:* Rawson, K. A., and Kintsch, W. (2005). Rereading effects depend on time of test. *Journal of Educational Psychology, 97*(1), p. 74.

mentioned in Excerpt 4.5, this correction formula is always used when a split-half reliability estimate is computed. The Spearman-Brown correction is needed because (a) reliability tends to be higher for longer tests (and lower for shorter tests) and (b) the process of splitting a test in half creates two "forms" of the test, each of which is only 50 percent as long as the full-length instrument. The Spearman-Brown correction formula "boosts" the correlation coefficient upwards so as to undo the "damage" caused by splitting the test in half.

KR 20

\* A second approach to assessing internal consistency is called **Kuder-Richardson #20,** or simply **K-R 20.** This procedure, like the split-half procedure, uses data from a single test that has been given once to a single group of respondents. After the full test is scored, the researcher simply puts the obtained data into a formula that provides the K-R 20 reliability coefficient. The end result is somewhat like a split-half reliability, but better. That's because the split-half approach to assessing internal consistency yields a result that can vary depending upon which items are put in the odd-numbered slots and which ones are placed in the even-numbered slots. In other words, if the items that go together to make up a full test are "scrambled" in terms of the way they are ordered, this will likely affect the value of the split-half reliability coefficient. Thus, whenever the split-half procedure is used to assess the reliability of a measuring instrument, we don't know whether the resulting reliability coefficient is favorable (i.e., high) or unfavorable (i.e., low) as compared with what would have been the case if the items had been ordered differently.

With K-R 20, the end result is guaranteed to be neither favorable nor unfavorable. That's the case because the formula for K-R 20 was designed to produce a result that's equivalent to what you would get if you (1) scramble the order of the test items over and over again until you had all possible orders, (2) compute a split-half reliability coefficient for each of these forms of the test, and (3) take the mean value of those various coefficients. Of course, the researcher who wants to obtain the K-R 20 coefficient does not have to go to the trouble to do these three things. A simple little formula is available that brings about the desired end result almost instantaneously.

In Excerpt 4.7, we see an example of how K-R 20 results are often reported in published research reports.

### EXCERPT 4.7 • *Kuder-Richardson 20 Reliability*

After rounding, the KR-20 estimates were the same across different samples and sub-samples but different for the sections: .91 for the LC section, .93 for the RC section and .96 for the total score.

*Source:* Zhang, S. (2006). Investigating the relative effects of persons, items, sections, and languages on TOEIC score dependability. *Language Testing, 23*(3), p. 359.

A third method for assessing internal consistency is referred to as **coefficient alpha,** as **Cronbach's alpha,** or simply as **alpha.** This technique is identical to K-R 20 whenever the instrument's items are scored in a dichotomous fashion (e.g., "1" for correct, "0" for incorrect). However, alpha is more versatile because it can be used with instruments made up of items that can be scored with three or more possible values. Examples of such a situation include (1) a four-question essay test, where each examinee's response to each question is evaluated on a 0–10 scale or (2) a Likert-type questionnaire where the five response options for each statement extend from "strongly agree" to "strongly disagree" and are scored with the integers 5 through 1. Excerpts 4.8 and 4.9 show two instances in which Cronbach's alpha was used to evaluate internal consistency. These excerpts demonstrate the versatility of Cronbach's technique for assessing internal consistence, for the two instruments had very different scoring systems. Whereas the instrument in Excerpt 4.8 had "1" or "0" scores (to indicate correct or incorrect responses to test questions), the instrument in Excerpt 4.9 utilized a 7-point Likert-type response format aimed at assessing the respondents' attitudes.

### EXCERPTS 4.8–4.9 • *Coefficient Alpha Reliability*

The final exam consisted of 40 multiple-choice questions (Cronbach's alpha = 0.70).

*Source:* Gijbels, D., Van De Watering, G., Dochy, F., and Van Den Bossche, P. (2005). The relationship between students' approaches to learning and the assessment of learning outcomes. *European Journal of Psychology of Education, 20*(4), p. 331.

------------------------------------------------------------------------

The SWLS is comprised of five items (e.g., "In most ways my life is close to my ideal."), which are rated on a 7-point scale, from 1, "strongly disagree" to 7, "strongly agree." Answers to the five items are averaged, yielding a single measure of global life satisfaction. . . . The Cronbach's alpha calculated for the SWLS was .84 in the current study.

*Source:* Degges-White, S., and Myers, J. E. (2006). Transitions, wellness, and life satisfaction: Implications for counseling midlife women. *Journal of Mental Health Counseling, 28*(2), p. 140.

### Interrater Reliability

Researchers sometimes collect data by having raters evaluate a set of objects, pictures, applicants, or whatever. To quantify the degree of consistency among the raters, the researcher will compute an index of **interrater reliability.** Five popular procedures for doing this include a percent-agreement measure, Pearson's correlation, Kendall's coefficient of concordance, Cohen's kappa, and the intraclass correlation.

The simplest measure of interrater reliability involves nothing more than a percentage of the occasions where the raters agree in the ratings they assign to

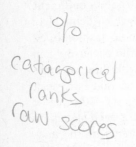

%
catagorical
ranks
raw scores

whatever is being rated. In Excerpt 4.10, we see an example of this approach to interrater reliability. With 11 questions administered to 25 students on two occasions (pretest and posttest), there were 275 instances where each of the two raters assigned a 0 or 1 or 2 to a student's answer. As indicated in the excerpt, the two raters assigned the exact same score 84 percent of the time.

### EXCERPT 4.10 • *Percent Agreement*

A subset of students from the experimental group was interviewed both before and after the intervention (n = 25) regarding their understanding of ways to think about history and historical thinking. . . . A scoring rubric (using a 3-point scale) was developed to analyze students' level of understanding for each of the 11 questions, resulting in a possible score of 22. The entire set of interviews was independently scored by me and by an undergraduate student who was unfamiliar with the design or purpose of the study (percentage of exact agreement = 84).

*Source:* De La Paz, S. (2005). Effects of historical reasoning instruction and writing strategy mastery in culturally and academically diverse middle school classrooms. *Journal of Educational Psychology, 97*(2), p. 149.

r = Pearsons
c̄ raw
scores

The second method for quantifying interrater reliability uses Pearson's product-moment correlation. Whereas the percent-agreement procedures can be used with data that are categorical, ranks, or raw scores, Pearson's procedure can be used only when the raters' ratings are raw scores. In Excerpt 4.11, we see an example of Pearson's correlation being used to assess the interrater reliability among three raters.

Kendall's procedure is appropriate for situations where each rater is asked to rank the things being evaluated. If these ranks turn out to be in complete agreement

### EXCERPT 4.11 • *Using Pearson's r to Assess Interrater Reliability*

Eighty-three employer interviews were conducted and scored. . . . Three rehabilitation professionals were trained in scoring the surveys [and] we calculated the interrater correlations (Pearson's *r*) by comparing the scores of each pair of raters. The correlations were as follows:

Rater 1 with Rater 2 = .90
Rater 1 with Rater 3 = .85
Rater 2 with Rater 3 = .89

*Source:* Gilbride, D., Vandergoot, D., Golden, K., and Stensrud, R. (2006). Development and validation of the employer openness survey. *Rehabilitation Counseling Bulletin, 49*(2), p. 84.

across the various evaluators, then the **coefficient of concordance** will turn out equal to $+1.00$. To the extent that the evaluators disagree with one another, Kendall's procedure will yield a smaller value. In Excerpt 4.12, we see a case in which Kendall's coefficient of concordance was used.

## EXCERPT 4.12 • *Kendall's Coefficient of Concordance*

Both sets of participants [immigrants and employment recruiters] were asked: Please rank these statements, from (1) agree with most to (4) agree with least. If an immigrant comes to a new country, they should: "Adopt the new culture and keep their own culture as well"; "Adopt the new culture and put their own culture in the background"; "Keep their own culture and put the new culture in the background"; and, "They should ignore both their own culture and the new culture and look after themselves." . . . For the rank data as a whole (i.e., across all four acculturation styles), Kendall's Coefficient of Concordance $\omega = .561$.

*Source:* Mace, K. A., Atkins, S., Fletcher, R., and Carr, S. C. (2005). Immigrant job hunting, labour market experiences, and feelings about occupational satisfaction in New Zealand: An exploratory study. *New Zealand Journal of Psychology, 34*(2), pp. 102–103.

Kendall's coefficient of concordance establishes how much interrater reliability exists among ranked data. **Cohen's kappa** accomplishes the same purpose when the data are nominal (i.e., categorical) in nature. In other words, kappa is designed for situations where raters classify the items being rated into discrete categories. If all raters agree that a particular item belongs in a given category, and if there is a total agreement for all items being evaluated (even though different items end up in different categories), then kappa assumes the value of $+1.00$. To the extent that raters disagree, kappa assumes a smaller value.

To see a case in which Cohen's kappa was used, consider Excerpt 4.13. In the study that provided this excerpt, interviews were conducted with 100 elderly individuals, some of whom had been diagnosed with Alzheimer's disease. During

## EXCERPT 4.13 • *Cohen's Kappa*

Each possible self was coded into 1 of 17 domains, with hoped-for and feared selves coded separately. . . . To determine interrater reliability for this study, a trained second rater blind to the cognitive status of the participant randomly selected 20% of the data for recoding. Cohen's kappa was used to assess agreement across all domains for hoped-for (.88) and feared (.84) responses.

*Source:* Cotrell, V., and Hooker, K. (2005). Possible selves of individuals with Alzheimer's Disease. *Psychology and Aging, 20*(2), p. 287.

the interview, each participant was asked to look into the future and describe "future selves" (i.e., an image of themselves later in life), some of which were desired and some not (referred to as "hoped-for" and "feared" future selves, respectively). The domains for the two kinds of future selves were categorical and thus fully nominal in nature. Cohen's kappa was used to see how consistently the two raters put the participants' future selves into the same domain.

The final method for assessing interrater reliability to be considered here is called **intraclass correlation.** Abbreviated ICC, the intraclass correlation is a multipurpose statistical procedure, as it can be used for either correlational or reliability purposes. Even if we restrict our thinking to reliability, ICC is still versatile. Earlier in this chapter, we saw a case where the intraclass correlation was used to estimate test-retest reliability. Now, we consider how ICC can be used to assess interrater reliability.

Intraclass correlation is similar to the other reliability procedures we have considered in terms of the core concept being dealt with (consistency), the theoretical limits of the data-based coefficient (0 to 1.00), and the desire on the part of the researcher to end up with a value as close to 1.00 as possible. It differs from the other reliability procedures in that several ICC procedures exist. The six most popular of these procedures are distinguished by two numbers put inside parentheses following the letters ICC. For example, ICC (3,1) designates one of the six most frequently used versions of intraclass correlation. The first of the two numbers indicates which of three possible statistical models has been assumed by the researchers to underlie their data. The second number indicates whether the researchers are interested in the reliability of a single rater (or, one-time use of a measuring instrument) or in the reliability of the mean score provided by a group of raters (or, the mean value produced by using a measuring instrument more than once). The second number within the parentheses will be a 1 for the first of these two cases; if interest lies in the reliability of means, the second number will be a value greater than 1 that designates how many scores are averaged together to generate each mean.

I will not attempt to differentiate any further among the six main cases of ICC. Instead, I simply want to point out that researchers should explain in their research reports (1) which of the six ICC procedures was used and (2) the reason(s) behind the choice made. You have a right to expect clarity regarding these two issues because the ICC-estimated reliability coefficient can vary widely depending on which of the six available formulas is used to compute it.

In Excerpts 4.14 and 4.15, we see two examples where the intraclass correlation was used to assess interrater reliability. Notice that the researchers associated with the second of these excerpts indicate which of the six main types of ICC they used—model 2 for a single rater. Because the coefficient provided by ICC can vary widely depending on which of the six main formulas are used to obtain the intraclass correlation, we have a right to think more highly about the information in the

**Research
Navigator.c⊕m**

Intraclass
correlation

## EXCERPTS 4.14–4.15 • *Intraclass Correlation*

For this variable [treatment plan elaboration], coders were instructed to rate how well the clinician explained or developed the treatment plan. The following scale was used: 0 = insufficient information, 1 = very little elaboration, 2 = little elaboration, 3 = moderate elaboration, 4 = high elaboration. An ICC of .86 was achieved, which shows excellent reliability.

*Source:* Eells, T. D., Lombart, K. G., Kendjelic, E. M., Turner, L. C., and Lucas, C. P. (2005). The quality of psychotherapy case formulations: A comparison of expert, experienced, and novice cognitive-behavioral and psychodynamic therapists. *Journal of Consulting and Clinical Psychology, 73*(4), p. 583.

Interrater reliability was assessed for each of the items with an intraclass correlation coefficient (ICC[2,1]), for the raw (timed) scores and the converted scores.

*Source:* Williams, G. P., Greenwood, K. M., Robertson, V. J., Goldie, P. A., and Morris, M. E. (2006). High-Level Mobility Assessment Tool (HiMAT): Interrater reliability, retest reliability, and internal consistency. *Physical Therapy, 86*(3), p. 397.

second excerpt. It would have been even nicer if the authors of Excerpt 4.15 had explained why they chose ICC(2,1) instead of other variations of this reliability procedure.

### The Standard Error of Measurement

Some researchers, when discussing reliability, will present a numerical value for the **standard error of measurement.** Often abbreviated as **SEM,** the standard error of measurement can be used to estimate the range within which a score would likely fall if a given measured object were to be remeasured. To illustrate, suppose an intelligence test is administered to a group of children, and also suppose that Tommy ends up with an IQ score of 112. If the SEM associated with the IQ scores in this group were equal to 4, then we would build an interval for Tommy (by adding 4 to 112 and subtracting 4 from 112) that would extend from 108–116. This interval, or **confidence band,** would help us interpret Tommy's IQ because we could now say that Tommy would likely score somewhere between 108 and 116 if the same intelligence test were to be readministered and if Tommy didn't change between the two testings.[5]

[5]By creating an interval via the formula "score±SEM," we end up with a 68 percent confidence band. If we doubled or tripled the SEM within this little formula, we would end up with a 95 percent or a 99 percent confidence band, respectively.

In a very real sense, the standard error of measurement can be thought of as an index of consistency that is inversely related to reliability. To the extent that reliability is high, the SEM will be small (and vice versa). There is one other main difference between these two ways of assessing consistency. Reliability coefficients are tied to a scale that extends from 0 to 1.00, and in this sense they are completely "metric free." In contrast, an SEM is always tied to the nature of the scores generated by a test, and in this sense it is not "metric free." Simply stated, the continuum for reliability coefficients has no units of measurement, whereas the SEM is always "in" the same measurement units as are the scores around which confidence bands are built.

In Excerpt 4.16, we see a case in which the standard error of measurement was computed for each of five different scales on a measuring instrument called the Contextual Needs Assessment. In providing their rule-of-thumb for estimating "true scores," the researchers are acknowledging that the CNA's scores are not infallible. (A 95 percent confidence band would extend from 10–14 points above an earned score to 10–14 points below that same score. With the maximum score being 80 on any of the CNA's scales, this would be a wide confidence band.)

### EXCERPT 4.16 • *Standard Error of Measurement*

Each Scale on the CNA has a possible maximum score of 80 points, 10 points for each of the 8 situations. The standard error of measurement for the scales fell between 4.86 for Freedom and 6.65 for Belonging. The standard error fell reasonably close for all other scales to establish a "rule of thumb" true score estimate of between 5 and 7 points.

*Source:* Brown, T., and Swenson, S. (2005). Identifying basic needs: The Contextual Needs Assessment. *International Journal of Reality Therapy, 24*(2), p. 8.

### Warning about Reliability

Before we turn to the topic of validity, there are five important warnings about reliability to which you should become sensitive. It would be nice if all researchers were also aware of these five concerns; unfortunately, that is not the case.

First of all, keep in mind that different methods for assessing reliability consider the issue of consistency from different perspectives. Thus a high coefficient of stability does not necessarily mean that internal consistency is high (and vice versa). Even within the internal consistency category, a high value for split-half reliability does not necessarily mean that Kuder-Richardson #20 would be equally high for the same data. The various methods for assessing reliability accomplish different purposes, and the results do not necessarily generalize across methods. Because of this, I like to see various approaches to reliability used within the same study.

My second warning concerns the fact that reliability coefficients really apply to data and not to measuring instruments. To understand the full truth of this claim, imagine that a test designed for a college-level class in physics is administered twice to a group of college students, producing a test-retest reliability coefficient of .90. Now, if that same test is administered on two occasions to a group of first grade students (with the same time interval between test and retest), the coefficient of stability would not be anywhere near .90. (The first graders would probably guess at all questions, and the test-retest reliability for this younger group most likely would end up close to 0.00.) Try to remember, therefore, that reliability is conceptually and computationally connected to the data produced by the *use* of a measuring instrument, not to the measuring instrument as it sits on the shelf.

Excerpts 4.17 and 4.18 illustrate the fact that reliability is a characteristic of data, not the instrument that produces the data. Reliability can vary across groups that vary in gender, age, health status, profession, or any number of other characteristics.

### EXCERPTS 4.17–4.18 • *Different Reliabilities from Different Samples*

The coefficient alpha for the RN composite ranges from .83 to .91 across ethnic groups. . . .

*Source:* Nelson, J. R., Stage, S. A., and Epstein, M. H. (2005). Effects of a prereading intervention on the literacy and social skills of children. *Exceptional Children, 72*(1), p. 36.

---

The third subscale, dietary restraint, which consists of five items, had an internal consistency of 0.70 for boys and 0.87 for girls at baseline.

*Source:* Wade, T. D., Davidson, S., and O'Dea, J. A. (2003). A preliminary controlled evaluation of a school-based media literacy program and self-esteem program for reducing eating disorder risk factors. *International Journal of Eating Disorders, 33*(4), p. 375.

Some researchers realize that reliability is a property of scores produced by the administration of a measuring instrument (rather than a property of the printed instrument itself). With this in mind, they not only cite reliability coefficients obtained by previous researchers who used the same instrument, but also gather reliability evidence *within* their own investigation. This practice is not widely practiced, unfortunately. Most of the time, researchers simply reiterate the reliability evidence gathered earlier by previous researchers who developed or used the same instrument. Those researchers who take the extra time to assess the reliability of the data gathered in their own investigation deserve credit for knowing that reliability ought to be reestablished in any current study. In Excerpt 4.19, we see an example of this good practice.

## EXCERPT 4.19 • *Assessing Reliability within the Researcher's Study*

A scale developed by Procidano and Heller (1983) was used to evaluate the qualitative characteristics of social support provided to the students by their peers and families. . . . In the study carried out by Procidano and Heller, Cronbach's alpha of perceived peer support and perceived family support were found to be 0.88 and 0.90 respectively. In the current study, the values were found to be 0.85 and 0.91 respectively.

*Source:* Kukulu, K., Buldukoglu, K., Kulakaç, Ö., and Köksal, C. D. (2006). The effects of locus of control, communication skills and social support on assertiveness in female nursing students. *Social Behavior & Personality: An International Journal, 34*(1), p. 33.

My next warning calls on you to recognize that any reliability coefficient is simply an estimate of consistency. If a different batch of examinees or raters are used, you should expect the reliability coefficient to be at least slightly different—even if the new batch of examinees or raters contains people who are highly similar to the original ones. If the groups are small, there would probably be more fluctuation in the reliability coefficient than if the groups are large. Accordingly, place more faith in the results associated with large groups. Regardless of how large the group of examinees or raters is, however, give credit to researchers who use the word *estimated* in conjunction with the word *reliability*.

My next-to-last warning concerns estimates of internal consistency. If a test is administered under great time pressure, the various estimates of internal consistency—split-half, K-R 20, and coefficient alpha—will be spuriously high (i.e., too big). Accordingly, do not be overly impressed with high internal consistency reliability coefficients if data have been collected under a strict time limit or if there is no mention as to conditions under which the data were collected.

Finally, keep in mind that reliability is not the only criterion that should be used to assess the quality of data. A second important feature of the data produced by measuring instruments (or raters) has to do with the concept of validity. The remaining portion of this chapter is devoted to a consideration of what validity means and how it is reported.

## Validity

Whereas the best one-word synonym for reliability is consistency, the core essence of **validity** is captured nicely by the word *accuracy*. From this general perspective, a researcher's data are valid to the extent that the results of the measurement process are accurate. Stated differently, a measuring instrument is valid to the extent that it measures what it purports to measure.

In this portion of the chapter, we first will consider the relationship between reliability and validity. Next, we will examine several of the frequently used procedures for assessing validity. Finally, I will offer a few warnings concerning published claims that you may see about this aspect of data quality.

### The Relationship between Reliability and Validity

It is possible for a researcher's data to be highly reliable even though the measuring instrument does not measure what it claims to measure. However, an instrument's data must be reliable if they are valid. Thus high reliability is a necessary but not sufficient condition for high validity. A simple example may help to make this connection clear.

Suppose a test is constructed to measure the ability of fifth-grade children to solve arithmetic word problems. Also suppose that the test scores produced by an administration of this test are highly reliable. In fact, let's imagine that the coefficient of stability turns out equal to the maximum possible value, $+1.00$. Even though the data from our hypothetical test demonstrate maximum consistency over time, the issue of accuracy remains unclear. The test may be measuring what it claims to measure—math ability applied to word problems. On the other hand, it may be that this test really measures reading ability.

Now, reverse our imaginary situation. Assume for the moment that all you know is that the test is valid. In other words, assume that this newly designed measuring instrument does, in fact, produce scores that accurately reflect the ability of fifth graders to solve arithmetic word problems. If our instrument produces scores that are valid, then those scores, of necessity, must also be reliable. Stated differently, accuracy requires consistency.

### Different Kinds of Validity

In published articles, researchers often present evidence concerning a specific kind of validity. Validity takes various forms because there are different ways in which scores can be accurate. To be a discriminating reader of the research literature, you need to be familiar with the purposes and statistical techniques associated with the popular validity procedures. The three most frequently used procedures are content validity, criterion-related validity, and construct validity.

Research
Navigator.c⦿m

Content validity

*Content Validity.*    With certain tests, questionnaires, or inventories, an important question concerns the degree to which the various items collectively cover the material that the instrument is supposed to cover. This question can be translated into a concern over the instrument's **content validity.** Normally, an instrument's standing with respect to content validity is determined simply by having experts carefully compare the content of the test against a syllabus or outline that specifies the instrument's claimed domain. Subjective opinion from such experts establishes—or doesn't establish—the content validity of the instrument.

In Excerpt 4.20, we see a case in which content validity is discussed by a team of researchers. As you will see, these researchers were extremely thorough in their effort to assess—and improve—the content validity of the new measuring instrument they had developed.

validity =
coefficient

***Criterion-Related Validity.***     Researchers sometimes assess the degree to which their new instruments provide accurate measurements by comparing scores from the new instrument with scores on a relevant criterion variable. The new instrument under investigation might be a short, easy-to-give intelligence test, and in this case the criterion would probably be an existing reputable intelligence test (possibly the *Stanford-Binet*). Or, maybe the new test is an innovative college entrance exami-

### EXCERPT 4.20 • *Content Validity*

The WHS was designed to measure the construct of hope and the three components (goals, pathways, and agency) pertaining to work and work-related issues. . . . After we made changes from the initial pilot sample data, we sent a copy of the 24-item WHS to each of three expert reviewers to establish content validity. All three reviewers were counseling psychologists and had both scholarly and clinical experience with issues related to work and career counseling. Additionally, one of these reviewers was also a contributor to Snyder's (2000) *Handbook of Hope: Theory, Measures, and Applications,* and another was an expert in test construction and item analysis. We asked the reviewers to evaluate each proposed item of the WHS and to specifically address (a) whether the item was essential, useful but not essential, or not necessary; (b) whether the item reflected the pathways, goals, or agency component of hope theory; (c) concerns about or bias apparent in this item; and (d) any other items that we should consider.

We compared the responses of the reviewers to determine which items had been consistently identified as either pathways, goals, or agency items. The reviewers agreed on the aspect of hope represented by 14 of the 24 items. We maintained all of these items, incorporating reviewer suggestions for language changes. For example, we changed "I have faith in the future" to "I am confident that things will work out for me in the future" in response to one reviewer's suggestion that the first version was too general to adequately address a respondent's sense of his or her own future and another reviewer's comment that faith could be interpreted as religious faith. We independently reviewed the 10 items that the expert reviewers did not rate consistently. We retained 5 of the 10 as written after we agreed independently with each other and one of the reviewers. We made changes to 4 items to more clearly identify them as reflecting a single component of the theoretical structure of hope. We dropped 1 item and replaced it with a new item to maintain balance across the three components.

*Source:* Juntunen, C. L., and Wettersten, K. B. (2006). Work hope: Development and initial validation of a measure. *Journal of Counseling Psychology, 53*(1), p. 97.

nation; hence, the criterion variable would be a measure of academic success in college (possibly GPA). The validity of either of those new tests would be determined by (1) finding out how various people perform on the new test and on the criterion variable, and (2) correlating these two sets of scores. The resulting *r* is called the **validity coefficient,** with high values of *r* indicating high validity.

**Research Navigator.c⊛m**

Concurrent validity

There are two kinds of criterion-related validity. If the new test is administered at about the same time that data are collected on the criterion variable, then the term **concurrent validity** is used to designate the kind of validity being investigated. Continuing the first example provided in the preceding paragraph, if people were given the new and existing intelligence tests with only a short time interval between their administrations, the correlation between the two data sets would speak to the issue of concurrent validity. If, however, people were given the new test years before they took the criterion test, then *r* would be a measure of **predictive validity.**

In Excerpts 4.21 and 4.22, we see cases where the expressed concern of the researchers was with concurrent and predictive validity. In each of these excerpts, note that a single bivariate correlation coefficient—most likely Pearson's *r*—was used to evaluate the **criterion-related validity** of the tests being investigated. Note also that the criterion variable is not explicitly named in either excerpt. For example, in Excerpt 4.21 was the criterion variable the ILS Sequential and Global scale or was it the PT? You will have no problem answering a question like this if you simply remember that data on the criterion variable come from the test used to evaluate the quality of the measuring instrument under investigation. Keeping this in mind, you

### EXCERPTS 4.21–4.22 • *Concurrent and Predictive Validity*

This study suggests that there are good reasons to question the usefulness of the ILS Sequential and Global scale. First because of its low internal reliability and, second, because of its low correlation ($r = -.08$) with the PT, a measure of a similar construct. Thus the Sequential-Global scale of the ILS can be said to lack concurrent validity with the PT.

*Source:* Genovese, J. E. C. (2005). The Index of Learning Styles: An investigation of its reliability and concurrent validity with the Preference Test. *Individual Differences Research,* 2(3), p. 173.

--------------------------------------------------------------------------------

The predictive validity of RBANS Total Score for stroke inpatients was supported by its strong correlation [$r = .72$] with a measure of cognitive disability at follow-up, 12 months later.

*Source:* Larson, E. B., Kirschner, K., Bode, R., Heinemann, A., and Goodman, R. (2005). Construct and predictive validity of the Repeatable Battery for the Assessment of Neuropsychological Status in the evaluation of stroke patients. *Journal of Clinical & Experimental Neuropsychology,* 27(1), p. 28.

should be able to discern that PT was the criterion instrument in Excerpt 4.21 while an unnamed measure of cognitive disability was the criterion in Excerpt 4.22.

In Excerpt 4.23, we see a case where the generic term *criterion-related validity* was used. When you encounter passages like this, you may have to make a guess as to whether reference is being made to concurrent validity or to predictive validity. Sometimes, as with Excerpt 4.23, there are not many clues to use when trying to decide which type of criterion-related validity is being discussed. Here, I would guess that it is concurrent validity, for I suspect scores on the CSR and measurements of goniometric flexibility were collected in close temporal proximity.

### EXCERPT 4.23 • *Criterion-Related Validity*

The chair sit-and-reach (CSR) assesses lower-body flexibility, primarily the hamstring. . . . Criterion validity was established by the good correlation between goniometric-measured flexibility and the CSR ($r = 0.76$ for men, $r = 0.81$ for women).

*Source:* Taylor-Piliae, R. E., Haskell, W. L., Stotts, N. A., and Froelicher, E. S. (2006). Improvement in balance, strength, and flexibility after 12 weeks of Tai Chi exercise in ethnic Chinese adults with cardiovascular disease risk factors. *Alternative Therapies in Health & Medicine, 12*(2), p. 52.

*Construct Validity.*    Many measuring instruments are developed to reveal how much of a personality or psychological construct is possessed by the examinees to whom the instrument is administered. To establish the degree of **construct validity** associated with such instruments, the test developer will typically do one or a combination of three things: (1) provide correlational evidence showing that the construct has a strong relationship with certain measured variables *and* a weak relationship with other variables, with the strong and weak relationships conceptually tied to the new instrument's construct in a logical manner; (2) show that certain groups obtain higher mean scores on the new instrument than other groups, with the high- and low-scoring groups being determined on logical grounds *prior to* the administration of the new instrument; or (3) conduct a factor analysis on scores from the new instrument.

Excerpt 4.24 provides an example of the first of these approaches to construct validity. This excerpt deserves your close attention because it contains a clear explanation of how correlational evidence is examined for the purpose of establishing **convergent validity** and **discriminant** (divergent) **validity.**

It is not always easy to demonstrate that a measuring instrument is involved in a network of relationships where certain of those relationships are strong while others are weak. However, claims of construct validity are more impressive when evidence regarding both convergent *and* discriminant validity is provided.

Research
Navigator.c⊕m

Convergent
validity
Discriminant
validity

## EXCERPT 4.24 • *Construct Validity Using Correlations*

Convergent and divergent validity were evaluated by determining the association between scores on the CQOLC-K and on other rating scales completed at the same time. Convergent validity was supported by moderate to strong correlations ($r = 0.39$–$0.58$) between the CQOLC-K and the SF-36 MCS total score and sub-scale scores (i.e., emotional role, mental health, social functioning, and vitality); and by correlations between the CQOLC-K and the BDI ($r = 0.50$ and $0.60$). In contrast, divergent validity was supported by the weaker or negligible correlations ($r = 0.16$–$0.30$) between the CQOLC-K and the SF-36 PCS total and subscale scores (i.e. physical functioning, physical role, bodily pain and general health).

*Source:* Rhee, Y. S., Shin, D. O., Lee, M. K., Yu, H. J., Kim, J. W., Kim, S. O., Lee, R., Lee, Y. O., Kim, N. S., and Yun, Y. H. (2005). Korean version of the Caregiver Quality of Life Index–Cancer (CQOLC–K). *Quality of Life Research, 14*(3), p. 901.

Of course, not all measuring instruments are created to deal with personality or psychological constructs, and even those that have been can be validated with noncorrelational evidence. When you *do* encounter validation evidence like that illustrated in Excerpt 4.24, give some "bonus points" (in your evaluation) to those researchers who have utilized the two-pronged approach.

In Excerpt 4.25, we see an example of the group comparison approach to construct validity. Here, the evidence for construct validity came from showing that a group of experienced surgeons could perform better than a group of novice surgeons in using the new virtual reality training device that was being evaluated.

## EXCERPT 4.25 • *Construct Validity Using Comparison Groups*

In order to evaluate construct validity, it was tested whether the measured parameters of a task in the VR trainer (time, collisions, and path length) could discriminate between experienced surgeons (>100 endoscopic procedures) and novices (no experience with endoscopic surgery). . . . [Results showed that] the performance of experts was significantly better than that of the novices on all parameters.

*Source:* Verdaasdonk, E. G. G., Stassen, L. P. S., Monteny, L. J., and Dankelman, J. (2006). Validation of a new basic virtual reality simulator for training of basic endoscopic skills. *Surgical Endoscopy, 20*(3), pp. 514, 516.

The third procedure frequently used to assess construct validity involves a sophisticated statistical technique called **factor analysis.** Although I will not discuss the details of factor analysis here, I want you to see an illustration of how the results of such an investigation are typically summarized. I don't expect you

**EXCERPT 4.26 • *Construct Validity Using Factor Analysis***

---

### *Construct Validity: Factor Structure*

A principal components factor analysis with oblimin rotation was conducted. . . . The factor solution was determined using the scree plot method. . . . It was decided that the factors extracted would only comprise items with a factor load greater than .35. The factor solution was composed of 36 items grouped into 5 factors that accounted for 42.86% of the variance. . . . Factor 1, *Assertiveness* (eigenvalue = 8.31), accounted for 12.42% of the variance and included 16 items about making complaints; defense of one's rights and interests; rejecting unreasonable requests; and asking service staff (waiters, shop assistants, etc.), family and acquaintances (grandparents, neighbors, etc.), and strangers in the street for information. Factor 2, *Heterosexual Relationships* (eigenvalue = 2.34), accounted for 11.29% of the variance and was composed of seven items about heterosexual relationships (having a date, giving compliments, etc.). Factor 3, *Public Speaking* (eigenvalue = 1.68), accounted for 7.71% of the variance and comprised five items in which the adolescent has to act in front of a large group of people or an audience. Factor 4, *Family Relationships* (eigenvalue = 1.65), accounted for 6.07% of the variance and was composed of four items about assertion, particularly in the family environment. Factor 5, *Close Friendships* (eigenvalue = 1.45), accounted for 5.37% of the variance and included four items about giving thanks, apologizing, and handling criticism with close friends of the opposite sex.

*Source:* Inglés, C. J., Hidalgo, M. D., and Méndez, F. X. (2005). Interpersonal Difficulties in Adolescence: A new self-report measure. *European Journal of Psychological Assessment, 21*(1), pp. 14–16.

---

to understand everything in Excerpt 4.26; my only purpose in presenting it is to alert you to the fact that construct validity is often assessed statistically using factor analysis.

## *Warnings about Validity Claims*

Before concluding our discussion of validity, I want to sensitize you to a few concerns regarding validity claims. Because researchers typically have a vested interest in their studies, they are eager to have others believe that their data are accurate. Readers of research literature must be on guard for unjustified claims of validity and for cases where the issue of validity is not addressed at all.

First, remember that reliability is a necessary but not sufficient condition for validity. Accordingly, do not be lulled into an unjustified sense of security concerning the accuracy of research data by a technical and persuasive discussion of consistency. Reliability and validity deal with different concepts, and a presentation of reliability coefficients—no matter how high—should not cause one's concern for validity to evaporate.

Next, keep in mind that validity (like reliability) is really a characteristic of the data produced by a measuring instrument and not a characteristic of the measuring instrument itself.[6] If a so-called valid instrument is used to collect data from people who are too young or who cannot read or who lack any motivation to do well, then the scores produced by that instrument will be of questionable validity. The important point here is simply this: The people used by a researcher and the conditions under which measurements are collected must be similar to the people and conditions involved in validation studies before you should accept the researcher's claim that the research data are valid because those data came from an instrument having "proven validity."

My third warning concerns content validity. Earlier, I indicated that this form of validity usually involves a subjective evaluation of the measuring instrument's content. Clearly, this evaluation ought to be conducted by individuals who possess (1) the technical expertise to make good judgments as to content relevance and (2) a willingness to provide, if necessary, negative feedback to the test developer. When reporting on efforts made to assess content validity, researchers should describe in detail who examined the content, what they were asked to do, and how their evaluative comments turned out.

With respect to criterion-related and construct validity, a similar warning seems important enough to mention. With these approaches to assessing validity, scores from the instrument being validated are correlated with the scores associated with one or more "other" variables. If the other variables are illogical or if the validity of the scores associated with such variables is low, then the computed validity coefficients conceivably could make a truly good instrument look as if it is defective. Thus, regarding the predictive, concurrent, or construct validity of a new measuring instrument, the researcher should first discuss the quality of the data that are paired with the new instrument's data.

My next-to-last warning concerns the fact that the validity coefficients associated with criterion-related or construct probes are simply estimates, not definitive statements. Just as with reliability, the correlation coefficients reported to back up claims of validity would likely fluctuate if the study were to be replicated with a new batch of examinees. This is true even if the test-takers in the original and replicated studies are similar. Such fluctuations can be expected to be larger if the validity coefficients are based on small groups of people; accordingly, give researchers more credit when their validity investigations are based on large groups.

Finally, keep in mind that efforts to assess predictive and concurrent validity utilize correlation coefficients to estimate the extent to which a measuring instrument can be said to yield accurate scores. When construct validity is dealt with by assessing an instrument's convergent/discriminant capabilities or by conducting a factor analysis, correlation again is the vehicle through which validity is revealed. Because correlation plays such a central role in the validity of these kinds of

---

[6]This is true for all varieties of validity except content validity.

investigations, it is important for you to remember the warnings about correlation that were presented near the end of Chapter 3. In particular, do not forget that $r^2$ provides a better index of a relationship's strength than does $r$.

## Three Final Comments

Within this discussion of reliability and validity, I have not addressed a question that most likely passed through your mind at least once as we considered different procedures for assessing consistency and accuracy. That question is simply, "How high do the reliability and validity coefficients need to be before we can trust the results and conclusions of the study?" Before leaving this chapter, I want to answer this fully legitimate question.

For both reliability and validity, it would be neat and tidy if there were some absolute dividing point (say, .50) that separates large from small coefficients. Unfortunately, no such dividing point exists. In evaluating the reliability and validity of data, the issue of large enough has to be answered in a *relative* manner. The question that the researcher (and you) should ask is, "How do the reliability and validity of data associated with the measuring instrument(s) used in a given study compare with the reliability and validity of data associated with other available instruments?" If the answer to this query about relative quality turns out to be "pretty good," then you should evaluate the researcher's data in a positive manner—even if the absolute size of reported coefficients leaves lots of room for improvement.

The second of my three final comments concerns the possible use of multiple methods to assess instrument quality. Since there is no rule or law that prohibits researchers from using two or more approaches when estimating reliability or validity, it is surprising that so many research reports contain discussions of only *one* kind of reliability and (if validity is discussed at all) only *one* kind of validity. That kind of research report is common because researchers typically overlook the critical importance of having good data to work with and instead seem intent on quickly analyzing whatever data have been collected. Give credit to those few researchers who present multiple kinds of evidence when discussing reliability and validity.

My last general comment about reliability and validity is related to the fact that data quality, by itself, does not determine the degree to which a study's results can be trusted. It's possible for a study's conclusions to be totally worthless even though the data analyzed possess high degrees of reliability and validity. A study can go down the tubes despite the existence of good data if the wrong statistical procedure is used to analyze data, if the conclusions extend beyond what the data legitimately allow, or if the design of the study is deficient. Reliability and validity are important concepts to keep in mind as you read technical reports of research investigations, but other important concerns must be attended to as well.

## Review Terms

| | |
|---|---|
| Accuracy | Equivalent-forms reliability |
| Alpha | Factor analysis |
| Alternate-forms reliability | Internal consistency reliability |
| Coefficient alpha | Interrater reliability |
| Coefficient of concordance | Intraclass correlation |
| Coefficient of equivalence | Kuder-Richardson #20 (K-R 20) |
| Coefficient of stability | Parallel-forms reliability |
| Cohen's kappa | Predictive validity |
| Concurrent validity | Reliability |
| Consistency | Reliability coefficient |
| Construct validity | Spearman-Brown |
| Content validity | Split-half reliability coefficient |
| Convergent validity | Standard error of measurement (SEM) |
| Criterion-related validity | Test-retest reliability coefficient |
| Cronbach's alpha | Validity |
| Discriminant validity | Validity coefficient |

## The Best Items in the Companion Website

1. An interactive online quiz (with immediate feedback provided) covering Chapter 4.
2. Ten misconceptions about the content of Chapter 4.
3. An online resource entitled "Multitrait-Multimethod."
4. An email message about convergent and discriminant validity sent from the author to his students to help them understand these two measurement concepts.
5. Chapter 4's best paragraph.

To access chapter objectives, practice tests, weblinks, and flashcards, visit the companion website at www.ablongman.com/huck5e.

Research Navigator.c⊛m

## Fun Exercises inside Research Navigator

1. **How reliable is measured empathy in medical residents over a one-year time period?**

   In this study, nearly 100 medical internists completed the *Jefferson Scale of Physician Empathy* during their residence. Of these interns, 41 had their empathy measured on two occasions: at the beginning of their first year and then again a year later. Pearson's product-moment correlation was used to assess the reliability of these 41 pairs of scores. After presenting the value of $r$, the researchers asserted "this magnitude of test-retest reliability over [a] one-year interval supports the conclusion that the empathy scores remained stable during this time period." How large do you think that test-retest reliability was? After making a guess, locate the PDF version of the research report in the Nursing, Health, and Medicine database of ContentSelect and read (on page 71) the last paragraph of the "Results" section.

S. Mangione, G. C. Kane, J. W. Caruso, J. S. Gonnella, T. J. Nasca, & M. Hojat. Assessment of empathy in different years of internal medicine training. *Medical teacher*. Located in the NURSING, HEALTH, AND MEDICINE database of ContentSelect.

### 2. How valid is a 10-item instrument for measuring alcohol withdrawal symptoms?

The data in this study came from 60 patients receiving alcohol withdrawal treatment in a London psychiatric hospital. These individuals were evaluated with the SAWS, a 10-item self-report instrument designed to measure alcohol withdrawal symptoms. (This assessment instrument is quite simple; the patient simply indicates, using a scale of 0 to 3, how severe each of 10 conditions—such as sweating or tremors—has been within the past 24 hours.) To assess concurrent validity, 46 of the patients were also measured with the CIWA-Ar, another more complicated procedure for assessing alcohol withdrawal symptoms. After reporting the correlation between the SAWS and the CIWA-Ar, the researchers said, "since the SAWS and the CIWA-Ar have both been designed to measure the same phenomena, a substantial degree of correlation between the two scores is to be expected." You might be surprised to see the actual size of the validity coefficient! To see what it was, locate the PDF version of the research report in the Biology database of ContentSelect and then read the last full paragraph on page 42.

M. Gossop, F. Keaney, D. Stewart, E. J. Marshall, & J. Strang. A Short Alcohol Withdrawal Scale (SAWS): Development and psychometric properties. *Addiction Biology*. Located in the BIOLOGY database of ContentSelect.

**Review Questions and Answers begin on page 513.**

# CHAPTER 5

# Foundations of Inferential Statistics

In Chapters 2 through 4, we considered various statistical procedures that are used to organize and summarize data. At times, the researcher's sole objective is to describe the people (or things) in terms of the characteristic(s) associated with the data. When that is the case, the statistical task is finished as soon as the data are displayed in an organized picture, are reduced to compact indices (e.g., the mean and standard deviation), are described in terms of distributional shape, are evaluated relative to the concerns of reliability and validity, and, in the case of a bivariate concern, are examined to discern the strength and direction of a relationship.

In many instances, however, the researcher's primary objective is to draw conclusions that extend beyond the specific data that are collected. In this kind of study, the data are considered to represent a sample—and the goal of the investigation is to make one or more statements about the larger group of which the sample is only a part. Such statements, when based upon sample data but designed to extend beyond the sample, are called *statistical inferences*. Not surprisingly, the term **inferential statistics** is used to label the portion of statistics dealing with the principles and techniques that allow researchers to generalize their findings beyond the actual data sets obtained.

In this chapter, we will consider the basic principles of inferential statistics. We begin by considering the simple notions of sample, population, and scientific guess. Next, we take a look at eight of the main types of samples used by applied researchers. Then we consider certain problems that crop up to block a researcher's effort to generalize findings to the desired population. Finally, a few tips are offered concerning specific things to look for as you read professional research reports.

## Statistical Inference

Whenever a statistical inference is made, a **sample** is first extracted (or is considered to have come from) a larger group called the **population.** Measurements are then taken on the people or objects that compose the sample. Once these measurements are summarized—for example, by computing a correlation coefficient—an educated guess is made as to the numerical value of the same statistical concept (which, in our example, would be the correlation coefficient) in the population. This educated guess as to the population's numerical characteristic is the **statistical inference.**

If measurements could be obtained on all people (or objects) contained in the population, statistical inference would be unnecessary. For instance, suppose the coach of the girls' basketball team at a local high school wants to know the median height of 12 varsity team members. It would be silly for the coach to use inferential statistics to answer this question. Instead of the coach making an educated guess as to the team's median height (after seeing how tall a few of the girls are), it would be easy to measure the height of each member of the varsity team and then obtain the precise answer to the question.

In many situations, researchers cannot answer their questions about their populations as easily as could the coach in the basketball example. Two reasons seem to account for the wide use of inferential statistics. One of these explanations concerns the measurement process while the other concerns the nature of the population. Because inferential statistics are used so often by applied researchers, it is worthwhile to pause for a moment and consider these two explanations as to why only portions of populations are measured, with educated guesses being made on the basis of the sample data.

First of all, it is sometimes too costly (in dollars and/or time) to measure every member of the population. For example, the intelligence of all students in a high school cannot be measured with an individual intelligence test because (1) teachers would be upset by having each student removed from classes for two consecutive periods to take the test and (2) the school's budget would not contain the funds needed to pay a psychologist to do this testing. In this situation, it would be better for the principal to make an educated guess about the average intelligence of the high school students than to have no data-based idea whatsoever as to the students' intellectual capabilities. The principal's guess about the average intelligence is based on a sample of students taken from the population made up of all students in the high school. In this example, the principal is sampling from a **tangible population** because each member of the student body could end up in the sample and be tested.

The second reason for using inferential statistics is even more compelling than the issue of limited funds and time. Often, the population of interest extends into the future. For example, the high school principal in the previous example probably would like to have information about the intellectual capabilities of the school's student body so improvements in the curriculum could be made. Such changes are made on the assumption that next year's students will not be dissimilar from this year's students. Even if the funds and time could be found to administer an individual intelligence test to every student in the school, the obtained data would be viewed as coming from a *portion* of the population of interest. That population is made up of students who attend the school now *plus* students who will follow in their footsteps. Clearly, measurements cannot be obtained from all members of such a population because a portion of the population has not yet "arrived on the scene." In this case, the principal creates an **abstract population** to fit an existing sample.

Several years ago, I participated as a subject in a study to see if various levels of consumed oxygen have an effect, during strenuous exercise, on blood composition. The researcher who conducted this study was interested in what took place physiologically during exercise on a stationary bicycle among nonsedentary young men between the ages of 25 and 35. That researcher's population was not just active males who were 25–35 years old at the time of the investigation. The population was defined to include active males who *would be* in this age range at the time the research summary got published—approximately 18 months following the data collection. Inferential statistics were used because the subjects of the investigation were considered to be a representative sample of a population of similar individuals that extended into the future.

To clarify the way statistical inference works, consider the two pictures in Figure 5.1. These pictures are identical in that (1) measurements are taken only on the people (or objects) that compose the sample; (2) the educated guess, or inference, extends *from* the sample *to* the population; and (3) the value of the population characteristic is not known (nor ever can be known as a result of the inferential process). Although these illustrations show that the inference concerns the mean, the pictures could have been set up to show that the educated guess deals with the median, the variance, the product-moment correlation, or any other statistical concept.

As you can see, the only differences between the two pictures involve the solid versus dotted nature of the larger circle and the black arrows. In the top picture, the population is tangible in nature, with each member within the larger circle available for inclusion in the sample. When this is the case, the researcher actually begins with the population and then ends up with the sample. In Figure 5.1, the lower picture is meant to represent the inferential setup in which the sequence of events is reversed. Here, the researcher begins with the sample and then creates an abstract population that is considered to include people (or objects) like those included in the sample.

Excerpts 5.1 and 5.2 illustrate the distinction between tangible and abstract populations. In the first of these excerpts, the population was made up of 2,033 students in third, fourth, and fifth grade in a North Carolina community. This was a tangible population because (a) every student in the population had a unique name or ID number and (b) any of those individual students could have ended up in the sample. In Excerpt 5.1, you will see the term **sampling frame.** Generally speaking, a sampling frame is simply a list that enumerates the things—people, animals,

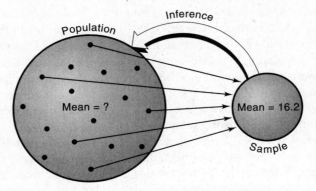

(a) Sampling from a tangible population

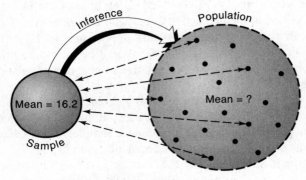

(b) Creation of an abstract population
to fit an existing sample

**FIGURE 5.1**   *Two Kinds of Sample/Population Situations*

objects, or whatever—in the population. In a very real sense, there must be a sampling frame for any tangible population.

In Excerpt 5.2, we see a study in which the population was abstract. No sampling frame was referred to by the researchers because there wasn't one. The 90 students who composed the sample were not "pulled from" (i.e., drawn out of) a larger group; instead, they got into the sample because they voluntarily responded to a posted advertisement. Because the researchers associated with Excerpt 5.2 used inferential statistics with the data collected from those 90 students, it's clear that they wanted to generalize the study's findings beyond those specific students. The relevant population cannot be realistically defined as the full student body at the University of Chicago, for it's highly like that (a) only some of the University's students saw the posted information about the study and (b) only some of those who saw it volunteered to be in the study. Thus, the population in this study was abstract because it existed only hypothetically as a larger "mirror image" of the sample.

### EXCERPTS 5.1–5.2 • *Tangible and Abstract Populations*

The primary sample [involved] students in the third through fifth grades in a community bordering a major urban center in North Carolina. . . . The sampling frame for the study was all third- through fifth-grade students attending the seven public elementary schools in the community (n = 2,033). From the sampling frame, school district evaluation staff generated a random sample of 700 students.

*Source:* Bowen, N. K. (2006). Psychometric properties of the Elementary School Success Profile for Children. *Social Work Research, 30*(1), p. 53.

-------------------------------------------------------------------------------------

*Participants.* Ninety University of Chicago students were recruited using posted advertisements and were paid two dollars for participating in this 15-min experiment.

*Source:* Burson, K. A., Larrick, R. P., and Klayman, J. (2006). Skilled or unskilled, but still unaware of it: How perceptions of difficulty drive miscalibration in relative comparisons. *Journal of Personality and Social Psychology, 90*(1), p. 63.

## The Concepts of Statistic and Parameter

When researchers engage in inferential statistics, they must deal with four questions *before* they can make their educated guess, or inference, that extends from the sample to the population:

1. What is/are the relevant population(s)?
2. How will a sample be extracted from each population of interest, presuming the population(s) is/are tangible in nature?
3. What characteristic of the sample people, animals, or objects will serve as the target of the measurement process?
4. What will be the study's statistical focus?

The first of these four questions is completely up to the researcher and will be dictated by the study's topical focus. The second question will be considered in detail in the next section. The third question, of course, is answered when the researcher decides what to study.[1] The notion of a measurement process is also involved in this question, thus making the issues of reliability and validity (covered in Chapter 4) important to consider when judging whether the researcher did an adequate job in measuring the subjects. This brings us to the fourth question, a concern for the statistical focus of the inference.

---

[1] You may, at times, disagree with the researcher as to whether the characteristic of the people, animals, or objects in the population is important. Nevertheless, I doubt that you will ever experience difficulty determining what variables were examined. A clear answer to this question is usually contained in the article's title, the statement of purpose, and/or the discussion of dependent variables.

After the researcher has measured the sample on the variable(s) of interest, there are many alternative ways in which the data can be summarized. The researcher could compute, for example, a measure of central tendency, a measure of variability, a measure of skewness, or a measure of relationship. But even within each of these broad categories, the researcher has alternatives as to how the data will be summarized. With central tendency, for example, the researcher might decide to focus on the median rather than on the mean or the mode. If relationship is the issue of interest, a decision might be made to compute Pearson's product-moment correlation coefficient rather than other available correlational indices. The term **statistical focus** is used simply to indicate the way in which the data are summarized.

Regardless of how a researcher decides to analyze the sample data, there will always be two numerical values that correspond to the study's statistical focus. One of these is "in" the sample—and it can be computed as soon as the sample is measured. This numerical value is called the **statistic.** The second value that corresponds to the study's statistical focus is "in" the population, and it is called the **parameter.** The parameter, of course, can never be computed because measurements exist for only a portion of the people, animals, or objects that compose the population.

Because researchers often use symbols to represent the numerical values of their statistics (and sometimes use different symbols to represent the unknown values of the corresponding parameters), it is essential that you become familiar with the symbols associated with inferential statistics. To assist you in doing this, I have developed a chart (Table 5.1) that shows the most frequently used symbols for the statistic and parameter that correspond to the same statistical focus. As you can

**TABLE 5.1**   *Symbols Used for Corresponding Statistics and Parameters*

| *Statistical Focus* | *Statistic* *(in the sample)* | *Parameter* *(in the population)* |
|---|---|---|
| Mean | $\overline{X}$ or $M$ | $\mu$ |
| Variance | $s^2$ | $\sigma^2$ |
| Standard deviation | $s$ | $\sigma$ |
| Proportion | $p$ | $P$ |
| Product-moment correlation* | $r$ | $\rho$ |
| Rank-order correlation | $r_s$ | $\rho_s$ |
| Size of group† | $n$ | $N$ |

*Unfortunately, the symbol $\rho$ is used to designate the value of the product-moment correlation in the relevant population. This is the letter rho from the Greek alphabet. In Chapter 3, we saw that Spearman's rank-order correlation is also referred to as rho.

†In many articles, the symbol $N$ is used to indicate the size of the *sample*. It would be better if the symbol $n$ could be used instead of $N$ when researchers give us information about their sample sizes.

easily see, Roman letters are used to represent statistics whereas Greek letters stand for parameters.

Now that I have clarified the notions of statistic and parameter, I can be a bit more parsimonious in my definition of inferential statistics. When engaged in inferential statistics, a researcher uses information concerning the known value of the sample statistic to make an educated guess as to the unknown value of the population parameter. If, for example, the statistical focus is centered on the mean, then information concerning the known value of $\overline{X}$ is used to make a scientific guess as to the value of $\mu$.

## Types of Samples

The nature of the sample used by a researcher as a basis for making an educated guess as to the parameter's value obviously has an influence on the inferential process. To be more specific, the nature of the sample will influence either (1) the accuracy of the inferential guess or (2) the definition of the population toward which the inferential guess is directed. To help you understand the way in which the sample can affect the inferential process in these two ways, I need to distinguish among eight kinds of samples that fall into two main categories: probability samples and nonprobability samples.

### Probability Samples

If all members of the population can be specified prior to drawing the sample, if each member of the population has at least some chance of being included in the sample, and if the probability of any member of the population being drawn is known, then the resulting sample is referred to as a **probability sample.** The four types of probability samples that we will consider are called *simple random samples, stratified random samples, systematic samples,* and *cluster samples.* As you read about each of these samples, keep in mind the illustration presented in Figure 5.1a.

***Simple Random Samples.***   With a **simple random sample,** the researcher, either literally or figuratively, puts the names of all members of the population into a hat, shuffles the hat's contents, and then blindly selects out a portion of the names to determine which members of the total group will or won't be included in the sample. The key feature of this kind of sample is an equal opportunity for each member of the population to be included in the sample. It is conceivable, of course, that such a sample could turn out to be grossly unrepresentative of the population (because the sample turns out to contain the population members that are, for example, strongest or most intelligent or tallest). It is far more likely, however, that a simple random sample will lead to a measurement-based statistic that approximates the value of the parameter. This is especially true when the sample is large rather than small.

In Excerpts 5.3 and 5.4, we see examples of simple random samples being used in applied research studies. Because there are different kinds of random samples that can be drawn from a tangible population, these researchers deserve credit for using the word *simple* to clarify exactly what type of random sampling procedure was used in their studies.

### EXCERPTS 5.3–5.4 • *Simple Random Samples*

A simple random sample of 350 adults aged 18 and over was drawn from the R. L. Polk Directory of names and addresses of Oklahoma City residents.

*Source:* Welch, M. R., Tittle, C. R., and Grasmick, H. G. (2006). Christian religiosity, self-control and social conformity. *Social Forces, 84*(3), p. 1608.

--------------------------------------------------------------------------------

Four different secondary schools were randomly selected (based on the simple random sampling technique) from the list of daily secondary schools in Penang Island.

*Source:* Chwen, J. C., Seong, C. T., and Wan, M. F. (2005). Are learning styles relevant to virtual reality? *Journal of Research on Technology in Education, 38*(2), p. 128.

Research Navigator.com

Sratified random sample

**Stratified Random Samples.**     To reduce the possibility that the sample might turn out to be unrepresentative of the population, researchers will sometimes select a **stratified random sample.** To do this, the population must first be subdivided into two or more parts based upon the knowledge of how each member of the population stands relative to one or more stratifying variables. Then, a sample is drawn so as to mirror the population percentages associated with each segment (or stratum) of the population. Thus if a researcher knew that the population contained 60 percent males and 40 percent females, a random sample stratified on gender would end up containing six males for every four females.

An example of a stratified random sample is presented in Excerpt 5.5. Notice how the population of young adults in Angola's capital city was initially stratified by the nine sections (i.e., municipalities) of the city. From each of these strata, households were selected (most likely, at random), with the number of households from each municipality being proportional to its population size. By using this stratified random sampling procedure, the researcher made sure that the final sample had the correct proportionate representation of households in each of Luanda's nine municipalities.

### EXCERPT 5.5 • *Stratified Random Samples*

The purpose of this study was to identify determinants of condom use among adolescents and young adults in Angola. We analyzed data from a recent survey [administered to] 2,419 males and females aged 15–24 who lived in Luanda, the capital of Angola. It used a stratified random sample that included all nine municipalities of Luanda province, each representing a stratum. The number of households selected for interviewing in each stratum was proportional to its population size.

*Source:* Prata, N. (2005). Gender and relationship differences in condom use among 15–24-year-olds in Angola. *International Family Planning Perspectives, 31*(4), pp. 193–194.

In some studies in which stratified random samples are used, researchers will make the size of the sample associated with one or more of the strata larger than that strata's proportionate slice of the population. This **oversampling** in certain strata is done for one of three reasons: (1) anticipated difficulty in getting people in certain strata to participate in the study, (2) a desire to make comparisons between strata (in which case there are advantages to having equal strata sizes in the sample, even if those strata differ in size in the population), and (3) a need to update old strata sizes, when using archival data, because of recent changes in the characteristics of the population. In Excerpt 5.6, we see an example of a stratified random sample that involved oversampling for the second of these three reasons.

### EXCERPT 5.6 • *Oversampling in Stratified Random Samples*

The sampling frame was stratified by race/ethnicity and level of restrictiveness of treatment setting (i.e., home vs. aggregate care setting). From the sampling frame of 12,662 children, 3,417 were randomly selected. . . . To ensure adequate sample size for subgroup analysis, particular groups were purposely oversampled (e.g., Asian/Pacific Islanders and youth in alcohol/drug treatment).

*Source:* McCabe, K. M., Lucchini, S. E., Hough, R. L., Yeh, M., and Hazen, A. (2005). The relation between violence exposure and conduct problems among adolescents: A prospective study. *American Journal of Orthopsychiatry, 75*(4), p. 578.

Research
Navigator.c⊕m

Systematic
Sample

**Systematic Samples.**   A third type of probability sample is called a systematic sample. This type of sample is created when the researcher goes through an ordered list of members of the population and selects, for example, every fifth entry on the list to be in the sample. (Of course, the desired size of the sample and the number of entries on the list determine how many entries are skipped following the selection of each entry to be in the sample.) So long as the starting position on the list is determined randomly, each entry on the full list has an equal chance of ending up in the sample. Thus if the researcher decides to generate a sample by select-ing every fifth entry, the first entry selected for the sample should not arbitrarily be the entry at the top of the list (or the one positioned in the fifth slot); instead, a random decision should determine which of the first five entries goes into the sample.

Excerpt 5.7 exemplifies the use of a systematic sample. Notice that the starting point for this systematic sample was chosen at random. That identified which of the first three members of the social work society would be included in the sample. Then, every third member on the SSWR list (past the starting point) was selected until the full sample size of 309 individuals was reached.

**EXCERPT 5.7 • *Systematic Samples***

A random sample of 309 members [of the Society for Social Work and Research] was selected for participation using a systematic sampling with a random start in which every third SSWR member was chosen.

*Source:* Apgar, D. H., and Congress, E. (2005). Authorship credit: A national study of social work educators' beliefs. *Journal of Social Work Education, 41*(1), pp. 103–104.

*Cluster Samples.*     The last of the four kinds of probability sampling to be discussed here involves what are called cluster samples. When this technique is used to extract a sample from a population, the researcher first develops a list of the clusters in the population. The clusters might be households, schools, litters, car dealerships, or any other groupings of the things that make up the population. Next, a sample of these clusters is randomly selected. Finally, data are collected from each person, animal, or thing that is in each of the clusters that have been randomly selected, or data are collected from a randomly selected subset of the members of each cluster.

In Excerpt 5.8, we see an example of a cluster sample. In this study, each "cluster" was a school. As indicated in the excerpt, six schools were initially selected (at random) from within each geographical area; then, six classes were randomly se-lected from each school. Thus, the students who ended up in the sample were drawn randomly from within the clusters. This technique of cluster sampling made it much easier for the researchers to collect their study's data than would have been the case if a simple random sample had been taken from the population of 74,318 students.

It is worthwhile to compare Excerpt 5.8 with Excerpt 5.5; there is an important yet subtle difference between the sampling procedures used in these two excerpts. In Excerpt 5.5, the area of Luanda was first stratified into nine municipalities and then individual households were randomly selected from within each municipality. In Ex-cerpt 5.8, the population of Murcia was also stratified (into five sections). Note, how-ever, that students were not directly and randomly selected from within each of

## EXCERPT 5.8 • *Cluster Samples*

The reference population was high school pupils from the Murcia region of Spain. . . . According to the school census there was a total of 74,318 subjects, 63,329 enrolled in 77 public schools and 10,989 in 30 private schools. . . . A cluster random sampling was carried out throughout the geographical areas of the region of Murcia: center, north, south, east, and west. Thirty-two schools, 24 public and 8 private, were randomly selected to represent all geographical areas. Each geographical area was represented by an average of six schools. Once the schools were selected, six classes were randomly chosen, with approximately 140 subjects per school.

*Source:* Inglés, C. J., Hidalgo, M. D., and Méndez, F. X. (2005). Interpersonal difficulties in adolescence: A new self-report measure. *European Journal of Psychological Assessment, 21*(1), p. 13.

Murcia's areas. Instead, six schools were. This meant that only those students from the selected clusters (i.e., from each region's six schools) had a chance to be in the study.

### Nonprobability Samples

In many research studies, the investigator does *not* begin with a finite group of persons, animals, or objects in which each member has a known, nonzero probability of being plucked out of the population for inclusion in the sample. In such situations, the sample is technically referred to as a **nonprobability sample.** Occasionally, as in Excerpt 5.9, an author will tell us directly that one or more nonprobability samples served as the basis for the inferential process. Few authors do this, however, and so you need to be able to identify this kind of sample from the description of the study's subject pool.

## EXCERPT 5.9 • *Nonprobability Samples*

A nonprobability sample was recruited from community sources and medical facilities in areas served by the University of Georgia, the University of Pittsburgh, and the University of Texas Southwestern Medical Center in Dallas.

*Source:* Beach, S. R., Schulz, R., Williamson, G. M., Miller, L. S., Weiner, M. F., and Lance, C. E. (2005). Risk factors for potentially harmful informal caregiver behavior. *Journal of the American Geriatrics Society, 53*(2), p. 256.

Although inferential statistics can be used with nonprobability samples, extreme care must be used in generalizing results from the sample to the population. From the research write-up, you probably will be able to determine who (or what) was in the sample that provided the empirical data. Determining the larger group to whom such inferential statements legitimately apply is usually a much more difficult task.

We will now consider four of the most frequently seen types of nonprobability samples. These are called purposive samples, convenience samples, quota samples, and snowball samples.

***Purposive Samples.*** In some studies, the researcher starts with a large group of potential subjects. To be included in the sample, however, members of this large group must meet certain criteria established by the researcher because of the nature of the questions to be answered by the investigation. Once these screening criteria are employed to determine which members of the initial group wind up in the sample, the nature of the population at the receiving end of the "inferential arrow" is different from the large group of potential subjects with which the researcher started. The legitimate population associated with the inferential process is either (1) the portion of the initial group that satisfied the screening criteria, presuming that only a subset of these acceptable people (or objects) were actually measured or (2) an abstract population made up of people (or objects) similar to those included in the sample, presuming that each and every "acceptable" person (or object) was measured. These two notions of the population, of course, are meant to parallel the two situations depicted earlier in Figure 5.1.

Excerpt 5.10 illustrates the way researchers will sometimes use and describe their **purposive samples.** In this passage, notice how the researchers set up six criteria for determining whether or not a resident of the Pine Ridge Indian Reservation was qualified to be in the sample. By listing these inclusion and exclusion criteria (and by using the term *purposive sample*), the researchers helped their readers avoid the mistake of generalizing the study's findings to all residents of the Pine Ridge Indian Reservation.

### EXCERPT 5.10 • *Purposive Samples*

A purposive sample was drawn from a WIC program located on the Pine Ridge Indian Reservation in South Dakota. . . . Inclusion criteria were self-described AI/AN women, age 19 years or older, and parent of child or children enrolled in WIC. Exclusion criteria were women who were unable to read or understand spoken English, and women who were currently pregnant (due to the potentially confounding effect of pregnancy on physical activity behavior).

*Source:* Fahrenwald, N. L., and Shangreaux, P. (2006). Physical activity behavior of American Indian mothers. *Orthopaedic Nursing, 25*(1), p. 24.

It should be noted that the research report from which Excerpt 5.10 was taken contained a detailed description of the American Indian women who supplied this study's data. That description (not shown in this excerpt) focused on several demographic characteristics other than those used as inclusion or exclusion screening criteria. Such descriptions are exceedingly important in studies involving purposive samples, for the relevant populations associated with nonprobability samples are abstract rather than tangible. As pointed out earlier, the nature of an abstract population is determined by who or what is in the sample. Accordingly, if the characteristics of the sample are not known, how can anyone describe the population to which the inference is directed?

***Convenience Samples.*** In some studies, no special screening criteria are set up by the researchers to make certain that the individuals in the sample possess certain characteristics. Instead, the investigator simply collects data from whoever is available or can be recruited to participate in the study. Such data-providing groups, if they serve as the basis for inferential statements, are called **convenience samples.**

The population corresponding to any convenience sample is an abstract (i.e., hypothetical) population. It is considered by the researcher to include individuals (or objects) similar to those included in the sample. Therefore, the sample-population relationship brought about by convenience samples is always like that pictured earlier in Figure 5.1b.

Excerpts 5.11 and 5.12 illustrate the use of convenience samples. In these excerpts, the researchers clearly label the kind of sample they used. Not all researchers are so forthright.

### EXCERPTS 5.11–5.12 • *Convenience Samples*

A convenience sample of 50 adults over age 18 and known by the researchers in the form of co-workers, friends, and family members was recruited for the study.

*Source:* Greenwald, B. (2006). A pilot study evaluating two alternate methods of stool collection for the Fecal Occult Blood Test. *MEDSURG Nursing, 15*(2), p. 91.

-------------------------------------------------------------------------------------

A convenience sample of 200 female employees from three Ontario health care centers participated in the study.

*Source:* Williams, A., Franche, R., Ibrahim, S., Mustard, C. A., and Layton, F. R. (2006). Examining the relationship between work-family spillover and sleep quality. *Journal of Occupational Health Psychology, 11*(1), p. 29.

It should be noted that the statements presented in Excerpts 5.11 and 5.12 do not constitute the full description of the convenience samples used in these studies. In each case, the researchers provided extremely detailed descriptions of the individuals from whom data were gathered. Unfortunately, many researchers put us in a quandary by not providing such descriptions. Unless we have a good idea of who is in a convenience sample, there is no way to conceptualize the nature of the abstract population toward which the statistical inferences are aimed.

*Quota Samples.*      The next type of nonprobability sample that we will consider is called a **quota sample.** Here, the researcher decides that the sample should contain X percent of a certain kind of person (or object), Y percent of a different kind of person (or object), and so on. Then, the researcher simply continues to hunt for enough people/things to measure within each category until all predetermined sample slots have been filled.

In Excerpt 5.13, we see an example of a quota sample. In this investigation, the researchers wanted a predetermined number of their research participants to fall into each of several demographic categories based on age, race, and gender. These were the quotas. The researchers then went out and recruited people for the study, with the freedom to recruit almost anyone they located who fit the demographic criteria, until the various quota goals were met.

## EXCERPT 5.13 • *Quota Samples*

Because the study's goal was to examine the way women of all ages respond to sports media and report feelings of body dissatisfaction, a quota sample was used. Researchers in three areas—the Northeast, the Deep South, and the Southwest—determined their area's representation with regard to age, race, and gender. A matrix was created for each region that identified the percentage of respondents needed in each category, such as Black women between 35 and 50 or Hispanic women between 18 and 29, to represent the population of each region. An overall $N$ of 660 males and females was the target; therefore, each researcher computed the percentage needed for each demographic group based on an $N$ of 220 per region.

Finally, researchers went into the field, provided with instruments with a cover sheet attached that described the gender, approximate age, and race of the participant they were to recruit for the study. Researchers were told participants could be recruited from anywhere in the state or region as specified on their coversheet, but undergraduate students were not to be recruited. They continued to recruit participants until data was collected from all target groups.

*Source:* Bissell, K. L. (2004). What do these messages really mean? Sports media exposure, sports participation, and body image distortion in women between the ages of 18 and 75. *Journalism & Mass Communication Quarterly, 81*(1), p. 112.

On the surface, quota samples and stratified random samples seem to be highly similar. There is, however, a big difference. To obtain a stratified random sample, a finite population is first subdivided into sections and then a sample is selected randomly from each portion of the population. When combined, those randomly selected groups make up the stratified random sample. A quota sample is also made up of different groups of people that are combined. Each subgroup, however, is not randomly extracted from a different stratum of the population; rather, the researcher simply takes whoever comes along until all vacant sample slots are occupied. As a consequence, it is often difficult to know to whom the results of a study can be generalized when a quota sample serves as the basis for the inference.

**Research Navigator.com**

Snowball sample

***Snowball Samples.*** A snowball sample is like a two-stage convenience or purposive sample. First, the researcher locates a part of the desired sample by turning to a group that is conveniently available or to a set of individuals who possess certain characteristics deemed important by the researcher. Then, those individuals are asked to help complete the sample by going out and recruiting family members, friends, acquaintances, or coworkers who might be interested (and who possess, if a purposive sample is being generated, the needed characteristics). Excerpt 5.14 illustrates how this technique of snowballing is sometimes used in research studies.

### EXCERPT 5.14 • *Snowball Samples*

A diverse group of 224 women, aged 35 to 65, was recruited through a variety of means and volunteered to participate in the study. Notices were placed on electronic listservs with predominantly adult female memberships including high school alumni listservs, college alumni and active student listservs, and special interest listservs that included midlife women and lesbian women. . . . Snowball sampling was used by having participants contact other midlife women and inviting them to participate.

*Source:* Degges-White, S., and Myers, J. E. (2006). Transitions, wellness, and life satisfaction: Implications for counseling midlife women. *Journal of Mental Health Counseling, 28*(2), p. 137.

## The Problems of Low Response Rates, Refusals to Participate, and Attrition

If the researcher uses a probability sample, there will be little ambiguity about the destination of the inferential statement that is made—as long as the researcher clearly defines the *population* that supplied the study's subjects. Likewise, there will be little ambiguity associated with the target of inferential statements based upon nonprobability samples—as long as the *sample* is fully described. In each case, however, the inferential process becomes murky if data are collected from less than 100 percent of the individuals (or objects) that comprise the sample. In this section, we need to consider three frequently seen situations in which inferences are limited because only a portion of the full sample is measured.

### Response Rates

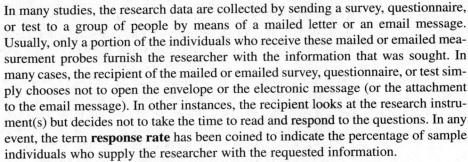

**Research
Navigator.c⊕m**
Response rate

In many studies, the research data are collected by sending a survey, questionnaire, or test to a group of people by means of a mailed letter or an email message. Usually, only a portion of the individuals who receive these mailed or emailed measurement probes furnish the researcher with the information that was sought. In many cases, the recipient of the mailed or emailed survey, questionnaire, or test simply chooses not to open the envelope or the electronic message (or the attachment to the email message). In other instances, the recipient looks at the research instrument(s) but decides not to take the time to read and respond to the questions. In any event, the term **response rate** has been coined to indicate the percentage of sample individuals who supply the researcher with the requested information.

In Excerpts 5.15, 5.16, and 5.17, we see three cases in which response rates were reported in recent studies. In the first two of these excerpts, the response rate was far below the optimum value of 100 percent. Response rates like these are not uncommon. Some researchers attempt to justify their low response rates by saying that "it is normal to have a low response rate in mailed surveys" or that some so-called research authority says that "a response rate of 30 percent or more is adequate." You should be wary of such attempts to justify low response rates. Clearly, the statistical inferences in these studies extend only to individuals who are similar to those who returned completed surveys.

### EXCERPTS 5.15–5.17 • *Response Rates*

One hundred six of the 360 questionnaires were returned, a response rate of 29%.

*Source:* Nordquist, G. (2006). Patient insurance status and do-not-resuscitate orders: Survival of the richest? *Journal of Sociology & Social Welfare, 33*(1), p. 81.

---

Accounting for the e-mails that did not reach the recipients, the response rate was approximately 15%.

*Source:* Reiss, R., Schoenig, G., and Wright, G. (2006). Development of factors for estimating swimmers' exposures to chemicals in swimming pools. *Human & Ecological Risk Assessment, 12*(1), p. 142.

---

The final sample included 701 individuals. The overall response rate for eligible participants was 89% (701/787).

*Source:* Grzywacz, J. G., Arcury, T. A., Bell, R. A., Wei, L., Suerken, C. K., Smith, S. L., and Quandt, S. A. (2006). Ethnic differences in elders' home remedy use: Sociostructural explanations. *American Journal of Health Behavior, 30*(1), p. 41.

Adequate response rates rarely show up in studies where the researcher simply sits back and waits for responses from people who have been mailed just once a survey, questionnaire, or test. As Excerpts 5.18, 5.19, and 5.20 show, researchers can do certain things both before and after the measuring instrument is mailed in an effort to achieve a high response rate. Researchers (like those associated with these three excerpts) who try to get responses from everyone in the target sample deserve credit for their efforts; on the other hand, you ought to downgrade your evaluation of those studies in which little or nothing is done to head off the problem of ending up with a poor response rate.

### EXCERPTS 5.18–5.20 • *Working to Get a Good Response Rate*

At the seventh week, we sent a follow-up letter to thank the respondents and to remind the nonrespondents to complete and return their questionnaires. The follow-up letter generated 66 additional usable responses.

*Source:* Zhao, J. J., Truell, A. D., Alexander, M. W., and Hill, I. B. (2006). "Less success than meets the eye?" The impact of Master of Business Administration education on graduates' careers. *Journal of Education for Business, 81*(5), p. 263.

----------

Participants were offered $20 to complete the [mailed] materials and became eligible for drawings totaling another $1,500 (no proxy reports by caregivers or family members were accepted).

*Source:* Krause, J. S., and Broderick, L. (2006). Relationship of personality and locus of control with employment outcomes among participants with spinal cord injury. *Rehabilitation Counseling Bulletin, 49*(2), p. 112.

----------

When these [reminder] letters did not have any noticeable effect on the response rate, we telephoned the non-responding principals. . . . Then, we sent a second reminder to the non-responding schools by telefax. In some cases, we delivered 3rd copies of the questionnaires personally. A few weeks later, we made reminder telephone calls to the outstanding schools. For 24 schools, we made arrangements to personally collect the completed questionnaires.

*Source:* Mathews, C., Boon, H., Flisher, A. J., and Schaalma, H. P. (2006). Factors associated with teachers' implementation of HIV/AIDS education in secondary schools in Cape Town, South Africa. *AIDS Care, 18*(4), p. 391.

Most researchers who collect data through the mail or via the Internet want their findings to generalize to individuals like those in the *full* group to whom the measuring instrument was originally sent, not just individuals like those who send back completed instruments. To get a feel for whether less-than-perfect response rates ought to restrict the desired level of generalizability, researchers sometimes conduct a midstream ministudy to see whether a **nonresponse bias** exists. As indicated in Excerpts 5.21 and 5.22, there are different ways to check on a possible nonresponse bias. The methods exemplified by the first of these excerpts are easier to execute, but they provide the least impressive evidence as to the existence of any nonresponse bias. In contrast, the method illustrated in Excerpt 5.22 is difficult to accomplish; it is, however, the best approach for investigating possible nonresponse bias.

### EXCERPTS 5.21–5.22 • *Checking for Nonreponse Bias*

Nonresponse bias was addressed by comparing the demographics of participants in the final study to those of individuals contacted at each phase of recruitment. No substantial differences emerged between participants and nonparticipants in terms of gender and age distribution or education levels.

*Source:* Russell, C. A., and Stern, B. B. (2006). Consumers, characters, and products: A Balance model of sitcom product placement effects. *Journal of Advertising, 35*(1), p. 12.

---

The response rate, however, was below our expectation. We used two procedures to explore issues related to non-response bias. First, there were several identical items (e,g,, previous visitation, time spent onsite, fee attitude questions) that we used in both the onsite and mailback surveys. We compared the responses of nonrespondents to those of respondents for both the onsite and mailback questionnaires. No significant differences between respondents and non-respondents were observed. We then conducted a follow-up telephone survey of non-respondents to test for potential non-response bias as well as to further explore reasons why respondents had not returned their survey instruments. . . . Again, we observed no significant differences between the telephone and mailback samples on all items.

*Source:* Kyle, G. T., Mowen, A. J., Absher, J. D., and Havitz, M. E. (2006). Commitment to public leisure service providers: A conceptual and psychometric analysis. *Journal of Leisure Research, 38*(1), pp. 86–87.

### Refusal to Participate

In studies where individuals are asked to participate, some people may decline. Such **refusals to participate** create the same kind of problem that is brought about by low response rates. In each case, valid inferences extend only to individuals similar to those who actually supplied data, not to the larger group of individuals who were *asked* to supply data. In Excerpt 5.23, we see a case in which nearly 60 percent of the potential subjects chose not to participate.

### EXCERPT 5.23 • *Refusals to Participate*

Participants were 38 children (17 boys, 21 girls) aged between 7 and 9 years ($M = 8.4$; range = 7-5 months to 9-4). Children were from working- or middle-class backgrounds, and were drawn from two primary schools in the north of England. Letters were sent to the parents of all children aged between 7 and 9 years in both schools seeking consent to participate in the study. Around 40% of the parents approached agreed for their children to take part.

*Source:* Meins, E., Fernyhough, C., Johnson, F., and Lidstone, J. (2006). Mind-mindedness in children: Individual differences in internal-state talk in middle childhood. *British Journal of Developmental Psychology, 24*(1), p. 184.

Just as some researchers perform a check to see whether a less-than-optimal response rate affects the generalizability of results, certain investigators will compare those who agree to participate with those who decline. If no differences are noted, a stronger case exists for applying inferential statements to the full group of individuals invited to participate (and others who are similar) rather than simply to folks similar to those who supplied data. Researchers who make this kind of comparison in their studies deserve bonus points from you as you critique their investigations. Conversely, you have a right to downgrade your evaluation of a study if the researcher overlooks the possible problems caused by refusals to participate.

### Attrition[2]

In many studies, less than 100 percent of the subjects remain in the study from beginning to end. In some instances, such attrition arises because the procedures or data-collection activities of the investigation are aversive, boring, or costly to the participant. In other cases, forgetfulness, schedule changes, or changes in home location explain why certain individuals become dropouts. Regardless of the causal forces that bring about the phenomenon of **attrition,** it should be clear why attrition can affect the inferential process.

Excerpt 5.24 illustrates the problems that can be caused by attrition. Of the 251 male participants who were in this study when it began, more than 50 percent dropped out before the final point of data collection. The researchers deserve high marks for noting this high level of attrition and for pointing out that their findings should not be generalized beyond their study's sample. As you read or listen to other research reports, you will inevitably encounter studies in which the researchers are not so candid about attrition. In many cases, the researcher simply is unaware of the

[2]The problem of attrition is sometimes referred to as **mortality.**

potential problems caused by attrition; in other cases, the researcher knows about such problems but chooses not to call attention to a deficiency in the study.

### EXCERPT 5.24 • *Attrition*

Data were collected at intake, at one month, and at three months after completing an assigned intervention using the Sexual Risk Questionnaire (SRQ). . . . Of the 251 men who completed an assigned intervention, about a fifth (19%) failed to return for a 1-month assessment and more than half (54%) for a 3-month assessment. . . . Conclusions also cannot be generalized beyond the sample [partly because] attrition in the evaluation study was relatively high and it was not random. Therefore, findings cannot be generalized to those least likely to complete intervention sessions or follow-up assessments.

*Source:* Williams, M. L., Bowen, A. M., Timpson, S. C., Ross, M. W., and Atkinson, J. S. (2006). HIV prevention and street-based male sex workers: An evaluation of brief interventions. *AIDS Education & Prevention, 18*(3), pp. 207, 210, 214.

When attrition occurs in a study, it may be possible for the researcher to check for an attrition bias. The purpose and procedures in doing this mirror the goal and technique in checking for a response bias. In Excerpt 5.25, we see an example of an attrition rate that was quite high (34 percent), in which the researchers checked to see if this attrition was potentially damaging to the study. Notice that the check of a possible attrition bias revealed that those who dropped out of the study were different in several respects from those who stayed in.

### EXCERPT 5.25 • *Checking for Attrition Bias*

The 171 participants who did not return for their two follow-up visits represent a significant attrition rate (34%). A comparison of demographic and baseline measures indicated that the two groups [those who stayed in the study versus those who did not] differed on age, BMI, when diagnosed, language used in the DLC class attended, ethnicity (Caucasian, non-Caucasian dichotomy), HbA1c, PCS, MCS, and symptoms of depression (CES-D).

*Source:* Maljanian R., Grey, N., Staff, I., and Conroy, L. (2005). Intensive telephone follow-up to a hospital-based disease management model for patients with diabetes mellitus. *Disease Management, 8*(1), p. 18.

## A Few Warnings

As we approach the end of this chapter, I'd like to offer a handful of warnings about the inferential connection between samples and populations. I highly suggest that you become sensitive to these issues, because many professional journals contain articles in which the researcher's conclusions seem to extend far beyond what the inferential process legitimately allows. Unfortunately, more than a few researchers get carried away with the techniques used to analyze their data—and their technical reports suggest that they gave little or no consideration to the nature of their samples and populations.

My first warning has to do with *a possible mismatch between the source of the researcher's data and the destination of the inferential claims.* Throughout this chapter, we have emphasized the importance of a good match between the sample and the population. Be on guard when you read or listen to research reports, because the desired fit between sample and population may leave much to be desired. Consider, for example, the information presented in Excerpt 5.26.

### EXCERPT 5.26 • *Mismatch between Sample and Intended Population*

The population of interest in this study included traditional-aged female undergraduate students. Participants were recruited from a midsized university in the Southeast. All were volunteers who completed questionnaires during classes in counseling, human development and family studies, communications, and humanities. . . . A total of 272 female undergraduate students completed questionnaires for this study. Data from 82 participants were excluded from the primary analyses: four participants' questionnaires were incomplete, 68 participants were not European American, 6 women identified themselves as bisexual, and 4 women identified themselves as "exclusively or primarily homosexual."

*Source:* Sinclair, S. L. (2006). Object lessons: A theoretical and empirical study of objectified body consciousness in women. *Journal of Mental Health Counseling, 28*(1), pp. 53–54.

The major concern you ought to have with the passage in Excerpt 5.26 is the vast difference between the declared population of interest and the actual sample. The researcher's intent was to use sample data and inferential statistics as a basis for making claims about "traditional-aged female undergraduate students." However, data were collected from a sample of students attending a single midsized university, and several potential participants were tossed out of the sample because of their ethnicity or sexual preference. These features of the sample made it impossible for the study's findings to be generalized to the stated population of interest.

My next warning has to do with the *size of the sample.* If you don't know much about the members of the sample or how the researcher obtained the sample, then the inferential process cannot operate successfully—no matter how large the sample might be. Try to remember, therefore, that it is the quality of the sample (rather than its size) that makes statistical inference work. Proof of this claim can be seen during national elections when pollsters regularly predict with great accuracy who will win elections even though the samples used to develop these predictions are relatively small.

My third warning concerns the term *random*. Randomness in research studies is usually considered to be a strong asset, but you should not be lulled into thinking that an investigation's results can be trusted simply because the term *random* shows up in the method section of the write-up. Consider, for example, the material presented in Excerpts 5.27 and 5.28.

**EXCERPTS 5.27–5.28 •** *The Word "Random"*

To specify the two key informants from each of the 500 firms, the firms were telephoned and requested to select one midlevel manager randomly (e.g., sales, marketing, research-and-development [R&D] department manager) and one top executive (e.g., chief executive officer, general manager). The key informants were carefully chosen to ensure that they had the knowledge and background to complete the questionnaire in a thoughtful manner.

*Source:* Luo, X., Slotegraaf, R. J., and Pan, X. (2006). Cross-functional "coopetition": The simultaneous role of cooperation and competition within firms. *Journal of Marketing, 70*(2), p. 71.

As the prison was divided in sections, a sampling by section took place, selecting inmates randomly within each section [and then] the randomly selected inmates were invited to [participate]. . . . From the 436 invited inmates, 254 completed and returned the questionnaires (response rate 58.2%).

*Source:* Koulierakis, G., Power, K. G., Gnardellis, C., and Agrafiotis, D. (2003). HIV/Aids related knowledge of inmates in Greek prisons. *Addiction Research & Theory, 11*(2), pp. 107, 108.

In Excerpt 5.27, we are told that the two key informants within each of the 500 firms were chosen randomly. This seems unlikely for two reasons. First, the selection of the mid-level managers and top executives was done by someone within each firm after receiving a phone call and being asked to select these individuals. I seriously doubt that all of the recipients of those phone calls (or even most of them!) knew what must be done to select something—which, in this case, was a person from each of two categories—in a true random fashion. Second, because the manager and the executive were "carefully chosen to ensure that they had the knowledge and background to complete the questionnaire in a thoughtful manner," a conscious decision was probably made to select them in a nonrandom fashion. Simply stated, the notions of "key informant" and "random selection" are logically incompatible.

In Excerpt 5.28, we again see the word *randomly* used, this time to describe prison inmates who served as this study's research participants. In this instance, I think the researchers actually selected a random sample of 436 inmates from the larger set of individuals incarcerated at Korydallos Prison in Greece. But did the researchers' *data* come from a random sample? No. That's because less than 60 percent of the randomly selected inmates completed the questionnaires they were given. Accurate inferences can be based on samples that are made up of small portions of their corresponding populations. That is not possible, however, when initial randomness is destroyed by nonresponse bias.

To clarify that their random samples are truly random, researchers should describe the procedures used to extract samples from their relevant populations. They should do this because the question of whether or not a sample is a random sample can be answered only by considering the procedure used to select the sample. As indicated earlier in the chapter, one not-too-sophisticated procedure for getting a random sample is to draw slips of paper from a hat. Random samples can also be produced by flipping coins or rolling dice to determine which members of the population end up in the sample.

Most contemporary researchers do not draw their random samples by rolling dice, flipping coins, or drawing slips of paper from a hat. Instead, they utilize either a printed **table of random numbers** or a set of **computer-generated random numbers.** To identify which members of the population get into the sample, the researcher first assigns unique ID numbers (such as 1, 2, 3, etc.) to the members of the population. Then, the researcher turns to a table of random numbers (or a set of computer-generated random numbers) where the full set of ID numbers will appear in a scrambled order. Finally, the ID numbers that appear at the top of the list (e.g., 27, 4, 9) designate which members of population get into the sample.

In Excerpts 5.29 and 5.30, we see how easy it is for a researcher to indicate that a random sample was selected via a table of random numbers or computer-generated random numbers. These authors deserve credit for clarifying exactly how their random samples were created. All researchers should follow these good examples!

**Research Navigator.com**

Computer-generated random numbers

**EXCERPTS 5.29–5.30** • *Using a Table of Random Numbers and Computer-Generated Random Numbers*

At each selected house, interviewers asked the initial contact to list all eligible inhabitants (persons living in that house who were 18 years of age or older). A random numbers table was then used to select one inhabitant from this list.

*Source:* Bolton, P., Wilk, C. M., and Ndogoni, L. (2004). Assessment of depression prevalence in rural Uganda using symptom and function criteria. *Social Psychiatry & Psychiatric Epidemiology, 39*(6), p. 443.

---

The 22 students in the placement failure group were compared with a computer generated randomly selected group of 66 (14.6% of 474 students) who had not failed a placement.

*Source:* Ryan, M., Cleak, H., and McCormack, J. (2006). Student performance in field education placements: The findings of a 6-year Australian study of admission data. *Journal of Social Work Education, 42*(1), p. 76.

The final warning I wish to provide is really a repetition of a major concern expressed earlier in this chapter. Simply stated, an empirical investigation that incorporates inferential statistics is worthless unless there is a detailed description of the population or the sample. No matter how carefully the researcher describes the measuring instruments and procedures of the study, and regardless of the levels of appropriateness and sophistication of the statistical techniques used to analyze the data, the results will be meaningless unless we are given a clear indication of the population from which the sample was drawn (in the case of probability samples) or the sample itself (in the case of nonprobability samples). Unfortunately, too many researchers get carried away with their ability to use complex inferential techniques when analyzing their data. I can almost guarantee that you will encounter technical write-ups in which the researchers emphasize their analytical skills to the near exclusion of a clear explanation of where their data came from or to whom the results apply. When you come across such studies, give the authors *high* marks for being able to flex their "data analysis muscles"—but *low* marks for neglecting the basic inferential nature of their investigations.

To see an example of a well-done description of a sample, consider Excerpt 5.31. Given this relatively complete description of the 211 individuals who formed this study's sample, you have a much better sense of the population to which the statistical inferences can be directed. After reading the material in Excerpt 5.31, go back and take a look at Excerpt 5.2 (which constitutes the full description of the sample used in that study). In which case do you have a better sense of the kind of people included in the sample?

## EXCERPT 5.31 • *Detailed Description of a Sample*

Participants ranged in age from 17 to 62 ($M = 24.88$, $SD = 9.6$). Twenty-six percent of the participants were men ($n = 54$), and 74% of them were women ($n = 157$). Forty-nine percent of the respondents were African American ($n = 104$), with 43% ($n = 91$) Caucasian, 2% ($n = 4$) Hispanic/Latino, 3% ($n = 5$) Asian American, and 3% ($n = 5$) unidentified. Most of the participants were employed part-time (37%, $n = 77$), with 33% ($n = 70$) unemployed and 12% ($n = 26$) employed full-time. We assessed the disability status of the student participants by asking one question: whether they had a disability. All individuals with disabilities in this study were found eligible for services through the state/federal vocational rehabilitation program and were receiving services through the agency. Fifty-four percent of the clients ($n = 44$) were diagnosed with cognitive disabilities, 14% ($n = 11$) with psychological disabilities, and 30% ($n = 24$) with physical disabilities.

*Source:* Strauser, D. R. (2006). Examining the moderating effect of disability status on the relationship between trauma symptomatology and select career variables. *Rehabilitation Counseling Bulletin, 49*(2), p. 93.

## Review Terms

| | |
|---|---|
| Abstract population | Quota sample |
| Attrition | Refusals to participate |
| Convenience sample | Response rate |
| Inferential statistics | Sample |
| Mortality | Simple random sample |
| Nonprobability sample | Statistic |
| Nonresponse bias | Statistical inference |
| Oversampling | Statistical focus |
| Parameter | Stratified random sample |
| Population | Table of random numbers |
| Probability sample | Tangible population |
| Purposive sample | |

## The Best Items in the Companion Website

1. An interactive online quiz (with immediate feedback provided) covering Chapter 5.
2. Ten misconceptions about the content of Chapter 5.
3. An email message sent from the author to his students to help them understand the difference between tangible and abstract populations.
4. A poem about questionnaires (written by a famous statistician).
5. The best passage from Chapter 5 (selected by the author).

To access chapter objectives, practice tests, weblinks, and flashcards, visit the companion website at www.ablongman.com/huck5e.

Research Navigator.c⊕m

## Fun Exercises inside Research Navigator

1. **What is the ethnic composition of a national probability sample of children aged 18 to 36 months?**

   In this U.S. study, parents of young children were interviewed concerning the language development of their children. The 278 children who were the focus of this study were carefully selected to be a representative probability sample of all similarly aged children living in the continental United States. Stratified random sampling was used in an effort to achieve this goal, with 94.4 percent of the targeted parents agreeing to participate. As you would guess, the gender split in the sample was quite even (with 51 percent being girls). Focus now, however, on the sample's ethnic composition. There were four ethnic categories: African American, Latino/Hispanic, White, and Other (Asian or mixed). Choose any one of these ethnic categories and guess its percentage "slice" of the sample. To find out how accurate your guess is, locate the PDF version of the research report in the Communication Sciences and Disorders database of ContentSelect and look (on page 736) at Table 1.

L. Rescoria & T. M. Achenbach. Use of the Language Development Survey (LDS) in a national probability sample of children 18 to 36 months old. *Journal of Speech, Language, and Hearing Research.* Located in the COMMUNICATION SCIENCES AND DISORDERS database of ContentSelect.

## 2. Illicit psychostimulants on the college campus: Who uses them and why?

In this study, a sample of college students completed anonymous questionnaires through which they provided information about demographic variables, personality variables, and their use or nonuse of illicit drugs. Summarizing their findings in the journal article's "Discussion" section, the authors said this: "The present study suggests that abuse of stimulants, both prescription and illegal, may be a significant problem on U.S. college campuses. Roughly a third of the college students surveyed reported illicit use of prescription amphetamines." OK. Let's now back up a bit. How many colleges and universities do you think supplied the sample of students used in this study? And what kind of sampling do you think the researchers used? To find out the answers to these two not-so-trivial questions, locate the PDF version of the research report in the Nursing, Health, and Medicine database of ContentSelect and read (on page 284) the section entitled "Participants." You may be quite surprised at what you find!

K. G. Low & A. E. Gendaszek. Illicit use of amphetamines among college students: A preliminary study. *Psychology, Health, and Medicine.* Located in the NURSING, HEALTH, AND MEDICINE database of ContentSelect.

**Review Questions and Answers begin on page 513.**

# Estimation

In the previous chapter, we laid the foundation for our consideration of inferential statistics. We did that by considering the key ingredients of this form of statistical thinking and analysis: population, sample, parameter, statistic, and inference. In this chapter, we now turn our attention to one of the two main ways in which researchers use sample statistics to make educated guesses as to the values of population parameters. These procedures fall under the general heading **estimation.**

This chapter is divided into three main sections. First, the logic and techniques of *interval estimation* are presented. Next, we examine a second, slightly different way in which estimation works; this approach is called *point estimation*. Finally, I offer a few tips to keep in mind as you encounter research articles that rely on either of these forms of estimation.

Before beginning my discussion of estimation, I need to point out that the two major approaches to statistical inference—estimation and hypothesis testing—are similar in that the researcher makes an educated guess as to the value of the population parameter. In that sense, both approaches involve a form of guesswork that might be construed to involve estimation. Despite this similarity, the term *estimation* has come to designate just one of the two ways in which researchers go about making their educated guesses about population parameters. The other approach, hypothesis testing, is discussed in Chapters 7 and 8.

## Interval Estimation

To understand how **interval estimation** works, you must become familiar with three concepts: sampling errors, standard errors, and confidence intervals. In addition, you must realize that a confidence interval can be used with just about any statistic that is computed on the basis of sample data. To help you acquire these skills, we begin with a consideration of what is arguably the most important concept associated with inferential statistics: sampling error.

### Sampling Error

When a sample is extracted from a population, it is conceivable that the value of the computed statistic will be identical to the unknown value of the population parameter. Although such a result is possible, it is far more likely that the statistic will turn out to be different from the parameter. The term **sampling error** refers to the magnitude of this difference.

To see an example of sampling error, flip a coin 20 times, keeping track of the proportion of times the outcome is heads. I'll consider your 20 coin flips to represent a sample of your coin's life history of flips, with that total life history being the population. I will also assume that your coin is unbiased and that your flipping technique does not make a heads outcome more or less likely than a tails outcome. Given these two simple assumptions, I can assert that the parameter value is known to be .50. Now, stop reading, take out a coin, flip it 20 times, and see how many of your flips produce a heads outcome.

I do not know, of course, how your coin-flipping exercise turned out. When *I* flipped my coin (a nickel) 20 times, however, I *do* know what happened. I ended up with 13 heads and 7 tails, for a statistic of .65. The difference between the sample's statistic and the population's parameter is the sampling error. In my case, therefore, the sampling error turned out to be .15.[1]

If you end up observing 10 heads in your 20 coin flips, the sampling error would be equal to zero. Such a result, however, is not likely to occur. Usually, the sample statistic will contain sampling error and fail to mirror exactly the population parameter. Most of the time, of course, the size of the sampling error will be small, thus indicating that the statistic is a reasonably good approximation of the parameter. Occasionally, however, a sample will yield a statistic that is quite discrepant from the population's parameter. That would be the case if you get 19 or 20 heads (or tails) when flipping a coin 20 times.

It should be noted that the term sampling error does *not* indicate that the sample has been extracted improperly from the population or that the sample data have been improperly summarized. (I ended up with a sampling error of .15 even though I took a random sample from the population of interest and even though I carefully summarized my data.) When sampling error exists, it is attributable not to any mistake being made but rather to the natural behavior of samples. Samples generally do not turn out to be small mirror images of their corresponding populations, and statistics usually do not turn out equal to their corresponding parameters. Even with proper sampling techniques and data analysis procedures, sampling error ought to be expected.

In my example dealing with 20 coin flips, we knew what the parameter's value was equal to. In most inferential situations, however, the researcher will know the numerical value of the sample's statistic but not the value of the population's parameter.

---

[1] I computed the sampling error by subtracting .50 from .65.

This situation makes it impossible for the researcher to compute the precise size of the sampling error associated with any sample, but it does not alter the fact that sampling error should be expected. For example, suppose I gave you a coin that was known *only by me* to be slightly biased. Imagine that it would turn up heads 55 percent of the time over its life history. If I asked you to flip this coin 20 times and then make a guess as to the value of the coin's parameter value, you should expect sampling error to occur. Hence, not knowing the parameter value (and thus not being able to compute the magnitude of any sample's sampling error) should not affect your expectation that the statistic and the parameter are at least slightly unequal.[2]

### *Sampling Distributions and Standard Errors*

Most researchers extract a single sample from any population about which they want to make an educated guess. Earlier, for example, I asked you to take a sample of 20 flips of your coin's coin-flipping life history. It is possible, however, to *imagine* taking more than one sample from any given population. Thus I can imagine taking multiple samples from the coin I flipped that gave us, in the first sample, an outcome of .65 (that is, 65 percent heads).

When I imagine taking multiple samples (each made up of 20 flips) from that same coin, I visualize the results changing from sample to sample. In other words, whereas I obtained a statistic of .65 in my first sample, I would not be surprised to find that the statistic turns out equal to some other value for my second set of 20 flips. If a third sample (of 20 flips) were to be taken, I would not be surprised to discover that the third sample's statistic assumes a value different from the first two samples' statistics. If I continued (in my imagination) to extract samples (of 20 flips) from that same coin, I would eventually find that values of the statistic (1) would begin to repeat, as would be the case if I came across another sample that produced 13 heads, and (2) would form a distribution having tails that extend away from the distribution's modal value.

The distribution of sample statistics alluded to in the preceding paragraph is called a **sampling distribution,** and the standard deviation of the values that make up such a distribution is called a **standard error.** Thus a standard error is nothing more than an index of how variable the sample statistic is when multiple samples of the same size are drawn from the same population. As you recall from Chapter 2, variability can be measured in various ways; the standard error, however, is always conceptualized as being equal to the standard deviation of the sampling distribution of the statistic (once we imagine that multiple samples are extracted and summarized).[3]

[2]If a population is perfectly homogenous, the sampling error will be equal to 0. If the population is heterogeneous but an enormously large sample is drawn, here again the statistic will turn out equal to the parameter once that statistic is rounded to one or two decimal places. Both of these situations, however, are unrealistic. Researchers typically are involved with heterogeneous populations and base their statistical inferences on small samples where $n < 50$.

[3]Even though the concepts of standard deviation and standard error are closely related, they are conceptually quite different. A standard deviation indicates the variability inside a single set of actual data points; a standard error, in contrast, indicates how variable the sample statistic is from sample to sample.

Figure 6.1 contains the sampling distribution that we would end up with if we took many, many samples (of 20 flips per sample) from a fair coin's population of potential flips, with the statistical focus being the proportion of heads that turn up within each sample. The standard deviation of this sampling distribution is equal to about .11. This standard error provides a numerical index of how much dispersion exists among the values on which the standard deviation is computed; in this case, each of those values corresponds to the proportion of heads associated with one of our imaginary samples.

The standard error indicates the extent to which the statistic fluctuates, from sample to sample, around the value of the parameter. The standard error, therefore, provides a measure of how much sampling error is likely to occur whenever a sample of a particular size is extracted from the population in question. To be more

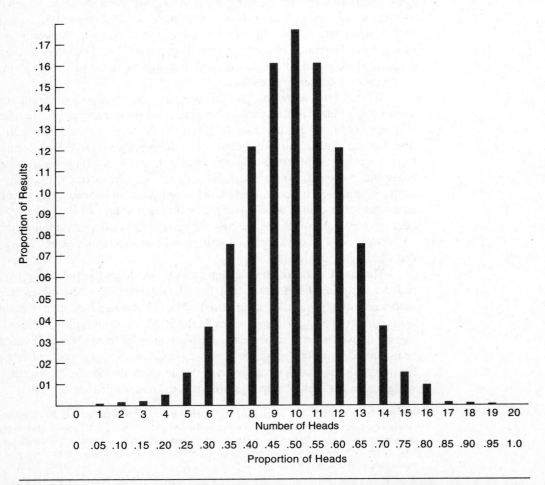

**FIGURE 6.1**   *Sampling Distribution of Number/Proportion of Heads in 20 Flips of a Fair Coin*

specific, the chances are about 2 out of 3 that the sampling error will be smaller than the size of the standard error (and about 1 in 3 that the sampling error will be larger than the size of the standard error). If the standard error is small, therefore, this would indicate that we should expect the statistic to approximate closely the value of the parameter. On the other hand, a large standard error would indicate that a larger discrepancy between the statistic and parameter is to be anticipated.

Earlier, I said that researchers normally extract only one sample from any given population. Based on my earlier statement to that effect (and now my reiteration of that same point), you may be wondering how it is possible to know what the standard error of the sampling distribution is equal to in light of the fact that the researcher would not actually develop a sampling distribution like that shown in Figure 6.1. The way researchers get around this problem is to use their sample data to estimate the standard error. I will not discuss the actual mechanics that are involved in doing this; rather, I simply want you to accept my claim that it *is* possible to do this.[4]

In my earlier example about a coin being flipped 20 times, the statistical focus was a proportion. Accordingly, the standard error (of .11) illustrated in Figure 6.1 is the standard error *of the proportion*. In some actual studies, the researcher's statistical focus will be a proportion, as has been the case in my coin-flipping example. In many studies, however, the statistical focus is something other than proportion. When reading journal articles, I find that the overwhelming majority of researchers focus their attention on means and correlation coefficients. There are, of course, other ways to "attack" a data set, and I occasionally come across articles in which the median, the variance, or the degree of skewness represents a study's statistical focus. Regardless of the statistical focus selected by the researcher, the standard error concept applies so long as the study involves inferential statistics.

Consider, for example, the short passage contained in Excerpt 6.1. As you can see, this excerpt comes from a study that involved the collection of physiological data on a group of individuals who ran a high-altitude marathon. The data here deal with heart rate (HR), and the researchers provided a mean HR for their eight runners plus an index of the sampling variability. Because the mean is the statistical focus, that index is called the standard error of the mean (SEM).

By providing (in Excerpt 6.1) information as to the estimated SEM associated with the marathon runners' heart rate, the researchers were alerting their readers to the fact that their data allowed them to compute sample statistics, not population parameters. In other words, each SEM in this short passage cautions us not to consider the means to be equal to $\mu$. If a different group of distance runners (like the ones used in this study) were to be plucked out of the same area of Peru, the mean heart rate for the new group of runners would probably turn out equal to some value other than 169.8.

---

[4]For example, when I use my single sample of 20 coin flips (13 heads, 7 tails) to estimate the standard error of the theoretical sampling distribution, I obtain the value of .1067. This estimated standard error of the proportion approximates the true value, .1118, that corresponds to the full sampling distribution shown in Figure 6.1.

**EXCERPT 6.1 • *Estimated Standard Error of the Mean***

Results were expressed as mean ± standard error of the mean (SEM). . . . Mean HR maintained during the marathon was 169.8 ± 5.3 bpm, which represented 89.0 ± 3.1% of the maximum theoretical heart rate (220 − age) and 94.4 ± 3.5% of the maximal HR assessed during the $VO_{2max}$ test. The fastest time of our subjects was 02:46:24 h and the slowest was 03:20:00 h.

*Source:* Cornolo, J., Brugniaux, J. V., Macarlupu, J., Privat, C., Leon-Velarde, F., & Richalet, J. (2005). Autonomic adaptations in Andean trained participants to a 4220-m altitude marathon. *Medicine and Science in Sports and Exercise, 37*(12), pp. 2150, 2151.

Excerpt 6.2 contains another example where information on the standard error of the mean was presented, this time in a table. In the study associated with this excerpt, the researchers investigated childhood abuse among female and male gambling addicts who were in treatment for their pathological desire to gamble. The table in Excerpt 6.2 shows a portion of a larger table that appeared in the research report and that summarized a variety of demographic characteristics of the gamblers who were studied.

In Excerpt 6.2, the presence of standard errors (in parentheses next to each mean) makes it clear that the researchers who conducted this study considered their female and male gamblers to be samples, not populations. If the researchers had been interested only in the 77 women and 72 men from whom data were gathered, it would have been illogical to compute standard error values. (The fact that these

**EXCERPT 6.2 • *Estimated Standard Error of the Mean in a Table***

**TABLE 1   *Demographic Characteristics***

| *Characteristic* | *Women* | *Men* |
|---|---|---|
| No. of participants | 77 | 72 |
| Age | 48.7 (1.2) | 46.6 (1.4) |
| Education (years) | 13.8 (0.2) | 14.1 (0.3) |
| Days of alcohol use in past month | 2.9 (0.7) | 2.7 (0.7) |
| Age started gambling | 24.6 (1.6) | 15.6 (0.9) |
| Age at onset of gambling problems | 39.3 (1.5) | 31.8 (1.5) |
| Age first sought gambling treatment | 45.4 (1.3) | 39.9 (1.3) |

*Note:* Tabled values represent means and standard errors (in parentheses).

*Source:* Petry, N. M., and Steinberg, K. L. (2005). Childhood maltreatment in male and female treatment-seeking pathological gamblers. *Psychology of Addictive Behaviors, 19*(2), p. 228. (Modified slightly for presentation here.)

female and male gamblers were viewed as samples was also made clear in the research report when inferential statistical procedures were used to compare the 77 women and 72 men to see if there was a statistically significant difference between them on a variety of variables, including those shown in Excerpt 6.2.)

The SEM values in Excerpts 6.1 and 6.2 give us a feel for how much variability we should expect to see if these studies were to be replicated, with the new samples in the replication studies being pulled out of the same abstract populations as were the marathon runners (in Excerpt 6.1) or the gamblers (in Excerpt 6.2). Consider, for example, the ages of the 77 female gamblers involved in the second of these excerpts. Because the standard error of the mean associated with the mean age of those women was quite small (1.2 years), another sample of 77 female gamblers would have about the same mean age, presuming that the population associated with this new sample is identical to the population actually associated with Excerpt 6.2. I wouldn't expect the new sample's mean to be exactly 48.7; however, I wouldn't expect it to be too different from that.

In Excerpt 6.3, we see a case where SEM values are presented in a bar graph. In this interesting study, each bar corresponds to a different sample involved in an

**EXCERPT 6.3 • *Estimated Standard Error of the Mean in a Bar Graph***

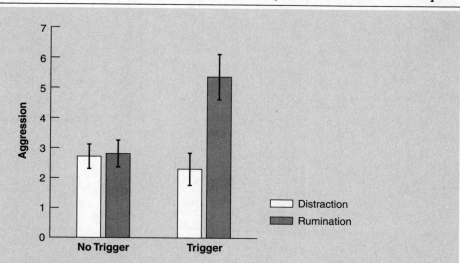

**FIGURE 2**    *Effects of triggering event and rumination on aggression after an initial provocation (Study 2). Aggression was measured using the number of grams of hot sauce that participants gave a confederate (who hated spicy food) to consume. Vertical bars denote plus or minus one standard error.*

*Source:* Bushman, B. J., Bonacci, A. M., Pedersen, W. C., Vasquez, E. A., and Miller, N. (2005). Chewing on it can chew you up: Effects of rumination on triggered displaced aggression. *Journal of Personality and Social Psychology, 88*(6), p. 975.

experiment focused on aggression. Two of the four groups were forced to experience a minor annoyance (referred to as a "trigger"). Then, one of the "trigger" groups and one of the "no trigger" groups was distracted while the other group within each pair was led to "ruminate." Finally, all members of the four groups had their aggression measured. The height of each bar corresponds to each sample's mean, and the vertical line that overlaps the top of each bar is a graphical indication of that group's SEM.

Excerpt 6.4 contains a graph showing how two groups of adolescent males performed on an acoustical test of voice quality both before and after a two-hour reading session. The boys in the experimental group read aloud; those in the control group read silently. As you can see, a vertical line passes through each of the six means displayed for each of the two groups. These vertical lines represent the estimated standard error of the mean.

**EXCERPT 6.4 •** *Estimated Standard Error of the Mean in a Line Graph*

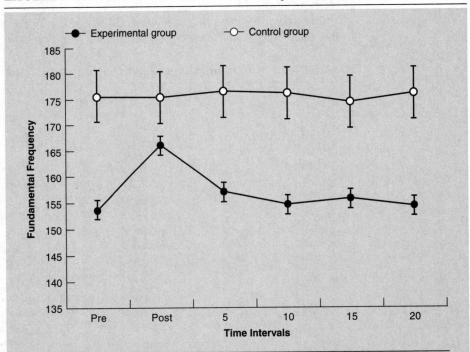

**FIGURE 1** *Average reading fundamental frequencies (Hz) and standard error of the means for both participant groups, recorded before, immediately after, and at each additional 5-min increment for 20 min following the experimental task.*

*Source:* Kelchner, L. N., Toner, M. M., and Lee, L. (2006). Effects of prolonged loud reading on normal adolescent male voices. *Language, Speech, and Hearing Services in Schools, 37,* p. 101.

In Excerpt 6.5, we see a passage that closely resembles the one presented earlier in Excerpt 6.1. In both cases, several means are presented, each accompanied by an estimated standard error. In the excerpt we looked at earlier, the abbreviation SEM was used to explain the meaning of the numbers (each preceded by a $\pm$ sign) that immediately followed each mean. Here, in Excerpt 6.5, the abbreviation SE is used. These two excerpts provide yet another case where different abbreviations or symbols are used by different researchers to refer to the same statistical concept. To understand research reports, you must develop the ability to see through such surface differences.

### EXCERPT 6.5 • *Estimated Standard Error of the Mean in the Text*

The means of the mathematics and reading scores for the higher achieving mathematics group were 7.00 ($SE = 0.30$) and 6.43 ($SE = 0.29$), respectively, and for the lower achieving group they were 3.86 ($SE = 0.10$) and 4.00 ($SE = 0.26$), respectively. There were 6 girls and 8 boys in the higher achieving group, and 8 girls and 6 boys in the lower achieving group.

*Source:* Cook, J. L., and Rieser, J. J. (2005). Finding the critical facts: Children's visual scan patterns when solving story problems that contain irrelevant information. *Journal of Educational Psychology, 97*(2), p. 230.

### Confidence Intervals

Researchers who report standard errors along with their computed sample statistics deserve to be commended. This practice helps to underscore the fact that sampling error is very likely to be associated with any sample mean, with any sample standard deviation, with any sample correlation coefficient, and with any other statistical summary of sample data. By presenting the numerical value of the standard error (as in Excerpts 6.1, 6.2, and 6.5) or by putting a line segment through the statistic's position in a graph (as in Excerpts 6.3 and 6.4), researchers help us to remember that they are only making educated *guesses* as to parameters.

Although standard errors definitely help us when we try to understand research results, a closely related technique helps us even more. As the title of this section indicates, we now wish to talk about **confidence intervals.** My fourfold objective here is to show what a confidence interval looks like, to explain how confidence intervals are built, to clarify how to interpret confidence intervals properly, and to point out how confidence intervals carry with them a slight advantage over standard errors.

*Confidence Intervals: What They Look Like.*   A confidence interval is simply a finite interval of score values on the dependent variable. Such an interval is constructed by adding a specific amount to the computed statistic (thereby obtaining the upper limit of

Research
Navigator.c⬡m

Confidence
intervals

the interval) and by subtracting a specific amount from the statistic (thereby obtaining the lower limit of the interval). In addition to specifying the interval's upper and lower limits, researchers will always attach a percent to any interval that is constructed. The percentage value selected by the researcher will invariably be a high number, such as 90 percent or 95 percent or 99 percent.[5]

In technical research reports, confidence intervals are typically presented in one of three ways. Excerpts 6.6 and 6.7 illustrate how confidence intervals will sometimes be reported within the text of the research report. Although both of these excerpts present 95 percent confidence intervals, notice that these presentations differ in that the confidence intervals are built around correlation coefficients in Excerpt 6.6 but around percentages in Excerpt 6.7. Also notice that the confidence interval built around the $r$ of $-.09$ in the first of these excerpts extends from $-.31$ to $+.14$. The presentation in the excerpt is potentially confusing, as it might cause you to think that the confidence interval extends from $-.31$ to $-.14$. That cannot be true, for the sample statistic (in this case $-.09$) *always* will be positioned between the end points of the confidence interval that's built around it.

### EXCERPTS 6.6–6.7 • *Confidence Intervals Reported in the Text*

For simple pictures, appraised ability did not significantly predict interest ($r = -.09$, *ns*, 95% confidence interval [CI] $= -.31-.14$). For complex pictures, however, appraised ability significantly predicted interest ($r = .41$, $p < .001$, 95% CI $= .21-.58$).

*Source:* Silvia, P. J. (2005). What is interesting? Exploring the appraisal structure of interest. *Emotion, 5*(1), p. 95.

Most participants in the control condition (79%, 95% confidence interval 61%–92%) and in the incentive condition (84%, 95% confidence interval $=$ 66%–95%) believed they could taste the difference between the two drinks—substantially more than the 50% of uninformed participants in the pretest who could distinguish the two drinks.

*Source:* Epley, N., Keysar, B., Van Boven, L., and Gilovich, T. (2004). Perspective taking as egocentric anchoring and adjustment. *Journal of Personality and Social Psychology, 87*(3), p. 332.

The second place you will see confidence intervals is in tables. Excerpt 6.8 illustrates this reporting strategy. In this excerpt, take a look at the two confidence intervals in the table's bottom row. Notice that the Phase 1 and Phase 3 percentages are almost identical (32.4 versus 32.3). Also notice that the confidence interval built

---

[5]The vast majority of researchers set up 95% confidence intervals. If you read enough research reports, you may come across 90% and 99% confidence intervals; however, you will likely consider them to be "exceptions to the rule" because they are used so infrequently.

**EXCERPT 6.8** • *Confidence Intervals Reported in a Table*

**TABLE 2** *Prevalence and Severity of Self-Reported Depression Among Phase 1 and Phase 3 MSSC Respondents*

| | Phase 1 | | Phase 3 | |
|---|---|---|---|---|
| | % | 95% CI | % | 95% CI |
| Self-reported depression | 50.2 | 46.4–54.1 | 49.3 | 44.1–54.5 |
| Severity of depression | | | | |
|     Very big | 19.5 | 16.5–22.6 | 16.3 | 12.5–20.2 |
|     Moderate | 16.3 | 13.4–19.1 | 19.5 | 15.3–23.6 |
|     Not very big | 14.3 | 11.6–17.0 | 13.3 | 9.7–16.8 |
| Been to physician for depression | 34.1 | 30.4–37.7 | 34.4 | 29.4–39.3 |
| Been to emergency room for depression | 5.7 | 3.9–7.5 | 5.4 | 3.0–7.7 |
| Hospitalized because of depression | 7.2 | 5.2–9.2 | 5.6 | 3.2–8.0 |
| Unable to do routine activities because of depression | 32.4 | 28.8–36.0 | 32.3 | 27.4–37.2 |

*Source:* Mitra, M., Wilber, N., Allen, D., and Walker, D. K. (2005). Prevalence and correlates of depression as a secondary condition among adults with disabilities. *American Journal of Orthopsychiatry, 75*(1), p. 81.

around the Phase 3 percentage is wider than the one built around the Phase 1 percentage. (By "wider," I simply mean that there is a greater distance between the interval's end points.) This discrepancy between the interval widths is caused by the sample size being larger at Phase 1 than Phase 3. The actual *n*s were 656 and 355, respectively. In general, small sample sizes lead to wider confidence intervals, and this point is illustrated nicely in Excerpt 6.8.

The third way researchers sometimes report confidence intervals is through a picture. To see an example of this way of presenting information on confidence intervals, take a look at Excerpt 6.9. In the study associated with this excerpt, 119 individuals diagnosed as having acute schizophrenia were first evaluated in terms of their levels of depressions. Based on this evaluation, four subgroups were created. Next, two different rating scales (the CDRS and HDRS) were used to assess each patient's level of depression. The heights of the four bars on the left correspond to the means earned by the four subgroups when evaluated by the CDRS; likewise, the four bars on the right show the means earned by these same individuals when evaluated by the HDRS. As indicated in the graph, the vertical error bars display the 95 percent confidence intervals for the four groups on each rating scale. These confidence intervals help keep us alert to the fact that the eight means in Excerpt 6.9 are sample statistics, not population parameters.

**EXCERPT 6.9 • *Confidence Intervals Reported in a Graph***

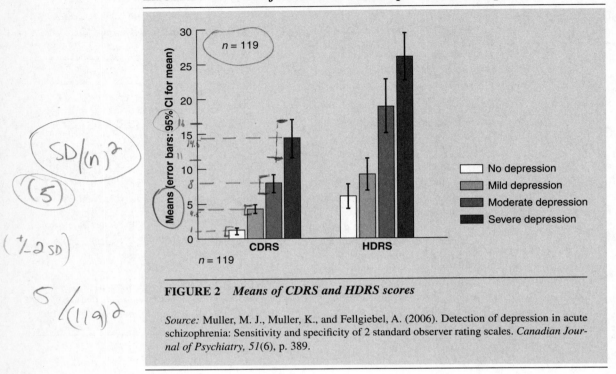

**FIGURE 2**   *Means of CDRS and HDRS scores*

*Source:* Muller, M. J., Muller, K., and Fellgiebel, A. (2006). Detection of depression in acute schizophrenia: Sensitivity and specificity of 2 standard observer rating scales. *Canadian Journal of Psychiatry, 51*(6), p. 389.

Before leaving this section, note that the confidence intervals reported in Excerpts 6.6 through 6.9 were constructed to help interpret a variety of sample statistics: means, percentages, and correlation coefficients. These particular excerpts were specifically selected not only because they illustrate different procedures for reporting confidence intervals but also because they help to underscore the point that confidence intervals can be constructed around *any* sample statistic.

***The Construction of Confidence Intervals.***     The end points of a confidence interval are not selected by the researcher magically making two values appear out of thin air. Rather, the researcher first makes a decision as to the level of confidence that is desired (usually 95 or 99). Then, the end points are computed by means of a joint process that involves the analysis of sample data (so as to obtain the estimated standard error of the statistic) that is then multiplied by a tabled numerical value.[6]

[6]For example, if we were to build a 95 percent confidence interval around the mean in Excerpt 6.2 that corresponds to the age of the 77 women who were in the sample, we would multiply the estimated standard error of 1.2 times 1.99, with the second of these numbers coming from a *t*-table. The product, 2.39, would then be added to and subtracted from the mean of 48.7 to establish the "ends" of our confidence interval.

Although you do not need to know the various formulas used to construct confidence intervals, you should be cognizant of the fact that a scientific approach is taken to the creation of any confidence interval. Moreover, you should be aware of three factors that affect the length of any confidence interval. These factors are the level of confidence selected by the researcher, the degree of homogeneity within the sample, and the size of the sample. If other things are held constant, the distance between the end points of a confidence interval will be smaller to the extent that (1) the researcher selects a lower level of confidence, (2) the sample is homogeneous, and (3) the sample is large. Because short (i.e., narrow) intervals that have a high level of confidence associated with them are more helpful in inferential statistics, researchers typically try to base their confidence intervals on large samples.

It should be noted that the length of a confidence interval is also affected by the nature of the statistic computed on the basis of sample data. For example, confidence intervals built around the mean will be shorter than those constructed for the median. The same situation holds true for Pearson's product-moment correlation coefficient as compared with Spearman's rho. This may explain, in part, why $\bar{X}$s and $r$s are seen so frequently in the published literature.

***The Proper Interpretation of Confidence Intervals.***     Confidence intervals are often misinterpreted to designate the probability that population parameters lie somewhere between the intervals' upper and lower limits. For example, many people (including more than a few researchers) would look at the end points of the second 95 percent confidence interval presented in Excerpt 6.6 and conclude that there is a .95 probability (i.e., a 95 percent chance) that the population parameter, $\rho$, lies somewhere between .21 and .58. Confidence intervals should *not* be interpreted in this fashion.

After a sample has been extracted from a population and then measured, the confidence interval around the sample's statistic either will or will not "cover" the value of the parameter. Hence, the probability that the parameter lies between the end points of a confidence interval is either 0 or 1. Because of this fact, a confidence interval should never be considered to specify the chances (or probability) that the parameter is "caught" by the interval.

The proper way to interpret a confidence interval is to *imagine* that (1) many, many samples of the same size are extracted from the same population and (2) a 95 percent confidence interval is constructed separately around the statistic computed from each sample's data set. Some of these intervals would "capture" the parameter—that is, the interval's end points would be such that the parameter would lie within the interval. On the other hand, some of these confidence intervals would *not* capture the parameter. Looked at collectively, it would turn out that 95 percent of these 95 percent confidence intervals contain the parameter. Accordingly, when you see a 95 percent confidence interval, you should consider that the chances are 95 out of 100 that the interval you are looking at is one of those that does, in fact, capture the parameter. Likewise, when you encounter a 99 percent confidence interval, you can say to yourself that the chances are even higher (99 out of 100) that the interval in front of you is one of the many possible intervals that would have caught the parameter.

***The Advantage of Confidence Intervals over Estimated Standard Errors.***   As I indicated in a previous section, a confidence interval is determined by first computing and then using the value of the estimated standard error. Researchers should be commended for providing either one of these inferential aids to their readers, for it is unfortunately true that most researchers supply their readers with neither standard errors nor confidence intervals for any of the sample statistics that are reported. Nevertheless, confidence intervals carry with them a slight advantage that is worth noting.

When a confidence interval is computed, it will be labeled as to its level of confidence. (As exemplified by Excerpts 6.6 through 6.9, researchers usually build 95 percent confidence intervals.) In contrast, standard error intervals rarely are labeled as to their level of confidence. Given the fact that standard error intervals usually have a confidence level of about 68 percent, they are apt to be misinterpreted and thought to be better than they really are.

Consider, for example, the information on heart rate (HR) shown earlier in Excerpt 6.1. If you use the number that follows the $\pm$ symbol to create the ends of an interval, you end up with an interval for the HR variable that extends from 164.5 to 175.1 beats per minute. That interval, however, is *not* a 95 percent confidence interval. (The confidence interval actually extends from 157.27 to 182.33.) You could approximate a 95 percent confidence interval by *doubling* the SEM number and then moving above and below the sample mean by that amount to establish your guess as to the end points of the confidence interval. However, doing this works accurately only when the sample *n* is at least 30.

## Point Estimation

When engaged in interval estimation, a researcher will (1) select a level of confidence (e.g., 95 percent), (2) analyze the sample data, (3) extract a number out of a statistical table, and (4) scientifically build an interval that surrounds the sample statistic. After completing these four steps, the researcher makes an educated guess as to the unknown value of the population parameter. In making this guess, the researcher ends up saying, "My data-based interval extends from _____ to _____, and the chances are _____ out of 100 that this interval is one of the many possible intervals (each based on a different sample) that would, in fact, contain the parameter between the interval limits."

A second form of estimation is called **point estimation,** and here again an educated guess is made, on the basis of sample data, as to the unknown value of the population parameter. With this second kind of estimation, however, the activities and thinking of the researcher are much simpler. With point estimation, no level of confidence needs to be selected, no statistical table needs to be consulted, and no interval needs to be created. Instead, the researcher simply computes the statistic on the basis of the sample data and then posits that the unknown value of the population parameter is the same. Thus the researcher who uses this guessing technique ends up saying, "Since the sample-based statistic turned out equal to _____, my best guess is that the value of the parameter is also equal to that particular value."

Point estimation, of course, is likely to produce statements that are incorrect. Because of the great likelihood of sampling error, the value of the statistic will rarely match the value of the parameter. For this reason, interval estimation is generally considered to represent a more logical way of making educated guesses as to parameter values than is point estimation.

Despite the fact that point estimation disregards the notion of sampling error, researchers often can be seen making pinpoint guesses as to parameter values. Consider, for example, the material contained in Excerpts 6.10 and 6.11.

### EXCERPTS 6.10–6.11 • *Point Estimation*

When instructed to start walking back and forth at their preferred speed immediately after the light was dimmed, participants typically started off slowly. Thus, a point estimate of relative group mean speed after 3 s was 0.85, indicating a speed reduction of 15%.

*Source:* Moe-Nilssen, R., Helbostad, J. L., Åkra, T., Birkedal, L., and Nygaard, H. A. (2006). Modulation of gait during visual adaptation to dark. *Journal of Motor Behavior, 38*(2), p. 122.

-------------------------------------------------------------------------------

According to a study conducted by the Child Trends . . . an average of 77.4 percent of parents are actively involved in the students' academia in grades K–5, but only 67.4 percent of parents are actively involved in grades 6–8, and the percentage of parents actively involved drops to an even lower percentage rate of 56.8 when their children enter high school in grades 9–12.

*Source:* Cordry, S., and Wilson, J. D. (2004). Parents as First Teacher. *Education, 125*(1), p. 57.

In Excerpt 6.10, we are told directly that the mean speed (of 0.85) was a point estimate. You will occasionally see statements such as this where the term point estimate is used. However, you are far more likely to see statements that include one or more point estimates, based on sample data, *without* the researcher using the term point estimate. An example of this common practice appears in Excerpt 6.11. As indicated in the excerpt, the three reported percentages came from a study. Even if those percentages were based on hundreds or thousands of parents (or even hundreds of thousands of parents), they still are sample statistics, not population parameters.

*Many* researchers engage in point estimation in the discussion of the measuring instruments used to collect data. As was indicated in Chapter 4, these discussions often involve the presentation of reliability and validity coefficients.

Give yourself a pat on the back if you recall, within that discussion, my claim that such coefficients are only estimates. If a different sample of examinees were to provide the data for the assessment of reliability and/or validity, the obtained coefficients most likely would fluctuate. Sampling error would account for such fluctuation.

Although it is possible to build confidence intervals around reliability and validity coefficients, researchers rarely do this. Instead, point estimates are typically provided. This is a common practice, even in cases where the researcher recognizes that the computed reliability and/or validity coefficients are only estimates. Consider, for example, Excerpts 6.12 and 6.13.

**EXCERPTS 6.12–6.13 • *Point Estimates of Reliability and Validity***

Split-half reliability for this sample was .86.

*Source:* Wrobleski, K. K., and Snyder, C. R. (2005). Hopeful thinking in older adults: Back to the future. *Experimental Aging Research, 31*(2), p. 223.

- - - - - - - - - - - - - - - - - - - - - - - - - - - - - - - - - - - - - - - - - - - - - - - - - - - - - - - - -

With the help of students, 225 couples (married or living together for at least 3 years) were recruited to participate on a voluntary and anonymous basis in a study of marital satisfaction. The mean age of this sample was 40.5. . . . The second question addressed concerned the similarity of the PFB and the DAS. The correlation between these two scales is high for both women and men ($r = .79$). This high correlation indicates that there is a good convergent validity between these two scales.

*Source:* Rossier, J., Rigozzi, C., Charvoz, L., and Bodenmann, G. (2006). Marital satisfaction: Psychometric properties of the PFB and comparison with the DAS. *Swiss Journal of Psychology—Schweizerische Zeitschrift für Psychologie—Revue Suisse de Psychologie, 65*(1), p. 61.

In each of these excerpts, notice that the word *sample* is used. Accordingly, the reliability coefficient in Excerpt 6.12 and the validity coefficient in Excerpt 6.13 are point estimates, not parameters. You need to keep these examples in mind when you come across the reliability and validity evidence researchers will include in their research reports. Unfortunately, many researchers use their sample data to compute reliability and validity coefficients and then discuss their findings as if they have discovered "the truth, the whole truth, and nothing but the truth." Rarely do researchers present such coefficients and then talk about the likely sampling error associated with their obtained indices of reliability and validity.

In Excerpts 6.14 and 6.15, we see cases in which confidence intervals were built around sample-based reliability and validity coefficients. (Because the data used in the first of these excerpts were nominal whereas the data in Excerpt 6.15 were ordinal, we again see that the notion of a confidence interval can be applied to just about any sample statistic.) The researchers who conducted these studies deserve high praise for recognizing that their reliability and validity coefficients were sample statistics, not population parameters.

**EXCERPTS 6.14–6.15 •** *Confidence Intervals Built around Reliability and Validity Coefficients*

The test-retest reliability for the categorization of participants as active, insufficiently active, or sedentary was $\kappa = 0.62$ (95% CI: 0.48, 0.76).

*Source:* Lynch, B. M., Owen, N., Newman, B., Pakenham, K., Leggett, B., Dunn, J., and Aitken, J. F. (2006). Reliability of a measure of prediagnosis physical activity for cancer survivors. *Medicine and Science in Sports and Exercise, 38*(4), p. 717.

- - - - - - - - - - - - - - - - - - - - - - - - - - - - - - - - - - - - - - - - - - - - - - - - - - - - - - - - - - - - - - - - - - - - -

Regarding predictive validity, the correlation between mEFAP performance on admission and Barthel Index and Rivermead Mobility Index scores at discharge was moderate to good (Spearman's $r = -0.52$, 95% CI $-0.72, -0.25$, and $-0.78$, 95% CI $-0.88, -0.62$, respectively).

*Source:* Liaw, L., Hsieh, C., Lo, S., Lee, S., Huang, M., and Lin, J. (2006). Psychometric properties of the modified Emory Functional Ambulation Profile in stroke patients. *Clinical Rehabilitation, 20*(5), p. 432.

Although the likelihood of sampling error causes the practice of point estimation to seem quite ill-founded, this form of statistical inference deserves to be respected for two reasons. These two supportive arguments revolve around (1) the role played by point estimation in interval estimation and (2) the reliance on point estimation by more advanced scientific disciplines (such as physics). Let's consider briefly each of these reasons why it would be unwise to look upon point estimation with complete disrespect.

When engaged in interval estimation, the researcher builds a confidence interval that surrounds the sample statistic. Point estimation is relied on in two ways when such intervals are constructed. First of all, the pinpoint value of the sample statistic is used as the best single estimate of the population parameter. The desired interval is formed by adding a certain amount to the statistic and subtracting a certain amount from the statistic. Hence, the value of the statistic, as a *point estimate* of the parameter, serves as the foundation for each and every confidence interval that is constructed.

Interval estimation draws on point estimation in a second manner. To be more specific, the amount that is added to (and subtracted from) the statistic in order to obtain the interval's upper and lower limits is based on a point estimate of the population's variability. For example, when a confidence interval is constructed around a sample mean, the distance between the end points of the interval is contingent on, among other things, a *point estimate* of the population standard deviation. Likewise, whenever a confidence interval is built around a sample proportion, the length of the interval cannot be specified until the researcher first uses *point estimation* to guess how variable the population is.

From a totally different perspective, the practice of point estimation deserves to be respected. Certain well-respected scientists assert that as a discipline advances and becomes more scientifically rigorous, point estimation is turned to with both increased frequency and greater justification.

## *Warnings Concerning Interval and Point Estimation*

As we wrap up this chapter, I would like to provide four cautionary comments concerning the techniques of estimation. The first three of these warnings concern interval estimation while the fourth is relevant to both kinds of estimation techniques: point and interval. You will be a better consumer of the research literature if you will keep these final points in mind.

First of all, be aware that the second of two numbers separated by a plus-and-minus sign can represent any of three things. In other words, if you see the notation $63 \pm 8$, be careful before you guess what the 8 signifies. It might be the standard deviation, it might be an estimated standard error, or it might be half the distance to the end points of a confidence interval. Excerpts 2.23 and 6.1 illustrate two of these three possibilities. Researchers will almost always clarify the meaning of such statements within a table or figure, or in the text of the research article. Take the time to look and read before jumping to any conclusions.

A second warning concerns the fact that sample data allow a researcher to *estimate* the standard error of the statistic, not to *determine* that standard error in a definitive manner. Excerpts in this chapter illustrate how researchers sometimes forget to use the word *estimated* prior to the phrase *standard error.* Keep in mind that the researcher will never know for sure, based on the sample data, how large the standard error is; it can only be estimated.

The third warning concerns, once again, confidence intervals. The sample statistic, of course, will always be located between the upper and lower limits of the confidence interval—but it will *not* always be located halfway between the interval's end points. When confidence intervals are built around a sample mean, it is true that $\bar{X}$ will turn out to be positioned at the midpoint of the interval. When confidence intervals are constructed for many other statistics (e.g., $r$, $s$, and $s^2$), however, one "side" of the interval will be longer than the other "side."[7] Whenever

---

[7]The degree to which such confidence intervals appear to be lopsided is inversely related to sample size. If $n$ is large enough, the statistic will be positioned in the middle of the interval.

a confidence interval is built around a proportion (or percent), the same thing will happen unless the value of the statistic is .50 (i.e., 50 percent).

My final warning applies to both interval estimation and point estimation—and this is by far the most important of my end-of-chapter cautionary comments. Simply stated, the entire process of estimation requires that the data used to form the inference come from a *random* sample. For the techniques of estimation to work properly, therefore, there must be a legitimate connection between the sample and population such that either (1) the former is actually extracted, randomly, from the latter (with no refusals to participate, mortality, or response rate problems); or (2) the population, if hypothetical, is conceptualized so as to match closely the nature of the sample. Without such a link between sample and population, neither form of estimation can be expected to function very well.

## Review Terms

Confidence interval      Sampling distribution
Estimation      Sampling error
Interval estimation      Standard error
Point estimation

## The Best Items in the Companion Website

1. An interactive online quiz (with immediate feedback provided) covering Chapter 6.
2. Ten misconceptions about the content of Chapter 6.
3. An online resource entitled "Sampling Distributions."
4. An email message about a "dead even" political race sent from the author to his students.
5. Two jokes, one about probability and the other about statisticians screwing in light bulbs.

To access chapter objectives, practice tests, weblinks, and flashcards, visit the companion website at www.ablongman.com/huck5e.

Research
Navigator.com

## Fun Exercises inside Research Navigator

1. **How long do surgical implants for back pain last before replacement is needed?**

   This study focused on 70 individuals with severe and chronic back pain. Each of these individuals had a device called a "spinal cord stimulation" (SCS) surgically implanted. The positive finding of this investigation was the fact that most patients reported lower levels of back pain following the implantation of the SCS device. The negative finding was the frequent need for a follow-up surgery to repair or replace the SCS device. The median time from initial implantation to the first revision surgery was 36 months. Because the 70 patients were considered to be a sample rather than a population, a 95 percent confidence interval was placed around this median. This CI extended from 24 to 60 months. Based on the median value and the end points of the CI, what kind of skewness (positive or negative) do you think the time-to-revision data had? To find out, locate the PDF version of the research report in the Nursing, Health, and Medicine database of ContentSelect and look at Figure 3 on page 100.

A. D. Kay, M. D. McIntyre, W. A. Macrea, & T. R. K. Varma. Spinal cord stimulation—A long-term evaluation in patients with chronic pain. *British Journal of Neurology.* Located in the NURSING, HEALTH, AND MEDICINE database of ContentSelect.

2. **How often do nurses and nurse assistants fail to record children's growth data?**

In this study, the researchers looked at a random sample of 149 medical charts of children who had been seen at the Yale-New Haven Hospital Primary Care Center. Each chart was examined for several purposes, one of which was to see if the nurse or nurse practitioner (who first saw the child) followed instructions by recording the child's height, weight, and (for very young children) head circumference. On 31 (21%) of the charts, at least one of these three expected growth measurements was unrecorded. A 95 percent confidence interval extended from 14.5 percent to 27.5 percent. Do you think the three measurements—height, weight, and head circumference—were unrecorded at the same rate, or do you think one of them was the main culprit? To find out, locate the PDF version of the research report in the Communication Sciences and Disorders database of ContentSelect, look at Table 2 (on page 100), and examine the unplotted percentages for the overall sample.

R. S. Chen & R. N. Shiffman. Assessing growth patterns—Routine but sometimes overlooked. *Clinical Pediatrics.* Located in the COMMUNICATION SCIENCES AND DISORDERS database of ContentSelect.

**Review Questions and Answers begin on page 513.**

# CHAPTER 7

# Hypothesis Testing

In Chapter 6, we saw how the inferential techniques of estimation can assist researchers when they use sample data to make educated guesses about the unknown value of population parameters. Now, we turn our attention to a second way in which researchers engage in inferential thinking. This procedure is called **hypothesis testing.**

Before we turn our attention to the half-dozen elements of hypothesis testing, I'd like to reiterate something I said near the beginning of Chapter 5. In order for inferential statistics to begin, the researcher must first answer four preliminary questions: (1) What is/are the relevant population(s)? (2) How will a sample be extracted from the population(s) of interest? (3) What characteristic(s) of the sample people, animals, or objects will serve as the target of the measurement process? (4) What is the study's statistical focus—or stated differently, how will the sample data be summarized so as to obtain a statistic that can be used to make an inferential statement concerning the unknown parameter? In this chapter, I will assume that these four questions have been both raised and answered by the time the researcher starts to apply the hypothesis testing procedure.

To help you understand the six-step version of hypothesis testing, I first will simply list the various steps in their proper order (that is, the order in which a researcher ought to do things when engaged in this form of statistical inference). After presenting an ordered list of the six steps, I then will discuss the function and logic of each step.

*Hypothesis – a proposed explanation for an observable phenomenon*

## An Ordered List of the Six Steps

Whenever researchers use the six-step version of the hypothesis testing procedure, they will

1. State the null hypothesis. *Ho*
2. State the alternative hypothesis. *Ha*
3. Select a level of significance. *α*
4. Collect and summarize the sample data.
5. Refer to a criterion for evaluating the sample evidence.
6. Make a decision to discard/retain the null hypothesis.
   *reject or fail to reject*

It should be noted that there is no version of hypothesis testing that involves fewer than six steps. Stated differently, it is outright impossible to eliminate any of these six ingredients and have enough left to test a statistical hypothesis.

## A Detailed Look at Each of the Six Steps

As indicated previously, the list of steps we just presented is arranged in an ordered fashion. In discussing these steps, however, we now will look at these six component parts in a somewhat jumbled order: 1, 6, 2, 4, 5, and then 3. My motivation in doing this is not related to sadistic tendencies! Rather, I am convinced that the function and logic of these six steps can be understood far more readily if we purposely chart an unusual path through the hypothesis testing procedure. Please note, however, that the six steps will now be rearranged only for pedagogical reasons. If I were asked to apply these six steps in an actual study, I would use the ordered list as my guide, not the sequence to which we now turn.

*= no relationship between two measures*
*Phenomenon*
*= or treatment has no effect*

### Step 1: The Null Hypothesis

When engaged in hypothesis testing, a researcher begins by stating a **null hypothesis.** If there is just one population involved in the study, the null hypothesis is a pinpoint statement as to the unknown quantitative value of the parameter in the population of interest. To illustrate what this kind of null hypothesis might look like, suppose that (1) we conduct a study in which our population contains all full-time students enrolled in a particular university, (2) our variable of interest is intelligence, and (3) our statistical focus is the mean IQ score. Given this situation, we could set up a null hypothesis to say that $\mu = 100$. This statement deals with a population *parameter,* it is *pinpoint* in nature, and *we* made it.

The symbol for null hypothesis is $H_0$, and this symbol is usually followed by (1) a colon, (2) the parameter symbol that indicates the researcher's statistical focus, (3) an equal sign, and (4) the pinpoint numerical value that the researcher has

Research
Navigator.c⊕m

Null hypothesis

↓

*Ho:*
*statistical*
*focus*
*=*
*pinpoint*
*numerical*
*value*

*Null hypothesis*
*statistical focus*
*pinpoint value*

selected. Accordingly, we could specify the null hypothesis for our imaginary study by stating $H_0$: $\mu = 100$.

If our study's statistical focus involved something other than the mean, we would have to change the parameter's symbol so as to make $H_0$ consistent with the study's focus. For example, if our imaginary study were to be concerned with the variance among students' heights, the null hypothesis would need to contain the symbol $\sigma^2$ rather than the symbol $\mu$. Or, if we were concerned with the product-moment correlation between the students' heights and weights, the symbol $\rho$ would have to appear in $H_0$.

With respect to the pinpoint numerical value that appears in the null hypothesis, researchers have the freedom to select any value that they wish to test. Thus in our example dealing with the mean IQ of university students, the null hypothesis could be set up to say that $\mu = 80$, $\mu = 118$, $\mu = 101$, or $\mu =$ any specific value of our choosing. Likewise, if our study focused on the variance, we could set up $H_0$, the null hypothesis, to say that $\sigma^2 = 10$ or that $\sigma^2 =$ any other positive number of our choosing. And in a study having Pearson's product-moment correlation coefficient as its statistical focus, the null hypothesis could be set up to say that $\rho = 0.00$ or that $\rho = -.50$ or that $\rho = +.92$ or that $\rho =$ any specific number between $-1.00$ and $+1.00$.

The only statistical restrictions on the numerical value that appears in $H_0$ are that it (1) must lie somewhere on the continuum of possible values that correspond to the parameter and (2) cannot be fixed at the upper or lower limit of that continuum, presuming that the parameter has a lowest and/or highest possible value. These restrictions rule out the following null hypotheses:

$$H_0: \sigma^2 = -15 \qquad H_0: \rho = +1.30$$
$$H_0: \sigma^2 = 0 \qquad H_0: \rho = -1.00$$

because the variance has a lower limit of 0 while Pearson's product-moment correlation coefficient has limits of $\pm 1.00$.

Excerpts 7.1 and 7.2 show how researchers sometimes talk about their null hypotheses. In the first of these excerpts, it is clear that correlation is the statistical focus in each of the two null hypotheses. If either of these null hypotheses had been expressed in symbols rather than in words, it would have taken the form $H_0: \rho = 0.00$, where $\rho$ would represent the correlation in the population of "lecturer practitioners" in nursing. In the first null hypothesis, the two variables involved in this correlation would be experience and stress; in the second null hypothesis, the two variables would be experience and burnout.

In Excerpt 7.2, the statistical focus of the null hypothesis is the mean. That is made clear by the inclusion of the symbol $\mu$. As you can see, there are two $\mu$s in this null hypothesis. That is because there were two populations involved in this study, 10-year-old girls and 11-year-old girls. The symbol $\mu$, of course, corresponds to the mean score on some variable of interest. As indicated in the excerpt, the

**EXCERPTS 7.1–7.2 • *The Null Hypothesis***

The null hypotheses addressed were:

1. There is no correlation between LPs' experience index and their occupational stress (measured by OSI sub-scale indices).
2. There is no correlation between LPs' experience index and their burnout (measured by MBI sub-scale indices).

*Source:* Willamson, G. R., Webb, C., and Abelson-Mitchell, M. (2004). Developing lecturer practitioner roles using action research. *Journal of Advanced Nursing, 47*(2), p. 155.

----

Null hypothesis 2: There is no significant difference in mean throw distance for age groups, i.e., $H_0: \mu_{10} = \mu_{11}$, where

$$\mu_{10} = \text{mean distance of throw of 10-year-old girls}$$
$$\mu_{11} = \text{mean distance of throw of 11-year-old girls.}$$

*Source:* Salonia, M. A., Chu, D. A., Cheifetz, P. M., and Friedhoff, G. C. (2004). Upper-body power as measured by medicine-ball throw distance and its relationship to class level among 10- and 11-year-old female participants in club gymnastics. *Journal of Strength & Conditioning Research, 18*(4), p. 699.

researchers wanted to compare the two groups of girls in terms of how far they could throw a medicine ball.

Earlier, I indicated that every null hypothesis must contain a pinpoint numerical value. From what is stated in Excerpt 7.1 (or from what I have already said about that excerpt's null hypothesis), it is clear that the pinpoint number in this excerpt's $H_0$ is zero. But what about Excerpt 7.2? This excerpt's null hypothesis also has a pinpoint number, but it's hidden. If two things are equal, there is no difference between them, and the notion of no difference is equivalent to saying that a zero difference exists. Accordingly, the null hypothesis shown in Excerpt 7.2 could be rewritten $H_0: \mu_{10} - \mu_{11} = 0$, where the subscripts 10 and 11 designate the ages of the two populations of girls.

Although researchers have the freedom to select any pinpoint number they wish for $H_0$, a zero is often selected when two or more populations are being compared. When this is done, the null hypothesis becomes a statement that there is no difference between the populations. Because of the popularity of this kind of null hypothesis, people sometimes begin to think that a null hypothesis *must* be set up as a "no difference" statement. This is both unfortunate and wrong. When two populations are compared, the null hypothesis can be set up with any pinpoint value the researcher wishes to use. (For example, in comparing the mean height of men and women, we could set up a legitimate null hypothesis that stated

$H_0$: $\mu_{men} - \mu_{women} = 2$ inches.) When the hypothesis testing procedure is used with a single population, the notion of "no difference," applied to parameters, simply doesn't make sense. How could there be a difference, zero or otherwise, when there is only one $\mu$ (or only one $\rho$, or only one $\sigma^2$, etc.)?

In Excerpts 7.3 and 7.4, we see two additional null hypotheses. In the first of these excerpts, the null hypothesis stated that two population proportions were equal. If we let the capital letter $P$ stand for population proportion, we can express the null hypothesis of Excerpt 7.3 like this: $H_0$: $P_{1995} = P_{2001}$. The subscripts here serve to distinguish the two different populations of interest to the researchers in this study.[1]

## EXCERPTS 7.3–7.4 • *Two Additional Null Hypotheses*

The researchers tabulated frequencies and percentages and used a $z$-test for the equality of two population proportions to test the null hypothesis that the two population proportions (1995 respondents compared to 2001 respondents) were equal.

*Source:* Oster-Aaland, L. K., Sellnow, T. L., Nelson, P. E., and Pearson, J. C. (2004). The status of service learning in departments of communication: A follow-up study. *Communication Education, 53*(4), p. 351.

-----

The null hypothesis was that there would be no intra-group (within-group) difference between the results obtained at baseline and after interventions 5, 9, and at 1 month after intervention 9 for Groups 1 and 2:

$$H_0: \mu_1 = \mu_2 = \mu_3 = \mu_4$$

*Source:* Dimou, E. S., Brantingham, J. W., and Wood, T. (2004). A randomized, controlled trial (with blinded observer) of chiropractic manipulation and achilles stretching vs. orthotics for the treatment of plantar fasciitis. *Journal of the American Chiropractic Association, 41*(9), p. 33.

Excerpt 7.4 shows a null hypothesis that involves four population means. The four $\mu$s in this null hypothesis do not correspond to four different groups; instead, these $\mu$s represent the performance of a single population measured at four points in time. Thus, the subscripts on the $\mu$s correspond to the first point in time (baseline), the second point in time (after intervention 5), and so on. This null hypothesis was actually used twice in the study, because there were two groups of people with a foot problem called plantar fasciitis. People in one of the groups were treated with chiropractic manipulation and Achilles stretching; people in the other group received shoe inserts. This null hypothesis was investigated separately for each of these two groups.

-----

[1]In Chapter 17, we will consider in depth statistical tests that focus on percentages.

Before we leave our discussion of the null hypothesis, it should be noted that $H_0$ does *not* always represent the researcher's personal belief, or hunch, as to the true state of affairs in the population(s) of interest. In fact, the vast majority of null hypotheses are set up by researchers in such a way as to *disagree* with what they actually believe to be the case. We will return to this point later (when we formally consider the research hypothesis). For now, however, all I want to do is alert you to the fact that the $H_0$ associated with any given study probably is *not* an articulation of the researcher's honest belief concerning the population(s) being studied.

### Step 6: The Decision Regarding $H_0$

At the end of the hypothesis testing procedure, the researcher will do one of two things with $H_0$. One option is for the researcher to take the position that the null hypothesis is probably false. In this case, the researcher **rejects** $H_0$. The other option available to the researcher is to refrain from asserting that $H_0$ is probably false. In this case, a **fail-to-reject** decision is made.

If, at the end of the hypothesis testing procedure, a conclusion is reached that $H_0$ is probably false, the researcher will communicate this decision by saying one of four things: that $H_0$ was rejected, that a statistically significant finding was obtained, that a **reliable difference** was observed, or that $p$ is less than a small decimal value (e.g., $p < .05$). In Excerpts 7.5 through 7.7, we see examples of how researchers will sometimes communicate their decision to disbelieve $H_0$.

**EXCERPTS 7.5–7.7 • *Rejecting* the Null Hypothesis**

The null hypothesis was rejected.

*Source:* Nogueras, D. J. (2006). Occupational commitment, education, and experience as a predictor of intent to leave the nursing profession. *Nursing Economic\$, 24*(2), p. 90.

---

The comparison group scored significantly higher on the scale "I Want to Be a Scientist" than the experimental group.

*Source:* Barnett, M., Lord, C., Strauss, E., Rosca, C., Langford, H., Chavez, D., and Deni, L. (2006). Using the urban environment to engage youths in urban ecology field studies. *Journal of Environmental Education, 37*(2), p. 8.

---

Among the respondents, White users [of the drug ecstasy] reported more days of use during the past 90 days ($p < 0.05$) than users from other racial/ethnic groups.

*Source:* Sterk, C. E., Theall, K. P., and Elifson, K. W. (2006). Young adult ecstasy use patterns: Quantities and combinations. *Journal of Drug Issues, 36*(1), p. 220.

Just as there are different ways for a researcher to tell us that $H_0$ is considered to be false, there are various mechanisms for expressing the other possible decision concerning the null hypothesis. Instead of saying that a fail-to-reject decision has been reached, the researcher may tell us that $H_0$ was tenable, that $H_0$ was **accepted,** that no reliable differences were observed, that no significant difference was found, that the result was not significant (often abbreviated as *ns* or *NS*), or that $p$ is greater than a small decimal value (e.g., $p > .05$). Excerpts 7.8 through 7.11 illustrate these different ways of communicating a fail-to-reject decision.

**EXCERPTS 7.8–7.11 • *Failing to Reject the Null Hypothesis***

Our analysis of walking failed to demonstrate a significant difference between healthy elderly fallers and non-fallers walking freely under single-task conditions.

*Source:* Toulotte, C., Thevenon, A., Watelain, E., and Fabre, C. (2006). Identification of healthy elderly fallers and non-fallers by gait analysis under dual-task conditions. *Clinical Rehabilitation, 20*(3), p. 274

---

Therefore, the null hypothesis was accepted.

*Source:* Rouse, W. J., and Hollomon, H. L. (2005). A comparison of student test results: Business and marketing education National Board Certified Teachers and non-national Board Certified Teachers. *Delta Pi Epsilon Journal, 47*(3), p. 138.

---

Participants were selected such that the three experimental groups did not differ in age, $F(2, 54) < 1$, *ns*.

*Source:* van der Sluis, S., van der Leij, A., and de Jong, P. F. (2005). Working memory in Dutch children with reading- and arithmetic-related LD. *Journal of Learning Disabilities, 38*(3), p. 210.

---

The main effect of gender was not significant, $F(1, 20) = 1.2$, $p > .05$.

*Source:* Andersen, G. J., and Enriquez, A. (2006). Aging and the detection of observer and moving object collisions. *Psychology and Aging, 21*(1), p. 79.

It is especially important to be able to decipher the language and notation used by researchers to indicate the decision made concerning $H_0$. This is because most researchers neither articulate their null hypotheses nor clearly state that they used the hypothesis testing procedure. Often, the only way to tell that a researcher has used this kind of inferential technique is by noting what happened to the null hypothesis.

$H_a$ or $H_1$

### Step 2: The Alternative Hypothesis

Near the beginning of the hypothesis testing procedure, the researcher must state an **alternative hypothesis.** Referred to as $H_a$ (or as $H_1$), the alternative hypothesis takes the same form as the null hypothesis. For example, if the null hypothesis deals with the possible value of Pearson's product-moment correlation in a single population (e.g., $H_0: \rho = +.50$), then the alternative hypothesis must also deal with the possible value of Pearson's correlation in a single population. Or, if the null hypothesis deals with the difference between the means of two populations (perhaps indicating that $\mu_1 = \mu_2$), then the alternative hypothesis must also say something about the difference between those populations' means. In general, therefore, $H_a$ and $H_0$ are identical in that they must (1) deal with the same number of populations, (2) have the same statistical focus, and (3) involve the same variable(s).

The only difference between the null and alternative hypothesis is that the possible value of the population parameter included within $H_a$ will always differ from what is specified in $H_0$. If the null hypothesis is set up so as to say $H_0: \rho = +.50$, then the alternative hypothesis might be set up to say $H_a: \rho \neq +.50$; or, if a researcher specifies, in Step 1, that $H_0: \mu_1 = \mu_2$, we might find that the alternative hypothesis is set up to say $H_a: \mu_1 \neq \mu_2$.

Excerpt 7.12 contains an alternative hypothesis, labeled $H_a$, as well as the null hypothesis with which it was paired. Notice that both $H_0$ and $H_a$ deal with the same population and have the same statistical focus (the mean). If expressed symbolically, these two hypotheses would have looked identical to the $H_0$ and $H_a$ shown in the final sentence of the previous paragraph. Expressed in that manner, the $\mu$s appearing in both $H_0$ and $H_a$ would be representing admission rates.

### EXCERPT 7.12 • *The Alternative Hypothesis*

$H_0$ = no difference between the mean reductions in admission rates of the two populations
$H_a$ = the population means are different

*Source:* Smith, R. B. (2001). Gatekeepers and sentinels: Their consolidated effects on inpatient medical care. *Evaluation Review, 25*(3), p. 293.

As was indicated in the previous section, the hypothesis testing procedure terminates (in Step 6) with a decision to either reject or fail to reject the null hypothesis. In the event that $H_0$ is rejected, $H_a$ represents the state of affairs that the researcher will consider to be probable. In other words, $H_0$ and $H_a$ always represent two opposing statements as to the possible value of the parameter in the population(s) of interest. If, in Step 6, $H_0$ is rejected, then belief shifts *from $H_0$ to $H_a$*.

Stated differently, if a reject decision is made at the end of the hypothesis testing procedure, the researcher will reject $H_0$ *in favor of* $H_a$.

Although researchers have flexibility in the way they set up alternative hypotheses, they normally will set up $H_a$ either in a **directional** fashion or in a **nondirectional** fashion.[2] To clarify the distinction between these options for the alternative hypothesis, let's imagine that a researcher conducts a study to compare men and women in terms of intelligence. Further suppose that the statistical focus of this hypothetical study is on the mean, with the null hypothesis asserting that $H_0$: $\mu_{men} = \mu_{women}$. Now, if the alternative hypothesis is set up in a nondirectional fashion, the researcher will simply state $H_a$: $\mu_{men} \neq \mu_{women}$. If, on the other hand, the alternative hypothesis is stated in a directional fashion, the researcher will specify a direction in $H_a$. This could be done by asserting $H_a$: $\mu_{men} > \mu_{women}$ *or* by asserting $H_a$: $\mu_{men} < \mu_{women}$.

The directional/nondirectional nature of $H_a$ is highly important within the hypothesis testing procedure. The researcher will need to know whether $H_a$ was set up in a directional or nondirectional manner in order to decide whether to reject (or to fail to reject) the null hypothesis. No decision can be made about $H_0$ unless the directional/nondirectional character of $H_a$ is clarified.

In most empirical studies, the alternative hypothesis is set up in a nondirectional fashion. Thus if I had to guess what $H_a$ would say in studies containing the null hypotheses presented here on the left, I would bet that the researchers had set up their alternative hypotheses as indicated on the right.

| Possible $H_0$ | Corresponding nondirectional $H_a$ |
|---|---|
| $H_0$: $\mu = 100$ | $H_a$: $\mu \neq 100$ |
| $H_0$: $\rho = +.20$ | $H_a$: $\rho \neq +.20$ |
| $H_0$: $\sigma^2 = 4$ | $H_a$: $\sigma^2 \neq 4$ |
| $H_0$: $\mu_1 - \mu_2 = 0$ | $H_a$: $\mu_1 - \mu_2 \neq 0$ |

Researchers typically set up $H_a$ in a nondirectional fashion because they do not know whether the pinpoint number in $H_0$ is too large or too small. By specifying a nondirectional $H_a$, the researcher permits the data to point one way or the other in the event that $H_0$ is rejected. Hence, in our hypothetical study comparing men and women in terms of intelligence, a nondirectional alternative hypothesis would allow us to argue that $\mu_{women}$ is probably higher than $\mu_{men}$ (in the event that we reject the $H_0$ because $\overline{X}_{women} > \overline{X}_{men}$); or such an alternative hypothesis would allow us to argue that $\mu_{men}$ is probably higher than $\mu_{women}$ (if we reject $H_0$ because $\overline{X}_{men} > \overline{X}_{women}$).

---

[2]A directional $H_a$ is occasionally referred to as a *one-sided* $H_a$; likewise, a nondirectional $H_a$ is sometimes referred to as a *two-sided* $H_a$.

Occasionally, a researcher will feel so strongly (based on theoretical consideration or previous research) that the true state of affairs falls on one side of $H_0$'s pinpoint number that $H_a$ is set up in a directional fashion. So long as the researcher makes this decision prior to looking at the data, such a decision is fully legitimate. It is, however, totally inappropriate for the researcher to look at the data first and then subsequently decide to set up $H_a$ in a directional manner. Although a decision to reject or fail to reject $H_0$ could still be made after first examining the data and then articulating a directional $H_a$, such a sequence of events would sabotage the fundamental logic and practice of hypothesis testing. Simply stated, decisions concerning how to state $H_a$ (and how to state $H_0$) must be made without peeking at any data.

When the alternative hypothesis is set up in a nondirectional fashion, researchers sometimes use the phrase **two-tailed test** to describe their specific application of the hypothesis testing procedure. In contrast, directional $H_a$s lead to what researchers sometimes refer to as **one-tailed tests.** Inasmuch as researchers rarely specify the alternative hypothesis in their technical write-ups, the terms *one-tailed* and *two-tailed* help us to know exactly how $H_a$ was set up. For example, consider Excerpts 7.13 and 7.14. Here, we see how researchers sometimes use the term *two-tailed* or *one-tailed* to communicate their decisions to set up $H_a$ in a nondirectional or directional fashion.

Research
Navigator.com

One-tailed test
Two-tailed test

### EXCERPTS 7.13–7.14 • *Two-Tailed and One-Tailed Tests*

Two-tailed tests were used for all analyses.

*Source:* Baker, D. W., Cameron, K. A., Feinglass, J., Thompson, J. A., Georgas, P., Foster, S., Pierce, D., and Hasnain-Wynia, R. (2006). A system for rapidly and accurately collecting patients' race and ethnicity. *American Journal of Public Health, 96*(3), p. 533.

---

Directional (one-tailed) tests were used because improvement was hypothesized over sequential treatment sessions.

*Source:* Storchheim, L. F., and O'Mahony, J. F. (2006). Compulsive behaviours and levels of belief in obsessive–compulsive disorder: A case-series analysis of their interrelationships. *Clinical Psychology & Psychotherapy, 13*(1), p. 70.

If $H_a$ is set up in a directional manner, the null hypothesis can be expressed as an **inexact $H_0$.** This type of null hypothesis functions exactly like the kind of $H_0$ we have been considering, so it really does not matter whether $H_0$ takes the form of an inexact statement or an exact statement. Nonetheless, I feel it necessary to illustrate what an inexact $H_0$ looks like so you are not thrown into a tizzy if you ever see one in a research report.

Suppose a researcher wants to compare a sample of high school students against a sample of college students in terms of their vocabulary. Further suppose that our hypothetical researcher can look ahead into the hypothesis testing procedure and knows that the alternative hypothesis in Step 2 will be set up in a directional manner to say $H_a$: $\mu_{college} > \mu_{high\ school}$. If the researcher knows from the beginning that $H_a$ will be directional, then the null hypothesis (in Step 1) could be set up to say $H_0$: $\mu_{college} \leq \mu_{high\ school}$. This null hypothesis is inexact because it does not contain a pinpoint numerical value for the population parameter (as would be the case if the null hypothesis were to be set up to say $H_0$: $\mu_{college} - \mu_{high\ school} = 0$). Instead, this inexact $H_0$ says that the mean vocabulary among college students is equal to or lower than the mean vocabulary among high school students, with lower being anything from a tiny amount to an enormous difference.

Excerpt 7.15 provides an illustration of an inexact null hypothesis. If this $H_0$ had been expressed symbolically, it would have taken the form $H_0$: $\rho \leq 0.00$. It is worth noting that the null hypothesis, when set up to be inexact, does not overlap whatsoever with the alternative hypothesis. This is due to the general requirement that $H_0$ and $H_a$ be mutually exclusive.

### EXCERPT 7.15 • *An Inexact Null Hypothesis (and Its Alternative Hypothesis)*

$H_0$: The relationship between social performance and financial performance in the commercial banking industry is either zero or negative.
$H_a$: The relationship between social performance and financial performance in the commercial banking industry is positive.

*Source:* Simpson, W. G., and Kohers, T. (2002). The link between corporate social and financial performance: Evidence from the banking industry. *Journal of Business Ethics, 35*(2), p. 102.

In terms of the ultimate reject or fail-to-reject decision reached by the researcher, it makes absolutely no difference whether the null hypothesis is set up to be exact or inexact. I prefer to articulate any null hypothesis as an exact $H_0$, because this is consistent with the notion that the null hypothesis is a *point* on a numerical continuum, with the alternative hypothesis represented by either (1) the rest of that continuum, both above and below the null point, if $H_a$ is nondirectional, or (2) the segment of the continuum that lies on just one side of the null point, if $H_a$ is directional. Certain authors have a preference for conceptualizing $H_0$ in an inexact manner, thereby equating $H_0$ to one of those two segments. It really doesn't matter which definition of $H_0$ is used. (If $H_a$ is nondirectional, however, there is no option. In that more common situation, $H_0$ must be exact.)

## *Step 4: Collection and Analysis of Sample Data*

So far, we have covered Steps 1, 2, and 6 of the hypothesis testing procedure. In the first two steps, the researcher states the null and alternative hypotheses. In Step 6, the researcher will either (1) reject $H_0$ in favor of $H_a$ or (2) fail to reject $H_0$. We now turn our attention to the principal stepping-stone that is used to move from the beginning points of the hypothesis testing procedure to the final decision.

Inasmuch as the hypothesis testing procedure is, by its very nature, an empirical strategy, it should come as no surprise that the researcher's ultimate decision to reject or to retain $H_0$ is based on the collection and analysis of sample data. No crystal ball is used, no Ouija board is relied on, and no eloquent argumentation is permitted. Once $H_0$ and $H_a$ are fixed, only scientific evidence is allowed to affect the disposition of $H_0$.

The fundamental logic of the hypothesis testing procedure can now be laid bare because the connections between $H_0$, the data, and the final decision are as straightforward as what exists between the speed of a car, a traffic light at a busy intersection, and a lawful driver's decision as the car approaches the intersection. Just as the driver's decision to stop or to pass through the intersection is made after observing the color of the traffic light, the researcher's decision to reject or to retain $H_0$ is made after observing the sample data. To carry this analogy one step further, the researcher will look at the data and ask, "Is the empirical evidence inconsistent with what one would expect if $H_0$ were true?" If the answer to this question is yes, then the researcher has a green light and will reject $H_0$. On the other hand, if the data turn out to be consistent with $H_0$, then the data set serves as a red light telling the researcher not to discard $H_0$.

Because the logic of hypothesis testing is so important, let us briefly consider a hypothetical example. Suppose a valid intelligence test is given to a random sample of 100 males and a random sample of 100 females attending the same university. If the null hypothesis had first been set up to say $H_0: \mu_{male} = \mu_{female}$ and if the data reveal that the two sample means (of IQ scores) differ by only two points, the sample data would be consistent with what we expect to happen when two samples are selected from populations having identical means. Clearly, the notion of sampling error could fully explain why the two $\overline{X}$s might differ by two IQ points even if $\mu_{male} = \mu_{female}$. In this situation, no empirical grounds exist for making the data-based claim that males at our hypothetical university have a different IQ, on the average, than do their female classmates.

Now, let's consider what would happen if the difference between the two sample means turns out to be equal to 40 (rather than 2) IQ points. If the empirical evidence turns out like this, we would have a situation where the data are inconsistent with what one would expect if $H_0$ were to be true. Although the concept of sampling error strongly suggests that neither sample mean will turn out exactly equal to its population parameter, the difference of 40 IQ points between $\overline{X}_{males}$ and $\overline{X}_{females}$ is quite improbable if, in fact, $\mu_{males}$ and $\mu_{females}$ are equal. With results such as this, the researcher would reject the arbitrarily selected null hypothesis.

To drive home the point I'm trying to make about the way the sample data influence the researcher's decision concerning $H_0$, let's shift our attention to a real study that had Pearson's correlation as its statistical focus. In Excerpt 7.16, the hypothesis testing procedure was used to evaluate two bivariate correlations based on data that came from watching 40 pairs of children at play (with a sibling) and then talking with each child about conflicts that arose during the play. The two variables that were correlated were age of the child and the degree to which the child denied responsibility for an interpersonal conflict with his or her siblings. The correlation between these two variables was computed separately for each of two groups of children: younger siblings (who were between 3.5 and 5.3 years old) and their older siblings (who were between 5.5 and 8.9 years old).

**EXCERPT 7.16 • *Rejecting $H_0$ When the Sample Data Are Inconsistent with $H_0$***

For younger siblings, age was not related to denials, $r = -.02$, *ns*. However, for older siblings the relation was significant, $r = -.63$, [thus] indicating that as the age of older siblings increased (from 5.5 to 8.9), older siblings became considerably less likely to rely on denials.

*Sources:* Wilson, A. E., Smith, M. D., Ross, H. S., and Ross, M. (2004). Young children's personal accounts of their sibling disputes. *Merrill-Palmer Quarterly, 50*(1), p. 53.

In the study associated with Excerpt 7.16, the hypothesis testing procedure was used separately to evaluate each of the two sample *r*s. In each case, the null hypothesis stated $H_0$: $\rho = 0.00$. The sample data, once analyzed, yielded correlations of $-.02$ and $-.63$. The first of these *r*s ended up being quite close to the pinpoint number in $H_0$, 0.00. The small difference between the null number and $-.02$ can easily be explained by sampling error. In other words, if the correlation in the population were truly equal to 0.00, it would not be surprising to have a sample *r* (with $n = 20$) that deviates from 0.00 but by only a small amount. Accordingly, the null hypothesis concerning the age-denial correlation for the young children was not rejected, as indicated by the notation *ns*.

The second correlation in Excerpt 7.16 turned out to be quite different from the null hypothesis number of 0.00. Statistically speaking, the *r* of $-.63$ was so inconsistent with $H_0$ that sampling error alone was considered to be an inadequate explanation for why the observed correlation was so far away from the pinpoint number in the null hypothesis. Although we would expect some discrepancy between 0.00 and the data-based value of *r* even if $H_0$ were true, we would *not* expect this big of a difference. Accordingly, the null hypothesis concerning the age-denial correlation for the older children was rejected, as indicated by the phrase "the relation was significant."

In Step 4 of the hypothesis testing procedure, the summary of the sample data will always lead to a single numerical value. Being based on the data, this number is technically referred to as the **calculated value.** (It is also called the **test statistic.**) Occasionally, the researcher's task in obtaining the calculated value involves nothing more than computing a value that corresponds to the study's statistical focus. This was the case in Excerpt 7.16, where the statistical focus was Pearson's correlation coefficient and where the researcher needed to do nothing more than compute a value for $r$.

In most applications of the hypothesis testing procedure, the sample data are summarized in such a way that the statistical focus becomes hidden from view. For example, consider Excerpts 7.17 and 7.18. In the first of these excerpts, the calculated value was labeled $F$ and it turned out equal to 4.267. In Excerpt 7.18, the calculated value was $t$, and this time it turned out equal to $-0.48$. In each of these excerpts, the statistical focus was the mean.

**EXCERPTS 7.17–7.18 • *The Calculated Value***

Men on average published 5.50 ($SD = 5.20$) articles over the course of 3 years, and the average for women was 4.66 ($SD = 4.18$) articles, $F(1, 534) = 4.267$, $p < .05$.

*Source:* Sellers, S. L., Smith, T., Mathiesen, S. G., and Perry, R. (2006). Perceptions of professional social work journals: Findings from a national survey. *Journal of Social Work Education, 42*(1), p. 146.

The children who listened to the musical story were less accurate ($M = 14.13$, $SD = 24.17$) than the children who listened to the spoken version of the story ($M = 17.50$, $SD = 21.33$). This difference, however, was not statistically significant ($t(40) = -0.48$, $p > .05$).

*Source:* Noguchi, L. K. (2006). The effect of music versus nonmusic on behavioral signs of distress and self-report of pain in pediatric injection patients. *Journal of Music Therapy, 43*(1), p. 27.

In each of these excerpts, two sample means were compared. In Excerpt 7.17, the mean of 5.50 was compared against the mean of 4.66. In Excerpt 7.18, the means were 14.13 and 17.50. Within each of these studies, the researchers put their sample data into a formula that produced the calculated value. The important thing  to notice in these excerpts is that in neither case does the calculated value equal the difference between the two means being compared. In Chapter 10, we'll consider $t$-tests and $F$-tests in more detail, so you should not worry now if you do not currently comprehend everything that is presented in these excerpts. They are shown solely to illustrate the typical situation in which the statistical focus of a study is *not* reflected directly in the calculated value.

Before computers were invented, researchers would always have a single goal in mind when they turned to Step 4 of the hypothesis testing procedure. That goal was the computation of the data-based calculated value. Now that computers are widely available, researchers still are interested in the magnitude of the calculated value derived from the data analysis. Contemporary researchers, however, are also interested in a second piece of information generated by the computer. This second item is the data-based *p*-value.

Whenever researchers use a computer to perform the data analysis, they will either (1) tell the computer what the null hypothesis is going to be or (2) accept the computer's built-in default version of $H_0$. The researcher will also specify whether $H_a$ is directional or nondirectional in nature. Once the computer knows what the researcher's $H_0$ and $H_a$ are, it can easily analyze the sample data and compute the probability of having a data set that deviates as much or more from $H_0$ as does the data set being analyzed. The computer informs the researcher as to this probability by means of a statement that takes the form *p* = _____, with the blank being filled by a single decimal value somewhere between 0 and 1.

Excerpts 7.19 and 7.20 illustrate nicely how a *p*-value is like a calculated value in that either one can be used as a single-number summary of the sample data. As you can see, two sample percentages were compared in Excerpt 7.19, while two correlation coefficients were computed in Excerpt 7.20. In the first of these excerpts, the researchers used a *p*-value to assess the likelihood, under the null hypothesis, of getting two percentages that differed as much or more than the two percentages actually observed (34 versus 20). The researchers associated with Excerpt 7.20 did the same

**EXCERPTS 7.19–7.20 • *Using p as the Calculated Value***

Women receiving radiation therapy are more likely to have reduced shoulder mobility one year after breast cancer diagnosis (34% women had loss of range of motion compared with 20% who did not receive radiation therapy, $P = 0.03$).

*Source:* Internal, M. E., Freeman, J. L., Zhang, D. D., Jansen, C., Ostir, G., Hatch, S. S., and Goodwin, J. S. (2006). The relationship between depressive symptoms and shoulder mobility among older women: Assessment at one year after breast cancer diagnosis. *Clinical Rehabilitation, 20*(6), p. 518.

---

Age was not significantly correlated with pre-test scores, $r = -0.13, n = 111$, $P = 0.16$, nor improvement, $r = -0.02, n = 110, P = 0.85$.

*Source:* Law, A. V., and Shapiro, K. (2005). Impact of a community pharmacist-directed clinic in improving screening and awareness of osteoporosis. *Journal of Evaluation in Clinical Practice, 11*(3), p. 253.

sort of thing, because they used a $p$-value to determine how likely it would be, assuming the null hypothesis to be true, to end up with a sample correlation as large or larger than each of their computed $r$s. Within both of these excerpts, each $p$ functioned as a measure of how inconsistent the sample data were compared with what we'd expect to happen if $H_0$ were true.

Be sure to note that there is an *inverse* relationship between the size of $p$ and the degree to which the sample data deviate from the null hypothesis. In Excerpt 7.19, the $p$-value would have been larger than 0.03 if the two percentages had been closer together (or smaller than 0.03 if those percentages had been even further apart). In Excerpt 7.20, the $p$-value would have been smaller if the $r$s had been further away from zero (or smaller if the $r$s had turned out even lower than they did).

## Step 5: The Criterion for Evaluating the Sample Evidence

After the researcher has summarized the study's data, the next task involves asking the question "Are the sample data inconsistent with what would likely occur if the null hypothesis were true?" If the answer to this question is "yes," then $H_0$ will be rejected; on the other hand, a negative response to this query will bring forth a fail-to-reject decision. Thus as soon as the sample data can be tagged as consistent or inconsistent (with $H_0$), the decision in Step 6 is easily made. "But how," you might ask, "does the researcher decide which of these labels should be attached to the sample data?"

If the data from the sample(s) are in perfect agreement with the pinpoint numerical value specified in $H_0$, then it is obvious that the sample data are consistent with $H_0$. (This would be the case if the sample mean turned out equal to 100 when testing $H_0: \mu = 100$, if the sample correlation coefficient turned out equal to 0.00 when testing $H_0: \rho = 0.00$, etc.) Such a situation, however, is unlikely. Almost always, there will be a discrepancy between $H_0$'s parameter value and the corresponding sample statistic.

In light of the fact that the sample statistic (produced by Step 4) is almost certain to be different from $H_0$'s pinpoint number (specified in Step 1), the concern over whether the sample data are inconsistent with $H_0$ actually boils down to the question "Should the observed difference between the sample evidence and the null hypothesis be considered to be a big difference or a small difference?" If this difference (between the data and $H_0$) is judged to be large, then the sample data will be looked on as being inconsistent with $H_0$ and, as a consequence, $H_0$ will be rejected. If, on the other hand, this difference is judged to be small, the data and $H_0$ will be looked on as consistent with each other and, therefore, $H_0$ will not be rejected.

To answer the question about the sample data's being either consistent or inconsistent with what one would expect if $H_0$ were true, a researcher can use either of two simple procedures. As you will see, both of these procedures involve comparing a single-number summary of the sample evidence against a criterion number. The single-number summary of the data can be either the calculated value or the $p$-value. Our job now is to consider what each of these data-based indices is compared against and what kind of result forces researchers to consider their samples as representing a large or a small deviation from $H_0$.

One available procedure for evaluating the sample data involves comparing the calculated value against something called the **critical value.** The critical value is nothing more than a number extracted from one of many statistical tables developed by mathematical statisticians. Applied researchers, of course, do not close their eyes and point to just any entry in a randomly selected table of critical values. Instead, they must learn which table of critical values is appropriate for their studies and also how to locate the single number within the table that constitutes the correct critical value.

As a reader of research reports, you do not have to learn how to locate the proper table that contains the critical value for any given statistical test, nor do you have to locate, within the table, the single number that allows the sample data to be labeled as being consistent or inconsistent with $H_0$. The researcher will do these things. Occasionally, the critical value will be included in the research report, as exemplified in Excerpts 7.21 through 7.23.

### EXCERPTS 7.21–7.23 • *The Critical Value and the Decision Rule*

Results indicated that subjects in the treatment group had significantly higher post-test self-concept scores than the control group (obtained $t$ of 6.58 is greater than the critical $t$-value of 1.96 with $df = 66$ at alpha level of .05).

*Source:* Egbochuku, E. O., and Obiunu, J. J. (2006). The effect of reciprocal peer counseling in the enhancement of self-concept among adolescents. *Education, 126*(3), p. 504.

----------

Marital status has a noticeable but not significant influence on students' use of their time for economic activities. This is because the chi-square value of 4.19 is less than the critical value of 5.99 at .05 level of probability.

*Source:* Ogonor, B. O., and Nwadiani, M. (2006). An analysis of non-instructional time management of undergraduates in southern Nigeria. *College Student Journal, 40*(1), pp. 209–210.

----------

The hypothesis testing for hierarchical regression analysis (Cohen et al., 2003) found that the computed $F(5, 288) = 3.10$ was greater than the critical $F(5, 288) = 2.25$. Therefore, the hypothesis of this study was supported. The conclusion was to reject the null hypothesis at an alpha of .05.

*Source:* Pluta, D. J., and Accordino, M. P. (2006). Predictors of return to work for people with psychiatric disabilities: A private sector perspective. *Rehabilitation Counseling Bulletin, 49*(2), p. 105.

Once the critical value is located, the researcher will compare the data-based summary of the sample data against the scientific dividing line that has been extracted from a statistical table. The simple question being asked at this point is whether the calculated value is larger or smaller than the critical value. With most tests (such as $t$, $F$, chi-square, and tests of correlation coefficients), the researcher will follow a decision rule that says to reject $H_0$ if the calculated value is at least as large as the critical value. With a few tests (such as $U$ or $W$), the decision rule tells the researcher to reject $H_0$ if the calculated value is smaller than the critical value. You do not need to worry about which way the decision rule works for any given test because this is the responsibility of the individual who performs the data analysis. The only things you need to know about the comparison of calculated and critical values are (1) that this comparison allows the researcher to decide easily whether to reject or fail to reject $H_0$ and (2) that some tests use a decision rule that says to reject $H_0$ if the calculated value is larger than the critical value, whereas other tests involve a decision rule that says to reject $H_0$ if the calculated value is smaller than the critical value.

The researchers associated with Excerpts 7.21, 7.22, and 7.23 helped the readers of their research reports by specifying not only the critical value but also the nature of the decision rule that was used when the calculated value was compared against the critical value. In most research reports, you will not see either of these things; instead, you will only be given the calculated value. (On rare occasions, you won't even see the calculated value.) As indicated previously, however, you should not be concerned about this because it is the researcher's responsibility to obtain the critical value and to know which way the decision rule operates. When reading most research reports, all you can do is trust that the researcher did these two things properly.

The second way a researcher can evaluate the sample evidence is to compare the data-based $p$-value against a preset point on the 0-to-1 scale on which the $p$ must fall. This criterion is called the **level of significance,** and it functions much as does the critical value in the first procedure for evaluating sample evidence. Simply stated, the researcher compares his or her data-based $p$-value against the criterion point along the 0-to-1 continuum so as to decide whether the sample evidence ought to be considered consistent or inconsistent with $H_0$. The decision rule used in this second procedure is always the same: If the data-based $p$-value is equal to or smaller than the criterion, the sample is viewed as being *in*consistent with $H_0$; if, on the other hand, $p$ is larger than the criterion, the data are looked on as being consistent with $H_0$.

I will discuss the level of significance in more depth in the next section, since it is a concept that must be dealt with by the researcher no matter which of the two procedures is used to evaluate the sample data. (With the second procedure, the level of significance *is* the criterion against which the data-based $p$-value is compared; with the first procedure, the level of significance influences the size of the critical value against which the calculated value is compared.) Before we leave this

Research
Navigator.c⊕m

Level of
significance

section, however, I need to point out that the same decision will be reached regarding $H_0$ no matter which of the two procedures is used in Step 5 of the hypothesis testing procedure. For example, suppose a researcher conducts an $F$-test and rejects $H_0$ because the calculated value is larger than the critical value. If that researcher were to compare the data-based $p$ against the level of significance, it would be found that the former is smaller than the latter, and the same decision about $H_0$ would be made. Or, suppose a researcher conducts a $t$-test and fails to reject $H_0$ because the calculated value is smaller than the critical value. If that researcher were to compare the data-based $p$ against the level of significance, it would be found that the former is larger than the latter, and the same fail-to-reject decision would be made.

## Step 3: Selecting a Level of Significance

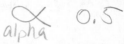

After the data of a study are collected and summarized, the six-step hypothesis testing procedure allows absolutely no subjectivity to influence, or bias, the ultimate decision that is made concerning the null hypothesis. This goal is accomplished by reliance on a scientific cutoff point to determine whether the sample data are consistent or inconsistent with $H_0$. By referring (in Step 5) to a numerical criterion, it becomes clear whether or not sampling error provides, by itself, a sufficient explanation for the observed difference between the single-number summary of the researcher's data (computed in Step 4) and $H_0$'s pinpoint numerical value (articulated in Step 1). If the single-number summary of the data is found to lie on $H_a$'s side of the criterion number (or if the data-based $p$ lands on $H_a$'s side of the level of significance), a decision (in Step 6) is made to reject $H_0$ in favor of $H_a$ (set forth in Step 2); on the other hand, if the calculated value lands on $H_0$'s side of the critical value (or if the data-based $p$ lands on $H_0$'s side of the level of significance), a fail-to-reject decision is made.

Either the critical value or the level of significance serves as a scientific cutoff point that determines what decision will be made concerning the null hypothesis. The six-step hypothesis testing procedure not only allows the researcher to do something that affects the magnitude of this criterion—*it actually forces the researcher to become involved in determining how rigorous the criterion will be.* The researcher should not, as I have pointed out, do anything like this after the data have been collected and summarized. However, the researcher *must* do something prior to collecting data that has an impact on how large or small the criterion number will be.

After the null and alternative hypotheses have been set up, but before any data are collected, the researcher must select a level of significance. This third step of the hypothesis testing procedure simply asks the researcher to select a positive decimal value of the researcher's choosing. Although the researcher has the freedom to select any value between 0 and 1 for the level of significance, most researchers select a small number such as .10, .05, or .01. The most frequently selected number is .05.

Before explaining how the researcher-selected level of significance influences the size of the critical value, I need to alert you to the fact that not all researchers use the phrase *level of significance* to designate the decimal number that must be specified in Step 3. Instead of indicating, for example, that the level of significance is set equal to .05, some researchers will state that "the **alpha level** ($\alpha$) is set equal to .05," others will assert that "$p = .05$," and still others will indicate that "$H_0$ will be rejected if $p < .05$." Likewise, a decision to use the .01 level of significance might be expressed using statements such as "alpha = .01," "$\alpha = .01$," or "results will be considered significant if $p < .01$."

In Excerpts 7.24 through 7.28, we see different ways in which researchers report what level of significance was selected within their studies.

If the single-number summary of the sample data is a *p*-value, the pragmatic value of the level of significance is clear. In this situation, *p* is compared directly

**EXCERPTS 7.24–7.28 • *The Level of Significance***

A significance level of .05 was used for all statistical analyses.

*Source:* Mangione, K. K., Craik, R. L., Tomlinson, S. S., and Palombaro, K. M. (2005). Can elderly patients who have had a hip fracture perform moderate- to high-intensity exercise at home? *Physical Therapy, 85*(8), p. 734.

-----

We used an alpha level of .05 for all analyses.

*Source:* Elias, S. M., and Cropanzano, R. (2006). Gender discrimination may be worse than you think: Testing ordinal interactions in power research. *Journal of General Psychology, 133*(2), p. 124.

-----

The level of significance was set at $p < 0.05$.

*Source:* Davids, J. R., Peace, L. C., Wagner, L. V., Gidewall, M. A., Roberson, W. M., and Blackhurst, D. W. (2006). Validation of the Shriner's Hospital for Children Upper Extremity Evaluation (SHUEE) for children with hemiplegic cerebral palsy. *Journal of Bone & Joint Surgery, 88*(2), p. 328.

-----

An $\alpha$ of 0.05 was selected for tests of significance.

*Source:* Sloka, J. S., Pryse-Phillips, W., and Stefanelli, M. (2006). The relation between menarche and the age of first symptoms in a multiple sclerosis cohort. *Multiple Sclerosis, 12*(3), p. 334.

-----

For all the analyses reported below, the level of confidence for rejecting a null hypothesis was 0.05.

*Source:* Pichette, F. (2005). Time spent on reading and reading comprehension in second language learning. *Canadian Modern Language Review, 62*(2), p. 252.

against $\alpha$ to determine whether or not $H_0$ should be rejected. But even if the single-number summary of the sample data is a calculated value, the level of significance still performs a valuable, pragmatic function. This is because a critical value cannot be located (in Step 5) unless the level of significance has first been set. As indicated in our earlier discussion of Step 4, there are many tables of critical values. Once the proper table is located, the researcher still has the task of locating the single number within the table that will serve as the critical value. The task of locating the critical value is easy, so long as the level of significance has been specified.[3]

Although the level of significance plays an important pragmatic role within the six-step hypothesis testing procedure, the decimal number selected in Step 3 is even more important from a different perspective. When I introduced the concept of the null hypothesis and when I talked about the reject or fail-to-reject decision that researchers will make regarding the null hypothesis, I was careful to use language that did *not* suggest that $H_0$ is ever *proven* to be true or false by means of hypothesis testing. Regardless of the decision made about $H_0$ after the calculated and critical values (or $p$ and $\alpha$) are compared, it is possible that the wrong decision will be reached. If $H_0$ is rejected in Step 6, it is conceivable that this action represents a mistake, since $H_0$ may actually be true. Or, if $H_0$ is not rejected, it is conceivable that *this* action represents a mistake, since $H_0$ may actually be an inaccurate statement about the value of the parameter in the population(s).

In light of the fact that a mistake can conceivably occur regardless of what decision is made at the end of the hypothesis testing procedure, two technical terms have been coined to distinguish between these potentially wrong decisions. A **Type I error** designates the mistake of rejecting $H_0$ when the null hypothesis is actually true. A **Type II error,** on the other hand, designates the kind of mistake that is made if $H_0$ is not rejected when the null hypothesis is actually false. The following chart may help to clarify the meaning of these possible errors.

*ERRORS*

|  |  | Is $H_0$ Really True? | |
|---|---|---|---|
|  |  | Yes | No |
| **Researcher's Decision** | Reject $H_0$ | Type I Error | Correct Decision |
|  | Fail-to-Reject $H_0$ | Correct Decision | Type II Error |

[3]With certain tests, researchers cannot locate the critical value unless they also know (1) whether their test is one- or two-tailed in nature and (2) how many degrees of freedom are connected with the sample data. I will discuss the concept of degrees of freedom in later chapters.

Beyond its pragmatic utility in helping the researcher locate the critical value (or in serving as the criterion against which the data-based $p$ is compared), the level of significance is important because it establishes the probability of a Type I error. In other words, the selected alpha level determines the likelihood that a true null hypothesis will be rejected. If the researcher specifies, in Step 3, that $\alpha = .05$, then the chances of rejecting a true null hypothesis become equal to 5 out of 100. If, on the other hand, the alpha level is set equal to .01 (rather than .05), then the chances of rejecting a true null hypothesis would become equal to 1 out of 100. The alpha level, therefore, directly determines the probability that a Type I error will be committed.[4]

After realizing that the researcher can fully control the likelihood of a Type I error, you may be wondering why the researcher does not select an alpha level that would dramatically reduce the possibility that a true $H_0$ will be rejected. To be more specific, you may be inclined to ask why the alpha level is not set equal to .001 (where the chance of a Type I error becomes equal to 1 out of 1,000), equal to .00001 (where the chance of Type I error becomes equal to 1 out of 100,000), or even equal to some smaller decimal value. To answer this legitimate question, we must consider the way in which a change in the alpha level has an effect on both Type I error risk *and* Type II error risk.

If the alpha level is changed, it's as if there is an apothecary scale in which the two pans hanging from opposite ends of the balance beam contain, respectively, Type I error risk and Type II error risk. The alpha level of a study could be changed so as to decrease the likelihood of a Type I error, but this change in alpha will simultaneously have an opposite effect on the likelihood of a Type II error. Hence, researchers rarely move alpha from the more traditional levels of .05 or .01 to levels that would greatly protect against Type I errors (such as .0001) because such a change in the alpha level would serve to make the chances of a Type II error unacceptably high.

In Excerpts 7.29, 7.30, and 7.31, we see three cases where a connection is drawn between the selected level of significance and the likelihood of a Type I error and/or a Type II error. The third group of researchers deserve your respect for having explained why they chose the levels of significance they did. Far too many researchers, without thinking, set alpha equal to .05 simply because this is the most popular level of significance. If they weighed the risks of Type I and Type II errors in their own studies, they might choose some level of significance other than .05.

Near the beginning of this chapter, I pointed out that $H_0$ is normally set up so as to disagree with the researcher's personal hunch regarding the population parameter(s) focused on in the study. For example, if a researcher thinks that a new pill will reduce the mean stress level among students preparing to take their final examinations, a study might be set up involving an experimental group and a placebo group. Within this study, the researcher's null hypothesis would probably be set up to say that the pill has no effect on stress (i.e., $H_0$: $\mu_{\text{experimental}} = \mu_{\text{placebo}}$).

[4]As you will see later, the alpha level defines the probability of a Type I error only if (1) important assumptions underlying the statistical test are valid and (2) the hypothesis testing procedure is used to evaluate only *one* null hypothesis.

**EXCERPTS 7.29–7.31 •** *Alpha and the Risk of Type I and Type II Errors*

A type I error level of 5% was chosen for statistical significance.

*Source:* Sadri, H., MacKeigan, L. D., Leiter, L. A., and Einarson, T. R. (2005). Willingness to pay for inhaled insulin: A contingent valuation approach. *Pharmaco Economics, 23*(1), p. 1220.

---

For all tests of significance, the alpha error level was set at $p = .05$.

*Source:* Nagata, H., Dalton, P., Doolittle, N., and Breslin, P. A. S. (2005). Psychophysical isolation of the modality responsible for detecting multimodal stimuli: A chemosensory example. *Journal of Experimental Psychology: Human Perception and Performance, 31*(1), p. 102.

---

In order to balance a legitimate concern about the potential for Type I error with concern about Type II error, particularly given the small sample size, we set alpha at .05 for the hypotheses tested.

*Source:* Woodhouse, S. S., Schlosser, L. Z., Crook, R. E., Ligiéro, D. P., and Gelso, C. J. (2003). Client attachment to therapist: Relations to transference and client recollections of parental caregiving. *Journal of Counseling Psychology, 50*(4), p. 405.

In light of the fact that researchers typically like to reject $H_0$ to gain empirical support for their honest hunches, and in light of the fact that a change in the level of significance has an impact on the likelihood of Type II errors, you now may be wondering why the researcher does not move alpha in the opposite direction. It is true that a researcher would decrease the chance of a Type II error by changing alpha—for example, from .05 to .40—since such a change would make it more likely that $H_0$ would be rejected. Researchers do not use such high levels of significance simply because the scientific community generally considers Type I errors to be more dangerous than Type II errors. In most disciplines, few people would pay attention to researchers who reject null hypotheses at alpha levels higher than .20, because such levels of significance are considered to be too lenient (i.e., too likely to yield reject decisions that are Type I errors).

The most frequently seen level of significance, as illustrated earlier in Excerpts 7.24 through 7.31, is .05. This alpha level is considered to represent a happy medium between the two error possibilities associated with any application of the six-step hypothesis testing procedure. If, however, a researcher feels that it is more important to guard against the possibility of a Type I error, a lower alpha level (such as .01 or .001) will be selected. On the other hand, if it is felt that a Type II error would be more dangerous than a Type I error, then a higher alpha level (such as .10 or .15) will be selected. Excerpts 7.32 and 7.33 illustrate how (and why) researchers sometimes set alpha equal to something other than .05. In Excerpt 7.32, the

**EXCERPTS 7.32–7.33 • *Reasons for Using Alpha Levels Other Than .05***

Although the level of significance of a statistical test is generally set at 0.05 by convention, [our study's objectives] justified the acceptability of a higher Type I error rate, resulting in greater statistical power. The alpha level for statistical tests in this study was set a priori at 0.10.

*Source:* Gall, J. (2006). Orienting tasks and their impact on learning and attitudes in the use of hypertext. *Journal of Educational Multimedia and Hypermedia, 15*(1), p. 15.

A Bonferroni approach to control for Type I error across the 10 correlations indicated that a *p* value of less than .005 (.05/10 = .005) was required for significance.

*Source:* Wrobleski, K. K., and Snyder, C. R. (2005). Hopeful thinking in older adults: Back to the future. *Aging Research, 31*(2), p. 223.

researcher wanted to guard against making Type II errors (by making sure his statistical tests had high "power"), so he set the level of significance equal to .10 rather than .05. In contrast, the researchers in Excerpt 7.33 wanted to guard against making Type I errors when statistically evaluating their study's 10 different correlation coefficients, so they changed the level of significance from .05 to .005 by making a "Bonferroni" adjustment. In the next chapter, we will consider both power and the Bonferroni adjustment. For now, the only thing you need to know is that not all alpha levels are set equal to .05.

Before concluding our discussion of the level of significance, I need to clarify two points of potential confusion. To accomplish this goal, I want to raise and then answer two questions: "Does the alpha level somehow determine the likelihood of a Type II error?" and "If $H_0$ is rejected, does the alpha level indicate the probability that $H_0$ is true?"

The first point of potential confusion concerns the relationship between alpha and Type II error risk. Since alpha does, in fact, determine the likelihood that the researcher will end up rejecting a true $H_0$, and since it is true that a change in alpha affects the chance of a Type I error *and* the chance of a Type II error (with one increasing, the other decreasing), you may be tempted to expect the level of significance to dictate Type II error risk. Unfortunately, this is not the case. The alpha level specified in Step 3 does influence Type II error risk, but so do other features of a study such as sample size, population variability, and the reliability of the measuring instrument used to collect data.

The second point of potential confusion about the alpha level again concerns the decision reached at the end of the hypothesis testing procedure. If a study's $H_0$ is rejected in Step 6, it is *not* proper to look back to see what alpha level was specified in Step 3 and then interpret that alpha level as indicating the probability that

$H_0$ is true. For example, if a researcher ends up rejecting $H_0$ after having set the level of significance equal to .05, you cannot legitimately conclude that the chances of $H_0$ being true are less than 5 out of 100. The alpha level in any study indicates only what the chances are that the forthcoming decision will be a Type I error. If alpha is set equal to .05, then the chances are 5 out of 100 that $H_0$ will be rejected *if $H_0$ is actually true.* Statisticians sometimes try to clarify this distinction by pointing out that the level of significance specifies "the probability of a reject decision, given a true $H_0$" and *not* "the probability of $H_0$ being true, given a reject decision."

## Results That Are Highly Significant and Near Misses

As indicated earlier, the level of significance plays a highly important role in hypothesis testing. In a very real sense, it functions as a dividing line. Statistical significance is positioned on one side of that line, the lack of statistical significance on the other. That dividing line is clearly visible if the researcher decides to reject or fail-to-reject $H_0$ by comparing the data-based *p* against the level of significance. But even when the procedure for deciding $H_0$'s fate involves comparing the data-based calculated value against a tabled critical value, the level of significance is still involved. That's because $\alpha$ influences the size of the critical value.

Because the level of significance plays such an important role—both pragmatically and conceptually—in hypothesis testing, it often is included when the decision about $H_0$ is declared. With the level of significance set at .05 (the most popular $\alpha$-level), a decision to reject $H_0$ is often summarized by the notation $p < .05$, while a decision not to reject $H_0$ is summarized by the notation $p > .05$. Earlier, you saw such notational summaries in Excerpts 7.7, 7.11, 7.17, and 7.18.

Many researchers do not like to summarize their results by reporting simply that the null hypothesis either was or was not rejected. Instead, they want their readers to know how much of a discrepancy existed between the data-based *p* and the level of significance (or between the data-based calculated value and the critical value). In doing this, the researcher's goal is to provide evidence as to how strongly the data challenge $H_0$. In other words, these researchers want you to know if they beat the level of significance by a wide margin (presuming that $H_0$ was rejected) or if they just missed beating $\alpha$ (presuming that $H_0$ was retained).

Consider Excerpts 7.34 and 7.35. In the first of these excerpts, the researchers presented three *p*s, each of which turned out to be smaller than .000001. In Excerpt 7.35, the researcher reports a single *p* that turned out equal to .0000003. Instead of simply summarizing their results by saying "$p < .05$," these researchers wanted to show us that they beat the .05 level of significance "by a mile." Further evidence of that presumed motivation for reporting these unusually low *p* values is the phrase **highly significant** in Excerpt 7.34.

Although *p*-values like those shown in Excerpts 7.34 and 7.35 are not seen very often in research reports, I can assure you that you will frequently encounter

Research
Navigator.c⊕m
Highly significant

## EXCERPTS 7.34–7.35 • *Rejecting the Null Hypothesis with Room to Space*

The effect of question was highly significant ($p < 0.000001$), as was the effect of class ($p < 0.000001$). There was also a highly significant interaction between question and class ($p < 0.000001$).

*Source:* Massie, R., and Dillon, H. (2006). The impact of sound-field amplification in mainstream cross-cultural classrooms: Part 2 Teacher and child opinions. *Australian Journal of Education, 50*(1), p. 82.

-----

In the national study, those who met the diagnostic criteria for eating disorders ($n = 24$) had significantly ($F1,993 = 27.0, p = .0000003$) lower scores on the SCQ ($M = 130, SD = 22.5$) compared to those without eating disorders ($M = 152, SD = 20.4$). . . .

*Source:* Ghaderi, A. (2005). Psychometric properties of the Self-Concept Questionnaire. *European Journal of Psychological Assessment, 21*(2), p. 144.

$p$-less-than statements where the numerical value is smaller than .05. You regularly will see $p < .01$, you will come across $p < .001$ quite often, and you will see $p < .0001$ every now and then. Such statements do *not* indicate that the researcher initially set the level of significance equal to .01, .001, or .0001.

Many researchers use an approach to hypothesis testing that involves reporting the most impressive $p$-statement that honestly describes their data. They first check to see they have statistical significance at the .05 level. If they do, then they know they at least can say $p < .05$. They next check to see if the sample data would have been significant at the .01 level, had this been the selected alpha level. If the answer is yes, they then check again, this time to see if the data are significant at the .001 level. This process continues until either (1) the data cannot beat a more rigorous level of significance or (2) the researcher does not want to check further to see if $p$ might beat an even more impressive $\alpha$. It is clear that this approach to hypothesis testing was used in Excerpt 7.36.

Researchers often test more than one null hypothesis in the same study. In the research reports for these investigations, it is usually the case that certain results are summarized via the statement $p < .05$, other results are summarized via the statement $p < .01$, and still other results are summarized via the statement $p < .001$. (Recently, I read a research report in which four different $p$-statements—$p < .05$, $p < .01$, $p < .005$, and $p < .001$—were connected to the results presented in a single table.) In any one of these studies, it is highly unlikely that the researcher decided at the outset to use different alpha levels with the different null hypotheses being tested. Rather, it's far more probable that all $H_0$s were initially tested with $\alpha$

## EXCERPT 7.36 • *Reporting p < .0001 in Conjunction with a .05 Alpha Level*

The *p*-value was considered significant at $p < 0.05$. . . . Overall results indicated teachers' knowledge of SCD improved significantly after the intervention. Before the session, 73% of questions were answered correctly, and this rate increased to 83% afterward, $p = 0.0001$.

*Source:* King, A. A., Tang, S., Ferguson, K. L., and DeBaun, M. R. (2005). An education program to increase teacher knowledge about sickle cell disease. *Journal of School Health, 75*(1), p. 13.

set equal to .05, with the researcher then revising $\alpha$ (as indicated in the previous paragraph) so that more impressive *p*-statements could be presented.

Now, let us shift gears and consider what happens if the data-based *p* is larger than the initially specified level of significance. If *p* is much larger than $\alpha$, the situation is clear: the null hypothesis cannot be rejected. At times, however, *p* turns out to be just slightly larger than $\alpha$. For example, *p* might turn out equal to .07 when $\alpha$ is set at .05. Many researchers consider this to be a near miss, and they will communicate this observation via certain commonly seen phrases. When *p* fails to beat $\alpha$ by a small amount, researchers often say that they achieved *marginal significance,* that their findings *approached significance,* that there was a *trend toward significance,* or that the results indicate *borderline significance.* In Excerpts 7.37 and 7.38, we see two examples of this.

## EXCERPTS 7.37–7.38 • *Just Barely Failing to Reject the Null Hypothesis*

Younger adults' mnemonic usage ratings were numerically higher than were the older adults' ratings, which implied that younger adults use memory aids somewhat less frequently than do older adults, a marginally significant difference ($p = .06$).

*Source:* Cherry, K. E., and Brigman, S. (2005). Memory failures appraisal in younger and older adults: Role of individual difference and event outcome variables. *Journal of Genetic Psychology, 166*(4), p. 445.

For the subsample taking cholesterol medications, mean HDL levels for the adherers and nonadherers approached significance (52.0 vs. 44.3 mg/dl, respectively; $p = .06$).

*Source:* Hill-Briggs, F., Gary, T. L., Bone, L. R., Hill, M. N., Levine, D. M., and Brancati, F. L. (2005). Medication adherence and diabetes control in urban African Americans with type 2 diabetes. *Health Psychology, 24*(4), p. 353.

It should be noted that some researchers use an approach to hypothesis testing that has two clear rules: (1) choose the level of significance at the beginning of the study and then never change it, and (2) consider any result, summarized by $p$, to lie on one side or the other side of $\alpha$, with it making no difference whatsoever whether $p$ is a smidgen or a mile away from $\alpha$. According to this school of thought, the *only* thing that matters is whether $p$ is larger or smaller than the level of significance.

Consider, for example, Excerpts 7.39 and 7.40. The data-based $p$s in these studies turned out equal to .052 and .049, respectively. Even though each $p$ was extremely close to the common $\alpha$ level used in both studies, .05, notice that the result in the first study was declared not significant whereas the result in the second study was referred to as being significant.

**EXCERPTS 7.39–7.40 •** *An All-or-Nothing Approach to Hypothesis Testing*

The number of dreams of each group was approximately equal (young women = 193, older women = 203), and although the older women reported more home dreams and the young women more laboratory dreams, this difference in distribution did not reach significance, $\chi^2(1, N = 396) = 3.79, p = .052$.

*Source:* St-Onge, M., Lortie-Lussier, M., Mercier, P., Grenier, J., and De Koninck, J. (2005). Emotions in the diary and REM dreams of young and late adulthood women and their relation to life satisfaction. *Dreaming, 15*(2), p. 121.

---

Phobic patients' STAI scores dropped significantly across Session 1 (46.6) to Session 2 (42.7), $t(20) = 1.73, p = .049. \ldots$

*Source:* Alpers, G. W., Wilhelm, F. H., and Roth, W. T. (2005). Psychophysiological assessment during exposure in driving phobic patients. *Journal of Abnormal Psychology, 114*(1), p. 134.

## A Few Cautions

Now that you have considered the six-step hypothesis testing procedure from the standpoint of its various elements and its underlying rationale, you may be tempted to think that it will be easy to decipher and critique any research report in your field that has employed this particular approach to inferential statistics. I hope, of course, that this chapter has helped you become more confident about making sense out of statements such as these: "A two-tailed test was used," "A rigorous alpha level was employed to protect against the possibility of a Type I error," and "The results were significant ($p < .01$)." Before I conclude this chapter, however, it is important that I alert you to a few places where misinterpretations can easily be made by the consumers of research literature (and by researchers themselves).

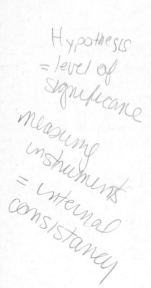

Hypothesis
= level of
significance

measuring
instrument
= internal
consistency

## Alpha

The word *alpha* (or its symbol $\alpha$) refers to two different concepts. Within the hypothesis testing procedure, alpha designates the level of significance selected by the researcher. In discussions of measuring instruments, alpha means something entirely different. In this context, alpha refers to the estimated internal consistency of data from the questionnaire, inventory, or test being discussed. Note that alpha must be a *small* decimal number in hypothesis testing in order to accomplish the task of protecting against Type I errors. In contrast, alpha must be a *large* decimal number in order to document high reliability.

## The Importance of $H_0$

Earlier in this chapter, I presented excerpts from various journal articles wherein the null hypothesis was clearly specified. Unfortunately, most researchers do not take the time or space to indicate publicly the precise nature of $H_0$. They don't do this because they presume that their readers will understand what the null hypothesis was in light of the number of samples involved in the study, the nature of the measurements collected, and the kind of statistical test used to analyze the data.

Right now, you may feel that you will never be able to discern $H_0$ unless it is specifically articulated. However, after becoming familiar with the various statistical tests used to analyze data, you will find that you can make accurate guesses as to the unstated null hypotheses you encounter. Many of the chapters in this book, beginning with Chapter 9, will help you acquire this skill.

This skill is important to have because the final decision of the hypothesis testing procedure always has reference to the point of departure. Researchers never end up by rejecting (or failing to reject) in the abstract; instead, they *always* will terminate the hypothesis testing procedure by rejecting (or failing to reject) a *specific* $H_0$. Accordingly, no decision to reject should be viewed as important unless we consider what specifically has been rejected.

On occasion, the hypothesis testing procedure is used to evaluate a null hypothesis that could have been rejected from the very beginning, strictly on the basis of common sense. Although it is statistically possible to test such an $H_0$, no real discovery is made by rejecting something that was known to be false from the outset. To illustrate, consider Excerpt 7.41.

The material in Excerpt 7.41 is, perhaps, a truly classic case of the hypothesis testing procedure resulting in a statistically significant finding that was fully guaranteed to be produced because of the way the two comparison groups were formed. The researcher deserves credit for stating that the "it is not surprising" that the two groups were found to be significantly different. On the other hand, what is also surprising is why in the world the two groups were compared in the first place.

I cannot exaggerate the importance of the null hypothesis to the potential meaningfulness of results that come from someone using the hypothesis testing

## EXCERPT 7.41 • *Rejecting an Unimportant $H_0$*

The participants were divided into two reading proficiency groups (i.e., the more proficient and less proficient groups) based on the total test scores on the two reading comprehension tests. The 21 participants whose scores were higher than the average score (12.5 points) were put in "the more proficient group," and the remaining 21 participants whose scores were lower than the average were put in the "less proficient group." The mean and standard deviation (*SD*) of the total reading comprehension test scores for the more proficient group were 15.7 and 1.9, respectively. The mean and *SD* of the total reading comprehension test scores for the less proficient group were 9.2 and 2.0, respectively. It is not surprising that the result of an independent group's *t* test indicated that the more proficient group significantly outperformed the less proficient group on the reading comprehension tests ($df = 40, t = 10.934, p < .001$).

*Source:* Kondo-Brown, K. (2006). How do English L1 learners of advanced Japanese infer unknown Kanji words in authentic texts? *Language Learning, 56*(1), pp. 125–126.

procedure. Remember that a reject decision, by itself, is not indicative of a useful finding. Such a result could be easily brought about simply by setting up, in Step 1, an outrageous $H_0$. Consequently, you should always be interested in not only the ultimate decision reached at the end of the hypothesis testing procedure but also the target of that decision—$H_0$.

### The Ambiguity of the Word Hypothesis

In discussing the outcomes of their data analyses, researchers will sometimes assert that their results support the hypothesis (or that the results do not support the hypothesis). But which hypothesis is being referred to?

As you now know, the hypothesis testing procedure involves two formal hypotheses, $H_0$ and $H_a$. In addition, the person conducting the study may have a hunch (i.e., prediction) as to how things will turn out. Many researchers refer to such hunches as their *hypotheses*. Thus, within a single study, there can be three different hypotheses![5] Usually, the full context of the research report will help to make clear which of these three hypotheses stands behind any statement about the hypothesis. At times, however, you will need to read very carefully to accurately understand what the researcher found.

[5]The researcher's hunch will differ from *both* $H_0$ and $H_a$ if the alternative hypothesis is set up to be nondirectional even though the researcher's prediction is directional. This situation is not uncommon. Many researchers have been taught to conduct two-tailed tests—even though they have a directional hunch—in order to allow the data to suggest that reality is on the flip side of their hunch. (In using a one-tailed test, this could never happen.)

To illustrate why I offer this caution, consider the two short sentences in Excerpt 7.42. As you can see, the final word in the first sentence is *hypothesis*. But which hypothesis is it: the null hypothesis, the alternative hypothesis, or the researchers' hunch (i.e., the **research hypothesis**)? After reading Chapter 9, you will be in a position to guess, with high confidence, that it is not the null hypothesis. Now, we're down to two choices, the alternative hypothesis and the research hypothesis. I'm going to guess that it's the research hypothesis. (After you read Chapter 9, I think you'll see why I made this guess.) The point of this little guessing game is simply to point out, through an example, that you must be careful when you come across the word *hypothesis*. It does *not* always mean the same thing.

**EXCERPT 7.42 • *The Ambiguity of the Word Hypothesis***

The results of this study supported the hypothesis. That is, time use efficiency was positively related to conscientiousness.

*Source:* Kelly, W. E., and Johnson, J. L. (2005). Time use efficiency and the five-factor model of personality. *Education, 125*(3), p. 513.

## When *p* Is Reported to Be Equal to or Less Than Zero

Whenever sample data are analyzed by a computer for the purpose of evaluating a null hypothesis, a *p*-value will be produced. This *p* is a probability, and it can end up being any number between 0 and 1. As you now know, a small value of *p* causes $H_0$ to be rejected. The researcher takes that action because a small *p* signifies that a true $H_0$ population situation would not likely produce a randomly selected data set that, when summarized, is at least as far away from $H_0$'s pinpoint number as is the researcher's actual data set. In most of the excerpts of this chapter, the *p* turned out to be very low. In one case, *p* was equal to .049; in another, *p* was reported to be equal to .03. We even saw one instance where *p* turned out equal to .0000003.

Occasionally, as illustrated in Excerpts 7.43 and 7.44, you will encounter cases where the reported *p*-value is equal to or less than zero. Such *p*s are misleading, for they do not mean that an imaginary population defined by $H_0$ had no chance whatsoever (or less than no chance) to produce sample data like that obtained by the researcher. Rather, such *p*-statements are created when exceedingly small computer-generated *p*-values (e.g., *p* = .00003) are rounded off to a smaller number of decimal places. It's important to know this to avoid falling into the trap of thinking that $H_0$ is proven to be wrong in those cases where *p* is reported to be zero or less than zero.

## EXCERPTS 7.43–7.44 • *Reporting p as Being Equal to or Less Than Zero*

Support was associated with the pattern of sexual activity, controlling for background characteristics ($F = 6.4$, $df = 3,711$, $p = .000$).

*Source:* Darling, N., Palmer, R. F., and Kipke, M. D. (2005). Do street youths' perceptions of their caregivers predict HIV-risk behavior? *Journal of Family Psychology, 19*(3), p. 461.

---

The reading speed at the beginning of training was correlated with the reading speed at the end of training ($r = 0.571$, $p < .000$).

*Source:* Goodrich, G. L., Kirby, J., Wood, J., and Peters, L. (2006). The Reading Behavior Inventory: An outcome assessment tool. *Journal of Visual Impairment & Blindness, 100*(3), p. 166.

## The Meaning of Significant

If the null hypothesis is rejected, the researcher may assert that the results are **significant.** Since the word *significant* means something different when used in casual everyday discussions than when it is used in conjunction with the hypothesis testing procedure, it is crucial that you recognize the statistical meaning of this frequently seen term. Simply stated, a statistically significant finding may not be very significant at all.

In our everyday language, the term *significant* means important or noteworthy. In the context of hypothesis testing, however, the term *significant* has a totally different meaning. Within this inferential context, a significant finding is simply one that is not likely to have occurred if $H_0$ is true. So long as the sample data are inconsistent with what one would expect from a true null situation, the statistical claim can be made that the results are significant. Accordingly, a researcher's statement to the effect that the results are significant simply means that the null hypothesis being tested has been rejected. It does *not* necessarily mean that the results are *important* or that the absolute difference between the sample data and $H_0$ was found to be *large*.

Whether or not a statistically significant result constitutes an important result is influenced by (1) the quality of the research question that provides the impetus for the empirical investigation and (2) the quality of the research design that guides the collection of data. I have come across journal articles that summarized carefully conducted empirical investigations leading to statistically significant results, yet the studies seemed to be quite insignificant. Clearly, to yield important findings, a study must be dealing with an important issue.

But what if statistically significant results *are* produced by a study that focuses on an important question? Does this situation mean that the research findings are important and noteworthy? The answer, unfortunately, is no. As you will see in the next chapter, it is possible for a study to yield statistically significant results even though there is a tiny difference between the data and the null hypothesis. For example, in a recent study reported in the *Journal of Applied Psychology,* the researcher tested $H_0$: $\rho = 0$ within the context of a study dealing with correlation.

After collecting and analyzing the sample data, this null hypothesis was rejected, with the report indicating that the result was "significant at the .001 level." The sample value that produced this finding was −.03!

Even if the issue being investigated is crucial, I cannot consider a correlation of −.03 to be very different in any meaningful way from the null value of 0. (With $r = -.03$, the proportion of explained variance is equal to .0009.) As you will soon learn, a large sample can sometimes cause a trivial difference to end up being statistically significant—and that is precisely what happened in the correlational study to which I am referring. In that investigation, there were 21,646 individuals in the sample. Because of the gigantic sample, a tiny correlation turned out to be statistically significant. Although significant in a statistical sense, the $r$ of −.03 was clearly insignificant in terms of its importance.

## Review Terms

| | |
|---|---|
| Accept | Reliable difference |
| Alpha level | Research hypothesis |
| Alternative hypothesis | Significant |
| Calculated value | Test statistic |
| Critical value | Two-tailed test |
| Directional | Type I error |
| Fail to reject | Type II error |
| Hypothesis testing | $\alpha$ |
| Level of significance | $H_0$ |
| Nondirectional | $H_a$ |
| Null hypothesis | *ns* |
| One-tailed test | *p* |
| Reject | .05 |

## The Best Items in the Companion Website

1. An email message sent from the author to his students entitled "Learning about Hypothesis Testing Is NOT Easy!"
2. An interactive online quiz (with immediate feedback provided) covering Chapter 7.
3. Ten misconceptions about the content of Chapter 7.
4. Chapter 7's best passage (selected by the author).
5. An interactive online resource called "Type I Errors."

To access chapter objectives, practice tests, weblinks, and flashcards, visit the companion website at www.ablongman.com/huck5e.

## Fun Exercises inside Research Navigator

### 1. Are college students more aggressive if they listen to more music?

In this study, 243 undergraduate college students were measured in terms of two music variables (what kind they liked and how often they listened) and several personality variables (such as aggression). In one set of their analyses, the researchers computed five separate Pearson $r$s, correlating frequency of listening with five personality variables (aggression, trust, self-esteem, attitudes toward women, and assault). Each of these sample correlation coefficients was evaluated using the hypothesis testing procedure. (As is usually the case, the researchers who conducted these five tests did not specify the null hypothesis; instead, they are counting on you to know that in each case $H_0$ specified a zero correlation in the population.) How do you think these five tests turned out? Do you think all five null hypotheses were rejected, just some of them, or none of them? To find out, locate the PDF version of the research report in the Communication database of ContentSelect and read the last paragraph on page 33.

A. M. Rubin, D. V. West, & W. S. Mitchell. Differences in aggression, attitudes toward women, and distrust as reflected in popular music preferences. *Media Psychology.* Located in the COMMUNICATION database of ContentSelect.

### 2. Are smokers or nonsmokers better workers?

To see whether smokers differ from nonsmokers in work quality, the researchers of this study collected job performance and discipline data on 136 hotel employees. Using a $t$-test, they applied the hypothesis testing procedure nine times to compare the smokers ($n = 65$) versus the nonsmokers ($n = 71$) on each of the study's nine dependent variables: job knowledge, work quality, tardiness, and so on. Though not articulated in the research report, the null hypothesis in each of these $t$-tests stated that the population mean for the smoking group was equal to the population mean for the nonsmoking group. (We know that the alternative hypothesis was nondirectional because the researchers pointed out that their tests were "two-tailed.") Do you think any of the nine null hypotheses was rejected? If so, which of the comparison groups—smokers or nonsmokers—do you think had the better sample mean? To find out, locate the PDF version of the research report in the Psychology database of ContentSelect, look at Table 1, and then read (on page 344) the two paragraphs in the "Results" section.

P. C. Morrow & T. Leedle. A comparison of job performance and disciplinary records of smokers and nonsmokers. *Journal of Psychology.* Located in the PSYCHOLOGY database of ContentSelect.

**Review Questions and Answers begin on page 513.**

# Effect Size, Power, CIs, and Bonferroni

In Chapter 7, we considered the basic six-step version of hypothesis testing procedure. Although many researchers use that version of hypothesis testing, there is a definite trend toward using a seven-step or nine-step procedure when testing null hypotheses. In this chapter, we will consider the extra step(s) associated with these approaches to hypothesis testing. In addition, this chapter includes two related topics: the connection between hypothesis testing and confidence intervals, and the problem of an inflated Type I error rate brought about by multiple tests conducted simultaneously.

## *The Seven-Step Version of Hypothesis Testing*

As you will recall from the previous chapter, the elements of the simplest version of hypothesis testing are as follows:

1. State the null hypothesis ($H_0$).
2. State the alternative hypothesis ($H_a$).
3. Select a level of significance ($\alpha$).
4. Collect and analyze the sample data.
5. Refer to a criterion for evaluating the sample evidence.
6. Reject or fail to reject $H_0$.

To these six steps, many researchers add a seventh step. Instead of ending the hypothesis testing procedure with a statement about $H_0$, these researchers return to their sample data and perform one of two additional analyses. Regardless of which specific analysis is applied to the data, the purpose of the seventh step is the same:

to go beyond the decision made about $H_0$ and say something about the *degree* to which the sample data turned out to be incompatible with the null hypothesis.

Before discussing what researchers do when they return to their data in Step 7 of this (slightly expanded) version of hypothesis testing, I want to explain why competent researchers take the time to do this. Simply stated, they do this because a result that is deemed to be statistically significant can be, at the same time, completely devoid of *any* practical significance whatsoever. This is because there is a direct relationship between the size of the sample(s) and the probability of rejecting a false null hypothesis. If the pinpoint number in $H_0$ is wrong, large samples increase the likelihood that the result will be statistically significant—even if $H_0$ is very, very close to being true. In such situations, a decision to reject $H_0$ in favor of $H_a$ is no great accomplishment due to the fact that $H_0$ is "off" by such a small amount.

In Excerpts 8.1 and 8.2, this critically important distinction between **statistical significance** and **practical significance** is discussed.[1] In the first of these excerpts, notice that the researchers state that their finding had "practical significance as well as statistical significance." (Later in this chapter, we'll consider the statistically based justification for this statement: "substantial effect sizes.") In Excerpt 8.2, note that the researchers point out that their findings lack practical significance despite the fact

*(handwritten margin note: rH sample ← Size of type II error)*

**Research Navigator.com**
Statistical significance
Practical significance

### EXCERPTS 8.1–8.2 • *Statistical Significance versus Practical Significance*

Results support the appropriate use of guidance and reflection for interactive multimedia games. . . . It is worthwhile to note that guidance and reflection produced substantial effect sizes under certain circumstances indicating that the effects have practical significance as well as statistical significance.

*Source:* Moreno, R., and Mayer, R. E. (2005). Role of guidance, reflection, and interactivity in an agent-based multimedia game. *Journal of Educational Psychology, 97*(1), pp. 117, 127.

- - - - - - - - - - - - - - - - - - - - - - - - - - - - - - - - - - - - - - - - - - - - - - - - - - - - - - - - -

In general, the PD group members, with their mild hypokinetic dysarthria, exhibited a faster speaking rate in the connected speech passages than the control group. Although statistically significant, these mean differences were less than $1/2$ syllable/s for both reading passages and were therefore not regarded as representing profound performance differences in speaking rate.

*Source:* Caviness, J. N., and Evidente, V. (2006). Analysis of high-frequency electroencephalgraphic-electrornyographic coherence elicited by speech and oral nonspeech tasks in Parkinson's Disease. *Journal of Speech, Language, and Hearing Research, 49*(2), p. 430.

[1]The term *clinical significance,* used frequently within medical research, means the same thing as practical significance.

that their data produced statistically significant results. It would be nice if all research reports contained statements like the ones in these two excerpts. Unfortunately, many researchers seem concerned with just one thing: statistical significance. This is dangerous because it is quite possible (as illustrated by Excerpt 8.2) for a study's results to be significant in a statistical sense without being important (i.e., significant) in a practical fashion.

We now will look briefly at two different procedures that researchers use in executing the seventh step of hypothesis testing. These procedures are similar in that they (a) provide a kind of insight into the study's data that is not captured at all by a *p*-level or a decision to reject or fail to reject $H_0$ and (b) take the form of a single numerical value. These two procedures are quite different in some other ways, and I will therefore discuss them as "Step 7a" and "Step 7b" as we continue now our discussion of hypothesis testing.

## Step 7a: Compute a Measure of Effect Size

Researchers who are sensitive to the distinction between statistical significance and practical significance will often add a seventh step to the basic version of hypothesis testing by computing a measure of effect size. Simply stated, measures of **effect size** give us a yardstick for assessing practical significance. Whereas the null hypothesis might be rejected in a study comparing two ways of treating a disease, an effects size index allows us to see whether the differential impact of the two treatments should be thought of as small or medium or large. Or, in a study involving the correlation of two variables that declares *r* to be significantly different from zero, a measure of effect size allows the researcher to talk about the pure strength of measured relationship, beyond saying simply that it is statistically significant.

Several different procedures for measuring effect size have been created because not all studies have the same statistical focus. Sometimes the statistical focus is on one or more correlations, sometimes it is on one or more means, and sometimes it is on one or more percentages. Moreover, different measures of effect size have been created for any given statistical focus (e.g., correlation). This situation is somewhat like what we encountered in the second half of Chapter 3. Just as there are many different kinds of bivariate correlations, there are several different ways that researchers measure effect size.

Because I will discuss many of these different effect size measures in later chapters, we will not consider them in detail at this point. Here, my two-fold goal is simply to introduce you to the names of a few of these statistical procedures and to show you that they are used by applied researchers. Unfortunately, I must add that that many, many researchers pay no attention whatsoever to the concept of practical significance. Accordingly, the excerpts that I present here come from studies wherein the researchers went "an extra mile" in an effort to have a better-than-average research report.

Excerpts 8.3 through 8.6 contain brief passages that illustrate the use of four different measures of effect size. These passages are quite different in that the first one deals with a correlation, the second one deals with the means of a single group measured twice, the third one deals with the means of three groups measured just once, and the fourth one deals with the percentages of two groups. Despite these differences, in each case the researcher team computed a measure of effect size. If you look closely, you will see the value of having indices of effect size. Look at the *p*-values in these studies. If those were the only things you could look at, you might draw the conclusion that each of these four findings (and especially the first, third, and fourth ones) revealed something big and important. However, the effect size in every case was either small or medium, thus suggesting the statistically significant findings did *not* have impressive practical significance.

↑effect
(large)
=↑effect

## EXCERPTS 8.3–8.6 • *Effect Size*

Consistent with our hypothesis, a significant correlation was found between the patient and therapist Confident Collaboration scales ($r = 0.37$, $p < 0.001$; medium effect size).

*Source:* Clemence, A. J., Hilsenroth, M. J., Ackerman, S. J., Strassle, C. G., and Handler, L. (2005). Facets of the therapeutic alliance and perceived progress in psychotherapy: Relationship between patient and therapist perspectives. *Clinical Psychology & Psychotherapy, 12*(6), p. 448.

-------------------------------------------------------------------------------------------------

On the WJ Letter-Word Identification subtest, which served as the test of far transfer, the PDF/GR participants made significant gains, $t(10) = 2.47$, $p < .05$, $d = .53$. The effect size for these gains was medium.

*Source:* Manset-Williamson, G., and Nelson, J. M. (2005). Balanced, strategic reading instructions for upper-elementary and middle school students with reading disabilities: A comparative study of two approaches. *Learning Disability Quarterly, 28*(1), p. 69.

-------------------------------------------------------------------------------------------------

Type of vignette also was significant, $F(2, 174) = 13.59$, $p < .001$, with a medium effect size ($f = .34$; Cohen, 1988).

*Source:* Nabors, L. A., and Lehmkuhl, H. D. (2005). Young adults' perceptions of children with cerebral palsy. *Rehabilitation Psychology, 50*(3), p. 294.

-------------------------------------------------------------------------------------------------

A chi square comparison of age versus presence was significant, $\chi^2(7, N = 293) = 19.1$, $p = .0079$, with a small effect size, Cramer's $V = .255$.

*Source:* Ukrainetz, T. A., Justice, L. M., Kaderavek, J. N., Eisenberg, S. L., Gillam, R. B., and Harm, H. M. (2005). The development of expressive elaboration in fictional narratives. *Journal of Speech, Language & Hearing Research, 48*(6), p. 1370.

*The stats*
*ability to*
*reject Ho*
*if indeed*
*is false.*

### Step 7b: Conduct a Post Hoc Power Analysis

A statistical test's **power** is its ability to reject the null hypothesis if, in fact, the null hypothesis is false. One place where power becomes an issue is in those situations where a researcher applies a statistical test and ends up not rejecting $H_0$. Perhaps such a result came about because the null hypothesis is true, and if that's the case, then it is altogether proper that the statistical test yield a nonsignificant result. However, there is a second explanation that might stand behind the researcher's decision to fail to reject $H_0$. Maybe the null hypothesis is false, but the researcher's statistical test lacks sufficient power to detect the true state of affairs represented by the sample data.

If the six-step version of hypothesis testing indicates that $H_0$ should not be rejected, some researchers will add a seventh step that involves conducting a little investigation to see if the statistical test had adequate power. When researchers do this, they are said to be conducting a **post hoc power analysis.** In Excerpt 8.7, we see an example of this.

### EXCERPT 8.7 • A Post Hoc Power Analysis

Since there was no significant difference in vastus lateralis and vastus medialis obliquus EMG activity among taping conditions, a post hoc power analysis for the ANOVA was conducted. Based on the sample size of the study ($n = 30$), the power analysis revealed that the study has sufficient power (80%) to detect a relative 'medium to large' intervention effect size.

*Source:* Janwantanakul, P., and Gaogasigam, C. (2005). Vastus lateralis and vastus medialis obliquus muscle activity during the application of inhibition and facilitation taping techniques. *Clinical Rehabilitation, 19*(1), pp. 15–16.

*Type II.*
*20*
*(7)*
*power*
*100   80*

In the study associated with Excerpt 8.7, the researchers measured the muscle activity in people's thighs to see one or the other of two different taping procedures of the thigh, as compared with a third condition that involved no taping at all, might differentially affect the thigh muscle. When the comparison of the three conditions yielded a nonsignificant result, the researchers conducted a power analysis to see if their statistical result might be a Type II error. As indicated in Excerpt 8.7, this power analysis indicated that the researchers had an 80 percent chance to detect differences among the three conditions, presuming that the differences (if there were any) were medium to large in size. Because statistical power and the likelihood of a Type II error are complementary (i.e., they must always add up to 100 percent), the researchers in Excerpt 8.7 were reporting that they had a 20 percent chance of making a Type II error. This level of Type II error risk is considered acceptable in most studies, and that is why the researchers stated that their statistical test had "sufficient" power.

In Excerpt 8.8, we see another example of a post hoc power analysis. Again, this power analysis was conducted because the statistical tests turned out to be nonsignificant. Unlike what we saw in Excerpt 8.7, the power analysis here indicated that the statistical tests were not sensitive enough to detect important differences, if such differences really existed. As reported by the researchers, the computed power levels were .55 and .62 for the two tests that were conducted. If you first change these decimal numbers into percentages and then subtract from 100, you can see that there was a 45 percent chance of a Type II error in one test and a 38 percent chance in the other.

### EXCERPT 8.8 • *Another Post Hoc Power Analysis*

The effect sizes (eta squared) for these group differences were 0.117 and 0.139, respectively. A post hoc power analysis indicated that this sample size ($N$ = 36), with two-tailed tests and alpha = .05, yields statistical power of .55 and .62, respectively, for effect sizes of this magnitude. . . . A number of methodological factors limit the strength of conclusions that can be drawn from this study. [In particular, the sample size] was small. Statistical power was correspondingly reduced, and the increased chance of Type II error should be considered carefully—especially before concluding that positive bonds with fathers, or bonds of any type with mothers, are not important in influencing daughters' science self-efficacy.

*Source:* Scott, A. B., and Mallinckrodt, B. (2005). Parental emotional support, science self-efficacy, and choice of science major in undergraduate women. *Career Development Quarterly, 53*(3), pp. 267, 270.

The second half of Excerpt 8.8 is important because it points to the connection between sample size and statistical power. These two features of the hypothesis testing procedure are directly related. Presuming that nothing else about a study is changed, an increase in the sample size will bring about an increase in power; conversely, a decrease in sample size causes power to go down. Since power and **Type II error risk** are like the opposite sides of a single coin, there is an inverse relationship between sample size and the likelihood of a Type II error. Hold everything else constant and make the sample size larger, and such a change will cause the chance of a Type II error to go down. Decrease the sample size and the likelihood of a Type II error will go up.

There are three importance statistical concepts mentioned in Excerpt 8.8: power, sample size, and the chance of a Type II error. You'll be better able to decipher and critique research reports if you know well the connection between these three concepts. I say that because you are bound to come across research reports in which the authors claim that no differences exist or that variables are not related, with these claims based on statistical tests that did not reveal any statistically significant differences or relationships. If the sample sizes in such studies are small, I hope you'll entertain the possibility that the research "findings" are incorrect and represent a Type II error brought about by inadequate statistical power.

## The Nine-Step Version of Hypothesis Testing

Although many researchers still utilize the six-step and seven-step versions of hypothesis testing, there is a definite trend toward using a nine-step approach. Six of the steps of this more elaborate version of hypothesis testing are identical to the six basic elements considered in Chapter 7, while the other three steps are related to the concepts of effect size, power, and sample size considered in the earlier portion of this chapter. Listed in the order in which the researcher will deal with them, the various elements of the nine-step version of hypothesis testing are as follows:

          **1.** State the null hypothesis, $H_0$.
          **2.** State the alternative hypothesis, $H_a$.
          **3.** Specify the desired level of significance, $\alpha$.
(new) **4.** Specify the effect size, ES.
(new) **5.** Specify the desired level of power.
(new) **6.** Determine the proper size of the sample(s).
          **7.** Collect and analyze the sample data.
          **8.** Refer to a criterion for assessing the sample evidence.
          **9.** Make a decision to discard/retain $H_0$.

The steps in the first third and final third of this nine-step version of hypothesis testing are identical to the six steps we discussed in Chapter 7. We will focus here only on Steps 4, 5, and 6. Although our discussion of these three steps will, in some ways, seem redundant considering the material presented earlier in this chapter, there is an important way in which the seven- and nine-step versions of hypothesis testing differ. In the seven-step approach considered earlier in this chapter, the researcher executes the six basic steps and then adds a seventh step. That seventh step involves returning to the sample data *after* the reject/retain decision has been made. In contrast, the nine-step version of hypothesis testing requires that the researcher specify the effect size, specify the desired power, and then determine the size of the sample(s) *before* any data are collected.

### Step 4: Specification of the Effect Size

Unfortunately, the term effect size has two meanings. We saw one of these earlier in this chapter when we considered the first option researchers have for adding a seventh step to the basic bare-bones kind of hypothesis testing. Now, we must consider a different notion of effect size. In our present discussion, the effect size refers to a priori specification of what constitutes the smallest study "finding" that the researcher considers to be "worth talking about." Perhaps a picture will help you understand this new notion of effect size. You'll need a pen or pencil; this is going to be a picture that *you* draw.

Draw a line segment about 12 inches long. Mark the far left end of your line with this four-word sentence: "$H_0$ is totally true." At the far right end of your line, write these six words: "$H_0$ is false by a mile." Now, put a big dot somewhere on this line such that it divides the line into two parts. The portion of the line that's located to the left of the dot represents situations where the null hypothesis is false but only false to a trivial degree. It might help if you put the label "trivial" on that side of the line. The portion of the line to the right of the dot represents situations where the null hypothesis is false by an amount that deserves to be thought of as "big" or "noteworthy." You might want to put the label "important" on this segment of your line. As you may have guessed, the dot on this line represents the kind of effect size that we now want to consider.

To illustrate what an effect size is and how it gets selected, suppose a researcher uses the hypothesis testing procedure in a study where there is one population, where the data are IQ scores, where the statistical focus is on the mean, and where the null and alternative hypotheses are $H_0$: $\mu = 100$ and $H_a$: $\mu > 100$, respectively. In this hypothetical study, the continuum of possible false null cases, as specified by $H_a$, extends from a value that is just slightly greater than 100 (say, 100.1) to whatever the maximum earnable IQ score is (say, 300). The researcher might decide to set 110 as the effect size. By so doing, the researcher would be declaring that (1) the true $\mu$ is judged to be only trivially different from 100 if it lies anywhere between 100 and 110, while (2) the difference between the true $\mu$ and 100 is considered to be important so long as the former is at least 10 points greater than $H_0$'s pinpoint value of 100.

Researchers specify an effect size in one of two ways. On the one hand, the researcher can specify a **raw effect size.** On the other, he or she can specify a **standardized effect size.** Specifying a raw effect size is the better strategy, but it is often more difficult (or impossible) to do this. Standardized effect sizes are easy to specify, but they are not as good despite the fact that the word *standardized* gives the impression of scientific superiority.

The process of specifying a raw effect size was illustrated in the hypothetical IQ study we recently considered. In that example, the raw effect size would be equal to an IQ of 110. Because the null hypothesis in that study was set equal to 100, the researcher could alternatively say that the effect size is equal to 10 IQ points (i.e., the difference between 110 and 100). Regardless of how the researcher might report what he or she has done, this process leads to a raw effect size because the researcher began by specifying the "line of demarcation" between trivial and nontrivial outcomes directly on the score continuum of the study's dependent variable.

Because the nine-step version of hypothesis testing requires that the researcher be able to estimate the degree of variability in the population(s) involved in the study, and because this is often difficult to do because the researcher may have no idea how to make a reasonable guess as to the size of $\sigma$, standardized effect sizes (rather than raw effect sizes) can be used. When using standardized effect sizes, researchers refer to established "criteria." For most statistical procedures, the standardized effect size criteria are numerical values that indicate what is considered to be a "small" effect, a "medium" effect, and a "large" effect. In choosing one of these standardized effect sizes, the researcher thinks about his or her study and then poses this three-part question:

> In the study I am going to conduct, do I want my statistical test to be sensitive to (and thus be able to detect) only a large effect, if that's what's truly "out there" in the real world? Or, do I want my study to have the added sensitivity that would allow it to detect either a large effect or a medium-sized effect? Or, is it important for my study to have the high-level sensitivity that would allow it to detect not just large and medium effects but small effects as well?

The criteria for small, medium, and large standardized effect sizes vary depending on the kind of statistical test the researcher is using. For example, if the researcher is going to compare two group means via a *t*-test, the criteria are .2, .5, and .8 for small, medium, and large effect sizes, respectively, but if the researcher is going to compute a correlation coefficient, the standardized effect sizes that define small, medium, and large *r*s are .1, .3, and .5, respectively. When we consider different test procedures in Chapters 9 through 18, I will point out what the standardized effect size criteria are for each test procedure. At this point, all you need to know is that (1) the nine-step version of hypothesis testing requires an a priori effect size specification, and (2) researchers have the option of specifying a raw effect size or a standardized effect size.

Excerpts 8.9 and 8.10 illustrate the two kinds of effect sizes we have been considering. In Excerpt 8.9, the researchers used a standardized effect size by selecting .5. In Excerpt 8.10, the researchers conducted a study using Pearson's *r*. Here, a raw effect size was used because the researchers decided on their own that $\rho$ would be consider trivial if it was smaller than $-.38$.

## Step 5: Specification of the Desired Level of Power

The researcher's next task within the nine-step hypothesis testing procedure is to specify the level of power that is desired for rejecting $H_0$ if $H_0$ is off by an amount equal to the previously established effect size. Power is a probability value and can range from 0 to 1.0. Only high values are considered, however, because the complement of power is the probability of a Type II error.

The researcher does not know, of course, exactly how far off-target the null hypothesis is (or even if it is wrong at all). The specified effect size is simply the

### EXCERPTS 8.9–8.10 • *A Priori Power Analysis*

We used the random sampling procedure in SPSS to generate a sample of 90 cases. We arrived at a sample size of 90 cases based on an a priori power analysis using GPOWER, v2 software. We [wanted] adequate power (Cohen, 1988, suggested a minimum of .8). We set the criteria for medium effect size at .5.

*Source:* Ryan, J. P., and Yang, H. (2005). Family contact and recidivism: A longitudinal study of adjudicated delinquents in residential care. *Social Work Research, 29*(1), p. 33.

----------------------------------------------------------------

For a priori calculation of the required sample size, the computer program GPOWER (Faul & Erdfelder, 1992) was employed. The calculation was based on the correlation between active coping and sperm concentration found in previous research ($r = -0.38$; Pook et al., 2000). Considering this effect size, the conventional alpha (0.05), a one-tailed test and the conventional power (0.80), a total sample of 39 subjects was needed.

*Source:* Pook, M., Tuschen-Caffier, B., Kubek, J., Schill, W., and Krause, W. (2005). Personality, coping and sperm count. *Andrologia, 37*(1), p. 31.

researcher's judgment as to what would or wouldn't constitute a meaningful deviation from the null case. Note, however, that if the null hypothesis is wrong by an amount that is greater than the specified effect size, then the actual probability of rejecting $H_0$ will be larger than the specified power level. Thus the power level selected in Step 5 represents the lowest acceptable power for any of the potentially true $H_a$ conditions that are considered to be meaningfully different from $H_0$.

To see illustrations of how researchers report desired levels level of power, take another look at Excerpts 8.9 and 8.10. In both excerpts, the researchers indicate that they wanted to have a minimum power level of .80 in their studies. In other words, they wanted to have at least an 80% chance of rejecting the null hypothesis—and thus no more than a 20 percent chance of making a Type II error—if the true state of affairs in each study's population differed from $H_0$ by any amount equal to or larger than the specified effect size. These two excerpts nicely illustrate the widely-held opinion that power should be no lower than .80.

Before leaving our discussion of statistical power, we need to address a question that you may have formulated. Inasmuch as power is a good thing to have for trying to detect situations in which $H_0$ is false by an amount at least equal to the effect size, why doesn't the researcher specify a power equal to .95 or .99 or even .999? There are two reasons why such high power values are rarely seen in applied research studies. First, they would place unreasonable demands on researchers when they move to Step 6 and compute the sample size required to provide the desired power. Second, extremely high power increases the probability that trivial deviations from $H_0$ will be labeled as statistically significant. For these two reasons, power levels higher than .90 are rarely seen.

## Step 6: Determination of the Needed Sample Size

After stating $H_0$ and $H_a$, after selecting a level of significance, and after specifying the effect size and the desired power, the researcher then uses a formula, a specially prepared table, or a computer program to determine the size of the sample(s) needed in the study (**sample size determination**). No judgment or decision-making comes into play at this point in the nine-step version of hypothesis testing, since the researcher simply calculates or looks up the answer to a very pragmatic question: How large should the sample be? At this point (and also in Steps 7–9), the researcher functions like a robot who performs tasks in a routine fashion without using much brain power.

To see the kinds of things researchers say when they talk about having computed their sample sizes in a power analysis, take one final look at Excerpts 8.9 and 8.10. The second of these excerpts is especially worth reviewing because it illustrates how researchers will often indicate the main "ingredients" for the recipe that determines the needed sample size. Note that this excerpt contains an indication of (1) the selected level of significance, (2) the desired level of statistical power, (3) the chosen effect size, and (4) whether the test is one-tailed or two-tailed.

In Excerpt 8.11, we see a case where a researcher used a larger sample size than that indicated by the a priori power analysis that was conducted. In survey research, this situation is not atypical. After determining the needed sample size, the researcher will make a guess at the likely response rate. Then, the initial sample size is increased so as to compensate for the probable event that not all of the surveys will be completed and returned. Researchers do this same sort of thing in studies where they anticipate individuals dropping out of the investigation after the study commences.

## EXCERPT 8.11 • *Sample Size Determination in Survey Research*

An a priori power analysis with an effect size of .30, an alpha level of .05, and a power of .80 indicated that a sample size of 350 participants was required to detect group differences. Assuming a 60% to 65% return rate (Dillman, 2000) the total required sample was approximated at 575.

*Source:* Ipsen, C., Arnold, N. L., and Colling, K. (2005). Self-employment for people with disabilities. *Journal of Disability Policy Studies, 15*(4), p. 232.

As we finish our discussion of the nine-step version of hypothesis testing, I want to underscore the primary advantage of this approach to evaluating any null hypothesis. The eventual results of the statistical test become easier to interpret after the researcher has successfully wrestled with the issue of what ought to be viewed as a meaningful deviation from $H_0$, and after the sample size has been computed so as to create the desired level of power (or the power computed on the basis of the available sample). In contrast, the six-step version of hypothesis testing can lead to a highly ambiguous finding.

If no consideration is given to the concepts of effect size and power, the researcher may end up very much in the dark as to whether (1) a fail-to-reject decision is attributable to a trivial (or zero) deviation from $H_0$ *or* is attributable to the test's insensitivity to detect important non-null cases due to a small sample size, or (2) a reject decision is attributable to $H_0$ being false by a nontrivial amount *or* is attributable to an unimportant non-null case being labeled *significant* simply because the sample size was so large. In Excerpts 8.12 and 8.13, we see examples of how murky results can be produced when the six-step approach to hypothesis testing is used. In Excerpt 8.12, the researchers tell us, in essence, that the statistically insignificant results may have been caused by insufficient power. In Excerpt 8.13, we see a research team that obtained statistically significant results but admits, in essence, that the initial findings may have been caused by an overly large sample size making the statistical tests too sensitive.

## EXCERPTS 8.12–8.13 • *Problems Caused by Small and Large Samples*

After matching the two groups on the degree of diffuse structural brain atrophy, we found that neither the direct parametric comparison of neuropsychological tests nor the pattern analysis demonstrated significant differences between TBI and ABI groups. . . . The major limitation of this study was the small sample size, as negative findings may simply be a reflection of insufficient power to detect genuine between-groups differences.

*Source:* Hopkins, R. O., Tate, D. F., and Bigler, E. D. (2005). Anoxic versus traumatic brain injury: Amount of tissue loss, not etiology, alters cognitive and emotional function. *Neuropsychology, 19*(2), pp. 238, 240.

---

For the 2-way analysis of variance model, the study sample provided statistical power of >90% to detect main effects of 0.20 standard deviation units. Thus, the sample size provided ample statistical power to detect the existence of small effects. For this reason, it is possible that effects that are statistically significant are too small to warrant clinical intervention.

*Source:* Croghan, I. T., Bronars, C., Patten, C. A., Schroeder, D. R., Nirelli, L. M., Thomas, J. L., Clark, M. M., Vickers, K. S., Foraker, R., Lane, K., Houlihan, D., Offord, K. P., and Hurt, R. D. (2006). Is smoking related to body image satisfaction, stress, and self-esteem in young adults? *American Journal of Health Behavior, 30*(3), p. 330.

The advantage of the nine-step (or seven-step) approach to hypothesis testing is *not* that the researcher will be able to know whether the decision reached about $H_0$ is right or wrong. Regardless of the approach used, a reject decision might be correct or it might constitute a Type I error, and similarly a fail-to-reject decision might be correct or it might be a Type II error. The advantage of having effect size and power built into the hypothesis testing procedure is twofold: On the one hand, the researchers know and control, on an a priori basis, the probability of making a Type II error, and on the other hand, they set up the study so that no critic can allege that a significant result, if found, was brought about by an overly sensitive test (or that a nonsignificant result, if found, was produced by an overly insensitive test).[2]

## Hypothesis Testing Using Confidence Intervals

Researchers can, if they wish, engage in hypothesis testing by means of using one or more confidence intervals, rather than by comparing a calculated value against a critical value or by comparing a *p*-level against $\alpha$. Although this approach to hypothesis testing is not used as often as the approaches discussed in Chapter 7, it is important for you to understand what is going on when a researcher uses confidence intervals within the context of hypothesis testing.

Whenever confidence intervals are used in this manner, it should be noted that everything about the hypothesis testing procedure remains the same except the way the sample data are analyzed and evaluated. To be more specific, this alternative approach to hypothesis testing involves the specification of $H_0$, $H_a$, and alpha, and the final step will involve a reject or fail-to-reject decision regarding $H_0$. The concepts of Type I and Type II errors are still relevant, as are the opportunities to specify effect size and power and to compute the proper sample size if the nine-step version of hypothesis testing is being used.

As indicated in Chapter 7, calculated and critical values usually are numerical values that are metric-free. Such calculated and critical values have no meaningful connection to the measurement scale associated with the data. Although it is advantageous for the researcher to use metric-free calculated and critical values, such values provide little insight as to why $H_0$ ultimately is rejected or not rejected. The advantage of confidence intervals is that they help to provide that insight.

The way confidence intervals are used within hypothesis testing is easy to explain. If there is just a single sample involved in the study, the researcher will take the sample data and build a confidence interval around the sample statistic. Instead of computing a calculated value, the researcher computes an interval, with the previously specified alpha level dictating the level of confidence associated with the interval (an $\alpha$ of .05 calls for a 95 percent interval, an $\alpha$ of .01 calls for a 99 percent interval, etc.). Instead of then turning to a critical value, the researcher turns to

---

[2]In saying this, I assume that the hypothetical critic agrees with the researcher's decisions about $H_0$, $H_a$, $\alpha$, and the effect size.

Chapter 8

*means*

$$H_0 = X$$

*if X is
w/i the interval
fail to reject*

*outside of interval
reject*

the null hypothesis and compares the confidence interval against the pinpoint number contained in $H_0$. The decision rule for the final step is straightforward: If the null number is outside the confidence interval, $H_0$ can be rejected; otherwise, $H_0$ must be retained.

Excerpt 8.14 illustrates the confidence interval approach to hypothesis testing. This excerpt comes from a study in which medical interns were measured in terms of their on-call napping behavior. This excerpt deals with a correlation that was computed using data collected for four weeks from 38 interns. The two variables were (1) the amount of time spent napping during on-call work periods and (2) the amount of time, during these same periods, the intern's pager was "covered" (meaning that calls would be automatically forwarded to someone else). The correlational null hypothesis that was tested said $H_0$: $\rho = 0$, where $\rho$ was the correlation in the population. As you can see, the sample correlation turned out equal to +.69. When a 95 percent confidence interval was built around this value for $r$, the interval extended from +.52 to +.80. Since 0, the pinpoint number from $H_0$, is not included within this interval, the null hypothesis was rejected.

**EXCERPT 8.14 • *A Confidence Interval Approach to Hypothesis Testing***

Protected sleep time, or the minutes that an intern's pager was "covered," was significantly associated with on-call sleep (Pearson $r = 0.69$ [95% CI, 0.52 to 0.80]; $P < 0.001$).

*Source:* Arora, V., Dunphy, C., Chang, V. Y., Ahmad, F., Humphrey, H. J., and Meltzer, D. (2006). The effects of on-duty napping on intern sleep time and fatigue. *Annals of Internal Medicine, 144*(1), p. 795.

*Correlations
if Ø is contained
fail to reject*

*if Ø is outside
reject*

A confidence interval can also be used to determine whether two samples differ sufficiently to allow the researchers to reject a null hypothesis that says the corresponding populations have the same parameter value. Excerpt 8.15 illustrates how this is done. In the study associated with this excerpt, there were two groups of patients who had neck injuries caused by "whiplash." One group received supervised treatment twice a week at a rehabilitation center; the other group did unsupervised home therapy. Three months after treatment ended, the two groups were compared with respect to the percentage of individuals that had improved in terms of the consumption of analgesics, with the null hypothesis being that the study's two populations have the same rate of improvement. As indicated in Excerpt 8.15, there was a 25 percent difference between the two groups' "improvement rates," and a 95 percent confident interval built around this figure (25%) extended from .003 to .497. Because this interval did not overlap 0, the two groups in the study were said to be significantly different.

**EXCERPT 8.15 • *Using a Confidence Interval to Compare Two Groups***

At the three-month follow-up there was a significant difference between groups with regard to the use of analgesics ($P < 0.05$). In the supervised group 35% were improved, considering the use of analgesics, compared with 10% in the home training group which corresponds to a difference of 25% (95% CI was 0.003–0.497).

*Source:* Bunketorp, L., Lindh, M., Carlsson, J., and Stener-Victorin, E. (2006). The effectiveness of a supervised physical training model tailored to the individual needs of patients with whiplash-associated disorders—a randomized controlled trial. *Clinical Rehabilitation, 20*(3), p. 212.

Before completing our discussion of the confidence-interval approach to hypothesis testing, I need to alert you (once again) to the difference between a confidence interval and a standard error interval.[3] Many researchers who compute calculated and critical values within one of the more traditional approaches to hypothesis testing will summarize their sample data in terms of values of the statistic plus or minus the standard error of the statistic. Intervals formed by adding and subtracting the standard error to the sample statistic do *not* produce alpha-driven confidence intervals. Instead, the result is a 68 percent interval. (Alpha-driven confidence intervals will typically be 95 percent intervals.)

## Adjusting for an Inflated Type I Error Rate

In Chapter 7, I indicated that the researchers have direct control over the probability that they will make a Type I error when making a judgment about $H_0$. (Type I errors, you will recall, occur when true null hypotheses are rejected.) This control is exerted when the researcher selects the level of significance. As long as the underlying assumptions of the researcher's statistical test are tenable, the alpha level selected in Step 3 of the hypothesis testing procedure instantly and accurately establishes the probability that a true $H_0$ will be rejected.

The fact that $\alpha$ dictates Type I error risk holds true *only* for situations where researchers use the hypothesis testing procedure just once within any given study. In many studies, however, more than one $H_0$ is tested. In Excerpt 8.16, we see an illustration of this common practice of applying the hypothesis testing procedure multiple times within the same study. As you can see, four correlation coefficients appear in this excerpt. The $p$-values, one presented for each of the computed $r$s, indicate that the hypothesis testing procedures was used here four times, once for each $r$.

---

[3]The difference between confidence intervals and standard errors was first covered in Chapter 6.

## EXCERPT 8.16 • *Hypothesis Testing Used More than Once*

The pattern of correlations among the scales mirrors the pattern obtained with samples of older children using the original CPIC; the Conflict Properties scale was moderately correlated with the Threat scale, $r = .48$, $p < .05$, whereas the correlations of the Self-Blame scale with the Conflict Properties, $r = .20$, $p < .05$, and Threat scales, $r = .23$, $p < .05$, were more modest. . . . Children's scores on the Conflict Properties scale were moderately correlated with their mothers' reports of interparental conflict on the CTS, $r = .46$, $p < .05$.

*Source:* McDonald, R., and Grych, J. H. (2006). Young children's appraisals of interparental conflict: Measurement and links with adjustment problems. *Journal of Family Psychology,* *20*(1), p. 93.

When the hypothesis testing procedure is applied multiple times within the same study, the alpha level used within each of these separate tests specifies the Type I error risk that would exist if that particular test were the only one being conducted. However, with multiple tests being conducted in the study, the actual probability of making a Type I error somewhere within the set of tests *exceeds* the alpha level used within any given test. The term **inflated Type I error risk** is used to refer to this situation in which the alpha level used within each of two or more separate tests understates the likelihood that at least one of the tests will cause the researcher to reject a true $H_0$.

A simple example may help to illustrate the problem of an inflated Type I error rate. Suppose you were given a fair die and told to roll it on the table. Before you toss the die, also suppose that the person running this little game tells you that you will win $10 if your rolled die turns out to be anything but a six. If you get a six, however, you must fork over $50. With an unloaded die, this would be a fair bet, for your chances of winning would be 5/6 while the chances of losing would be 1/6.

But what if you were handed a pair of fair dice and asked to roll both members of the pair simultaneously, with the rule being that you would win $10 if you can avoid throwing an evil six but lose $50 if your roll of the dice produces a bad outcome. This would not be a fair bet for you, for the chances of avoiding a six are $5/6 \times 5/6 = 25/36$, a result that is lower than the 5/6 value needed to make the wager an even bet in light of the stakes ($10 versus $50). If you were handed five pairs of dice and were asked to roll them simultaneously, with the same payoff arrangement in operation (i.e., win $10 if you avoid a six, otherwise lose $50), you would be at a terrific disadvantage. With 10 of the six-sided cubes being rolled, the probability of your winning the bet by avoiding a six anywhere in the full set of results is equal to approximately .16. You would have a 16 percent chance of winning $10 versus an 84 percent chance of losing $50. That would be a very good arrangement for your opponent!

As should be obvious, the chances of having an evil six show up at least once increase as the number of dice being thrown increases. With multiple dice involved in our hypothetical game, there would be two ways to adjust things to make the wager equally fair to both parties. One adjustment would involve changing the stakes. For example, with two dice being rolled, the wager could be altered so you would win $11 if you avoid a six or lose $25 if you don't. The other kind of adjustment would involve tampering with the two little cubes so as to produce a pair of loaded dice. With this strategy, each die would be weighted such that its chances of ending up as something other than a six would be equal to a tad more than 10/11. This would allow two dice to be used, in a fair manner, with the original stakes in operation ($10 versus $50).

When researchers use the hypothesis testing procedure multiple times, an adjustment must be made somewhere in the process to account for the fact that at least one Type I error somewhere in the set of results increases rapidly as the number of tests increases. Although there are different ways to effect such an adjustment, the most popular method is to change the level of significance used in conjunction with the statistical assessment of each $H_0$. If the researcher wants to have a certain level of protection against a Type I error anywhere within his or her full set of results, then he or she would make the alpha level more rigorous within each of the individual tests. By so doing, it's as if the researcher is setting up a fair wager in that the claimed alpha level will truly match the study's likelihood of yielding a Type I error.

The most frequently used procedure for adjusting the alpha level is called the **Bonferroni technique,** and it is quite simple for the researcher to apply or for consumers of research to understand. When there is a desire on the part of the researcher to hold the Type I error in the full study equal to a selected value, the alpha levels for the various tests being conducted must be chosen such that the sum of the individual alpha levels is equivalent to the full-study alpha criterion. This is usually accomplished by simply dividing the desired Type I error risk for the full study by the number of times the hypothesis testing procedure is going to be used. Excerpt 8.17 illustrates nicely how the Bonferroni technique works.

Research
Navigator.com

Bonferroni
technique

### EXCERPT 8.17 • *The Bonferroni Adjustment Procedure*

An alpha of .05 was used for all statistical tests. The Bonferroni correction was used, however, to reduce the chance of committing a Type I error. Therefore, given that five statistical tests were conducted, the adjusted alpha used to reject the null hypothesis was .05/5 or alpha = .01.

*Source:* Cumming-McCann, A. (2005). An investigation of rehabilitation counselor characteristics, white racial attitudes, and self-reported multicultural counseling competencies. *Rehabilitation Counseling Bulletin, 48*(3), pp. 170–171.

When using the Bonferroni technique, researchers typically indicate the size of the adjusted alpha used to evaluate each null hypothesis that was set up and tested. As you now know, that adjusted alpha is computed in a simple fashion by dividing the desired overall Type I error risk by the number of tests being conducted. The term **experimentwise error rate** refers to this desired studywide Type I error risk. In Excerpt 8.18, we see this term being used in a study where the researchers used the hypothesis testing procedure 10 times. This excerpt contains a little formula that nicely shows how the level of significance used when testing individual null hypotheses ($\alpha'$) must be lowered in order to keep the experimentwise error rate ($\alpha$) equal to a desired size.

### EXCERPT 8.18 • *Experimentwise Error Rate*

The Bonferroni method was used to insure that the overall experimentwise error rate did not exceed $\alpha = 0.05$. This was done by using a significance level for each individual test equal to $\alpha' = \alpha/n$, where $n = 10$ is the number of variables tested.

*Source:* Donali, E., Brettum, P., Øyvind, K., Løvik, J. E., Lyche-Solheim, A., and Anderson, T. (2005). Pelagic response of a humic lake to three years of phosphorus addition. *Canadian Journal of Fisheries and Aquatic Sciences, 62*(2), p. 325.

Since the Bonferroni technique leads to a more rigorous alpha level for each of the separate tests being conducted, each of those tests becomes more demanding. In other words, Bonferroni-adjusted alpha levels (as compared with an unadjusted level of significance) create a situation wherein the sample data must be even more inconsistent with null expectations before the researcher is permitted to reject $H_0$. If the researcher makes a decision about $H_0$ by comparing the data-based *p*-value against the adjusted alpha, that alpha criterion will be smaller and therefore harder to beat. Or, if each test's calculated value is compared against a critical value, the researcher will find that the Bonferroni technique has created a more stringent criterion. Thus it does not make any difference which of these two paths the researcher takes in moving from the sample data to the ultimate decision about the null hypothesis. Either way, more protection against Type I errors is brought about by making it harder for the researcher to reject $H_0$.

Excerpts 8.19 and 8.20 illustrate nicely how the Bonferroni technique brings about a more demanding assessment of each study's set of statistical comparisons. In the first of these excerpts, the researchers started out with the popular .05 level of significance. Because there were three tests being conducted in their study, the Bonferroni technique brought about a revised level of significance of .017. For any of the three tests in that study to yield a statistically significant result, its *p*-level had to "beat" (i.e., end up lower than) .017. In Excerpt 8.20, we see the same thing happened. The Bonferroni technique lowered the level of significance to .0002. This

**EXCERPTS 8.19–8.20 • *Why Bonferroni Makes It Harder to Reject $H_0$***

Using the Bonferroni approach to control for Type I error across the three comparisons, a *p* value of less than .017 was required for significance.

*Source:* Dornburg, C. C., and McDaniel, M. A. (2006). The cognitive interview enhances long-term free recall of older adults. *Psychology and Aging, 21*(1), p. 198.

---

Due to the number of correlations being performed, a Bonferroni correction was applied to reduce the possibility of a Type I error, so that the null hypothesis was rejected if $p < .0002$.

*Source:* Carlisle, A. C. S., John, A. M. H., Fife-Schaw, C., and Lloyd, M. (2005). The self-regulatory model in women with rheumatoid arthritis: Relationships between illness representations, coping strategies, and illness outcome. *British Journal of Health Psychology, 10*(4), p. 576.

meant that the sample data, in any one of the individual tests, would need to be *extremely* "at odds with" the null hypothesis before $H_0$ could be rejected.

It may seem odd that researchers who want to reject their null hypothesis choose to apply the Bonferroni technique and thereby make it more difficult to accomplish their goal. However, researchers who use the Bonferroni technique are not doing something stupid, self-defeating, or inconsistent with their own objectives. Although the Bonferroni technique does, in fact, create a more demanding situation for the researcher, it does not function to pull something legitimate out of reach. Instead, this technique serves the purpose of helping the researcher pull in the reins so he or she is less likely to reach out and grab something that, in reality, is nothing at all. The Bonferroni technique, of course, does not completely eliminate the chance that a Type I error will be made. But it does eliminate the problem of an *inflated* Type I error risk.

Although the Bonferroni procedure is the most frequently used technique for dealing with the inflated Type I error problem, other procedures have been developed to accomplish the same general procedure. One of these is formally called the Sidak modification of Dunn's procedure. If you come across a research report in which it has been used, you are likely to see it referred to by its "nickname," the **Dunn-Sidak modification.**

## A Few Cautions

As we come to the close of our two-chapter treatment of hypothesis testing, I want to offer a few more cautions that should assist you as you attempt to make sense out of the technical write-ups of empirical investigations. These tips (or warnings!) are different from the ones provided at the end of Chapter 7, so you may profit from a review of what I said there. In any event, here are four more things to keep in mind when you come across statistical inferences based on the hypothesis testing procedure.

### Two Meanings of the Term Effect Size

When the seven-step version of hypothesis testing is used, the researcher may opt (in Step 7a) to compute an effect size. We saw several examples of this being done in Excerpts 8.3 through 8.6. Or, that same researcher might opt (in Step 7b) to conduct a post hoc power analysis. As illustrated nicely by Excerpt 8.8, a post hoc power analysis necessitates that the researcher compute an effect size measure. The important thing to note is that the effect size involved in Step 7a or 7b of the hypothesis testing procedure is based on the sample data. This kind of effect size is *computed* using the evidence gathered in the researcher's study.

When the nine-step version of hypothesis testing is employed, a different kind of effect size comes into play. Within this strategy, researchers *specify* (rather than compute) the effect size, and this is done prior to the collection and examination of any data. When researchers specify the effect size in Step 4 of the nine-step version of hypothesis testing, they are not making a predictive statement as to the magnitude of the effect that will be found once the data are analyzed. Rather, they are indicating through Step 4 the minimum size of an effect that they consider to have practical significance. Most researchers hope that the magnitude of the true effect size will exceed the effect size specified prior to the collection of any data.

It is unfortunate that the same term—effect size—is used by researchers to refer to two different things. However, a careful consideration of context ought to clarify which kind of effect size is being discussed. If reference is made to the effect size within the research report's method section (and specifically when the sample size is being discussed), then it is likely that the nine-step version of hypothesis testing was used, with the effect size being a judgment call as to the dividing line between trivial and important findings. If, on the other hand, reference is made to the effect size during a presentation of the obtained results, that effect size is probably a data-based measure of how false the null hypothesis seems to be.

### "Small," "Medium," and "Large" Effect Sizes

Regardless of whether a researcher's effect size is computed (in a post hoc sense) from the sample data or specified in the planning stages of the study (to help determine the needed sample size), it is not uncommon for the researcher to refer to the effect size as being "small," "medium," or "large." As I indicated earlier in this chapter, criteria have been developed that help to define these standardized effect sizes. For example, the popular effect size standards for correlations indicate that .1, .3, and .5 represent small, medium, and large effect sizes, respectively.

Unfortunately, the criteria for small, medium, and large effect sizes vary depending on the study's statistical focus and the kind of effect size that is computed or specified. For example, if the effect size $d$ is used in conjunction with a study that compared two sample means, the criteria for standardized effect sizes say .2 is small, .5 is medium, and .8 is large. Clearly, these criteria are different from the ones cited in the previous paragraph for a correlation coefficient.

In an effort to help you keep things straight when it comes to the criteria for standardized effect sizes, I will put a small chart into several of the following chapters. Each of these charts will show the names for the effect size measures associated with the statistical tests discussed in a given chapter, and then the criteria for small, medium, and large will be presented. The information in these charts may prove useful to you, because it is not unusual to see a research report that contains a computed effect size (such as $d$) with absolutely no discussion about its meaning.

### The Simplistic Nature of the Six-Step Version of Hypothesis Testing

Most researchers test null hypotheses with the six-step version of the hypothesis testing procedure. This is unfortunate because the important distinction between statistical and practical significance is not addressed in any way whatsoever by this simplistic approach to testing null hypotheses. Consequently, the outcome is ambiguous no matter what decision is reached about $H_0$. A reject decision may have been caused by a big difference between the single-number summary of the sample evidence and the pinpoint number in $H_0$; however, that same decision may have come about by a small difference being magnified by a giant sample size. Likewise, a fail-to-reject decision might be the result of a small difference between the sample evidence and the null hypothesis; however, the researcher's decision not to reject $H_0$ may have resulted from a big difference that was camouflaged by a small sample size.

To see examples of these two undesirable scenarios described in the previous paragraph, take another look at Excerpts 8.12 and 8.13. Before doing that, however, please formulate an answer to each of the two questions I'd like to ask you. In Excerpt 8.12, the researchers first indicated that their study did not reveal any statistically significant finding. They then articulated what they believed was "the major limitation" of their study. Can you guess what that limitation was? In Excerpt 8.13, the researchers stated that what they discovered was "too small to warrant clinical intervention." What feature of the study was primarily responsible for the caution that the statistically significant results didn't have very much practical significance? OK. Now see if your answers are correct.

It is relatively easy for a researcher to conduct a study using the basic six-step version of hypothesis testing. It is harder to use the nine-step version. Nevertheless, there is a giant pay-off (for the researcher and for those who read the research report) if the researcher (1) decides, in the planning stage of the study, what kind of results would represent trivial deviations from the null hypothesis versus results that others would say are important, and (2) uses this belief within the context of an a priori power analysis to determine how large the samples should be. When you come across a research report indicating that these two things were done, give that study's researcher(s) some big, big bonus points!

Despite its limitations, the basis six-step version of hypothesis testing is widely used. Whenever you encounter a researcher who has used this more simplistic version of hypothesis testing, *you* will have to be the one who applies the important seventh step. Although you probably will not be able to conduct a post hoc power analysis, there are certain things you *can* do.

If a correlation coefficient is reported to be statistically significant, look at the size of the $r$ and ask yourself what kind of relationship (weak, moderate, or strong) was revealed by the researcher's data. Better yet, square the $r$ and then convert the resulting coefficient of determination into a percentage; then make your own judgment as to whether a small or large amount of variability in one variable is being explained by variability in the other variable. If the study focuses on means rather than correlations, look carefully at the computed means. Ask yourself whether the observed difference between two means represents a finding that has practical significance.

I cannot overemphasize my warning that you can be (and will be) misled by many research claims if you look only at $p$ statements when trying to assess whether results are important. Most researchers use the simple six-step version of hypothesis testing, and the only thing revealed by this procedure is a yes or no answer to the question, "Do the sample data deviate from $H_0$ more than we would expect by chance?" Even if a result is statistically significant with $p < .0001$, it may be the case that the finding is completely devoid of *any* practical significance!

### Inflated Type I Error Rates

My final caution is simply a reiteration of something I said earlier in this chapter. This has to do with the heightened chance of a Type I error when multiple tests are conducted simultaneously. This is a serious problem in scientific research, and this caution deserves to be reiterated.

Suppose a researcher measures each of several people on seven variables. Also suppose that the true correlation between each pair of these variables is exactly 0.00 in the population associated with the researcher's sample. Finally, suppose our researcher computes a value for $r$ for each pair of variables, tests each $r$ to see if it is significantly different from 0.00, and then puts the results into a correlation matrix. If the .05 level of significance is used in conjunction with the evaluation of each $r$, the chances are greater than 50–50 that at least one of the $r$s will turn out to be significant. In other words, even though the alpha level is set equal to .05 for each separate test that is conducted, the collective Type I error risk has ballooned to over .50 due to the fact that 21 separate tests are conducted.

My caution here is simple. Be wary of any researcher's conclusions if a big deal is made out of an unreplicated single finding of significance when the hypothesis testing procedure is used simultaneously to evaluate many null hypotheses. In contrast, give researchers extra credit when they apply the Bonferroni technique to hold down their studywide Type I error risk.

## Review Terms

Bonferroni technique

Dunn-Sidak modification

Effect size (raw and standardized)

Inflated Type I error risk

Large standardized effect size

Medium standardized effect size

Power

Practical significance

Sample size determination

Small standardized effect size

Statistical significance

Type II error risk

## The Best Items in the Companion Website

1. An email message sent from the author to his students entitled "Binoculars and Significance."
2. An interactive online quiz (with immediate feedback provided) covering Chapter 8.
3. Ten misconceptions about the content of Chapter 8.
4. An email message sent by the author to his students concerning the seven-step and nine-step versions of hypothesis testing.
5. An interactive online resource called "Statistical Power."

To access chapter objectives, practice tests, weblinks, and flashcards, visit the companion website at www.ablongman.com/huck5e.

Research Navigator.c⊕m

## Fun Exercises inside Research Navigator

1. **Does "strategy training" help stroke patients with daily living activities?**

    A stroke patient with apraxia either doesn't know what to do or knows what to do but not how to do it. To see whether a new treatment might help such patients, the researchers randomly assigned 113 stroke patients to two groups. Those in one group received traditional occupational therapy, in which the focus was on improving motor behavior skills. Those in the other group received cognitive "strategy training" in addition to the usual occupational therapy. Data on the main dependent variable in this study came from observers who assessed each patient's ability to perform four tasks (e.g., put on a shirt or blouse). After computing the effect size ($d$) to contrast the two groups' improvement over the eight-week period of the study, the researchers reported that the strategy training had "a small to medium" effect. How large do you think their computed $d$ was? To find out, locate the PDF version of the research report in the Nursing, Health, and Medicine database of ContentSelect, go to page 559, and read the first paragraph in the section entitled "Outcome."

M. Donkervoort, J. Dekker, F. C. Stehmann-Saris, & B. G. Deelman. Efficacy of strategy training in left hemisphere stroke patients with apraxia: A randomised clinical trial. *Neuropsychological Rehabilitation.* Located in the NURSING, HEALTH, AND MEDICINE database of ContentSelect.

2.  **Comparing males versus females (on a spatial abilities task) and BESD versus $d$ (as an index of practical significance).**

In this study, males and females were compared in terms of their ability to perform a paper-and-pencil spatial task. Gender groups were compared at each of three age levels: 9, 13, and 21 to 35. At each age level, there was a statistically significant difference between males and females in their mean rate of correct responding. To see if each of these gender differences was also significant in a practical sense, the researchers computed two measures of effect size: Cohen's $d$ and something called BESD. (This latter measure is computed as the simple difference between the percentage of each group located above the combined median of the two groups pooled together.) To find out (1) which gender group was superior at each age level and (2) whether $d$ and BESD indicated the same thing, locate the PDF version of the research report in the Biology database of ContentSelect, read the bottom two paragraphs on page 214, and look at Tables 2 and 3.

E. Govier & G. Salisbury. Age-related sex differences in performance on a side-naming spatial task. *Psychology, Evolution, and Gender.* Located in the BIOLOGY database of ContentSelect.

**Review Questions and Answers begin on page 513.**

# Statistical Inferences Concerning Bivariate Correlation Coefficients*

In Chapter 3, we considered several descriptive techniques used by researchers to summarize the degree of relationship that exists between two sets of scores. In this chapter we will examine how researchers deal with their correlation coefficients inferentially. Stated differently, the techniques to be considered here are the ones used when researchers have access only to sample data but wish to make educated guesses as to the nature of the population(s) associated with the sample(s). As you will see shortly, the techniques used most frequently to do this involve hypothesis testing. Occasionally, however, inferential guesses are made through the use of confidence intervals.

We begin this chapter with a consideration of the statistical tests applied to various bivariate correlation coefficients, along with an examination of the typical ways researchers communicate the results of their analyses. I will also point out how the Bonferroni technique is used in conjunction with tests on correlation coefficients, how researchers compare two (or more) correlation coefficients to see if they are significantly different, and how statistical tests can be applied to reliability and validity coefficients. Finally, I will provide a few tips designed to help you become a more discerning consumer of research claims that emanate from studies wherein inferential statistics are applied to correlation coefficients.

## Statistical Tests Involving a Single Correlation Coefficient

Later in this chapter, we will consider the situation in which data are analyzed to see if a significant difference exists between two or more correlation coefficients. Before doing that, however, we need to consider the simpler situation where the researcher has a single sample and a single correlation coefficient. Although simple in nature because only one sample is involved, the inferential techniques focused on in the first part of this chapter are used far more frequently than the ones that involve comparisons between/among correlation coefficients.

### The Inferential Purpose

Figure 9.1 has been constructed to help clarify what researchers are trying to do when they apply an inferential test to a correlation coefficient. I have set up this picture to make it consistent with a hypothetical study involving Pearson's product-moment correlation. However, by changing the symbols that are included, we could make our picture relevant to a study wherein any other bivariate correlation coefficient is tested.

As Figure 9.1 shows, a correlation coefficient is computed on the basis of data collected from a sample. Although the sample-based value of the correlation coefficient is easy to obtain, the researcher's primary interest lies in the corresponding value of the correlation in the population from which the sample has been drawn. However, the researcher cannot compute the value of the correlation coefficient in the population because only the objects (or persons) in the sample can be measured. Accordingly, an inference (i.e., educated guess) about the parameter value of the correlation is made on the basis of the known value of the statistic.

The nature of the inference that extends from the sample to the population could take one of two forms depending on whether the researcher wishes to use the techniques of estimation or to set up and evaluate a null hypothesis. Near the

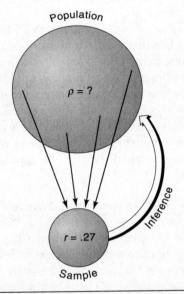

**FIGURE 9.1** *The Inferential Purpose of a Test on a Correlation Coefficient*

end of the chapter, we will examine the way confidence intervals are sometimes used to make inferences about correlation coefficients. We first turn our attention to the way researchers set up, evaluate, and report what happens to correlational null hypotheses.

### The Null Hypothesis

When researchers are concerned about the relationship between two variables in a single population but can collect data only from a sample taken from that population, they are likely to attack their inferential question by means of hypothesis testing. In doing this, a null hypothesis serves as the hub around which all other statistical elements revolve.

In dealing with a single correlation, the null hypothesis will simply be a pinpoint statement as to a possible value of the correlation in the population. Although researchers have the freedom to choose any value between $-1.00$ and $+1.00$ for inclusion in $H_0$, typically researchers will set up their correlational null hypothesis to say that there is, in the relevant population, a zero correlation between the two variables of interest. In Excerpt 9.1, we see an example where the notion of no relationship appeared in a stated null hypothesis.

### EXCERPT 9.1 • *The Null Hypothesis for Testing Correlations*

Correlation analyses were used to test the first and second null hypotheses using the Pearson product moment correlation.

- $H_{01}$, There is no relationship between the period of existence of workforce diversity programs and the level of diversity present in the workforce.
- $H_{02}$, No relationship exists between the number of training hours and the extent of reported backlash.

*Source:* Whittenburg, C. E. (2001). The relationship of selected variables on diversity programs in Fortune 250 manufacturing firms. *Journal of Industrial Teacher Education, 38*(2), p. 86.

In Excerpts 9.2 and 9.3, we see two cases where the researchers alluded to the correlational null hypothesis after conducting their data analyses. Note the final four words in the first excerpt and the final five words in the second excerpt. In the full research reports associated with these studies, the null hypothesis was not discussed beyond what is presented in these excerpts. If the researchers in either study had stated it formally, such a statement would have taken the form $H_0: \rho = 0.00$.

Because the correlational null hypothesis is usually set up to say that a zero correlation exists in the population, most researchers do not explicitly state the $H_0$ that is tested but rather take for granted that recipients of their research reports will

**EXCERPTS 9.2–9.3 • *Indication That Test on r Used Null Value of Zero***

These correlations are presented in Table 3 [not shown here] where it can be seen that only two of the 18 correlations were significantly different from zero.

*Source*: Salthouse, T. A., and Siedlecki, K. L. (2005). Reliability and validity of the divided attention questionnaire. *Aging, Neuropsychology & Cognition, 12*(1), p. 95.

---

However, when we computed separate correlations for each sample, we found the pre- and post-correlation was .028 for the intervention group, which is not significantly different from zero.

*Source:* Gersten, R., Baker, S. K., Smith-Johnson, J., Dimino, J., and Peterson, A. (2006). Eyes on the prize: Teaching complex historical content to middle school students with learning disabilities. *Exceptional Children, 72*(3), p. 275.

know that the inferential conclusions refer to a null hypothesis of no relationship. Consider, for example, Excerpts 9.4 and 9.5. In each case, the sample $r$ presented in the report was compared against the null value of zero—even though the tested $H_0$ never appeared in the technical write-ups.

**EXCERPTS 9.4–9.5 • *Tests on r without Any Reference to the Null Value of Zero***

However, through correlational analysis, a positive correlation emerged between FNE and post-test stress, $r = .26$, $p < .05$.

*Source*: Karakashian, L. M., Walter, I., Christopher, A. N., and Lucas, T. (2006). Fear of negative evaluation affects helping behavior: The bystander effect revisited. *North American Journal of Psychology, 8*(1), p. 25.

---

The correlation between age and PCC ($r = .272$) was not statistically significant ($p > .05$).

*Source:* Flipsen, P., Hammer, J. B., and Yost, K. M. (2005). Measuring severity of involvement in speech delay: Segmental and whole-word measures. *American Journal of Speech-Language Pathology, 14*(4), p. 302.

In light of the fact that very few researchers either state the null hypothesis when applying a test to a sample correlation coefficient or refer to $H_0$'s pinpoint number when discussing their results, you frequently will be forced into the position of having to guess what a researcher's $H_0$ was. In these situations, a safe bet is that $H_0$ was a statement of no relationship in the population. If researchers set up a null hypothesis that specifies a population correlation different from zero, I am confident that they will specify $H_0$'s pinpoint number.

### Deciding If r Is Statistically Significant

In conducting a statistical test on a single correlation coefficient, the value of $r$ usually functions as the data-based calculated value. As you will soon see, statistical tests on means, variances, or percentages involve calculated values that are different from the means, variances, or percentages computed from the sample(s). But with correlations, the sample-based correlation coefficient is, in its raw form, the calculated value.

When the sample value of $r$ is considered to be the calculated value, there are two ways to determine whether it is statistically significant. If the data have been analyzed on a computer or Internet website, then the data-based value of $p$ can be compared against the level of significance. If $p$ is equal to or smaller than $\alpha$, the null hypothesis will be rejected. In Excerpt 9.6, you can see this decision-making approach in operation.

Excerpt 9.7 illustrates the second method for determining whether a sample $r$ is statistically significant. If the data have not been analyzed such that a data-based $p$ is available, the researcher can compare the sample value of $r$ against a tabled critical value. If the former equals or exceeds the latter, $H_0$ will be rejected. On occasion (but not often), you will come across a research report that includes the tabled critical value. An example of such a situation is presented in Excerpt 9.7. The single sentence in this excerpt was positioned beneath a correlation matrix that contained 21 correlation coefficients. To tell which of the correlation

### EXCERPTS 9.6–9.7 • *Two Ways to Decide If r Is Statistically Significant*

To assess statistical significance, we chose an alpha level of .05 for all analyses ($p < .05$). . . . We found the relationship between CI intensity and verbal fluency to be nonsignificant ($r = -.19, p = .13$).

*Source:* Davidson, J., Lee-Archer, S., and Sanders, G. (2005). Dream imagery and emotion. *Dreaming, 15*(1), p. 40.

------

For correlations greater than .07, $p < .05$; for correlations greater than .13, $p < .01$; for correlations greater than .28, $p < .001$; all two-tailed.

*Source:* Conner, M., Sandberg, T., McMillan, B., and Higgins, A. (2006). Role of anticipated regret, intentions and intention stability in adolescent smoking initiation. *British Journal of Health Psychology, 11*(1), p. 93.

coefficients were significant (and at what level), the researchers as well as the readers of their research report had to compare each *r* against critical values shown in Excerpt 9.7.

### One-Tailed and Two-Tailed Tests on r

Most researchers conduct their tests on *r* in a two-tailed fashion. That's because they would like to know, as best they can, whether there is a positive or a negative correlation in the population of interest. Sometimes, however, researchers will use a one-tailed test to evaluate a sample *r*. In Excerpts 9.8 and 9.9, we see examples of these two options for testing any *r*.

**EXCERPTS 9.8–9.9 • *Two-Tailed and One-Tailed Tests on r***

The Pearson product–moment correlation for the interviewer's rating of academic potential with GPA in the one-on-one interview format was statistically significant at $r = .82$, p $<$ .001, two-tailed, $n = 40$.

*Source:* Tran, T., and Blackman, M. C. (2006). The dynamics and validity of the group selection interview. *Journal of Social Psychology, 146*(2), p. 193.

As predicted, we found a significant correlation between the numbers of facial expressions across situations ($r = .74$, $p <$ .01, one-tailed).

*Source:* Frank, M. G., and Ekman, P. (2004). Appearing truthful generalizes across different deception situations. *Journal of Personality and Social Psychology, 86*(3), p. 492.

Unlike Excerpts 9.8 and 9.9, the typical research report dealing with tested correlations will not indicate whether *r* was evaluated in a one-tailed or two-tailed fashion. That's the case with most of the excerpts in this chapter, because there usually is not even a hint as to whether the alternative hypothesis was nondirectional (with $H_a$: $\rho \neq 0.00$) or directional (with $H_a$ stating either $\rho > 0.00$ or $\rho < 0.00$). Why is this the case?

Because the vast majority of researchers conduct their tests on *r* in a two-tailed fashion, researchers presume that you will understand this even if they don't say so directly. Therefore, you should guess that any test on *r* was conducted in a two-tailed manner unless the researcher says otherwise. When researchers perform a one-tailed test on *r*, they will be sure to point this out (as was the case in Excerpt 9.9).

### Tests on Specific Kinds of Correlation

Up until this point, we have been discussing tests of correlation coefficients in the generic sense. However, there is no such thing as a generic correlation. When correlating two sets of data, a specific correlational procedure must be used, with the choice usually being influenced by the nature of variables and/or the level of measurement of the researcher's instruments. As you will recall from Chapter 3, there are many different kinds of bivariate correlations: Pearson's, Spearman's, biserial, point biserial, phi, tetrachoric, and so on.

With any of the various correlation procedures, a researcher can apply the hypothesis testing procedure. When researchers report having tested $r$ without specifying the type of correlation that was computed, you should presume that $r$ represents Pearson's product-moment correlation. Thus, it's a good guess that the correlations presented or referred to in Excerpts 9.1 through 9.9 were all Pearson $r$s. In Excerpts 9.10 through 9.13, we now see illustrations of other kinds of bivariate correlation coefficients being subjected to inferential testing.

### EXCERPTS 9.10–9.13 • *Tests on Specific Kinds of Correlation*

These rankings produced a Spearman's rho of .649, and this statistic was significant at the .01 level.

*Source:* Ward, M. A. (2006). Information systems technologies: A public-private sector comparison. *Journal of Computer Information Systems, 46*(3), p. 53.

---

The relationship between BUMP-R scores and the family type (adoptive or biological) was further examined and found to be significant by a point-biserial correlation, $r_{pb}(10) = -.569, p = 0.054$.

*Source:* Smit, E. M., Delpier, T., Tarantino, S. F., and Anderson, M. L. (2006). Caring for adoptive families: Lessons in communication. *Pediatric Nursing, 32*(2), p. 140.

---

We computed a phi coefficient to estimate the degree of relationship between the intervention score and posttest score. A moderate relationship was found between these scores ($r = .29, p < .05, n = 48$).

*Source:* Fernandez-Berrocal, P., and Santamaria, C. (2006). Mental models in social interaction. *Journal of Experimental Education, 74*(3), p. 235.

---

The majority (81.77%) of the sexually abstinent teens reported that they go home after school, compared to 61.8% of sexually active teens, who go elsewhere (Cramer's V = .148, $p = .027$).

*Source:* Vélez-Pastrana, M. C., Gonzádez-Rodríguez, R. A., and Borges-Hernández, A. (2005). Family functioning and early onset of sexual intercourse in Latino adolescents. *Adolescence, 40*(160), p. 785.

# Tests on Many Correlation Coefficients (Each of Which Is Treated Separately)

In most of the excerpts presented so far in this chapter, inferential interest was focused on a single correlation coefficient. Although some researchers set up only one correlational null hypothesis (because each of their studies involves only one correlation coefficient), most researchers have two or more correlations that are inferentially tested in the same study. Our objective now is to consider the various ways in which such researchers present their results, to clarify the fact that a separate $H_0$ is associated with each correlation coefficient that is computed, and to consider the way in which the Bonferroni adjustment technique can help the researcher avoid the problem of an inflated Type I error risk.

## Tests on the Entries of a Correlation Matrix

Research
Navigator.c⊛m

Correlation matrix

As we saw in Chapter 3, a **correlation matrix** is an efficient way to present the results of a correlational study in which there are three or more variables and a correlation coefficient is computed between each possible pair of variables.[1] Typically, each of the entries within the correlation matrix will be subjected to an inferential test. In Excerpt 9.14, we see an illustration of this situation.

### EXCERPT 9.14 • *Tests of Many rs in a Correlation Matrix*

**TABLE 3    Correlation of Undergraduates' Responses to the PDSR and Other Measures (Study 3)**

| Measure | 1 | 2 | 3 | 4 |
|---------|-----|-----|-----|-----|
| 1. SIAS | — | | | |
| 2. PCL | .52** | — | | |
| 3. PSWQ | .48** | .55** | — | |
| 4. PDSR | .17** | .26** | .32** | — |

*Note:* PDSR = Panic Disorder Self-Report; SIAS = Social Interaction Anxiety Scale; PCL = PTSD Checklist; PSWQ = Penn State Worry Questionnaire.

\*\*$p < .01$.

*Source:* Newman, M. G., Holmes, M., Zuellig, A. R., Kachin, K. E., Behar, E. (2006). The reliability and validity of the Panic Disorder Self-Report: A new diagnostic screening measure of panic disorder. *Psychological Assessment, 18*(1), p. 55.

---

[1]Whenever a correlation coefficient is computed, it is really not the variables per se that are being correlated. Rather, it is the measurements of one variable that are correlated with the measurements of the other variable. This distinction is not a trivial one because it is possible for a low correlation coefficient to grossly underestimate a strong relationship that truly exists between the two variables of interest. Poor measuring instruments could create this anomaly.

The correlation matrix in Excerpt 9.14 contains six bivariate correlations that were computed among the four variables. Each of the resulting $r$s was subjected to a separate statistical test, and in each case the null hypothesis was a no-relationship statement about the population associated with the single sample of undergraduates used in the investigation. As you can see, each of the six correlations turned out to be significant with $p < .01$.

### Tests on Several Correlation Coefficients Reported in the Text

Research write-ups often present the results of tests on many correlation coefficients in the text of the article rather than in a table. Excerpts 9.15 and 9.16 illustrate this approach to summarizing the results of inferential tests on multiple correlations.

**EXCERPTS 9.15–9.16 • *Tests on Several rs with Results in the Text***

Whether a teacher expelled a child in the past 12 months was related positively to both teachers' job stress (as measured by the Job Demands survey; $r = .24$, $P < .01$) and depressive symptoms (as measured by the CES-D Total; $r = .23$, $P < .05$).

*Source:* Gilliam, W. S., and Shabar, G. (2006). Preschool and child care expulsion and suspension: Rates and predictors in one state. *Infants & Young Children: An Interdisciplinary Journal of Special Care Practices, 19*(3), p. 238.

- - - - - - - - - - - - - - - - - - - - - - - - - - - - - - - - - - - - - - - - - - - - - - - - - - - -

A significant positive correlation was also found between the Hostile Intent subscale of the CATS and the SDQ behavioral problem score . . .; however, this was only the case for the AD group, $r(34) = .602$, $p < .01$, and NC group, $r(30) = .428$, $p < .05$, with no significant correlation found in the AS group, $r(29) = .244$, $p > .05$.

*Source:* Farrugia, S., and Hudson, J. (2006). Anxiety in adolescents with Asperger Syndrome: Negative thoughts, behavioral problems, and life interference. *Focus on Autism & Other Developmental Disabilities, 21*(1), p. 31.

In Excerpt 9.15, we see the results of tests on two correlations. Note that each of these correlations came from data on a single group of individuals. Excerpt 9.16 presents the results of tests on three correlations. As you can see, each of these three correlations came from data collected from a different group of people.

### The Bonferroni Adjustment Technique

In Chapter 8, I explained why researchers will sometimes use the **Bonferroni technique** to adjust their level of significance. As you will recall, the purpose of doing this is to hold down the chances of a Type I error when multiple tests are conducted. I also hope that you remember the simple mechanics of the Bonferroni technique: Simply divide the desired studywide Type I error risk by the number of tests being conducted.

In Excerpts 9.17 and 9.18, we see two examples in which the Bonferroni technique was used in conjunction with correlation coefficients. Both of these excerpts are worth considering.

**EXCERPTS 9.17–9.18 •** *Use of the Bonferroni Correction with Tests on Several Correlation Coefficients*

A Bonferroni approach to control for Type I error across the 10 correlations indicated that a p value of less than .005 (.05/10 = .005) was required for significance.

*Source:* Wrobleski, K. K., and Snyder, C. R. (2005). Hopeful thinking in older adults: Back to the future. *Experimental Aging Research, 31(*2), p. 223.

- - - - - - - - - - - - - - - - - - - - - - - - - - - - - - - - - - - - - - - - - - - - - - - - - - - - - - - - - - - - - - -

The alpha level was adjusted by dividing the customary alpha level of .05 by the number of correlations tested (21). Based on the resulting alpha level of .002, only six of the 21 correlations were significant.

*Source:* Niehuis, S. (2005). Alternative monitoring predictors: When the grass looks greener on the other side. *North American Journal of Psychology, 7(*3), pp. 424–425.

Excerpt 9.17 provides a nice review as to why the Bonferroni technique is used and how it works. In Excerpt 9.18, notice that the Bonferroni procedure reduced the level of significance from .05 to .002. This may strike you as an overly severe change in the alpha level. However, if a researcher uses the hypothesis testing procedure several times (as was the case in Excerpt 9.18), the actual Type I error risk become greatly inflated if the level of significance is not made more rigorous. The researchers associated with both of these excerpts would deserve bonus points in our evaluation of these studies because they recognized that they needed to "pay a price" for testing multiple correlations.

When you come across the report of a study that presents the results of inferential tests applied to several correlation coefficients, try to remember that the conclusions drawn can be radically different depending on whether or not some form of Bonferroni adjustment technique is used. For example, consider once again Excerpt 9.16. The researchers report that the second of their three correlations (.428) was significant at the .05 level. However, if the Bonferroni adjustment procedure had been used (because tests were conducted on three correlations), the null hypothesis associated with this correlation would have been retained rather than rejected.

## Tests of Reliability and Validity Coefficients

As indicated in Chapter 4, many of the techniques for estimating reliability and validity rely totally or partially on one or more correlation coefficients. After computing these indices of instrument quality, researchers sometimes apply a statistical test to determine whether or not their reliability and validity coefficients are significant. Excerpts 9.19 and 9.20 illustrate such tests.

### EXCERPTS 9.19–9.20 • *Tests of Reliability and Validity Coefficients*

Test–retest reliability was high ($r = .78$, $p < .001$), indicating considerable stability in PPVT–III scores over a 6-month period.

*Source:* Huaqing Qi, C., Kaiser, A. P., Milan, S., and Hancock, T. (2006). Language performance of low-income African American and European American preschool children on the PPVT-III. *Language, Speech, & Hearing Services in Schools, 37*(1), p. 10.

-------------------------------------------------------------------------------------------------

Support for concurrent validity was found ($r = .31$, $p < .0001$).

*Source:* Boyd, H. C., and Helms, J. E. (2005). Consumer entitlement theory and measurement. *Psychology & Marketing, 22*(3), p. 279.

When you come across a research report in which reliability and validity coefficients are tested for significance, be careful to focus your attention on the size of the coefficient (which should be large) as well as the reported $p$-level (which may be quite small). For example, in Excerpt 9.19, it is nice to know that the reported test-retest reliability coefficient turned out to be significantly different from zero (with $p < .001$); however, what's also important is the size of the stability coefficient, which in this case is respectable at .78. Look at what happens, however, when we consider both $p$ and $r$ in Excerpt 9.20. Here, the $p$ looks good (since it is less than .0001) but the validity coefficient of .31 appears quite inadequate. This result provides proof that it is possible for a reliability or validity coefficient to end up being statistically significant even though it is unimpressive in terms of its absolute size.

## Statistically Comparing Two Correlation Coefficients

At times, researchers will have two correlation coefficients that they wish to compare. The purpose of such a comparison is to determine whether a significant difference exists between the two $r$s, with the null hypothesis being a statement of no difference between the two correlations in the population(s) associated with the study. For such tests, a no-difference $H_0$ is fully appropriate.

Figure 9.2 is designed to help you distinguish between two similar but different situations where a pair of correlation coefficients is compared. In Figure 9.2(a),

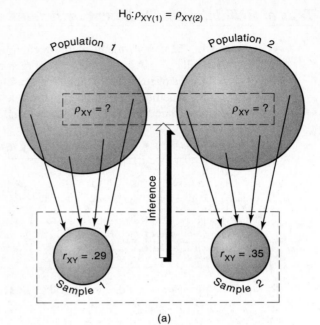

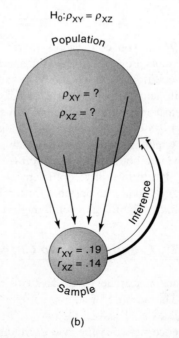

**FIGURE 9.2    *Two Kinds of Inferential Situations Involving Two Correlations***

we see that a sample is drawn from each of two populations, with a bivariate correlation coefficient computed, in each sample, between the same pair of variables. In this picture, I have labeled these variables as $X$ and $Y$; the two variables might be height and weight, running speed and swimming speed, or any other pair of variables. The null hypothesis is that correlation between $X$ and $Y$ has the same value in each of the two populations. Notice that the single inference here is based on both groups of sample data and is directed toward the *set* of populations associated with the study.

In Figure 9.2(b), we see that a single sample is drawn from one population, but two correlation coefficients are computed on the basis of the sample data. One correlation addresses the relationship between variables $X$ and $Y$ while the other correlation is concerned with the relationship between variables $X$ and $Z$. The null hypothesis in this kind of study is that the parameter value of the correlation between $X$ and $Y$ is equal to the parameter value of the correlation between $X$ and $Z$. Based on the sample's pair of correlation coefficients, a single inference is directed toward the unknown values of the pair of correlations in the population.

Excerpts 9.21 and 9.22 illustrate the two situations depicted in Figure 9.2. In the first of these excerpts, the correlation between two variables (CRA and composite thought disorder) from one group of patients was compared with the correlation between these same two variables from a different group of patients. In Excerpt 9.22, we again see that two correlation coefficients were statistically compared. Here, however, the situation was different. In this case, the individuals in a single group were measured on three variables—work hope, goals, and optimism.

### EXCERPTS 9.21–9.22 • *Statistical Comparison of Two Correlation Coefficients*

As predicted, an increase in CRA was associated with a decrease in composite thought disorder. This correlation was significant and negative for introjective patients ($r = -.38$, $p = .02$) and insignificant for anaclitic patients ($r = .08$, *ns*). The difference between these correlations in anaclitic and introjective patients was statistically significant ($z = -2.09$, $p < .02$, two-tailed).

*Source:* Fertuck, E. A., Bucci, W., Blatt, S. J., and Ford, R. Q. (2004). Verbal representation and therapeutic change in anaclitic and introjective inpatients. *Psychotherapy: Theory, Research, Practice, Training, 41*(1), p. 21.

-------------------------------------------------------------------------------------------

Results show . . . the correlation between the WHS [Work Hope Scale] and the Goals scale ($r = .62$) was not significantly higher than the correlation between the WHS and optimism ($r = .53$), $t(221) = 1.69$, $p > .05$.

*Source:* Juntunen, C. L., and Wettersten, K. B. (2006). Work hope: Development and initial validation of a measure. *Journal of Counseling Psychology, 53*(1), p. 100.

Correlations were computed between work hope and each of the other variables, and then these two *r*s were statistically compared.

In Excerpt 9.21, the two correlations were compared by means of a statistical test that's called a *z-test*.[2] In Excerpt 9.22, a *t-test* was used to make the correlational comparison. You do not need to know anything about these statistical tests except one very important thing. In each case, the null hypothesis being evaluated was that the population values associated with the two sample correlations were identical. Stated symbolically, $H_0$: $\rho_1 = \rho_2$. In Excerpt 9.22, the two correlations (.62 and .53) were both fairly large and probably would have been significant if individually tested against a no-relationship null hypothesis. However, because those two *r*s were close together, there was no statistically significant difference between them.

## The Use of Confidence Intervals around Correlation Coefficients

When researchers subject a data-based correlation coefficient to an inferential statistical procedure, they will probably do so via hypothesis testing. All of the excerpts presented so far in this chapter have been taken from studies in which this testing strategy was used. It is possible, however, for a researcher to deal inferentially with a correlation coefficient simply by placing a confidence interval around the sample value of *r*. Oddly, few researchers do this.

As was indicated previously, confidence intervals can be used *within* the context of hypothesis testing. In applying inferential tests to correlation coefficients, most researchers do not place confidence intervals around their sample values of *r*, but a few do. We see an illustration of this use of confidence intervals in Excerpt 9.23.

In Excerpt 9.23, notice that the confidence interval extends from .26 to .30. Thus, the full CI lies on the positive side of 0.00. Because the CI did not overlap zero, the researcher rejects the null hypothesis, as indicated by the notation $p < .05$. That null hypothesis was never mentioned in the research report, but it took the form $H_0$: $\rho = 0.00$, as is usually the case when a single correlation coefficient is tested.

### EXCERPT 9.23 • *Use of Confidence Intervals to Test r*

The correlation between perceived intelligence and actual intelligence was .28 (95% confidence interval [CI] = 0.26–0.30, $p < .05$), suggesting a moderate correlation between the two constructs.

*Source:* Jaccard, J., Dodge, T., and Guilamo-Ramos, V. (2005). Metacognition, risk behavior, and risk outcomes: The role of perceived intelligence and perceived knowledge. *Health Psychology, 24*(2), p. 166.

---

[2]The term **Fisher's *r*-to-*z* transformation** is often used to describe the test that's conducted to see if two correlations are significantly different from each other.

## *Cautions*

I feel obligated to end this chapter by suggesting a few cautions that you should keep in mind when trying to decipher (and critique) research reports based on correlation coefficients. As you will see, my comments here constitute a reiteration of some of the points presented at the end of Chapter 3 as well as some of the points offered at the conclusions of Chapters 7 and 8.

### *Relationship Strength, Effect Size, and Power*

Many researchers seem to get carried away with the *p*-levels associated with their correlation coefficients and thus seem to forget that the estimated strength of a relationship is best assessed by squaring the sample value of *r*. Discovering that a correlation coefficient is significant may not really be very important—even if the results indicate $p < .01$ or $p < .001$—unless the value of $r^2$ is reasonably high. The result may be significant in a statistical sense (thus indicating that the sample data are not likely to have come from a population characterized by $H_0$), but it may be quite insignificant in a practical sense.

Consider Excerpt 9.24. Each of the three correlation coefficients in this excerpt was tested, and in each case the *r* was found to be significantly different from 0.00. The researchers are correct in what they say in the excerpt's final two sentences. Nevertheless, I can't help but think that they focused more on the statistical result that said $p < .05$ rather than on the size and strength of the three bivariate *r*s.

### EXCERPT 9.24 • *Incorrect Focus on p Rather Than r*

There was a significant correlation (p < .05) between career commitment and appropriate duties (*r* = .08), supervision by peers (*r* = .06), and stress (*r* = −.11). Higher levels of commitment were related to higher levels of appropriate duties and supervision from peers. Lower levels of commitment were related to higher levels of stress.

*Source:* Baggerly, J., and Osborn, D. (2006). School counselors' career satisfaction and commitment: Correlates and predictors. *Professional School Counseling, 9*(3), pp. 200–201.

To see an example in which the important distinction between statistical significance and practical significance *was* kept in mind, take a look at Excerpt 9.25. In this excerpt, notice that the researchers used the terms "small" and "very small" to describe the first three of the four correlations. Clearly, researchers there were paying more attention to the coefficients of determination than to the actual values of the correlation coefficients.

**EXCERPT 9.25 • *Expressed Concern for the Strength of Statistically Significant Correlations***

The correlation between actual and perceived oral sex was .33 ($p < .001$), .25 ($p < .001$) between actual and perceived vaginal intercourse, .10 ($p = .005$) between actual and perceived anal sex, and .06 ($p = .098$) between actual and perceived number of sexual partners. These results suggest a small to moderate relationship between actual and perceived oral sex and vaginal intercourse ($r^2$ values of .11 and .06, respectively) but a very small relationship between actual and perceived anal sex and number of sexual partners ($r^2$ values of .01 and .004, respectively).

*Source:* Martens, M. P., Page, J. C., Mowry, E. S., Damann, K. M., Taylor, K. K., and Cimini, M. D. (2006). Differences between actual and perceived student norms: An examination of alcohol use, drug use, and sexual behavior. *Journal of American College Health, 54*(5), p. 298.

In Chapter 8, I pointed out how researchers can apply a seven-step version of hypothesis testing by computing a measure of effect size or by conducting a post hoc power analysis. These strategies can be used with correlation coefficients. In fact, we saw the first of these two things done in Excerpt 9.25 where the researchers computed the coefficient of determination for each *r*.

In Excerpt 9.26, we see a case in which a group of researchers compared their obtained phi coefficient against some common effect size criteria. (These criteria have been duplicated and put into Table 9.1, because these criteria apply to any of the correlational procedures we have considered.) Because the researcher's sample value of phi (.57) was larger than the criterion value of .50, the researchers felt justified in saying that their computed correlation suggested a "strong relationship."

**EXCERPT 9.26 • *Using Effect Size Criteria with Correlation***

The obtained Phi of .57 indicates a strong relationship between the Self-Directed IEP intervention and students starting the meeting (e.g., Cohen, 1988). (We used the following to determine the magnitude of the Phi effect size: .10 = small effect, .30 = moderate effect, .50 = large effect.)

*Source:* Martin, J. E., Van Dycke, J. L., Christensen, W. R., Greene, B. A., Gardener, J. E., and Lovett, D. L. (2006). Increasing student participation in IEP meetings: Establishing the self-directed IEP as an evidenced-based practice. *Exceptional Children, 72*(3), p. 307.

As indicated by the note under Table 9.1, researchers should not blindly use the common effect size criteria for evaluating correlation coefficients. Depending upon the specific context of a given study, it might be appropriate to think of a

**TABLE 9.1**    *Effect Size Criteria for Correlations*

| Small | Medium | Large |
|---|---|---|
| $r = .1$ | $r = .3$ | $r = .5$ |

*Note:* These standards for judging relationship strength are quite general and should be changed to fit the unique goals of any given research investigation.

relationship as being "strong" when a correlation coefficient turns out to be .30 or .40 or to think of a correlation as "weak" even if it turns out to be .60 or .70. For example, if Pearson's *r* is being used to estimate test-retest reliability, a correlation coefficient of .50 would *not* be looked upon as strong evidence of desirable stability over time. And, in some fields of study where two variables have appeared independent, a new investigation (perhaps using better measuring instruments) yielding a correlation of .20 might well cause researchers to think that the new study's correlation is quite high. Although the effect size criteria for correlations are convenient and easy to use, give credit to those researchers who explain *why* these criteria either do or don't fit their particular studies.

The second thing researchers sometimes do in the last stage of the seven-step version of hypothesis testing focused on a correlation is to conduct a post hoc power analysis. In doing this, the goal usually is to see if the study had sufficient power to "find significance" in the situation where the sample correlation(s) turned out to be nonsignificant. Excerpt 9.27 illustrates this kind of post hoc power analysis.

## EXCERPT 9.27 • *A Post Hoc Power Analysis*

We conducted a post hoc power analysis on the intercorrelations to better interpret our findings, given the dearth of significant relationships, and the small sample size. None of the nonsignificant correlations possessed adequate (i.e., 80%) power.

*Source:* Cook, J. M., Elhai, J. D., Cassidy, E. L., Ruzek, J. I., Ram, G. D., and Sheikh, J. I. (2005). Assessment of trauma exposure and post-traumatic stress in long-term care veterans: Preliminary data on psychometrics and post-traumatic stress disorder prevalence. *Military Medicine, 170*(10), p. 864.

Although researchers can demonstrate a concern for relationship strength by discussing effect size, by computing $r^2$, or by conducting a post hoc power analysis, they can do an even better job if they use the nine-step version of hypothesis testing. As I hope you remember from Chapter 8, this involves setting up the study so that it will have the desired power and the proper sample size. When a researcher's study is focused on one or more correlation coefficients, it is quite easy to add these extra tasks to the basic six-step version of hypothesis testing.

In Excerpt 9.28, we see an example of an a priori power analysis being conducted for a study dealing with correlations. As indicated in this excerpt, the researchers' preliminary power analysis indicated that they would need a sample size of 85 in order to have the desired minimum power of .80 to detect meaningful correlations at the .05 level of significance. In this study, the dividing line between trivial and meaningful $r$s was specified by the researchers when they selected, for the power analysis, an effect size of $r = .30$.

### EXCERPT 9.28 • *An A Priori Power Analysis*

A power analysis for correlation methods based on a medium effect size ($r = 0.30$), alpha of 0.05 and power of 0.80 determined the required sample size of 85. Subsequently, a convenience sample ($n = 108$) was recruited from patients ($n = 412$) undergoing elective cardiac or orthopaedic surgery during a 3 month period at a major Australian tertiary hospital. . . . The final sample ($n = 86$) was composed of male ($n = 53$) and female ($n = 33$), cardiac ($n = 57$) and orthopaedic ($n = 29$) surgical patients who met the [inclusion criteria].

*Source:* Griffiths, M. F., and Peerson, A. (2005). Risk factors for chronic insomnia following hospitalization. *Journal of Advanced Nursing, 49*(3), p. 247.

When you come across a study in which the appropriate sample size was determined prior to the collection of any data, give the researcher some bonus points for taking the time to set up the study with sensitivity to both Type I *and* Type II errors. When you come across a study in which the power associated with the test(s) conducted on the correlation coefficient(s) is computed in a post hoc sense, give the researcher only a few bonus points. And when you come across a study in which there is no mention whatsoever of statistical power, award *yourself* some bonus points for detecting a study that could have been conducted better than it was.

### Linearity and Homoscedasticity

Tests on Pearson's $r$ are conducted more frequently than tests on any other kind of correlation coefficient. Whenever tests on Pearson's $r$ are conducted, two important assumptions about the population must hold true in order for the test to function as it was designed. One of these important prerequisite conditions is referred to as the linearity assumption. The other is referred to as the equal variance assumption (or, alternatively, as the assumption of homoscedasticity).

The assumption of **linearity** states that the relationship in the population between the two variables of interest must be such that the bivariate means fall on a straight line. The assumption of **homoscedasticity** states that (1) the variance of the $Y$ variable around $\mu_y$ is the same regardless of the value of $X$ being considered and (2) the variance of the $X$ variable around $\mu_x$ is constant regardless of the value of $Y$ being considered. If a population is characterized by a curvilinear relationship between $X$ and $Y$ and/or characterized by heteroscedasticity, the inferential test on

Pearson's *r* will provide misleading information concerning the existence and strength of the relationship in the population.

The easiest way for a researcher to check on these two assumptions is to look at a scatter diagram of the sample data. If the data in the sample appear to conform to the linearity and equal variance assumptions, then the researcher can make an informed guess that linearity and homoscedasticity are also characteristics of the population. In that situation, the test on *r* can then be performed. If a plot of the data suggests, however, that either of the assumptions is untenable, then the regular test on *r* should be bypassed in favor of one designed for curvilinear or unequal variance conditions.

As a reader of the research literature, my preference is to be able to look at scatter diagrams so I can judge for myself whether researchers' data sets appear to meet the assumptions that underlie tests on *r*. Because of space limitations, however, technical journals rarely permit such visual displays of the data to be included. If scatter diagrams cannot be shown, then it is my feeling that researchers should communicate in words what *they* saw when they looked at their scatter diagrams.

Consider Excerpt 9.29. In the study associated with this excerpt, the researchers measured 72 individuals having neck pain on several variables (such as age, pain intensity, and effectiveness of medication). Bivariate correlations were computed among these variables in an attempt to identify factors that might be related to the patients' physical disorder. Before computing the correlations and testing the *r*s to see which correlations were statistically significant, the researchers checked their data to see if the assumptions of linearity and normality were tenable.

### EXCERPT 9.29 • *Expressed Concern for Linearity and Normality*

Before conducting correlational analyses, scatter plots were examined and the residual error for the linear model between each set of variables was calculated. By examining the distribution of the residual errors for each bivariate comparison, the linear model was found to be appropriate for all comparisons except those which involved the duration of the symptoms. Pearson's product-moment correlations and coefficients of determination ($r^2$) were calculated between variables where the assumptions of linearity and bivariate normality were met.

*Source:* Clair, D., Edmondston, S., and Allison, G. (2004). Variability in pain intensity, physical and psychological function in non-acute, non-traumatic neck pain. *Physiotherapy Research International, 9*(1), pp. 46–47.

I feel that too many researchers move too quickly from collecting their data to testing their *r*s to drawing conclusions based upon the results of their tests. Few take the time to look at a scatter diagram as a safety maneuver to avoid misinterpretations caused by curvilinearity or heteroscedasticity. I applaud the small number of researchers who take the time to perform this extra step.

## Causality

When we initially looked at correlation from a descriptive standpoint in Chapter 3, I pointed out that a correlation coefficient usually should not be interpreted to mean that one variable has a causal impact on the other variable. Now that we have considered correlation from an inferential standpoint, I want to embellish that earlier point by saying that a correlation coefficient, even if found to be significant at an impressive alpha level, normally should not be viewed as addressing any cause-and-effect question.

In Excerpt 9.30, we see a situation in which a team of researchers warns their readers that correlation does not usually indicate causality. Take a close look at the second and final sentences of this excerpt. Not only do the researchers alert readers to the danger of drawing causal thoughts from a correlation, they also indicate why this can be problematic. As they point out, the causal force that brings about a relationship between two variables might not be one of those variables influencing the other variable; instead, there might be a third variable that has a causal impact on the first two.

### EXCERPT 9.30 • Correlation and Causality

A limitation of our study is its cross-sectional nature. The presence of a correlation does not establish the causal direction of that relationship. People may have changed the way they regulate their emotions as a consequence of their condition. In support of the causal potential of emotion regulation are previous prospective and experimental studies, which have shown that emotion regulation is able to influence perceived health [yet] our data cannot verify this causality. The associations found in this study may also be the consequence of some third variable such as neuroticism or extraversion.

*Source:* van Middendorp, H., Geenen, R., Sorbi, M. J., Hox, J. J., Vingerhoets, A. J. J. M., van Doornen, L. J. P., and Bijlsma, J. W. J. (2005). Styles of emotion regulation and their associations with perceived health in patients with rheumatoid arthritis. *Annals of Behavioral Medicine, 30*(1), pp. 51–52.

## Attenuation

The inferential procedures covered in this chapter assume that the two variables being correlated are each measured without error. In other words, these procedures are designed for the case where each variable is measured with an instrument that has perfect reliability. While this assumption may have full justification in a theoretical sense, it certainly does not match the reality of the world in which we live. To the best of my knowledge, no researcher has ever measured two continuous variables and ended up with data that were perfectly reliable.

When two variables are measured such that the data have less than perfect reliability, the measured relationship in the sample data will systematically underestimate the strength of the relationship in the population. In other words, the computed correlation coefficient will be a **biased estimate** of the parameter if either or both of the variables are measured without error-free instruments. The term **attenuation** has been coined to describe this situation, where, using the product-moment correlation as an example, measurement error causes $r$ to systematically underestimate $\rho$.

Once you come to understand the meaning (and likely occurrence) of attenuation, you should be able to see why statistical tests that yield fail-to-reject decisions are problematic in terms of interpretation. If, for example, a researcher computes Pearson's $r$ and ends up not rejecting $H_0$: $\rho = 0.00$, this outcome *may* have come about because there is a very weak (or possibly no) relationship between the two variables in the population. On the other hand, the decision not to reject $H_0$ *may* have been caused by attenuation masking a strong relationship in the population.

In Chapter 4, we spent a great deal of time considering various techniques used by researchers to estimate the reliability of their measuring instruments. That discussion now becomes relevant to our consideration of inferential reports on correlation coefficients. If a researcher's data possess only trivial amounts of measurement error, then attenuation becomes only a small concern. On the other hand, reports of only moderate reliability coupled with correlational results that turn out nonsignificant leave us in a quandary as to knowing anything about the relationship in the population.

If researchers have information concerning the reliabilities associated with the measuring instruments used to collect data on the two variables being correlated, they can use a formula that adjusts the correlation coefficient to account for the suspected amount of unreliability. When applied, this **correction-for-attenuation** formula will always yield an adjusted $r$ that is higher than the uncorrected, raw $r$. In Excerpt 9.31, we see an example where a group of researchers conducted a correlational study and used the correction-for-attenuation formula.

**Research Navigator.com**

Correction-for-attenuation

## EXCERPT 9.31 • *Correlation Coefficients and Attenuation*

Consistent with Hypothesis 1, . . . experience ratings were positively correlated with amusement facial behavior ($r = .73$). Amusement experience and facial behavior were positively correlated with SCL, cardiovascular activation, and somatic activity ($r$s ranged from .22 to .51). . . . Disattenuated correlations were considerably greater than correlations not corrected for measurement error (the disattenuated $r$ between experience and facial behavior correlation was .87; all other disattenuated $r$s ranged from .25 to .89).

*Source:* Mauss, I. B., Levenson, R. W., McCarter, L., Wilhelm, F. H., and Gross, J. J. (2005). The tie that binds? Coherence among emotion experience, behavior, and physiology. *Emotion, 5*(2), p. 183.

Attenuation, of course, is not the only thing to consider when trying to make sense out of a correlation-based research report. Several of these other relevant considerations have been addressed within our general discussion of cautions. Two points are worth reiterating, each now connected to the concept of reliability. First, it is possible that a correlation coefficient will turn out to be statistically significant even though $H_0$ is true and even though highly reliable instruments are used to collect the sample data; do not forget that Type I errors *do* occur. Second, it is possible that a correlation coefficient will turn out to be nonsignificant even when $H_0$ is false and even when highly reliable data have been collected; do not forget about the notion of Type II errors and power.

## Review Terms

Attenuation                     Correlation matrix
Biased estimate                 Fisher's *r*-to-*z* transformation
Bonferroni technique            Homoscedasticity
Correction for attenuation      Linearity

## The Best Items in the Companion Website

1. An interactive online quiz (with immediate feedback provided) covering Chapter 9.
2. Nine misconceptions about the content of Chapter 9.
3. An email message sent from the author to his students entitled "Significant Correlations."
4. Four e-articles illustrating the use of hypothesis testing with correlations.
5. A delightful poem "A Word on Statistics."

To access chapter objectives, practice tests, weblinks, and flashcards, visit the companion website at www.ablongman.com/huck5e.

Research
Navigator.com

## Fun Exercises inside Research Navigator

**1. Are attractive people more "socially connected"?**

In this study, each of 125 college students submitted 20 photos to answer the question "Who are you?" For the central part of the study, each participant's photos were rated by a set of judges so as to determine two scores for the participant: (1) his or her physical attractiveness and (2) his or her social connectedness. (Social connectedness was rated high if a photo showed the participant with others, if people were smiling, and so on; social attractiveness was rated low if the photo showed the participant alone, if no people were in the photo, or if there were two or more people who looked unhappy.) These two sets of scores were correlated, and the resulting *r* was tested for significance. If you had to guess the value of *r* and also guess whether it turned out to be statistically significant, what would your guesses be? To find out if your guesses are good ones, locate the PDF version of the research report in the Psychology database of ContentSelect and read the second paragraph of the "Results and Discussion" section.

S. J. Dollinger. Physical attractiveness, social connectedness, and individuality: An autophotographic study. *Journal of Psychology*. Located in the PSYCHOLOGY database of ContentSelect.

## 2. Who eats more: those who do or don't have their lower-level needs met?

A group of adults ranging in age from 21 to 79 years old filled out two questionnaires. One of these, the *Basic Need Satisfaction Inventory* (BNSI), measures people's perceived satisfaction with meeting different kinds of needs: basic physiological needs, safety/security, love and belonging, self-esteem, and self-actualization. (As you may have noticed, these needs correspond with Maslow's hierarchy of needs.) The other questionnaire, the *Emotional Eating Scale* (EES), measures the degree to which people eat as a response to emotional states. The main finding of this study was connected to the statistically significant correlation between the composite scores of these two measures. Do you think it was a positive or negative correlation? To find out, locate the PDF version of the research report in the Nursing, Health, and Medicine database of ContentSelect and read the last full sentence on page 697.

G. M. Timmerman & G. J. Acton. The relationship between basic need satisfaction and emotional eating. *Issues in Mental Health Nursing*. Located in the NURSING, HEALTH, AND MEDICINE database of ContentSelect.

**Review Questions and Answers begin on page 513.**

# 10

# Inferences Concerning
# One or Two Means

In the previous chapter, we saw how inferential statistical techniques can be used with correlation coefficients. Now, we turn our attention to the procedures used to make inferences with means. A variety of techniques are used by applied researchers to deal with their sample means, and we will consider many of these inferential procedures here and in several of the following chapters. Multiple chapters are needed to deal with this broad topic because the inferential procedures used by researchers vary according to (1) how many groups of scores are involved, (2) whether underlying assumptions seem tenable, (3) how many independent variables come into play, (4) whether data on concomitant variables are used to increase power, and (5) whether people are measured under more than one condition of the investigation.

In this introductory chapter on inferences concerning means, we will restrict our focus to the cases in which the researcher has computed either just one sample mean or two sample means. I will illustrate how statistical tests are used in studies where interest lies in one or two means and the way interval estimation is sometimes used in such studies. Near the end of this chapter, we will consider the assumptions that underlie the inferential procedures covered in this chapter, and we will also examine the concept of "overlapping distributions." With this overview now under your belt, let us turn to the simplest inferential situation involving means: the case where there is a single mean.

## Inferences Concerning a Single Mean

If researchers have collected data from a single sample and if they wish to focus on $\overline{X}$ in an inferential manner, one (or both) of two statistical strategies will be implemented. On the one hand, a confidence interval can be built around the sample mean. On the other hand, a null hypothesis can be set up and then evaluated by means of the hypothesis testing procedure.

### The Inferential Purpose

Figure 10.1 has been constructed to help clarify what researchers are trying to do when they use the mean of a sample as the basis for building a confidence interval or for assessing a null hypothesis. As this figure shows, $\overline{X}$ is computed on the basis of data collected from the sample. Although the sample-based value of the mean is easy to obtain, primary interest lies in the corresponding value of $\mu$, the population mean.[1] However, the researcher cannot compute the value of $\mu$ because only the objects in the sample can be measured. Accordingly, an inference (i.e., educated guess) about the unknown value of the population parameter, $\mu$, is made on the basis of the known value of the sample statistic, $\overline{X}$.

In summarizing their empirical investigations, many researchers discuss their findings in such a way that the exclusive focus seems to be on the sample data. The thick arrow in Figure 10.1 will help you remember that the different inferential techniques to which we now turn our attention are designed to allow a researcher to say something about the *population* involved in the study, not the sample. If concern rested with the sample, no inferential techniques would be necessary.

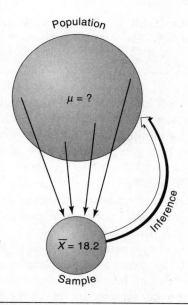

**FIGURE 10.1**   *The Inferential Purpose When One Sample's Mean Is Computed*

[1] If the researcher's data come from a probability sample, then $\mu$ represents the mean of the study's *tangible* population. On the other hand, if the data come from a convenience or purposive sample (or some other form of nonprobability sample), then $\mu$ represents the mean of the study's *abstract* population.

### Interval Estimation

Research
Navigator.com

Confidence
interval

Of the two basic ways of applying inferential statistics to a sample mean, the **confidence interval** procedure is simpler. All the researcher will do in implementing this inferential strategy is (1) make a decision as to the level of confidence that will be associated with the interval to be built and (2) build the interval around $\overline{X}$ by using a formula that incorporates information from the sample (e.g., $\overline{X}$, *SD,* and *n*) as well as a numerical value extracted from a statistical table. The result will be an interval that extends equally far above and below the sample value of $\overline{X}$.

In Excerpt 10.1, we see a case in which a 95 percent confidence interval was placed around a sample mean. In a sense, this CI gives us a feel for how trustworthy the sample mean is. If this study were to be replicated, with another sample taken from the same population, we would expect sampling error to cause the mean age of people in the replicated study to be different from the mean age of this study's sample. But how much variation should we expect? The CI gives us a range within which we would expect to find that next sample mean.

*[handwritten: class 11/16]*
*[handwritten: CI built around the mean]*
*[handwritten: an estimate]*

### EXCERPT 10.1 • *Confidence Interval around a Single Mean*

*[handwritten: sample mean]*

The mean age in the sample was 56.6 years (95% CI 54.7–58.5) with a median age of 60 years.

*Source:* Grill, E., Lipp, B., Boldt, C., Stucki, G., and Koenig, E. (2005). Identification of relevant ICF categories by patients with neurological conditions in early post-acute rehabilitation facilities. *Disability & Rehabilitation, 27*(7/8), p. 461.

When looking at a confidence interval, some people make a big mistake in interpreting what it means. This mistake is thinking that a 95% CI indicates the range for the middle 95% of the scores used to generate the CI. By looking at Excerpt 10.1, you can see why this is an incorrect interpretation of this or any CI. Whereas the CI around the sample mean extends from 54.7 to 58.5, the median was 60. If the middle 95 percent of the scores fell inside the CI, then the median would also have to be positioned somewhere inside that interval. But it isn't. That's because a 95% CI does *not* indicate the range of scores for all but the highest and lowest $2\frac{1}{2}$ percent of the scores!

As you may recall from Chapter 8, it is technically wrong to interpret this (or other) CI by saying or thinking that there is a 95% chance that the population mean lies somewhere between the end points of the CI. Instead, you need to imagine (1) that many samples are drawn randomly from the same population, (2) that a separate CI is built for each sample, and (3) that each CI is examined to see if it has captured the population mean. With these three things in mind, the correct way to interpret a 95% CI is to say or think that it is one of many (actually 95%) CIs that would, in fact, overlap $\mu$ rather than one of the few (actually 5%) that would not.

Excerpt 10.2 again illustrates how researchers build confidence intervals around means, except here the results are presented in a table. This excerpt comes from a study in which the researchers asked 6- to 7-year-old children and 10- to 11-year-old children to evaluate two sets of traits regarding characters in a story. (In evaluating the traits, the children chose faces that had large or small smiles or frowns, with these options translated into a 0–4 scale.)

## EXCERPT 10.2 • *Confidence Intervals around Means*

**TABLE 1**   *Emotion Response Scores from Study 1*

| Traits | Age Group | |
| --- | --- | --- |
| | *Younger children* | *Older children* |
| Smart/Honest | M = 3.46 (0.62) | M = 3.39 (0.63) |
| | CI = 3.23–3.70 | CI = 3.16–3.63 |
| Outgoing/Nervous | M = 2.05 (0.88) | M = 1.63 (1.01) |
| | CI = 1.70–2.41 | CI = 1.27–1.98 |

*Note.* Standard deviations are shown in parentheses. CI = 95% confidence intervals.

*Source:* Heyman, G. D., and Legare, C. H. (2005). Children's evaluation of sources of information about traits. *Developmental Psychology, 41*(4), p. 638. (Modified slightly for presentation here.)

There are two things to note about Excerpt 10.2. First, each sample mean is positioned in the middle of the confidence interval that was built around it. Second, the CIs on the bottom row of the excerpt are wider than the CIs on the top row. This difference in CI width was caused by differences in the standard deviations. These CIs illustrate the fact that if other things are held constant, there is a direct relationship between interval width and the degree of variability in the raw scores.

Because the number of young children involved in the study associated with Excerpt 10.2 was equal to the number of older children, you cannot see here the connection between interval width and sample size. However, there is a connection. If other things are held constant, larger sample sizes produce CIs that are narrower, whereas CIs based on smaller $n$s are wider. This relationship between $n$ and CI width ought to seem reasonable to you. Simply stated, estimates based on more data are likely to be more accurate than estimates based on small amounts of data.

## Tests Concerning a Null Hypothesis

When researchers have a single sample (and thus a single population) and have inferential interest in the mean, they can approach the data by means of the hypothesis testing procedure. When this strategy is used, a null hypothesis must be articulated. In this kind of research situation, the null hypothesis will take the form

$$H_0: \mu = a$$

where $a$ stands for a pinpoint numerical value selected by the researcher.

After specifying $H_0$, researchers will proceed to apply the various steps of the inferential testing strategy they have decided to follow. Regardless of which strategy is used, researchers assess the discrepancy between the sample mean and $H_0$'s pinpoint value; if the difference between $\overline{X}$ and $H_0$'s $\mu$-value is large enough, $H_0$ will be rejected and viewed as not likely to be true due to the small value of $p$ associated with the sample data.

There are several available test procedures that can be used to analyze the data of a one-sample study wherein the statistical focus is the mean. The two most popular of these test procedures are the **$t$-test** and the **$z$-test**. These two ways of testing the discrepancy between $\overline{X}$ and $H_0$'s $\mu$-value are identical in logic and have the same decision rule when comparing the calculated value against the critical value.[2] The only difference between the two tests is that the $z$-test yields a calculated value that is slightly larger than it ought to be (and a $p$-value that is slightly smaller than it ought to be). However, the amount of the bias is trivial when the sample size is at least 30.

Excerpts 10.3 and 10.4 illustrate how researchers will often present their results when they have a single sample and conduct a $z$-test or a $t$-test to evaluate a

**Research Navigator.com**

*t*-test
*z*-test

### EXCERPTS 10.3–10.4 • *Use of z or t to Test the Mean of a Single Sample*

One-sample $z$ tests were conducted to examine the difference between the sample means and the normative means. . . . Significant mean differences largely showed higher than expected means on measures of intellectual ability and general language (CELF-3), but lower scores on tests of memory and phonologic awareness (QUIL).

*Source:* Northcott, E., Connolly, A. M., Berroya, A., Sabaz, M., McIntyre, J., Christie, J., Taylor, A., Batchelor, J., Bleasel, A. F., Lawson, J. A., Bye, A. M. E. (2005). The neuropsychological and language profile of children with benign rolandic epilepsy. *Epilepsia, 46*(6), pp. 925, 926.

-------------------------------------------------------------------------------------

The stuttering sample ($N = 63$, mean anxiety $= 38.5$) was shown to be significantly more anxious than the nonstuttering controls ($N = 102$, population mean anxiety $= 35.8$) using a one-sample $t$ test, $t(62) = 2.23$, $p < .05$.

*Source:* Craig, A., Hancock, K., Tran, Y., and Craig, M. (2003). Anxiety levels in people who stutter: A randomized population study. *Journal of Speech, Language, and Hearing Research, 46*(5), p. 1202.

---

[2]This decision rule says to reject $H_0$ if the calculated value is as large as or larger than the critical value; otherwise, the null hypothesis should not be rejected.

null hypothesis of the form $H_0$: $\mu = a$. In the first of these excerpts, the pinpoint number from the null hypothesis is not shown. However, it was equal to the mean score on the norms. In Excerpt 10.4, the null hypothesis took the form $H_0$: $\mu = 35.8$, with that level of anxiety chosen because it was the mean of the 102 nonstuttering individuals who served as the "norm group" against which the sample of 63 stutterers was compared.

Near the end of Excerpt 10.4, notice that a number is positioned inside a set of parentheses located between the letter $t$ and the calculated value of 2.23. This number, which in this particular excerpt is 62, is technically referred to as the **degrees of freedom** (which is often abbreviated *df*) for the *t*-test that was performed.[3] If you add 1 to the *df* number of a one-sample *t*-test, you get a number that equals the size of the sample. Take a minute and check Excerpt 10.4 to see if this little method for determining *n* works.

## Inferences Concerning Two Means

If researchers want to compare, using inferential statistics, two samples in terms of the mean scores, they can utilize a confidence interval approach to the data or an approach that involves setting up and testing a null hypothesis. We will consider the way in which estimation can be used with two means after we examine the way in which two means can be compared through a tested $H_0$. Before we do either of these things, however, I must draw a distinction between two 2-group situations: those that involve independent samples and those that involve correlated samples.

### Independent versus Correlated Samples

Whether two samples are considered to be independent or correlated is tied to the issue of the nature of the groups *before* data are collected on the study's dependent variable. If the two groups have been assembled in such a way that a logical relationship exists between each member of the first sample and one and only one member of the second sample, then the two samples are **correlated samples.** On the other hand, if no such relationship exists, the two samples are **independent samples.**

Correlated samples come into existence in one of three ways. If a single group of people is measured twice (e.g., to provide pretest and posttest data), then a relationship exists in the data because each of the pretest scores goes with one and only one of the posttest scores, since both come from measuring the same research participant. A second situation that produces correlated samples is **matching.** Here, each person in the second group is recruited for the study because he or she is a good match for a particular individual in the first group. The matching could be done in terms of height, IQ, running speed, or any of a multitude of possible matching variables. The matching variable, however, is never the same as the dependent variable that will be measured and then used to compare the two samples. The third

[3]There is no *df* value in Excerpt 10.3 because *z*-tests do not utilize the *df* concept.

situation that produces correlated samples occurs when biological twins are split up, with one member of each pair going into the first sample and the other member going into the second group. Here, the obvious connection that ties together the two samples is genetic similarity.

When people, animals, or things are measured twice or when twin pairs are split up, it is fairly easy to sense which scores are paired together and why such pairing exists. When a study involves matching, however, things are slightly more complicated. That is because two data-based variables are involved. The data on one or more of these variables are used to create pairs of people such that the two members of any pair are as similar as possible on matching variables. Once the matched pairs are formed, then new data are examined on the dependent variable of interest to see if the two groups of individuals differ *on the dependent variable.* For example, a researcher might create matched pairs of students who have low academic self-concept, randomly split up the pairs to form an experimental group (that receives tutoring) and a control group (that does not), and then compare the two groups in terms of how they perform at the end of the term on a final course examination. In this hypothetical study, the matching variable would be academic self-concept (with these scores discarded after being used to form matched pairs); the scores of primary interest—that is, the scores corresponding to the dependent variable—would come from the final course examination.

If the two groups of scores being compared do not represent one of these three situations (pre–post, matched pairs, or twins), then they are considered to be independent samples. Such samples can come about in any number of ways. People might be assigned to one of two groups using the method of simple randomization, or possibly they end up in one or the other of two groups because they possess a characteristic that coincides with the thing that distinguishes the two groups. This second situation is exemplified by the multitude of studies that compare males against females, students who graduate against those who don't graduate, people who die of a heart attack versus those who don't, and so on. Or, maybe one of the two groups is formed by those who volunteer to undergo some form of treatment whereas the other group is made up of folks who choose not to volunteer. A final example (of the ones to be mentioned) would be created if the researchers simply designate one of two intact groups to be their first sample, which receives something that might help them, while the second intact group is provided with nothing at all or maybe a placebo.

In Excerpts 10.5 and 10.6, we see descriptions of data sets that represent independent and correlation samples. It's easy to tell that the data in the first of these studies should be thought of as independent samples due to the fact that the sample sizes are different. (Whenever $n_1$ is different from $n_2$, it's impossible to have each score in one of the data sets paired logically with one of the scores in the second data set.) The two data sets in Excerpt 10.6 were correlated because the 13 individuals in the first group were matched with 13 individuals who then formed the second group. Note that these two groups were matched on two variables, age and gender.

## EXCERPTS 10.5–10.6 • *Independent and Correlated Samples*

Eligible participants were parents of toddlers enrolled in the Children's Toddler School (CTS) who . . . had been enrolled in the program for a minimum of six months. They included parents of 37 children with Autism Spectrum Disorders (ASD) and 23 typically developing children (TDC).

*Source:* Baker-Ericzen, M. J., Brookman-Frazee, L., and Stahmer, A. (2005). Stress levels and adaptability in parents of toddlers with and without autism spectrum disorders. *Research and Practice for Persons with Severe Disabilities, 30*(4), p. 196.

---

Participants were 13 adult and adolescent individuals who stuttered (11 males) and 13 control participants who were matched for age (age range for speakers who stuttered = 14–48 years; age range for control participants = 15–50 years) and gender.

*Source:* Godinho, T., Ingham, R. J., Davidow, J., and Cotton, J. (2006). The distribution of phonated intervals in the speech of individuals who stutter. *Journal of Speech, Language & Hearing Research, 49*(1), p. 163.

Research
Navigator.c⊕m

Matched samples
Paired samples

Although this was not done in either of the two excerpts we have just considered, researchers sometimes indicate explicitly that their data came from independent samples or correlated samples. When they do so, you will have no trouble knowing what kind of samples were used. However, they may use terms other than independent samples and correlated samples. Correlated samples are sometimes referred to as **paired samples, matched samples, dependent samples,** or **within samples,** while independent samples are sometimes called **unpaired samples, unmatched samples,** or **uncorrelated samples.**

To understand exactly what researchers did in comparing their two groups, you must develop the ability to distinguish between correlated samples and independent samples. The language used by the researchers will help to indicate what kind of samples were involved in the study. If a descriptive adjective is not used, you will have to make a judgment based on the description of how the two samples were formed.

### The Inferential Purpose

Before we turn our attention to the way researchers typically summarize studies that focus on two sample means, I want to underscore the fact that these comparisons of means are inferential in nature. Figure 10.2 is designed to help you visualize this important point.

Panel A in Figure 10.2 represents the case where the means of two independent samples are compared. Panel B represents the case where two correlated samples of data are compared in terms of means. (In panel B, the dotted chains that extend from population 1 to population 2 are meant to denote the pairing or matching that is characteristic of correlated samples.)

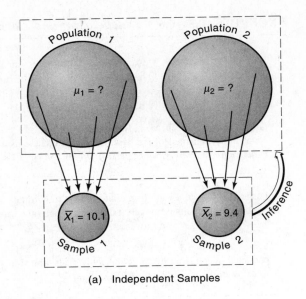

(a)   Independent Samples

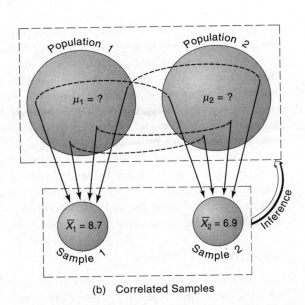

(b)   Correlated Samples

**FIGURE 10.2**   *Two Different Kinds of Inferential Situations Involving Two Means*

Two points about Figure 10.2 need to be highlighted. First, in both the independent-samples situation and in the correlated-samples situation, inferential statements are made about populations, not samples. Unfortunately, researchers often discuss their results as if the samples were the total focus of their investigations. If you keep Figure 10.2 in mind when you are dealing with these research summaries, you can (and should) correct the discussion by having all conclusions apply to the study's populations.

My second point regarding Figure 10.2 concerns the fact that the statistical inference, in panel A and in panel B, extends from the full set of sample data to the study's *pair* of populations. Separate inferences are not made from each sample to its corresponding population because the purpose is to make a comparison between two things. The focus here is on how $\mu_1$ compares with $\mu_2$, and thus the inferential arrow in each picture points to the dotted box surrounding both populations involved in the study.

### *Setting Up and Testing a Null Hypothesis*

The null hypothesis for the two-sample case having a focus on means can be expressed in the same form regardless of whether the samples are independent or correlated. The most general way to write the null hypothesis is to state

$$H_0: \mu_1 - \mu_2 = a$$

where $a$ represents any pinpoint number the researcher wishes to use in $H_0$. In most studies, researchers decide to set up a no-difference null hypothesis, and they accomplish this goal by saying $H_0: \mu_1 - \mu_2 = 0$. An alternative way to express the notion of no difference is to say $H_0: \mu_1 = \mu_2$.

Unfortunately, the null hypothesis is rarely stated in studies where two means are inferentially compared using a statistical test (or in other studies, for that matter). Evidently, most researchers assume that their readers will be able to discern the null hypothesis from the discussion of the research hypothesis and/or the way the sample data are summarized. A good rule of thumb to use when trying to decipher research reports is to presume that a test of two means revolved around a no-difference $H_0$ unless it is explicitly stated that some other kind of null hypothesis was set up.

After the sample data are collected, summarized, and analyzed, the results of the statistical comparison of the two $\overline{X}$s will be presented within the text of the report and/or in a table. Excerpts 10.7 and 10.8 illustrate the way results are typically presented, with the first and second studies involving independent and correlated samples, respectively. In the first of these excerpts, the two sample means (4.94 and 4.90) were too close together to permit the null hypothesis to be rejected. Just the opposite happened in Excerpt 10.8; here, the two sample means (25.6 and 39.2) were so far apart that the $t$-test was significant.

In both Excerpts 10.7 and 10.8, the null hypothesis being tested could be expressed as $H_0: \mu_1 = \mu_2$, with the subscripts attached to the $\mu$s standing for the first and second comparison group in each study. Of course, the $\mu$s in this symbolic expression of $H_0$ would not represent the same variable. In Excerpt 10.7, the $\mu$s would correspond with prior experience with teams; in Excerpt 10.8, they would represent the beliefs mental health trainees have about women ($\mu_1$) and about men ($\mu_2$).

## EXCERPTS 10.7–10.8 • *Comparison of Two Sample Means Using a t-Test*

Cohort 1 consisted of 94 students . . . . Cohort 2 consisted of 113 students. . . . Cohorts were similar with respect to their previous team experiences, based on a self-rating at the start of each year on a 10-item team experience questionnaire. These team experience ratings were averaged for each participant. Mean team experience levels for Cohort 1 ($M = 4.94$, $SD = 0.58$) and Cohort 2 ($M = 4.90$, $SD = 0.62$) did not differ significantly ($t(205) = 0.40$, $p > .05$).

*Source:* Prichard, J. S., Bizo, L. A., and Stratford, R. J. (2006). The educational impact of team-skills training: Preparing students to work in groups. *British Journal of Educational Psychology, 76*(1), p. 125.

The mental health trainees filled out the DRIQ regarding the degree to which women and the degree to which men would have difficulty talking about emotional topics with their intimate partners. A paired *t*-test of the beliefs of mental health trainees about women ($M = 25.6$, $SD = 11.3$) versus men ($M = 39.2$, $SD = 10.6$) was significant, $t(103) = -9.8$, $p < .001$, supporting the notion that mental health trainees endorsed this dimension of the stereotype.

*Source:* Vogel, D. L., Wester, S. R., Heesacker, M., Boysen, G. A., and Seeman, J. (2006). Gender differences in emotional expression: Do mental health trainees overestimate the magnitude? *Journal of Social & Clinical Psychology, 25*(3), p. 315.

In each of the excerpts we have just considered, the two sample means were compared by a *t*-test. The *t*-test is a versatile statistical tool, because it can be used when a study's statistical focus is on a variety of other things (e.g., proportions and regression coefficients). Nevertheless, *t*-tests probably are used more often with means than anything else.

Note that the authors of Excerpts 10.7 and 10.8, in reporting their *t*-test results, provide information as to the degrees of freedom associated with the tests that were conducted. These *df* values are useful because they allow us to know how much data each *t* was based on. When *t*-tests are conducted to compare the means of two independent samples, the total amount of data can be determined by adding 2 to the *t*-test's *df*. When *t*-tests are used to see if a significant difference exists between the means of two correlated samples of data, you can determine how many pairs of data were used by adding 1 to the *t*-test's *df*. Armed with this knowledge, we can verify that there were a total of 207 individuals involved in the study associated with Excerpt 10.7, and we can determine (on our own) that there were 104 mental health trainees involved in the study associated with Excerpt 10.8.

Although a statistical test comparing the two means can be conducted using a *t*-test, it can also be accomplished by means of a **z-test** or an **F-test**. The *z*-test provides a result that is slightly biased in the sense that its probability of resulting in a Type I error is greater than the level of significance (with this bias being more pronounced when the sample sizes are small). The *F*-test, on the other hand, is not biased. The *F*-test's conclusion regarding $H_0$ will always be identical to the conclusion reached by a *t*-test. Hence, it really doesn't matter whether researchers compare their two means using a *t*-test or an *F*-test.

In light of the fact that (1) some researchers opt to use an *F*-test when comparing two means and (2) the results of an *F*-test are typically presented in a way that requires an understanding of concepts not yet addressed, I feel obliged to comment briefly about *F*-test results. Here I will focus attention exclusively on the use of *F*-tests to compare the means of two independent samples. In a later chapter, I will show how *F*-tests can be used with correlated samples.

To begin our discussion of *F*-tests applied to the means of two independent samples, consider the material in Excerpt 10.9. In this excerpt, note that there were two groups being compared, that the focus was on the mean score on the OPTS (53.19 for women and 47.24 for men), and that a statistically significant difference was found between these sample means, as indicated by the notation $p < .05$ at the end of the excerpt. Also note that the calculated value turned out equal to 5.62 and that this value is referred to as *F*.

### EXCERPT 10.9 • *Comparison of Means from Two Independent Samples Using an F-Test*

A one-way ANOVA was used to assess gender differences. Women gave higher mean ratings of positive traits about obese people on the OPTS ($M = 53.19$, $SD = 8.77$) than men ($M = 47.24$, $SD = 9.50$), $F(1, 53) = 5.62, p < .05$.

*Source:* Puhl, R. M., Schwartz, M. B., and Brownell, K. D. (2005). Impact of perceived consensus on stereotypes about obese people: A new approach for reducing bias. *Health Psychology, 24*(5), p. 520.

In Excerpt 10.9, also note that there are two degrees of freedom values presented along with the calculated value. The *df*s appear within a set of parentheses immediately to the right of the *F*, and they are separated by a comma. *F*-tests always have a pair of *df* values associated with them, and in this case the *df* values are equal to 1 and 53.

The *df* values presented along with the results of an *F*-test can be used to discern the amount of data used to make the statistical comparison. When an *F*-test is used as in Excerpt 10.9 to compare the means of two independent samples, all you need to do to determine the amount of data used is add the two *df* values together and then add 1 to the resulting sum. Thus in this study the calculated value of 5.62 was based on a total of 55 pieces of data. Since each piece of data corresponded to a particular person and his or her score on the OPTS, we know that there were 55 people involved in this study.

Sometimes, a table will be used to present the results of the kind of *F*-test we have been discussing. An example of such a table is contained in Excerpt 10.10. In the study associated with this excerpt, 91 teachers from Korea responded to a 35-item questionnaire in which they shared their attitudes toward children's language development. Each question used a 7-point Likert scale (7 = strongly agree, 1 = strongly disagree), and each teacher's score was determined by adding responses to the 35 items. These scores were then used to compare two subgroups of teachers, those with and without experience in using a teaching method called "whole language."

**EXCERPT 10.10 • *F-Test Comparison of Two Sample Means with Results Presented in an ANOVA Summary Table***

**TABLE 5    *Teachers' Beliefs Related to Children's Literacy by Prior Learning about Whole Language***

| Learning about WL | N | M | SD | Minimum Value | Maximum Value |
|---|---|---|---|---|---|
| Prior learning | 66 | 190.66 | 18.80 | 150.00 | 232.00 |
| No prior learning | 25 | 172.24 | 20.16 | 136.00 | 227.00 |

**TABLE 6    *One-Way ANOVA for Teachers' Beliefs Related to Children's Literacy by Prior Learning about Whole Language***

| Source | df | Sum of Squares | Mean Squares | F Ratio |
|---|---|---|---|---|
| Between Groups | 1 | 6156.532 | 6156.532 | 16.74*** |
| Within Groups | 89 | 32741.227 | 367.879 | |
| Total | 90 | 38897.758 | | |

*** $p < 0.001$

*Source:* Yoo, S. Y. (2005). The study of early childhood teachers' beliefs related to children's literacy at South Korea. *Reading Improvement, 42*(3), p. 141.

The first thing to note about Excerpt 10.10 is the researcher's use of the acronym **ANOVA** in reference to the statistical analysis that was conducted in the second of the two tables. This acronym stands for the phrase **analysis of variance.** This phrase is misleading, for it probably would lead an uninformed reader to think that the statistical focus was on variances. However, as you will see, the analysis of variance focuses on *means*.

The main thing going on in Excerpt 10.10 is a statistical comparison of the two sample means (190.66 and 172.24) shown in Table 5. Note that this table also contains descriptive information concerning each group's size, standard deviation, and range of scores. If you take a minute to examine this descriptive information, you will note that the two groups had different numbers of teachers in them, that the two standard deviations were approximately the same size, and that the "prior learning" group had higher high and low scores.

The outcome of the inferential test comparing the two means shown in Excerpt 10.10 is presented in Table 6. The calculated value is presented at the far right in the column labeled *F* Ratio. This data-based value, 16.74, turned out to be significant, as indicated by the note beneath the table. Thus, the two sample means differed by an amount that was beyond the limits of chance sampling, presuming that $\mu_{prior\ learning}$ and $\mu_{no\ prior\ learning}$ were equal. The null hypothesis, therefore, was rejected.

There are three *df* values presented in the analysis of variance table. On the row labeled "Between Groups," the *df* value is equal to 1; this will always be the case when two sample means are being compared. The *df* value on the row labeled "Within Groups" is found first by subtracting 1 from each sample size and then by adding the resulting figures [(66 − 1) + (25 − 1) = 89]. Note that the sum of the *df*s for the "Between groups" and "Within groups" rows is equal to 90, one less than the total number of people used in the analysis.

The column of numbers to the right of the *df* numbers is labeled Sum of Squares (but in other ANOVA summary tables you will see it labeled with the abbreviation *SS*). These numbers come from a statistical analysis of the sample data, and there is really no way to make sense out of this column of the analysis of variance table. The next column is labeled Mean Squares (which often is abbreviated *MS*). The first of these values was found by dividing the first row's Sum of Squares by that row's *df* (6156.532 ÷ 1 = 6156.532). In a similar fashion, the second row's Mean Square was found by dividing 32741.227 by 89. Finally, the calculated value for the *F* column was computed by dividing the "Between Groups" Mean Square by the "Within Groups" Mean Square (6156.532 ÷ 367.879 = 16.74).

In one sense, all of the numbers in the *df,* Sum of Squares, and Mean Squares columns of the analysis of variance table are used solely as stepping stones to obtain the calculated value. The top two *df* values are especially important, however, because the size of the appropriate critical value depends on these two *df* values (along with the selected level of significance). When the statistical analysis is being performed on a computer, the researcher's decision to reject or not reject $H_0$ will be made by looking at the *p*-value provided by the computer (rather than by comparing the calculated *F* against the critical value). The computer's *p*-value, however, is influenced by the "between" and "within" *df* values (as well as by $\alpha$ and the computed *F*). Accordingly, the three most important numbers in the table are the first two values in the *df* column and the single number in the *F* column.

## Interval Estimation with Two Means

As noted in Chapter 8, confidence intervals can be used to deal with a null hypothesis that a researcher wishes to test. Or, the confidence interval can be set up in studies where no test is being conducted on any $H_0$, with interest instead residing strictly in the process of interval estimation. Regardless of the researcher's objective, it is important to be able to decipher the results of a study in which the results are presented using a confidence interval around the difference between two means.

Consider Excerpt 10.11. Within this excerpt, notice how there is just one confidence interval, not two. Instead of building a separate CI around each of the two sample means (30.8 and 41.7), a single CI was built around 10.9, the *difference* between the two means. Because this CI did not overlap 0, the researchers were able to say that a significant difference existed in the mean age of the two comparison groups. The null hypothesis—that $\mu_1 = \mu_2$—was rejected.

**EXCERPT 10.11 • *Using a Confidence Interval to Do Hypothesis Testing with Two Means***

The aim of this study was to analyze the effect of the broadcast of a television documentary wherein an adolescent girl is interviewed about her suicide plan and subsequently dies by suicide. National suicide rates during the 8 weeks prior to the program and the 4 weeks following it were compared to the same periods in the previous year. . . . Figure 1 [not shown here] shows the mean age of the suicide attempters/completers in the weeks before and after the broadcast in 2001 and 2000. The only week in which a significant difference was observed was the eighth week of the promotion, just prior to the broadcast, for suicide attempters (in 2001—mean 30.8 years, $SD = 13.2$, $n = 13$; in 2000—mean 41.7 years, $SD = 14.1$, $n = 22$; $p = .032$). The difference in mean age was 10.9 years (95% CI 1.61–20.19).

*Source:* Shoval, G., Zalsman, G., Polakevitch, J., Shtein, N., Sommerfeld, E., Berger, E., and Apter, A. (2005). Effect of the broadcast of a television documentary about a teenager's suicide in Israel on suicidal behavior and methods. *Crisis: The Journal of Crisis Intervention and Suicide Prevention, 26*(1), pp. 20, 23.

## Multiple Dependent Variables

If data are collected from one or two samples on two or more dependent variables, researchers with inferential interest in their data may build several confidence intervals or set up and test several null hypotheses, one for each dependent variable. A quick look at a few excerpts from recent studies will illustrate how researchers often talk about such analyses.

### Results Presented in the Text

In Excerpts 10.12 and 10.13, we see two examples of how researchers often discuss what they discovered when they compared two groups on multiple dependent variables. While both studies involved two means per comparison, note how a *t*-test was

**EXCERPTS 10.12–10.13 • *Comparing Two Means on Multiple Dependent Variables***

Female participants ($M = 99.19$, $SD = 14.56$) scored higher than males ($M = 90.80$, $SD = 15.07$) on the Sociotropy scale, $t(170) = 3.69$, $p < .001$. Female participants ($M = 16.72$, $SD = 3.41$) also scored slightly higher than males ($M = 15.58$, $SD = 4.03$) on the Perfectionism/Self-criticism scale, $t(170) = 2.01$, $p < .05$. There were no significant gender differences in mean BDI-II, Need for Control, or Defensive Separation scores.

*Source:* Frewen, P. A., and Dozois, D. J. (2006). A self-worth appraisal of life events and Beck's congruency model of depression vulnerability. *Journal of Cognitive Psychotherapy*, 20(2), p. 234.

----

Analysis of variance revealed significant difference between the two groups with the humor condition having higher ratings for overall opinion of the lesson, $F(1, 92) = 21.02$, $p < .001$; how well the lesson communicated the information, $F(1, 92) = 54.86$, $p < .001$; and rating of the instructor, $F(1, 92) = 43.33$, $p < .001$.

*Source:* Garner, R. L. (2006). Humor in pedagogy: How ha-ha can lead to aha! *College Teaching*, 54(1), p. 179.

used in Excerpt 10.12, whereas an *F*-test was used in Excerpt 10.13. Note also that you can use the degrees of freedom to determine how many individuals were involved in each study. In the study associated with the first excerpt, there was a total of 170 + 2, or 172, female and male participants. In the study associated with Excerpt 10.13, there were 1 + 92 + 1, or 94, individuals involved.

## Results Presented in a Table

Excerpt 10.14 illustrates how a table can be used to convey the results of a two-sample comparison of means on several dependent variables. The numerical values in the *t*-test column are the calculated values that resulted from a comparison of the two means on each row. Hence, the first calculated value of 2.91 came from a comparison of 6,388 and 5,952. As you can see, five *t*-tests were conducted, and the information in the right-hand column tells us that the null hypothesis (of equal population means) was rejected in four of these five tests.

When reading research reports, try to remember that you can use the reported *df* numbers to help you understand the way the study was structured, how many groups got compared, and how many participants were involved. Excerpt 10.14 is a bit unusual in that the two sample sizes are presented in the table's title. If that information had not been presented, we could have figured out how many individuals were involved in this study by adding 2 to the number 221 that's located in parentheses next to the *t* at the top of the next-to-last column.

## EXCERPT 10.14 • *Results of Several t-Tests in a Table*

**TABLE 2**   *Cognitive Performance as Measured by Composite Factor Scores in 107 Hypertensive and 116 Normotensive Older Adults*

| Factor | Hypertensive | | Normotensive | | t(221) | p |
|---|---|---|---|---|---|---|
| | M | SD | M | SD | | |
| Speed of Cognition | 6,388 | 1,211 | 5,952 | 1,025 | 2.91 | <.01 |
| Executive Function | 148 | 297 | 263 | 269 | −2.99 | <.01 |
| Episodic Memory | 220 | 52 | 241 | 40 | −3.12 | <.01 |
| Continuity of Attention | 92 | 2 | 92 | 2 | −0.58 | .57 |
| Working Memory | 160 | 34 | 175 | 22 | −4.13 | <.001 |

*Note:* Factor scores are as shown in Table 2 except for picture recognition accuracy, which was included in the Episodic Memory factor, and spatial memory accuracy, which was included in the Working Memory factor. The hypertensive group had impaired performance in all measures except Continuity of Attention. For Speed of Cognition, a higher score indicates poorer performance.

*Source:* Saxby, B. K., Harrington, F., McKeith, I. G., Wesnes, K., and Ford, G. A. (2003). Effects of hypertension on attention, memory, and executive function in older adults. *Health Psychology*, *22*(6), p. 590.

Knowing how to use *df* numbers, of course, is not the most important skill to have when it comes to *t*- or *F*-tests. Clearly, it's more important for you to know what these tests compare, what the null hypothesis is, and what kind of inferential error might be made. Even though *df* numbers are *not* of critical importance, it's worth the effort to learn how to use them as an aid to interpreting what went on in the studies you read.

### Use of the Bonferroni Adjustment Technique

When a researcher sets up and tests several null hypotheses, each corresponding to a different dependent variable, the probability of having at least one Type I error pop up somewhere in the set of tests will be higher than indicated by the level of significance used in making the individual tests. As indicated in Chapter 8, this problem is referred to as the *inflated Type I error problem*. There are many ways to deal with this problem, but the most common strategy is the application of the **Bonferroni adjustment technique.**

In Excerpts 10.15 and 10.16, we see two examples of the Bonferroni adjustment technique. The first of these excerpts is helpful because it explains how the Bonferroni procedure works. Knowing this, you should be able to look at Excerpt 10.16 and work backwards from the information that's provided so as to determine what level of significance those researchers started out with *before* they adjusted it.

## EXCERPTS 10.15–10.16 • *Use of the Bonferroni Adjustment Technique*

For each group [those with traumatic brain injury; those with spinal cord injury], paired *t* tests were then conducted comparing patients' and clinicians' PCL scores on each of the 3 disability spheres to determine whether patients' self-evaluations differ significantly from those of their clinicians (hypothesis 2). A Bonferroni correction was applied (.05/6 = .008).

*Source:* Trahan, E., Pépin, M., and Hopps, S. (2006). Impaired awareness of deficits and treatment adherence among people with traumatic brain injury or spinal cord injury. *Journal of Head Trauma Rehabilitation, 21*(3), p. 231.

---

Independent-sample *t* tests were used for group comparisons of each measure. . . . A Bonferroni correction for nine comparisons ($\alpha = .0056$) was used to determine significance.

*Source:* Rosen, K. M., Kent, R. D., Delaney, A. L., and Duffy, J. R. (2006). Parametric quantitative acoustic analysis of conversation produced by speakers with dysarthria and healthy speakers. *Journal of Speech, Language & Hearing Research, 49*(2), p. 402.

In Excerpts 10.15 and 10.16, the Bonferroni adjustment procedure was used in conjunction with *t*-tests that compared two means. It should be noted that the Bonferroni technique is quite versatile. It can be used in studies where two sample means are compared with an *F*-test, or where the means of a single sample's multiple dependent variables are each tested to see if it differs from some appropriate comparison value. When we consider other kinds of statistical tests in later chapters, you will see that this procedure for handling the inflated Type I error problem can be used there as well.

### A Pseudo-Bonferroni Adjustment

Some researchers who have multiple dependent variables attempt to hold down their total Type I error risk by using a crude technique referred to here as the **pseudo-Bonferroni adjustment procedure.** This procedure works as follows: The researchers take the normal level of significance and change it to a popular but more rigorous level. For example, researchers who normally would set alpha equal to .05 if there were just one dependent variable might decide to use an alpha level of .01 to compensate for the inflated Type I error risk caused by multiple dependent variables.

When multiple tests are conducted, a change in the alpha level (e.g., from .05 to .01) does, in fact, bring about greater control of Type I errors. I refer to it as a pseudo-Bonferroni technique, however, because the studywide risk of falsely rejecting one or more true null hypotheses rarely will be equal to the desired (in most cases) .05 level. It might be higher than that; it might be lower.

Excerpt 10.17 illustrates the use of the pseudo-Bonferroni technique. In this instance, the adjusted alpha levels were more rigorous that would have been the case if the normal Bonferroni adjustment procedure had been used. (That's because there

### EXCERPT 10.17 • *A Pseudo-Bonferroni Correction*

Four factor scores were computed from each Likert scale (i.e., Scale 1—current attainment level and Scale 2—importance). . . . Paired *t* tests were then conducted comparing respondents' ratings on the two Likert scales for each of the four factors. Alpha-level was set at $p < .01$ for the four factor paired *t* tests. Any subsequent paired *t* test comparisons of individual survey items were conducted only if the original factor paired *t* test was deemed to be statistically significant. An alpha-level of $p < .01$ was set for subsequent paired *t* tests for individual survey items to minimize the potential for any spurious significance (i.e., Type I errors, based on the number of multiple comparisons made).

*Source:* Michaels, C. A., and McDermott, J. (2003). Assistive technology integration in special education teacher preparation: Program coordinators' perceptions of current attainment and importance. *Journal of Special Education Technology, 18*(3), p. 32.

were four *t*-tests conducted initially and then 22 more after it was discovered that the first four were significant.) In many other studies, the pseudo-Bonferroni technique leads to gross underprotection of Type I errors.

## Effect Size Assessment and Power Analyses

When dealing with one or two means using hypothesis testing, many researchers give no evidence that they are aware of the important distinction between statistical significance and practical significance. Those researchers seem content simply to reject or to fail to reject the null hypotheses that they assess, with impressive *p*-levels sometimes reported along with calculated values when the sample data "beat" the conventional .05 alpha level by a wide margin. A few researchers, however, make an effort to provide insight into their results or to set up their studies with systematic control over the probability of Type II errors. In Chapter 8, I discussed in general terms the way researchers can accomplish these goals. Now, I wish to illustrate how researchers actually do these things in studies where there is inferential interest in one or two means.

In Excerpt 10.18, we see a case where a researcher computed an **effect size** index, *d,* for the correlated-samples *t*-test that had revealed a statistically significant difference between the mean reading speeds measured at a study's first and final training sessions. This illustrates one way in which researchers can execute the seven-step version of hypothesis testing. Notice that the researchers say that their effect size turned out to be "large." This was the justification for the researchers stating that the increase in reading speed not only was significant in a statistical sense but also significant in a clinical (i.e., practical) sense.

Excerpts 10.19 and 10.20 show how researchers can assess effect size via two measures that are analogous to the $r^2$ that is often computed from a bivariate

ResearchNavigator.com

Effect size

## EXCERPT 10.18 • *Effect Size Assessment with d*

The increase in reading speed from the first training session (an average of 34 words per minute, wpm) to the last training session (an average of 71 wpm) was significant ($t = 7.445$, $p < .000$). . . . The effect size (Cohen, 1988) for this increase was ($d = 1.01$), which is considered large and indicates that the intervention had clinical, as well as statistical, significance.

*Source:* Goodrich, G. L., Kirby, J., Wood, J., and Peters, L. (2006). The Reading Behavior Inventory: An outcome assessment tool. *Journal of Visual Impairment & Blindness, 100*(3), p. 165.

## EXCERPTS 10.19–10.20 • *Effect Size Assessment with Eta Squared and Omega Squared*

The ANOVA for the eight-item conceptual test also indicated a significant effect, $F(1, 69) = 8.81$, $MSE = 44.03$, $p < .05$. The restricted CP group answered significantly more items correctly than the unrestricted CP group. The strength of the relationship between level of CP restriction and conceptual recognition was moderate, as assessed by eta squared, with level of restriction accounting for 11.3% of the variance in conceptual recognition.

*Source:* Igo, L. B., Bruning, R., and McCrudden, M. T. (2005). Exploring differences in students' copy-and-paste decision making and processing: A mixed-methods study. *Journal of Educational Psychology, 97*(1), pp. 105, 107.

-------------------------------------------------------------------

A one-way ANOVA with APOE group as the independent variable revealed a significant difference in recognition scores, $F(1, 30) = 5.01$, $p = .03$, $\omega^2 = .11$, with the $\epsilon 4-$ participants performing better than the $\epsilon 4+$ participants.

*Source:* Driscoll, I., McDaniel, M. A., and Guynn, M. J. (2005). Apolipoprotein E and prospective memory in normally aging adults. *Neuropsychology, 19*(1), p. 31.

Research
Navigator.c⊕m

Eta squared

correlation. These measures are called **eta squared** and **omega squared.** After comparing two means via a *t*-test or an *F*-test, these measures provide an index of the proportion, or percentage, of variability in the study's dependent variable that is associated with (or explained by) the study's grouping variable.

In Excerpt 10.19, the researchers provide the meaning of the eta squared number (.113) that they had computed. As they pointed out, 11.3 percent of the variability in the participants' scores on the dependent variable, conceptual recognition, could be explained by participants being in one or the other of the two groups. In Excerpt 10.20, the computed value of omega squared (.11) was reported, and the researchers later referred to this as a proportion-of-variance measure.

In Excerpt 10.18, the researchers referred to their effect size measure ($d$) as being "large." In Excerpt 10.19, that set of researchers referred to their effect size measure (eta squared) as being "moderate." Because researchers frequently use the terms "small," "medium," and "large" when talking about their effect size measures, it's important for you to know what criteria they are using to make these judgments.

Table 10.1 contains the established criteria for small, medium, and large effect sizes for seven different measures that researchers use. In Excerpts 10.18, 10.19, and 10.20, we have looked at cases where three of these measures were used by applied researchers. You are likely to encounter the other four if you read research reports from several different academic disciplines. As you can see from Table 10.1, there are two versions of eta squared and two versions of omega squared. The two versions of each measure differ in terms of the way "explained variance" is conceptualized and in terms of the formula used to compute each measure. Despite these differences, the criteria remain the same for judging whether a measured effect size is small, medium, or large.

In terms of effect size measures, there are two additional things you need to know. First, the computed value for any of these measures is based on sample data, which means that the actual effect size in the relevant populations is only estimated. Because of this, it is proper for researchers to place confidence intervals around their computed effect size so as to make clear that they are sample statistics and not population parameters. Second, neither researchers nor you should blindly use the values in Table 10.1 when interpreting effect size indices. Depending upon the specific context of a given study, it might be fully appropriate to deviate from these general "rules of thumb." For this reason, give credit to those researchers who explain *why* these criteria either do or don't fit their particular studies.

Instead of estimating effect size, some researchers conduct a post hoc **power analysis** as a way of trying to add clarity to their initial findings. Usually, this is done after a comparison of two sample means has yielded a nonsignificant result. In conducting a post hoc power analysis, the researcher enters the known facts about the study (e.g., sample sizes, level of significance, means, and *SD*s) into a formula that

Research
Navigator.c☻m

Power analysis

**TABLE 10.1** *Effect Size Criteria for Comparing Two Means*

| Effect Size Measure | Small | Medium | Large |
|---|---|---|---|
| $d$ | .20 | .50 | .80 |
| Eta ($\eta$) | .10 | .24 | .37 |
| Eta Squared ($\eta^2$) | .01 | .06 | .14 |
| Omega Squared ($\omega^2$) | .01 | .06 | .14 |
| Partial Eta Squared ($\eta_p^2$) | .01 | .06 | .14 |
| Partial Omega Squared ($\omega_p^2$) | .01 | .06 | .14 |
| Cohen's $f$ | .10 | .25 | .40 |

*Note:* These standards for judging relationship strength are quite general and should be changed to fit the unique goals of any given research investigation.

determines how much power there was to detect differences as large as or larger than the estimated effect size. If the power is adequate (i.e., at or above 80 percent), the researcher will likely argue that nonsignificant results were *not* caused by Type II errors. On the other hand, if the power shows up as being inadequate, the researcher will usually say something to the effect that "something important may well be out there, but my study lacked the needed sensitivity to detect it."

Excerpt 10.21 provides an excellent illustration of a post hoc power analysis. In this study, the researchers were unable to replicate the findings of an earlier study. Once the results of the post hoc power analysis indicated that these researchers had sufficient power in their *t*-test comparisons, they have the evidence needed to argue that their nonsignificant findings most likely are not cases of Type II errors.

### EXCERPT 10.21 • *Post Hoc Power Analysis*

We failed to replicate Wang and Spelke's (2000) finding of greater configuration error in the disoriented condition than in the eyes-closed condition in each of the seven experiments reported here. Because we were unable to duplicate their results, it is reasonable to ask whether our experiments had sufficient power to detect an effect of disorientation on configuration error, if one were present. . . . We computed power by adapting the procedures recommended by Cohen (1988, pp. 48–50) for a two-sample, repeated-measures, directional *t* test at a .05 alpha level [and] the results of the postexperiment power analysis suggest that our failure to find a detrimental effect of disorientation on configuration error was not attributable to a lack of power.

*Source:* Holmes, M. C., and Sholl, M. J. (2005). Allocentric coding of object-to-object relations in overlearned and novel environments. *Journal of Experimental Psychology: Learning, Memory, and Cognition, 31*(5), pp. 1082–1083.

In the four excerpts we have just considered, the researchers' computation of effect size indices and of power were all performed *after* the data in each study had been gathered. As pointed out in Chapter 8, however, it is possible to conduct a power analysis *before* any data are collected. The purpose of such an analysis is to determine how large the sample(s) should be so as to have a known probability of rejecting $H_0$ when $H_0$ is false by an amount at least as large as the researcher-specified effect size.

In Excerpt 10.22, we see what goes into, and what comes out of, an a priori power analysis. In doing this power analysis, the researchers first decided that their statistical focus would be the mean, that they would compare their sample means with an independent-samples *t*-test, that they would use the .05 level of significance, and that they wanted to have at least an 85 percent chance of rejecting the null hypothesis (of equal population means) if the true $\mu_1 - \mu_2$ difference (in angulation improvement) between short-arm casts and long-arm casts is as large as or larger than 4°. After making these decisions, the power analysis indicated that the researchers would need about 50 individuals in each group to achieve the desired level of power.

### EXCERPT 10.22 • *An A Priori Power Analysis*

An a priori power calculation was done to determine group size. It was determined that, with approximately fifty patients in each group, there was at least an 85% chance (statistical power) of detecting a mean difference of $\geq 4°$ in the change in angulation, from the postreduction to the final assessment, between cast groups. An alpha value of 0.05 and an independent Student $t$ test were used in this calculation.

*Source:* Webb, G. R., Galpin, R. D., and Armstrong, D. G. (2006). Comparison of short and long arm plaster casts for displaced fractures in the distal third of the forearm in children. *Journal of Bone and Joint Surgery,* American Volume, *88*(1), p. 11.

## Underlying Assumptions

When a statistical inference concerning one or two means is made using a confidence interval or a $t$-, $F$-, or $z$-test, certain assumptions about the sample(s) and population(s) are typically associated with the statistical technique applied to the data. If one or more of these assumptions are violated, then the probability statements attached to the statistical results may be invalid. For this reason, well-trained researchers (1) are familiar with the assumptions associated with the techniques used to analyze their data and (2) take the time to check out important assumptions before making inferences from the sample mean(s).

For the statistical techniques covered thus far in this chapter, there are four underlying assumptions. First, each sample should be a random subset of the population it represents. Second, there should be "independence of observations" (meaning that a particular person's score is not influenced by what happens to any other person during the study). Third, each population should be normally distributed in terms of the dependent variable being focused on in the study. And fourth, the two populations associated with studies involving two independent samples or two correlated samples should each have the same degree of variability relative to the dependent variable.

The assumptions dealing with the randomness and independence of observations are methodological concerns, and researchers rarely talk about either of these assumptions in their research reports. The other two assumptions, however, are often discussed by researchers. To be a discerning consumer of the research literature, you will need to know when the **normality assumption** and **equal variance assumption** should be considered, what is going on when the normality and equal variance assumptions are tested, what researchers will do if they find that their data violate these assumptions, and under what conditions a statistical test will be "robust" to violations of the normality or equal variance assumption. This section is intended to provide you with this knowledge.

Researchers should consider the normality and equal variance assumptions *before* they evaluate their study's primary $H_0$. Assumptions should be considered first because the statistical test used to evaluate the study's $H_0$ may not function the way it is supposed to function if the assumptions are violated. In a sense, then, checking on the assumptions is like checking to see if there are holes in a canoe (or whether your companion has attached an outboard motor) before getting in and paddling out to the middle of a lake. Your canoe simply won't function the way it is supposed to if it has holes or has been turned into a motorboat.

When the normality or equal variance assumption is examined, the researcher will use the sample data to make an inference from the study's sample(s) to its population(s). This inference is similar to the one that the researcher wishes to make concerning the study's primary $H_0$, except that assumptions do not deal with the mean of the population(s). As their names suggest, the normality assumption deals with distributional shape whereas the equal variance assumption is concerned with variability. Often, the sample data will be used to test these assumptions. In such cases the researcher will apply all of the steps of the hypothesis testing procedure, starting with the articulation of a null hypothesis and ending with a reject or fail-to-reject decision. In performing such tests, researchers will hope that the null hypothesis of normality or of equal variance will *not* be rejected, for then they will be able to move ahead and test the study's main null hypothesis concerning the mean(s) of interest.

Excerpts 10.23 and 10.24 illustrate how the normality and equal variance assumptions are sometimes tested by applied researchers.[4] In each of these excerpts,

**EXCERPTS 10.23–10.24 • *Testing the Normality and Equal Variance Assumptions***

An independent *t*-test was conducted to determine if there was a significant difference between the mathematics self-efficacy of students enrolled in Intermediate Algebra and Calculus I as measured by the MSES. A two-sample Kolmogorov-Smirnov Test was conducted to validate the assumption of normality. The results indicated ($p = .580$) that the data were indeed normal, thereby allowing for the use of the two-sample *t*-test.

*Source:* Hall, J. M., and Ponton, M. K. (2005). Mathematics self-efficacy of college freshman. *Journal of Developmental Education, 8*(3), p. 28.

The variances were not significantly different from each other ($F = .88$, n.s.), and a *t*-test assuming equal variances revealed a significant difference between the means ($t = 5.69$, $p < .01$, $df = 9$, two-tailed).

*Source:* Shizuka, T., Takeuchi, O., Yashima, T., and Yoshizawa, K. (2006). A comparison of three- and four-option English tests for university entrance selection purposes in Japan. *Language Testing, 23*(1), p. 43.

---

[4]In Excerpt 10.23, the researcher used the Kolmogorov–Smirnov test to check on the normality assumption. There are other available test procedures (e.g., the chi square goodness-of-fit test) that do the same thing. In Excerpt 10.24, there is no mention of the specific tests used to check on the equal variance assumption. While many such test procedures exist, Levene's test seems to be used more than the others.

notice that the null hypothesis for the assumption was not rejected. That was the desired result, for the researchers were then permitted to do what they were really interested in, a comparison of their two sample *means.*

The assumption of equal variances is often referred to as the **homogeneity of variance assumption.** This term is somewhat misleading, however, since it may cause you to think that the assumption specifies homogeneity *within* each population in terms of the dependent variable. That is not what the assumption means. The null hypothesis associated with the equal variance assumption says that $\sigma_1^2 = \sigma_2^2$. This assumption can be true even when there is a large degree of variability within each population. "Homogeneity of variance" exists if $\sigma_1^2$ is equal to $\sigma_2^2$, regardless of how large or small the common value of $\sigma^2$.

If a researcher conducts a test to see if the normality or equal variance assumption is tenable, it may turn out that the sample data do not argue against the desired characteristics of the study's populations. That was the case in Excerpts 10.23 and 10.24. But what happens if the test of an assumption suggests that the assumption is not tenable?

In the situation where the sample data suggest that the population data do not conform with the normality and/or equal variance assumptions, there are three options available to the researcher. These options include (1) using a special formula in the study's main test so as to "compensate" for the observed lack of normality or heterogeneity of variance, (2) changing each raw score by means of a data transformation designed to reduce the degree of nonnormality or heterogeneity of variance, thereby permitting the regular *t*-test, *F*-test, or *z*-test to be used when the study's main test focuses on the study's mean(s), or (3) using a test procedure other than *t, F,* or *z*—one that does not involve such rigorous assumptions about the populations. Excerpts 10.25, 10.26, and 10.27 illustrate these three options.

Excerpt 10.25 represents option 1, for a special version of the *t*-test (called Welch's *t*-test) has built-in protection against violations of the equal variance assumption. Excerpt 10.26 shows option 2, the strategy of transforming the data and then using the regular test procedure to compare the group means. Here, a square root transformation was used. In Excerpt 10.27, the researchers wanted to use a paired *t*-test to make comparisons of pretest and posttest means on several dependent variables. However, in those cases where their data violated the normality assumption, the researchers chose option 3; instead of using the paired *t*-test, the researchers used a nonparametric test that does not assume normality.

As illustrated by Excerpt 10.26, **data transformations** are sometimes used by researchers in an effort to make variances more similar or to create data sets that more closely approximate the normal distribution. Many transformations have been designed to help researchers accomplish these goals. In Excerpt 10.26, for example, the square root transformation was used. In Excerpt 10.28, we see two

## EXCERPTS 10.25–10.27 • *Options When Assumptions Seem Untenable*

I used Levene's test of equality of error variances to identify unequal error variances. When necessary, I conducted Welch's *t* test to confirm any statistically significant group differences, thus controlling for the inequality in variances.

*Source:* Leighton, J. (2006). Teaching and assessing deductive reasoning skills. *Journal of Experimental Education, 74*(2), p. 120.

----

Since the homogeneity test for change scores was significant, $F(3, 77) = 5.72$, $p < .001$, for these [paired *t*-test] analyses the change scores were subjected to a square-root transformation in order to reduce the impact of extreme scores (see Howell, 1997).

*Source:* Falomir-Pichastor, J. M., Mugny, G., and Invernizzi, F. (2006). Smokers' (dis)satisfaction, persuasive constraint, and influence of expert and non-expert sources. *Swiss Journal of Psychology, 65*(1), p. 12.

----

Data were first analysed as to whether a normal distribution was present by means of a Kolmogorov–Smirnov test. Comparisons before and after treatment period for clinical and subjective/objective sleep variables were performed by paired *t*-test or the Wilcoxon signed rank test as appropriate.

*Source:* Kaynak, D., Kiziltan, G., Kaynak, H., Benbir, G., and Uysal, O. (2005). Sleep and sleepiness in patients with Parkinson's disease before and after dopaminergic treatment. *Journal of Neurology, 12*(3), p. 201.

histograms that show how nicely the square root transformation can accomplish the goal of converting a highly skewed distribution of raw scores into a transformed data set that looks fairly normal.

When researchers are interested in comparing the means of two groups, they will often bypass testing the assumption of equal variances if the two samples are equally big. This is done because studies in theoretical statistics have shown that a test on means will function very much as it should even if the two populations have unequal amounts of variability, as long as $n_1 = n_2$. In other words, *t*-, *F*-, and *z*-tests are strong enough to withstand a violation of the equal variance assumption if the sample sizes are equal. Stated in statistical "jargoneze," equal *n*s make these tests **robust** to violations of the homogeneity of variance assumption.

**EXCERPT 10.28** • *Reducing Skewness via a Data Transformation*

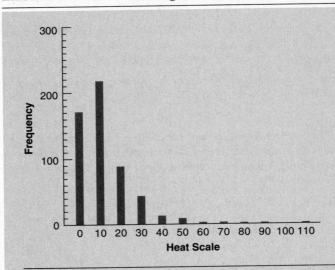

**FIGURE 1** *Frequency distribution for Heat Illness Symptom Scale.*

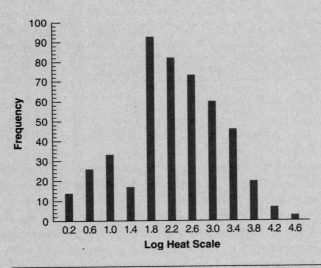

**FIGURE 2** *Frequency distribution for Log-transformed scale.*

*Source:* Coris, E. E., Walz, S. M., Duncanson, R., Ramirez, A. M., and Roetzheim, R. G. (2006). Heat Illness Symptom Index (HISI): A novel instrument for the assessment of heat illness in athletes. *Southern Medical Journal, 99*(4), pp. 343–344.

# *Comments*

Before concluding our consideration of inferences regarding one or two means, I want to offer five warnings that will, if you heed them, cause you to be a more informed recipient of research results. These warnings are concerned with (1) outcomes where the null hypothesis is not rejected, (2) outcomes where $H_0$ is rejected, (3) the typical use of *t*-tests, (4) practical significance, and (5) research claims that seem to neglect the possibility of a Type I or a Type II error.

## *A Nonsignificant Result Does Not Mean $H_0$ Is True*

In Chapter 7, I indicated that a null hypothesis should *not* be considered to be true simply because it is not rejected. Researchers sometimes forget this important point, especially when they compare groups in terms of pretest means. In making this kind of comparison, researchers usually hope that the null hypothesis will *not* be rejected, because then they can consider the comparison groups to have been the same at the beginning of the study. I'd like to mention three reasons why it's dangerous to think that $H_0$ is true if it's not rejected.

The context for my three comments is a hypothetical study. Imagine that we have two groups, E and C (experimental and control), with pretest data available on each person in each group. Let's also imagine that the sample means, $\overline{X}_E$ and $\overline{X}_C$, turn out equal to 16 and 14, respectively. Finally, imagine that a *t*-test or *F*-test is used to compare the two $\overline{X}$s, with the result being that the null hypothesis ($H_0$: $\mu_E = \mu_C$) is not rejected because $p_{\text{two-tailed}} > .05$.

The first reason for not accepting $H_0$ in this hypothetical study is purely logical in nature. If the null hypothesis had been set up to say that $H_0$: $\mu_E - \mu_C = 1$, a fail-to-reject decision also would have been reached. That is also what would have happened if $H_0$'s pinpoint number had been set equal to any other value between 0 and +4.0. Since the data support multiple null hypotheses that could have been set up (and that are in conflict with each other), there is no scientific justification for believing that any one of them is right while the others are wrong.

The second reason for not accepting $H_0$ Hconcerns data quality. In Chapter 9, I discussed attenuation and pointed out how measuring instruments that have less than perfect reliability can function to mask a true nonzero relationship that exists between two variables. The same principle applies to inferential tests that focus on things other than correlation coefficients, such as means. In our hypothetical study, data produced by a measuring instrument with low reliability could lead to a fail-to-reject decision; with a more reliable instrument, the sample means—even if they again turn out equal to 16 and 14—might end up producing a $p$ that's lower than .05! Thus, our hypothetical study may have produced a nonsignificant finding because of unreliability in the data, not because $H_0$: $\mu_E = \mu_C$.

A final consideration that mitigates against concluding that $\mu_E = \mu_C$ when $H_0$ is retained has to do with statistical power. As I have pointed out on several occasions, there is a direct relationship between sample size and the probability of detecting a situation in which $H_0$ is false. Thus, the failure to find a statistically significant finding in our hypothetical study may have been caused by $ns$ that were too small. Perhaps $\mu_E$ and $\mu_C$ differ greatly, but our study simply lacked the statistical sensitivity to illuminate that situation.

For these three reasons (logic, reliability, and statistical power), be on guard for unjustified claims that $H_0$ is true following a decision not to reject $H_0$.

## Overlapping Distributions

Suppose a researcher compares two groups of scores and finds that there is a statistically significant difference between $\overline{X}_1$ and $\overline{X}_2$. Notice that the significant difference exists between the *means* of the two groups. Be on guard for research reports in which the results are discussed without reference to the group means, thus creating the impression that every score in one group is higher than every score in the second group. Such a situation is *very* unlikely.

To illustrate what I mean by **overlapping distributions,** consider once again the information presented in Excerpt 10.10. In that excerpt, we saw that the mean score for 66 teachers who had prior knowledge of whole language learning was 190.66, whereas the mean score for the 25 teachers without such knowledge was 172.24. These two sample means were compared with an ANOVA $F$-test, and it turned out that there was a statistically significant difference between the group means. The null hypothesis of equal population means was rejected with $p < 0.001$.

Did all members of the group with prior knowledge about whole language learning earn higher scores than anyone in the group that lacked such knowledge? The evidence contained in Excerpt 10.10 allows us to answer this question with a resounding "no." Return to Excerpt 10.10 and take a look at the high and low scores of each group. Specifically compare the high score in the group of 25 teachers against the low score in the group of 66 teachers. Even if the high and low scores in each group had not been presented, the standard deviations (along with the means) would have suggested that the two distributions of scores overlapped. That's because the two group means were 18.42 points apart while the two standard deviations were 18.80 and 20.16.

Be on guard for researchers who make a comparison between two different groups (or between a single group that's measured twice), who reject the null hypothesis, and who then summarize their findings by saying something like "girls outperformed boys" or "the treatment produced higher scores than did the control" or "participants improved between pretest and posttest." Such statements are often seen in the abstracts of research reports. When you see these phrases, be sure to insert the three words "on the average" at the beginning of the researcher's summary.

Also keep in mind that overlapping distributions are the rule, not the exception, in research investigations.

## The Typical Use of t-Tests

In this chapter, you have seen how a *t*-test can be used to evaluate a null hypothesis dealing with one or two means. You will discover that *t*-tests can also be used when the researcher's statistical focus is on things other than means. For example, a *t*-test can be used to see if a correlation coefficient is significantly different from zero or if there is a significant difference between two correlations. (Excerpt 9.22 illustrates the second of these cases.) For this reason, it is best to consider a *t*-test to be a general tool that can be used to accomplish a variety of inferential goals.

Although a *t*-test can focus on many things, it is used most often when the researcher is concerned with one or two means. In fact, *t*-tests are used so frequently to deal with means that many researchers equate the term *t-test* with the notion of a test focusing on the mean(s). These researchers use a modifying phrase to clarify how many means are involved and the nature of the samples, thus leading to the terms *one-sample t-test, independent-samples t-test, correlated-samples t-test, matched t-test, dependent-samples t-test,* and *paired t-test.* When any of these terms is used, a safe bet is that the *t*-test being referred to had the concept of mean as its statistical focus.

## Practical Significance versus Statistical Significance

Earlier in this chapter, you saw how researchers can do certain things in an effort to see whether a statistically significant finding is also meaningful in a practical sense. Unfortunately, many researchers do not rely on computed effect size indices, strength-of-association measures, or power analyses to help them avoid the mistake of "making a mountain out of a molehill." They simply use the six-step version of hypothesis testing and then get excited if the results are statistically significant.

Having results turn out to be statistically significant can cause researchers to go into a trance in which they willingly allow the tail to wag the dog. That's what happened, I think, to the researchers who conducted a study comparing the attitudes of two groups of women. In their technical report, they first indicated that the means turned out equal to 67.88 and 71.24 (on a scale that ranged from 17 to 85) and then stated "despite the small difference in means, there was a significant difference."

To me, the final 11 words of the previous paragraph conjure up the image of statistical procedures functioning as some kind of magic powder that can be sprinkled on one's data and transform a molehill of a mean difference into a mountain that deserves others' attention. However, statistical analyses lack that kind of magical power. Had the researchers who obtained those means of 67.88 and 71.24 not been blinded by the allure of statistical significance, they would have focused their attention on the small difference and not the significant difference. And had they done this, their final words would have been "although there was a significant difference, the difference in means was small."

Estimates of effect size and power analyses can help keep researchers (and you) alert to the important distinction between practical significance and statistical significance. However, do not be reluctant to use your own knowledge (and common sense) when it comes to judging the "meaningfulness" of statistical results. In some cases, you will be able to make confident decisions on your own as to whether a "big difference" exists between two sample means. You ought to be able to do that when you examine Excerpt 10.29.

### EXCERPT 10.29 • *Practical Significance: Is This Mean Difference "Big"?*

To examine the difference between the parents' perceptions of their involvement and the children's perceptions of the parents' involvement, a matched pairs *t* test was used. The mean score for the parents' perception of parental involvement was $M = 4.86$ (on a Likert scale of 1–6), and the mean for the children's perception of parental involvement was $M = 4.61$. A statistical difference was shown between the two means ($t = 2.41, df = 76, p = .02$), indicating that the parents were rating their perceived level of involvement as greater than how their children were rating their perceived parents' level of involvement.

*Source:* Gibson, D. M., and Jefferson, R. N. (2006). The effect of perceived parental involvement and the use of growth-fostering relationships on self-concept in adolescents participating in Gear Up. *Adolescence, 41*(161), p. 118.

## Type I and Type II Errors

My final comment concerns the conclusion reached whenever the hypothesis testing procedure is used. Because the decision to reject or fail to reject H₀ is fully inferential in nature (being based on sample data), there is *always* the possibility that a Type I or Type II error will be committed. You need to keep this in mind as you read technical research reports, as most researchers do not allude to the possibility of inferential error as they present their results or discuss their findings. In certain cases, the researcher simply presumes that you know that a Type I or Type II error may occur whenever a null hypothesis is tested. In other cases, the researcher unfortunately may have overlooked this possibility in the excitement of seeing that the statistical results were congruent with his or her research hypothesis.

Consider Excerpt 10.30. The researchers associated with this study deserve high praise for indicating that their findings may have been the result of inferential error. With full clarity, they point out that they may have made a Type I error and/or a Type II error. Frankly, I wish there were some sort of law that forced all researchers to follow the example shown here.

When reading research reports, you will encounter many articles in which the researchers will talk as if they have discovered something definitive. The researchers' assertions typically reduce to the claim that "the data confirm our expectations, so now we have proof that our research hypotheses were correct." Resist the

**EXCERPT 10.30 • *The Possibility of Inferential Error***

> Matched paired *t* tests were used to analyze data for the first 2 aims of the study (assessing knowledge and attitudes related to advance directives and assessing acculturation). . . . The significant findings could have a type I error, and the nonsignificant findings could have a type II error.
>
> *Source:* McAdam, J. L., Stotts, N. A., Padilla, G., and Puntillo, A. (2005). Attitudes of critically ill Filipino patients and their families toward advance directives. *American Journal of Critical Care, 14*(1), pp. 21, 24.

temptation to bow down in front of such researchers and accept everything and anything they might say, simply because they have used fancy statistical techniques when analyzing their data. Remember that *inferences* are *always* involved whenever (1) confidence intervals are placed around means or differences between means and (2) null hypotheses involving one or two means are evaluated. Nothing is *proven* by any of these techniques, regardless of how bold the researchers' claims might be.

## *Review Terms*

| | |
|---|---|
| Analysis of variance | *MS* |
| Confidence interval | Omega squared |
| Correlated samples | Overlapping distributions |
| Dependent samples | Paired samples |
| *df* | Power analysis |
| Effect size | Pseudo-Bonferroni adjustment procedure |
| Eta squared | Robust |
| *F*-test | *SS* |
| Homogeneity of variance assumption | *t*-test |
| Independent samples | *z*-test |
| Matched samples | |

## *The Best Items in the Companion Website*

1. An interactive online quiz (with immediate feedback provided) covering Chapter 10.
2. Nine misconceptions about the content of Chapter 10.
3. An email message sent from the author to his students entitled "A Little *t*-Test Puzzle."
4. One of Chapter 10's best passages: "Inference and Proof."
5. Two good jokes about statistics.

To access chapter objectives, practice tests, weblinks, and flashcards, visit the companion website at www.ablongman.com/huck5e.

## *Fun Exercises inside Research Navigator*

### 1. Do men with high or low sperm counts engage in more "active coping" behavior?

A group of 55 infertile men in Germany provided data on this study's two variables: sperm concentrations and "active coping style." The data on coping style came from a questionnaire that dealt with such issues as accepting responsibility, seeking social support, and problem solving. The data on sperm concentration came from semen analyses. For one of their analyses, the researchers first created high and low subgroups on the basis of sperm count, and then they used an ANOVA *F*-test to compare these subgroups with respect to their mean scores on active coping. What do you think this *F*-test revealed? To find out, locate the PDF version of the research report in the Nursing, Health, and Medicine database of ContentSelect and take a look (near the top of page 251) at the middle row of Table 1.

M. Pook, W. K. Rause, & B. Rohrle. A validation study on the negative association between an active coping style and sperm concentration. *Journal of Reproductive & Infant Psychology.* Located in the NURSING, HEALTH, AND MEDICINE database of ContentSelect.

### 2. What do college men and women think about housewives and househusbands?

In this study, 328 female and 196 male college students took a questionnaire about housewives and househusbands. The questionnaire contained 35 statements such as "Men who are househusbands are not 'real' men." The students responded to each statement on a five-point Likert-type scale ranging from *strongly disagree* (1) to *strongly agree* (5). Five scores were derived from each student's responses to the questionnaire, one each for the four subscales (negative perceptions of househusbands, negative effect on spousal relationships, negative perceptions of housewives, and psychological effects) and one based on the full instrument. A separate *t*-test was used to compare the mean scores for men and women on each of the four subscales and on the composite score. As you would probably guess, most of these *t*-tests revealed a statistically significant difference, with the male mean always reflecting a more traditional perspective. Let's focus on one of those significant results, the one dealing with negative effect on spousal relations. On the 1-to-5 scale, how far apart do you think the male and female means were? After making a guess, locate the PDF version of the research report in the Psychology database of ContentSelect and take a look (on page 648) at Table 2. You may be quite surprised at what you see!

D. K. Wentworth & R. M. Chell. The role of househusband and housewife as perceived by a college population. *Journal of Psychology.* Located in the PSYCHOLOGY database of ContentSelect.

**Review Questions and Answers begin on page 513.**

# Tests on Three or More Means Using a One-Way ANOVA

In Chapter 10, we considered various techniques used by researchers when they apply inferential statistics within studies focusing on one or two means. I now wish to extend that discussion by considering the main inferential technique used by researchers when their studies involve three or more means. The popular technique used in these situations is called analysis of variance and it is abbreviated **ANOVA.**

As I pointed out in the preceding chapter, the analysis of variance can be used to see if there is a significant difference between two sample means. Hence, this particular statistical technique is quite versatile. It can be used when a researcher wants to compare two means, three means, or any number of means. It is also versatile in ways that will become apparent in later chapters.

The analysis of variance is an inferential tool that is widely used in many disciplines. Although a variety of statistical techniques have been developed to help applied researchers deal with three or more means, ANOVA ranks first in popularity. Moreover, there is a big gap between ANOVA and whatever ranks second!

In the current chapter, we will focus our attention on the simplest version of ANOVA, something called a one-way analysis of variance. I will begin with a discussion of the statistical purpose of a one-way ANOVA, followed by a clarification of how a one-way ANOVA differs from other kinds of ANOVA. Then, we will turn our attention to the way researchers present the results of their one-way ANOVAs, with examples to show how the Bonferroni adjustment technique is used in conjunction with one-way ANOVAs, how the assumptions underlying a one-way ANOVA are occasionally tested, and how researchers sometimes concern themselves with power analyses, measures of association, and effect size. Finally, I will offer a few tips that should serve to make you better able to decipher and critique the results of one-way ANOVAs.

# The Purpose of a One-Way ANOVA

**Research
Navigator.c⊕m**
One-way ANOVA

*[handwritten note in margin]* ≥3 inferential statement r/t means of the population

When a study has been conducted in which the focus is centered on three or more groups of scores, a **one-way ANOVA** permits the researcher to use the data in the samples for the purpose of making a single inferential statement concerning the means of the study's populations. Regardless of how many samples are involved, there is just one inference that extends from the set of samples to the set of populations. This single inference deals with the question, "Are the means of the various populations equal to one another?"

In Figure 11.1 I have tried to illustrate what is going on in a one-way ANOVA. There are three things to notice about this picture. First, I have drawn our picture for the specific situation where there are three comparison groups in the study; additional samples and populations can be added to parallel studies that have four, five, or more comparison groups. Second, there is a single inference made from the full set of sample data to the group of populations. Finally, the focus of the inference is on the population means, even though each sample is described in terms of $\overline{X}$, *SD,* and *n.*

Although you will never come across a journal article that contains a picture like that presented in Figure 11.1, I hope that my picture will help you to understand what is going on when researchers talk about having applied a one-way ANOVA to their data. Consider, for example, Excerpt 11.1, which comes from a study focused on grade inflation in business courses at a small private college in the northeastern United States. Each year, some of the business courses at this college were taught by full-time tenured professors, others were taught by full-time untenured professors, and still others were taught by adjunct professors who were not full-time faculty members. Over the span of a year, the mean of the grades

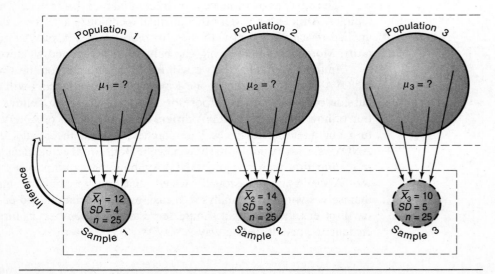

**FIGURE 11.1** *Illustration of a One-Way ANOVA's Inferential Objective*

assigned by the professors in each of these three categories was computed, thereby giving a grade point average (for the year) for each particular kind of faculty member. This was done each year for two decades, thus providing 20 GPAs for the tenured professor category, 20 GPAs for the untenured professor category, and 20 GPAs for the adjunct professor category. The 20 mean GPAs associated with each faculty category became the sample data for the category.

**EXCERPT 11.1 • *Typical Data Used in a One-Way ANOVA***

**TABLE 1**  *Descriptive Statistics of Grade Point Averages by Faculty Category*

| Category | Sample size | M | SD |
|---|---|---|---|
| Adjunct | 20 | 2.8268 | 0.1366 |
| Nontenured | 20 | 2.7363 | 0.1066 |
| Tenured | 20 | 2.6872 | 0.0816 |
| Total | 60 | 2.7501 | 0.1233 |

*Source:* Kezim, B., Pariseau, S. E., and Quinn, F. (2005). Is grade inflation related to faculty status? *Journal of Education for Business, 80*(6), p. 360.

After looking at the picture in Figure 11.1, you should be able to look at Excerpt 11.1 and discern what the researchers were trying to accomplish by using a one-way ANOVA. Each of the first three rows of data in this excerpt, of course, corresponds to one of the three samples involved in this study. Connected to each of these samples was an abstract population (i.e., a larger group of faculty members who teach business courses at small private colleges). The researchers' goal was to use the data from all three samples to make a single inference concerning the means of those populations. The statistical question dealt with by the one-way ANOVA could be stated as: "In light of the empirical information available in the samples, is it reasonable to think that the mean grade point average is the same across the three populations?"

As you can see, the sample means in Excerpt 11.1 turned out to be different from each other. Based on the fact that the $\bar{X}$s in this study were dissimilar, you might be tempted to think that there was an easy answer to the inferential question being posed. However, the concept of sampling error makes it *impossible* to simply look at the sample means, see differences, and then conclude that the population means are also different. Possibly, the population means are identical, with the sample means being dissimilar simply because of sampling error. Or, maybe the discrepancy between the $\bar{X}$s *is* attributable to dissimilarities among the population means. A one-way ANOVA helps researchers to decide, in a scientific manner, whether the sample means are far enough apart to place their eggs into the second of these two possible baskets.

## The Distinction between a One-Way ANOVA and Other Kinds of ANOVA

In this chapter we are focusing our attention on the simplest kind of ANOVA, the kind that is referred to as a **one-way ANOVA,** as a **one-factor ANOVA,** or as a **simple ANOVA.** Since there are many different kinds of analysis variance, it is important to clarify the difference between the kind that we are considering in this chapter and the more complex kinds of ANOVA that will be discussed in later chapters. (Some of the more complex kinds of analysis of variance have the labels "two-way ANOVA," "randomized blocks ANOVA," "repeated measures ANOVA," and "multivariate ANOVA.")

Although all ANOVAs are alike in that they focus on means, they differ in three main respects: the number of independent variables, the number of dependent variables, and whether the samples are independent or correlated. In terms of these distinguishing characteristics, a one-way ANOVA has *one* independent variable, it focuses on *one* dependent variable, and it involves samples that are *independent.* It is worthwhile to consider each of these defining elements of a one-way ANOVA because researchers sometimes use the term *ANOVA* by itself without the clarifying adjective *one-way.*

When we say that there is just one independent variable, this means that the comparison groups differ from one another, prior to the collection and analysis of any data, in one manner that is important to the researcher. The comparison groups can differ in terms of a qualitative variable (e.g., favorite TV show) or in terms of a quantitative variable (e.g., number of siblings) but there can be only one characteristic that defines how the comparison groups differ. Since the terms **factor** and **independent variable** mean the same thing within the context of analysis of variance, this first way in which a one-way ANOVA differs from other ANOVAs can be summed up in this manner: A one-way ANOVA has a single factor (that is, one independent variable).

Excerpt 11.2 comes from a study involving 489 new teachers and teacher trainees in China. The researchers divided these individuals into four groups based on a consideration of each person's "stage" of development as a prospective or new teacher. Stage 1 was for teacher trainees who had completed just the general

### EXCERPT 11.2 • *The Independent and Dependent Variables in a One-Way ANOVA*

A one-way ANOVA was computed to compare the self-estimation across the four levels of professional development. The independent variable was Professional Development Stage (General-Prep Students, Prestudent-Teaching Students, Initial-Licensure Teachers, Inservice Educators). The dependent variable was score on the Basic Computer Skills Survey (of 120 possible).

*Source:* Song, J., Liang, G., Liu, G., Walls, R. T., Li, G., Wang, Z., and Yin, A. H. (2005). Are teachers in China ready to teach in the 21st century? *Journal of Technology and Teacher Education, 13*(2), p. 204.

preparation portion of their educational curriculum; Stage 2 was for teacher trainees who had completed their teaching curriculum but had not yet done any student teaching; Stage 3 was for individuals who had completed all of their training and were about ready to be licensed; Group 4 was for teachers who had just completed their first year of teaching. A one-way ANOVA was used to see if differences existed among these groups in terms of computer skills. As stated in Excerpt 11.2, the independent (i.e., grouping) variable was called professional development stage.

As illustrated by Excerpt 11.2, some researchers will identify explicitly the independent variable associated with their one-way ANOVA. However, many researchers choose not to do this and instead presume that their readers can figure out what the independent variable was based on a description of samples used in the study. By the end of this chapter, I feel confident that you'll have little difficulty identifying the independent variable in any one-way ANOVA you encounter.

As you might suspect, a two-way ANOVA has two independent variables, a three-way ANOVA has three independent variables, and so on. In later chapters, we will consider some of these more complex ANOVAs. In this chapter, however, we will restrict our focus to the kind of ANOVA that has a single independent variable.

Even if there is just one independent variable within a study in which the analysis of variance is applied, the ANOVA may or may not be a one-way ANOVA. The second criterion that distinguishes one-way ANOVAs from many other kinds of ANOVAs has to do with the number of dependent variables involved in the analysis. With a one-way ANOVA, there is always just one dependent variable. (If there are two or more dependent variables involved in the same analysis, then you are likely to see the analysis described as a multivariate ANOVA, or MANOVA.)

The **dependent variable** corresponds to the measured characteristic of people, animals, or things from whom or from which data are gathered. For example, in the study from which Excerpt 11.1 was taken, the dependent variable was the year's grade point average of the grades assigned by professors to students in the business courses. In that excerpt, the table's title lets us know that the dependent variable had to do with grades. In Excerpt 11.2, the researchers came right out and told us what their dependent variable was.

The third distinguishing feature of a one-way ANOVA concerns the fact that the comparison groups are independent (rather than correlated) in nature. As you will recall from the discussion in Chapter 10 of independent versus correlated samples, this means that (1) the people or animals who provide the scores in any given group are different from those who provide data in any other comparison group and (2) there is no connection across comparison groups because of matching or because several triplets or litters were split up (with one member of each family being put into each of the comparison groups). It is possible for an ANOVA to be applied to the data that come from correlated samples, but I will delay my discussion of that form of analysis until later in the book.

In Excerpt 11.3, we see a case in which the researchers refer to their study's independent variable as being the **between-subjects variable.** The adjective *between subjects* is used by researchers when they want to clarify that comparisons are being

### EXCERPT 11.3 • *A Between-Subjects Variable*

To explore the differences among the group means for the various characteristics, we also conducted a one-way analysis of variance (ANOVA) with good teaching (i.e., a composite score of the individual characteristics) as the dependent variable and group (i.e., second graders, preservice teachers, and inservice teachers) as the between-subjects variable.

*Source:* Murphy, P. K., Delli, L. A. M., and Edwards, M. N. (2004). The good teacher and good teaching: Comparing beliefs of second-grade students, preservice teachers, and inservice teachers. *Journal of Experimental Education, 72*(2), p. 79.

made with data that have come from independent samples. (In Chapter 14, you will encounter one-way ANOVAs used in studies where the data come from correlated samples, and you'll see that the independent variables in those studies are considered to be *within subjects* in nature.) Since each of the one-way ANOVAs discussed in this chapter involves data collected from separate groups of individuals who have not been matched in any way, every independent variable we encounter here could be considered to be a between-subjects independent variable.

Now, we turn our attention to the specific components of a one-way ANOVA. We begin that effort with a consideration of the one-way ANOVA's null and alternative hypotheses.

## The One-Way ANOVA's Null and Alternative Hypotheses

The null hypothesis of a one-way ANOVA is always set up to say that the mean score on the dependent variable is the same in each of the populations associated with the study. The null hypothesis is usually written by putting equal signs between a set of $\mu$s, with each $\mu$ representing the mean score within one of the populations. For example, if there were four comparison groups in the study, the null hypothesis would be $H_0: \mu_1 = \mu_2 = \mu_3 = \mu_4$.

If you recall my claim (in Chapter 7) that every null hypothesis must contain a pinpoint parameter, you may now be wondering how the symbolic statement at the end of the preceding paragraph qualifies as a legitimate null hypothesis since it doesn't contain any pinpoint number. In reality, there is a pinpoint number contained in that $H_0$ but it is simply hidden from view. If the population means are all equal to one another, then there is no variability among those means. Therefore, we can bring $H_0$'s pinpoint number into plain view by rewriting the null hypothesis as $H_0: \sigma_\mu^2 = 0$. As we said earlier, however, you are more likely to see $H_0$ written with Greek mus and equal signs and no pinpoint number (e.g., $H_0: \mu_1 = \mu_2 = \mu_3$) rather than with a sigma squared set equal to zero.

## EXCERPTS 11.4–11.5 • *The Null Hypothesis in a One-Way ANOVA*

$H_0$: $\mu_P = \mu_S = \mu_A$

*Source:* Chang, Y. (2006). A study on the motivations of ports seeking to diversify their operations in Taiwan. *Journal of American Academy of Business, 8*(1), p. 109.

----------------------------------------------------------------

A one-way ANOVA was performed [and] indicated that the null hypothesis of equal population means cannot be rejected.

*Source:* Prendergast, G., Shi, Y., and West, D. (2001). Organizational buying and advertising agency-client relationships in China. *Journal of Advertising, 30*(2), p. 66.

In Excerpts 11.4 and 11.5, we see examples of one-way ANOVA null hypotheses that have appeared in research summaries. Notice that these two excerpts are similar in that each null hypothesis deals with its study's population means. Moreover, both null hypotheses have been set up to say that there are no differences among the population means.

The researchers associated with Excerpts 11.4 and 11.5 deserve high praise for taking the time to articulate the null hypothesis associated with their one-way ANOVAs. The vast majority of researchers do not do this. They tell us about the data they collected and what happened in terms of results, but they skip over the important first step of hypothesis testing. Perhaps they assume that readers will know what the null hypothesis was.

In hypothesis testing, of course, the null hypothesis must be accompanied by an alternative hypothesis. This $H_a$ will always say that at least two of the population means differ. Using symbols to express this thought, we get $H_a$: $\sigma_\mu^2 \neq 0$. Unfortunately, the alternative hypothesis is rarely included in technical discussions of research studies. Again, researchers evidently presume that their readers are familiar enough with the testing procedure being applied and familiar enough with what goes on in a one-way ANOVA to know what $H_a$ is without being told.

## *Presentation of Results*

The outcome of a one-way ANOVA is presented in one of two ways. Researchers may elect to talk about the results within the text of their report and to present an ANOVA **summary table.** On the other hand, they may opt to exclude the table from the report and simply describe the outcome in a sentence or two of the text. (At times, a researcher wants to include the table in the report but is told by the journal editor to delete it due to limitations of space.)

Once you become skilled at deciphering the way results are presented within an ANOVA summary table, I am confident that you will have no difficulty interpreting results presented within a "tableless" report. For this reason, I begin each of the next two sections with a consideration of how the results of one-way ANOVAs are typically presented in tables. I have divided this discussion into two sections because some reports contain the results of a single one-way ANOVA while other reports present the results of many one-way ANOVAs.

### Results of a Single One-Way ANOVA

In Excerpt 11.6, we see the ANOVA summary table for the data presented in Excerpt 11.1. As you may recall, that earlier excerpt, and now this new one, come from a study wherein the researchers wanted to know if different kinds of professors (full-time tenured, full-time untenured, and part-time adjunct) assign, on average, the same level of grades to students. You might want to take a quick look at Excerpt 11.1 before proceeding.

**EXCERPT 11.6 • Results from a One-Way ANOVA Presented in a Table**

**TABLE 4   ANOVA Results of Grade Point Average by Faculty Category**

| Source | Sum of squares | df | MS | F | p |
|---|---|---|---|---|---|
| Between groups | 0.201 | 2 | 0.100 | 8.209 | .001 |
| Within groups | 0.697 | 57 | 0.012 | | |
| Total | 0.898 | 59 | | | |

Source: Kezim, B., Pariseau, S. E., and Quinn, F. (2005). Is grade inflation related to faculty status? *Journal of Education for Business, 80*(6), p. 360.

In Excerpt 11.6, the number 8.209 is the calculated value, and it is positioned in the column labeled *F*. That calculated value was obtained by dividing the **mean square** (*MS*) on the "Between groups" row of the table (0.100) by the mean square on the "Within groups" row of the table (0.012). Each row's *MS* value was derived by dividing that row's sum of squares (*SS*) value by its *df* value.[1] Those *SS* values came from an analysis of the sample data. The *df* values, on the other hand, came from simply counting the number of groups, the number of people within each group, and the total number of participants—with 1 subtracted from each number to obtain the *df* values presented in the table.[2]

The first two *df* values determined the size of the critical value against which 8.209 was compared. (That critical value, at the .05 level of significance, was equal to 3.16.) Most likely, a computer used the *df* values of 2 and 57 to determine the critical

[1]A mean square is never computed for the total row of a one-way ANOVA or for the total row of any other kind of ANOVA.

[2]The within *df* was computed first by subtracting 1 from each of the three sample sizes, and then by adding the three $n - 1$ values.

value, and then the computer said that $p$ was smaller than .001. It's possible, however, that the researcher used the two $df$ values to look up the size of the critical value in a statistical table located in the back of a statistics book. Such tables allow researchers to see how big the critical values are at the .05, .01, and .001 levels of significance.

Whereas the $df$ numbers in a one-way ANOVA have a technical and theoretical meaning (dealing with things called central and noncentral $F$ distributions), those $df$ numbers can be useful to *you* in a very practical fashion. To be more specific, you can use the first and the third $df$ to help you understand the structure of a completed study. To show you how this is done, let's focus on Excerpts 11.6 and 11.1. By adding 1 to the between groups $df$, you can determine, or verify, there were $2 + 1 = 3$ groups in this study. By adding 1 to the total $df$, you can figure out that there were $59 + 1 = 60$ professors who had their "grade point averages" used as data in this study.

One other feature of Excerpt 11.6 is worth noting. In the far right-hand column, the researchers report that the probability associated with their calculated $F$ value was .001. This small decimal number most likely was *not* the researchers' level of significance. In their article, the researchers did not indicate their alpha level. Nevertheless, I would guess that they started out with $\alpha = .05$. They then followed the practice (discussed earlier in Chapter 8) of reporting $p$-levels that are precise and that show the degree to which the sample data are inconsistent with the null hypothesis. By reporting $p < .001$, the researchers are saying that the three population means, if identical, would have been *very* unlikely to yield sample means as dissimilar as those actually associated with this study's three comparison groups.

In Excerpt 11.7, we see a one-way ANOVA summary table from a different research report. The ANOVA summary table here resembles the one you saw in Excerpt 11.6, except here the column of $df$ values is positioned as the first (rather than the second) column of numbers. Also note that no row for "Total" appears at the bottom of the table. Consequently, if you want to determine how many people were involved as research participants in the study associated with Excerpt 11.7, you need to add together the $df$ values for the "Between" and "Within" rows ($2 + 27 = 29$ total $df$) and then add 1 ($29 + 1 = 30$ participants).

## EXCERPT 11.7 • *Another Set of Results for a One-Way ANOVA*

**TABLE 4**  *ANOVA for Delayed L2 Word Retrieval*

| Source | df | SS | MS | F |
|---|---|---|---|---|
| Between | 2 | 84.867 | 42.433 | 6.027* |
| Within | 27 | 190.10 | 7.041 | |

*$p < 0.01$

*Source:* de la Fuente, M. J. (2006). Classroom L2 vocabulary acquisition: Investigating the role of pedagogical tasks and form-based instruction. *Language Teaching Research, 10*(3), p. 277.

In the two ANOVA summary tables displayed in Excerpts 11.6 and 11.7, the second row of numbers was labeled "Within groups" and "Within," respectively. I would be remiss if I did not warn you that a variety of terms are used by different researchers to label this row of a one-way ANOVA summary table. On occasion, you are likely to see this row referred to as *Error, Residual,* or *Subjects within groups.* Do not let these alternative labels throw you for a loop. If everything else about the table is similar to the two tables we have just examined, then you should presume that the table you are looking at is a one-way ANOVA summary table.

Because the calculated *F*-value and the *p*-value are considered by most researchers to be the two most important numbers in a one-way ANOVA summary table, those values will sometimes be pulled out of the summary table and included in a table containing the comparison group means and standard deviations. By doing this, space is saved in the research report because only one table is needed rather than two. Had this been done in Excerpt 11.1, a note might have appeared beneath Table 1 saying "$F(2, 57) = 8.209, p < .001$." Since this note indicates the *df* for between groups and within groups, you could use these numbers to determine how many people were involved in the study if the sample sizes are not included in the table. A note like this will not contain *SS* or *MS* values, but you really don't need them to understand the study's structure or its results.

Although the results of a one-way ANOVA are sometimes presented in a table similar to those we have just considered, more often the outcome of the statistical analysis simply will be talked about in the text of the report, with no table included. In Excerpts 11.8 and 11.9, we see two illustrations of a one-way ANOVA being summarized in one or two sentences.

These two excerpts are similar in that each one indicates what the independent and dependent variables were. In Excerpt 11.8, the independent variable was

**EXCERPTS 11.8–11.9 • *Results of One-Way ANOVAs Discussed in the Text of the Research Report***

One-way analysis of variance (ANOVA) indicated that [there were] no significant differences in general SRL between the four methods of instruction, $F(3, 82) = 2.36$, $p > .05$.

*Source:* Kramarski, B., and Mizrachi, N. (2006). Online discussion and self-regulated learning: Effects of instructional methods on mathematical literacy. *Journal of Educational Research, 99*(4), p. 225.

--------------------------------------------------------------

The three diagnostic groups differed significantly on levels of anxiety as measured by the SCAS total score, $F(2, 90) = 10.89, p < .05$.

*Source:* Farrugia, S., and Hudson, J. (2006). Anxiety in adolescents with Asperger Syndrome: Negative thoughts, behavioral problems, and life interference. *Focus on Autism and Other Developmental Disabilities, 21*(1), p. 29.

instructional method, because that's how the comparison groups differed prior to the collection of the study's data. The dependent variable was represented by the data. Those data were scores on the general SRL. In Excerpt 11.9, the independent and dependent variables were diagnostic group and anxiety level, respectively. The two excerpts are also similar in that each one indicates, through words and *p*s, what happened to the null hypothesis. Finally, each excerpt contains the one-way ANOVA's calculated value. Those calculated values were 2.36 and 10.89.

Excerpts 11.8 and 11.9 are also similar in that two numbers appear in parentheses next to each *F*. These are the *df* values taken from the between groups and within groups rows of the one-way ANOVA summary table. By adding 1 to the first of these *df* values, you can verify or determine how many groups were compared. To figure out or verify how many people were involved in each study, you must add the two *df* values together and then add 1 to the sum. Thus the studies associated with these two excerpts were based on 86 and 93 individuals, respectively.

## Results of Two or More One-Way ANOVAs

Data are often collected on two or more dependent variables in studies characterized by at least three comparison groups, a concern for means, and a single independent variable. Although such data sets can be analyzed in various ways, many researchers choose to conduct a separate one-way ANOVA for each of the multiple dependent variables. Accordingly, we ought to look at some of the different ways researchers present their results when more than one one-way ANOVA has been conducted.

In Excerpt 11.10, we see a table that contains the results of two separate one-way ANOVAs. Since the column headings in this table are nearly identical to those you saw earlier in Excerpts 11.6 and 11.7, and since the row labels for each of these two ANOVAs are also familiar (Between Groups and Within Groups), you ought to

**EXCERPT 11.10** • *Results of Two One-Way ANOVAs Combined in One Table*

**TABLE 2** *One-Way ANOVA for Communication of Benefits*

| Source | Sum of Squares | df | Mean Square | F | p |
|---|---|---|---|---|---|
| **TRADITIONAL** | | | | | |
| Between groups | 1.88 | 2 | .94 | 5.25 | .01 |
| Within Groups | 75.38 | 421 | .18 | | |
| Total | 77.26 | 423 | | | |
| **NONTRADITIONAL** | | | | | |
| Between groups | 1.98 | 2 | .99 | 3.21 | .04 |
| Within Groups | 130.16 | 422 | .31 | | |
| Total | 132.14 | 424 | | | |

*Source:* Jennings, M., Werbel, J. D., and Power, M. L. (2003). The impact of benefits on graduating student willingness to accept job offers. *Journal of Business Communication, 40*(4), p. 297.

have little or no difficulty determining that (1) the means of three samples were compared in each of these ANOVAs and (2) each analysis involved data from over 400 research participants.

Before leaving Excerpt 11.10, I'd like to point out something important that holds true for any presentation of results that contains the statistical outcome of two or more statistical tests. In such a presentation, a distinct null hypothesis is associated with each outcome that turned out to be either statistically significant or statistically nonsignificant. Hence, two null hypotheses were connected to Excerpt 11.10. Each null hypothesis would look the same on the surface: $H_0: \mu_1 = \mu_2 = \mu_3$. They differed, however, with respect to the data represented by the $\mu$s.

In the study associated with Excerpt 11.10, business students were asked to fill out a questionnaire containing a variety of potential benefits associated with a new job. Some of the benefits were "traditional" (such as medical insurance) while others (such as membership in an offsite fitness center) were "nontraditional." Each student rated each benefit on a 4-point Likert scale to indicate its likely impact on accepting a job offer. The three samples of this study came into existence because the business students were randomly assigned to one of three forms of the survey. These forms differed in the degree of information provided about the benefits. Thus, the study's independent variable was connected to the three forms of the questionnaire, and we could think of that independent variable as "Amount of Information Provided."

Now that you understand what went on in the study associated with Excerpt 11.10, let's again consider the null hypotheses. For the first one-way ANOVA, dealing with traditional benefits, the first $\overline{X}$ is related to the data collected on traditional benefits from those students who received the low-detail version of the questionnaire. If you focus your thoughts on the population of individuals represented by the sample of research participants who received the low-detail questionnaire, then $\mu_1$ is the mean rating that would be given to traditional benefits by that population. The other two means in the null hypothesis, $\mu_2$ and $\mu_3$, should be thought of in a similar fashion. The three $\mu$s in the second null hypothesis, dealing with non-traditional benefits, should be thought of in the same manner.

Now consider Excerpt 11.11. The table in this excerpt presents the results of three one-way ANOVAs, each conducted on the data associated with one of the scales listed on the left side of the table. The data for these ANOVAs came from female juniors and seniors in college majoring in three kinds of disciplines: male-dominated fields, female-dominated fields, and "gender-balanced" fields. The women in this study responded to several questions focused on the experience of gender discrimination using a 4-point scale where 1 and 4 meant "never" or "often," respectively. In Excerpt 11.11, note that there are no *SS* or *MS* values presented for any of the ANOVAs.

In many research reports, the results of more than one one-way ANOVA are presented without any ANOVA summary table(s). We now turn our attention to an example where multiple one-way ANOVA results are discussed in the text of the report. Excerpt 11.12 illustrates this common reporting technique. As you read through this passage, you ought to be able to determine (1) how many null

**EXCERPT 11.11 • A Table with Results from Three One-Way ANOVAs without Sums of Squares or Mean Squares**

**TABLE 1**  *Differences in Student Behavior Scales According to Gender Enrollment Patterns of Students*

| | Gender Enrollment Patterns | | | | |
|---|---|---|---|---|---|
| Scale | Female Majority M (SD) n | Male Majority M (SD) n | Male/Female Enrollment M (SD) n | df Between/ Within Groups | F |
| Behaviors of Male Classmates | 1.84 (.64) 124 | 2.13 (.58) 123 | 2.01 (.57) 84 | 2/328 | 7.21* |
| Silencing Behaviors | 1.85 (.61) 122 | 1.72 (.60) 112 | 1.88 (.76) 71 | 2/302 | 1.73 |
| Sexually Offensive Behaviors | 1.91 (.72) 137 | 1.83 (.62) 121 | 1.87 (.67) 78 | 2/333 | .472 |

*Note:* Students were given a 4-point scale (1 = never; 2 = rarely; 3 = sometimes; and 4 = often) to rate the frequency with which they experienced the behaviors.

$*p < .001$

*Source:* Allan, E., and Madden, M. (2006). Chilly classrooms for female undergraduate students: A question of method? *Journal of Higher Education, 77*(4), p. 693.

**EXCERPT 11.12 • Results of Several One-Way ANOVAs Presented in the Text**

Practitioners from a variety of EI [early intervention] disciplines were represented in the sample, which consisted of service coordinators ($n = 9$), occupational therapists ($n = 14$), physical therapists ($n = 20$), speech-language pathologists ($n = 11$), early childhood teachers ($n = 15$), and others (including nurses, supervisors, and social workers; $n = 9$). . . . Based on a one-way analysis of variance (ANOVA), group differences between the disciplines were found to be statistically significant on each factor of the ATCS: Use and Application, $F(5, 72) = 3.49, p < .01$; Accessing Information/Support, $F(5, 71) = 2.55, p < .05$; and Assessment, $F(5, 72) = 5.82$, $p < .01$.

*Source:* Moore, H. W., and Wilcox, M. J. (2006). Characteristics of early intervention practitioners and their confidence in the use of assistive technology. *Topics in Early Childhood Special Education, 26*(1), pp. 17, 20.

hypotheses were tested, (2) what decision was made regarding each $H_0$, (3) what the dependent variables were, (4) how many comparison groups were involved in each analysis, and (5) how many individuals were in the study.

### The Bonferroni Adjustment Technique

In the preceding section, we looked at three examples where separate one-way ANOVAs were used to assess the data from multiple dependent variables. When a researcher has a situation such as this, there will be an inflated Type I error risk unless something is done to compensate for the fact that multiple tests are being conducted. In other words, if the data associated with each of several dependent variables are analyzed separately by means of a one-way ANOVA, the probability of incorrectly rejecting at least one of the null hypotheses is greater than the common alpha level used across the set of tests. (If you have forgotten what I mean by an inflated Type I error risk, return to Chapter 8 and read again the little story about the two gamblers, dice, and the bet about rolling, or not rolling, a six.)

Several statistical techniques are available for dealing with the problem of an inflated Type I error risk. Among these, the **Bonferroni adjustment procedure** appears to be the most popular choice among applied researchers. As you will recall from our earlier consideration of this procedure, the researcher compensates for the fact that multiple tests are being conducted by making the alpha level more rigorous on each of the separate tests.

In Excerpt 11.13, we see an example of the Bonferroni technique being used in a study where nine one-way ANOVAs were used, one for each of the different dependent variables involved in the study. In this excerpt and in most other applications of the Bonferroni adjustment, the desired studywide alpha level is divided by the number of tests being conducted, and then that revised alpha becomes the common criterion against which each test's $p$ is compared. In Excerpt 11.13, the researchers wanted the Type I error risk for their set of nine one-way ANOVAs to be no greater than .05. Therefore, they divided .05 by nine and then rounded off the result to .005. This revised alpha level then became the criterion for evaluating the

### EXCERPT 11.13 • *The Bonferroni Adjustment Used in Conjunction with a One-Way ANOVA*

Nine one-way between-groups analysis of variance (ANOVAs) were conducted to examine differences across orientation grouping on the perceived benefits of exercise. These analyses used an adjusted probability value of p = .005 to reduce risk of Type I error.

*Source:* Zizzi, S. J., Keeler, L. A., and Watson II, J. C. (2006). The interaction of goal orientation and stage of change on exercise behavior in college students. *Journal of Sport Behavior, 29*(1), p. 102.

*p*-level produced by each of the individual ANOVAs. Most researchers use the Bonferroni procedure in this fashion.

If a researcher considers certain of the study's dependent variables to be of primary concern while other dependent variables are viewed as being of secondary concern, the Bonferroni procedure may be used with a slight twist. Instead of using the same reduced alpha level to evaluate the results of all tests, the researcher has the option of varying the degree to which the alpha level is reduced for the different tests being conducted. Suppose, for example, that a researcher conducts a study in which a one-way ANOVA is applied separately to each of four dependent variables. Instead of setting alpha at .0125 for each of these tests, the researcher could conduct the two primary tests with $\alpha = .02$ and conduct the two secondary tests with $\alpha = .005$. (Using this varying-alpha version of the Bonferroni procedure gives the researcher more power on those tests deemed to be of greater importance.) Any combination of alphas is permitted so long as the sum of the separate alphas does not exceed the desired studywide Type I error risk.

There is no law, of course, that directs all researchers to deal with the problem of an inflated Type I error risk when multiple one-way ANOVAs are used, each with a different dependent variable. Furthermore, there are circumstances where it would be unwise to take any form of corrective action. Nevertheless, I believe that you should value more highly those reports wherein the researcher either (1) does something (e.g., uses the Bonferroni procedure) to hold down the chances of a Type I error when multiple tests are conducted or (2) explains why nothing was done to deal with the inflated Type I error risk. If neither of these things is done, you have a right to downgrade your evaluation of the study.

## Assumptions of a One-Way ANOVA

In Chapter 10, we considered the four main assumptions associated with *t*-tests, *F*-tests, and *z*-tests: independence, randomness, normality, and homogeneity of variance. My earlier comments apply as much now to cases in which a one-way ANOVA is used to compare three or more means as they did to cases in which two means are compared using a *t*-, *F*-, or *z*-test. In particular, I hope you recall the meaning of these four assumptions and my point about how these tests are robust to the equal variance assumption when the sample sizes of the various comparison groups are equal.

Many researchers who use a one-way ANOVA seem to pay little or no attention to the assumptions that underlie the *F*-test comparison of their sample means. Consequently, I encourage you to feel better about research reports that (1) contain discussions of the assumptions, (2) present results of tests that were conducted to check on the testable assumptions, (3) explain what efforts were made to get the data in line with the assumptions, and/or (4) point out that an alternative test having fewer assumptions than a regular one-way ANOVA *F*-test was used. Conversely, I encourage you to lower your evaluation of research reports that do none of these things.

Take a look at Excerpt 11.14. In this study, the researchers used a one-way ANOVA. Before doing so, however, they screened their data in to see if the normality assumption was tenable. It is not clear what "preliminary analyses" were used to detect the skewness in the data. Perhaps this was done by means of a visual inspection of the data or by the computation of an index of skewness. The researchers are clear, however, in saying that a "normal probability plot" indicated that the normality assumption was violated. Because of this, they transformed their data. After doing this, the researchers evidently rechecked the normality assumption, for they say that the transformation "rectified these problems."

### EXCERPT 11.14 • *Testing for Normality*

One-way analyses of variance (ANOVA) were performed. . . . Preliminary analyses indicated that the distributions of positioning errors [i.e., scores that served as each ANOVA's dependent variable] were positively skewed, and a normal probability plot indicated that the variables failed to meet the assumption of normality. Performing log transforms on the dependant variables from these tests rectified these problems.

*Source:* Kristjansson E., Dall'Alba, P., and Jull, G. (2003). A study of five cervicocephalic relocation tests in three different subject groups. *Clinical Rehabilitation, 17*(7), p. 771.

The researchers associated with Excerpt 11.14 set a good example by demonstrating a concern for the normality of their populations. Unfortunately, most researchers give no indication that they thought about the **normality assumption.** Perhaps they are under the mistaken belief that the *F*-test is always robust to violations of this assumption. Or perhaps they simply are unaware of the assumption. In any event, I salute the researchers associated with Excerpt 11.14 for checking their data before conducting a one-way ANOVA.

Excerpt 11.15 illustrates how the **homogeneity of variance assumption** can be tested. Notice that the results of this probe were nonsignificant. This is what the researchers were hoping would happen when they tested this assumption. They

Research
Navigator.c⊛m

Homogeneity of
variance
assumption

### EXCERPT 11.15 • *Testing the Equal Variance Assumption*

The GMNH, GMH, and HC groups had mean full-scale *T* scores of 41.2 ($s = 4.5$), 46.1 ($s = 11.1$), and 44.9 ($s = 14.4$), respectively. Although the variances appear different from each other in the descriptive data, the Levene's Test of Equality of Error Variances revealed that the homogeneity-of-variance assumption was met ($F(2, 40) = 2.33, p = .11$). The groups were compared [in terms of their means] using a one-way analysis of variance (ANOVA), and they did not significantly differ from each other at the .05 alpha level.

*Source:* Boyle, S. W., Church, W. T., Byrnes, E. C., and Byrnes, E. (2005). Migraine headaches and anger. *Best Practice in Mental Health: An International Journal, 1*(1), p. 54.

wanted to retain the null hypothesis of equal population variances so they could move forward and compare their sample means with a one-way ANOVA.

Sometimes, preliminary checks on normality and the equal variance assumption suggest that the populations are not normal and/or have unequal variances. When this happens, researchers have three options. They can (1) identify and eliminate outliers, presuming that such scores are the source of the problem, (2) transform their sample data in an effort to reduce nonnormality and/or stabilize the variances, or (3) switch from the one-way ANOVA $F$-test to some other test that does not have such rigorous assumptions. In Excerpts 11.16 and 11.17, we see cases in which researchers employed the second and third of these options, respectively.

### EXCERPTS 11.16–11.17 • *Options When Assumptions Seem Untenable*

We found inequality of variances of all [dolphin] whistle parameters except Beginning Frequency ($F = 2.05$, d.f. $= 2$, $P = 0.13$) among three populations by Bartlett's test for homogeneity of variances. We then transformed all whistle parameters to near normality by a Box-Cox transformation. . . . One-way ANOVA was used for comparisons of all whistle parameters after transformation.

*Source:* Morisaka, T., Shinohara, M., Nakahara, F., and Akamatsu, T. (2005). Geographic variations in the whistles among three Indo-Pacific bottlenose dolphin Tursiops aduncus populations in Japan. *Fisheries Science, 71*(3), p. 569.

-------------------------------------------------------------------------------------------------

A Bartlett's test . . . suggested that the differences among the standard deviations for the groups were significant. Thus, a non-parametric ANOVA (Kruskal-Wallis test) was performed. . . .

*Source:* de la Fuente, M. J. (2006). Classroom L2 vocabulary acquisition: Investigating the role of pedagogical tasks and form-focused instruction. *Language Teaching Research, 10*(3), p. 278.

Of the four assumptions associated with a one-way ANOVA, the one that is neglected most often is the **independence assumption.** In essence, this assumption says that a particular person's score should not be influenced by the measurement of any other people or by what happens to others in the execution phase of the study. This assumption would be violated if different groups of students (perhaps different intact classrooms) are taught differently, with each student's exam score being used in the analysis.

In studies where groups are a necessary feature of the investigation, the recommended way to adhere to the independence assumption is to have the **unit of analysis** (i.e., the scores that are analyzed) be each group's mean rather than the scores from the individuals in the group. In Excerpt 11.18, we see a case in which a team of researchers did just this. In their study, data were gathered from 351 third-grade children spread out across 24 classrooms. Instead of putting each student's

Research
Navigator.c✦m

Unit of analysis

**EXCERPT 11.18** • *The Unit of Analysis*

Twenty-four third-grade teachers from seven urban schools volunteered to participate. Stratifying so that each condition was represented approximately equally in
each school, we randomly assigned 8 teachers to each condition: control, SBTI, and
expanded SBTI. . . . Student participants were the 351 children in these classrooms
who were present for each of the pretests and posttests. . . . Because teachers were
assigned randomly to conditions, we used teacher as the unit of analysis. . . .

*Source:* Fuchs, L. S., Fuchs, D., Finelli, R., Courey, S. J., and Hamlett, C. L. (2004). Expand-
ing schema-based transfer instruction to help third graders solve real-life mathematical problems. *American Educational Research Journal, 41*(2), pp. 425, 433.

scores into the ANOVAs that were conducted to compare three different kinds of
instruction, the data that went into those analyses were the classroom means, one
per teacher. This was the proper thing to do, because scores that come from students
who are together in a classroom together cannot be considered to be independent.

## Statistical Significance versus Practical Significance

Researchers who use a one-way ANOVA can do any of three things to make their
studies more statistically sophisticated than would be the case if they use the crude
six-step version of hypothesis testing. The first two options involve doing something
after the sample data have been collected and analyzed to obtain the *F*-ratio. Here,
the researcher can either estimate the **effect size** or conduct a **post hoc power analysis.** The third option involves doing something on the front end of the study, not the
tail end. With this option, the researcher can conduct an **a priori power analysis.**

Unfortunately, only a minority of the researchers who use a one-way ANOVA
take the time to perform any form of analysis designed to address the issue of
**practical versus statistical significance.** In my opinion, too many researchers simply use the simplest version of hypothesis testing to test their one-way ANOVA's
$H_0$. They collect the amount of data that time, money, or energy will allow, and then
they anxiously await the outcome of the analysis. If their *F*-ratios turn out significant, these researchers quickly summarize their studies, with emphasis put on the
fact that "significant findings" have been obtained.

I encourage you to upgrade your evaluation of those one-way ANOVA
research reports in which the researchers demonstrate that they were concerned
about practical significance as well as statistical significance. Examples of such
concern appear in Excerpts 11.19, 11.20, and 11.21. In each case, the effect size
associated with the ANOVA was estimated. As you can see, the effect size measures
used in these studies were partial eta squared, omega squared, and Cohen's *f.*

In Excerpts 11.19 and 11.20, notice the terms "medium effect size" and "large
effect." The researchers used these terms in an effort to interpret their effect size
estimates. Most likely, they used the relevant information in Table 11.1 as a guide when

## EXCERPTS 11.19–11.21 • *Estimating the Effect Size*

A one-way ANOVA contrasted the overall mean scores of the two elementary and one middle school included in the sample, with effect size measured by partial eta squared $(\eta_p^2)$. . . . Results indicate significant differences across the three schools, $F(2,77) = 3,927$, $p < .05$, $\eta_p^2 = .09$, reflecting a medium effect size (Cohen, 1987).

*Source:* Safran, S. P. (2006). Using the effective behavior supports survey to guide development of schoolwide positive behavior support. *Journal of Positive Behavior Interventions, 8*(1), p. 6.

----

For the first set of analyses, we conducted a series of one-way analyses of variance (ANOVAs) with type of transcript read by participants used as an independent variable. Participants' ratings . . . varied depending on which transcript participants read: $F(2, 171) = 10.30$, $MSE = 2.68$, $\omega^2 = .10$; $F(2, 171) = 9.70$, $MSE = 1.99$, $\omega^2 = .09$; $F(2, 171) = 14.45$, $MSE = 2.45$, $\omega^2 = .14$. The omega-squared values indicate that, on average, manipulating the type of transcript read by participants had a large effect (Cohen, 1988).

*Source:* Lampinen, J. M., Judges, D. P., Odegard, T. N., and Hamilton, S. (2005). The reactions of mock jurors to the Department of Justice guidelines for the collection and preservation of eyewitness evidence. *Basic & Applied Social Psychology, 27*(2), p. 159.

----

A one-way ANOVA carried out on the performance data from the RSVP task in Experiments 1–5 revealed no significant difference in performance on this concurrent primary task across all the five experiments for either the percentages of correct responses, $F(4, 59) = 2.13$, $MSE = 133.3$, *ns*, Cohen's $f = 0.18$, or the RT data, $F(4, 59) = 0.80$, $MSE = 2558$, *ns*, Cohen's $f = 0.11$.

*Source:* Ho, C., and Spence, C., (2005). Assessing the effectiveness of various auditory cues in capturing a driver's visual attention. *Journal of Experimental Psychology: Applied, 11*(3), p. 169.

----

**TABLE 11.1**   *Effect Size Criteria for a One-Way ANOVA*

| Effect Size Measure | Small | Medium | Large |
|---|---|---|---|
| Eta $(\eta)$ | .10 | .24 | .37 |
| Eta Squared $(\eta^2)$ | .01 | .06 | .14 |
| Omega Squared $(\omega^2)$ | .01 | .06 | .14 |
| Partial Eta Squared $(\eta_p^2)$ | .01 | .06 | .14 |
| Partial Omega Squared $(\omega_p^2)$ | .01 | .06 | .14 |
| Cohen's $f$ | .10 | .25 | .40 |

*Note:* These standards for judging relationship strength are quite general and should be changed to fit the unique goals of any given research investigation.

trying to judge whether the estimated effect size number deserved the label "small" or "medium" or "large." (This table does not include any information about $d$, for this measure of effect size cannot be used when three or more means are compared.)

In Excerpt 11.22, we see an example of a post hoc power analysis following their one-way ANOVA. Notice how the power turned out to be far under the desired minimum level of .80. Because of that finding, the researchers say that they could not "assert the validity of the null hypothesis." If this study's sample sizes had been larger, statistical power would have been higher. So a good question to direct toward the researchers is simply this, "Why didn't you think of power before rather than after you collected and analyzed your data?"

In Excerpt 11.23, we see a case in which a team of researchers performed a power analysis to determine the needed sample size for their one-way ANOVA. In this excerpt, notice that the researcher had to specify an effect size and a desired

### EXCERPT 11.22 • *Post Hoc Power Analysis*

The one-way ANOVA on knowledge acquisition did not find significant differences across the five conditions, $F(4, 45) = 2.39$, $ns$, $MSE = .48$, Cohen's $f = .46$. With the current sample size, the probability of rejecting the null hypothesis, where there is a large effect (Cohen's $f = .40$ according to Cohen, 1977), is only .56. Therefore, although the groups did not differ significantly, we cannot assert the validity of the null hypothesis, as power is not equal to or greater than .80 (Cohen, 1977).

*Source:* Charman, S. C., and Howes, A. (2003). The adaptive user: An investigation into the cognitive and task constraints on the generation of new methods. *Journal of Experimental Psychology: Applied, 9*(4), p. 244.

### EXCERPT 11.23 • *Determining the Needed Sample Size*

We distributed these transcripts to a convenience sample of 150 participants drawn from a basic undergraduate course at a large university in the Southwestern U.S. In selecting this sample size, our assumptions were that there should be apparent differences between computer generated and human generated transcripts, and that the differences should become more clear with additional text for comparison. Assuming a moderate-to-strong effect size ($f = .325$) and three treatment groups with $\alpha = .05$, $n = 150$ provides power $> 0.95$ (based on calculations by GPOWER; Erdfelder, Faul, & Buchner, 1996). . . . To test for the effects of transcript length, we analyzed ratings for computer generated transcripts and human-group transcripts with separate one-way ANOVAs, with transcript size as the treatment.

*Source:* Corman, S. R., and Kuhn, T. (2005). The detectability of socio-egocentric group speech: A quasi-Turing test. *Communication Monographs, 72*(2), p. 126.

power level in order to determine the sample size. These three things—*f*, power, and *n*—represent the middle three elements of the nine-step version of the hypothesis testing procedure that we considered earlier in Chapter 8.

# Cautions

Before concluding this chapter, I want to offer a few tips that will increase your skills at deciphering and critiquing research reports based on one-way ANOVAs.

## Significant and Nonsignificant Results from One-Way ANOVAs

When researchers say that they have obtained a statistically significant result from a one-way ANOVA, this means that they have rejected the null hypothesis. Because you are unlikely to see the researchers articulate the study's $H_0$ (in words or symbols) or even see them use the term *null hypothesis* in discussing the results, it is especially important for you to remember (1) that a significant $F$ means $H_0$ has been rejected, (2) what the one-way ANOVA $H_0$ stipulates, and (3) how to interpret correctly the decision to reject $H_0$.

Although a one-way ANOVA can be used to compare the means of two groups, this chapter has focused on the use of one-way ANOVAs to compare three or more means. If the data lead to a significant finding when more than two means have been contrasted, it means that the sample data are not likely to have come from populations having the same $\mu$. This one-way ANOVA result does not provide any information as to how many of the $\mu$ values are likely to be dissimilar, nor does it provide any information as to whether any specific pair of populations are likely to have different $\mu$ values. The only thing that a significant result indicates is that the variability among the full set of sample means is larger than would be expected if all population means were identical.

Usually, a researcher wants to know more about the likely state of the population means than is revealed by a one-way ANOVA. To be more specific, the typical researcher wants to be able to make comparative statements about pairs of population means, such as "$\mu_1$ is likely to be larger than $\mu_2$ but $\mu_2$ and $\mu_3$ cannot be looked on as different based on the sample data." To address these concerns, the researcher must move past the significant ANOVA $F$ and apply a subsequent analysis. In the next chapter, we will consider such analyses, which are called, understandably, post hoc or follow-up tests.

Since you probably will be given information regarding the means that were compared by the one-way ANOVA, you may be tempted, if a significant result has been obtained, to consider each mean to be significantly different from every other mean. Refrain!

To gain an understanding of this very important point, consider once again Excerpt 11.11. In that excerpt, the results of three one-way ANOVAs are presented along with the three sample means compared by each ANOVA. The three means compared in the first one-way ANOVA were 1.84, 2.13, and 2.01, and the $F$-test yielded statistical significance. This result indicates that the null hypothesis of equal population means was rejected. Hence, it is legitimate to think that $H_0: \mu_1 = \mu_2 = \mu_3$ is not true. However, it is *not* legitimate to look at the first row of results in Excerpt 11.11 and think that the mean of 1.84 is significantly different from 2.01, or to think that the mean of 2.01 is significantly different from 2.13. A one-way ANOVA simply does not provide such information.[3]

You must also be on guard when it comes to one-way ANOVAs that yield non-significant $F$s. As I have pointed out now on several occasions, a fail-to-reject decision should not be interpreted to mean that $H_0$ is true. Unfortunately, many researchers make this inferential mistake when comparison groups are compared in terms of mean scores on a pretest. The researchers' goal is to see whether the comparison groups are equal to one another at the beginning of their studies, and they mistakenly interpret a nonsignificant $F$-test to mean that no group began with an advantage or a disadvantage.

One-way ANOVAs, of course, can produce a nonsignificant $F$-value when groups are compared on things other than a pretest. Consider once again Excerpt 11.11. The second of the three ANOVAs (where the dependent variable was silencing behaviors) yielded a nonsignificant $F$ of 1.73. Similarly, the third ANOVA (dealing with sexually offensive behaviors) turned out to be nonsignificant. These two results should *not* be interpreted to mean that students like those involved in this study—female undergraduate juniors and seniors—perceive the same level of silencing and sexually offensive behaviors, from other students, regardless of the gender composition of the course being taken. In other words, neither you nor the researchers who conducted this study should draw the conclusion that $\mu_1 = \mu_2 = \mu_3$ because the $p$-value associated with the ANOVA $F$ turned out to be larger than the selected level of significance. A one-way ANOVA, if nonsignificant, cannot be used to justify such an inference.

### Confidence Intervals

In Chapter 10, you saw how a confidence interval can be placed around the difference between two sample means. You also saw how such confidence intervals can be used to test a null hypothesis, with $H_0$ rejected if the null's pinpoint numerical value lies beyond the limits of the interval. As we now conclude our consideration of how researchers compare three or more means with a one-way ANOVA, you may be wondering why I haven't said anything in this chapter about the techniques of estimation.

When a study's focus is on three or more means, researchers will occasionally build a confidence interval around each of the separate sample means. This is done in situations where (1) there is no interest in comparing all the means together at one time or (2) there is a desire to probe the data in a more specific fashion after the null hypothesis of equal population means has been rejected. Whereas researchers some-

[3]Surprisingly, a significant $F$ does not necessarily indicate that a statistically significant difference exists between the largest and smallest sample means.

times use interval estimation (on individual means) in lieu of or as a complement to a test of the hypothesis that all $\mu$s are equal, they do not use interval estimation as an alternative strategy for testing the one-way ANOVA null hypothesis. Stated differently, you are not likely to come across research studies where a confidence interval is put around the variance of the sample means in order to test $H_0: \sigma_\mu^2 = 0$.

## Other Things to Keep in Mind

If we momentarily lump together the current chapter with the ones that preceded it, it is clear that you have been given a slew of tips or warnings designed to help you become a more discerning recipient of research-based claims. Several of the points are important enough to repeat here.

**1.** The mean is focused on in research studies more than any other statistical concept. In many studies, however, a focus on means does not allow the research question to be answered because the question deals with something other than central tendency.

**2.** If the researcher's interest resides exclusively in the group(s) from which data are collected, only descriptive statistics should be used in analyzing the data.

**3.** The reliability and validity of the researcher's data are worth considering. To the extent that reliability is lacking, it is difficult to reject $H_0$ even when $H_0$ is false. To the extent that validity is lacking, the conclusions drawn will be unwarranted because of a mismatch between what is truly being measured and what the researcher thinks is being measured with a one-way ANOVA.

**4.** With a one-way ANOVA, nothing is proven regardless of what the researcher concludes after analyzing the data. Either a Type I error or a Type II error always will be possible no matter what decision is made about $H_0$.

**5.** The purpose of a one-way ANOVA is to gain an insight into the population means, not the sample means.

**6.** Those researchers who talk about (and possibly test) the assumptions underlying a one-way ANOVA deserve credit for being careful in their utilization of this inferential technique.

**7.** A decision not to reject the one-way ANOVA's $H_0$ does not mean that all population means should be considered equal.

**8.** Those researchers who perform a power analysis (either before or after conducting their one-way ANOVAs) or compute effect size indices (following the application of a one-way ANOVA) are doing a more conscientious job than are those researchers who fail to do anything to help distinguish between statistical significance and practical significance.

**9.** The Bonferroni procedure helps to control the risk of Type I errors in studies where one-way ANOVAs are conducted on two or more dependent variables.

**10.** The *df* values associated with a one-way ANOVA (whether presented in an ANOVA summary table or positioned next to the calculated *F*-value in the text of the research report) can be used to determine the number of groups and the total number of subjects involved in the study.

## A Final Comment

We have covered a lot of ground in this chapter. We've looked at the basic ingredients that go into any one-way ANOVA, seen different formats for showing what pops out of this kind of statistical analysis, considered underlying assumptions, and observed how conscientious researchers will make an effort to discuss practical significance as well as statistical significance. You may have assimilated everything presented in this chapter, you may have assimilated only the highlights (with a review perhaps in order), or you may be somewhere between these two extremes. Regardless of how well you can decipher research reports based on one-way ANOVAs at this point, you need to leave this chapter with a crystal clear understanding of one exceedingly important point. Unless you heed the advice embodied in this final comment, you're likely to lose sight of the forest for all the trees.

A one-way ANOVA (like any other statistical analysis) cannot magically transform a flawed study into a sound one. And where can a study be flawed the most? The answer to this question is unrelated to *F*-tests, equal variance assumptions, effect size indices, or Bonferroni adjustments. That's because the potential worth of any study is connected, first and foremost, to the research question that sets the data collection and analysis wheels in motion. If the research question is silly or irrelevant, a one-way ANOVA cannot make the study worthwhile. Hence, don't be impressed by researchers who use one-way ANOVAs *until* you have first considered the merits of the research questions being addressed.

If you would like to see an example of a silly one-way ANOVA, consider Excerpt 11.24. As indicated in this excerpt, a one-way ANOVA was used to compare three groups of individuals. The independent variable concerned the kind of people

**EXCERPT 11.24 • *An Unnecessary One-Way ANOVA***

In the present investigation, we compared the morphosyntactic productions of a group of children with SLI, an older MLU-matched group of children with DS, and an MLU-matched group of younger children developing language typically. . . . Mean values for MLU across the three groups were 4.07 morphemes for the TL group, 3.83 morphemes for the DS group, and 3.95 morphemes for the SLI group. A one-way ANOVA was used to detect differences between the groups on MLU. No significant differences between the groups were found, $F(2,26) = 1.81, p = .18$.

*Source:* Eadie, P. A., Fey, M. E., Douglas, J. M., and Parsons, C. L. (2002). Profiles of grammatical morphology and sentence imitation in children with specific language impairment and Down syndrome. *Journal of Speech, Language, and Hearing Research, 45*(2), pp. 722–723.

in each group. One group was made up of children who had a specific language impairment (SLI), the second group was made up of children with Down syndrome (DS), and the third group of was made up of children with typical language development (TL). The final two sentences of this excerpt indicate that a one-way ANOVA was used to compare these three groups in terms of MLU, a measure of speech that was operationally defined as the mean length of utterances.

However, consider closely how the three comparison groups were formed. As indicated in Excerpt 11.24, the three groups were matched on MLU. The success of this matching is evident in the similarity of the MLU means: 3.83, 3.95, and 4.07. Although other parts of this research report may have dealt with interesting issues, two obvious questions must be asked relative to the one-way ANOVA summarized in Excerpt 11.24. Because of the matching strategy used to form the three groups, wasn't it known from the very beginning that the three groups did not differ in terms of MLU, the variable used to do the matching? If so, wasn't the one-way ANOVA completely unnecessary?

## Review Terms

ANOVA
Between groups
Bonferroni adjustment procedure
Dependent variable
*df*
Error
Factor
*f*
*F*
Homogeneity of variance assumption
Independent variable
Mean square

Normality assumption
One-factor ANOVA
One-way ANOVA
Post hoc power analysis
Practical significance
   versus statistical significance
Simple ANOVA
Source
Sum of squares
Summary table
Unit of analysis
Within groups

## The Best Items in the Companion Website

1. An interactive online quiz (with immediate feedback provided) covering Chapter 11.
2. Eight misconceptions about the content of Chapter 11.
3. An email message sent from the author to his students entitled "A Closed Hydraulic System."
4. The author-selected best passage from Chapter 11: "One-Way ANOVAs and What's Really Important."
5. An interactive online resource entitled "One-Way ANOVA (a)."

To access chapter objectives, practice tests, weblinks, and flashcards, visit the companion website at www.ablongman.com/huck5e.

## *Fun Exercises inside Research Navigator*

**1. Are college sophomores, juniors, or seniors more confident about their problem-solving abilities?**

In this Canadian study, 158 college students majoring in physiotherapy completed the *Heppner Problem Solving Inventory* (PSI) during the first week of the academic year. This instrument does not measure problem-solving ability; rather, it evaluates one's *confidence* in being successful when engaged in problem-solving tasks. After scoring the PSI, the researchers used a one-way ANOVA to compare the mean scores of the sophomore ($n = 56$), junior ($n = 53$), and senior ($n = 49$) participants. Four one-way ANOVAs were conducted, one on the PSI total scores and one on each of its three subscales. What do you think these ANOVAs revealed? After you formulate your guess, locate the PDF version of the research report in the Nursing, Health, and Medicine database of ContentSelect, look at Figure 3 (on page 21), and then read (on page 20) the second paragraph of the research report's "Results" section.

J. Wessel, J. Loomis, S. Rennie, P. Brook, J. Hoddinott, & M. Aherne. Learning styles and perceived problem-solving ability of students in a baccalaureate physiotherapy programme. *Physiotherapy Theory and Practice.* Located in the NURSING, HEALTH, AND MEDICINE database of ContentSelect.

**2. Do better Sumo wrestlers have different kinds of bodies?**

In this study, the physical characteristics of four different groups of professional Sumo wrestlers were compared. These four groups were drawn from different competitive "leagues" of the sport, with the first group ($n = 7$) from the top two leagues, the second group ($n = 12$) from the third-ranked league, the third group ($n = 12$) from the fourth- and fifth-ranked leagues, and the fourth group ($n = 5$) from the bottom two leagues. A one-way ANOVA compared the means of these four samples on each of several dependent variables, including height, weight, and percent body fat. Regarding these three variables, two of the *F*-tests were nonsignificant while one turned out $p < .01$. On which variable—height, weight, or percent body fat—do you think the ANOVA null hypothesis was rejected? After making your guess, locate the PDF version of the research report in the Biology database of ContentSelect and then look at Table 2 at the top of page 181.

K. Hattori, K. Kondo, T. Abe, S. Tanake, & F. Fukunaga. Hierarchical differences in body composition of professional Sumo wrestlers. *Annals of Human Biology.* Located in the BIOLOGY database of ContentSelect.

**Review Questions and Answers begin on page 513.**

# 12

# Post Hoc and Planned Comparisons

In the previous chapter, we examined the setting, purpose, assumptions, and outcome of a one-way analysis of variance that compares three or more groups. In this chapter, we turn our attention to two categories of inferential procedures that are closely related to the one-way ANOVA. As with a one-way ANOVA, the procedures looked at in this chapter involve one independent variable, one dependent variable, no repeated measures, and a focus on means.

The two classes of procedures considered here are called **post hoc comparisons** and **planned comparisons.** One set of these procedures—the post hoc kind—was developed because a one-way ANOVA $F$, if significant, does not provide any specific insight into what caused the null hypothesis to be rejected. To know that all population means are probably not equal to one another is helpful, but differing scenarios fit the general statement that not all $\mu$s are identical. For example, with three comparison groups, it might be that two $\mu$s are equal but the third is higher, or maybe two $\mu$s are equal but the third is lower, or it could be that all three $\mu$s are different. By using a post hoc procedure, the researcher attempts to probe the data to find out which of the possible non-null scenarios is most likely to be true.

*why do a post hoc →*

The second class of procedures considered in this chapter involves planned comparisons. These procedures were developed because researchers sometimes pose questions that cannot be answered by rejecting or failing to reject the null hypothesis of the more general one-way ANOVA $H_0$. For example, a researcher might wonder whether a specific pair of $\mu$s is different, or whether the average of two $\mu$s is different from a third $\mu$. In addition to allowing researchers to answer specific questions about the population means, planned comparisons have another desirable characteristic. Simply stated, the statistical power of the tests used to answer specific, preplanned questions is higher than is the power of the more generic $F$-test from a one-way ANOVA. In other words, planned comparisons allow a researcher

*important*

to deal with specific, a priori questions with less risk of a Type II error than does a two-step approach involving an ANOVA $F$-test followed by post hoc comparisons.

Researchers use post hoc comparisons more often than they do planned comparisons. For this reason, we will first consider the different test procedures and reporting schemes used when a one-way ANOVA yields a significant $F$ and is followed by a post hoc investigation. We then will turn our attention to what researchers do when they initially set up and test planned comparisons instead of following the two-step strategy of conducting a one-way ANOVA followed by a post hoc analysis. Finally, we will look at the unusual situation where planned comparisons are conducted along with a one-way ANOVA, with no post hoc investigation conducted to help explain what caused the ANOVA $F$ to turn out significant.

## Post Hoc Comparisons

### Definition and Purpose

There is confusion among researchers as to what is or is not a post hoc test. I have come across examples where researchers conducted a post hoc investigation but used the term *planned comparisons* to describe what they did. I have also come across research reports where planned comparisons were conducted by means of a test procedure that many researchers consider to be post hoc in nature. To help you avoid getting confused when you read research reports, I want to clarify what does and does not qualify as a post hoc investigation.

If a researcher conducts a one-way ANOVA and uses the outcome of the $F$-test to determine whether additional specific tests should be conducted, then I will refer to the additional tests as being **post hoc** in nature. As this definition makes clear, the defining criterion of a post hoc investigation has nothing to do with the name of the test procedure employed, with the number of tests conducted, or with the nature of the comparisons made. The only thing that matters is whether the ANOVA $F$-test must first be checked to see if further analysis of the data set is needed.

In turning to a post hoc investigation, the researcher's objective is to better understand why the ANOVA yielded a significant $F$. Stated differently, a post hoc investigation helps the researcher understand why the ANOVA $H_0$ was rejected. Since the $H_0$ specifies equality among all population means, you might say that a set of post hoc comparisons is designed to help the researcher gain insight into the pattern of $\mu$s. As we indicated at the outset of this chapter, the ANOVA $F$ can turn out to be significant for different reasons—that is, because of different possible patterns of $\mu$s. The post hoc analysis helps researchers in their efforts to understand the true pattern of the population means.

In light of the fact that empirical studies are usually driven by research hypotheses, it is not surprising to find that post hoc investigations are typically conducted to find out whether such hypotheses are likely to be true. Furthermore, it should not be surprising that differences in research hypotheses lead researchers to do different things in their post hoc investigations. Sometimes, for example, researchers set up their post hoc investigations to compare each sample mean against every other sample mean. On other occasions they use their post hoc tests to compare the mean associated with each of several experimental groups against a control group's mean, with no comparisons made among the experimental groups. On rare occasions, a post hoc investigation is implemented to compare the mean of one of the comparison groups against the average of the means of two or more of the remaining groups. I will illustrate each of these post hoc comparisons later in the chapter.

### Terminology

Various terms are used in a synonymous fashion to mean the same thing as the term **post hoc test.** The three synonyms that show up most often in the published literature are **follow-up test, multiple comparison test,** and **a posteriori test.** Excerpts 12.1 through 12.4 show how some of these terms have been used.

You may come across a research report in which the term *contrast* appears. The word **contrast** is synonymous with the term **comparison.** Hence, post hoc contrasts are nothing more than post hoc comparisons. Follow-up contrasts are nothing more than follow-up comparisons. A posteriori contrasts are nothing more than a posteriori comparisons.

It is also worth noting that the $F$-test used in the preliminary ANOVA is sometimes referred to as the **omnibus $F$-test.** This term seems appropriate because the ANOVA's $H_0$ involves *all* of the population means. Since post hoc (and planned) investigations often use $F$-tests to accomplish their objectives, it is helpful when researchers use the term *omnibus* (when referring to the ANOVA $F$) to clarify which $F$ is being discussed. Excerpt 12.5 illustrates the use of this term.

Finally, the terms *pairwise* and *nonpairwise* often pop up in discussions of post hoc (and planned) comparisons. The term **pairwise** simply means that groups are being compared two at a time. For example, pairwise comparisons among three groups labeled A, B, and C would involve comparisons of A versus B, A versus C, and B versus C. With four groups in the study, a total of six pairwise comparisons would be possible.

A **nonpairwise** (or **complex**) **comparison** involves three or more groups, with these comparison groups divided into two subsets. The mean score for the data in each subset is then computed and compared. For example, suppose there are four comparison groups in a study: A, B, C, and D. The researcher might be interested in comparing the average of groups A and B against the average of groups C and D. This would be a nonpairwise comparison, as would a comparison between the first group and the average of the final two groups (with the second group omitted from the comparison).

**EXCERPTS 12.1–12.4 • *The Term Post Hoc and Its Synonyms***

Post hoc tests showed that the three HPS groups were all significantly different from each other in the mean level of mania.

*Source:* Hofmann, B. U., and Meyer, T. D. (2006). Mood fluctuations in people putatively at risk for bipolar disorders. *British Journal of Clinical Psychology, 45*(1), p. 108.

---

One-way analysis of variance (ANOVA) and a . . . multiple comparison test were used to assess the significance of the differences between the schizophrenic inpatients, the nonschizophrenic inpatients, and the community controls.

*= Post hoc*

*Source:* Hadjez, J., Stein, D., Gabbay, U., Bruckner, J., Meged, S., Barak, Y., Elizur, A., Weizman, A., and Rotenberg, V. S. (2003). Dream content of schizophrenic, nonschizophrenic mentally ill, and community control adolescents. *Adolescence, 38*(150), pp. 335–336.

---

Follow-up tests were conducted to evaluate the three pairwise differences among the means for rhythmic suffixes.

*Post hoc*   *AB AC BC*

*Source:* Jarmulowicz, L. (2006). School-aged children's phonological production of derived English words. *Journal of Speech, Language & Hearing Research, 49*(2), p. 299.

---

A one-way Analysis of variance (ANOVA) was used. . . . Whenever ANOVA resulted in significant F-values (P < 0.05), a posteriori comparison of means . . . was conducted to determine the location of significant differences. *Post hoc*

*Source:* Muli, J. (2005). Spatial variation of benethic macroinvertebrates and the environmental factors influencing their distribution in Lake Victoria, Kenya. *Aquatic Ecosystem Health and Management, 8*(2), pp. 150, 151.

**EXCERPT 12.5 • *The Omnibus F-Test***

A one-way ANOVA with Class Rank as the factor variable also had a significant omnibus *F*-test for self-efficacy.

*Source:* Brown, U. J., Jara, U., and Braxton, E. (2005). College students and AIDS awareness: The effects of condom perception and self efficacy. *College Student Journal, 39*(1), p. 186.

In Excerpts 12.6 and 12.7, we see cases in which reference was made to the use of pairwise and nonpairwise (complex) comparisons. Of these two types of comparisons, the pairwise kind is used widely by applied researchers whereas the nonpairwise is used only rarely.

## EXCERPTS 12.6–12.7 • *Pairwise and Nonpairwise Comparisons*

We used one-way analysis of variance (ANOVA). . . . Pairwise comparisons were performed [if the *F* was] found to be statistically significant in the ANOVA.

*Source:* Crane, H. M., Van Romplaey, S., Dillingham, P. W., Herman, E., Diehr, P., and Kitahata, M. M. (2006). A single-item measure of health-related quality-of-life for HIV-infected patients in routine clinical care. *AIDS Patient Care & STDs, 20*(3), p. 164.

---

We hypothesized that people in the uncertain condition would maintain their positive mood the longest and thus would report a better mood than people in the certain or control conditions. As seen in Table 1 [not shown here], this hypothesis was confirmed. A planned comparison (that assigned a weight of 2 to the mean in the uncertain condition and −1 to the means in the certain and control conditions) was significant, $F(1, 28) = 8.95, p = .006$.

*Source:* Wilson, T. D., Centerbar, D. B., Kermer, D. A., and Gilbert, D. T. (2005). The pleasures of uncertainty: Prolonging positive moods in ways people do not anticipate. *Journal of Personality and Social Psychology, 88*(1), p. 8.

## Test Procedures Frequently Used in Post Hoc Analyses

A wide array of statistical procedures is available for making post hoc comparisons. Many of these you are unlikely to see, simply because they are not used very often. Three procedures are used by a few researchers, and thus you may come across **Fisher's LSD test, Duncan's multiple range test,** or the **Newman-Keuls test.** The three most frequently used procedures are called the **Bonferroni test,** the **Tukey test,** and **Scheffé test.** Excerpts 12.8 through 12.10 show how researchers will indicate that they have chosen to use these three popular tests.

You may have been surprised to see, in Excerpt 12.9, that the Bonferroni procedure can be used to conduct post hoc tests. But it can. Suppose there are four comparison groups (A, B, C, and D) in a study, suppose that a one-way ANOVA has yielded a significant *F*, and finally suppose that the researcher uses $\alpha = .05$. A post hoc investigation involving the Bonferroni test would involve a set of six independent-samples *t*-tests within which each group's mean being compared with every other group's mean, two at a time ($M_A$ vs. $M_B$, $M_A$ vs. $M_C$, and so on), with these post hoc tests conducted at a reduced alpha level of .017 (i.e., .05/3). Using the Bonferroni procedure is logically equivalent to using it in a two-group study where six *t*-tests are conducted because there are six dependent variables.

Instead of dealing with the problem of an inflated Type I error risk by adjusting the level of significance (as is done when the Bonferroni technique is applied), the Fisher, Duncan, Newman-Keuls, Tukey, and Scheffé procedures make an adjustment in the size of the critical value used to determine whether an observed

### EXCERPTS 12.8–12.10 • *Test Procedures Frequently Used in Post Hoc Investigations*

A one-way analysis of variance with a Tukey post hoc analysis was used to determine if any significant differences were present between the estimated target displacements calculated by each of the 3 indentation techniques and the gold standard.

*Source:* Kawchuk, G. N., Liddle, T. R., Fauvel, O. R., and Johnston, C. (2006). The accuracy of ultrasonic indentation in detecting simulated bone displacement: A comparison of three techniques. *Journal of Manipulative & Physiological Therapeutics, 29*(2), p. 129.

-----

One-way analyses of variance (ANOVAs) with Bonferroni post hoc comparisons were used to analyze the data.

*Source:* van der Leij, A., and Morfidi, E. (2006). Core deficits and variable differences in Dutch poor readers learning English. *Journal of Learning Disabilities, 39*(1), p. 80.

-----

One-way ANOVAs were conducted to determine if these groups differed in their ratings of classroom climate. Significant differences between groups were examined using post-hoc tests (Scheffe's).

*Source:* Allan, E. J., and Madden, M. (2006). Chilly classrooms for female undergraduate students: A question of method? *Journal of Higher Education, 77*(4), p. 691.

difference between two means is significant. To compensate for the fact that more than one comparison is made, larger critical values are used. However, the degree to which the critical value is adjusted upward varies according to which test procedure is used.

When the critical value is increased only slightly (as compared with what would have been the critical value in the situation of a two-group study), the test procedure is considered to be **liberal.** On the other hand, when the critical value is increased greatly, the test procedure is referred to as being **conservative.** Liberal procedures provide less control over Type I errors, but this disadvantage is offset by increased power (i.e., more control over Type II errors). Conservative procedures do just the opposite; they provide greater control over Type I error risk but do so at the expense of lower power (i.e., higher risk of Type II errors).

The Fisher LSD test procedure is the most liberal of the test procedures, because it makes no adjustment for the multiple tests being conducted. In a very real sense, it is just like comparing every pair of means with a *t*-test. On the other end of the liberal–conservative continuum is the Scheffé test. It has enormous protection against Type I errors, because it was designed for the situation where the researcher wishes to make all possible pairwise comparisons *plus* all possible nonpairwise comparisons. Few researchers need or want that level of protection! The other test procedures (such as Bonferroni and Tukey) lie between these two liberal–conservative extremes.

Excerpt 12.11 shows what can happen when there is or isn't control exerted over Type I error risk. In this study, the means of six samples were compared twice in a post hoc analysis, with the same set of 15 pairwise comparisons made in each investigation. In the first post hoc investigation, regular *t*-tests were applied to make each pairwise comparison. In the second investigation, the inflated Type I error risk was controlled by means of the Bonferroni procedure. Take a look at these two sets of results.

### EXCERPT 12.11 • *Why Holding Down Type I Error Risk Matters*

There were significant differences between RN level of education [Diploma, ADN, BSN, MSN, PhD, and Other Doctorate] and RN occupational commitment to the nursing profession $(F(5, 900) = 3.56, p = 0.00)$. Post hoc analyses showed that RNs with graduate degrees had greater commitment to the nursing profession than did those RNs with diploma or undergraduate degrees. However, using Bonferroni post hoc correction, the only statistically significant group difference that remained was between the BSN and MSN, such that the MSN had higher occupational commitment scores (MSN, $M = 67.81$, BSN, $M = 65.35$).

*Source:* Nogueras, D. J. (2006). Occupational commitment, education, and experience as a predictor of intent to leave the nursing profession. *Nursing Economic$*, *24*(2), p. 90.

You are likely to come across two additional test procedures that are used in post hoc investigations. These tests have special purposes compared with the ones we have considered so far. One of these procedures is Dunnett's test; the other one is called Tamhane's test.

**Dunnett's test** makes pairwise comparisons, as do the other test procedures we have considered. However, Dunnett's test does not pair every mean with every other mean. Instead, the Dunnett test compares the mean of a particular group in the study against each of the remaining group means. This procedure might be used, for example, if a researcher cares only about how each of several versions of an experimental treatment affects the dependent variable, compared with a control (or placebo) condition. In Excerpt 12.12, we see a case where the Dunnett test was used in just this manner.

The second of our two "special case" test procedures is **Tamhane's post hoc test.** This test has been created so researchers can make pairwise comparisons among group means in the situation where the equal variance assumption seems untenable. Excerpt 12.13 illustrates the use of the Tamhane test.

## EXCERPTS 12.12–12.13 • *The Dunnett and Tamhane Tests*

The difference in response to test drugs and control was evaluated using one-way analysis of variance followed by Dunnett's *t*-test. . . . [Results showed that] MEO extract at doses of 50, 100, and 150 mg/kg decreased the propulsion of charcoal meal through the gastrointestinal tract, as compared with the control group.

*Source:* Perianayagam, J. B., Narayanan, S., Gnanasekar, G., Pandurangan, A., Raja, S., Rajagopal, K., Rajesh, R., Vijayarajkumar, P., and Vijayakumar, S. G. (2005). Evaluation of antidiarrheal potential of emblica officinalis. *Pharmaceutical Biology, 43*(4), pp. 374, 375.

--------------------------------------------------------------------------------

A one-way ANOVA showed significant differences between groups ($F(7, 165) = 46.031; p < .001$). Since the Levene statistic indicated unequal variances, a Tamhane *post hoc* test was conducted. . . .

*Source:* Roever, C. (2006). Validation of a web-based test of ESL pragmalinguistics. *Language Testing, 23*(2), p. 245.

## The Null Hypotheses of a Post Hoc Investigation

In the next section, we will look at the different ways researchers present the results of their post hoc analyses. In those presentations, you will rarely see reference made, through symbols or words, to the null hypotheses that are associated with the test results. Consequently, you need to remember that all of the post hoc procedures are inferential in nature and are concerned with null hypotheses.

In any post hoc analysis, at least two contrasts will be investigated, each involving a null hypothesis. For example, in a study involving three groups (A, B, and C) and pairwise comparisons used to probe a significant result from a one-way ANOVA, three null hypotheses would be tested: $H_0$: $\mu_A = \mu_B$, $H_0$: $\mu_A = \mu_C$ and $H_0$: $\mu_B = \mu_C$.[1] With a similar analysis involving four groups, there will be six null hypotheses. With Dunnett's test, there will be one fewer null hypothesis than there are comparison groups.

The purpose of a post hoc analysis is to evaluate the null hypothesis associated with each contrast that is investigated. As I have pointed out several times, many applied researchers seem to forget this exceedingly important point. They often talk about their findings with reference only to their sample means, and they discuss their results in such a way as to suggest that they have proven something in

--------------------------------------------------------------------------------

[1]Although the null hypotheses of a post hoc investigation theoretically can be set up with something other than zero as $H_0$'s pinpoint number, you are unlikely to ever see a researcher test anything except no-difference null hypotheses in a post hoc analysis.

a definitive manner. When they do so, they are forgetting that their "discoveries" are nothing more than inferences regarding unseen population means, with every inference potentially being nothing more than a Type I or Type II error.

## Presentation of Results

Researchers sometimes summarize the results of their post hoc investigations through the text of the technical report. Usually it is not difficulty to figure out what the researcher has concluded when results are presented in this fashion. Sometimes, however, you must read carefully. Consider, for example, Excerpt 12.14. In the study associated with this excerpt, three one-way ANOVAs were involved, one for each of the study's dependent variables. Because each of these ANOVAs yielded a significant $F$, three post hoc investigations were conducted. See if you can figure out what the dependent variables were, what the independent variable was (and how many comparison groups there were) in each ANOVA, and how many pairwise comparisons were made following each ANOVA?[2]

### EXCERPT 12.14 • *Results of a Post Hoc Investigation*

These [one-way ANOVAs] revealed a significant difference between age groups for verbatim responses to consistent presentations, $F(2, 58) = 10.13, p < .05$, and inconsistent presentations, $F(2, 58) = 4.15, p < .05$, and for substitution errors in response to inconsistent presentations, $F(2, 58) = 5.13, p < .05$. A Tukey's post hoc test revealed that for verbatim responses, there was a significant difference for consistent presentations between the young and older groups ($p < .05$) and between the middle and older groups ($p < .05$) and for inconsistent presentations between the young and middle groups ($p < .05$). For substitution errors, there was a significant difference for inconsistent presentations between the young and older groups ($p < .05$) and between the middle and older groups ($p < .05$).

*Source:* Ziegler, F., Mitchell, P., and Currie, G. (2005). How does narrative cue children's perspective taking? *Developmental Psychology, 41*(1), pp. 117–118.

If you take another look at Excerpt 12.14, you'll notice that the researchers say that they used "a Tukey's post hoc test" after the ANOVAs turned out to be significant. Actually, there are several versions of the Tukey post hoc test

---

[2]The dependent variables were verbatim responses to consistent presentations, verbatim responses to inconsistent presentations, and substitution errors in response to inconsistent presentations; the independent variable was age (with three groups: young, middle, and old); there were three pairwise comparisons following each ANOVA.

procedure, and researchers will often specify which particular Tukey test they used. Excerpts 12.15, 12.16, and 12.17 show reference to Tukey HSD, the Tukey–Kramer test, and Tukey-B. For all practical purposes, you can consider these different versions of Tukey's test to be nearly equivalent.

When the results of a post hoc analysis are presented graphically, one of three formats is typically used. These formats involve (1) a table of means with attached letters, (2) a table of means with one or more notes using group labels and less than or greater than symbols, and (3) a figure containing lines drawn above vertical bars. Although different formats are employed for displaying the results, these three formats are identical in that they reveal where significant differences were found among the comparison groups.

The first format for presenting post hoc results is a table in which *letters are attached to group means.* Such a table appears in Excerpt 12.18.

The table shown in Excerpt 12.18 contains a row of three means, with each of these means coming from one of the three comparison groups involved in the study. After an omnibus *F*-test had yielded a significant result, pairwise comparisons were made among these means using the Bonferroni test procedure. The results of the post hoc investigation are indicated by means of subscript letters attached to the group means. If you examine the note beneath the table, you will see

### EXCERPTS 12.15–12.17 • *Different Versions of Tukey's Test Procedure*

Post-hoc Tukey HSD (Honestly Significant Differences) tests were conducted when significant one-way ANOVA results were obtained with the demographic data.

*Source:* Trépanier, L. L., Rourke, S. B., Bayoumi, A. M., Halman, M. H., Krzyzanowski, S., and Power, C. (2005). The impact of neuropsychological impairment and depression on health-related quality of life in HIV-infection. *Journal of Clinical & Experimental Neuropsychology, 27*(1), p. 8.

------------------------------------------------------------

Follow-up tests were conducted to evaluate the three pairwise differences among the means for rhythmic suffixes. The Tukey–Kramer method was used to account for the unequal group sizes.

*Source:* Jarmulowicz, L. (2006). School-aged children's phonological production of derived English words. *Journal of Speech, Language & Hearing Research, 49*(2), p. 299.

------------------------------------------------------------

Follow up tests using Tukey-B comparisons indicated that the mean score of children with no imaginary companions was significantly lower than that of children with invisible imaginary companions and children with personified objects.

*Source:* Gleason, T. R. (2004). Imaginary companions: An evaluation of parents as reporters. *Infant & Child Development, 13*(3), p. 205.

**EXCERPT 12.18 • *Results of a Post Hoc Investigation Presented in a Table with Letters Attached to Group Means***

**TABLE 4** *Means and Standard Deviations of PDSS-SR Scores for SCID-Diagnosed Panic Disordered Community Participants and PDSR-Identified Panic Disordered and Non-Panic Disordered Students*

| Measure | PDSR-Identified non-panic-disordered students ($n = 388$) | PDSR-Identified panic-disordered students ($n = 49$) | SCID-Identified panic-disordered community participants ($n = 27$) |
|---|---|---|---|
| PDSS-SR | | | |
| *M* | $1.50_a$ | $9.39_b$ | $11.15_b$ |
| *SD* | 2.25 | 5.32 | 5.08 |

*Note.* Differing subscripts indicate significant differences between means, $p < .001$. Like subscripts indicate nonsignificant differences between means. PDSS-SR = Panic Disorder Severity Scale—Self Report; SCID = Structured Clinical Interview for *DSM-IV*; PDSR = Panic Disorder Self Report.

*Source:* Newman, M. G., Holmes, M., Zuellig, A. R., Kachin, K. E., and Behar, E. (2006). The reliability and validity of the Panic Disorder Self-Report: A new diagnostic screening measure of panic disorder. *Psychological Assessment, 18*(1), p. 55.

that the researchers provided their readers with instructions as to what the small letters mean.

When looking at a table in which the results of a post hoc investigation are shown via letters attached to the means, you need to read the note that explains what the letters mean. It's important to do this because all authors do not set up their tables in the same way. In some tables, the same letter attached to any two means indicates that the tested null hypothesis was *not* rejected; in other tables, common letters indicate that the tested null hypothesis *was* rejected. Excerpt 12.18 provides an example of the first (and more typical) situation. The second (less typical) situation can be illustrated best by these words that I recently saw in a note positioned beneath a table: "means sharing the same subscript were all significant at $p < .05$."

The second method for summarizing the results of a post hoc investigation also involves a table of group means, as did the first method. Instead of attaching letters to those means, however, the second method involves (1) an ordering of abbreviations or numbers that represent the group means and (2) the use of the symbols $>$, $<$, and $=$ (positioned within those group abbreviations or numbers) to indicate the findings of the pairwise comparisons. Excerpt 12.19 illustrates this method.

**EXCERPT 12.19** • *Another Table Showing the Results of a Post Hoc Investigation*

**TABLE 1** *Multidimensional Personality Questionnaire Brief Form Higher Order Factor Scale Scores by Cluster Group*

| | Cluster | | | | | | | |
| | Low pathology (Cluster 1)[a] | | Externalizing (Cluster 2)[b] | | Internalizing (Cluster 3)[c] | | | Pairwise |
| Measure | M | SD | M | SD | M | SD | F(2, 202) | contrast |
|---|---|---|---|---|---|---|---|---|
| PEM | 49.7 | 11.0 | 42.5 | 8.2 | 28.6 | 5.9 | 126.3 | 1 > 2 > 3 |
| NEM | 50.9 | 8.2 | 69.9 | 6.8 | 65.3 | 6.8 | 114.4 | 2 > 3 > 1 |
| CON | 49.4 | 8.8 | 38.4 | 8.8 | 44.6 | 8.7 | 22.9 | 1 > 3 > 2 |

*Note.* All $F$ ratios listed are significant at $p < .003$. Total sample sizes for all analyses was 205. PEM = Positive Emotionality; NEM = Negative Emotionality; CON = Constraint. [a]$n = 66$. [b]$n = 51$. [c]$n = 88$.

*Source:* Miller, M. W., Greif, J. L., and Smith, A. A. (2003). Multidimensional Personality Questionnaire profiles of veterans with traumatic combat exposure: Externalizing and internalizing subtypes. *Psychological Assessment, 15*(2), p. 209. (Adapted slightly for presentation here.)

In Excerpt 12.19, there are three comparison groups, each of which is referred to as a "cluster." These three groups of individuals were compared on each of three measures (the PEM, NEM, and CON) with separate one-way ANOVAs. After each ANOVA yielded a significant $F$, Tukey's HSD post hoc test was applied. The results of each post hoc investigation are presented in the far right-hand column. The notation in that column for the NEM measure indicates that Tukey's test found that the mean from the Cluster 2 individuals was significantly higher than the mean from the Cluster 3 individuals, with the mean of the Cluster 1 individuals being significantly lower than both of the other means.

Sometimes a researcher will use a graph of some type to help others "see" what was discovered in a post hoc investigation. Excerpt 12.20 contains an example of this helpful strategy. In this case, each of the three means was found to be significantly different from the other two. If only one or two of the three pairwise comparisons had been significant, the researchers would have noted this by means of a note beneath the figure or a set a subscript letters attached to the bars.

**EXCERPT 12.20** • *Use of a Bar Graph to Show Results of a Post Hoc Investigation*

Counting backward significantly reduced motion aftereffect duration, $F(2, 16) = 25.69$, $MSE = 30.01$, $p < .01$. Tukey–Kramer post hoc analysis showed that all three conditions—control (passive observation), counting backward in 2s, and counting backward in 12s—differed from each other at the $p < .05$ level. Aftereffect durations are plotted by condition in Figure 5.

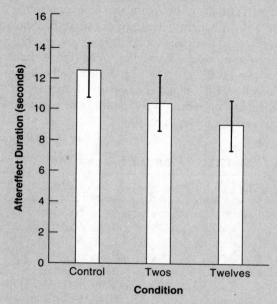

**FIGURE 5**  *Motion aftereffect durations by condition, averaged across participants in Experiment 3 for counting backward in 2s and 12s. Error bars show standard errors.*

*Source:* Houghton, R. J., Macken, W. J., and Jones, D. M. (2003). Attentional modulation of the visual motion aftereffect has a central cognitive locus: Evidence of interference by the postcategorical on the precategorical. *Journal of Experimental Psychology: Human Perception and Performance, 29*(4), p. 737.

## Planned Comparisons

So far we have considered the comparison of group means using a two-step strategy that involves conducting a one-way ANOVA followed by a post hoc investigation. Researchers can, if they wish, bypass the ANOVA *F*-test and move directly to one or more specific comparisons of particular interest. Such comparisons among

Research
Navigator.c🌐m

Planned
comparisons

means (without reliance on a green light from a significant omnibus *F*-test) are called **planned comparisons**.[3] Although planned comparisons are used less frequently than post hoc comparisons, they show up in the research literature often enough to make it important for you to recognize and understand this kind of statistical test on means.

Excerpts 12.21 and 12.22 illustrate the use of a planned comparisons. In the study associated with Excerpt 12.21, there were three comparison groups: ballet dancers, modern dancers, and nondancers. Members of all three of these groups were measured on two dependent variables that are referred to in the excerpt as the FNE and the PSN. Although the researchers used the nondancers in certain of the study's analyses (e.g., when all three groups were compared with a one-way ANOVA), there was particular interest in comparing the ballet dancers and the modern dancers on the FNE and PSN. Consequently, the researchers compared these two groups directly with a planned comparison. In Excerpt 12.22, we see that the planned comparisons of interest were contrasts between each of the study's experimental groups and the control group.

## EXCERPTS 12.21–12.22 • *Planned Comparisons*

In sum, the present study tested the accuracy of the stereotypes that the two types of dancers had of each other and compared dancers' stereotypes to those of nondancers. . . . The ballet dancers were an average of 19.8 years old. . . . Modern dancers were an average of 20.1 years old. . . . [There were] 34 in the final nondancer group (average age 20.12). . . . Our specific hypotheses about ballet and modern dancers justified planned comparisons with independent-samples *t*-tests. . . . As seen in Table 1 [not shown here], ballet dancers scored significantly higher than modern dancers on FNE, $t(87) = -3.06, p = .003, d = -0.65$; and PSN, $t(87) = -2.59, p = .01, d = -0.57$.

*Source:* Clabaugh, A., and Morling, B. (2004). Stereotype accuracy of ballet and modern dancers. *Journal of Social Psychology, 144*(1), pp. 35, 36, 37, 39.

- - - - - - - - - - - - - - - - - - - - - - - - - - - - - - - - - - - - - - - - - - - - - - - - - - - -

Hypothesis 1 proposed that increases in category salience would result in enhanced social identification with the relevant category. This hypothesis was tested separately for each focus of identification using one-way ANOVAs. . . . More important, however, were planned comparisons between those conditions that were expected to vary compared with the control group.

*Source:* van Dick, R., Wagner, U., Stellmacher, J., and Christ, O. (2005). Category salience and organizational identification. *Journal of Occupational & Organizational Psychology, 78*(2), p. 280.

---

[3]The term *a priori comparison* means the same thing as *planned comparison*.

Excerpt 12.23 illustrates the use of planned nonpairwise comparisons. In the study from which this excerpt was taken, four groups of individuals were compared in terms of brain activity (as measured by a PET scan) as the individuals completed a series of tasks involving fast-action decision making. As indicated in the excerpt, the four comparison groups were defined by drug use. Two of the groups included current drug addicts. In one of these groups, the drug of choice was amphetamine; those in the other group were opiate users. The third group was made up of former amphetamine/opiate users who had been abstinent for at least a year. The fourth group contained individuals who had no history of drug use. Each of the four groups was composed of both men and women.

**EXCERPT 12.23 • *Planned Pairwise and Nonpairwise Comparisons***

Four groups, each consisting of 15 participants, were compared: chronic amphetamine users, chronic opiate users, ex-drug users who had been long-term amphetamine/opiate users but are abstinent from all drugs of abuse for at least 1 year, and healthy matched controls without a drug-taking history. . . . Three planned comparisons were conducted: the three drug user groups compared to controls, current users versus ex-drug users, and amphetamine users contrasted with opiate users.

*Source:* Ersche, K. D., Fletcher, P. C., Lewis, S. J. G., Clark, L., Stocks-Gee, G., London, M., Deakin, J. B., Robbins, T. W., and Sahakian, B. J. (2005). Abnormal frontal activations related to decision-making in current and former amphetamine and opiate dependent individuals. *Psychopharmacology, 180*(4), pp. 612, 617.

Of the three planned contrasts mentioned in Excerpt 12.23, the first two were nonpairwise comparisons. The null hypothesis associated with the first of these contrasts could be expressed in one of two ways, as $H_0$: $\mu_{user} = \mu_{nonuser}$ or as $H_0$: $(\mu_{amphetamine} + \mu_{opiate} + \mu_{ex\text{-}user})/3 = \mu_{nonuser}$. To test this null hypothesis, the researchers compared the mean of the 45 current/former drug users with the mean of the 15 nonusers. The second contrast's null hypothesis could be expressed as $H_0$: $\mu_{user(current)} = \mu_{ex\text{-}user}$ or as $H_0$: $(\mu_{amphetamine} + \mu_{opiate})/2 = \mu_{ex\text{-}user}$. This null hypothesis was tested by comparing the mean of the 30 amphetamine/opiate users with the mean of the 15 ex-users. The third of the three planned comparisons was pairwise in nature, and its null hypothesis took the form $H_0$: $\mu_{amphetamine} = \mu_{opiate}$. For this final comparison, the mean of the 15 amphetamine users was compared with the mean of the 15 opiate users.

## Comments

As we come to the end of this chapter on planned and post hoc comparisons, there are a few final things to consider. If you take the time to consider these end-of-chapter issues, you will be better able to decipher and critique research reports. These issues are positioned here at the end of the chapter because each of them has relevance to both post hoc and planned comparisons.

### Terminology

Earlier in this chapter, you encountered six technical terms: post hoc, planned, comparison, contrast, pairwise, and nonpairwise. (A seventh term, **a priori,** appeared in a footnote.) We now need to consider two additional terms: "1 *df F*-test" and "orthogonal." After you add these two terms to your working vocabulary, you'll be able to understand just about any research report wherein the researchers discuss their post hoc and planned comparisons.

In reading discussions of post hoc and planned comparisons, you are likely to come across the term **one-degree-of-freedom *F*-test.** This term pops up every so often when nonpairwise contrasts are conducted via *F*-tests, and it simply refers to the fact that the first of the two *df* values of such an *F*-test will always be 1 no matter how many groups are involved in the comparison being made. Thus, if a study involves groups of blonds, brunettes, and redheads, the researcher might want to pool together the blonds and the brunettes and compare that combined group's mean against the mean of the redheads. An *F*-test used to do this would have a between-groups *df* equal to 1.

My hair color example, of course, is quite artificial. To see an example of this special kind of *F*-test, take another look at Excerpt 12.7. In the study associated with that excerpt, there were three comparison groups. Nevertheless, the first of the two *df* numbers attached to the *F* is a 1, not a 2.

The second new term for us to consider is **orthogonal.** As illustrated in Excerpt 12.24, researchers occasionally use the term *orthogonal* when discussing the contrasts that they tested.

### EXCERPT 12.24 • *Orthogonal Comparisons*

We conducted two planned orthogonal comparisons: Non-bullies were compared to identified bullies (self-reported and peer-nominated) and then self-reported bullies were compared to peer-nominated bullies.

*Source:* Cole, J. C. M., Cornell, D. G., and Sheras, P. (2006). Identification of school bullies by survey methods. *Professional School Counseling, 9*(4), p. 308.

In a researcher's planned (or post hoc) investigation, two contrasts are said to be orthogonal to one another if the information yielded by one contrast is new and different (i.e., independent) from what is revealed by the other contrast. For example, with three groups in a study (A, B, and C), a contrast comparing group A against the average of groups B and C would be orthogonal to a contrast

*[handwritten margin note:]* independent comparisons of more than 2 groups

comparing group B against group C because knowing how the first contrast turned out would give you no clue as to how the second contrast will turn out.

## Assumptions

The various planned and post hoc test procedures mentioned earlier in this chapter will function as they are supposed to function only if four underlying assumptions hold true for the populations and samples involved in the study. These assumptions are the same ones that underlie a one-way ANOVA *F*-test, and they are referred to by the terms *randomness, independence, normality,* and *homogeneity of variance.* I hope you remember the main points that I made in Chapter 11 about these assumptions.

Although the various test procedures covered so far in this chapter generally are robust to the normality assumption, the same point cannot be made regarding the equal variance assumption—especially in situations where the sample sizes are dissimilar. If researchers conduct planned comparisons, they ought to talk about the issue of assumptions. If the study's sample sizes vary, a test should be applied to assess the homogeneity of variance assumption. With a post hoc investigation, the assumptions should have been discussed in conjunction with the omnibus *F*-test; those assumptions do not have to be discussed or tested a second time when the researcher moves from the one-way ANOVA to the post hoc comparisons.

If the equal variance assumption is tested and shown to be untenable (in connection with planned comparisons or with the one-way ANOVA), the researcher will likely make some form of adjustment when a priori or post hoc contrasts are tested. This adjustment might take the form of a data transformation, a change in the level of significance employed, or a change in the test procedure used to compare means. If the latter approach is taken, you are likely to see the Welch test applied to the data (because the Welch model does not assume equal population variances).

Many of the test procedures for making planned or post hoc comparisons were developed for the situation in which the various samples are the same size. When used with samples that vary in size, researchers may indicate that they used a variation of one of the main techniques. For example, Kramer's extension of Duncan's multiple range test simply involves a modification of the regular Duncan test procedure to make it usable in studies in which the *n*s vary. Don't let such extensions or modifications cause you to shy away from deciphering research reports in the same way you would if the regular planned or post hoc test had been used.

## The Researcher's Choice of Test Procedure

As I pointed out near the outset of this chapter, the various post hoc procedures differ in terms of how liberal or conservative they are. Ideally, a researcher ought to choose among these procedures after considering the way they differ in terms of power and control of Type I errors. Realistically, however, the decision to use a particular test procedure is probably influenced most by what computer programs are available for doing the data analysis or by what procedure was emphasized in a specific textbook or by a specific instructor.

In Excerpt 12.25, a pair of researchers did the right thing: they explained *why* they chose the test procedure they used to make multiple comparisons among means. As indicated in this excerpt, there were two reasons why they used the Scheffé test: variability among their sample sizes and a desire to use a conservative procedure. By selecting a procedure that was conservative (rather than liberal), these researchers demonstrated a concern for holding down the possibility of a Type I error.

### EXCERPT 12.25 • *Explaining Why a Test Procedure Was Used*

The Scheffé method was chosen because of its versatility in handling comparison means that are based on unequal cell sizes [and also] it is the most conservative of the post-hoc tests; so, it is less likely than any other post-hoc approach to indicate that a given comparison is statistically significant. . . .

*Source:* Sue-Chan, C., and Latham, G. P. (2004). The relative effectiveness of external, peer, and self-coaches. *Applied Psychology: An International Review, 53*(2), p. 268.

Regardless of the reasons why the researcher chooses to use a particular test procedure, you are in full control of how *you* interpret the results presented in the research report. If a researcher uses a test procedure that is too liberal or too conservative for *your* taste, remember that you have the undisputed right to accept only a portion of the researcher's full set of conclusions. Or, you may want to reject *everything* that is "discovered" in the research study because your position on the liberal/conservative continuum is quite different from that of the researcher who performed the data analysis.

## Statistical Significance versus Practical Significance

We have considered the distinction between statistical significance and practical significance in earlier chapters. My simple suggestion at this point is to keep this distinction in mind when you come into contact with the results of planned and post hoc comparisons.

In Excerpt 12.26, we see a case in which the measure *d* was used to estimate the effect size for each of the two pairwise comparisons that turned out to be statistically significant. The researchers who conducted the study associated with Excerpt 12.26 deserve high praise for demonstrating an awareness that statistical significance does not necessarily signify practical significance. Unfortunately, most researchers conduct their post hoc and planned comparisons without performing a

## EXCERPT 12.26 • *Concern for Practical Significance in a Post Hoc Investigation*

The ANOVA results show that the mean MTEBI scores of low, moderate, and high math anxiety groups were significantly different, $F(2, 61) = 20.117, p < .001$. According to the Tukey's HSD tests, the mean differences in MTEBI scores between the low and moderate anxiety groups ($p < .001; d = 1.25$) and between the low and high anxiety groups ($p < .001; d = 1.89$) were found to be statistically significant. Large effect sizes from these comparisons indicate the practical significance of the mean differences.

*Source:* Bursal, M., and Paznokas, L. (2006). Mathematics anxiety and preservice elementary teachers' confidence to teach mathematics and science. *School Science & Mathematics, 106*(4), p. 176.

power analysis and without computing effect size estimates. When you come across studies like that associated with Excerpt 12.26, upgrade your evaluation of the researchers' work.

As exemplified by Excerpt 12.26, researchers often use terms such as "small," "medium," or "large" to describe their estimated effect sizes. When they do this, they are using a set of criteria for interpreting *d* that are widely used by researchers in many different disciplines. Those criteria for comparing two means were presented earlier in Chapter 10. If you refer to Table 10.1, you'll be able to tell whether the use of the term "large" in Excerpt 12.26 was justified.

### Other Test Procedures

In this chapter, we have considered several test procedures that researchers use when comparing means within planned and post hoc investigations. The excerpts we have considered demonstrate the popularity of the Tukey and Bonferroni test procedures. However, we have seen additional excerpts that illustrate the use of other test procedures, such as Tamhane's test, Scheffé's test, and Dunnett's test. All of these procedures help hold down the chances of a Type I error when two or more contrasts are evaluated.

Although a variety of test procedures have received our attention in this chapter, there are additional test procedures that we have not discussed. The tests mentioned in the preceding paragraph are the ones I believe you will encounter most often when you read research reports. However, you may come across one or more techniques not discussed in this text. If this happens, I hope you will not be thrown by the utilization of a specific test procedure different from those considered here. If you understand the general purpose served by the planned and post hoc tests we *have* considered, I think you will have little difficulty understanding the purpose and results of similar test procedures that we have *not* considered.

## Review Terms

| | |
|---|---|
| A posteriori test | Multiple comparison test |
| A priori | Newman-Keuls test |
| Comparison | Nonpairwise (or complex) comparison |
| Complex comparison | Omnibus $F$-test |
| Conservative | One-degree-of-freedom $F$-test |
| Contrast | Orthogonal |
| Duncan's multiple range test | Pairwise comparison |
| Dunnett test | Planned comparisons |
| Fisher's LSD test | Post hoc comparisons |
| Follow-up test | Scheffé test |
| Liberal | Tukey test |

## The Best Items in the Companion Website

1. An interactive online quiz (with immediate feedback provided) covering Chapter 12.
2. Eight misconceptions about the content of Chapter 12.
3. An email message sent from the author to his students entitled "Seemingly Illogical Results."
4. Two funny jokes about statisticians.
5. One of the best passages from Chapter 12: "Your Right to Be Liberal or Conservative."

To access chapter objectives, practice tests, weblinks, and flashcards, visit the companion website at www.ablongman.com/huck5e.

## Fun Exercises inside Research Navigator

Research Navigator.com

### 1. What is the quality of life for those who are HIV-positive?

In an effort to validate the Italian version of an HIV quality-of-life questionnaire, a team of researchers divided a sample of HIV-positive individuals into three subgroups: "asymptomatic" (no evidence of a problem), "symptomatic" (evidence of minor problems), and "AIDS" (evidence of major problems). After the people in these three categories took the quality-of-life questionnaire, a one-way ANOVA was used to compare the three group means on each of the instrument's many scales. If the omnibus $F$ turned out to be significant on any of the scales, pairwise comparisons were made within the context of a post hoc investigation. Your job is to think about this study and then make a guess as to which test procedure was used to make the pairwise comparisons. After formulating your guess, locate the PDF version of this article in the Nursing, Health, and Medicine database of ContentSelect, look at Table 5 (on page 412), and then read the "statistical analysis" section on page 407.

E. Starace, L. Cafaro, N. Abrescia, A. Chirianni, C. Izzo, P. Rucci, & G. deGirolamo. Quality of life assessment in HIV-positive persons: Application and validation of the WHOQOL-HIV, Italian Version. *AIDS Care.* Located in the NURSING, HEALTH, AND MEDICINE database of ContentSelect.

## 2.  Can you catch mistakes in a published article?

The central purpose of this study was to compare four groups of elderly individuals—English-speaking Alzheimer's patients, English-speaking normal controls, Spanish-speaking Alzheimer's patients, and Spanish-speaking normal controls—in terms of their ability to perform two tasks often included in an intelligence test. Before the researchers discussed those results, however, they presented the findings of four one-way ANOVAs that compared the groups on two demographic variables and two screening variables. Because the omnibus *F*-test from each of these one-way ANOVAs turned out significant, a post hoc investigation was conducted so as to make all possible pairwise comparisons. To see if you have an "eagle-eye" for catching mistakes, first find this research report in the Nursing, Health, and Medicine database of ContentSelect. Next, take a look at Table 1 at the bottom of page 360. Finally, see if you can find something wrong with one of the table's numbers and one of the letters that are used as superscripts to convey the results of the post hoc tests.

T. Argüelles, D. Loewenstein, & S. Argüelles. The impact of the native language of Alzheimer's disease and normal elderly individuals on their ability to recall digits. *Aging & Mental Health.* Located in the NURSING, HEALTH, AND MEDICINE database of ContentSelect.

**Review Questions and Answers begin on page 513.**

# 13

# Two-Way Analyses of Variance

In Chapters 10 and 11, we saw how one-way ANOVAs can be used to compare two or more sample means in studies involving a single independent variable. In this chapter, I want to extend our discussion of analysis of variance to consider how this extremely popular statistical tool is used in studies characterized by two independent variables. It should come as no surprise that the kind of ANOVA to be considered here is referred to as a two-way ANOVA. Since you may have come across the term *multivariate analysis of variance* or the abbreviation *MANOVA*, it is important to clarify that this chapter does not deal with multivariate analyses of variance. The first letter of the acronym *MANOVA* stands for the word multivariate, but the letter *M* indicates that multiple dependent variables are involved in the same unitary analysis. Within the confines of this chapter, we will look at ANOVAs that involve multiple independent variables but only one dependent variable. Accordingly, the topics in this chapter (along with those of earlier chapters) fall under the general heading **univariate analyses.**

## Similarities between One-Way and Two-Way ANOVAs

Like any one-way ANOVA, a two-way ANOVA focuses on group means. (As you will soon see, a minimum of four $\overline{X}$s are involved in any two-way ANOVA.) Because it is an inferential technique, any two-way ANOVA is actually concerned with the set of $\mu$ values that correspond to the sample means that are computed from the study's data. The inference from the samples to the populations will be made through the six-, seven-, or nine-step version of hypothesis testing. Statistical assumptions may need to be tested, and the research questions will dictate whether planned and/or post hoc comparisons are used in conjunction with (or in lieu of) the two-way ANOVA. Despite these similarities between one-way and two-way ANOVAs, the kind of ANOVA to which we now turn is substantially different from the kind we examined in Chapter 11.

## The Structure of a Two-Way ANOVA

Before we discuss what kinds of research questions can be answered by a two-way ANOVA, it is essential that you understand how a two-way ANOVA is structured. Therefore, I now will explain (1) how factors and levels come together to form cells, (2) how randomization is used to "fill" the ANOVA's cells with the people, animals, or things from which data are eventually collected, and (3) why this chapter deals exclusively with two-way ANOVAs having "between-subjects" factors.

### Factors, Levels, and Cells

A two-way ANOVA always involves two independent variables. Each independent variable, or **factor,** is made up of, or defined by, two or more elements called **levels.** When looked at simultaneously, the levels of the first factor and the levels of the second factor create the conditions of the study to be compared. Each of these conditions is referred to as a **cell.**

To help you see how factors, levels, and cells form the basic structure of any two-way ANOVA, let's consider a recent study that involved death, the dentist, and the desire to have children. In this study, the researchers first asked each of 38 male and 38 female undergraduate college students to write a brief essay. For half of each gender group, the students were told to explain how they felt when thinking about going to the dentist and to describe what would happen to them when they did. For the remaining students, the phrase "going to the dentist" was replaced by the phrase "your own death." After each student completed the essay, the researchers presented a task (identical for everyone) that was designed to distract the students from the initial essay that had been written. Finally, each student was asked how many children he or she would like to have (with options being any whole number between 0 and 6).

The table in Excerpt 13.1 provides a kind of picture of the study we are considering, and it permits us to see the factors, levels, and cells of this particular two-way ANOVA. In this excerpt's table, the term *Mortality Salience* labels the two main rows, while the term *Gender* labels the two main columns. These are the two independent variables, or factors, involved in this study. The specific rows and columns indicate the levels that went together to make up the two factors. Thus the factor of Mortality Salience was made up of two levels, Dentist and Death, while the Gender factor was made up of two levels, Women and Men. If you take either row of Table 1 and combine it with either of the columns, you end up with one of the four cells associated with this particular two-way ANOVA. Each of these cells represents the "home" of one of the subgroups of 19 college students.

*2×2 Levels = 4 cells*

**EXCERPT 13.1 • *Factors, Levels, and Cells***

**TABLE 2   *Procreation Strivings as Indicated by the Number of Desired Children as a Function of Mortality Salience and Gender***

|  |  |  | **GENDER** | |
|---|---|---|---|---|
|  |  |  | **Women** | **Men** |
|  | Dentist | M | 2.74 | 2.13 |
|  |  | SD | 1.17 | 1.03 |
|  |  | n | 19 | 19 |
| **MORTALITY** |  |  |  |  |
| **SALIENCE** | Death | M | 2.37 | 2.87 |
|  |  | SD | 1.23 | 1.33 |
|  |  | n | 19 | 19 |

*Source:* Wisman, A., and Goldenberg, J. (2005). From the grave to the cradle: Evidence that mortality salience engenders a desire for offspring. *Journal of Personality and Social Psychology, 89*(1), p. 52. (Modified slightly for presentation here.)

*IV or factors*

*DV = desired # of children*

Within each cell shown in Excerpt 13.1, you will see a mean and a standard deviation. These two numerical values constitute a summary of the scores on the dependent variable—desired number of children—collected from the 19 college students who were associated with each of the four cells. These data, of course, were very important to the two-way ANOVA that was conducted in conjunction with this study. The factors, levels, and cells provided the structure for the two-way ANOVA; without data on the dependent variable, however, there would have been no way to probe any of the research questions of interest.

As indicated earlier, all two-way ANOVAs involve two factors. Researchers will tell you what factors were involved in their studies, but they are not consistent in their descriptions. Sometimes factors are called *independent variables*, sometimes they are called *main effects*, and sometimes they are not called anything. Such variations in the way researchers label the two factors of their two-way ANOVAs are illustrated in Excerpts 13.2 through 13.4.

When describing their two-way ANOVAs, most researchers indicate how many levels were in each factor. They do this by using terms such as 2 × 2 ANOVA, 2 × 4 ANOVA, 3 × 5 ANOVA, and 2 × 3 ANOVA. When such notation is used, the first of the two numbers that precede the acronym ANOVA specifies how many levels went together to make up the first factor, while the second number indicates how many levels composed the second factor. Excerpts 13.5 and 13.6 illustrate the use of this kind of notation.

*Levels → IV*

## EXCERPTS 13.2–13.4 • *The Factors of a Two-Way ANOVA*

We conducted separate ANOVAs on each item with age and ability as factors.

*Source:* Reese, C., and Cherry, K. E. (2006). Effects of age and ability on self-reported memory functioning and knowledge of memory aging. *Journal of Genetic Psychology, 167*(2), p. 233.

---

A two-way ANOVA, with treatment and student type as the independent variables, showed that . . . .

*Source:* Saddler, B., and Graham, S. (2005). The effects of peer-assisted sentence-combining instruction on the writing performance of more and less skilled young writers. *Journal of Educational Psychology, 97*(1), p. 46.

---

A two-way ANOVA was calculated in order to determine whether there were any differences regarding educational track and gender across the dependent variables used in the study.

*Source:* Kristensson, P., and Ohlund, L. S. (2005). Swedish upper secondary school pupils' sense of coherence, coping resources and aggressiveness in relation to educational track and performance. *Scandinavian Journal of Caring Sciences, 19*(1), p. 81.

## EXCERPTS 13.5–13.6 • *Delineating a Two-Way ANOVA's Dimensions*

A $2 \times 3$ factorial analysis of variance was used to test this hypothesis.

*Source:* Ogiegbaen, S. E. A. (2006). Assessment of teachers' perception of instructional media use in colleges of education in southern Nigeria. *International Journal of Instructional Media, 33*(2), p. 210.

---

In order to determine any difference in civic competency between high school-aged children, scores on the test of civic competency were analyzed by means of a $4 \times 2$ (ethnicity $\times$ disability) factorial analysis of variance.

*Source:* Hamot, G. E., Shokoohi-Yekta, M., and Sasso, G. M. (2005). Civic competencies and students with disabilities. *Journal of Social Studies Research, 29*(2), p. 38.

The researchers who are most helpful in describing their two-way ANOVAs are the ones who indicate not only the names of the factors and the number of levels in each factor but also the names of the levels. An example of this kind of description appears in Excerpt 13.7.

Based on the information contained in Excerpt 13.7, you can and should create a picture (either on paper or in your mind) like the one presented earlier in

## EXCERPT 13.7 • *Naming Factors and Levels*

> To examine whether food moderates the impact of death primes on the judgment of social transgressions, a 3 × 4 ANOVA was performed with prime condition (death, fail, neutral) and food conditions (no food, unpleasant, neutral, pleasant) as the factors.
>
> *Source:* Hirschberger, G., and Ein-Dor, T. (2005). Does a candy a day keep the death thoughts away? The terror management function of eating. *Basic & Applied Social Psychology*, 27(2), p. 182.

Excerpt 13.1. Here, however, the picture would have three rows, four columns, and 12 cells. Collectively, the three rows would be labeled prime condition, with the specific rows being death, fail, and neutral. Collectively, the four columns would be labeled food condition, with the terms no food, unpleasant, neutral, and pleasant used to name the specific columns.[1]

Shortly, we will consider the null hypotheses that are typically tested when researchers use a two-way ANOVA, and we also will look at the different reporting schemes used by researchers to report the results of such tests. I cannot overemphasize how important it is to understand the concepts of factor, level, and cell before considering what a two-way ANOVA tries to accomplish. Stated differently, if you can't create a picture that shows the structure of a researcher's two-way ANOVA, there is no way you will be able to understand the results or evaluate whether the researcher's claimed discoveries are supported by the empirical data.

### Active versus Assigned Factors and the Formation of Comparison Groups

All two-way ANOVAs are the same in that the levels of the two factors jointly define the cells. However, there are different ways to "fill" each cell with the things (people, animals, or objects) from which measurements will be taken. In any given study, one of three possible procedures for forming the comparison groups will be used depending on the nature of the two factors. Since any factor can be classified as being "assigned" or "active" in nature, a two-way ANOVA could be set up to involve two assigned factors, two active factors, or one factor of each type.

An **assigned factor** deals with a characteristic of the things being studied that they "bring with them" to the investigation. In situations where the study focuses on people, for example, such a factor might be gender, handedness, birth order, intellectual capability, color preference, GPA, or personality type. If the study focused on dogs, an assigned factor might be breed, size, or age. The defining element of an

---

[1]The picture of Excerpt 13.7 could be set up with rows corresponding to food condition and columns corresponding to prime condition. If we set it up that way, there would be four rows and three columns. With two-way ANOVAs, it makes no difference whether a particular factor is used to define the picture's rows or columns.

assigned factor is that a person's (or animal's) status for this kind of independent variable is determined by the nature of that person (or animal) on entry into the study.

The second kind of factor is called an **active factor.** Here, a participant's status on the factor is determined within the investigation. This is because active factors deal with conditions of the study that are under the control of the researcher. Simply put, this means that the researcher can decide, for any participant, which level of the factor that participant will experience. Examples of active factors include type of diet, time allowed to practice a task, gender of the counselor to whom the participant is assigned, and kind of reward received following the occurrence of desirable behavior. The hallmark of these and all other active factors is the researcher's ability to decide which level of the factor any participant will experience during the investigation.

*[handwritten margin note: Determined w/i the investigation by the investigator]*

If a two-way ANOVA involves two assigned factors, the researcher simply will put the available participants into the various cells of the ANOVA design based on the characteristics of the participants. This situation is exemplified by Excerpt 13.6. In that study dealing high school students, the two factors were ethnicity and disability. Each of the students was put into one of the study's eight cells entirely based on the student's ethnicity and disability status.

If the factors of a two-way ANOVA are both active, the researcher will form the comparison groups by randomly assigning participants to the various cells of the design. This is what happened in the study that supplied Excerpt 13.7. In that investigation, 149 undergraduate students were randomly assigned to the study's 12 cells. Depending on which ANOVA cell a student ended up in, he or she had to write a brief essay on their emotions when thinking about their own death, failing an exam, or watching television. After the essay was written, each student's food condition dictated what was provided: a piece of candy, a bitter and unpleasant candy lookalike, a cracker, or nothing. Thus, it was the researchers who decided which level of each factor would be given to any participant. In that sense, the researchers had control over each of the study's independent variables.

If a two-way ANOVA involves one active factor and one assigned factor, the researcher will form the comparison groups by taking the participants who share a particular level on the assigned factor and randomly assigning them to the various levels of the active factor. This procedure for forming comparison groups was used in the study from which Excerpt 13.3 was drawn. In that study, 44 fourth-grade children were first identified as being skilled or not skilled in terms of their writing ability. Both a standardized test and teacher input were used to assign each child into one or the other of these two levels of the student type factor. Then, the 22 skilled students were randomly assigned to one of the two kinds of instructional procedures involved in the study; in a similar fashion, the 22 unskilled students were also randomly assigned to the two instructional methods. Collectively, those instructional methods were called the ANOVA's treatment factor. The thing to notice about this study is that the assigned nature of the student type factor meant that the 44 students had to be randomly assigned to the treatments from *within* each level of the student type factor.

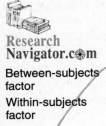

Research
Navigator.c⊕m
**Between-subjects
factor**
**Within-subjects
factor**

*Between
Subject*

## Between-Subjects and Within-Subjects Factors

Each of the factors in a two-way ANOVA can be described as being either between subjects or within subjects in nature. The distinction between these two kinds of factors revolves around the simple question, "Are the study's participants measured under (i.e., have exposure to) just one level of the factor, or are they measured repeatedly across (and thus exposed to) all levels of the factor?" If the former situation exists, the factor is a between-subjects factor; otherwise, it is a within-subjects factor.

*Within Subjects*

To help clarify the difference between these two kinds of factors, let's consider a simple (yet hypothetical) study. Imagine that a researcher wants to see if a golfer's ability to putt accurately is influenced by whether or not the flag is standing in the hole and whether the golf ball's color is white or orange. Further imagine that 20 golfers agree to participate in our study, that all putts are made on the same green from the same starting spot 25 feet from the hole, and that putting accuracy (our dependent variable) is measured by how many inches each putted ball ends up away from the hole.

In our putting investigation, we might design the study so both of our independent variables (flag status and ball color) are between-subjects factors. If we did that, we'd create four comparison groups (each with $n = 5$) and have the golfers in each group putt under just one of the conditions of our study (e.g., putting an orange ball toward a flagless hole). Or, we might want to have both factors be within-subjects in nature. If that were our choice, we would have all 20 golfers putt under all four conditions of the study. There's also a third possibility. We could have one between-subjects factor and one within-subjects factor. For example, we could have all golfers putt both white and orange balls, with half of the golfers putting toward the hole with the flag in and the other half putting toward the hole with the flag out.

In this chapter, we will consider two-way ANOVAs involving two between-subjects factors. If a researcher indicates that he/she used a two-way ANOVA (without any specification as to the type of factors involved), you should presume that it's the kind of two-way ANOVA being discussed in this chapter. You can feel relatively confident doing this because most researchers use the generic phrase "two-way ANOVA" when both factors are of the between-subjects variety.[2] Occasionally, as illustrated in Excerpt 13.8, you'll see a clear indication that two between-subjects factors were involved in the ANOVA being discussed.

## Samples and Populations

*Samples = Cells*

The samples associated with any two-way ANOVA are always easy to identify. There will be as many samples as there are cells, with the subjects who share a common cell creating each of the samples. Thus there will be four distinct samples in any $2 \times 2$ ANOVA, six distinct samples in any $2 \times 3$ ANOVA, twelve distinct samples in any $3 \times 4$ ANOVA, and so on.

[2]If one or both of the factors are of the within-subjects variety, researchers will normally draw this to your attention by labeling the factor(s) in that way or by saying that they used a repeated-measures ANOVA, a mixed ANOVA, or a split-plot ANOVA. We will consider such ANOVAs in Chapter 14.

## EXCERPT 13.8 • *Between-Subjects Factors*

The number of distractive errors was analyzed with a two-way ANOVA with two between-subjects factors (age and education).

*Source:* Plumet, J., Gil, R., and Gaonac'h, D. (2005). Neuropsychological assessment of executive functions in women: Effects of age and education. *Neuropsychology, 19*(5), p. 570.

As is always the case in inferential statistics, a distinct population is associated with each sample in the study. Hence, the number of cells designates not only the number of samples (i.e., comparison groups) in the study, but also the number of populations involved in the investigation. While it is easy to tell how many populations are involved in any two-way ANOVA, care must be exercised in thinking about the nature of these populations, especially when one or both factors are active.

Simply put, each population in a two-way ANOVA should be conceptualized as being made up of a large group of people, animals, objects, or ideas that are similar to those in the corresponding sample represented by one of the cells. Suppose, for example, that the dart-throwing ability of college students is measured via a two-way ANOVA in which the factors are sex (male and female) and handedness (right and left). One of the four populations in this study would be right-handed male college students. Each of the other three populations in this study would be defined in a similar fashion by the combination of one level from each factor. If the four samples in this study were extracted from a larger group of potential participants, then each population would be considered tangible in nature. If, on the other hand, all available dart-throwers were used, then the populations would be abstract in nature.[3]

If a two-way ANOVA involves one or two active factors, the populations associated with the study will definitely be abstract in nature. To understand why this is true, consider once again the study from which Excerpt 13.1 was taken. As discussed earlier, that study involved undergraduate college students who first wrote an essay—either about going to the dentist or about their eventual death—and then indicated how many children they would like to have. The study's two factors were gender (women and men) and mortality salience (writing about the dentist or death).

In this study, the populations were abstract because they were characterized by college students like those who were in this study following application of the study's procedures. There undoubtedly were (and are) lots of college students similar to the ones who served as participants in this investigation. However, there probably was (or is) no one outside the study who wrote the dentist or death essay, then did the distracting task, and finally answered the question about desired number of children. Even if the college students in this study had been drawn from a larger, tangible population of potential participants, the four groups of actual participants became fully unique once they experienced the conditions of this experimental investigation.

---

[3]I discussed the difference between tangible and abstract populations in Chapter 5.

## Three Research Questions

To gain an understanding of the three research questions that are focused on by a two-way ANOVA, let's continue our examination of the study discussed near the beginning of this chapter concerning dentist, death, and the desired number of children. To facilitate our current discussion, I have reproduced here the original four cells' means of Excerpt 13.1, plus I have added four additional numbers that we'll need to consider. As you will recall, the means in this study reflect the college students' desired number of children on a 0-to-6 scale.

*[Handwritten annotations: Q3 Interaction of factors / cell means; Q2. Columns main effect means; Q1. Rows main effect means; 2×2 Rows columns IV]*

| | | Gender | | |
|---|---|---|---|---|
| | | Women IV | Men | |
| Mortality Salience IV | Dentist | 2.74 | 2.13 | 2.435 |
| | Death | 2.37 | 2.87 | 2.620 |
| | | 2.555 | 2.500 | |

When the researchers applied a two-way ANOVA to the data provided by the 76 college students, they obtained answers to three research questions. Although these three research questions were tied to the specific independent and dependent variables involved in this study, the nature of their questions was identical to the nature of the three research questions that are posed and answered in any two-way ANOVA. These three questions, in their generic form, can be stated as follows: (1) Is there a statistically significant main effect for the first factor? (2) Is there a statistically significant main effect for the second factor? (3) Is there a statistically significant interaction between the two factors?

The first research question asked whether there was a statistically significant main effect for Mortality Salience. To get a feel for what this first research question was asking, you must focus your attention on the **main effect means** for the Mortality Salience factor. These means, located on the right side of the box containing the four cells, turned out equal to 2.435 and 2.620. The first of these means is simply the overall mean for the 38 students who were asked to write about going to the dentist. (Since there were 19 women and 19 men in the top two cells, the top row's main effect mean is equal to the arithmetic average of 2.74 and 2.13.) The second main effect mean for the Mortality Salience factor is the overall mean for the 38 students who were asked to write about their own death. Those 38 students are located, so to speak, within the two cells on the bottom row of the box.

In any two-way ANOVA, the first research question asks whether there is a statistically significant **main effect** for the factor that corresponds to the rows of the two-dimensional picture of the study. Stated differently, the first research question is asking whether the main effect means associated with the first factor are further

Research
Navigator.c⊕m

Main effect

apart from each other than would be expected by chance. There will be as many such means as there are levels of the first factor. In the study we are considering, there were two levels (Dentist and Death) of the first factor (Mortality Salience), with the first research question asking whether the difference between 2.435 and 2.620 was larger than could be accounted for by chance. In other words, the first research question asked, "Is there a statistically significant difference between the mean number of desired children for college students who first write about going to the dentist versus similar students who write about their own ultimate death?"

The second research question in any two-way ANOVA asks whether there is a significant main effect for the factor that corresponds to the columns of the two-dimensional picture of the study. The answer to this question will be yes if the main effect means for the second factor turn out to be further apart from each other than would be expected by chance. In the study we are considering there are two such main effect means, one for Women and one for Men. These means turned out equal to 2.555 and 2.500, respectively. Simply put, the second research question in this study asked, "Is there a statistically significant difference between the mean number of desired children for male and female college students (after they write essays and perform the distraction task involved in this particular study)?"

The third research question in any two-way ANOVA asks whether there is a statistically significant **interaction** between the two factors involved in the study. As you will see, the interaction deals with cell means, not main effect means. Therefore, there will always be four means involved in the interaction of any $2 \times 2$ ANOVA, six means involved in any $2 \times 3$ ANOVA, and so on.

Interaction exists to the extent that the difference between the levels of the first factor changes when we move from level to level of the second factor. To illustrate, consider again the dentist and death study. The difference between mean number of desired children of women and men who wrote about the dentist was .61, with the mean in the upper left-hand cell (for women) being larger than the mean in the upper right-hand cell (for men). If this difference of .61 were to show up again when we examine the bottom row of cell means (with the same ordering of those means in terms of their magnitude), there would be absolutely no interaction. If this difference on the bottom row is either smaller or larger than .61 (or if it is .61 with a reverse ordering of the means), then interaction is present in the data.

When we look at the bottom row of cell means, we can see that the difference between them does not mirror what we saw on the top row of cell means. The difference on the bottom row is −.50, not .61. (The negative sign is needed because the larger mean on the bottom row is in the right-hand cell.) Hence, there is some interaction between the mortality salience and gender factors. But is the amount of interaction contained in the four cell means more than what one would expect by chance? If so, then it can be said that a statistically significant interaction exists between the study's two factors, Gender and Mortality Salience.

It should be noted that the interaction of a two-way ANOVA can be thought of as dealing with the difference between the levels of the row's factor as one moves from one level to another level of the column's factor, or it can be thought of as dealing with the difference between the levels of the column's factor as one moves from one level to another level of the row's factor. For example, in the study on desired number of children, the difference between the cell means in the left-hand column is .37 (with the upper mean being larger) whereas the difference between the means in the right-hand column is −.74, a negative value because the lower mean is larger. Although these two differences (.37 and −.74) are not the same as the differences discussed in the preceding two paragraphs (.61 and −.50), note that in both cases the difference between the differences is exactly the same: 1.11. My point here is simply that there is only one interaction in a two-way ANOVA; the order in which the factors are named (or used to compare cell means) makes no difference whatsoever.

## The Three Null Hypotheses (and Three Alternative Hypotheses)

There are three null hypotheses examined within a two-way ANOVA. One of these null hypotheses is concerned with the main effect of the row's factor, the second is concerned with the main effect of the column's factor, and the third is concerned with the interaction between the two factors. Rarely are these null hypotheses referred to in a research report. In Excerpt 13.9, however, we see a case where the researcher enumerated the main effect and interaction null hypotheses associated with his two-way ANOVA.

### EXCERPT 13.9 • The Three Null Hypotheses of a Standard Two-Way ANOVA

All main and interaction effects were assessed. The null hypotheses for main effects were as follows: (a) there will be no difference in applicant reactions to advertisements varied according to instructional program content (academic transfer, career education, compensatory education); and (b) there will be no difference in applicant reactions to advertisements varied according to job attribute content (intrinsic, extrinsic, work context). The null hypothesis for interaction effects was as follows: There will be no influence on applicant reactions to advertisements associated with the joint effects of instructional programs and job attributes.

*Source:* Winter, P. A. (1996). The application of marketing theory to community college faculty recruitment: An empirical test. *Community College Review, 24*(3), p. 6.

To explain how each of these null hypotheses should be conceptualized, I want to reiterate that the group of participants that supplies data for any cell of the two-way ANOVA is only a sample. As was pointed out earlier in this chapter, a population is connected to each cell's sample. Sometimes each of these populations will be concrete in nature, with participants randomly selected from a finite pool of potential participants. In many studies, each population will be abstract in nature, with the nature of the population tailored to fit the nature of the group within each cell and the condition under which data are collected from the participants in that group.

In the $2 \times 2$ ANOVA that dealt with gender, mortality salience, and the desired number of children, four populations were involved. As indicated earlier, each of these populations was abstract (rather than tangible). One of them should be conceptualized as being made up of women college students (like those used in the study) who first write an essay about going to the dentist, next perform a distraction task, and finally indicate how many children they would like to have. The other three populations should be conceptualized in this same way, with changes made in the focus of the essay (substituting death for dentist) and the gender of the students (substituting men for women). Each of these four populations is created, in our minds, to match the students and study conditions associated with each of the ANOVA's cells.

The first null hypothesis in any two-way ANOVA deals with the main effect means associated with the rows factor of the study. This null hypothesis asserts that the population counterparts of these sample-based main effect means are equal to each other. Stated in symbols for the general case, this null hypothesis is as follows: $H_0$: $\mu_{row1} = \mu_{row2} = \ldots = \mu_{bottom\ row}$. For the study dealing with the number of desired children, this null hypothesis took the form $H_0$: $\mu_{dentist} = \mu_{death}$.

The second null hypothesis in any two-way ANOVA deals with the main effect means associated with the columns factor. This null hypothesis asserts that the population counterparts of these sample-based main effect means are equal to each other. For the general case, the null hypothesis says $H_0$: $\mu_{column1} = \mu_{column2} = \ldots = \mu_{last\ column}$. For the study dealing with the number of desired children, this null hypothesis took the form $H_0$: $\mu_{women} = \mu_{men}$.

Before we turn our attention to the third null hypothesis of a two-way ANOVA, I need to clarify the meaning of the $\mu$s that appear in the null hypothesis for the main effects. Each of these $\mu$s, like the data-based sample mean to which it is tied, actually represents the average of cell means. For example, $\mu_{row1}$ is the average of the $\mu$s associated with the cells on row 1, while $\mu_{column1}$ is the average of the $\mu$s associated with the cells in column 1. Each of the other main effect $\mu$s similarly represents the average of the $\mu$s associated with the cells that lie in a common row or in a common column. This point about the main effect $\mu$s is important to note because (1) populations are always tied conceptually to samples and (2) the samples in a two-way ANOVA are located *in* the cells. Unless you realize that the main effect $\mu$s are conceptually derived from averaging cell $\mu$s, you might find yourself being misled into thinking that the number of populations associated with any two-way ANOVA can be determined by adding the number of main effect means to the number of cells. Hopefully, my earlier and current comments will help you to see that a two-way ANOVA has only as many populations as there are cells.

The third null hypothesis in a two-way ANOVA specifies that there is no interaction between the two factors. This null hypothesis deals with the cell means,

*NO*
*Interaction*
*between*
*a factors*

$H_0 : \mu_{jk} - \mu_{j'k}$
$= \mu_{jk'} - \mu_{j'k'}$

not the main effect means. This null hypothesis asserts that whatever differences exist among the population means associated with the cells in any given column of the two-way layout are equal to the differences among the population means associated with the cells in each of the other columns. Stated differently, this null hypothesis says that the relationship among the population means associated with the full set of cells is such that a single pattern of differences accurately describes what exists within any column.[4]

To express the interaction null hypothesis using symbols, we must first agree to let $j$ and $j'$ stand for any two different rows in the two-way layout, and to let $k$ and $k'$ stand for any two different columns. Thus the intersection of row $j$ and column $k$ designates cell $jk$, with the population mean associated with this cell being referred to as $\mu_{jk}$. The population mean associated with a different cell in the same column would be symbolized as $\mu_{j'k}$. The population means associated with two cells on these same rows, $j$ and $j'$, but in a different column, $k'$, could be symbolized as $\mu_{jk'}$ and $\mu_{j'k'}$, respectively. Using this notational scheme, we can express the interaction null hypothesis of any two-way ANOVA as follows:

$$H_0: \mu_{jk} - \mu_{j'k} = \mu_{jk'} - \mu_{j'k'}, \text{ for all rows and columns}$$
(i.e., for all combinations of both $j$ and $j'$, $k$ and $k'$)

To help you understand the meaning of the interaction null hypothesis, I have constructed sets of hypothetical population means corresponding to a $2 \times 2$ ANOVA, a $2 \times 3$ ANOVA, and a $2 \times 4$ ANOVA. In each of the hypothetical ANOVAs, the interaction null hypothesis is completely true.

| $\mu = 20$ | $\mu = 40$ |
|---|---|
| $\mu = 10$ | $\mu = 30$ |

| $\mu = 10$ | $\mu = 30$ | $\mu = 29$ |
|---|---|---|
| $\mu = 5$ | $\mu = 25$ | $\mu = 24$ |

| $\mu = 2$ | $\mu = 12$ | $\mu = 6$ | $\mu = 24$ |
|---|---|---|---|
| $\mu = 4$ | $\mu = 14$ | $\mu = 8$ | $\mu = 26$ |

Before turning our attention to the alternative hypotheses associated with a two-way ANOVA, it is important to note that each $H_0$ we have considered is independent from the other two. In other words, any combination of the three null hypotheses can be true (or false). To illustrate, I have constructed three sets of hypothetical population means for a $2 \times 2$ layout. Moving from left to right, we see a case in which only the row means differ, a case in which only the interaction null hypothesis is false, and a case in which the null hypotheses for both the row's main effect and the interaction are false:

[4]The interaction null hypothesis can be stated with references to parameter differences among the cell means within the various rows (rather than within the various columns). Thus the interaction null hypothesis asserts that whatever differences exist among the population means associated with the cells in any given row of the two-way layout are equal to the differences among the population means associated with the cells in each of the other rows.

| $\mu = 10$ | $\mu = 10$ |
|---|---|
| $\mu = 5$ | $\mu = 5$ |

| $\mu = 20$ | $\mu = 10$ |
|---|---|
| $\mu = 10$ | $\mu = 20$ |

| $\mu = 10$ | $\mu = 30$ |
|---|---|
| $\mu = 20$ | $\mu = 0$ |

Because the three null hypotheses are independent of each other, a conclusion drawn (from sample data) concerning one of the null hypotheses is specific to that particular $H_0$. The same data set can be used to evaluate all three null statements, but the data must be looked at from different angles in order to address all three null hypotheses. This is accomplished by computing a separate *F*-test to see if each $H_0$ is likely to be false.

If the researcher who conducts the two-way ANOVA evaluates each $H_0$ by means of hypothesis testing there will usually be three alternative hypotheses. Each $H_a$ is set up in a nondirectional fashion, and they assert that:

1. The row $\mu$s are *not* all equal to each other;
2. The column $\mu$s are *not* all equal to each other;
3. The pattern of differences among the cell $\mu$s in the first column (or the first row) *fails* to describe accurately the pattern of differences among the cell $\mu$s in at least one other column (row).

## Presentation of Results

The results of a two-way ANOVA can be communicated through a table or within the text of the research report. We begin our consideration of how researchers present the findings gleaned from their two-way ANOVAs by looking at the results of the study dealing with dentists, death, and number of children desired. We then consider how the results of several other two-way ANOVAs were presented. Near the end of this section, we will look at the various ways researchers organize their findings when two or more two-way ANOVAs have been conducted within the same study.

### Results of the Two-Way ANOVA Study

In the research report of the study dealing with gender, mortality salience, and the number of desired children, the findings were not presented in a two-way ANOVA summary table. If such a table had been prepared, it probably would have looked like Table 13.1

In Table 13.1, notice that this summary table is similar to the summary table for a one-way ANOVA in terms of (1) the number and names of columns included in the table, (2) each row's *MS* being computed by dividing the row's *df* into its *SS*,  (3) the total *df* being equal to one less than the number of participants used in the investigation, and (4) calculated values being presented in the *F* column. Despite these

*(handwritten in left margin: "like one way")*

**TABLE 13.1**    *ANOVA Summary Table for Gender and Mortality Salience Study*

| Source | df | SS | MS | F | p |
|---|---|---|---|---|---|
| Mortality Salience | 1 | .6503 | .6503 | .46 | ns |
| Gender | 1 | .0575 | .0575 | .04 | ns |
| Interaction | 1 | 5.8525 | 5.8525 | 4.09 | p < .05 |
| Within Groups | 72 | 102.8088 | 1.4279 | | |
| Total | 75 | 109.3691 | | | |

*(handwritten annotations on table: "main effect" bracketing the .46 and .04 rows; "Interaction" next to the 4.09 row)*

similarities, one-way and two-way ANOVA summary tables differ in that the latter contain five rows (rather than three) and three *F*-ratios (rather than one). Note that in the two-way summary table, the *MS* for the next-to-bottom row (which is usually labeled *error* or *within groups*) was used as the denominator in computing each of the three *F*-ratios: $.6503/1.4279 = .46$ (*ns*), $.0575/1.4279 = .04$ (*ns*), and $5.8525/1.4279 = 4.09$ ($p < .05$).

There are three values in the *F* column of a two-way ANOVA summary table because there are three null hypotheses associated with this kind of ANOVA. Each of the three *F*s addresses a different null hypothesis. The first two *F*s are concerned with the study's main effects; in other words, the first two *F*s deal with the two sets of main effect means. The third *F* deals with the interaction between the two factors, with the focus of this *F* being on cell means. In the ANOVA summary table, look at the results for the two main effects. The *F* on each of these rows was small and not significant. If you look again at the table I created to display the cell, row, and column means, you will see that the main effect means for each factor were quite similar. (The main effect means for Women and Men were nearly identical—2.555 and 2.500—and that is why the **main effect** *F* for Gender was smaller than the main effect *F* for Mortality Salience.) With *F*-tests in ANOVAs, a homogeneous set of means will cause the *F* to be small and nonsignificant. Statistically speaking, the observed difference between the column main effect means was not large enough to cast doubt on the Gender null hypothesis ($H_0: \mu_{women} = \mu_{men}$); likewise, the observed difference between the row main effect means was too small to cast doubt on the Mortality Salience null hypothesis ($H_0: \mu_{dentist} = \mu_{death}$).

In the ANOVA summary table, you can see that the interaction *F* turned out to be significant. As we noted earlier, there was some interaction in the sample data because the difference between the means for the women and men who wrote about going to the dentist ($2.74 - 2.13 = .61$) was not the same as the difference between the means for the women and men who wrote about their own death ($2.37 - 2.87 = -.50$). The two-way ANOVA considered the difference between these differences and declared that it was "beyond the limits of chance sampling." In other words, this degree of observed interaction in the sample data would not be expected if the four samples had come from populations in which there was no interaction. Accordingly, the interaction null hypothesis was rejected, as indicated by the notation $p < .05$ that appears next to the *F* of 4.09.

## Results from Various Two-Way ANOVA Studies

In Excerpt 13.10, we see the summary table from a study in which a $2 \times 2$ ANOVA was used. It is worth the effort to compare this table to Table 13.1 so as to identify differences in how the same kind of information can be presented, even for cases that are identical in terms of the number of levels and cells involved.

**EXCERPT 13.10 •** *Two-Way ANOVA Summary Table*

**TABLE 2**    *Two-Way Analysis of Variance Results for the SCL-90-R, GSI for Women and Men in the Earthquake Region*

| Source | Sum of squares | df | Mean square | F | p |
|---|---|---|---|---|---|
| Sex | 111929.97 | 1 | 111929.97 | 30.28 | .001* |
| Administration group | 13235.12 | 1 | 13235.12 | 3.58 | .059 |
| Sex × Admin. group | 355.50 | 1 | 355.50 | 0.96 | .757 |
| Error | 2066360.13 | 559 | 3696.53 | | |
| Total | 2190330.27 | 562 | 3897.39 | | |

*$p < .001$

*Source:* Kisac, I. (2006). Stress symptoms of survivors of the Marmara region (Turkey) earthquakes: A follow-up study. *International Journal of Stress Management, 13*(1), p. 122.

First, notice that the terms *Sum of squares* and *Mean square* are used to label two of the table's columns rather than the abbreviations *SS* and *MS*. The second thing to notice is that the column of *df* numbers is positioned to the right (rather than the left) of the column of *SS* numbers. Next, notice the names of the third and fourth rows of the table. Here in Excerpt 13.10, the third row is called "Sex × Admin. group" (rather than just "Interaction"), and the fourth row is called "Error" (instead of "Within Groups"). Finally, notice that the actual *p*-levels are provided in the right-hand column for the results that were not significant, whereas the abbreviation *ns* was used to convey this information in Table 13.1.

I have seen summary tables for $2 \times 2$ ANOVAs that differ in other ways from the two we have just considered. Sometimes there will be no column of *SS* numbers, and sometimes there will be no bottom row for Total. You are not at a disadvantage by not having these parts of the table, because you could (if you so desired) compute all five missing *SS* values and the *df* for total. The $df_{\text{Total}}$ is the most important of these items, for it allows you to determine how many individuals were involved in the study.

Despite the differences between Table 13.1 and Excerpt 13.10, these two ANOVA summary tables are similar in several respects. In each case, the title of the table reveals what the dependent variable was. In each case, the names of the first two rows reveal the names of the two factors. In each case, the *df* values for the main effect rows of the table allow us to know that there were two levels in each factor. In each case, the three *F*-values were computed by dividing the *MS* values on the first three rows by the *MS* value located on the fourth row (i.e., within groups or error). And in each case, three calculated *F*-values are presented, one of which addresses each of the three null hypotheses associated with the two-way ANOVA.

Not all two-way ANOVAs, of course, are of the 2 × 2 variety. In Excerpt 13.11, we see the summary table for a 2 × 5 ANOVA. Although there were two levels of the administration group factor and five levels of the education groups factor, this two-way ANOVA still produced three *F*-values, one for each main effect and one for the interaction between the two factors. This table, when considered with the ones we have already seen, shows that the "structure" and "internal workings" of a two-way ANOVA summary table are the same no matter how many levels there are in each of the two factors.

**EXCERPT 13.11 • *Summary Table for 2 × 5 ANOVA***

**TABLE 4**   *Two-Way Analysis of Variance Results for the SCL-90-R (GSI) Based on Educational Levels*

| Source | Sum of squares | df | Mean square | F | p |
|---|---|---|---|---|---|
| Education groups | 46097.12 | 4 | 11524.28 | 2.99 | .018* |
| Administration groups | 2191.13 | 1 | 2191.13 | 0.57 | .451 |
| Educ. group × Admin. group | 3455.28 | 4 | 863.82 | 0.22 | .925 |
| Error | 2126971.36 | 552 | 3853.21 | | |
| Total | 2188796.28 | 561 | | | |

*$p < .05$

*Source:* Kisac, I. (2006). Stress symptoms of survivors of the Marmara region (Turkey) earthquakes: A follow-up study. *International Journal of Stress Management, 13*(1), p. 123.

In reporting the outcome of their two-way ANOVAs, researchers often talk about the results within the text of the research report without including a summary table. In Excerpt 13.12, we see a case in which six sentences were used to summarize and interpret the results of a 2 × 2 ANOVA. This ANOVA came from a study involving college students who drink alcohol. The study's two factors were gender (male and female) and repressor status (repressors versus nonrepressors). The data in the two-way ANOVA were difference scores based on the college students' perceptions of how much others' drinking might harm them versus other students. This difference in perception was the dependent variable.

Based on the information in Excerpt 13.12, you should be able to figure out what the three null hypotheses were, what decision was reached regarding each $H_0$,

**EXCERPT 13.12 • *Results of a Two-Way ANOVA Presented in the Text***

The difference scores of [college students] who reported that they were drinkers served as the dependent measure in a 2 (gender) $\times$ 2 (repressor status) ANOVA. Significant main effects were found for both gender [$F(1, 321) = 5.43, p = .020$] and repressor status [$F(1, 321) = 6.95, p = .009$]. The gender $\times$ repressor status interaction was not significant. Repressors ($M = 2.05, SD = 1.87$) had significantly higher scores than nonrepressors ($M = 1.44, SD = 1.95$). Repressors perceived that others would be harmed by others' drinking more than that they themselves would be harmed by their own drinking to a larger extent than did nonrepressors. The same trend was found between the genders, such that women ($M = 1.78, SD = 2.04$) perceived a greater discrepancy than did men ($M = 1.29, SD = 1.74$).

*Source:* Shirachi, M., and Spirrison, C. L. (2006). Repressive coping style and substance use among college students. *North American Journal of Psychology, 8*(1), p. 108.

and how many college students supplied the researcher with the data analyzed by the two-way ANOVA.[5]

When there are two or more dependent variables in a study along with two independent variables, researchers often choose a strategy for data analysis that involves conducting a separate two-way ANOVA on the data from each dependent variable. Sometimes, separate summary tables like the ones you saw in Table 13.1 or Excerpts 13.10 or 13.11 will appear in the same table. When you come across such a table, you will have no difficulty interpreting the results. Sometimes, however, the results of separate two-way ANOVAs are combined into a single table that does not look at all like the "standard" two-way ANOVA summary table. Consider, for example, Excerpt 13.13.

Excerpt 13.13 differs what we saw in Excerpts 13.10 and 13.11 in three main respects. First, there are no numerical values shown for either sums of squares or mean squares. Second, neither of the summary tables in this excerpt has a row for "Total." Third, instead of providing a *p*-value for each of the three *F*-values in each two-way ANOVA, we are given indices of estimated effect size. (We'll talk more about effect size later in the chapter.) Despite these three differences, I hope you would able to discern what is "going on" in Excerpt 13.13 if you were to see it in a research report rather than in this book.

If multiple two-way ANOVAs are conducted, researchers often summarize the results within the text of their research reports without any tables. Excerpt 13.14 illustrates this popular reporting technique. Notice that the same two factors were involved in all three of the two-way ANOVAs discussed in Excerpt 13.14. The dependent variable, however, was different in each separate analysis.

---

[5]If you end up thinking that 323 students were involved in this study, try again.

**EXCERPT 13.13** • *Results of Two Two-Way ANOVAs in One Table*

**TABLE 8**    *Analysis of Variance for Intrateam Coordination Process*

| Dependent variable | Source (independent variable) | df | F | $\eta^2$ | MSE |
|---|---|---|---|---|---|
| Intrateam coordination (air to ground) | Strategy training (SP) | 1 | 0.55 | .01 | |
| | Coordination training (CP) | 1 | 1.60 | .03 | |
| | SP × CP interaction | 1 | 2.14 | .03 | |
| | Error | 60 | | | 0.51 |
| Intrateam coordination (air to air) | SP | 1 | 1.79 | .03 | |
| | CP | 1 | 0.52 | .01 | |
| | SP × CP interaction | 1 | 0.15 | .00 | |
| | Error | 60 | | | 0.73 |

*Source:* DeChurch, L. A., and Marks, M. A. (2006). Leadership in multiteam systems. *Journal of Applied Psychology, 91*(2), p. 321.

**EXCERPT 13.14** • *Results of Three Two-Way ANOVAs*

A two-way ANOVA was calculated in order to determine whether there were any differences regarding educational track and gender across the dependent variables used in the study. The statistics showed no significant effect of education orientation on the SOC variable, but an effect was found on gender [$F(1, 249) = 4.39$, $p < 0.04$]. The interaction between educational orientation and gender was not statistically significant. The same findings were observed for CRI as for SOC: no significant effect of educational orientation, a statistically significant gender effect [$F(1, 249) = 6.3, p < 0.02$] and no significant interaction between educational orientation and gender. For AQ, both educational orientation [$F(1, 249) = 5.39$, $p < 0.03$] and gender [$F(1, 249) = 4.80, p < 0.03$] reached statistical significance. However, there was no interaction between these two variables.

*Source:* Kristensson, P., and Ohlund, L. S. (2005). Swedish upper secondary school pupils' sense of coherence, coping resources and aggressiveness in relation to educational track and performance. *Scandinavian Journal of Caring Sciences, 19*(1), p. 81.

## Follow-Up Tests

If none of the two-way ANOVA *F*s turns out to be significant, no follow-up test will be conducted. On the other hand, if at least one of the main effects is found to be significant, or if the interaction null hypothesis is rejected, you may find that a follow-up investigation is undertaken in an effort to probe the data. We will consider first the follow-up tests used in conjunction with significant main effect *F*-ratios. Then, we will examine the post hoc strategy typically employed when the interaction *F* turns out to be significant.

### Follow-Up Tests to Probe Significant Main Effects

If the *F*-test for one of the factors turns out to be significant and if there are only two levels associated with that factor, no post hoc test will be applied. In this situation, the outcome of the *F*-test indicates that a significant difference exists between that factor's two main effect means, and the only thing the researcher needs to do to determine where the significant difference lies is to look at the two row (or two column) means. Whichever of the two means is larger is significantly larger than the other mean. If you take another look at Excerpt 13.12, you will see an example in which both main effects were significant in a 2 × 2 ANOVA. Because there were only two main effect means associated with each of the significant *F*s, the researchers interpreted these results directly. That interpretation is presented in the final three sentences of Excerpt 13.12, with a focus on the two sets of main effect means.

If the two-way ANOVA yields a significant *F* for one of the two factors, and if that factor involves three or more levels, the researcher is likely to conduct a **post hoc** investigation in order to compare the main effect means associated with the significant *F*. This is done for the same reasons that a post hoc investigation is typically conducted in conjunction with a one-way ANOVA that yields a significant result when three or more means are compared. In both cases, the omnibus *F* that turns out to be significant needs to be "probed" so as to allow the researcher (and others) to gain insight into the pattern of population means.

Excerpt 13.15 shows how a post hoc investigation can help to clarify the meaning of a significant main effect in a two-way ANOVA. In this excerpt, notice how Scheffé pairwise tests compared the three levels of the condition factor. The main effect for the other factor (preschool class) was also significant; however, no post hoc investigation was needed there because there were only two levels of that factor.

### EXCERPT 13.15 • A Post Hoc Investigation Following a Significant Main Effect

The results of a two-way analysis of variance of the recall for relevant items with preschool class and condition as between subjects variables yielded a main effect of preschool class, $F(1, 106) = 4.11, p < 0.05$ and of condition, $F(2, 106) = 8.26, p < 0.001$. The results from a post hoc test using Scheffé's method indicated that the mean recall of children in the corners condition was significantly greater than that of children in the walls and control condition, $p < 0.01$.

*Source:* Blumberg, F. C., and Torenberg, M. (2005). The effects of spatial configuration on preschoolers' attention strategies, selective attention, and incidental learning. *Infant & Child Development, 14*(3), p. 252.

If each of the factors in a two-way ANOVA turns out significant and if each of those factors contains three or more levels, then it is likely that a separate post hoc investigation will be conducted on each set of main effect means. The purpose of the two post hoc investigations would be the same: to identify the main effect means associated with each factor that are far enough apart to suggest that the corresponding population means are dissimilar. When both sets of main effect means are probed by means of post hoc investigations, the same test procedure (e.g., Tukey's) will be used to make comparisons among each set of main effect means.

### Follow-Up Tests to Probe a Significant Interaction

When confronted with a statistically significant interaction, researchers will typically do two things. First, they will *refrain* from interpreting the *F*-ratios associated with the two main effects. Second, post hoc tests will be conducted and/or a graph will be prepared to help explain the specific nature of the interaction within the context of the study that has been conducted. Before turning our attention to the most frequently used follow-up strategies employed by researchers after observing a statistically significant interaction, I want to say a word or two about what they *do not do*.

Once the results of the two-way ANOVA become available, researchers will usually first look to see what happened relative to the interaction *F*. If the interaction turns out to be nonsignificant, they will move their attention to the two main effect *F*s and will interpret them in accordance with the principles outlined in the previous section. If, however, the interaction turns out to be significant, little or no attention will be devoted to the main effect *F*-ratios. This is because conclusions based on main effects can be quite misleading in the presence of significant interactions.

To illustrate how the presence of interaction renders the interpretation of main effects problematic, consider the three hypothetical situations presented in Figure 13.1. The number within each cell of each diagram is meant to be a sample mean, the numbers to the right of and below each diagram are meant to be main

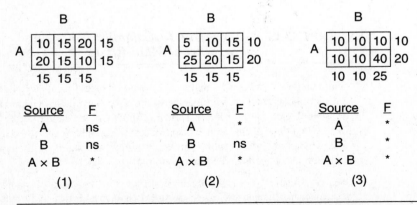

**FIGURE 13.1   *Hypothetical Results from Three Two-Way ANOVAs***

effect means (assuming equal cell sizes), and the abbreviated summary table provides the results that would be obtained if the samples were large enough or if the within-cell variability were small enough.

In situation 1, both main effect $F$s turn out nonsignificant. These results, coupled with the fact that there is no variability within either set of main effect means, might well lead one to think that the two levels of factor A are equivalent and to think that the three levels of factor B are equivalent. An inspection of the cell means, however, shows that those conclusions based on main effect means would cause one to overlook potentially important findings. The two levels of factor A produced different means at the first and third levels of factor B, and the three levels of factor B were dissimilar at each level of factor A.

To drive home this point about how main effect $F$s can be misleading when the interaction is significant, pretend that factor A is gender (males on the top row, females on the bottom row), that factor B is a type of headache medicine given to relieve pain (brands X, Y, and Z corresponding to the first, second, and third columns, respectively), with each participant asked to rate the effectiveness of his or her medication on a 0 to 40 scale (0 = no relief; 40 = total relief) 60 minutes after being given a single dose of one brand of medication. If one were to pay attention to the main effect $F$s, one might be tempted to conclude that men and women experienced equal relief and that the three brands of medication were equally effective. Such conclusions would be unfortunate because the cell means suggest strongly (1) that males and females differed, on the average, in their reactions to headache medications X and Z, and (2) that the three medications differed in the relief produced (with Brand X being superior for females, Brand Z being superior for males).

In the second of our hypothetical situations, notice again how the main effect $F$s are misleading because of the interaction. Now, the main effect of factor A is significant, and one might be tempted to look at the main effect means and draw the conclusion that males experienced less relief from their headache medicines than did females. However, inspection of the cell means clearly shows that no difference exists between males and females when given Brand Z. Again, the main effect $F$ for factor B would be misleading for the same reason as it would in the first set of results.

In the final hypothetical situation, both main effect $F$s are significant. Inspection of the cell means reveals, however, that the levels of factor A do not differ at the first or at the second levels of factor B, and that the levels of factor B do not differ at the first level of factor A. Within the context of our hypothetical headache study, the main effect $F$s, if interpreted, would lead one to suspect that females experienced more relief than males and that the three medicines differed in their effectiveness. Such conclusions would be misleading, for males and females experienced differential relief only when given Brand Z, and the brands seem to be differentially effective only in the case of females.

When the interaction $F$ turns out to be significant, the main effect $F$s must be interpreted with extreme caution—or not interpreted directly at all. This is why most researchers are encouraged to look at the interaction $F$ first when trying to make sense out of the results provided by a two-way ANOVA. The interaction $F$ serves as a guidepost that tells the researchers what to do next. If the interaction $F$ turns out to be *non*significant, this means that they have a green light and may proceed to interpret the $F$-ratios associated with the two main effects. If, however, the interaction $F$ *is* significant, this is tantamount to a red light that says "Don't pay attention to the main effect means but instead focus your attention on the cell means."

One of the strategies used to help gain insight into a statistically significant interaction is a **graph of the cell means.** In a moment, we will look at such a graph that was included in a recent research report. First, however, you need to become acquainted with the study.

In this study's experiment, the researchers randomly assigned 61 research participants (who were college students) to the four cells of a $2 \times 2$ between-subjects design. One of the two factors was called "Emotion," and this factor's two levels were "Anger" and "Gratitude." The other factor was called "Manipulation." One of second factor's levels was called "Priming (recall only)"; the other level of this factor was called "Emotion Induction (describe)."

In the first part of this two-stage study, the college students performed a simple task designed to elicit either feelings of gratitude or feelings of anger. Approximately one-fourth of the students were asked to write essays describing in detail someone who had made them feel a deep sense of gratitude and why they felt this way. Another fourth of the student group also wrote essays, except these students were asked to describe in detail the high level of anger they feel at someone and why. The other two groups did not write essays; instead, they were simply asked to recall an emotional event (without providing any specifics). One of these recall-only groups was asked to think about a time when they felt a deep sense of gratitude toward someone; the other group was told to think of a time when they got angry at someone.

In the second stage of this investigation, all 61 of the college students filled out a 10-item inventory designed to measure one's inclination to trust another person. Each item on the so-called trust inventory had a 7-point Likert scale with the end points being $1 = $ *not at all likely* and $7 = $ *very likely*. Each student's trust score was computed as the mean score across the 10 items of the inventory. The four cell means that went into the $2 \times 2$ ANOVA were presented in the research report, and they are reproduced here.

|  |  | **Manipulation** | |
|---|---|---|---|
|  |  | Priming (Recall only) | Emotion Induction (Describe in detail) |
| **Emotion** | Gratitude | 5.24 | 5.69 |
|  | Anger | 5.18 | 4.50 |

In Excerpt 13.16, we see a graph of the cell means from the study dealing with gratitude, anger, and trust. Most researchers set up their graphs like the one in Excerpt 13.16 in that (1) the ordinate represents the dependent variable, (2) the points on the abscissa represent the levels of one of the independent variables, and (3) the lines in the graph represent the levels of the other independent variable. In setting up such a graph, either of the two independent variables can be used to label the abscissa. For example, the researchers associated with Excerpt 13.16 could have put the factor Emotion and its two levels (Anger and Gratitude) on the baseline with the lines in the graph representing the two levels (Recall only; Describe in detail) of the Manipulation factor.

Notice how the graph in Excerpt 13.16 allows us to see whether or not an interaction exists. First recall that the absence of interaction means that the difference between the levels of one factor remains constant as we move from one level to another level of the other factor. Now look at Excerpt 13.16. In the graph, there is only a tiny difference between mean scores which define the left ends of the two lines. However, things change when we consider the right end points of these lines. Here,

**EXCERPT 13.16 • *The Graph of a Significant Interaction***

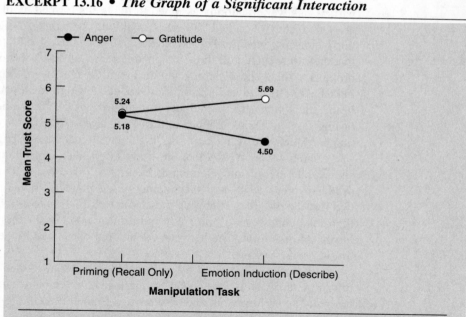

**FIGURE 1**   *Emotional states versus priming effects on trust, Study 2. Trust scale ratings range from 1 (least trusting) to 7 (most trusting).*

*Source:* Dunn, J. R., and Schweitzer, M. E. (2005). Feeling and believing: The influence of emotion on trust. *Journal of Personality and Social Psychology, 88*(5), p. 741.

there is more than a 1-point difference between the two means. Considered as a whole, this graph suggests that how the college students responded to the trust inventory was differentially influenced by whether they wrote a detailed essay about a gratitude or anger situation; on the other hand, mean scores on the trust inventory end up about the same if students were asked simply to recall a gratitude or anger event.[6]

The **graph of an interaction** can be and often is set up such that vertical bars (rather than dots above the baseline) represent the cell means. I will illustrate this popular reporting technique with a graph taken from a recent study in which data were analyzed using a $2 \times 2$ ANOVA. This graph will make more sense if I first provide a brief overview of the investigation.

In the study associated with this two-way ANOVA, 102 female college students were led to believe that they were involved in a taste test in which they would be evaluating the quality of a milkshake. Actually, the dependent variable in the study was measured by how much of the milkshake each student drank during the study. Each woman's milkshake was weighed at the beginning and at the end of the experimental session, and the difference in weight (in grams) was the way the researchers measured milkshake consumption.

Each of the study's two independent variables had two levels, and the research participants were randomly assigned to four cells formed by these factors and levels. One factor was called Salience Condition. The women assigned to one level of this factor tasted their milkshake under conditions designed to have them remember that they were on a diet; those assigned to the other level of this factor received no prompts to think about dieting, and thus their thoughts were directed entirely on the milkshake. The study's second factor was called Cognitive Load. All of the women in the study were given a number to memorize at the beginning of the milkshake-tasting session. Those assigned to the "low" level of this factor were given a 1-digit number to remember; those in the "high" level received a 9-digit number.

The two-way ANOVA of the study's milkshake-consumption data revealed a statistically significant interaction. Excerpt 13.17 contains the graph that the researchers prepared to show this interaction. As you look at this graph, be sure to notice that the difference between the amount of milkshake consumed under the two high-load conditions of the study (with means of 198.05 versus 109.08) is much larger than the difference between the amount consumed in the two low-load conditions (with means of 171.51 versus 164.43).

Another strategy used by researchers to help understand the nature of a significant interaction is a statistical comparison of cell means. Such comparisons will normally be performed in one of two ways. Sometimes all of the cell means will be compared simultaneously in a pairwise fashion using one of the test procedures discussed in Chapter 12. In other studies, cell means will be compared in a pairwise fashion one row and/or one column at a time using a post hoc strategy referred to

---

[6]Notice that the two lines in Excerpt 13.16 are not parallel. If the interaction $F$ turns out to be significant, this is because the lines in the graph are nonparallel to a degree that is greater than what one expects by chance. For this reason, some authors define interaction as a departure from parallelism.

**EXCERPT 13.17 • *Another Way to Graph an Interaction***

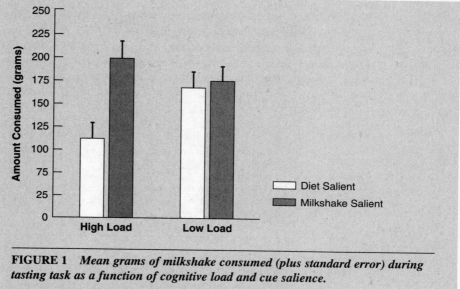

**FIGURE 1** *Mean grams of milkshake consumed (plus standard error) during tasting task as a function of cognitive load and cue salience.*

*Source:* Mann, T., and Ward, A. (2004). To eat or not to eat: Implications of the attentional myopia model for restrained eaters. *Journal of Abnormal Psychology, 113*(1), p. 94.

as a simple main effects analysis. In the following five paragraphs, excerpts from actual studies are used to illustrate each of these post hoc strategies.

When a researcher probes a statistically significant interaction via tests of simple main effects, the various levels of one factor are compared in such a way that the other factor is "held constant." This is accomplished by comparing the cell means that reside in individual rows and/or in individual columns of the two-dimensional arrangement of cell means. This strategy of making tests of simple main effects is illustrated in Excerpt 13.18.

The first thing to note about Excerpt 13.18 is that the two factors were called "school level" and "program type." The next thing to see is that the school type factor was made up of three levels (elementary school, middle school, and high school) while the program type factor involved two levels (general education and special education). You'll now need to use these "discoveries" to create a picture of the study. In my picture, I have a rectangle that contains three rows (for school level) and two columns (for program type). Finally, in looking at your picture, you need to realize that there was a group of teachers inside each of the six cells, with each teacher providing a score indicating the teacher's opinion of the importance of student self-control.

Because the interaction between school level and program type was significant, the researchers conducted tests of simple main effects. As you can see, they

Research
Navigator.c⊛m

Simple main
effects

## EXCERPT 13.18 • *Tests of Simple Main Effects*

Results of a two-way ANOVA with two between-groups factors (school level and program type) with self-control as the outcome variable produced a significant school level taught × program type interaction, $F(2, 539) = 4.62, p = .0102$. A simple effect for program type for elementary teachers was not significant nor was a simple effect for program type for middle school teachers. These findings indicated that general and special education teachers at the elementary and middle school levels shared similar views regarding the importance of self-control skills. A final simple effect for program type for high school teachers was significant, $F(1, 185) = 15.24, p = .0001$, effect size $(d) = .72$, with high school special education teachers viewing self control as significantly more important for school success as compared to high school general education teachers.

*Source:* Lane, K. L., Wehby, J. H., and Cooley, C. (2006). Teacher expectations of students' classroom behavior across the grade span: Which social skills are necessary for success? *Exceptional Children, 72*(2), p. 160.

did this by comparing, within each school level, the cell means for the two program types. In my picture, this amounts to comparing the two means on the top row, then comparing the two means on the middle row, and finally comparing the two means on the bottom row. My picture helps me understand what was being compared in each of the three tests of simple main effects.

The three tests of simple main effects conducted in Excerpt 13.18 are highly analogous to three independent-samples *t*-tests, because there were two means involved in each of the three tests. Instead of conducting the simple effects investigation to compare program type for each kind of school, the researchers could have compared the three school levels that had a common program type. Had the tests of simple main effects been conducted like this, there would have been just two tests, with each one being highly analogous to a one-way ANOVA. If the tests of simple main effects had been performed in this way and if one (or both) resulted in a significant *F*, the researchers then would likely make pairwise comparisons among the three cell means, perhaps with a test procedure like Tukey's HSD.

Sometimes two sets of tests of simple main effects are used to probe a statistically significant interaction. When this is done, one set of these post hoc tests compares cell means that lie in each row, and then a second set is used to compare the cell means that lie within each column. Excerpt 13.19 shows how tests of simple main effects can be applied in both directions to the cell means of a two-way ANOVA.

A third strategy exists for statistically comparing cell means. Instead of comparing the means that reside within individual rows and/or columns of the two-dimensional layout of a two-way ANOVA, some researchers conduct *all possible pairwise comparisons among the cell means*. In Excerpt 13.20, we see an example in which this approach was taken after the interaction null hypothesis was rejected.

## EXCERPT 13.19 • *Tests of Simple Main Effects Applied in Both Directions*

As Figure 1 [not shown here] shows, within the no-affirmation condition, coffee-drinkers ($M = 4.15$) were less accepting of the conclusions than were non-coffee-drinkers ($M = 6.22$), $F(1, 28) = 10.77, p < .01$. However, in the affirmation condition, coffee-drinkers ($M = 7.23$) were more accepting of the article's conclusions than were non-coffee-drinkers ($M = 5.81$), $F(1, 30) = 5.85, p < .05$. Examining the results somewhat differently shows that the effects of the affirmation were most beneficial to the relevant participants. For the non-coffee-drinkers, there was no difference between the affirmation condition ($M = 5.81$) and the non-affirmation condition ($M = 6.22$), $F(1, 31) < 1.00$, *ns*. However, for the coffee drinkers, the affirmation had clear beneficial effects. Affirmed coffee-drinkers were much more accepting of the article's conclusions ($M = 7.23$) than were nonaffirmed coffee-drinkers ($M = 4.15$), $F(1, 27) = 33.26, p < .001$. . . . Thus, for the coffee-drinking women, the self-affirmation reduced the defensive processing of the threatening message and persuaded them to accept that they should reduce their caffeine intake.

*Source:* Sherman, D. A. K., Nelson, L. D., and Steele, C. M. (2000). Do messages about health risks threaten the self? Increasing the acceptance of threatening health messages via self-affirmation. *Personality and Social Psychology Bulletin, 26*(9), p. 1050.

There were six cells involved in this study (because it was a 2 × 3 ANOVA), and it's clear that the Tukey test procedure was used to probe the significant interaction. It is not clear, however, how many pairwise comparisons were made. Based on the excerpt's last sentence, we know for sure that pairwise comparisons were made between one of the six cells (the women aged 50–59) with each of the other five cells. Those other five cells may have been compared, in a pairwise fashion, as well; however, we can't tell from the excerpt whether these additional 10 tests were conducted.

## EXCERPT 13.20 • *Pairwise Comparison of All Cell Means*

Two-way analysis of variance (ANOVA) was performed to test for differences in total CB&M score using age (30–39, 40–49, and 50–59 years) and gender as factors. In the event of a significant interaction, Tukey's post hoc comparisons were performed. . . . The two-way ANOVA conducted on the CB&M total scores indicated a significant main effect for age [$F(2, 84) = 20.70, p = .001$], a significant main effect for gender [$F(1, 84) = 11.66, p = .001$], and a significant age by gender interaction [$F(2, 84) = 7.72, p = .001$]. This interaction can be explained by the post hoc analyses that revealed that women in the age category 50 to 59 years had significantly lower scores than men or women in all other age and gender categories.

*Source:* Rocque, R., Bartlett, D., Brown, J., and Garland, S. J. (2005). Influence of age and gender of healthy adults on scoring patterns on the Community Balance and Mobility Scale. *Physiotherapy Canada, 57*(4), pp. 288–289.

# *Planned Comparisons*

In Chapter 12, we saw several cases in which planned comparisons were used instead of or in addition to a one-way ANOVA. (See Excerpts 12.21 through 12.24.) It should come as no surprise that such comparisons can also be used in conjunction with (or instead of) two-way ANOVAs. Not many researchers do this, but there are some who do. Consider, for example, Excerpt 13.21.

### EXCERPT 13.21 • *Planned Comparisons in a Two-Way ANOVA*

All data were analyzed in the context of a 2 × 2 between-subjects design with two levels of target-observer similarity (similar vs. dissimilar) and two levels of mental fatigue (high fatigue vs. low fatigue) unless otherwise stated. . . . Analysis of the perceived appropriateness of response ratings yielded a significant main effect for similarity condition. The target's response was seen as more appropriate for those in the similar versus the dissimilar condition, $F(1, 59) = 12.92$, $p < .001$, $MSE = 1.85$, $\eta^2 = .18$. To assess our two main predictions concerning perspective taking, two planned comparisons were conducted on the item assessing perceived appropriateness of response.[3] First, the effect of fatigue condition was assessed when participants were similar to the target. . . . A second planned comparison was conducted to test the effect of fatigue condition when participants were dissimilar to the target.

[3]We opted to calculate planned comparisons over traditional ANOVA interaction effect tests because the former were expected to provide a more powerful test of our predicted effects. ANOVA interaction tests tend to be most sensitive to a mirror-image interaction pattern and, because our predicted effects did not follow this pattern, planned comparisons were chosen as the most powerful test (Rosenthal & Rosnow, 1991).

*Source:* Nelson, D. W., Klein, C. T. F., and Irvin, J. E. (2003). Motivational antecedents of empathy: Inhibiting effects of fatigue. *Basic and Applied Social Psychology, 25*(1), pp. 41, 42.

In Excerpt 13.21, the researchers could have conducted a standard 2 × 2 ANOVA that would have produced two main effect *F*s and one interaction *F*. As you can see, they did, in fact, analyze the data to obtain one of those main effect *F*s. However, instead of conducting tests on the other main effect and the interaction, the researchers performed two planned comparisons. If you read the excerpt closely, you will see that each of these planned comparisons was just like a test of simple main effects that other researchers often perform to probe a significant interaction. What's different here is that no test was made of the interaction before these researchers compared the high fatigue individuals with the low fatigue individuals at each level of the target-observer similarity factor. The footnote in the excerpt explains why they did this.

The researchers associated with Excerpt 13.21 deserve credit for having specific plans in mind when they designed their study *and* when they analyzed their data. Their research questions guided their statistical analysis, and their analysis did not follow the conventional rules for making statistical comparisons in a two-way ANOVA. Far too many applied researchers erroneously think that (1) *F*-tests for main and interaction effects must be computed and (2) comparisons of cell means can be made only if the interaction is significant. This is unfortunate for several reasons, the main one being that planned comparisons of cell means can sometimes produce interesting findings that remain undetected by the standard *F*-tests of a two-way ANOVA.

## Assumptions Associated with a Two-Way ANOVA

*Randomness*
*independence*
*Normality*
*Homogeneity*
*of variance*

The assumptions associated with a two-way ANOVA are the same as those associated with a one-way ANOVA: randomness, independence, normality, and homogeneity of variance. As I hope you recall from the discussion of assumptions contained in Chapter 11, randomness and independence are methodological concerns; they are dealt with (or *should* be dealt with) when a study is set up, when data are collected, and when results are generalized beyond the participants and conditions of the researcher's investigation. Although the randomness and independence assumptions can ruin a study if they are violated, there is no way to use the study's sample data to test the validity of these prerequisite conditions.

The assumptions of normality and homogeneity of variance *can* be tested and in certain circumstances *should* be tested. The procedures used to conduct such tests are the same as those used by researchers to check on the normality and equal variance assumptions when conducting *t*-tests or one-way ANOVAs. Two-way ANOVAs are also similar to *t*-tests and one-way ANOVAs in that (1) violations of the normality assumption usually do not reduce the validity of the results, and (2) violations of the equal variance assumption are more problematic only when the sample sizes differ.

Since violations of the normality and equal variance are less disruptive to the *F*-tests of a two-way ANOVA when the *n*s are large and equal, many researchers will make an effort to set up the studies with equal cell sizes. Frequently, however, it is impossible to achieve this goal. On occasion, a researcher will start out with equal cell sizes but will end up with cell *n*s that vary because of equipment failure, subject dropout, or unusable answer sheets. On other occasions, the researcher will have varying sample sizes at the beginning of the study but will not want to discard any data so as to create equal *n*s because such a strategy would lead to a loss of statistical power. For either of these reasons, a researcher may end up with cell sizes that vary. In such situations, researchers will frequently concern themselves with the normality and homogeneity of variance assumptions.

In Excerpts 13.22 and 13.23, we see examples where the **normality assumption** and the **equal variance assumption** were tested. In these and other cases where assumptions are tested, researchers usually hope that the assumption's null hypothesis will not be rejected. When this is the case, they can proceed directly from these preliminary tests to their study's main tests. In Excerpt 13.22, we see a situation where Levene's test produced a nonsignificant result, a finding that was undoubtedly considered desirable by the researchers. In Excerpt 13.23, on the other

### EXCERPTS 13.22–13.23 • *The Normality and Equal Variance Assumptions*

Groups in this [2 × 3 ANOVA] study were near equal in size and met the assumption of homogeneity of variance as measured by the Levene test.

*Source:* Bentley, M. W., Stas, J. M., Johnson, J. M., Viet, B. C., and Garrett, N. (2005). Effects of preincisional ketamine treatment on natural killer cell activity and postoperative pain management after oral maxillofacial surgery. *AANA Journal, 73*(6), p. 429.

-----

A 2 × 2 between-subjects analysis of variance (ANOVA) was used to examine the influence of gender (male vs. female) and hearing status (impaired vs. partner) on total attributions. . . . Evaluation of assumptions indicated normal distribution of this variable and no outliers were present. Levene's test of homogeneity of error variances was significant ($p = 0.01$), indicating violation of the assumption of equality of error variances.

*Source:* Anderson, D. L., and Noble, W. (2005). Couples' attributions about behaviours modulated by hearing impairment: Links with relationship satisfaction. *International Journal of Audiology, 44*(4), pp. 200–201.

hand, the same test produced a "red flag" because the result provided evidence that the populations most likely did not have equal variance.

As indicated in Chapter 11, researchers have several options when it becomes apparent that their data sets are characterized by extreme nonnormality or heterogeneity of variance. One option is to apply a **data transformation** before testing any null hypotheses involving the main effect or cell means. In Excerpt 13.24, we see a case where this was done using a square root transformation. In other research reports, you are likely to see different kinds of transformations used (e.g., the log transformation and the arcsine transformation). Different kinds of transformations are available because nonnormality or heterogeneity of variance can exist in

### EXCERPT 13.24 • *Using a Data Transformation*

A two way analysis of variance (ANOVA) was performed for graft type (E-PHB, PHB-ALG, and PHB-GGF) and gap length (2 or 4 cm) and their interactions. The interaction term assessed whether the difference between the graft types varied with gap length. The normality assumption of the ANOVA was checked using the Shapiro-Francia W dash test and Bartletts test was used to check the equal variances assumptions. The assumptions from the analysis on the untransformed data were not valid, therefore a square root transformation of the data was carried out.

*Source:* Mohanna, P., Terenghi, G., and Wiberg, M. (2005). Composite PHB-GGF conduit for long nerve gap repair: A long-term evaluation. *Scandinavian Journal of Plastic & Reconstructive Surgery & Hand Surgery, 39*(3), p. 132.

different forms. It is the researcher's job, of course, to choose an appropriate transformation that accomplishes the desired objective of bringing the data into greater agreement with the normality and equal variance assumptions.

Well-trained researchers will indicate that they were aware of the assumptions underlying the *F*-tests of a two-way ANOVA. On occasion, you will see researchers say that their tests are **robust,** meaning that the assumptions are of little concern because the statistical tests have been found to operate as designed even if the assumptions are violated. Sometimes, the assumptions will be tested and found to be tenable. Not infrequently, data transformations will be used to bring the sample data into greater compatibility with assumptions. Finally, it is not uncommon to see a researcher assess the study's central null hypotheses with a test procedure that has less rigorous assumptions, either because the more rigorous assumptions associated with *F*-tests were tested and found to be untenable or because the researcher doesn't want to bother with test procedures that have lots of assumptions.

*Important*

If a researcher conducts a two-way ANOVA but does not say anything at all about the normality and equal variance assumptions, then you have a right—even an obligation—to receive the researcher's end-of-study claims with a big grain of salt. You have a right to do this because *F*-tests can be biased if the assumptions are violated. That **bias** can be positive or negative in nature, thus causing the ANOVA's *F*-tests to turn out either too large or too small, respectively. If the former problem exists, the computed *p*-value associated with a calculated *F*-value will be too small, thereby exaggerating how much the sample data deviate from null expectations. In this situation, the nominal alpha level will understate the probability of a Type I error. If the bias is negative, the *p*-values associated with computed *F*-values will be too large. This may cause the researcher to not reject one or more null hypotheses that would have been rejected if evaluated with unbiased *p*s.

## Estimating Effect Size and Conducting Power Analyses in Two-Way ANOVAs

As indicated in Chapter 8, various techniques have been developed to help researchers assess the extent to which their results are significant in a practical sense. It is worth repeating that such techniques serve a valuable role in quantitative studies wherein null hypotheses are tested; it is possible for a result to end up being declared statistically significant even though it is totally unimportant from a practical standpoint. Earlier, we saw how these techniques have been used in conjunction with *t*-tests and one-way ANOVAs. We now will consider their relevance to two-way ANOVAs.

A common strategy for demonstrating concern about practical significance in a two-way ANOVA is to estimate the effect size associated with the *F*-tests of the main effect and interaction null hypotheses. Researchers who do this will typically use one of three measures to estimate effect size: eta squared ($\eta^2$), omega squared ($\omega^2$), or **Cohen's *f*.** Excerpts 13.25 and 13.26 show how the first two of these indices were used in recent studies.

Research
Navigator.com

Effect size

**EXCERPTS 13.25–13.26** • *Estimating Effect Size with $\eta^2$ and $\omega^2$*

A 2 (authenticity: real vs. imagined) $\times$ 2 (recall: single vs. repeated) ANOVA with the number of words as dependent variable showed no significant main effect for authenticity, $F(1, 76) = 2.71, p = .10, \eta^2 = .03$. However, a significant main effect for recall was found, $F(1, 76) = 4.92, p < .05, \eta^2 = .03$, showing that children who had recalled the event four times gave more extensive statements ($M = 720.88, SD = 338.06$) than children who had recalled the event once ($M = 564.42, SD = 317.17$). The interaction effect was not significant, $F(1, 76) = 1.08, p = .30, \eta^2 = .01$.

*Source:* Granhag, P. A., Strömwall, L. A., and Landström, S. (2006). Children recalling an event repeatedly: Effects on RM and CBCA scores. *Legal & Criminological Psychology, 11*(1), p. 90.

---

The ANOVA indicated a significant effect for KR, $F(4, 105) = 2.54, p < .05, \omega^2 = .009$, and for period on watch, $F(3, 291) = 9.58, p < .001, \omega^2 = .06$. The interaction between these factors was not statistically significant ($p > .05$).

*Source:* Szalma, J. L., Hancock, P. A., Dember, W. N., and Warm, J. S. (2006). Training for vigilance: The effect of knowledge of results format and dispositional optimism and pessimism on performance and stress. *British Journal of Psychology, 97*(1), p. 122.

Instead of using a measure of association (such as **eta squared** or **omega squared**) to estimate effect size, many researchers will use *d*. This way of estimating effect size is restricted to the situation in which two means are being compared. Therefore, you'll likely see *d* used when the focus is on (1) the main effect means of a factor that has just two levels, (2) the main effect means (for a factor with more than two levels) that are compared in a pairwise fashion within a post hoc investigation, or (3) pairwise comparisons of cell means in tests of simple main effects. In Excerpt 13.27, we see *d* used to accomplish the second of these three goals.

**EXCERPT 13.27** • *Estimating Effect Size with d*

Results of the two-way ANOVA with two between-groups factors (school level taught and program type) revealed that the school level $\times$ program type interaction was not significant. The main effect of school level was significant, $F(2, 539) = 7.42, p = 0.0007$, with high school teachers rating assertion skills as significantly less important ($M = 8.26; SD = 3.77$) than did elementary [$M = 9.69; SD = 2.97$, effect size $(d) = 0.44$] or middle [$M = 8.90; SD = 3.66$, effect size $(d) = .17$] school teachers.

*Source:* Lane, K. L., Wehby, J. H., and Cooley, C. (2006). Teacher expectations of students' classroom behavior across the grade span: Which social skills are necessary for success? *Exceptional Children, 72*(2), p. 160.

When estimating the effect size of an omnibus *F*-ratio or the difference between two sample means, researchers ought to say something about the magnitude of the estimated effect. Unfortunately, you will come across research reports where this is not done. Because certain journals now require estimates of effect size to be presented, some researchers simply "jump through the hoop" to include such estimates when summarizing their studies. It's sad but true that in some cases these researchers don't say anything because they have no idea how to interpret their effect size estimates. They just throw them in to make their reports look good.

To make sure that *you* are not in the dark when it comes to interpreting measures of effect size computed for two-way ANOVA results, I have created Table 13.2. The top half of this table is identical to the information included earlier in Table 10.1. In the bottom half of Table 13.2, I have tried to indicate where you are likely to see the different effect size measures used with a two-way ANOVA. If you take another look at Excerpts 13.18 and 13.21, you will see examples of where two of these measures ($\eta^2$ and $d$) were used to help interpret tests of simple main effects and planned comparisons.

**TABLE 13.2**   *Effect Size Criteria for Two-Way ANOVAs*

### A. Criteria for Judging Magnitude of Estimated Effect Size

| Effect Size Measure | Small | Medium | Large |
|---|---|---|---|
| $d$ | .20 | .50 | .80 |
| Eta ($\eta$) | .10 | .24 | .37 |
| Eta Squared ($\eta^2$) | .01 | .06 | .14 |
| Omega Squared ($\omega^2$) | .01 | .06 | .14 |
| Partial Eta Squared ($\eta_p^2$) | .01 | .06 | .14 |
| Partial Omega Squared ($\omega_p^2$) | .01 | .06 | .14 |
| Cohen's $f$ | .10 | .25 | .40 |

### B. The Places Where Different Measures Are Typically Used

| Focus of Effect Size Estimation | Frequently Used Effect Size Measures | | | | |
|---|---|---|---|---|---|
| The main effect $F$ of a factor with $df = 2$ | $d$ | $\eta^2$ | $\omega^2$ | $\eta_p^2$ | $\omega_p^2$ |
| The main effect $F$ of factor with $df > 2$ | $\eta^2$ | $\omega^2$ | $\eta_p^2$ | $\omega_p^2$ | $f$ |
| The interaction $F$ | $\eta^2$ | $\omega^2$ | $\eta_p^2$ | $\omega_p^2$ | $f$ |
| Two means in a post hoc investigation | $d$ | $\eta^2$ | $\omega^2$ | $\eta_p^2$ | $\omega_p^2$ |
| A 1-$df$ $F$-test of a planned contrast | $d$ | $\eta^2$ | $\omega^2$ | $\eta_p^2$ | $\omega_p^2$ |

*Note.* These standards for judging effect size are quite general and should be changed to fit the unique goals of any given research investigation.

To demonstrate a concern for practical significance, certain researchers choose to conduct a **power analysis** in conjunction with their two-way ANOVAs. This can be done in the design phase of the study to determine the needed sample sizes for the two-way ANOVA to function as desired. A power analysis can also be conducted after a study has been completed, with the purpose here being to determine whether there was sufficient power to detect differences of a particular magnitude. These two kinds of power analyses are quite different in purpose, with the notion of effect size meaning different things in the two kinds of power analyses.

In Excerpt 13.28, we see an example of an a priori power analysis. The researchers who conducted this study deserve to be commended for taking the time to determine how large their sample sizes needed to be.

### EXCERPT 13.28 • *A Power Analysis to Determine Sample Size*

A priori power analysis was performed to determine the number of respondents necessary to detect a moderate effect size at the standard $\beta = .80$ level (Cohen, 1977). The number of respondents necessary to detect a moderate effect size in an independent sample $t$-test is 64 per sample; the number of respondents necessary for a $2 \times 2$ ANOVA is 33 per cell. Therefore, the experiment included a total of 134 respondents who were undergraduates at a large Midwestern university (41 males, 93 females).

*Source:* Sparks, G. G., Sherry, J., and Lubsen, G. (2005). The appeal of media violence in a full-length motion picture: An experimental investigation. *Communication Reports, 18*(1), p. 24.

In your reading of the research literature, you are likely to encounter many studies in which a two-way ANOVA functions as the primary data analytic tool. Unfortunately, many of the researchers who use this tool formally address only the concept of statistical significance, with the notion of practical significance automatically (and incorrectly) superimposed on each and every result that turns out to be statistically significant. Consequently, you must remain vigilant for instances of this unjustified and dangerous misinterpretation of results.

## The Inflated Type I Error Rate in Factorial ANOVAs

When data are subjected to a standard two-way ANOVA, three $F$-values are computed—one for each main effect and one for the interaction. If the same level of significance (e.g., .05) is used in assessing each $F$-value, you may have been thinking that the probability of a Type I error occurring somewhere among the three $F$-tests is greater than the alpha level used to evaluate each $F$-value. Accordingly, you may have been expecting me to point out how conscientious researchers make some form of adjustment to avoid having an inflated Type I error rate associated with their two-way ANOVAs.

Although it is clear that the computation of three $F$-values in a two-way ANOVA leads to a greater-than-alpha chance that one or more of the three null hypotheses will be incorrectly rejected, the vast majority of applied researchers do not adjust anything in an effort to deal with this "problem." This is because most applied researchers consider each $F$-test separately rather than look at the three $F$-tests collectively as a set. When the $F$-tests are viewed in that manner, the Type I error risk is *not* inflated, for the researcher's alpha level correctly specifies the probability that any given $F$-test will cause a true $H_0$ to be rejected.

When a given level of significance is used to evaluate each of the three $F$-values, it can be said that the **familywise error rate** is set equal to the alpha level. Each "family" is defined as the set of contrasts represented by an $F$-test and any post hoc tests that might be conducted if the $F$ turns out to be statistically significant. The familywise error rate is equal to the common alpha level employed to evaluate all three $F$-tests because the chances of a Type I error, *within each family*, are equal to the alpha level.

If a researcher analyzes the data from two or more dependent variables with separate two-way ANOVAs, you may find that the Bonferroni procedure is used to adjust the alpha level. In Excerpt 13.29, we see a case in which this was done. As you can see, the researchers associated with this study divided their desired study-wide alpha level by 3, the number of two-way ANOVAs they intended to conduct. Because this excerpt comes from the same research report that provided Excerpt 13.27, I am especially impressed with the careful approach these researchers demonstrated as they performed their statistical analyses. On the one hand, they adjusted their level of significance prior to doing their three two-way ANOVAs. On the other hand, they took the time to estimate the effect size of the statistically significant results yielded by their post hoc investigation.

### EXCERPT 13.29 • *The Bonferroni Adjustment*

Three 2-way analyses of variance (ANOVAs) were computed . . . to compare differences between program type (general vs. special education) and school level (elementary vs. middle vs. high school) with respect to teachers' expectations of students' social competence in the areas of self control, cooperation, and assertion skills. Composite scores for assertion, self-control, and cooperation domains served as dependent variables. The Bonferroni correction (0.05/3) was used to correct for Type I errors given that three separate ANOVAs were conducted.

*Source:* Lane, K. L., Wehby, J. H., and Cooley, C. (2006). Teacher expectations of students' classroom behavior across the grade span: Which social skills are necessary for success? *Exceptional Children, 72*(2), p. 159.

Researchers frequently conduct ANOVAs involving more than three factors. In such situations, the number of $F$-tests in the "standard" analysis increases dramatically as more and more factors are included. With three factors, for example, most researchers compute seven $F$-tests, whereas 16 $F$-tests are usually examined when there are four factors involved in the ANOVA. If a researcher uses one of these higher order factorial ANOVAs (with a single dependent variable), you are likely to see an alpha level of .05 used to evaluate each of the many $F$-tests computed. Thus the practice of using a familywise alpha (such as .05) is not restricted to two-way ANOVAs.

## A Few Warnings Concerning Two-Way ANOVAs

Before concluding this chapter, I want to offer a few cautionary comments that I hope you will tuck away in your memory bank and then bring up to consciousness whenever you encounter a research report based on a two-way ANOVA. Although I have touched on some of these issues in previous chapters, your ability to decipher *and* critique research summaries may well improve if I deliberately reiterate a few of those earlier concerns.

### Evaluate the Worth of the Hypotheses Being Tested

I cannot overemphasize how important it is to critically assess the worth of the hypotheses being tested within any study based on a two-way ANOVA. No matter how good the study may be from a statistical perspective and no matter how clear the research report is, the study cannot possibly make a contribution unless the questions being dealt with are interesting. In other words, the research questions that prompt the investigator to select the factors and levels of the two-way ANOVA must be worth answering and must have no clear answer before the study is conducted. If these things do not hold true, then the study has a fatal flaw in its foundation that cannot be overcome by large sample sizes, rigorous alpha levels, high reliability and validity estimates, impressive $F$-ratios that are statistically significant, elaborate post hoc analyses, tests of assumptions, and power analyses. The old saying that "you can't make a silk purse out of a sow's ear" is as relevant here as anywhere else.

### Remember That Two-Way ANOVAs Focus on Means

As with most $t$-tests and all one-way ANOVAs, the focus of a two-way ANOVA is on means. The main effect means and the cell means serve as the focal points of the three research questions associated with any two-way ANOVA. When the main effect and interaction $F$-tests are discussed, it is essential for you to keep in mind that conclusions should be tied to means.

I recently read a study (utilizing a two-way ANOVA) that evaluated the impact of an outdoor rock-climbing program on at-risk adolescents. There were two main dependent variables: alienation and personal control. The researchers asserted, in the abstract of the research report, that "after experiencing the climbing program, the experimental group was less alienated than its control counterparts" and "demonstrated a stronger sense of personal control than did the control group." Many people reading those statements would think that *everyone* in the experimental group scored lower on alienation and higher on personal power than *anyone* in the control group. However, the group means and standard deviations included in the research report—on both measures (alienation and personal power)—make it absolutely clear that some of the members of the control group had better scores than did some of the members in the experimental group.

Many researchers fail to note that their statistically significant findings deal with means, and the literal interpretation of the researchers' words says that all of the folks in one group outperformed those in the comparison group(s). If the phrase *on average* or some similar wording does not appear in the research report, make certain that you insert it as you attempt to decipher and understand the statistical findings. If you don't, you will end up thinking that comparison groups were far more different from one another than was actually the case.

## ✳ *Remember the Possibility of Type I and Type II Errors*

The third warning that I want to offer is not new. You have encountered it earlier in our consideration of *t*-tests and one-way ANOVAs. Simply stated, I want to encourage you to remember that regardless of how the results of a two-way ANOVA turn out, there is always the possibility of either a Type I or Type II error whenever a decision is made to reject or fail to reject a null hypothesis.

Based on the words used by many researchers in discussing their results, it seems to me that the notion of "statistical significance" is quite often amplified (incorrectly) into something on the order of a firm discovery—or even proof. Far too seldom do I see the word *inference* or the phrase *null hypothesis* in the technical write-ups of research investigations wherein the hypothesis testing procedure has been used. Although you do not have the ability to control what researchers say when they summarize their investigations, you most certainly *do* have the freedom to adjust the research summary to make it more accurate.

Sooner or later, you are bound to encounter a research report wherein a statement is made on the order of (1) "Treatment A works better than Treatment B" or (2) "Folks who possess characteristic X outperform those who possess characteristic Y." Such statements will come from researchers who temporarily forgot not only the difference between sample statistics and population parameters but also the ever-present possibility of an inferential error when a finding is declared either significant or nonsignificant. You can avoid making the mistake of accepting such statements as points of fact by remembering that no *F*-test *ever* proves anything.

### *Be Careful When Interpreting Nonsignificant F-tests*

In Chapter 7, I pointed out that it is wrong to consider a null hypothesis to be true simply because the hypothesis testing procedure results in a fail-to-reject decision. Any of several factors (e.g., small sample sizes, unreliable measuring instruments, or too much within-group variability) can cause the result to be nonsignificant, even if the null hypothesis being tested is actually false. This is especially true when the null hypothesis is false by a small amount.

Almost all researchers who engage in hypothesis testing have been taught that it is improper to conclude that a null hypothesis is true simply because the hypothesis testing procedure leads to a fail-to-reject decision. Nevertheless, many of these same researchers use language in their research reports suggesting that they have completely forgotten that a fail-to-reject decision does not logically permit one to leave a study believing that the tested $H_0$ is true. In your review of studies that utilize two-way ANOVAs (or, for that matter, any procedure for testing null hypotheses), remain vigilant for erroneous statements as to what a nonsignificant finding means.

### *Review Terms*

| | |
|---|---|
| Active factor | Graph of cell means |
| Assigned factor | Interaction |
| Biased *F*-test | Level |
| Cell | Main effect *F* |
| Cohen's *f* | Main effect mean |
| Data transformation | Normality assumption |
| Equal variance assumption | Omega squared |
| Eta squared | Post hoc tests |
| Factor | Power analysis |
| Familywise error rate | Simple main effect |
| Graph of an interaction | Univariate analysis |

### *The Best Items in the Companion Website*

1. An interactive online quiz (with immediate feedback provided) covering Chapter 13.
2. Nine misconceptions about the content of Chapter 13.
3. An email message sent from the author to his students entitled "Can One Cell Create an Interaction?"
4. An interactive online resource entitled "Two-Way ANOVA (a)."
5. One of the best passages from Chapter 13: "You Can't Make a Silk Purse Out of a Sow's Ear."

To access chapter objectives, practice tests, weblinks, and flashcards, visit the companion website at www.ablongman.com/huck5e.

Research
Navigator.c⊛m

## *Fun Exercises inside Research Navigator*

**1. Who admits to cheating more: undergraduate males or females? Younger or older undergraduates?**

As part of a study conducted in the UK, psychology students at four universities were administered a cheating questionnaire. In one analysis, the resulting data were subjected to a 2 (gender: male, female) × 2 (age: younger, older) ANOVA. The data that went into this two-way ANOVA were the scores on the cheating questionnaire. First, make a guess as to which of the ANOVA's three *F* tests turned out to be statistically significant. Then, locate the PDF version of the research report in the Education database of ContentSelect and read the first full paragraph on page 277 to find out what the two-way ANOVA actually revealed.

L. S. Norton, A. J. Tilley, S. E. Newstead, & A. Franklyn-Stokes. The pressures of assessment in undergraduate courses and their effect on student behaviours. *Assessment and Evaluation in Higher Education.* Located in the EDUCATION database of ContentSelect.

**2. Do different groups/genders have different attitudes toward rape victims?**

The *Attitudes toward Rape Victims Scale* (*ARVS*) was administered to three groups: upper-level undergraduates, Master's students in a counseling program, and professionals (who held a Master's or Doctoral degree) working as mental health practitioners. After subdividing each group on the basis of gender, the attitude scores were analyzed by a 2 × 3 ANOVA. Results showed that both main effects and the interaction were statistically significant. With high scores on the *ARVS* indicating more negative attitudes toward a rape victim, what do you think the tests of simple main effects revealed? (These tests were conducted "both directions," comparing the three groups for each gender and then comparing the two genders within each of the three groups.) After making a guess, refer to the PDF version of the research report in the Criminal Justice database of ContentSelect and check to see if you are correct by looking at the top paragraph on page of 922.

B. H. White & S. E. R. Kurpius. Attitudes toward rape victims. *Journal of Interpersonal Violence.* Located in the CRIMINAL JUSTICE database of ContentSelect.

**Review Questions and Answers begin on page 513.**

# Analyses of Variance
# with Repeated Measures

In this chapter, we consider three different ANOVAs that are characterized by repeated measures. In particular, the focus here is on one-way ANOVAs with repeated measures, two-way ANOVAs with repeated measures on both factors, and two-way ANOVAs with repeated measures on just one factor. Although there are other kinds of ANOVAs that involve repeated measures (e.g., a four-way ANOVA with repeated measures on all or some of the factors), the three types considered here are the ones you are most likely to encounter.

The one-way and two-way ANOVAs examined in this chapter are similar in many respects to the ANOVAs considered in Chapters 11 and 13. The primary difference between the ANOVAs of this chapter and those looked at in earlier chapters is that the ANOVAs to which we now turn our attention involve repeated measures on at least one factor. This means that the research participants will be measured once under each level (or combination of levels) of the factor(s) involved in the ANOVA.

Perhaps an example will help to distinguish between the ANOVAs considered in earlier chapters and their repeated measures counterparts examined in this chapter. If a researcher has a $2 \times 3$ design characterized by no repeated measures, each participant in the study can be thought of (1) as being located inside *one* of the six cells of the factorial design and (2) as contributing *one* score to the data set. In contrast, if a researcher has a $2 \times 3$ design characterized by repeated measures across both factors, each participant can be thought of (1) as being in *each of the six* cells and (2) as contributing *six* scores to the data set.

Before we turn our attention to the specific ANOVAs of this chapter, I'd like to make three introductory comments. First, each of the ANOVAs to be considered here will be univariate in nature. Even though participants are measured more than once within the same ANOVA, these statistical procedures are univariate in nature—not multivariate—because each participant provides only one score to the data set for each level or combination of levels of the factor(s) involved in the study. The ANOVAs of this chapter could be turned into multivariate ANOVAs if each participant were measured repeatedly within each cell of the design, with these within-cell repeated measurements corresponding to different dependent variables. Such multivariate repeated measures ANOVAs, however, are not considered in this chapter.

Second, it's important to understand the distinction between (1) two or more separate ANOVAs, each conducted on the data corresponding to a different dependent variable, with all data coming from the same participants, and (2) a single unified ANOVA in which there are repeated measures across levels of the factor(s) of the study. In Chapters 10, 11, and 13, you have seen many examples of multiple but separate ANOVAs being applied to different sets of data, each corresponding to a unique dependent variable. The ANOVAs to which we now turn our attention are different from those referred to in the preceding sentence in that the ones to be considered here always involve a single, consolidated analysis.

My final introductory point concerns different kinds of repeated measures factors. To be more specific, I want to distinguish between some of the different circumstances in a study that can create a **within-subjects factor.**[1] You will likely encounter three such circumstances as you read technical research reports.

One obvious way for a factor to involve repeated measures is for participants to be measured at different points in time. For example, a researcher might measure people before and after an intervention, with the factor being called *time* and its levels being called *pre* and *post.* Or, in a study focused on the acquisition of a new skill, the factor might be called *trials* (or *trial blocks*), with levels simply numbered 1, 2, 3, and so on. A second way for a factor to involve repeated measures is for participants to be measured once under each of two or more different treatment conditions. In such studies, the factor might well be called *treatments* or *conditions,* with the factor's levels labeled to correspond to the specific treatments involved in the study. A third kind of repeated measures factor shows up when the study's participants are asked to rate different things or are measured on different characteristics. Here, the factor and level names would be chosen to correspond to the different kinds of data gathered in the study.

In Excerpts 14.1 through 14.3, we see how different kinds of situations can lead to data being collected from each participant across levels of the repeated measures factor. Although the factors referred to in these excerpts are all within-subjects factors, they involve repeated measures for different reasons. In Excerpt 14.1, the data were collected at different *times;* in Excerpt 14.2, the data were collected under different *treatment conditions;* and in Excerpt 14.3, the data were collected on different *variables.*

---

[1]The terms *repeated-measures factor, within-subjects factor,* and *within-participants factor* are synonymous.

**EXCERPTS 14.1–14.3 • *Different Kinds of Repeated Measures Factors***

In this study [using ANOVA] the repeated-measures factor was time.

*Source:* Rodgers, M. D., and Emerson, R. W. (2005). Human factor analysis of long cane design: Weight and length. *Journal of Visual Impairment & Blindness, 99*(10), p. 625.

- - - - - - - - - - - - - - - - - - - - - - - - - - - - - - - - - - - - - - - - - - - - - - - - - - - - - - - -

Children learned words under three conditions: shape (SHP), function (FNC), and control (CTL). Spoken words labeled objects in all conditions, but shape gestures were paired with spoken words in the SHP condition and function gestures were paired with spoken words in the FNC condition. . . . Performance was subject to a one-way repeated measures ANOVA with three levels (condition).

*Source:* Capone, N. C., and McGregor, K. K. (2005). The effect of semantic representation on toddlers' word retrieval. *Journal of Speech, Language & Hearing* Research, *48*(6), pp. 1472, 1475.

- - - - - - - - - - - - - - - - - - - - - - - - - - - - - - - - - - - - - - - - - - - - - - - - - - - - - - - -

A one-way repeated-measures ANOVA was performed, with general IQ estimates for self, father, mother, grandfather, and grandmother as the five levels of the within-subjects factor.

*Source:* Furnham, A., Wytykowska, A., and Petrides, K. V. (2005). Estimates of multiple intelligences: A study in Poland. *European Psychologist, 10*(1), p. 55.

## *One-Way Repeated Measures ANOVAs*

When researchers use a one-way repeated measures ANOVA, they usually will tip you off that their ANOVA is different from the kind we considered in Chapters 10 and 11 (where no repeated measures are involved). They do this by including the phrase "repeated measures" or "within-subjects" or "within-participants" as a descriptor of their ANOVA or of their ANOVA's single factor. Examples of this practice appear in Excerpts 14.4, 14.5, and 14.6.

### *Purpose*

The purpose of a one-way repeated measures ANOVA is identical to the purpose of a one-way ANOVA not having repeated measures. In each case, the researcher is interested in seeing whether (or the degree to which) the sample data cast doubt on the null hypothesis of the ANOVA. That null hypothesis, for the within-subjects case as well as the between-subjects case, states that the $\mu$s associated with the different levels of the factor do not differ. Since the researcher who uses a one-way within-subjects ANOVA is probably interested in gaining an insight into how the $\mu$s differ, post hoc tests are normally used (as in a between-subjects ANOVA) if the overall null hypothesis is rejected and if three or more levels compose the ANOVA's factor.

To illustrate, suppose a researcher collects reaction-time data from six people on three occasions: immediately upon awakening in the morning, one hour after

## EXCERPTS 14.4–14.6 • *Different Labels for a One-Way Repeated Measures ANOVA*

Judgments of the critical cues within each problem were analyzed with one-way within subjects analysis of variance (ANOVA).

*Source:* White, P. A. (2005). Cue interaction effects in causal judgment: An interpretation in terms of the evidential evaluation model. *Quarterly Journal of Experimental Psychology: Section B, 58*(2), p. 115.

---

To check for variability in task performance across sessions, we performed one-way analyses of variance (ANOVAs) for repeated measurements on task performance for each session.

*Source:* Otzenberger, H., Gounot, D., Marrer, C., Namer, I. J., and Metz-Lutz, M. (2005). Reliability of individual functional MRI brain mapping of language. *Neuropsychology, 19*(4), p. 485.

---

To test these differences a one-way ANOVA was run using the four frequency level percentages as the within subject factor.

*Source:* Mochida, A., and Harrington, M. (2006). The Yes/No Test as a measure of receptive vocabulary knowledge. *Language Testing, 23*(1), p. 88.

awakening, and two hours after awakening. Each of the six people would be measured three times, with a total of 18 pieces of data available for analysis. In subjecting the data to a one-way repeated measures ANOVA, the researcher would be asking whether the three sample means, each based on six scores collected at the same time during the day, are far enough apart to call into question the null hypothesis that says all three population means are equivalent. In other words, the purpose of the one-way repeated measures ANOVA in this study would be to see if the average reaction time of folks similar to the six people used in the study varies depending on whether they are tested 0, 60, or 120 minutes after awakening.

It is usually helpful to think of any one-way repeated measures ANOVA in terms of a two-dimensional matrix. Within this matrix, each row corresponds to a different person and each column corresponds to a different level of the study's factor. A single score is entered into each cell of this matrix, with the scores on any row coming from the same person. Such a matrix, created for our hypothetical reaction-time study, is presented in Figure 14.1. Such illustrations normally do not appear in research reports. Therefore, you will need to create such a picture (in your mind or on a piece of scratch paper) when trying to decipher the results of a one-way repeated measures ANOVA. This will usually be easy to do because you will be given information as to the number of people involved in the study, the nature of the repeated measures factor, and the sample means that correspond to the levels of the repeated measures factor.

w/i
= Same
people
or
groups
measured
repeatedly

### Hours Since Awakening

|  | Zero | One | Two |
|---|---|---|---|
| Person 1 | 1.7 | 1.1 | 1.7 |
| Person 2 | 1.8 | 0.9 | 1.5 |
| Person 3 | 1.6 | 1.2 | 1.4 |
| Person 4 | 2.3 | 1.5 | 1.8 |
| Person 5 | 2.0 | 1.5 | 1.3 |
| Person 6 | 2.0 | 1.0 | 1.9 |
|  | $\bar{X} = 1.9$ | $\bar{X} = 1.2$ | $\bar{X} = 1.6$ |

*one way ANOVA   f test significance = Tukey or shuffe*

**FIGURE 14.1**   *Illustration of the Data Setup for the One-Way Repeated Measures ANOVA in the Hypothetical Reaction-Time Study*

Between
= group 0 hrs
≠ group 1 hr
≠ group 2 hrs

## Presentation of Results

The results of a one-way repeated measures ANOVA may be presented in an ANOVA summary table. In Table 14.1, I have prepared such a table for our hypothetical study on reaction time. This summary table is similar in some ways to the one-way ANOVA summary tables contained in Chapter 11, yet it is similar, in other respects, to the two-way ANOVA summary tables included in Chapter 13. Table 14.1 is like a one-way ANOVA summary table in that a single $F$-ratio is contained in the right-hand column of the table. (Note that this $F$-ratio is computed by dividing the $MS$ for the study's factor by the $MS$ for residual.) It is like a two-way ANOVA summary table in that (1) the row for people functions, in some respects, as a second factor of the study and (2) the numerical values on the row for residual are computed in the same way as if this were the interaction from a two-way ANOVA. (Note that the $df$ for residual is computed by multiplying together the first two $df$ values.) In fact, we could have used the term *hours* $\times$ *people* to label this row instead of the term *residual*.

2+1 = 3 levels of the factor

5+1 = 6 people

HRS x people

**TABLE 14.1**   *ANOVA Summary Table for the Reaction-Time Data Contained in Figure 14.1*

| Source | df | SS | MS | F |
|---|---|---|---|---|
| IV = Hours since awakening   groups | 2 | 1.48 | .74 | 16.34* |
| People   -1 | 5   +1=Subj | .47 | .09 |  |
| Residual | 10 | .45 | .05 |  |
| Total | 17 | 2.40 |  |  |

*$p < .001$.

scores of measurents ) 18-1
17+1 = 18 pros of data

IS A different between means

Regardless of whether Table 14.1 resembles more closely the summary table for a one-way ANOVA or a two-way ANOVA, it contains useful information for anyone trying to understand the structure and the results of the investigation. First, the title of the table indicates what kind of data were collected. Second, we can tell from the Source column that the study's factor was Hours since awakening. Third, the top two numbers in the *df* column inform us that the study involved three levels (2 + 1 = 3) of the factor and six people (5 + 1 = 6). Fourth, the bottom number in the *df* column indicates that a total of 18 pieces of data were analyzed (17 + 1 = 18). Finally, the note beneath the table reveals that the study's null hypothesis was rejected, with .01 being one of three things: (1) the original level of significance used by the researcher, (2) the revised alpha level that resulted from a Bonferroni or pseudo-Bonferroni adjustment, or (3) the most rigorous of the standard alpha levels (i.e., .05, .01, .001) that could be beaten by the data.

In our hypothetical study on reaction time, Table 14.1 indicates that the null hypothesis of equal population means is not likely to be true. To gain an insight into the pattern of the population means, a post hoc investigation would probably be conducted. Most researchers would set up this follow-up investigation such that three pairwise contrasts are tested, each involving a different pair of means ($\overline{X}_0$ versus $\overline{X}_1$, $\overline{X}_0$ versus $\overline{X}_2$, and $\overline{X}_1$ versus $\overline{X}_2$).

In Excerpt 14.7, we see the results of a real study that used a one-way repeated-measures ANOVA. The data summarized by this table came from 57 individuals who independently rated photographs of 17 buildings in San Francisco. The *F*- and *p*-values on the second row of the table indicate that the average scores for the various scenes differed more than would be expected by chance. Note that only one *F*-ratio appears in the ANOVA summary table, for there is only one true factor in this study, stimuli (i.e., photographs).

Although it is helpful to be able to look at the ANOVA summary table, researchers often must delete such a table from their reports because of space

### EXCERPT 14.7 • *Results of a One-Way Repeated Measures ANOVA Presented in a Summary Table*

**TABLE 1**    *Analysis of Variance*

| Source | SS | df | MS | F | p |
|--------|-----|-----|------|------|-------|
| Respondents | 1714 | 56 | 30.6 | | |
| Stimuli | 449 | 16 | 28.1 | 14.3 | < .001 |
| Residual | 1752 | 896 | 1.96 | | |
| Total | 3915 | 968 | | | |

*Source:* Stumps, A. E. (2000). Evaluating architectural design review. *Perceptual and Motor Skills, 90,* p. 269.

considerations. In Excerpt 14.8, we see how the results of a one-way repeated measures ANOVA were presented wholly within the text of the report. Note how a post hoc test was used to compare the three group means because (1) the omnibus $F$-test yielded a statistically significant result and (2) more than two means were being compared.

**EXCERPT 14.8 • *Results of a One-Way Repeated Measures ANOVA Presented without an ANOVA Summary Table***

A single factor (Expression: genuine/posed/neutral) within-subjects ANOVA on the mean evaluation scores revealed a main effect of expression, $F(2, 76) = 16.02$, $p < .0001$, $\eta_p^2 = .30$. Post hoc tests (Tukey HSD, $p < .05$) revealed that participants evaluated T-shirts paired with the genuine smile more positively than those paired with either the posed smile or neutral expression, these latter two not differing from one another ($Ms = 4.20$ vs. 3.35 and 3.26).

*Source:* Peace, V., Miles, L., and Johnston, L. (2006). It doesn't matter what you wear: The impact of posed and genuine expressions of happiness on product evaluation. *Social Cognition, 24*(2), p. 150.

Sometimes researchers will apply a one-way repeated measures ANOVA more than once within the same study. They do this for one of two reasons. On one hand, each participant in the study may have provided two or more pieces of data at each level of the repeated measures factor, with each of these scores corresponding to a different dependent variable. Given this situation, the researcher may utilize a separate one-way repeated measures ANOVA to analyze the data corresponding to each dependent variable. On the other hand, the researcher may have two or more groups of participants, with just one score collected from each of them at each level of the within-subjects factor. Here, the researcher may decide to subject the data provided by each group to a separate one-way repeated measures ANOVA. Excerpt 14.9 illustrates the first of these two situations.

**EXCERPT 14.9 • *Two One-Way Repeated Measures ANOVAs Used with Different Dependent Variables***

The sample here consisted of 20 participants whose frequencies of normal dream recall and lucid dream recall were recorded before, during and after a two week training program by using a dream questionnaire and a dream journal. A one-way repeated measures analysis of variance showed a significant increase in both dream recall frequency ($F_{2,38} = 22.09, p < .05$) and lucid dream recall frequency ($F_{2,38} = 5.96, p < .05$).

*Source:* Paulsson, T., and Parker, A. (2006). The effects of a two-week reflection-intention training program on lucid dream recall. *Dreaming, 16*(1), p. 22.

### The Presentation Order of Levels
### of the Within-Subjects Factor

The factor in a one-way repeated measures ANOVA can take one of three basic forms. In some studies, the within-subjects factor corresponds to time, with the levels of the factor indicating the different points in time at which data are collected. The second kind of within-subjects factor corresponds to different treatments or conditions given to or created for the participants, with a measurement taken on each person under each treatment or condition. The third kind of within-subjects factor is found in studies where each participant is asked to rate different things, take different tests, or in some other way provide scores on different dependent variables.

If the one-way repeated measures ANOVA involves data collected at different points in time, there is only one order in which the data can be collected. If, however, the within-subjects factor corresponds to treatment conditions or different dependent variables, then there are different ways in which the data can be collected. When an option exists regarding the order in which the levels of the factor are presented, the researcher's decision regarding this aspect of the study should be taken into consideration when *you* make a decision as to whether or not to accept the researcher's findings.

If the various treatment conditions, things to be rated, or tests to be taken are presented in the same order, then a systematic bias may creep into the study and function to make it extremely difficult—or impossible—to draw clear conclusions from the statistical results. The systematic bias might take the form of a **practice effect,** with participants performing better as they warm up or learn from what they have already done; a **fatigue effect,** with participants performing less well on subsequent tasks simply because they get bored or tired; or **confounding** with things that the participants do or learn outside the study's setting between the points at which the study's data are collected. Whatever its form, such bias can cause different treatment conditions (or the different versions of a measuring device) to look different when they are really alike or to look alike when they are really dissimilar.

To prevent the study from being wrecked by practice effects, fatigue effects, and confounding due to order effects, a researcher should alter the order in which the treatment conditions, tasks, questionnaires, rating forms, or whatever are presented to participants. This can be done in one of three ways. One design strategy is to randomize the order in which the levels of the within-subjects factor are presented. A second strategy is to utilize all possible presentation orders, with an equal proportion of the participants assigned randomly to each possible order. The third strategy involves counterbalancing the order in which the levels of the repeated measures factor are presented; here, the researchers make sure that each level of the factor appears equally often in any of the ordered positions.

In Excerpt 14.10, we see an example in which a set of researchers randomized and **counterbalanced** the order in which this study's participants received the three treatments (drinks containing different levels of caffeine). The **Latin square** referred to in this excerpt is simply an "ordering arrangement" that made sure that

**Research**
**Navigator.c⊛m**
Practice effect
Fatigue effect
Confounding

**Research**
**Navigator.c⊛m**
Counterbalanced

### EXCERPT 14.10 • *Two One-Way Repeated Measures ANOVAs Used with Different Dependent Variables*

Participants received three drinks containing 0 (placebo), 75 and 150 mg of caffeine hydrochloride BP (Merck, Darmstadt, Germany) on separate occasions. . . . On arrival at their first session on the first day, participants were randomly allocated to a treatment regime using a Latin square design which counterbalanced the order of treatments across the 3 active days of the study.

*Source:* Haskell, C. F., Kennedy, D. O., Wesnes, K. A., and Scholey, A. B. (2005). Cognitive and mood improvements of caffeine in habitual consumers and habitual non-consumers of caffeine. *Psychopharmacology, 179*(4), p. 817.

each of the three treatment conditions occurs equally often in the first, second, and final positions. For example, if we let the letters A, B, and C represent the three beverages used in this study, one-third of the study's participants would receive them in the order A-B-C. A different third of the participants would get the treatments in the order B-C-A. The order for the final third of the participants would be C-A-B.

### Carry-Over Effects

In studies where the repeated-measures factor is related to different kinds of treatments, the influence of one treatment might interfere with the assessment of how the next treatment works. If so, such a **carry-over effect** will interfere with the comparative evaluation of the various treatments. Even if the order of the treatments is varied, the disruptive influence of carry-over effects can make certain treatments appear to be more or less potent than they really are.

One way researchers can reduce or eliminate the problem of carry-over effects is to delay presenting the second treatment until after the first treatment has "run its course." In the caffeine study associated with Excerpt 14.10, there was a 48-hour time period between the days on which the caffeine drinks and performance tasks were administered. These so-called "washout" intervals were designed to allow the effects of each treatment to dissipate totally before another treatment was introduced.

### The Sphericity Assumption

In order for a one-way repeated measures ANOVA to yield an *F*-test that is valid, an important assumption must hold true. This is called the **sphericity assumption,** and it should be considered by *every* researcher who uses this form of ANOVA. Even though the same amount of data will be collected for each level of the repeated measures factor, the *F*-test of a one-way repeated measures ANOVA is *not* robust to

Research
Navigator.c⊛m

Sphericity

violations of the sphericity assumption. To be more specific, the $F$-value from this ANOVA will turn out to be too large to the extent that this assumption is violated.

The sphericity assumption says that the population variances associated with the levels of the repeated measures factor, in combination with the population correlations between pairs of levels, must represent one of a set of acceptable patterns. One of the acceptable patterns is for all the population variances to be identical and for all the bivariate correlations to be identical. There are, however, other patterns of variances and correlations that adhere to the requirements of sphericity.

The sample data collected in any one-factor repeated measures investigation can be used to test the sphericity assumption. This test was developed by J. W. Mauchly in 1940, and researchers now refer to it as the Mauchly sphericity test. If the application of **Mauchly's test** yields a statistically significant result (thus suggesting that the condition of sphericity does not exist), there are various things the researcher can do in an effort to help avoid making a Type I error when the one-way repeated measures ANOVA is used to test the null hypothesis of equal population means across the levels of the repeated measures factor. The two most popular strategies both involve using a smaller pair of $df$ values to determine the critical $F$-value used to evaluate the calculated $F$-value. This adjustment results in a larger critical value and a greater likelihood that a fail-to-reject decision will be made when the null hypothesis of the one-way repeated measures ANOVA is evaluated.

One of the two ways to adjust the $df$ values is to use a simple procedure developed by two statisticians, S. Geisser and S. W. Greenhouse. Their procedure involves basing the critical $F$-value on the $df$ values that would have been appropriate if there had been just two levels of the repeated measures factor. This creates a drastic reduction in the critical value's $df$s, because it presumes that the sphericity assumption is violated to the maximum extent. Thus the **Geisser-Greenhouse** approach to dealing with significant departures from sphericity creates a **conservative $F$-test** (since the true Type I error rate will be smaller than that suggested by the level of significance).

The second procedure for adjusting the degrees of freedom involves first using the sample data to estimate how extensively the sphericity assumption is violated. This step leads to $\varepsilon$, a fraction that turns out to be smaller than 1.0 to the extent that the sample data suggest that the sphericity assumption is violated. Then, the "regular" $df$ values associated with the $F$-test are multiplied by $\varepsilon$, thus producing adjusted $df$ values and a critical value that are tailor-made for the study being conducted. When researchers use this second procedure, they often report that they have used the **Huynh-Feldt correction.**

In Excerpts 14.11 and 14.12, we see two cases in which the researchers took corrective action after the sphericity assumption was tested and found not to be tenable. In the first of these excerpts, the Geisser-Greenhouse procedure was used. In Excerpt 14.12, the sample data were first examined to see how extensively the assumption was likely to be violated, and then the Huynh-Feldt correction was applied. In both of these studies, the degrees of freedom associated with the critical

**EXCERPTS 14.11–14.12** • *Dealing with the Sphericity Assumption Measures*

In order to determine whether differences among the means were significant, a one-way repeated measures ANOVA was conducted. The sphericity assumption of the ANOVA test was checked with Mauchly's sphericity test. In case of the violation of the sphericity assumption, adjustments were made to the ANOVA results using the Geisser–Greenhouse epsilon, which provides an F-test using a much more stringent criterion.

*Source:* Sakar, A., and Ercetin, G. (2005). Effectiveness of hypermedia annotations for foreign language reading. *Journal of Computer Assisted Learning, 21*(1), pp. 33–34.

-----------------------------------------------------------------------------------------------------

We analyzed constant error and variable error by using a one-way repeated measures analysis of variance (ANOVA; 20 levels of time) with Huynh-Feldt correction for violations of sphericity.

*Source:* Binsted, G., Rolheiser, T. M., and Chua, R. (2006). Decay in visuomotor representations during manual aiming. *Journal of Motor Behavior, 38*(2), p. 84.

value got smaller, thereby making the critical value larger. This change in the critical value eliminated the positive bias in the *F*-test that would have existed (due to a lack of sphericity) if the regular critical value had been used.

Regardless of which strategy is used to deal with the sphericity assumption, I want to reiterate my earlier statement that this is an important assumption for the ANOVAs being discussed in this chapter. If a researcher conducts a repeated measures ANOVA and does not say anything at all about the sphericity assumption, the conclusions drawn from that investigation probably ought to be considered with a *big* grain of salt. If the data analysis produces a statistically significant finding when no test of sphericity is conducted or no adjustment is made to the critical value's *df,* you have the full right to disregard the inferential claims made by the researcher.

## Two-Way Repeated Measures ANOVAs

We now turn our attention to ANOVAs that contain two repeated measures factors. As you will see, there are many similarities between this kind of ANOVA and the kind we examined in Chapter 13. However, there are important differences between two-way ANOVAs that do or don't involve repeated measures. For this reason, you need to be able to distinguish between these two kinds of analysis.

If researchers state that they have used a two-way ANOVA but say nothing about repeated measures, then you should presume that it is the kind of ANOVA we considered in Chapter 13. On the other hand, if researchers use the phrase "repeated measures," "within-subjects," or "within-participants" when describing each of their ANOVA's two factors, then you will need to remember the things you will learn in this section of the book. Excerpts 14.13 and 14.14 illustrate how researchers usually provide a tip-off that they used a two-way ANOVA with repeated measures.

### EXCERPTS 14.13–14.14 • *Different Labels for a Two-Way Repeated Measures ANOVA*

These data were analyzed with separate two-way within subjects ANOVAs.

*Source:* Dunn, J. M., Inderwies, B. R., Licata, S. C., and Pierce, R. C. (2005). Repeated administration of AMPA or a metabotropic glutamate receptor agonist into the rat ventral tegmental area augments the subsequent behavioral hyperactivity induced by cocaine. *Psychopharmacology, 179*(1), p. 177.

-------------------------------------------------------------------------------------------------

We conducted an analysis of variance (ANOVA) on the mean correct probe RTs with probe location (old, new) and SOA (150 ms, 450 ms, 750 ms, 1,050 ms) as repeated measures factors.

*Source:* Agter, F., and Donk, M. (2005). Prioritized selection in visual search through onset capture and color inhibition: Evidence from a probe-dot detection task. *Journal of Experimental Psychology: Human Perception and Performance, 31*(4), p. 725.

## Purpose

The purpose of a two-way repeated measures ANOVA is identical to the purpose of a two-way ANOVA not having repeated measures. In each case, the researcher uses inferential statistics to help assess three null hypotheses. The first of these null hypotheses deals with the main effect of one of the two factors. The second null hypothesis deals with the main effect of the second factor. The third null hypothesis deals with the interaction between the two factors.

Although two-way ANOVAs with and without repeated measures are identical in the number and nature of null hypotheses that are evaluated, they differ in two main respects. In terms of the way data are collected, the kind of two-way ANOVA considered in Chapter 13 requires that each participant be positioned in a single cell, with only one score per person going into the data analysis. In contrast, a two-way repeated measures ANOVA requires that each participant travel across all cells created by the two factors, with each person being measured once within *each* cell. For example, in a recent study, eight well-trained male athletes rode a bicycle on two occasions, each time for 100 miles. During one ride, the outside temperature was cold (0°C); during the other ride, it was much warmer (19°C). One of the study's dependent variables was heart rate, with measures taken just before each ride, immediately after each ride, and then again 24 hours after each ride. This study's two factors were temperature and time of measurement, and you should be able to imagine how each of the athletes was measured across the study's six cells.

The second main difference between two-way ANOVAs with and without repeated measures involves the ANOVA summary table. We will return to this second difference in the next section when we consider how researchers present the results of their two-way repeated measures ANOVAs. Right now, we need to concentrate on the three null hypotheses dealt with by this ANOVA and the way the necessary data must be collected.

To help you gain insight into the three null hypotheses of any two-way repeated measures ANOVA, let's consider an imaginary study. This study will involve the game "Simon," which is a battery-operated device with four colored buttons. After the player flips the start switch, a sequence of Simon's buttons lights up, with each light accompanied by a unique tone. The task of the person playing this game involves (1) watching and listening to what Simon does and then, after Simon stops, (2) pushing the same sequence of buttons that Simon just illuminated.

Suppose now that you are the player. If the red button on Simon lights up, you must press the red button. Then, if the red button lights up first followed by the green button, you must press these same two buttons in this same order to stay in the game. Every time you successfully mimic what Simon does, you receive a new string of lighted buttons that is like the previous one, except that the new sequence is one light longer. At first, it is easy for you to duplicate Simon's varied but short sequences. But after the sequences lengthen, you will find it more and more difficult to mimic Simon.

For my study, imagine that I have each of six people play Simon. The dependent variable will be the length of the longest sequence that the player successfully duplicates. (For example, if the player works up to the point where he or she correctly mimics an eight-light sequence but fails on the ninth light, that person's score would be 8.) After three practice rounds, I then ask each person to play Simon four times, each under a different condition defined by my study's two factors: tones and words. The two levels of the tones factor would be on and off, meaning that the Simon device would be set up either to provide the auditory cues or to be silent while the player played. The two levels of the word factor would be color names or people names. With color names, the player would be instructed to say out loud the color of the lights as Simon presents them in a sequence. (Those colors are red, blue, green, and yellow.) With people names, the player would be instructed to say out loud one of these names for each color: Ron for red, Barb for blue, Greg for green, and Yoko for yellow. Finally, imagine that I randomly arrange the order in which the four conditions of my study are ordered for each of the six Simon players.

Figure 14.2 contains the scores from my hypothetical study, with the order of each person's four scores arranged so as to fit accurately under the column headings. This figure also contains a 2 × 2 matrix of the four cell means, with the main effect means positioned on the right and bottom sides of the cell means.

As indicated earlier, there are three null hypotheses associated with any two-way repeated measures ANOVA. In our hypothetical study, the null hypothesis for the main effect of tones would state that there is no difference, in the populations associated with our samples, between the mean performance on the Simon game

|  | Color Names | | People Names | |
|---|---|---|---|---|
|  | Tones on | Tones off | Tones on | Tones off |
| Player 1 | 6 | 8 | 6 | 3 |
| Player 2 | 8 | 3 | 2 | 4 |
| Player 3 | 7 | 5 | 6 | 6 |
| Player 4 | 9 | 6 | 3 | 5 |
| Player 5 | 8 | 6 | 6 | 3 |
| Player 6 | 10 | 8 | 7 | 3 |
| *M* = | 8 | 6 | 5 | 4 |

*(handwritten left margin: each participant under each condition; 2×2)*

Words

|  | Colors | People | |
|---|---|---|---|
| Tones  On | 8 | 5 | 6.5 |
| Tones  Off | 6 | 4 | 5.0 |
|  | 7.0 | 4.5 | |

*(handwritten: Averages ... Averages; 2. 7.0  2. 4.5)*

---

**FIGURE 14.2** *A Picture Showing How the Data from the Simon Study Would Be Arranged*

*(handwritten left margin: 3 F's; 1. Ho difference between Row means; 2. Column means; 3. Interaction Rows x Colums)*

when players hear the tone cues as compared to when they don't hear the tone cues. In a similar fashion, the null hypothesis for the main effect of words would state that there is no difference, in the populations associated with our samples, between the mean performance on the Simon game when players say color words when trying to memorize each sequence as compared to when they say people's names. Finally, the interaction null hypothesis would state the positive (or negative) impact on players of having the tone cues is the same regardless of whether they are having to say color names or people names as Simon's buttons light up.

The lower portion of Figure 14.2 shows the four cell means and the two main effect means for each of the two factors. The null hypothesis for tones would be rejected if the means of 6.5 and 5.0 are found to be further apart from each other than we would expect by chance. Likewise, the null hypothesis for words would be rejected if the means of 7.0 and 4.5 are found to be further apart from each other than would be expected by chance. The interaction null hypothesis would be rejected if the difference between the cell means on the top row ($8 - 5 = 3$) varies more from the difference between the cell means on the bottom row ($6 - 4 = 2$) than would be expected by chance.

*(handwritten bottom right: Same as Two-way)*

Illustrations such as that presented in the upper portion of Figure 14.2 rarely appear in research reports. However, it is usually quite easy to construct pictures of cell means and main effect means. This picture-constructing task is easy because you almost always will be given information as to (1) the factors and levels involved in the study, (2) the nature of the dependent variable, and (3) the sample means. Having such a picture is highly important, for a study's results are inextricably tied to its table of cell and main effect means.

### Presentation of Results

Occasionally, the results of a two-way repeated measures ANOVA will be presented using an ANOVA summary table. In Table 14.2, I have prepared such a table for the Simon study.

The summary table shown in Table 14.2 is similar, in some very important ways, to the two-way ANOVA summary tables contained in Chapter 13. Most importantly, it contains three calculated $F$-values, one for the main effect of words, one for the main effect of tones, and one for the words-by-tones interaction. These three $F$-values speak directly to the null hypotheses discussed in the previous section.

There are two main differences between the summary table shown in Table 14.2 and the summary tables we examined in Chapter 13. First, there are three error rows in Table 14.2, whereas there is just one such row in the summary table for a two-way ANOVA without repeated measures. If you will look closely at the workings inside Table 14.2, you will see that the $MS$ for error 1 is used to obtain the calculated $F$-value for words, that the $MS$ for error 2 is used to obtain the calculated $F$-value for tones, and that the $MS$ for error 3 is used to obtain the calculated $F$-value for the interaction.[2]

**TABLE 14.2  ANOVA Summary Table of Performance Scores on Simon**

| Source | df | SS | MS | F |
|--------|----|----|----|----|
| Players | 5 | 15.5 | 3.1 | |
| Words | 1 | 37.5 | 37.5 | 19.74* |
| Error 1 | 5 | 9.5 | 1.9 | |
| Tones | 1 | 13.5 | 13.5 | 12.27** |
| Error 2 | 5 | 5.5 | 1.1 | |
| Words × tones | 1 | 1.5 | 1.5 | .29 |
| Error 3 | 5 | 25.5 | 5.1 | |
| Total | 23 | 108.5 | | |

*$p < .01$. **$p < .05$.

[2]The df numbers for these error rows are all equal to 5, but they were computed differently. Each was found by multiplying together the df for players and the df for the row immediately above the error being considered. For example, the df for error 2 was found by multiplying $df_{\text{Players}}$ by $df_{\text{Tones}}$.

The second difference between Table 14.2 and the ANOVA summary tables contained in Chapter 13 concerns the meaning of the *df* for total. As you can see, this *df* number is equal to 23. If this were a regular two-way ANOVA, you could add 1 to *df*~Total~ in order to figure out how many people were in the study. You can't do that here, obviously, because there were only six people who functioned as players in our Simon study, yet $df_{Total}$ is much larger than this. The problem gets solved completely when you realize that in all ANOVA summary tables, adding 1 to $df_{Total}$ gives you the total number of pieces of data that were analyzed. That is true for ANOVAs with and without repeated measures. If there are no repeated measures, then the number of pieces of data will be the same as the number of people (for each person provides, in those cases, just one score). When there *are* repeated measures, however, you must remember that adding 1 to the *df* for the top row of the summary table (not the bottom row) will allow you to know how many people were involved.

If you ever encounter a summary table like that presented in Table 14.2, do not overlook the valuable information sitting in front of you. From such a table, you can determine how many people were involved in the study ($5 + 1 = 6$), what the dependent variable was (performance on the Simon game), what the two factors were (tones and words) and how many levels made up each factor ($1 + 1 = 2$ in each case), how many total pieces of data were involved in the analysis ($23 + 1 = 24$), and which null hypotheses were rejected.

In Excerpt 14.15, we see how a team of researchers summarized the results of their two-way repeated measures ANOVA in the text of their report. Note that this passage is extremely similar to the textual summary of a two-way ANOVA without repeated measures. There are two factors (contrast and rate), separate *F*-tests of the two main effects (one of which was significant), and one *F*-test of the interaction (which turned out to be nonsignificant). Because there were four levels in the factor that was significant, the researchers conducted a post hoc investigation on the contrast main effect means.

### EXCERPT 14.15 • *Results of a Two-Way Repeated Measures ANOVA Presented without an ANOVA Summary Table*

A two-way repeated measures ($3 \times 4$) ANOVA was computed with contrast and rate as the two within-subject factors. This failed to show a significant effect for rate ($F(2,10) = 0.29$, $p = 0.75$) or an interaction between rate and contrast ($F(6,30) = 0.63$, $p = 0.70$) although there was a significant effect of contrast ($F(3,15) = 8.53$, $p < 0.005$). Post hoc *t*-tests for this factor showed significant differences ($p < 0.05$) between identification of date-gate and both fricative contrasts, but not between other minimal pair tests.

*Source:* Verschuur, C. A. (2005). Effect of stimulation rate on speech perception in adult users of the Med-El CIS speech processing strategy. *International Journal of Audiology, 44*(1), pp. 60–61.

Although the ANOVA discussed in Excerpt 14.15 resembles, in many ways, the kind of two-way ANOVA considered in Chapter 13, there is a subtle yet important difference. The $df$ values for the three $F$-tests are not the same. The first of the two $df$ numbers next to each $F$, of course, are not the same simply because there were three levels in one factor and four levels in the other factor. However, look at the second $df$ next to each $F$. These $df$s vary because there were three different values for $MS_{Error}$ involved in this analysis, each of which was used as the researchers (or a computer) calculated one of three $F$-ratios. Had this been a two-way ANOVA without repeated measures, just one $MS_{Error}$ would have been used to get all three of the $F$s, thus causing each $F$'s second $df$ to be equal to the same value.

Turning now to Excerpt 14.16, we see the summary of a $2 \times 3$ repeated measures ANOVA. This portion of the research report is important to read, because it shows another similarity between two-way ANOVAs with repeated measures and two-way ANOVAs without repeated measures. This similarity concerns what researchers typically do when the interaction turns out to be statistically significant. Note here that the significant interaction prompted the researchers to conduct tests of simple main effects, comparing the two measuring instruments at each walking speed. Because each of these tests of simple main effects involved just two means, a correlated $t$-test was used to make these comparisons. (Note that the significant $t$-test had 13 $df$, 1 less that the number of walkers involved in the study.)

### EXCERPT 14.16 • *Probing the Interaction of a Two-Way Repeated Measures ANOVA*

Participants were 14 community-dwelling adults with ABI and a related gait pattern impairment. . . . At the commencement of the protocol, the participant was asked to sit quietly for 5 min before walking back and forth for 6 min at a comfortable pace (CP). After a 5-min recovery, a 6-min brisk paced (BP) walk was completed, followed by a 9-min recovery and a 3-min walk at a fast pace (FP). . . . Throughout the protocol, participants wore two instruments that provided concurrent estimates of the intensity of each of the three walking trials. . . . The two measures of activity intensity (counts and oxygen consumption) were both converted to METs using the methods described previously and results are presented in Table 2 [not shown here]. Two-way repeated-measures ANOVA revealed a significant measurement instrument $\times$ walking speed interaction ($F(2,26) = 4.47, P < 0.05$). Simple main effects analysis of the interaction revealed no significant differences between measured [based on oxygen consumption] and predicted [based on counts] METs for either CP or BP walking. However, for FP, walking-predicted METs were significantly lower than measured ($t(13) = 2.175, P < 0.05$).

*Source:* Tweedy, S. M., and Trost, S. G. (2005). Validity of accelerometry for measurement of activity in people with brain injury. *Medicine and Science in Sports and Exercise, 37*(9), pp. 1475, 1477.

## The Presentation Order of Different Tasks

Earlier in this chapter, I indicated how a repeated measures factor can take one of three basic forms: different points in time, different treatment conditions, or different dependent variables. With a two-way repeated measures ANOVA, any combination of these three kinds of factors is possible. The most popular combinations, however, involve either (1) two factors, each of which is defined by different versions (i.e., levels) of a treatment, or (2) one treatment factor and one factor that involves measurements taken at different points in time.

When the levels of one or both factors in a two-way repeated measures ANOVA correspond with different treatment conditions or different dependent variables, those levels should not be presented to the research participants in the same order. If they were, certain problems (such as a practice effect or a fatigue effect) might develop. And if that happened, the meaning of the *F*-tests involving the repeated measures factor(s) would be muddied.

As indicated earlier in this chapter, researchers ought to use different presentation orders for the levels of factors that involve different treatments, tasks, or tests. In Excerpt 14.17, we see a case that illustrates the technique of randomizing the orders in which treatment conditions occur.

### EXCERPT 14.17 • *Different Presentation Orders in a Two-Way Repeated Measures ANOVA*

In the experiment, each search condition was presented in a separate block. . . . The order of the blocks was counterbalanced, and participants were given a practice session before each condition. . . . A two-way within-subjects analysis of variance (ANOVA), with condition and display size as its main variables, was used to compare the RTs for all conditions.

*Source:* Kunar, M. A., Humphreys, G. W., and Smith, K. J. (2003). Visual change with moving displays: More evidence for color feature map inhibition during preview search. *Journal of Experimental Psychology: Human Perception and Performance, 29*(4), pp. 781, 782.

## The Sphericity Assumption

The calculated *F*-values that are computed in a two-way repeated measure ANOVA will turn out to be too large unless the population variances and correlations that correspond to the sample data conform to one or more acceptable patterns. This is the case even though the sample variances and correlations in a two-way repeated measures ANOVA are based upon sample sizes that are equal (a condition brought about by measuring the same subjects repeatedly). Therefore it is important that researchers, when using this kind of ANOVA, attend to the assumption concerning population variances and correlations. This assumption is popularly referred to as the sphericity assumption.

Any of three strategies can be used when dealing with sphericity assumption. As is the case with a one-way repeated measures ANOVA, the researcher can (1) subject the sample data to Mauchly's test for sphericity, (2) bypass Mauchly's test and instead use the Geisser-Greenhouse conservative $dfs$ for locating the critical value needed to evaluate the calculated $F$-values, or (3) utilize the sample data to compute $\varepsilon$ (the index that estimates how badly the sphericity assumption is violated) and then reduce the critical value(s) $dfs$ to the extent indicated by the $\varepsilon$ index.

In the studies associated with Excerpts 14.15 and 14.16, there was no evidence in the research reports that the researcher attended to the important sphericity assumption. If they *had* done something, would it have made a difference? Let's consider what would have happened if these sets of researchers had used Geisser-Greenhouse conservative $dfs$ in their analyses. With this change, the significant $F$ in Excerpt 14.15 would still be significant, but now with $p < .05$ rather than $p < .005$. In Excerpt 14.16, the interaction $F$ would still be significant (with $p < .05$), but only by the slightest of margins. In these two studies, the significant results still would have been significant even if the Geisser-Greenhouse method for dealing with sphericity had been used. In other studies, significant differences might melt away if $F$-ratios are reevaluated with conservative $dfs$.

### *Practical versus Statistical Significance*

Throughout this book, I have tried to emphasize repeatedly the important point that statistical significance may or may not signify practical significance. Stated differently, a small $p$ does not necessarily indicate that a research discovery is big and important. In this section, I'd like to show that well-trained researchers who use two-way repeated measures ANOVAs do *not* use the simple six-step version of hypothesis testing.

There are several options available to the researcher who is concerned about the meaningfulness of his or her findings. These options can be classified into two categories: a priori and post hoc. In the first category, one option involves conducting an a priori power analysis for the purpose of determining the proper sample size. A second option in that category involves checking to see if there is adequate power for a fixed sample size that already exists. In the post hoc category, the two options involve using the study's sample data to estimate effect sizes or the power of the completed analysis.

In Excerpt 14.18, we see a case in which a post hoc strategy was used to address the issue of practical significance. The specific technique used in this study was the computation of partial eta squared. According to the criteria established for interpreting values of $\eta_p^2$, the value of .78 computed from the sample data represents a very, very large estimated effect size.

The criteria for judging effect size indices in a two-way repeated measures ANOVA are the same as the standards for these indices when they are computed for

## EXCERPT 14.18 • *Practical versus Statistical Significance*

We performed a two-way repeated measures analysis of variance (ANOVA) on these data with processing task (verbal, visuospatial) and set size (three, six, nine) as the factors. . . . The analysis revealed a main effect of task, $F(1, 74) = 261.82$, $p < .01$, $MSE = 92,908.53$, partial $\eta^2 = .78$, with slower RTs in the verbal processing task.

*Source:* Bayliss, D. M., Jarrold, C., Gunn, D. M., and Baddeley, A. D. (2003). The complexities of complex span: Explaining individual differences in working memory in children and adults. *Journal of Experimental Psychology: General, 132*(1), p. 77.

a two-way ANOVA without any repeated measures. As indicated in Chapter 13, the criteria for judging $\eta_p^2$ equate .01 with a small effect, .06 with a medium effect, and .14 with a large effect. Take another look at the value of $\eta_p^2$ in Excerpt 14.18 and you'll see why I said it represented a very, very large estimated effect size.

To see the criteria for judging the magnitude of other ways of estimating effect size, refer to Table 13.2. That table also shows which of these procedures are typically used in conjunction with tests on main effects, tests on interactions, and different kinds of post hoc tests.

## Two-Way Mixed ANOVAs

Research
Navigator.c⊕m

Two-way mixed
ANOVA

We now turn our attention to the third and final kind of ANOVA to be considered in this chapter. It is called a **two-way mixed ANOVA.** The word *mixed* is included in its label because one of the two factors is between subjects in nature while the other factor is within subjects.

### Labels for This Kind of ANOVA

Unfortunately, all researchers do not use the same label (that is, *two-way mixed ANOVA*) to describe the kind of ANOVA that has one between-subjects factor and one within-subjects factor. Therefore, the first thing you need to do relative to two-way mixed ANOVAs is familiarize yourself with the different ways researchers indicate that they have used this kind of ANOVA. If you don't do this, you might be looking at a study that involves a two-way mixed ANOVA and not even realize it.

When researchers use a two-way mixed ANOVA, some of them refer to it as a **two-way ANOVA with repeated measures on one factor.** Others call it an **ANOVA with one between-subjects factor and one within-subjects factor.** Occasionally it is called a **split-plot ANOVA** or a **two-factor between-within ANOVA.** In Excerpts 14.19 through 14.22, we see four different ways researchers chose to describe the two factor mixed ANOVA that they used.

**EXCERPTS 14.19–14.22 •** *Different Labels for a Two-Way Mixed Measures ANOVA*

A 3 (age) × 3 (trial) ANOVA was performed on the permanence scores with repeated measures on the last factor.

*Source:* Subbotsky, E. (2005). The permanence of mental objects: Testing magical thinking on perceived and imaginary realities. *Developmental Psychology, 41*(2), p. 310.

---

A 3 (type of prereading relevance instruction: physiology, space traveler, control) × 3 (type of text segment: physiology segment, space traveler segment, base text segment) mixed-model repeated measures analysis of variance (ANOVA) was conducted. Type of relevance instruction was presented between subjects; type of text segment was repeated within subjects.

*Source:* McCrudden, M. T., Schraw, G., and Kambe, G. (2005). The effect of relevance instructions on reading time and learning. *Journal of Educational Psychology, 97*(1), 91.

---

Therefore, a 2 × 2 repeated measures ANOVA was performed with group membership (treatment and control) as the between-participants factor, and pre- and posttest standard scores on the PPVT–III as the within-participants factor.

*Source:* van Kleeck, A.,Vander Woude, J., and Hammett, L. (2006). Fostering literal and inferential language skills in Head Start preschoolers with language impairment using scripted book-sharing discussions. *American Journal of Speech-Language Pathology, 15*(1), p. 89.

---

A 2 (certainty condition) × 2 (time) between–within analysis of variance (ANOVA) on the positive mood index revealed. . . .

*Source:* Wilson, T. D., Centerbar, D. B., Kermer, D. A., and Gilbert, D. T. (2005). The pleasures of uncertainty: Prolonging positive moods in ways people do not anticipate. *Journal of Personality and Social Psychology, 88*(1), p. 12.

## Data Layout and Purpose

To understand the results of a two-way mixed ANOVA, you must be able to conceptualize the way the data were arranged prior to being analyzed. Whenever you deal with this kind of ANOVA, try to think of (or actually draw) a picture similar to the one displayed in Figure 14.3. This picture is set up for an extremely small-scale study, but it illustrates how each participant is measured repeatedly across levels of the within-subjects factor but not across levels of the between-subjects factor. In this picture, of course, the between-subjects factor is gender and the within-subjects factor is time of day. The scores are hypothetical, and they are meant to

| Gender | | Time of Day | | |
|---|---|---|---|---|
| | | 8 A.M. | 2 P.M. | 8 P.M. |
| **Male** | Participant 1 | 6 | 3 | 8 |
| | Participant 2 | 7 | 6 | 8 |
| | Participant 3 | 4 | 2 | 10 |
| | Participant 4 | 8 | 5 | 10 |
| | Participant 5 | 5 | 4 | 9 |
| **Female** | Participant 6 | 8 | 5 | 9 |
| | Participant 7 | 6 | 6 | 7 |
| | Participant 8 | 8 | 4 | 8 |
| | Participant 9 | 7 | 4 | 9 |
| | Participant 10 | 6 | 6 | 7 |

**FIGURE 14.3** *Picture of the Data Layout for a 2 × 3 Mixed ANOVA*

reflect the data that might be collected if we asked each of five males and five females to give us a self-rating of his or her typical energy level (on a 0–10 scale) at each of three points during the day: 8 A.M., 2 P.M., and 8 P.M.

Although a two-way mixed ANOVA always involves one between-subjects factor and one within-subjects factor, the number of levels in each factor will vary from study to study. In other words, the dimensions and labeling of Figure 14.3 only match our hypothetical two-way mixed ANOVA in which there is a two-level between-subjects factor, a three-level within-subjects factor, and five participants per group. Our picture can easily be adapted to fit *any* two-way mixed ANOVA because we can change the number of main rows and columns, the number of mini-rows (to indicate the number of participants involved), and the terms used to reflect the names of the factors and levels involved in the study.

The purpose of a two-way mixed ANOVA is identical to that of a completely between-subjects two-way ANOVA or of a completely within-subjects two-way ANOVA. In general, that purpose can be described as examining the sample means to see if they are further apart than would be expected by chance. Most researchers take this general purpose and make it more specific by setting up and testing three null hypotheses. These null hypotheses, of course, focus on the populations relevant to the investigation, with the three null statements asserting that (1) the main effect means of the first factor are equal to one another, (2) the main effect means of the second factor are equal to one another, and (3) the two factors do not interact.

To help you understand these three null hypotheses, I have taken the data from Figure 14.3, computed main effect means and cell means, and positioned these means in the following picture:

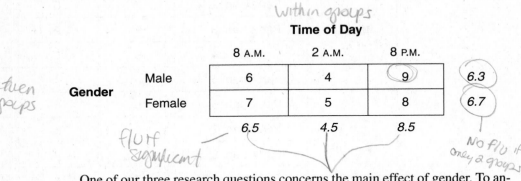

*within groups*

*Between groups*

*fluff significant*

*No flu if only 2 groups*

One of our three research questions concerns the main effect of gender. To answer this question, the mean of 6.3 (based on the 15 scores provided by the five males) will be compared against the mean of 6.7 (based on the 15 scores provided by the 5 females). The second research question, concerning the main effect of time of day, will be addressed through a statistical comparison of the column means of 6.5, 4.5, and 8.5 (each based on scores provided by all 10 participants). The third research question, dealing with the interaction between gender and time of day, will be dealt with by focusing on the six cell means (each based on five scores). This interaction question asks whether the change in the difference between the male and female means—which remains the same at 8 A.M. and 2 P.M. but then reverses itself at 8 P.M.—is greater than would be expected by chance sampling.

## Presentation of Results

If the results of a two-way mixed ANOVA are presented in an ANOVA summary table, three $F$-values will be presented—two for the main effects and one for the interaction—just as is the case in the ANOVA summary tables for completely between-subjects and completely within-subjects ANOVAs. However, the summary table for **mixed ANOVAs** is set up differently from those associated with the ANOVAs considered earlier. To illustrate these differences, I have analyzed the energy level data originally shown in Figure 14.3. The results of this two-way mixed ANOVA are found in Table 14.3.

As Table 14.3 shows, the summary table for a mixed ANOVA has an upper section and a lower section. These two sections are often labeled **between subjects** and **within subjects,** respectively. In the upper section, there will be two rows of information, one concerning the main effect of the between-subjects factor and the other for the error that goes with the between-subjects main effect. In the lower

**TABLE 14.3**   *ANOVA Summary Table of the Energy Level Data Shown in Figure 14.3*

| Source | df | SS | MS | F |
|--------|----|----|----|----|
| Between Subjects | 9 | | | |
| Gender | 1 | 0.83 | 0.83 | 0.50 |
| Error (between) | 8 | 13.34 | 1.67 | |
| Within Subjects | 20 | | | |
| Time of day | 2 | 80.00 | 40.00 | 28.17* |
| Gender × time of day | 2 | 6.67 | 3.33 | 2.35 |
| Error (within) | 16 | 22.66 | 1.42 | |
| Total | 29 | 123.50 | | |

*$p < .05$

section of the summary table, there will be three rows of information. The first of these rows is for the main effect of the within-subjects factor, the second is for the interaction between the two factors, and the third provides information for the within-subjects error term. As you can see from Table 14.3, the *MS* for the first error was used as a denominator in computing the *F*-value in the upper section of the summary table, while the *MS* for the second error was used as the denominator in computing the two *F*-values in the lower section.

Table 14.3 contains information that allows you to understand the structure of the study that provided the data for the two-way mixed ANOVA. To illustrate how you can extract this information from the table, pretend that you have not read anything about the study connected with Table 14.3. In other words, imagine that your first encounter with this study is this ANOVA summary table.

First of all, the *df* value for the between-subjects row of the table (9) allows you to know that data were gathered from 10 individuals. Second, the name of and the *df* value for the main effect in the upper portion of the table allow you to know that there were two groups in the study, with gender being the independent variable associated with this main effect. Third, the name of and *df* for the main effect in the lower portion of the table allow you to know that each of the 10 individuals was measured on three occasions, each being a particular time of the day. The table's title gives you a hint as to the kinds of scores used in this study, for you're told that this ANOVA was conducted on energy level data.

Table 14.3, of course, also contains the results of the ANOVA. To interpret these results, you now will need to look back and forth between the ANOVA summary table and the 2 × 3 table of cell and main effect means that we considered earlier. The first *F*-value (0.50) indicates that the two main effect means for males (6.3) and females (6.7) were not further apart from each other than we could expect by chance. Accordingly, the null hypothesis for gender was not rejected. The second *F*-value (28.17), on the other hand, shows that the null hypothesis for time of day was rejected. This finding came about because the main effect means of the within-subjects factor (6.5, 4.5, and 8.5) were further apart than could be expected by chance. The third $F$-value (2.35), for the interaction, was not statistically significant. Even though the differences between the male and female cell means were not constant across the data collection points during the day, the three male-female differences $(-1.0, -1.0, \text{and} +1.0)$ did not vary enough to call into question the interaction null hypothesis.

Now let's consider Excerpt 14.23 which comes from a published study that used a 2 × 2 mixed ANOVA. There are three important things to note about this excerpt's table. First, the table's title might make some people think that a regular two-way ANOVA had been conducted; hopefully, the information that's *inside* the table would cause you to realize that the ANOVA involved repeated measures on one factor. Second, each of the two error rows in Excerpt 14.23 is simply labeled "error." Even though these two error rows in Excerpt 14.23 carry the same label, it is important to note that they are not interchangeable. The *MS* associated with the first of these errors was used as the denominator in computing the $F$-value that appears in the upper section of the table; in contrast, the *MS* associated with the second of these error rows was used as the denominator in computing each of the two $F$-values that appear in the lower section of the table.[3]

**EXCERPT 14.23 • *Summary Table for Two-Way Mixed ANOVA***

**TABLE 6**   *Summary table for the two-way ANOVA*

| Source | SS | df | MS | F | Partial $\eta^2$ |
|---|---|---|---|---|---|
| Between-subjects effects | | | | | |
| Group | 1.83 | 1 | 1.83 | 0.07 | .00 |
| Error | 519.07 | 19 | 27.32 | | |
| Within-subjects effects | | | | | |
| Context | 77.40 | 1 | 77.40 | 43.16* | .69 |
| Context × Group | 0.07 | 1 | 0.07 | 0.85 | .00 |
| Error | 34.07 | 19 | 1.79 | | |

*Significant at $p < .001$.

*Source:* Kondo-Brown, K. (2006). How do English L1 learners of advanced Japanese infer unknown *Kanji* words in authentic texts? *Language Learning, 56*(1), p. 135.

[3]As illustrated in Table 14.3 and Excerpt 14.23, different terms are sometimes used to label the two rows that contain the *MS* values used as the denominators for the *F*s. You are likely to encounter ANOVA summary tables in which these two rows are labeled error 1 and error 2, error (a) and error (b), or error (b) and error (w). A few researchers label these error rows as "subjects within groups" and "_____ × subjects within groups," with the blank filled by the name of the within-subjects factor.

The third thing to note about Excerpt 14.23 is the information contained in the right-hand column. That information can help us interpret the meaningfulness of the *F*-ratio that was statistically significant.

Although it is helpful to be able to look at ANOVA summary tables when trying to decipher and critique research reports, such tables are usually not included in journal articles. Instead, the results are typically presented strictly within one or more paragraphs of textual material. To illustrate, consider Excerpt 14.24, wherein the results of a two-way mixed ANOVA are presented without a summary table.

**EXCERPT 14.24 •** *Results of a Two-Way Mixed ANOVA Presented without a Summary Table*

In addition, a 3 (ability) $\times$ 2 (trials) repeated measures ANOVA design was used to evaluate the relationship between students with disabilities, average writers, and talented writers and essay length at pretest and posttest. [Results] showed main effects for time of test, $F(1, 67) = 122.26$, $MSE = 3,034.68$, $p = .000$, and ability level, $F(2, 67) = 10.67$, $MSE = 9,116.07$, $p = .000$. The interaction between ability group and time was not significant. Two post hoc pairwise comparisons of means among students with disabilities, average writers, and talented writers were significant, controlling for Type I error across the three tests at the .05 level by using Holm's sequential Bonferroni procedure. These results indicated that students with disabilities wrote shorter papers than both average and talented writers, who wrote papers that were not significantly different in length.

*Source:* De La Paz, S. (2005). Effects of historical reasoning instruction and writing strategy mastery in culturally and academically diverse middle school classrooms. *Journal of Educational Psychology, 97*(2), pp. 149–150.

Excerpt 14.24 is worth looking at closely for two reasons. First, notice that the excerpt presents not just the size of the two significant *F*-ratios, but also the size of the two error terms from the ANOVA summary table. Both of these error terms are labeled *MSE*, so you've got to be somewhat of a detective to determine which one is the between-subjects error *MS* and which one is the within-subjects error *MS*. If you read closely and think about which factor involved repeated measures, you should be able to tell that the first of the two *MSE* values is the within-subjects mean square. (Here, as in most two-way mixed ANOVAs, the within-subjects mean square is smaller than the between-subjects mean square.)

The second reason for spending time with Excerpt 14.24 concerns the post hoc tests that were conducted. As with the other kinds of two-way ANOVAs that we considered earlier in this chapter and in Chapter 13, the statistically significant main effect for ability prompted the researchers to conduct a post hoc investigation focused on the ability main effect means. In this study, the researcher used the **Holm-sequential Bonferroni post hoc procedure.** There were three levels of the ability factor, and that meant there were three pairwise comparisons to make. Each of these comparisons was made with an independent-samples $t$-test. However, the alpha level for these tests was made more rigorous to head off the inflated Type I error problem.

If the regular **Bonferroni** procedure had been used in Excerpt 14.24, each of the three pairwise comparisons would have been tested with alpha set at .05/3, or .017. With the Holm-sequential Bonferroni procedure, the comparison yielding the smallest $p$ is first compared against the regular Bonferroni alpha level. Next, the comparison yielding the second smallest $p$ is compared against a slightly more lenient alpha level equal to .05/2, or .025. Finally, the third and last comparison would have its $p$ compared against an even more lenient $\alpha$, computed as .05/1, or .05. As you can see, there is a sequential change in the level of significance across the various tests, with the beginning point in the sequence being the regular Bonferroni-adjusted alpha level and the ending point being the unadjusted alpha level.

### Related Issues

Earlier in this chapter, I indicated how the levels of within-subjects factors sometimes can and should be presented to subjects in varying orders. That discussion applies to mixed ANOVAs as well as to fully repeated measures ANOVAs. Excerpt 14.25 shows how the technique of counterbalancing can be used to avoid the bias that might exist if the levels of the within-subjects factor are presented in the same order to all participants. By counterbalancing the order of the two priming conditions, the researchers arranged their study's trials so that on any given trial half of the participants were receiving control stimuli while the other half of the participants received IR stimuli. By doing this, the researchers made sure that priming condition was not confounded with trials.

**EXCERPT 14.25 •** *Altering the Order in Which the Levels of the*
*Within-Subjects Factor Are Presented*

A mixed design was employed. The between-subjects variable was age group (5- to 6-year-olds vs. 8- to 9-year-olds vs. 11- to 12-year-olds). The within-subjects variable was priming condition (control vs. IR). Half the trials in the experiment proper were control trials (in which the color of the prime distractors and the color of the target probe were unrelated), and half were IR trials (in which the color of the distractors in the previous display was the same as the subsequent target color). The distribution of stimuli across participants and conditions in the experiment was counterbalanced.

*Source:* Pritchard, V. E., and Neumann, E. (2004). Negative priming effects in children engaged in nonspatial tasks: Evidence for early development of an intact inhibitory mechanism. *Developmental Psychology, 40*(2), p. 194.

Research
Navigator.c⊕m
Sphericity

A second issue that you should keep in mind when examining the results of two-way mixed ANOVAs is the important assumption of **sphericity.** I discussed this assumption earlier when we considered fully repeated measures ANOVAs. It is relevant to mixed ANOVAs as well—but only the *F*-tests located in the within-subjects portion of the ANOVA summary are based upon the sphericity assumption. Thus the *F*-value for the main effect of the between-subjects factor is unaffected by a lack of sphericity in the populations connected to the study. In contrast, the *F*-values for the main effect of the within-subjects factor and for the interaction will be positively biased (i.e., turn out larger than they ought to) to the extent that the sphericity assumption is violated.

Well-trained researchers do not neglect the sphericity assumption when they use two-way mixed ANOVAs. Instead, they will do one of two things. One option is to adjust the degrees of freedom associated with the critical values (using the Geisser-Greenhouse or the Huynh-Feldt procedures), thereby compensating for possible or observed violation of the sphericity assumption. The other option is to apply Mauchly's test to the sample data to see if the assumption appears to be violated. In Excerpts 14.26 and 14.27, we see examples where researchers used these two options. Both sets of researchers deserve high marks for demonstrating a concern for the sphericity assumption.

### EXCERPTS 14.26–14.27 • *Options for Dealing with the Sphericity Assumption*

The three suggestibility measures were subjected to separate 3 (Age) × 5 (Category) repeated-measures ANOVAs. Geisser-Greenhouse corrections were applied to all effects that involved repeated measures and the effects reported were significant even with this correction.

*Source:* Shapiro, L. R., Blackford, C., and Chen, C. (2005). Eyewitness memory for a simulated misdemeanor crime: The role of age and temperament in suggestibility. *Applied Cognitive Psychology, 19*(3), p. 276.

Comparisons of pain scores between the placebo and morphine groups at T1 (baseline), T2, and T3 were conducted with a repeated-measures analysis of variance. The within-subjects factor was the pain score at T1, T2, and T3; the between-subjects factor was the treatment group (placebo versus morphine). Box's test of equality of covariance matrices and Mauchly's test of sphericity were verified before interpretation of results.

*Source:* Carbajal, R., Lenclen, R., Jugie, M., Paupe, A., Barton, B. A., and Anand, K. J. S. (2005). Morphine does not provide adequate analgesia for acute procedural pain among preterm neonates. *Pediatrics, 115*(6), p. 1495.

A third issue to keep in mind when you encounter the results of two-way mixed ANOVAs concerns the distinction between statistical significance and practical significance. I first talked about this distinction in Chapter 7, and I have tried to bring up this issue as often as possible since then. I have done this because far too many researchers conduct studies that yield one or more findings that have very little practical significance even though a very low probability level is associated with the calculated value produced by their statistical test(s).

As I indicated earlier in this chapter, the criteria for judging the magnitude of post hoc estimates of effect size (such as $d$ or $\eta^2$) are the same in a two-way mixed ANOVA as they are in a two-way ANOVA having no repeated measures. If you need to refresh your memory regarding these criteria, take a look at Table 13.2. That table also shows which of these procedures are typically used in conjunction with tests on main effects, tests on interactions, and different kinds of post hoc tests.

Most researchers who conduct two-way mixed ANOVAs fail to address the question of practical significance. However, some researchers do this—and they deserve credit for performing a more complete analysis of the study's data than is usually the case. In Excerpt 14.28, we see an illustration of this good practice.

### EXCERPT 14.28 • Concern for Practical Significance

Reading time data were analyzed using a 3 (type of prereading relevance instruction: topic, supporting, control) $\times$ 3 (sentence type: topic sentence, supporting sentence, base text) mixed-model repeated measures ANOVA on reading time per word. Type of relevance instruction was presented between subjects; sentence type was repeated within subjects. . . . The main effect for the type of relevance instruction variable reached significance, $F(2, 61) = 3.40$, $MSE = .036$, $p < .05$, indicating that there were significant differences in overall reading time across conditions. . . . The effect size for the main effect for the relevance instruction variable equaled .10 as measured by eta squared. This exceeds the criterion for a medium effect size. . . . The repeated main effect for the sentence type variable reached significance, $F(2, 122) = 8.74$, $MSE = .005$, $p < .001$, indicating that there were significant differences in reading times for different sentence types. . . . The effect size for the repeated main effect for the sentence type variable equaled .125 as measured by eta squared. This approximates the criterion for a large effect size. The interaction was not significant.

*Source:* McCrudden, M. T., Schraw, G., and Kambe, G. (2005). The effect of relevance instructions on reading time and learning. *Journal of Educational Psychology, 97*(1), p. 97.

## Three Final Comments

As we near the end of this chapter, I would like to close by making three final comments. In each case, I will argue that you need to be alert as you read or listen to formal summaries of research studies. This is necessary so you can (1) know for sure what kind of analysis the researcher *really* used, and (2) filter out unjustified claims from those that warrant your close attention. If you do not put yourself in a position to do these two things, you are likely to be misled by what is contained in the research reports that come your way.

### What Kind of ANOVA Was It?

In this chapter, we have considered three different kinds of ANOVAs: a one-way ANOVA with repeated measures, a two-way ANOVA with repeated measures on both factors, and a two-way ANOVA having repeated measures on just one factor. These three ANOVAs are different from each other, and they are also different from the one-way and two-way ANOVAs focused on in Chapters 11 and 13. Thus, for you to understand the structure and results of any one-way or two-way ANOVA, you need to know whether it did or did not involve repeated measures and, in the case of a two-way ANOVA having repeated measures, you need to know whether one or both of the factors involved repeated measures.

As indicated earlier, most researchers will clarify what kind of one-way or two-way ANOVA they have used. For example, if repeated measures are involved, they typically will use special terms—such as within-subjects or repeated measures—to describe the factor(s) in the ANOVA, or you may see the term *mixed* used to describe the kind of ANOVA considered near the end of this chapter. If no such term is used, this usually means that no repeated measures were involved.

Unfortunately, not all descriptions of one-way or two-way ANOVAs are clear as to the nature of its factor(s). At times, you'll be told that a one-way ANOVA was used when in reality it was a one-way ANOVA with repeated measures. Occasionally, this same thing will happen with two two-way ANOVAs. Or, you may be told that a two-way repeated measures ANOVA was used, thus causing you to think that there were two within-subjects factors, which will be wrong, because only one of the factors actually had repeated measures. To see an example of where the description of an ANOVA might mislead recipients of the research report, take another look at the title of the table in Excerpt 14.23.

Because the presence or absence of repeated measures does not affect the null hypothesis of a one-way ANOVA or the three null hypotheses of a two-way ANOVA, someone might want to argue that it really doesn't matter whether you can tell for sure if the factor(s) of the ANOVA had repeated measures. To that person I would ask just one simple question: "Do you know about the sphericity assumption and under what circumstances this assumption comes into play?"

### Practical versus Statistical Significance

At various points in this chapter, I have tried to help you understand that statistical significance does not always signify practical significance. I've tried to accomplish that objective by means of the words I have written and the excerpts I have chosen to include. Before you leave this chapter, you should take another look at four excerpts that we looked at during our consideration of ANOVAs having repeated measures. These are Excerpts 14.8, 14.18, 14.23, and 14.28.

There is a growing trend for researchers to do something in their studies, either as they choose their sample sizes or as they go about interpreting their results, so they and the recipients of their research reports do not make the mistake of thinking that statistical significance means big and important. However, you are bound to come across research claims that are based on the joint use of (1) one or more of the ANOVAs considered in this chapter and (2) the six-step version of hypothesis testing. When that happens, I hope you will remember two things. First, a very small $p$ may indicate that nothing big was discovered, only that a big sample can make molehills look like mountains, and, conversely, a large $p$ may indicate that something big was left undetected because the sample size was too small. The second thing to remember is that studies can be planned, using the nine-step version of hypothesis testing, such that neither of those two possible problems is likely to occur.

### The Possibility of Inferential Error

Many researchers discuss the results of their studies in such a way that it appears that they have discovered ultimate truth. Stated differently, the language used in many research reports suggests strongly that sample statistics and the results of inferential tests are being reified into population parameters and indisputable claims. At times, such claims are based on the kinds of ANOVA considered in this chapter.

You need to remember that the result of any $F$-test might be a Type I error (if the null hypothesis is rejected) or a Type II error (if the null hypothesis is retained). This is true even if the nine-step version of hypothesis testing is used, and even if attention is paid to all relevant underlying assumptions, and even if the data are collected in an unbiased fashion with valid and reliable measuring instruments from probability samples characterized by zero attrition, and even if all other good things are done so the study is sound. Simply stated, inferential error is *always* possible whenever a null hypothesis is tested.

### Review Terms

Between subjects
Bonferroni technique
Counterbalancing
Holm-sequential
 Bonferroni procedure
Mixed ANOVA

One between, one within ANOVA
Sphericity
Split-plot ANOVA
Two-way mixed ANOVA
Within subjects factor

## The Best Items in the Companion Website

1. An interactive online quiz (with immediate feedback provided) covering Chapter 14.
2. Ten misconceptions about the content of Chapter 14.
3. One of the best passages from Chapter 14: "Practical versus Statistical Significance in Mixed ANOVAs."
4. An online resource entitled "Within-Subjects ANOVA."
5. Two jokes about statistics.

To access chapter objectives, practice tests, weblinks, and flashcards, visit the companion website at www.ablongman.com/huck5e.

Research
Navigator.c⊕m

## Fun Exercises inside Research Navigator

1. **Do different conjunctions (*and* versus *or* versus *either/or*) in written material create different cognitive demands on college students?**

   In this experiment, college students read several short vignettes, each of which was followed by a sentence containing the word *and*, *or*, or *either/or*. Their task was to quickly determine whether or not each follow-up question was a legitimate "match" to the vignette to which it was paired. A separate 3 (conjunction: and, or, either/or) $\times$ 2 (match: yes, no) ANOVA with repeated measures on both factors was applied to the data for each of the two dependent variables: reaction time and accuracy. The results of these analyses suggested that one of the conjunctions was harder to deal with than the other two. Which one do you think it was? (Are you sure?) To find out if your guess is correct, refer to the PDF version of the research report in the Psychology database of ContentSelect and take a look at the first two paragraphs of the results along with Figures 1a and 1b.

   M. E. Pratarelli & A. Lawson. Conjunctive forms and conditional inference in questions and statements. *North American Journal of Psychology.* Located in the PSYCHOLOGY database of ContentSelect.

2. **Does the presence of a dog reduce stress for kids at the dentist's office?**

   To see if children's stress at the dental office could be reduced, the researchers of this study randomly assigned 40 children aged 7 to 11 to an experimental group ($n = 20$) and a control group ($n = 20$). Those in the experimental group were given a gentle and child-friendly Golden Retriever to be with them while they were in the dentist's office; those in the control group had no dog. Measures of stress were taken on two dependent variables at five points in time, with each set of data analyzed by means of a 2 (group) $\times$ 5 (time) mixed ANOVA. Data for one of the stress-related dependent variables came from ratings of a videotape of the child while he or she was in the dentist's office. Try to guess what the second dependent variable was. To find out if your guess is correct (and to see the results of this cute study), refer to the PDF version of the research report in the Nursing, Health, and Medicine database of ContentSelect. You'll find the second dependent variable described on page 143 and the main results for it presented on pages 145–147.

L. Gentes, B. Thaler, M. E. Megel, M. M. Baun, F. A. Driscoll, S. Beiraghi, & S. Agrawl. The effect of a companion animal on distress in children undergoing dental procedures. *Issues in Comprehensive Pediatric Nursing.* Located in the NURSING, HEALTH, AND MEDICINE database of ContentSelect.

**Review Questions and Answers begin on page 513.**

# The Analysis of Co...

In the previous five chapters, we looked at several different kinds of analysis of variance. We focused our attention on one-way and two-way ANOVAs, with consideration given to the situations where (1) each factor is between subjects in nature, (2) each factor is within subjects in nature, and (3) both between-subjects and within-subjects factors are combined in the same study. We closely examined five different kinds of ANOVAs that are distinguished from one another by the number and nature of the factors. In this book, these five ANOVAs have been referred to as a one-way ANOVA, a two-way ANOVA, a one-way repeated measures ANOVA, a two-way repeated measures ANOVA, and a two-way mixed ANOVA.

**Research Navigator.c☉m**

Analysis of covariance

We now turn our attention to an ANOVA-like inferential strategy that can be used instead of any of the ANOVAs examined or referred to in earlier chapters. This statistical technique, called the **analysis of covariance** and abbreviated by the six letters **ANCOVA,** can be used in any study regardless of the number of factors involved or the between-versus-within nature of the factor(s). Accordingly, the analysis of covariance is best thought of as an option to the analysis of variance. For example, if a researcher's study involves one between-subjects factor, data can be collected and analyzed using a one-way ANOVA *or* a one-way ANCOVA. The same option exists for any of the other four situations examined in earlier chapters. Simply stated, there is an ANCOVA counterpart to any ANOVA.

In Excerpts 15.1 through 15.3, we see how researchers typically indicate that their data were subjected to an analysis of covariance. Note how these excerpts illustrate the way ANCOVA can be used as an option to ANOVA regardless of the number of factors involved in the study or the between-versus-within nature of any factor.

analyzed ability beliefs with a one-way ANCOVA.

*Source:* Schlosser, A. E., White, T. B., and Lloyd, S. M. (2006). Converting web site visitors into buyers: How web site investment increases consumer trusting beliefs and online purchase intentions. *Journal of Marketing, 70*(2), p. 137.

---

Univariate 2 × 2 (Cue Type × Availability) analyses of covariance (ANCOVAs) were conducted to test for the main effects and interaction of the independent variables, with an a priori decision to covary baseline urge reports.

*Source:* MacKillop, J., and Lisman, S. A. (2005). Reactivity to alcohol cues: Isolating the role of perceived availability. *Experimental and Clinical Psychopharmacology, 13*(3), p. 232.

---

A two-way repeated measures analysis of covariance (ANCOVA) was used to formally compare the three groups (SCF, MTIF, and STIF), using four assessment periods (3, 6, 9, and 12 months) and a possible group-by-assessment interaction.

*Source:* Reimer, M. A., Slaugher, S., Donaldson, C., Currie, G., and Eliasziw, M. (2004). Special care facility compared with traditional environments for dementia care: A longitudinal study of quality of life. *Journal of the American Geriatrics Society, 52*(7), p. 1088.

## The Three Different Variables Involved in Any ANCOVA Study

In any of the ANOVAs considered in earlier chapters, there are just two kinds of variables: independent variables and dependent variables. The data analyzed in those ANOVAs, of course, represent the dependent variable; the factors correspond with the study's independent variables. We've seen how ANOVAs can involve more than one factor, factors made up of different numbers of levels, and different kinds of factors (i.e., between-subjects versus within-subjects factors); nevertheless, each and every factor in the ANOVAs considered in this book represents an independent variable. Thus such ANOVAs could be said to contain two structural ingredients: one or more independent variables and data on one dependent variable.

In any analysis of covariance, three rather than two kinds of variables are involved. Like the ANOVAs we have considered, there will be scores that correspond with the dependent variable and one or more factors that coincide with the study's independent variable(s). In addition, there will be a variable that is called the covariate.[1] Since the **covariate** is a variable on which the study's participants are measured, it is more similar to the study's dependent variable than to the independent variable(s). The covariate and dependent variables have entirely different functions

Research Navigator.com

Covariate

---

[1]The term *concomitant variable* is synonymous with the term *covariate variable*.

in any ANCOVA study, as the next section will make clear. Before discussing the covariate's function, however, let's consider a few real studies for the purpose of verifying that ANCOVA studies always have *three* structural ingredients.

Consider Excerpts 15.4 and 15.5, which come from studies involving one-way between subjects ANCOVAs. In the study from which Excerpt 15.4 was drawn, two groups of pregnant women (all of whom were drug addicts) were compared. The women in one group received a treatment called motivational enhancement treatment; the women in the other group received "standard care advice." The dependent variable was nicotine dependence (as measured by smoking frequency); the independent variable was treatment group. The covariate variable was a pretreatment baseline measure of smoking frequency. Excerpt 15.5 comes from a study that again compared two groups, students with and without learning disabilities. That distinction was the independent variable. The dependent variable was learning style, as measured by the Inventory of Learning Styles, and the covariate variable was GPA.

**EXCERPTS 15.4–15.5 • *The Three Kinds of Variables in Any ANCOVA Study***

We performed three one-way analyses of covariance procedures using treatment group (MET vs. SC) as the independent variable, post-treatment smoking as the dependent variable (i.e., self-reported cigarettes, CO ppm, cotinine–creatinine ratio ng/ml), and baseline level of smoking as a covariate.

*Source:* Haug, N. A., Svikis, D. S., and DiClemente, C. (2004). Motivational enhancement therapy for nicotine dependence in methadone-maintained pregnant women. *Psychology of Addictive Behaviors, 18*(3), p. 291.

---

Univariate analysis was performed to examine differences between groups (LD vs. NLD) as the independent variable, with total score on ILS measures as dependent measures, using GPA as a covariate variable.

*Source:* Heiman, T. (2006). Assessing the learning styles among students with and without learning disabilities at a distance-learning university. *Learning Disability Quarterly, 29*(1), p. 59.

## The Covariate's Role

Like the analysis of variance, the analysis of covariance allows researchers to make inferential statements about main and interaction effects. In that sense, these two statistical procedures have the same objective. However, an ANCOVA will be superior to its ANOVA counterpart in two distinct respects, so long as a good covariate is used.[2] To understand what is going on in an analysis of covariance, you need to understand this dual role of the covariate.

One role of the covariate is to reduce the probability of a Type II error when tests are made of main or interaction effects, or when comparisons are made within planned or post hoc investigations. As pointed out on repeated occasions in earlier chapters, this kind of inferential error is committed whenever a false null hypothesis is not rejected. Since the probability of a Type II error is inversely related to statistical **power,** I will restate this first role of the covariate by saying that an ANCOVA will be more powerful than its ANOVA counterpart, presuming that other things are held constant and that a good covariate has been used within the ANCOVA.

As you have seen, the $F$-tests associated with a standard ANOVA are computed by dividing the $MS$ for error into the $MS$s for main and interaction effects. If $MS_{error}$ can somehow be made smaller, then the calculated $F$s are larger, $p$s are smaller, and there's a better chance that null hypotheses will be rejected. When a good covariate is used within a covariance analysis, this is exactly what happens. Data on the covariate function to explain away a portion of within-group variability, resulting in a smaller value for $MS_{error}$. This mean square is often referred to as "error variance."

In Excerpt 15.6, we see a case in which a pair of researchers explain that they used the analysis of covariance because of its ability to increase power. In an ANOVA, the $MS_{error}$ is based upon the amount of variability within each group of scores. That variability can be caused by several things, but one of the main explanations is simply the individual differences among the people (or animals) in a given comparison group. By "taking into account" those individual differences, ANCOVA's $MS_{error}$ is reduced in size and statistical power goes up.

### EXCERPT 15.6 • *The First Role of the Covariate: Increased Statistical Power*

Analysis of covariance (ANCOVA) statistical tests were used because of their enhanced power to determine differences [by] taking into account individual differences on the covariate measure.

*Source:* Sallot, L. M., and Lyon, L. J. (2003). Investigating effects of tolerance-intolerance of ambiguity and the teaching of public relations writing: A quasi-experiment. *Journalism & Mass Communication Educator, 58*(3), p. 258.

In addition to its power function, the covariate in an analysis of covariance has another function. This second function can be summed up by the word *control.* In fact, some researchers will refer to the covariate of their ANCOVA studies as the *control variable.* Excerpt 15.7 illustrates nicely the fact that a covariate is sometimes

---

[2]The qualities of a "good" covariate will be described shortly.

used because of its control (or corrective) capability. It is worth noting, in this excerpt, that the covariate was used (to control for pretreatment group differences) even though the 66 patients were randomly assigned to the study's two comparison groups. It is also worth noting that the two comparison groups were found to differ significantly, at the time of the pretest, on two of the study's three dependent variables. Though random assignment is an excellent feature of studies designed to investigate cause-and-effect relationships, it does not (as illustrated by Excerpt 15.7) guarantee that comparison groups are identical.

### EXCERPT 15.7 • *The Second Role of the Covariate: Control*

The 66 patients who agreed to participate were randomly assigned to either the ATP group (*n* = 33) or the control group (*n* = 33). . . . Analysis of covariance was used to test the hypothesis that ESRD patients who participated in ATP would have better stress reduction, less depression and a higher quality of life than those who received only routine care. . . . In a between-group comparison of pretest scores, there were no significant differences in mean scores for quality of life; however, differences were found between the groups in terms of perceptions of stress and depression. A one-way analysis of covariance (ANCOVA) was used to control for these differences.

*Source:* Tsay, S., Lee, Y., and Lee, Y. (2005). Effects of an adaptation training programme for patients with end-stage renal disease. *Journal of Advanced Nursing, 50*(1), pp. 41, 43, 44.

The logic behind the control feature of ANCOVA is simple. The comparison groups involved in a study are likely to differ from one another with respect to one or more variables that the researcher may wish to hold constant. In an attempt to accomplish this objective, the researcher could use participants who have identical scores on the variable(s) where control is desired. That effort, however, would normally bring forth two undesirable outcomes. For one thing, only a portion of the available participants would actually be used, thus *reducing* the statistical power of inferential tests. Furthermore, the generalizability of the findings would be greatly restricted as compared with the situation where the analysis is based on a more heterogeneous group of people.

To bring about the desired control, ANCOVA adjusts each group mean on the dependent variable. Although the precise formulas used to make these adjustments are somewhat complicated, the rationale behind the adjustment process is easy to understand. If one of the comparison groups has an *above-average* mean on the *control variable* (as compared with the other comparison groups in the study), then that group's mean score on the *dependent variable* will be *lowered*. In contrast, any group that has a *below-average* mean on the *covariate* will have its mean score on the *dependent* variable *raised*. The degree to which any group's mean score on the dependent variable is adjusted depends on how far above or below average that group stands on the control variable. By adjusting the mean scores on the dependent variable in this fashion, ANCOVA provides the best estimates of how the comparison groups would have performed if they had all possessed identical means on the control variable(s).

To illustrate the way ANCOVA adjusts group means on the dependent variable, let's consider a recent study undertaken to see whether two methods of teaching reading differ in their ability to help struggling fifth-grade children improve their reading skills. Thirty-two children were randomly assigned to the two teaching methods, called TWA and RQ. Following this random assignment, the sixteen fifth graders in each group were taught five different reading lessons in small groups ($n = 4$).

In this study, data from the fifth graders were collected on several measures of reading comprehension as well as on two additional variables: self-efficacy and intrinsic motivation. Data on all of these variables were collected prior to the first reading lesson and then again after the five lessons had been taught. The second set of scores (i.e., from the posttest) represented the study's dependent variable, whereas the first set of scores (from the pretest) served as the control, or covariate, variable. In Excerpt 15.8, we see how the two groups performed on the self-efficacy measure.

As you can see from Excerpt 15.8, the two groups began the study with different mean scores on self-efficacy. With the mean pretest score for all 32 students being 3.125, it is clear that the 16 students in the TWA group started out, on the average, with a higher level of self-efficacy than did the 16 students in the RQ group. The range of possible scores on the self-efficacy measures was 1 to 5.

If the obtained posttest means on self-efficacy for the two groups had been directly compared (say, with an independent-samples $t$-test or $F$-test), a statistically significant result would be hard to interpret. That's because part or all of the posttest difference between the two groups might simply be a reflection of their different starting points.

To acknowledge the existence of the difference between the two groups on the covariate, ANCOVA adjusted the posttest means. If you examine the three sets of means in Excerpt 15.8, you'll easily see the basic logic of this adjustment procedure. The TWA group had an advantage at the outset, for its pretest mean (3.25) was higher than the grand average of both groups combined (3.125). Therefore that group's posttest mean was adjusted downward (from 3.19 to 3.09). The RQ group, in contrast, started out with a disadvantage, for its pretest mean (3.00) was lower than the grand average of all pretest scores. Consequently, the RQ group's posttest mean was adjusted upward (from 3.04 to 3.15). It is worth noting that the TWA group had the higher posttest mean but the lower adjusted posttest mean.

In *any* study, this is exactly how the control feature of ANCOVA works. Any group with an above-average mean on the covariate has its mean on the dependent

### EXCERPT 15.8 • *The "Control" Function of ANCOVA*

Thirty-two students from two urban elementary public schools who struggle with reading comprehension were randomly assigned to eight instructional groups of 4 students each. Four groups received an expository reading comprehension strategy—*T*hink before reading, think *W*hile reading, think *A*fter reading (TWA)—with SRSD instruction. . . . Four groups of 4 students served as a comparison, receiving instruction in an expository reading comprehension strategy for effective questioning, reciprocal questioning (RQ). . . . Written student responses, self-efficacy, and intrinsic motivation were tested using one-way ANCOVAs with pretest as the covariate.

**TABLE 4**   *Self Efficacy Means, Standard Deviations (in Parentheses), and Adjusted Means*

| Group | Pretest | Posttest | Adjusted posttest |
|-------|---------|----------|-------------------|
| TWA | 3.25 (0.34) | 3.19 (0.55) | 3.09 |
| RQ | 3.00 (0.40) | 3.04 (0.46) | 3.15 |

*Note:* TWA = think before reading, think while reading, think after reading approach; RQ = reciprocal questioning approach.

*Source:* Mason, L. H. (2004). Explicit self-regulated strategy development versus reciprocal questioning: Effects on expository reading comprehension among struggling readers. *Journal of Educational Psychology, 96*(2), p. 284. (Adapted slightly for presentation here.)

variable adjusted downward, while any group with a below-average mean on the covariate has its mean on the dependent variable adjusted upward. These **adjusted means** constitute the best estimates of how the two groups would have performed on the dependent variable if they had possessed identical means on the control (i.e., covariate) variable(s) used in the study.

Although the logic behind ANCOVA's adjustment of group means on the dependent variable is easy to follow, the statistical procedures used to make the adjustment are quite complicated. The formulas used to accomplish this goal will not be presented here, because you do not need to understand the intricacies of the adjustment formula in order to decipher and critique ANCOVA results. All you need to know is that the adjustment process involves far more than simply (1) determining how far each group's covariate mean lies above or below the grand covariate mean and (2) adding or subtracting that difference to that group's mean on the dependent variable. As proof of this, take another look at Excerpt 15.8. Each group's pretest mean in that study was precisely .125 points away from the grand pretest mean. However, the covariance adjustment caused less than this amount to be added to or subtracted from the posttest means.

Note that the two purposes of ANCOVA—increased power, on the one hand, and control of extraneous variables, on the other hand—occur simultaneously. If a researcher decides to use this statistical procedure solely to gain the increased power that ANCOVA affords, the means on the dependent variable will automatically be adjusted to reflect differences among the group means on the covariate variable. If, on the other hand, the researcher applies ANCOVA solely because of a desire to exert statistical control on a covariate variable, there will be, automatically, an increase in the statistical power of the inferential tests. In other words, ANCOVA accomplishes two objectives even though the researcher may have selected it with only one objective in mind.

At the beginning of this section, I stated that ANCOVA allows the researcher to make inferential statements about main and interaction effects in the populations of interest. Since you now know how data on the covariate variable(s) make it possible for the researcher to control one or more extraneous variables, I can now point out that ANCOVA's inferential statements are based on the adjusted means. The data on the covariate and the dependent variable are used to compute the adjusted means on the dependent variable, with ANCOVA's focus resting on these adjusted means whenever a null hypothesis is tested.

## Null Hypotheses

As typically used, ANCOVA will involve the same number of null hypotheses as would be the case in a comparable ANOVA. Hence, you will usually find that there will be one and three null hypotheses associated with ANCOVAs that have one and two factors, respectively. The nature of these ANCOVA null hypotheses is the same as the null hypotheses I talked about in earlier chapters when we considered various forms of ANOVA, except that the $\mu$s in any covariance $H_0$ must be considered to be adjusted means.[3]

Although null hypotheses rarely appear in research reports that contain ANCOVA results, sometimes researchers refer to them. Two examples to illustrate this are contained in Excerpts 15.9 and 15.10. Had the null hypotheses in these two studies been written out symbolically, the first one would have taken the form $H_0: \mu'_{Placebo} = \mu'_{Orlistar}$, and the second one would have stated $H_0: \mu'_{Green} = \mu'_{Blue} = \mu'_{Red} = \mu'_{White}$, where the symbol $\mu'$ stands for an adjusted population mean. Of course, the meaning of $\mu'$ would not be the same in these two null hypotheses, because the dependent variables in the two studies were quite different.

---

[3]In a completely randomized ANCOVA where each factor is active in nature, the adjusted population means on the dependent variable are logically and mathematically equal to the unadjusted population means.

**EXCERPTS 15.9–15.10 • *The Null Hypothesis in ANCOVA***

The null hypothesis—that the expected mean weight loss and change from baseline in $HbA_{1c}$ at the end of 1 year of double-blind treatment did not differ significantly between the placebo and orlistat treatments—was tested using ANCOVA.

*Source:* Kelley, D. E., Bray, G. A., Pi-Sunyer, F. X., and Klein, S. (2002). Clinical efficacy of orlistat therapy in overweight and obese patients with insulin-treated type 2 diabetes: A 1-year randomized controlled trial. *Diabetes Care, 25*(6), p. 1035.

-------------------------------------------------------------------------------------

The present study was designed to examine the effect of color on the performance of a target accuracy task (dart throwing). . . . A univariate ANCOVA indicated no significant differences ($p > .05$) between the performance means in the green, blue, red, and white conditions. . . . Based on the results of the present investigation, the null hypothesis that color would not produce significant performance differences on a dart throwing task could not be rejected.

*Source:* Araki, K., and Huddleston, S. (2002). The effect of color on a target accuracy task. *International Sports Journal, 6*(2), pp. 86, 90.

## The Focus, Number, and Quality of the Covariate Variable(s)

Suppose two different researchers each conduct a study in which they use the analysis of covariance to analyze their data. Further suppose that these two studies are conducted at the same point in time, in the same kind of setting, with the same independent variable(s) [as defined by the factor(s) and levels], and with the same measuring instrument used to collect data on the dependent variable from the same number and type of research participants. Despite all these similarities, these two ANCOVA studies might yield entirely different results because of differences in the focus, number, and quality of the covariate variable(s) used in the two investigations.

Regarding its focus, the covariate in many studies is set up to be simply an indication of each participant's status on the dependent variable at the beginning of the investigation. When this is done, the participant's scores on the covariate will be referred to as their pretest or baseline measures. Examples of this kind of covariate can be seen in Excerpts 15.7, 15.8, and 15.9. In one sense, this kind of ANCOVA study is simpler (but not necessarily of lower quality) because a single measuring instrument is used to collect data on both the covariate and the dependent variables.

There is no rule, however, that forces researchers to use pretest-type data to represent the covariate variable. In many studies, the covariate variable is entirely different from the dependent variable. For example, consider again Excerpt 15.5.

In that study, the dependent variable was total score on the ILS whereas the covariate variable was GPA.

Regardless of whether the covariate and dependent variables are the same or different, the adjustment process of ANCOVA is basically the same. First, the mean covariate score of all subjects in all comparison groups is computed. Next, each comparison group's covariate mean is compared against the grand covariate mean to see (1) if the former is above or below the latter, and (2) how much of a difference there is between these two means. Finally, each group's mean on the dependent variable is adjusted up or down (depending on whether the group was below or above average on the covariate), with larger adjustments made when a group's covariate mean is found to deviate further from the grand covariate mean.

The second way in which two ANCOVA studies might differ—even though they are identical in terms of independent and dependent variables, setting, and participants—concerns the number of covariate variables involved in the study. Simply stated, there can be one, two, or more covariate variables included in any ANCOVA study. Most often, only one covariate variable is incorporated into the researcher's study. Of the excerpts we have considered thus far, most came from studies wherein there was a single covariate variable. In Excerpt 15.11, we see a case in which two covariates were used. This study involved the comparison of two ways to teach a course in psychology, online versus in a classroom. The dependent variable was the grade earned by the student, and the two covariates measured pre-course ability levels. The term *quasi-independent variable* was used by the researcher to signal the fact that students were not randomly assigned to the two kinds of classes.

### EXCERPT 15.11 • *ANCOVA with Multiple Covariates*

Course grades expressed as a percentage were analyzed with a single factor between subjects analysis of covariance. The quasi-independent variable was Course Delivery with two levels (Online, Classroom). Covariates introduced into the analysis were HSGPA [high school grade point average] and SATC [SAT composite] scores.

*Source:* Edmonds, C. L. (2006). The inequivalence of an online and classroom based general psychology course. *Journal of Instructional Psychology, 33*(1), p. 17.

Although it might seem as if ANCOVA would work better when lots of covariate variables are involved, the researcher has to pay a price for each such variable. We will consider this point later in the chapter. For now, all I want you to know is that most ANCOVAs are conducted with only one or two covariate variables.

The third way two seemingly similar studies might differ concerns the quality of the covariate variable. Earlier, we considered the two roles of the covariate: power and control. Covariate data will not help in either regard if (1) an irrelevant covariate variable is used or (2) the covariate variable is relevant conceptually but measured in such a way that the resulting data are invalid or unreliable.

In order for a covariate variable to be conceptually relevant within a given study, it must be related to the study's dependent variable. In studies where measurements on the covariate variable are gathered via a pretest and then posttest scores (using the same measuring instrument) are used to represent the dependent variable, the conceptual relevance of the covariate is clear. When the covariate and dependent variables are different, it may or may not be the case that the covariate is worthy of being included in the ANCOVA. Later in this chapter, we will return to this issue of relevant covariate variables.

Even if the covariate *variable* selected by the researcher is sensible, the *measurement* of the variable must be sound. In other words, the data collected on the covariate variable need to be both reliable and valid. Earlier in this book, we considered different strategies available for estimating reliability and validity. Competent researchers use these techniques to assess the quality of their covariate data; moreover, they present evidence of such "data checks" within their research reports.

## Presentation of Results

Most researchers present the results of their ANCOVAs within the text of their research reports. Accordingly, we will now look at several passages that have been taken from recently published articles.

In Excerpt 15.12, we see the results of a one-way analysis of covariance. This passage is very similar to what you might see when a researcher uses a one-way ANOVA to compare the means of two groups. We're given information as to the independent and dependent variables, the calculated $F$-value, the sample means that were compared, and the decision about the null hypothesis ($p < .01$). Moreover, just like a one-way ANOVA, no follow-up test was needed because just two means were compared.

### EXCERPT 15.12 • *Results of a One-Way ANCOVA*

A pre- and postunit assessment of students' attitudes and beliefs about poetry [used] a 4-point Likert scale ranging from 1 (*strongly disagree*) to 4 (*strongly agree*). . . . I evaluated intervention effects with a one-way analysis of covariance (ANCOVA) in which pretest scores were used as covariates in the assessment of [group] differences between posttest scores. . . . An ANCOVA revealed significant differences between the control and experimental groups' interest and engagement with poetry, $F(1, 35) = 9.12, p < .01$. The control group's adjusted mean score ($M = 2.60, SE = .07$) was significantly lower than the experimental group's adjusted mean ($M = 2.89, SE = .07$) at the posttest.

*Source:* Eva-Wood, A. L. (2004). How think-and-feel-aloud instruction influences poetry readers. *Discourse Processes, 38*(2), pp. 181, 182.

There are two things about this passage that make it different from textual presentations of results following a one-way ANOVA. First, note that the two sample means are referred to as *adjusted means*. You'll never see sample means referred to this way in a one-way ANOVA. Second, note the *df* numbers next to the *F*-value. If this were a one-way ANOVA, you'd add those numbers together and then add 1 in order to figure out how many people were involved in the study. Because these results come from an ANCOVA, you must add 2 to the sum of $df_{Between}$ and $df_{Within}$ not 1. (This is because 1 degree of freedom is used up from the within-groups *df* for each covariate variable used in an ANCOVA study.) Knowing this, you can determine that the data for this one-way ANCOVA came from 38 individuals.

*[handwritten margin note: Add 2 to the sum of df]*

Now let's look at Excerpt 15.13. In this excerpt, we are given the results of four separate 2 × 2 ANCOVAs. Each analysis involved the same 82 research participants—4- and 5-year-old Head Start children—and the same two factors: Maltreatment Status (Yes or No, depending on whether each child had been neglected and/or physically abused by parents) and Treatment (Yes or No, depending on whether the child was randomly assigned to receive an innovative play strategy called Resilient Peer Treatment). Four ANCOVAs were needed because data had been gathered on four separate dependent variables: collaborative play, associative

## EXCERPT 15.13 • *Results of Four Two-Way ANCOVAs*

Eighty-two maltreated and nonmaltreated, socially withdrawn Head Start children were randomly assigned to either RPT [Resilient Peer Treatment] or attention-control (AC) conditions. Data were collected by teachers and independent observers blind to both maltreatment status and treatment condition. . . . Table 1 [not shown here] displays pre- and post-treatment means across groups for the Collaborative Play, Associative Play, Social Attention, and Solitary Play coding categories. . . . Two-way analyses of covariance (Treatment × Maltreatment status) were used to assess group difference at posttest, controlling for pretest levels. . . . Analyses of the Collaborative Play data indicated a significant main effect for treatment with the children assigned to the RPT intervention condition, evidencing higher levels of interactive play than the children in the control condition, $F(1, 77) = 39.1, p < .0001, \eta^2 = .36$. There was also a treatment main effect for the Solitary Play category, indicating the children in the RPT intervention condition displayed significantly less solitary play at posttest than the children in the control condition, $F(1, 77) = 13.7, p < .0001, \eta^2 = .15$. There were no significant main effects for maltreatment status or Treatment × Maltreatment status interaction effects for these two play categories. Also, no significant group differences were found for the Associative or Social Attention play categories.

*Source:* Fantuzzo, J., Manz, P., Atkins, M., and Meyers, R. (2005). Peer-mediated treatment of socially withdrawn maltreated preschool children: Cultivating natural community resources. *Journal of Clinical Child & Adolescent Psychology, 34*(2), pp. 320, 322.

play, social attention, and solitary play. Each of these ANCOVAs yielded three *F* values, two focused on main effects and one focused on the interaction between the two factors. In Excerpt 15.13, the researchers give us one main effect *F* from each of the first two analyses, but they don't present the other two *F*s from these AN-COVAs because they were not significant. In the excerpt's final sentence, the researchers indicate that none of the three *F*s in either of the other two ANCOVAs turned out to be statistically significant.

The researchers associated with the study that gave us Excerpt 15.13 did two things worth noting. One of these "good practices"—the estimation of effect size—can be seen in the excerpt. The other good practice followed by these researchers did not show up in Excerpt 15.13, but I'd like to give the researchers high marks for being alert to the possibility of an inflated Type I error risk in their study. I say that because the researchers used the Bonferroni adjustment procedure (changing $\alpha$ from .05 to .013) because they performed four separate ANCOVAs.

Turning now to Excerpt 15.14, we see the results of a two-way mixed AN-COVA. This set of results is worth examining for two reasons. As you will see, tests of simple main effects were conducted in order to probe the interaction. Second, this excerpt illustrates how competent researchers will pay attention to the assumptions that underlie the statistical procedures they use. Note the two actions these researchers took relative to underlying assumptions. First, they transformed their data so as to reduce nonnormality. Second, they used Geisser-Greenhouse conservative *df*s because they found that the sphericity assumption was violated.

## EXCERPT 15.14 • *Results of a Mixed ANCOVA*

We compared scores for the listeners with unimpaired hearing and the listeners with hearing loss using a repeated measures analysis of covariance. Because the group with unimpaired hearing was composed of younger listeners, age was entered into the model as a covariate. The dependent variable was test score, transformed from percentage correct to rationalized arcsine unit to normalize variance (Studebaker, 1985). The assumption of sphericity was violated, so the following results refer to the Greenhouse–Geisser adjusted degrees of freedom. Results indicated a significant Group $\times$ Condition interaction ($p = .013$). Next, we used Bonferroni-corrected means comparisons to compare the unimpaired-hearing and hearing-impaired groups within each test condition while controlling for age. There was no significant difference between groups for the 1-channel ($p = .095$) or 2-channel ($p = .166$) conditions. Performance was significantly better for the unimpaired-hearing listeners for the 4-channel ($p = .009$), 8-channel ($p < .0005$), and full ($p < .0005$) conditions.

*Source:* Souza, P. E., and Boike, K. T. (2006). Combining temporal-envelope cues across channels: Effects of age and hearing loss. *Journal of Speech, Language & Hearing Research, 49*(1), pp. 142–143.

# The Statistical Basis for ANCOVA's Power Advantage and Adjustment Feature

In an earlier section of this chapter, you learned that a good covariate variable is both conceptually related to the dependent variable and measured in such a way as to provide reliable and valid data. But how can researchers determine whether existing data (or new data that could be freshly gathered) meet this double criterion? Every researcher who uses ANCOVA ought to be able to answer this question whenever one or more covariate variables are incorporated into a study. With bad covariate variables, nothing of value comes in return for what is given up.

In order for ANCOVA to provide increased power (over a comparable ANOVA) and to adjust the group means, the covariate variable(s) must be correlated with the dependent variable. Although the correlation(s) can be either positive or negative in nature, ANCOVA will not achieve its power and adjustment objectives unless at least a moderate relationship exists between each covariate variable and the dependent variable. Stated differently, nuisance variability within the dependent variable scores can be accounted for to the extent that a strong relationship exists between the covariate(s) and the dependent variable.[4]

There are many ways to consider the correlation in ANCOVA, even when data have been collected on just one covariate variable. Two ways of doing this involve (1) looking at the correlation between the covariate and dependent variables for all participants from all comparison groups thrown into one large group, or (2) looking at the correlation between the covariate and dependent variables separately within each comparison group. The second of these two ways of considering the correlation is appropriate because ANCOVA makes its adjustments (of individual scores and of group means) on the basis of the pooled within-groups correlation coefficient.

One final point is worth making about the correlation between the covariate and dependent variables. Regarding the question of how large the pooled within-groups $r$ needs to be before the covariate can make a difference in terms of increasing power, statistical theory responds by saying that the absolute value of this $r$ should be at least .20. When $r$ is at least this large, the reduction in the error $SS$ compensates for $df$ that are lost from the error row of the ANCOVA summary table. If $r$ is between $-2.0$ and $+.20$, however, the effect of having a smaller number of error $df$ without a proportionate decrease in the error $SS$ is to make the error $MS$ larger, not smaller. That situation would bring about a reduction in power.[5]

---

[4]When two or more covariate variables are used within the same study, ANCOVA works best when the covariates are *unrelated* to each other. When the correlations among the covariate variables are low, each such variable has a chance to account for a different portion of the nuisance variability in the dependent variable.

[5]Although we have used $r$ in this paragraph, it is actually the population parameter $\rho$ that needs to exceed $\pm.20$ in order for ANCOVA to have a power advantage.

# Assumptions

The statistical assumptions of ANCOVA include all the assumptions that are associated with ANOVA, plus three that are unique to the situation where data on a covariate variable are used in an effort to make adjustments and increase power. All three of these unique-to-ANCOVA assumptions must be met if the analysis is to function in its intended manner, and the researcher (and you) should consider these assumptions whenever ANCOVA is used—even in situations where the comparison groups are equally large. In other words, equal *n*s do *not* cause ANCOVA to be robust to any of the assumptions we now wish to consider.

## The Independent Variable Should Not Affect the Covariate Variable

The first of these three new assumptions stipulates that the study's independent variable should not affect the covariate variable. In an experiment (where the independent variable is an active factor), this assumption clearly will be met if the data on the covariate variable are collected before the treatments are applied. If the covariate data are collected after the treatments have been applied, the situation is far murkier—and the researcher should provide a logical argument on behalf of the implicit claim that treatments do not affect the covariate. In nonexperimental (i.e., descriptive) studies, the situation is even murkier since the independent variable very likely may have influenced each subject's status on the covariate variable prior to the study. We will return to this issue—of covariance being used in nonrandomized studies—in the next major section.

To see an example of how the covariate can be affected by the independent variable in a randomized experiment, consider Excerpt 15.15. In this study, the data on the covariate variable (change scores over the 12-week duration of the study) were collected *after* the independent variable had been applied. Not only was there a possibility, therefore, that the independent variable affected covariate scores, the researchers seem to argue that this is exactly what happened!

## Homogeneity of Within-Group Correlations (or Regression Slopes)

The second unique assumption associated with ANCOVA stipulates that the correlation between the covariate and dependent variables is the same within each of the populations involved in the study. This assumption usually is talked about in terms of regression slopes rather than correlations, and hence you are likely to come across ANCOVA research reports that contain references to the **assumption of equal regression slopes** or to the **homogeneity of regression slope assumption.** The data of a study can be employed to test this assumption—and it should *always* be tested when ANCOVA is used. As is the case when testing other assumptions,

**EXCERPT 15.15 • *The Assumption That the Independent Variable Does Not Influence the Covariate Variable***

Subjects were randomly assigned to receive either 3g/day of E-EPA supplement in encapsulated form (three 500-mg capsules twice daily) or placebo (3g/day of medicinal liquid paraffin BP) in addition to the medication that they had been receiving. . . . The primary outcome measure was the percentage change in Positive and Negative Syndrome Scale total scores between baseline and 12 weeks. . . . An analysis of covariance using change in Positive and Negative Syndrome Scale total score as the dependent variable and change in dyskinesia score as a covariate was performed. . . . This study shows a significant advantage for E-EPA over placebo in the primary outcome measure [and] the results of the analysis of covariance suggest that reduction in Positive and Negative Syndrome Scale scores may at least in part be related to reduction in dyskinesia scores.

*Source:* Emsley, R., Myburgh, C., Oosthuizen, P., and van Rensburg, S. J. (2002). Randomized, placebo-controlled study of ethyl-eicosapentaenoic acid as supplemental treatment in schizophrenia. *American Journal of Psychiatry, 159*(9), pp. 1596–1597.

the researcher will be happy when the statistical test of the equal slopes assumption leads to a fail-to-reject decision. That outcome is interpreted as a signal that it is permissible to analyze the study's data using ANCOVA procedures.

Consider Excerpt 15.16. This excerpt shows how a team of researchers attended to most of the assumptions associated with the analysis of covariance before they used ANCOVA several times, once with each of their study's dependent variables. Move past the first sentence, however, and concentrate on the second and third sentences. What the researchers say in those sentences clearly indicates that (1) they

**EXCERPT 15.16 • *The Assumption of Equal Regression Slopes***

Before carrying out the main analyses using analysis of covariance, we conducted an evaluation of assumptions of normality, homogeneity of variance, reliability of the covariates, linearity, and homogeneity of regression slopes. All assumptions were satisfied except for a single violation of the assumption of homogeneity of regression slopes found between the job satisfaction posttest and covariate pretest scores. To address the violation of the assumption of homogeneity of regression slopes, we calculated a new job-satisfaction dependent variable involving change scores as suggested by Tabachnick and Fidell (2001, p. 303).

*Source:* Alford, W. K., Malouff, J. M., and Osland, K. S. (2005). Written emotional expression as a coping method in child protective services officers. *International Journal of Stress Management, 12*(2), pp. 182–183.

tested the assumption of equal regression slopes before conducting each ANCOVA and (2) they took appropriate corrective action when, in one of their tests of the equal slopes assumption, it became apparent that the assumption was violated.

If the equal-slopes $H_0$ is rejected, there are several options open to the researcher. In that situation, the data can be transformed and then the assumption can be tested again using the transformed data. Or, the researcher can turn to one of several more complicated analyses (e.g., the Johnson-Neyman technique) developed specifically for the situation where heterogeneous regressions exist. Or, the researcher can decide to pay no attention to the covariate data and simply use an ANOVA to compare groups on the dependent variable. These various options come into play only rarely, either because the equal-slopes assumption is not rejected when it is tested or because the researcher wrongfully bypasses testing the assumption.

### Linearity

The third assumption connected to ANCOVA (but not ANOVA) stipulates that the within-group relationship between the covariate and dependent variables should be linear.[6] There are several ways this assumption can be evaluated, some involving a formal statistical test and some involving visual inspections of scatter plots. (A special type of scatter diagram, involving plots of residuals, is used more frequently than plots of raw scores.) Regardless of how researchers might choose to assess the **linearity** assumption, we need to salute their efforts to examine their data to see if it is legitimate to conduct an analysis of variance.

Consider Excerpt 15.17. This passage is similar to the one we saw in Excerpt 15.16 in that attention is devoted to several of the assumptions that underlie an analysis of covariance. For our purposes now, first note what the covariate and dependent variables were in the study associated with Excerpt 15.17. Next, take a look

### EXCERPT 15.17 • *The Linearity Assumption*

The main analyses [included] an ANCOVA, as recommended by Tabachnick and Fidell (2001), to determine group differences in post-competition measures of positive affect (the dependent variable) controlling for the influence of a pre-competition measures of positive affect (the covariate). Assumptions of the statistics, including normality of the data, homogeneity of variance, linearity of relationship between the pre and post-competition measures of affect, and homogeneity of regression slopes, were met.

*Source:* Brown, L. J., and Malouff, J. M. (2005). The effectiveness of a self-efficacy intervention for helping adolescents cope with sport-competition loss. *Journal of Sport Behavior, 28*(2), p. 141.

---

[6]I first discussed the notion of linearity in Chapter 3; you may want to review that earlier discussion if you have forgotten what it means to say that two variables have a linear relationship.

at what follows the words "homogeneity of variance" in this excerpt's final sentence. These researchers deserve credit for attending to ANCOVA's linearity assumption.

### Other Standard Assumptions

As indicated earlier, the "standard" assumptions of ANOVA (e.g., normality, homogeneity of variance, sphericity) underlie ANCOVA as well. You should upgrade or downgrade your evaluation of a study depending on the attention given to these assumptions in the situations where $F$-tests are biased when assumptions are violated. Unfortunately, you are likely to come across *many* ANCOVA studies in which there is absolutely no discussion of linearity, equal regression slopes, normality, or homogeneity of variance.

## ANCOVA When Comparison Groups Are Not Formed Randomly

In a randomized experiment, the various population means on the covariate variable can be considered identical. This is the case because of the random assignment of research participants to the comparison groups of the investigation. Granted, the sample means for the comparison groups on the covariate variable will probably vary, but the corresponding population means are identical.

When ANCOVA is used to compare groups that are formed in a nonrandomized fashion, the population means on the covariate variable cannot be assumed to be equal. For example, if a study is set up to compare sixth-grade boys with sixth-grade girls on their ability to solve word problems in mathematics, a researcher might choose to make the comparison using ANCOVA, with reading ability used as the covariate variable. In such a study, the population means on reading ability might well differ between the two gender groups.

Although my concern over the equality or inequality of the covariate population means may initially seem silly (because of the adjustment feature of ANCOVA), this issue is far more important than it might at first appear. I say this because studies in theoretical statistics have shown that the ANCOVA's adjusted means turn out to be biased in the situation where the comparison groups differ with respect to population means on the covariate variable. In other words, the sample-based adjusted means on the dependent variable do not turn out to be accurate estimates of the corresponding adjusted means in the population when the population means on the covariate variable are dissimilar.

Because ANCOVA produces adjusted means, many applied researchers evidently think that this statistical procedure was designed to permit nonrandomly formed groups to be compared. Over the years, I have repeatedly come across research reports in which the researchers talk as if ANCOVA has the magical power to equate such groups and thereby allow valid inferences to be drawn from comparisons of adjusted means. Excerpts 15.18 and 15.19 illustrate this view held by many applied researchers that ANCOVA works well with nonrandomly formed groups. In the first of these excerpts, look at the final 11 words. In Excerpt 15.19, the researchers claim, in essence, that ANCOVA can control for initial group differences and "make up for" the inability to form groups randomly.

**EXCERPTS 15.18–15.19 •** *The Use of ANCOVA with Groups Formed without Random Assignment*

In this study a quasi-experimental research design was used. A quasi-experimental design has the appearance of a pretest-posttest randomized experiment but lacks random assignment (Babbie, 2001). . . . Posttests were analyzed with an analysis of covariance in order to adjust for any group differences on the pretests.

*Source:* Woullard, R., and Coats, L. T. (2004). The community college role in preparing future teachers: The impact of a mentoring program for preservice teachers. *Community College Journal of Research and Practice, 28*(7), pp. 614, 617.

---

Since there were differences between treatment groups at Time 1, before the treatments began—significant in trauma symptoms although not in other orientation—we performed analyses of covariance to determine the effects of treatments two months after the intervention ended, while statistically controlling for initial differences. . . . Lack of random assignment to conditions and possible variation in recruitment practices are methodological limitations of the study. We attempted to create a design that would enable us to deal with such methodological limitations, primarily by covariance analyses.

*Source:* Staub, E., Pearlman, L. A., Gubin, A., and Hagengimana, A. (2005). Healing, reconciliation, forgiving, and the prevention of violence after genocide or mass killing: An intervention and its experimental evaluation in Rwanda. *Journal of Social & Clinical Psychology, 24*(3), p. 321.

Besides ANCOVA's statistical inability to generate unbiased adjusted means when nonrandomly formed groups are compared, there is a second, logical reason why you should be on guard whenever you come across a research report in which ANCOVA was used in an effort to equate groups created without random assignment. Simply stated, the covariate variable(s) used by the researcher may not address one or more important differences between the comparison groups. Here, the problem is that a given covariate variable (or set of covariate variables) is limited in scope. For example, the covariate variable(s) used by the researcher might address knowledge but not motivation (or vice versa).

Consider, for example, the many studies conducted in schools or colleges in which one intact group of students receives one form of instruction while a different intact group receives an alternative form of instruction. In such studies, it is common practice to compare the two groups' posttest means via an analysis of covariance, with the covariate being IQ, GPA, or score on a pretest. In the summaries of these studies, the researchers will say that they used ANCOVA "to control for initial differences between the groups." However, it is debatable whether academic ability is reflected in any of the three covariates mentioned (or even in all three used jointly). In this and many other studies, people's motivation plays no small part in how well they perform.

In summary, be extremely cautious when confronted with research claims based upon the use of ANCOVA with intact groups. If an important covariate variable was overlooked by those who conducted the study, pay no attention whatsoever to the conclusions based upon the data analysis. Even in the case where data on all important covariate variables were collected and used, you *still* should be tentative in your inclination to buy into the claims made by the researchers.

Before you finish this section concerning ANCOVA and nonrandomly formed groups, take time to read Excerpts 15.20 and 15.21. They represent

EXCERPTS 15.20–15.21 • *Why ANCOVA with Nonrandomly Formed Groups Is Problematic*

In this study, forming groups by random assignment was not possible because it was necessary to work with the intact groups already formed by the schools. This fact made it impossible to assume that the population means on the pre-tests (potential covariates) were equal, as it would be possible to do with groups formed by random assignment. This assumption of equal population means is a requirement for using the analysis of covariance (ANCOVA) procedure.

*Source:* White, J. L., and Turner, C. E. (2005). Comparing children's oral ability in two ESL programs. *Canadian Modern Language Review, 61*(4), pp. 502–503.

---

Several limitations of the study [that used ANCOVA] need to be acknowledged. The natural clinical setting for this study was not readily conducive to the random assignment of patients to the experimental groups. It is possible that the patients who did not participate in the exercise program were less motivated, less compliant, and less ready to recover. It also is possible that the women who chose not to participate were more rigid with their exercise, and therefore more reluctant to engage in physical activity that did not adhere to their desired frequency, intensity, or quality. Finally, it is possible that there were some unknown systematic personality differences between the exercise and control group, which contributed to a self-selection bias, and in turn, may have interfered with treatment.

*Source:* Calogero, R. M., and Pedrotty, K. N. (2004). The practice and process of healthy exercise: An investigation of the treatment of exercise abuse in women with eating disorders. *Eating Disorders, 12*(4), p. 288.

exceptions to the rule, because the good thoughts expressed in these passages are seen quite rarely in research summaries. These researchers deserve high praise for understanding and pointing out that ANCOVA is *incapable* of equating nonrandomly formed groups.

## Related Issues

Near the beginning of this chapter, I asserted that any ANCOVA is, in several respects, like its ANOVA counterpart. We have already considered many of the ways in which ANOVA and ANCOVA are similar, such as the way post hoc tests are typically used to probe significant main effects and interactions. At this point, we ought to consider three additional ways in which ANCOVA is akin to ANOVA.

As with ANOVA, the Type I error rate will be inflated if separate ANCOVAs are used to analyze the data corresponding to two or more dependent variables. To deal with this problem, the conscientious researcher will implement one of several available strategies. The most frequently used strategy for keeping the operational Type I error rate in line with the stated alpha level is the **Bonferroni adjustment technique,** and it can be used with ANCOVA as easily as it can with ANOVA.

In Excerpt 15.22, we see a case in which the Bonferroni adjustment technique was used in conjunction with a two-way ANCOVA that was used three times. This was a longitudinal study, and the researchers wanted to see what happened to the same groups of children at the end of second grade, at the end of third grade, and at the end of fourth grade. In each of these analyses, the two between-subjects factors were gender and the type of kindergarten class (full-day or half-day) that the children had attended.

### EXCERPT 15.22 • *Use of the Bonferroni Adjustment Technique*

Our final choice was to conduct separate univariate ANCOVAs with appropriate Bonferroni adjustments to prevent inflation in the Type I error rate. For the reading-level analyses, we conducted three $2 \times 2$ ANCOVAs because reading achievement tests were given in the spring of the second, third, and fourth grades. The alpha level was set at .017 for each of the analyses.

*Source:* Wolgemuth, J. R., Cobb, R. B., Winokur, M. A., Leech, N., and Ellerby, D. (2006). Comparing longitudinal academic achievement of full-day and half-day kindergarten students. *Journal of Educational Research, 99*(5), p. 263.

The second issue that has a common connection to both ANOVA and ANCOVA is the important distinction between **statistical significance** and **practical significance.** Since it is possible, in either kind of analysis, for the data to produce a finding that is significant in a statistical sense but not in a practical sense, you should upgrade your evaluation of any ANCOVA study wherein the researcher conducts a power analysis or estimates the magnitude of observed effects. Because so many people mistakenly equate statistical significance and practical significance, let's take the time to consider three studies in which the researchers wisely tried to distinguish between these different concepts.

Earlier (in Excerpt 15.13), we saw an example in which eta squared was used to assess the practical significance of ANCOVA results. Now, in Excerpt 15.23, we see a case in which the issue of practical significance is addressed by means of a different way of estimating effect size. As you can see, the researchers here used $d$. They also use the terms "large" and "strong" when interpreting their two values of $d$.

**EXCERPT 15.23 • *Effect Size Estimation in ANCOVA***

On the WLPB-R Word Attack subtest, there was a significant difference between groups after adjusting for pretest performance, $F(1, 60) = 14.27, p < .001$, such that treatment group students demonstrated a greater ability to apply phonic and structural analysis skills to pronounce phonetically regular nonsense words in Spanish, and the effect size of this difference was large ($d = +0.85$). Moreover, on the WLPB-R Passage Comprehension subtest, there was a strong difference between groups after adjusting for pretest performance, $F(1, 60) = 8.46, p < .006$, with treatment students showing greater ability to supply missing words to demonstrate comprehension in a cloze procedure; the effect size of this difference was strong ($d = +0.55$).

*Source:* Vaughn, S., Thompson, L., Mathes, P. G., Cirino, P. T., Carlson, C. D., Pollard-Durodola, S. D., Cardenas-Hagan, E., and Francis, D. J. (2006). Effectiveness of Spanish intervention for first-grade English language learners at risk for reading difficulties. *Journal of Learning Disabilities, 39*(1), p. 65.

The criteria for judging effect size indices in any ANCOVA study are the same as the standards for these indices when they are computed for any ANOVA study. To see the criteria for judging the magnitude of $d$, $\eta^2$, and other ways of estimating effect size, refer to Table 13.2. That table also shows which of these procedures are typically used in conjunction with tests on main effects, tests on interactions, and different kinds of post hoc tests.

In Excerpt 15.24, we see a case in which a research team conducted an a priori power analysis in conjunction with their ANCOVA study. They did this in order to determine how large the study's sample sizes needed to be. If their sample sizes had been substantially larger than what the power analysis indicated, the study might have yielded a statistically significant finding without any practical significance. By using only 68 women in each of the study's "treatment arms," the researchers made it likely that statistical significance, if found, would be accompanied by clinical significance.

**EXCERPT 15.24** • *A Power Analysis to Determine Sample Size*

The sample size then was based on a covariance analysis of the BCSCS scores at course 4. The analysis used the BCSCS score at course 3 as a covariate and estimated the effect of viewing the videotape. The type I and type II errors were set to 0.05 (two-tail test) and 0.20, respectively. Actual sample size based on the interim analysis and power analysis provided that an estimated 68 women were required for each treatment arm.

*Source:* Nolte, S., Donnelly, J., Kelly, S., Conley, P., and Cobb, R. A. (2006). Randomized clinical trial of a videotape intervention for women with chemotherapy-induced alopecia: A gynecologic oncology group study. *Oncology Nursing Forum, 33*(2), p. 307.

Excerpt 15.25 illustrates the use of a post hoc power analysis in an ANCOVA study. This excerpt deserves your close attention. If you read it carefully, you'll note that the researchers ended up with "negative findings" (meaning that their null hypotheses were retained). Were these results caused by low power and thus the inability to detect group differences that would be considered of practical significance? The results of the power analysis suggest not. The researchers' defense for this claim is contained in the excerpt's final sentence.

**EXCERPT 15.25** • *A Post Hoc Power Analysis*

Use of the targeted drug during the intervention phase was analyzed separately within each study using analysis of covariance (ANCOVA), with two categorical between-subject factors (cannabis-use category and experimental treatment group) and one continuous covariate (each patient's baseline percentage of urine specimens positive for the targeted drug, arcsine-transformed to maintain homogeneity of variance). . . . Because the findings were generally negative, we performed *post hoc* power calculations for selected analyses. For the ANCOVAs on intervention-phase data, we used power tables for the $f$ effect–size measure. . . . Taking into account the presence of other factors in the ANCOVAs, the three studies (opiate, cocaine 1, and cocaine 2) each had power of 0.95 to detect effect sizes of $f = 0.40$, 0.44 and 0.35, respectively, for cannabis-use category. These are large-to-medium effects, equivalent to $r^2$ values of 0.14, 0.15 and 0.11. In other words, if cannabis-use category had accounted for 11% or more of the variance in use of the targeted drug (cocaine or illicit opiates), then the probability of our having failed to detect an association would be less than 0.05.

*Source:* Epstein, D. H., and Preston, K. L. (2003). Does cannabis use predict poor outcome for heroin-dependent patients on maintenance treatment? Past findings and more evidence against. *Addiction, 98*(3), p. 272, 273, 276.

The third point I want to make in this section is simple: Planned comparisons can be used in ANCOVA studies just as easily as they can be used in ANOVA studies. Excerpt 15.26 is a case in point. If you read this excerpt closely, you will discover that two different kinds of planned comparisons were conducted. One type was pairwise in nature; the other type was nonpairwise.

### EXCERPT 15.26 • *ANCOVA and Planned Comparisons*

Participants in each age group were randomly assigned to one of four strategy groups: *Writing (implicit organization), Categorization (explicit organization), Categorization + Writing (both explicit and implicit),* or *Control,* and were asked to study and recall a categorizable word list. . . . To test the strategy condition hypotheses, Age (3) × Condition (4) ANCOVAs were conducted on recall, categorization (ARC), self-efficacy, and task-specific control beliefs. . . . Planned contrasts were performed within each age group to test whether average performance improved more in the [combined] strategy compared to the control conditions and also to examine whether the strategy groups [individually] had higher efficacy and control beliefs compared to the control groups.

*Source:* Lachman, M. E., Andreoletti, C., and Pearman, A. (2006). Memory control beliefs: How are they related to age, strategy use and memory improvement? *Social Cognition, 24*(3), pp. 369, 370.

## A Few Warnings

Before concluding our discussion of ANCOVA, I want to offer a few warnings about deciphering research reports that present results from this form of statistical analysis. As you consider these comments, however, do not forget that ANCOVA legitimately can be thought of as a set of statistical procedures made possible by adding covariate data to an ANOVA-type situation. Because of this fact, all the tips and warnings offered at the conclusions of Chapters 10 through 14 should be kept in mind when you consider the results from a study that used ANCOVA. In addition to being aware of the concerns focused on in those earlier chapters, you should also remain sensitive to the following three unique-to-ANCOVA cautions when considering research claims based on covariance analyses.

### The Statistical Focus: Adjusted Means

In a covariance analysis, all *F*-tests (other than those concerned with underlying assumptions) deal with adjusted means on the dependent variable, not the unadjusted means. This holds true for the *F*-tests contained in the ANCOVA summary table, the *F*-tests involved in any planned comparisons, and the *F*-tests involved in any post hoc investigation. For this reason, adjusted means should be presented—either in a table or within the textual discussion—whenever the researcher attempts to explain the meaning of any *F*-test result. It is helpful, as we have seen, to have access to the means on the covariate variable and the unadjusted means on the dependent variable. However, the adjusted means on the dependent variable constitute the central statistical focus of any ANCOVA.

Unfortunately, many researchers fail to present the adjusted means in their research reports. When this happens, you are boxed into a corner in which you cannot easily decide for yourself whether a statistically significant finding ought to be considered significant in a practical sense. Since making this kind of decision is one of the things consumers of the research literature ought to do on a regular basis, I must encourage you to downgrade your evaluation of any ANCOVA-based study that fails to contain the adjusted means that go with the *F*-test(s) focused on by the researcher.

## The Importance of Underlying Assumptions

ANCOVA's *F*-tests that compare adjusted means function as they are supposed to function only if various underlying assumptions are valid. Moreover, the condition of equal sample sizes does not bring about a situation where the assumptions are rendered unimportant. In other words, equal *n*s do not cause ANCOVA to become robust to its underlying assumptions.

Whenever you consider research claims based on ANCOVA, check to see whether the researcher says anything about the statistical assumptions on which the analysis was based. Upgrade your evaluation of the research report when there is expressed concern over the assumption of equal regression slopes, the assumption of a linear relationship between the covariate and dependent variables, and the assumption that scores on the covariate variable are not influenced by the independent variable. If these assumptions are not discussed, you should downgrade your evaluation of the study.

If an assumption is tested, give the researchers some bonus credit if they use a lenient rather than rigorous alpha level in assessing the assumption's $H_0$. I say this because researchers deserve credit if they perform statistical tests in such a way that the "deck is stacked against them" in terms of what they would like to show. Since the typical researcher who uses ANCOVA wants the linearity and equal-slopes assumptions to be met, a lenient level of significance (such as .10, .15, .20, or even .25) gives the data more of a chance to reveal an improper situation than would be the case if alpha is set equal to .05, .01, or .001. When testing assumptions, Type II errors are generally considered to be more serious than errors of the first kind, and the level of significance should be set accordingly.

## ANCOVA versus ANOVA

My final warning has to do with your general opinion of ANCOVA-based studies as compared with ANOVA-based studies. Because ANCOVA is more complex (due to the involvement of a larger number of variables and assumptions), many consumers of the research literature hold the opinion that data-based claims are more trustworthy when they are based on ANCOVA rather than ANOVA. I strongly encourage you to *refrain* from adopting this unjustified point of view.

Although ANCOVA (as compared with ANOVA) does, in fact, involve more complexities in terms of what is involved both on and beneath the surface, it is an extremely delicate instrument. To provide meaningful results, ANCOVA must be used very carefully—with attention paid to important assumptions, with focus directed at the appropriate set of sample means, and with concern over the correct way to draw inferences from ANCOVA's $F$-tests. Because of its complexity, ANCOVA affords its users more opportunities to make mistakes than does ANOVA.

If used skillfully, ANCOVA can be of great assistance to applied researchers. If not used carefully, however, ANCOVA can be dangerous. Unfortunately, many people think of complexity as being an inherent virtue. In statistics, that is often *not* the case. As pointed out earlier in the chapter, the interpretation of ANCOVA $F$-tests is problematic whenever the groups being compared have been formed in a non-random fashion—and this statement holds true even if (1) multiple covariate variables are involved, and (2) full attention is directed to all underlying assumptions. In contrast, it would be much easier to interpret the results generated by the application of ANOVA to the data provided by participants who have been randomly assigned to comparison groups. Care is required, of course, whenever you attempt to interpret the outcome of *any* inferential test. My point is simply that ANCOVA, because of its complexity as compared to ANOVA, demands a higher—not lower—level of care on your part when you encounter its results.

## *Review Terms*

Adjusted means
Analysis of covariance
ANCOVA
Assumption of equal regression slopes
Bonferroni adjustment technique
Concomitant variable
Covariate variable

Homogeneity of regression
  slopes
Linearity
Power
Practical significance
Statistical significance

## *The Best Items in the Companion Website*

1. An interactive online quiz (with immediate feedback provided) covering Chapter 15.
2. Nine misconceptions about the content of Chapter 15.
3. One of the best passages from Chapter 15: "Are ANCOVA Studies Better Than ANOVA Studies?"
4. The first two e-articles.
5. The first of the two jokes, because it deals with the analysis of covariance.

To access chapter objectives, practice tests, weblinks, and flashcards, visit the companion website at www.ablongman.com/huck5e.

---

## *Fun Exercises inside Research Navigator*

---

### 1. Do reminders of death have a differential impact on college men versus college women?

In a three-stage experiment, 101 male and female college students first completed a questionnaire concerning their sensation-seeking behavior. Then they were randomly assigned to one of two groups. Those in one group were asked what they thought about their impending death; those in the other group were asked about watching TV. Finally, members of both groups completed a questionnaire dealing with the appeal of risk-taking behaviors (such as bungee jumping and hang gliding). Scores on sensation-seeking served as the covariate in a 2 (death/TV) × 2 (gender) ANCOVA. Results indicated that being reminded of death had an impact on one of the gender groups but not the other. Which group do you think was affected, and do you think the death reminder increased or decreased the appeal of risk-taking behaviors? To find out, locate the PDF version of the research report in the Helping Professions database of ContentSelect, read the three full paragraphs on page 126, and look at Table 1.

G. Hirschberger, V. Florian, M. Mikulincer, J. L. Goldenberg, & T. Pyszczynski. Gender differences in the willingness to engage in risky behavior. *Issues in Comprehensive Journal of Psychology.* Located in the HELPING PROFESSIONS database of ContentSelect.

### 2. In a study on college students' opinions about prayer and counselors, why wasn't the covariate used?

In this study, 67 college students were randomly assigned to two groups, both of which read a two-page vignette describing a counseling session. The vignettes were identical except for one sentence located near the end of the second page. In one vignette (given to one of the groups), the counselee mentioned prayer prior to the counselor disclosing the use of prayer. In the other vignette (given to the other group), the counselee never said anything about prayer and yet the counselor still disclosed the use of prayer. Evaluations of each vignette's counselor by the research participants served as the study's dependent variable. Religiosity scores, gathered from the vignette readers, were supposed to be used as the covariate within an ANCOVA comparison of the two groups. However, those religiosity scores were not used and the ANCOVA was not conducted. Why do you think the researchers made this decision? To find out, locate the PDF version of the research report in the Psychology database of ContentSelect and read (on page 273) the first two sentences of the second paragraph of the "Results."

S. J. Nyman & T. K. Daugherty. Congruence of counselor self-disclosure and perceived effectiveness. *Journal of Psychology.* Located in the PSYCHOLOGY database of ContentSelect.

---

**Review Questions and Answers begin on page 513.**

# Bivariate, Multiple, and Logistic Regression

In Chapter 3, we considered how bivariate correlation can be used to describe the relationship between two variables. Then, in Chapter 9, we looked at how bivariate correlations are dealt with in an inferential manner. In this chapter, our focus is on a topic closely related to correlation. This topic is called **regression.**

As you will see, three different kinds of regression will be considered here: **bivariate regression, multiple regression,** and **logistic regression.** Bivariate regression is similar to bivariate correlation, because both are designed for situations in which there are just two variables. Multiple and logistic regression, on the other hand, were created for cases in which there are three or more variables. Although many other kinds of regression procedures have been developed, the three considered here are by far the ones used most frequently by applied researchers.

The three regression procedures considered in this chapter are like correlation in that they are concerned with relationships among variables. Because of this, you may be tempted to think that regression is simply another way of talking about, or measuring, correlation. Resist that temptation! That's because these two statistical procedures differ in three important respects: their purpose, the way variables are labeled, and the kinds of inferential tests applied to the data.

The first difference between correlation and regression concerns the purpose of each technique. As indicated in Chapter 3, bivariate correlation is designed to illuminate the relationship, or connection, between two variables. The computed correlation coefficient may suggest that the relationship being focused on is direct and strong, or indirect and moderate, or so weak that it would be unfair to think of the relationship as being either direct or indirect. Regardless of how things turn out, each of the two variables is equally responsible for the nature and strength of the link between the two variables.

Whereas correlation concentrates on the relationship that exists *between* variables, regression focuses on the variable(s) that exist on one or the other *ends* of the link. Depending on which end is focused on, regression will be trying to accomplish one or the other of two goals. These two goals involve prediction on the one hand and explanation on the other.

In some studies, regression is utilized to **predict** scores on one variable based on information regarding the other variable(s). For example, a college might use regression in an effort to predict how well applicants will handle its academic curriculum. Each applicant's college GPA would be the main focus of the regression, with predictions made on the basis of available data on other variables (e.g., an entrance exam, the applicant's essay, and recommendations written by high school teachers). If used in this manner, regression's focus would be on the one variable toward which predictions are made: college GPA.

In other investigations, regression is used in an effort to **explain** why the study's people, animals, or things score differently on a particular variable of interest. For example, a researcher might be interested in why people differ in the degree to which they seem satisfied with life. If such a study were to be conducted, a questionnaire might be administered to a large group of individuals for the purpose of measuring life satisfaction. Those same individuals would also be measured on several other variables that might explain why some people are quite content with what life has thrown at them while others seem to grumble incessantly because they think life has been cruel and unfair to them. Such variables might include health status, relationships with others, and job enjoyment. If used in this manner, regression's focus would be on the variables that potentially explain why people differ in their levels of life satisfaction.

Excerpts 16.1 and 16.2 illustrate the two different purposes of regression. In the first of these excerpts, the clear objective was to use regression analyses to help predict the reading and spelling performance of young children, two markers of early literacy competence. In Excerpt 16.2, the goal was explanation, not prediction. Here, the researchers wanted to know which factors explain why some urban-dwelling African-American women with osteoarthritis (OA) or rheumatoid arthritis (RA) exercise more than others.

The second difference between regression and correlation concerns the labels attached to the variables. This difference can be seen most easily in the case in which data on just two variables have been collected. Let's call these variables A and B. In a correlation analysis, variables A and B have no special names; they are simply the study's two variables. With no distinction made between them, their location in verbal descriptions or in pictorial representations can be switched without changing what's being focused on. For example, once $r$ becomes available, it can be described as the correlation between A and B *or* it can be referred to as the correlation between B and A. Likewise, if a scatter diagram is used to show the relationship between the two variables, it doesn't matter which variable is positioned on the abscissa.

In a regression analysis involving A and B, an important distinction between the two variables must be made. In regression, one of the two variables needs to be

**EXCERPTS 16.1–16.2** • *The Two Purposes of Regression: Prediction and Explanation*

It is important to gather data on the effectiveness of the ELS [Early Literacy Support] in relation to other forms of intervention to enable schools to identify efficient and cost effective ways of preventing or overcoming difficulties in early literacy. In addition, an understanding of what predicts individual differences in children's responsiveness to the strategy is required so that modifications can be made to the curriculum in the light of children's special needs. . . . The correlation matrix [not shown here] suggests that reading and spelling at T2 are significantly predicted by all variables apart from receptive vocabulary at T1. However, given the association between predictor variables, the matrix does not allow us to identify the extent to which variables contribute unique variance to predicting reading and spelling. In order to do that, it is necessary to conduct regression analyses.

*Source:* Hatcher, P. J., Goetz, K., Snowling, M. J., Hulme, C., Gibbs, S., and Smith, G. (2006). Evidence for the effectiveness of the Early Literacy Support programme. *British Journal of Educational Psychology, 76,* pp. 353, 362.

-------------------------------------------------------------------------

The purpose of this study was to answer the following questions: (1) What factors explain physical activity and exercise behavior in urban adults with OA and RA who are predominantly African-American and female? and (2) Are the factors that explain physical activity and exercise behavior the same for people with OA and RA in this population? . . . Forward stepwise multiple linear regression was used to build a model of explanatory variables that best explained the variance in physical activity.

*Source:* Greene, B. L., Haldeman, G. F., Kaminski, A., Neal, K., Sam Lim, S., and Conn, D. L. (2006). Factors affecting physical activity behavior in urban adults with arthritis who are predominantly African-American and female. *Physical Therapy, 86*(4), pp. 512, 514.

identified as the **dependent variable** and the other variable must be seen as the **independent variable.**[1] This distinction is important because (1) the scatter diagram in bivariate regression always is set up such that the vertical axis corresponds with the dependent variable while the horizontal axis represents the independent variable and (2) the names of the two variables cannot be interchanged in verbal descriptions of the regression. For example, the regression of A on B is not the same as the regression of B on A.[2]

[1]The terms **criterion variable, outcome variable,** and **response variable** are synonymous with the term **dependent variable,** while the terms **predictor variable** or **explanatory variable** mean the same thing as **independent variable.**

[2]When the phrase "regression of _____ on _____" is used, the variable appearing in the first blank will be the dependent variable whereas the variable(s) appearing in the second blank will be the independent variable(s).

Excerpts 16.3 and 16.4 come from two studies that were quite different. In the first study, only two variables were involved in the single regression that was conducted. In the second excerpt, there was one dependent variable and four independent variables. Despite these differences, notice how the researchers associated with each excerpt clearly designate the status of each variable as being a dependent variable or an independent variable.

### EXCERPTS 16.3–16.4 • *Dependent and Independent Variables*

First, the subjects were divided into three groups, according to their resource levels (high, medium, or low), and then bivariate regressions were calculated for each resource level, with distress as the independent variable and suicidal ideation as the dependent variable.

*Source:* Lieberman, Z., Solomon, Z., and Ginzburg, K. (2005). Suicidal ideation among young adults: Effects of perceived social support, self-esteem, and adjustment. *Journal of Loss & Trauma, 10*(2), pp. 174–175.

To compare the predictive power of self-efficacy and SARS fear [as measured by the SARS Fear Scale subtests], we conducted a multiple regression analysis with CIES–R total as the dependent variable and perceived self-efficacy, SFS infection, SFS insecurity, and SFS instability as independent variables.

*Source:* Ho, S. M. Y., Kwong-Lo, R. S. Y., Mak, C. W. Y., and Wong, J. S. (2005). Fear of severe acute respiratory syndrome (SARS) among health care workers. *Journal of Consulting and Clinical Psychology, 73*(2), p. 347.

The third difference between correlation and regression concerns the focus of inferential tests and confidence intervals. With correlation, there is just one thing that can be focused on: the sample correlation coefficient. With regression, however, you will see that inferences focus on the correlation coefficient, the regression coefficient(s), the intercept, the change in the regression coefficient, and something called the odds ratio. We will consider these different inferential procedures as we look at bivariate regression, multiple regression, and logistic regression.

Although correlation and regression are not the same, correlational concepts serve as some (but not all) of regression's building blocks. With that being the case, you may wonder why this chapter is positioned here rather than immediately after Chapter 9. If this question has popped into your head, there is a simple answer. This chapter is located here because certain concepts from the analysis of variance and the analysis of covariance also serve as building blocks in some regression analyses. For example, researchers sometimes base their regression predictions (or explanations) on the interactions between independent variables. Also, regressions are sometimes conducted with one or more covariate variables controlled or held constant. Without knowing about interactions and covariates, you would be unable to understand these particular components of regression analyses.

We now turn our attention to the simplest kind of regression used by applied researchers. Take good mental notes as you study this material, for the concepts you will now encounter provide a foundation for the other two kinds of regression to be considered later in the chapter.

## Bivariate Regression

**Research
Navigator.c⊛m**

Bivariate
regression

The simplest kind of regression analysis is called **bivariate regression.** First, we need to clarify the purpose of and the data needed for this kind of regression. Then, we will consider scatter diagrams, lines of best fit, and prediction equations. Finally, we will discuss inferential procedures associated with bivariate regression.

### Purpose and Data

As you would suspect based on its name, bivariate regression involves just two variables. One of the variables will serve as the dependent variable while the other functions as the independent variable. The purpose of this kind of regression can be either prediction or explanation; however, bivariate regression is used most frequently to see how well scores on the dependent variable can be predicted from data on the independent variable.

To illustrate how bivariate regression can be used in a predictive manner, imagine that Sam, a 30-year-old weight lifter, has been plagued by a shoulder injury that for months has failed to respond to nonsurgical treatment. Consequently, arthroscopic surgery is scheduled to repair Sam's bad shoulder. Even though he knows that arthroscopic procedures usually permit a rapid return to normal activity, he would like to know how long he'll be out of commission following surgery. His presurgery question to the doctor is short and sweet: "When will I be able to lift again?" Clearly, Sam wants his doctor to make a prediction.

Although Sam's doctor might be inclined to answer this question concerning down time by telling Sam about the *average* length of convalescence for weight lifters following arthroscopic shoulder surgery, that's really not what Sam wants to know. Obviously, some people bounce back from surgery more quickly than do others. Therefore Sam wants the doctor to consider his (i.e., Sam's) individual case and make a prediction about how long he'll have to interrupt his training. If Sam's doctor has seen the results of a recent study dealing with weight lifters who had arthroscopic shoulder surgery, and if the doctor has a computer program that can perform a bivariate regression, he could provide Sam with a better-than-average answer to the question about postsurgical down time.

In the actual study conducted with people like Sam, there were 10 weight lifters who had shoulder injuries. Although data on several variables were collected in this real investigation, let's consider the data on just two: age and number of post-surgical days of down time. Excerpt 16.5 presents the data on these two variables.

**EXCERPT 16.5 • *Data on Two Variables***

**TABLE 1**  *Age and Postsurgical Time Away from Sport for 10 Weight Lifters*

| Patient | Age | Return to sport (days) |
|---------|-----|------------------------|
| 1 | 33 | 6 |
| 2 | 31 | 4 |
| 3 | 32 | 4 |
| 4 | 28 | 1 |
| 5 | 33 | 3 |
| 6 | 26 | 3 |
| 7 | 34 | 4 |
| 8 | 32 | 2 |
| 9 | 28 | 3 |
| 10 | 27 | 2 |

*Source:* Auge, W. K., and Fischer, R. A. (1998). Arthroscopic distal clavicle resection for isolated atraumatic osteolysis in weight lifters. *American Journal of Sports Medicine, 26*(2), p. 191. (Note: Table 1 was modified slightly for presentation here.)

## Scatter Diagrams, Regression Lines, and Regression Equations

The component parts and functioning of regression can best be understood by examining a scatter diagram. In Figure 16.1, such a picture has been generated using the data from Excerpt 16.5. There are 10 dots in this "picture," each positioned so as to reveal the age and postsurgical convalescent time for one of the weight lifters.

The scatter diagram in Figure 16.1 was set up with days of convalescence on the ordinate and age on the abscissa. These two axes of the scatter diagram were labeled like this because it makes sense to treat convalescence as the dependent variable. It is the variable toward which predictions will eventually be made for Sam and other weight lifters who are similar to those who supplied the data we are currently considering. Age, on the other hand, is positioned on the abscissa because it

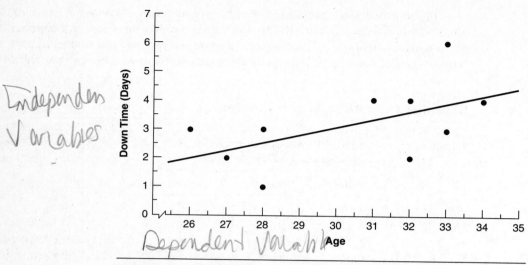

Independent Variables

Dependent Variable

**FIGURE 16.1**   *Regression Analysis Using Data in Excerpt 16.5*

is the independent variable. It is the variable that "supplies" data used to make the predictions.[3]

As you can see, a slanted line passes through the data points of the scatter diagram. This line is called the **regression line** or the **line of best fit,** and it will function as the tool our hypothetical doctor will use in order to predict how long Sam will have to refrain from lifting. As should be apparent, the regression line is positioned so as to be as close as possible to all of the dots. A special formula determines the precise location of this line; however, you do not need to know anything about that formula except that it is based on a statistical concept called *least squares.*[4]

Let's make a prediction for Sam, pretending now that we are his doctor. All we need to do is turn to the scatter diagram and take a little trip with our index finger or our eyes. Our trip begins on the abscissa at a point equal to Sam's age. (Remember, Sam is 30 years old.) We move vertically from that point up into the scatter diagram until we reach the regression line. Finally, we travel horizontally (to the left) from that point on the regression line until reaching the ordinate. Wherever this little trip causes us to end up on the ordinate becomes our prediction for Sam's down time. According to our information, our prediction is that Sam will be out of commission for approximately three days.

[3]Since we are dealing with regression (and not correlation), it would be improper to switch the two variables in the scatter diagram. The dependent variable always goes on the ordinate; the independent variable always goes on the abscissa.

[4]The *least squares principle* simply means that when the squared distances of the data points from the regression line are added together, they yield a smaller sum than would be the case for any other straight line that could be drawn through the scatter diagram's data points.

Notice that our prediction of Sam's down time would have been shorter if he had been younger and longer if he had been older. For example, we would have predicted about two days if he had been 26 years old, or four days if he had been 34. These alternative predictions for a younger or older Sam are brought about by the tilt of the regression line. Because there is a positive correlation between the independent and dependent variables, the regression line tilts from lower left to upper right.

**Research Navigator.c☀m**

Regression equation

Although it is instructive to see how predictions are made by means of a regression line that passes through the data points of a scatter diagram, the exact same objective can be achieved more quickly and more scientifically by means of something called the **regression equation.** In bivariate, linear regression, this equation always has the following form:

$$Y' = a + b \cdot X,$$

where $Y'$ stands for the predicted score on the dependent variable, $a$ is a constant, $b$ is the **regression coefficient,** and $X$ is the known score on the independent variable. This equation is simply the technical way of describing the regression line. For the data shown in Excerpt 16.5 (and Figure 16.1), the regression equation turns out like this:

$$Y' = -5.05 + (.27)X.$$

To make a prediction for Sam by using the regression equation, we simply substitute Sam's age for $X$ and then work out the simple math. When we do this, we find that $Y' = 3.05$. This is the predicted down time (in days) for Sam. The fact that this value is very similar to what we predicted earlier (when we took a trip through the scatter diagram) should not be at all surprising. That's because the regression equation is nothing more than a precise mechanism for telling us where we'll end up if, in a scatter diagram, we first move vertically from some point on the abscissa up to the regression line and then move horizontally from the regression line to the ordinate.

Whereas scatter diagrams and regression lines appear only rarely in research reports, regression equations show up quite frequently. In Excerpt 16.6, we see a case in point. As you can see from this passage, the regression equation was built so as to predict height from arm span. In this study, each person's height and arm span was measured in centimeters. Thus, the two numbers in the regression formula (0.87 and 20.54) must be interpreted as being in the scale of centimeters, not inches.

Let's use the regression equation presented in Excerpt 16.6 to make some height predictions. When I measure my own arm span, I find that it is equal to 175.1 cm. Using the regression equation, I find that my predicted height is equal to 20.54 + 0.87(175.1) = 172.88 cm. This predicted value turns out to be extremely close to my actual height of 172.70 cm. Now it's your turn. Get a metric measuring device, measure your arm span, and then use the regression formula in Excerpt 16.6 to calculate your predicted height. After doing this, check to see how closely your

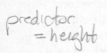

predictor
= height

### EXCERPT 16.6 • *The Regression Equation in Bivariate Regression*

The purpose of this study is to determine the accuracy of arm span as a measure of height in young and middle-age adults. . . . A convenience sample of 83 subjects was studied. Subjects were between the ages of 20 and 61 years, with a mean age of 41.63 years ($SD = 11.10$). Fifty-seven (69%) were women, and 26 (31%) were men. . . . The first analysis was a simple regression of height on arm span to determine how well arm span, alone, predicted height. The prediction equation is as follows: Height = 0.87 (arm span) + 20.54.

*Source:* Brown, J. K., Whittemore, K. T., and Knapp, T. R. (2000). Is arm span an accurate measure of height in young and middle-age adults? *Clinical Nursing Research, 9*(1), pp. 90–91.

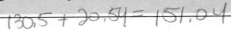

predicted height matches your actual height. You may be surprised (as I was) at how closely arm span predicts height!

It should be noted that there are two kinds of regression equations that can be created in any bivariate regression analysis. One of these is called an **unstandardized regression equation.** This is the kind we have considered thus far, and it has the form $Y' = a + b \cdot X$. The other kind of regression equation (that can be generated using the same data) is called a **standardized regression equation.** A standardized regression equation has the form $z'_y = \beta \cdot z_x$. These two kinds of regression equations differ in three respects. First, a standardized regression equation involves z-scores on both the independent and dependent variables, not raw scores. Second, the standardized regression equation does not have a constant (i.e., a term for *a*). Finally, the symbol $\beta$ is used in place of *b* (and is called a **beta weight** rather than a regression coefficient).

**Research Navigator.com**

Beta weight

### *Interpreting a, b, r, and r² in Bivariate Regression*

When used for predictive purposes, the regression equation has the form $Y' = a + bX$. Now that you understand how this equation works, let's take a closer look at its two main ingredients, *a* and *b*. In addition, let's now pin down the regression meaning of *r* and $r^2$.

Earlier, I referred to *a* as the "constant." Alternatively, this component of the regression equation is called the **intercept.** Simply stated, *a* indicates where the regression line in the scatter diagram would, if extended to the left, intersect the ordinate. It indicates, therefore, the value of $Y'$ for the case where $X = 0$. In many studies, it may be quite unrealistic (or downright impossible) for there to be a case where $X = 0$; nonetheless, $Y' = a$ when $b = 0$.

In Excerpt 16.6, the constant in the regression equation for the 83 people was equal to 20.54. That is not a very realistic number, for it indicates the predicted height for a person with zero arm span. Likewise, the value of *a* for the regression line in Figure 16.1 is equal to $-5.05$. This number is nonsensical, of course, for it indicates the predicted down time following surgery for a weight lifter whose age is 0! Clearly, *a* may be totally devoid of meaning within the context of a study's independent and dependent variables. Nevertheless, it has an unambiguous and not-so-nonsensical meaning within a scatter diagram, for *a* indicates the point where the regression line intercepts the ordinate.

The other main component of the regression is *b,* the regression coefficient. When the regression line has been positioned within the data points of a scatter diagram, *b* simply indicates the **slope** of that line. As you probably recall from your high school math courses, slope means "rise over run." In other words, the value of *b* signifies how many predicted units of change (either up or down) in the dependent variable there are for any one unit increase in the independent variable. In Figure 16.1, the regression equation has a slope equal to .27. This means that the predicted down time for our hypothetical patient Sam would be about one-fourth of a day longer if the surgery is put off a year.

When researchers use bivariate regression, they sometimes will focus on either *b* or $\beta$ more than anything else. Consider, for example, Excerpt 16.7. In the study associated with this excerpt, 50 individuals with multiple sclerosis were measured on three personality variables: existential (i.e., nonreligious) well-being (as measured by the EWB), perceived illness uncertainty (as measured by the MUIS), and psychosocial adjustment to illness (as measured by the PAIS-T). After dividing the full group of patients into high and low subgroups based on EWB scores, the researchers did a bivariate regression within each subgroup to investigate the connection between scores on the MUIS and PAIS-T. Notice how the researchers focused their attention on the beta weights when comparing the two subgroups of patients.

### EXCERPT 16.7 • *Focusing on the Regression Coefficient*

Scores on the EWB were first dichotomized into two groups around the distribution mean (high EWB $>$ 46, low EWB $<$ 46). [Bivariate] regression analyses for MUIS and PAIS-T scores were then conducted for each group (high vs. low) separately. Inspecting slope . . . indicated that for the high-EWB group, increase in MUIS scores resulted in no change to PAIS-T scores ($\beta = .015$). However, for those in the low-EWB group, increase in MUIS scores resulted in decrease in PAIS-T scores ($\beta = -.30$). In other words, whereas no relationship was found between uncertainty and overall psychosocial adjustment in participants who scored high on EWB, increased uncertainty was associated with decreased psychosocial distress for those who scored low on EWB.

*Source:* McNulty, K., Livneh, H., and Wilson, L. M. (2004). Perceived uncertainty, spiritual well-being, and psychosocial adaptation in individuals with multiple sclerosis. *Rehabilitation Psychology, 49*(2), pp. 94, 96.

When summarizing the results of a regression analysis, researchers will normally indicate the value of $r$ (the correlation between the independent and dependent variables) or $r^2$. You already know, of course, that such values for $r$ and $r^2$ measure the strength of the relationship between the independent and dependent variables. However, each has a special meaning, within the regression context, that is worth learning.

As you might expect, the value of $r$ will be high to the extent that the scatter diagram's data points are located close to the regression line. Though that is undeniably true, there is a more precise way to conceptualize the regression meaning of $r$. Once the regression equation has been generated, that equation could be used to predict $Y'$ for each person who provided the scores used to develop the equation. In one sense, that would be a very silly thing to do, for predicted scores are unnecessary in light of the fact that *actual* scores on the dependent variable are available for these people. However, by comparing the predicted scores for these people against their actual scores (both on the dependent variable), we would be able to see how well the regression equation works. The value of $r$ does exactly this. It quantifies the degree to which the predicted scores match up with the actual scores.

Just as $r$ has an interpretation in regression that focuses on the dependent variable, so it is with $r^2$. Simply stated, the coefficient of determination indicates the proportion of variability in the dependent variable that is "explained" by the independent variable. As illustrated in Excerpt 16.8, $r^2$ is usually turned into a percent when it is reported in research reports.

### EXCERPT 16.8 • *Variability in the Dependent Variable Explained by Variability in the Independent Variable*

Bivariate regression analysis carried out to model how drug and regimen choice vary with SBP [systolic blood pressure] indicated a moderate linear relationship in the study population: about 15% (Pearson product-moment correlation coefficient $r^2 = 0.148$) of the variance of drug and regimen decision made by the participating physicians were associated with SBP.

*Source:* Erhun, W. O., Agbani, E. O., and Bolaji, E. E. (2003). Managing hypertension with combination diuretics and methyldopa in Nigerian Blacks at the primary care level. *Clinical Drug Investigation, 23*(9), p. 585.

### Inferential Tests in Bivariate Regression

The data used to generate the regression line or the regression equation are typically considered to have come from a sample, not a population. Thus the component parts of a regression analysis—$a$, $b$, and $r$—are typically considered to be sample statistics, not population parameters. Accordingly, it should not come as a surprise that researchers conduct one or more inferential tests whenever they perform a regression analysis.

The most frequently conducted test focuses on $r$. The null hypothesis in such a test will probably be set up to say that the correlation in the population is equal to 0 (i.e., $H_0$: $\rho = 0$). This kind of test was discussed in Chapter 9, and the considerations raised there apply equally to tests of $r$ within the context of bivariate regression. In Excerpt 16.9, we see a case in which such a test was performed. Near the end of this excerpt, the researchers present the value of $r^2$ rather than $r$. If they had wanted to, they could have reported $r = .32$ in the place where they reported $r^2 = .10$. It doesn't matter, because a test of $r$ is mathematically equivalent to a test of $r^2$.

**EXCERPT 16.9 • *Testing r (or r²) for Significance in Bivariate Correlation***

To test the first research question, whether perceived support for challenging racism, sexism, and social injustice from key social actors is associated with the reflection component of critical consciousness among urban adolescents, inverted SDO sum scores were regressed on the total perceived support variable (the sum of perceived support for challenging racism, sexism, and social injustice). This simple regression was statistically significant, $F(1, 91) = 9.70, p < .01, r^2 = .10$, indicating that 10% of the reflection component of critical consciousness variance was accounted for by total support. . . .

*Source:* Diemer, M. A., Kauffman, A., Koenig, N., Trahan, E., and Hsieh, C. (2006). Challenging racism, sexism, and social injustice: Support for urban adolescents' critical consciousness development. *Cultural Diversity & Ethnic Minority Psychology, 12*(3), pp. 448, 452.

In bivariate regression, a test on $r$ is mathematically equivalent to a test on $b$ or $\beta$. Therefore, you will never see a case where both $r$ and $b$ (or $r$ and $\beta$) are tested, because these two tests would be fully redundant with each other. However, researchers have the freedom to have their test focus on $r$ or $b$ or $\beta$. In Excerpt 16.10, we see a case where a team of researchers chose to test $\beta$. The null hypothesis in

**EXCERPT 16.10 • *Testing the Beta Weight***

A bivariate regression analysis found that age was a small, but significant, predictor of PTGI scores ($\beta = .17, p < .05$).

*Source:* Morris, B. A., Shakespeare-Finch, J., Rieck, M., and Newbery, J. (2005). Multidimensional nature of posttraumatic growth in an Australian population. *Journal of Traumatic Stress, 18*(5), p. 581.

this kind of test says that the population value of the beta weight is $\hat{0}$. Stated differently, the null hypothesis in such tests is that the regression line has no tilt, thus meaning that the independent variable provides no assistance in predicting scores on the dependent variable.

## Multiple Regression

Research
Navigator.c⊛m

Multiple
regression

We now turn our attention to the most popular regression procedure of all, **multiple regression.** This form of regression involves, like bivariate regression, a single dependent variable. In multiple regression, however, there are two or more independent variables. Stated differently, multiple regression involves just one $Y$ variable but two, three, or more $X$ variables.[5]

In three important respects, multiple regression is identical to bivariate regression. First, a researcher's reason for using multiple regression is the same as the reason for using bivariate regression, either prediction (with a focus on the dependent variable) or explanation (with a focus on the independent variables). Second, a regression equation is involved in both of these regression procedures. Third, both bivariate and multiple regression almost always involve inferential tests and a measure of the extent to which variability among the scores on the dependent variable has been explained or accounted for.

Though multiple regression and bivariate regression are identical in some respects, they also differ in three extremely important ways. As you will see, multiple regression can be done in *different ways* that lead to different results, it can be set up to accommodate *covariates* that the researcher wishes to control, and it can involve (as predictor variables) one or more *interactions* between independent variables. Bivariate regression has none of these characteristics.

In upcoming sections, these three unique features of multiple regression will be discussed. We begin, however, with a consideration of the regression equation that comes from the analysis of data on one dependent variable and multiple independent variables. This equation functions as the most important stepping stone between the raw scores collected in a study and the findings extracted from the investigation.

### The Regression Equation

When a regression analysis involves one dependent variable and two independent variables, the regression equation takes the form

$$Y' = a + b_1 \cdot X_1 + b_2 \cdot X_2$$

---

[5]Recall that the dependent variable ($Y$) is sometimes referred to as the criterion, outcome, or response variable while the independent variable ($X$) is sometimes referred to as the predictor or explanatory variable.

where $Y'$ stands for the predicted score on the dependent variable, $a$ stands for the constant, $b_1$ and $b_2$ are regression coefficients, and $X_1$ and $X_2$ represent the two independent variables. In Excerpt 16.11, we see a regression equation that has this exact form.

### EXCERPT 16.11 • *A Regression Equation for the Case of Two Independent Variables*

The regression formula predicting overweight reduction was:

$$Y = 6.34 + 7.06X_1 = 4.17X_2$$

where $X_1$ is the change in eating between meals and $X_2$ is the change in eating while doing another activity.

*Source:* Golan, M., Fainaru, M., and Weizman, A. (1998). Role of behaviour modification in the treatment of childhood obesity with the parents as the exclusive agents of change. *International Journal of Obesity, 22*, p. 1221.

As indicated previously, multiple regression can accommodate more than two independent variables. In such cases, the regression equation will simply be extended to the right, with an extra term (made up of a new $b$ multiplied by the new $X$) added for each additional independent variable. The presence of these extra terms, of course, does not alter the fact that the regression equation contains only one $Y'$ term (located on the left side of the equation) and only one $a$ term (located on the right side of the equation).

Excerpt 16.12 illustrates what a multiple regression equation looks like when more than two independent variables are involved in the analysis. In the study

### EXCERPT 16.12 • *Regression Equation with Several Independent Variables*

In the first regression analysis, the predictor variables were the four attitude variables—*Enjoyment* ($X_1$), *Motivation* ($X_2$), *Importance* ($X_3$), and *Freedom from Anxiety* ($X_4$); and the response variable was *Time* ($Y$)—time spent on learning or using technologies. . . . The regression analysis generated a set of coefficients that were used to formulate the regression equation:

$$Y = -428.15 + 15.22\,(X_1) + 3.34(X_2) + 16.02(X_3) + 5.57\,(X_4)$$

*Source:* Liu, L., Maddux, C., and Johnson, L. (2004). Computer attitude and achievement: Is time an intermediate variable? *Journal of Technology and Teacher Education, 12*(4), pp. 599, 600.

associated with this excerpt, the researchers collected data from 609 college students enrolled in a three-semester computer technology course. To answer one of their questions, the researchers used a multiple regression analysis to see if certain attitudinal variables could predict how much time the students spent outside of class trying to improve their technology skills. In Excerpt 16.12, the researchers clarify which four attitudes were used as independent (i.e., predictor) variables. Note that the researchers refer to the dependent variable as the **response variable.**

In each of the regression equations shown in Excerpts 16.11 and 16.12, the algebraic sign between any two adjacent terms on the right side of the equation is positive. This means that the sign of every regression coefficient was positive. In some multiple regression equations, one of more of the $b$s will end up being negative. The sign of a regression coefficient simply indicates the nature of the relationship between that particular $X$ variable and the dependent variable. Thus, if the students in the study that gave us Excerpt 16.12 had also been measured on how extensively they were involved in extracurricular activities, I would expect this predictor variable's regression coefficient to have a negative sign in front of it, thereby implying an inverse relationship between involvement in extracurricular activities and time spent on the computer.

Regardless of whether the multiple regression is being conducted for predictive or explanatory purposes, the researcher is usually interested in comparing the independent variables to see the extent to which each one helps the regression analysis achieve its objective. In other words, there is usually interest in finding out the degree to which each independent variable contributes to successful predictions or valid explanations. Although you (as well as a fair number of researchers) may be tempted to look at the $b$s in order to find out how well each independent variable works, this should not be done because each regression coefficient is presented in the units of measurement used to measure its corresponding $X$. Thus if one of the independent variables in a multiple regression is height, its $b$ will differ in size depending on whether height measurements are made in centimeters, inches, feet, or miles.

To determine the relative importance of the different independent variables, the researcher needs to look at something other than an **unstandardized regression equation** like those we have seen thus far. Instead, a **standardized regression equation** can be examined. This kind of regression equation, for the case of three independent variables, would take the form

$$z'_y = \beta_1 \cdot z_{x1} + \beta_2 \cdot z_{x2} + \beta_3 \cdot z_{x3}.$$

As you will note, this equation presents the dependent and independent variables in terms of $z$, it has no constant term, and it uses the symbol $\beta$ instead of $b$. These $\beta$s are like standardized regression coefficients, and they are called **beta weights.**

Although standardized regression equations are rarely included in research reports, researchers often extract the beta weights from such equations and present the numerical values of these $\beta$s. In Excerpts 16.13 and 16.14, we see two instances in which this was done. Notice that the beta weights are referred to as "beta" in the first of these excerpts, while the symbol $\beta$ is used in the second excerpt.

Before concluding our discussion of regression equations, three important points need to be made. First, one or more of the independent variables in a regression analysis can be categorical in nature. For example, gender is often used in multiple regression to help accomplish the researcher's predictive or explanatory objectives. As you see the technique of multiple regression used in different studies, you are likely to see a wide variety of categorical independent variables included, such as marital status (single, married, divorced), highest educational degree (H.S. diploma, bachelor's degree, Master's degree, Ph.D.), and race (Black, White, Hispanic).

Second, researchers often include a term in the regression equation that represents the interaction between two of the study's independent variables. In Excerpt 16.15, we see such a case.

Researchers use interaction terms in multiple regression analyses for many different reasons. At times, the researcher is simply interesting in having $R^2$ be as large as possible. Putting an interaction term into the regression equation as a new independent variable may lead to an increase in the predictability of the dependent variable. Though this is done on occasion, most researchers use interactions in their regression analyses for a different reason.

### EXCERPTS 16.13–16.14 • *Beta Weights*

This study examined the relationship between student performance on collaborative learning group assignments and students' examination scores in statistics. . . . A multiple regression technique was used to analyze the data. . . . As revealed by a comparison of the standardized regression coefficients, group project 2 (*Beta* = .205) exerted an effect on final examination scores that was less than half that for the mean quiz score (*Beta* = .564).

*Source:* Delucchi, M. (2006). The efficacy of collaborative learning groups in an undergraduate statistics course. *College Teaching, 54*(2), pp. 244, 246.

----

We used a standard multiple regression analysis to test the efficacy of the original TPB variables and self-efficacy in predicting residents' intentions to follow the rules at youth shelters. . . . Two of the variables were significant predictors of intention. Self-efficacy, $\beta$ = .47, emerged as the strongest predictor of intention to follow the shelter rules; and subjective norm, $\beta$ = .34, emerged as another such significant predictor.

*Source:* Broadhead-Fearn, D., and White, K. M. (2006). The role of self-efficacy in predicting rule-following behaviors in shelters for homeless youth: A test of the theory of planned behavior. *Journal of Social Psychology, 146*(3), p. 316.

## EXCERPT 16.15 • *Interactions as Independent Variables*

In the first set of analyses, two multiple regression equations were created, and in both equations the criterion variable was customer satisfaction. With the first regression equation (the full equation), the predictor variables were provider occupation type (effect coded), courteous expressions, and an interaction term created by multiplying courteous expressions by service provider occupational level.

*Source:* Koermer, C. D. (2005). Service provider type as a predictor of the relationship between sociality and customer satisfaction. *Journal of Business Communication, 42*(3), p. 254.

The inclusion of an interaction term creates a situation in which the researcher can see if the regression equation works similarly for different levels of the variables involved in the interaction. Consider again Excerpt 16.15. In that study, the researcher could have conducted a simple bivariate regression to see if courteous expressions (from workers) predict customer satisfaction. By including service provider type as a second independent variable and the interaction (of service provider type with courteous expressions), the researcher had a chance to see whether the degree of association between courteous expressions and customer service varied across different types of service provider businesses. If so, then type of service provider could be called a **moderator variable.** Just as an interaction in a two-way ANOVA asks whether the main effect means of one of the factors describe well that factor's simple main effect means (at different levels of the other factor), an interaction term in a regression analysis asks whether the equation predicting the dependent variable stays the same for different categories of one of the variables involved in the interaction.

My third and final comment about regression equations is an important warning. Simply stated, be aware that the regression coefficients (or beta weights) associated with the independent variables can change dramatically if the analysis is repeated with one of the independent variables discarded or another independent variable added. Thus regression coefficients (or beta weights) do not provide a pure and absolute assessment of any independent variable's worth. Instead, they are "context dependent."

### Three Kinds of Multiple Regression

Different kinds of multiple regression exist because there are different orders in which data on the independent variables can be entered into the analysis. In this section, we will consider the three most popular versions of multiple regression. These are called simultaneous multiple regression, stepwise multiple regression, and hierarchical multiple regression.

In **simultaneous multiple regression,** the data associated with all independent variables are considered at the same time. This kind of multiple regression is

Research
Navigator.c⊛m
Simultaneous
multiple
regression

analogous to the process used in preparing vegetable soup where all ingredients are thrown into the pot at the same time, stirred, and then cooked together. In Excerpt 16.16, we see an example of simultaneous multiple regression.

### EXCERPT 16.16 • *Simultaneous Multiple Regression*

Simultaneous multiple regression analyses were conducted to further examine the extent to which Sport MPS subscales related in theoretically meaningful ways to Hewitt-MPS subscales. Each Sport-MPS subscale was separately entered as the dependent variable in regression analyses, with the three Hewitt MPS subscales simultaneously entered as the independent (or predictor) variables.

*Source:* Dunn, J. G. H., Dunn, J. C., Gotwals, J. K., Vallance, J. K. H., Craft, J. M., and Syrotuik, D. G. (2006). Establishing construct validity evidence for the Sport Multidimensional Perfectionism Scale. *Psychology of Sport & Exercise, 7*(1), p. 68.

Research
Navigator.c⊕m

Stepwise multiple
regression

The second kind of multiple regression analysis is analogous to the process of preparing a soup in which the ingredients are tossed into the pot based on the amount of each ingredient. Here the stock goes in first (because there's more of that than anything else), followed by the vegetables, the meat, and finally the seasoning. Each of these different ingredients is meant to represent an independent variable, with "amount of ingredient" equated to the size of the bivariate correlation between a given independent variable and the dependent variable. Here, in **stepwise multiple regression,** the computer determines the order in which the independent variables become a part of the regression equation. In Excerpt 16.17, we see an example of this kind of multiple regression.

Instead of preparing our vegetable soup by simply tossing everything into the pot at once or by letting the amount of an ingredient dictate its order of entry, we

### EXCERPT 16.17 • *Stepwise Multiple Regression*

To determine factors affecting academic performance as assessed by average mark at the end of the first year, stepwise multiple regression was first carried out with average mark as the dependent variable to discover which variables were related to academic performance. The following independent variables were entered: age category at entry (under 21, 21 to 25, over 25), gender, socio-economic class, A-Level points, father with/without degree, mother with/without degree, three life goal scores, three study approaches.

*Source:* Wilding, J., and Andrews, B. (2006). Life goals, approaches to study and performance in an undergraduate cohort. *British Journal of Educational Psychology, 76*(1), p. 177.

could put things into the pot on the basis of concerns regarding flavor and tenderness. If we wanted garlic to flavor everything else, we'd put it in first even though there's only a small amount of it required by the recipe. Similarly, we would hold back some of the vegetables (and not put them in with the others) if they are tender to begin with and we want to avoid overcooking them. **Hierarchical multiple regression** is like cooking the soup in this manner, for in this form of regression the independent variables are entered into the analysis in stages. Often, as illustrated in Excerpt 16.18, the independent variables that are entered first correspond with things the researcher wishes to control. After they are allowed to explain as much variability in the dependent variable as they can, then the other variables are entered to see if they can contribute above and beyond the independent variables that went in first.

### EXCERPT 16.18 • *Hierarchical Multiple Regression*

A hierarchical linear regression analysis was used to predict intention to engage in a binge drinking session over the next week. The independent variables were entered in three blocks: (i) age and gender, (ii) attitude, subjective norm, self-efficacy, and perceived control, and (iii) past binge drinking. In this way, it was possible to examine the predictive utility of the TPB [theory of planned behaviour] variables, controlling for the effects of age and gender, as well as the additional predictive utility of past behaviour.

*Source:* Norman, P. and Conner, M. (2006). The theory of planned behaviour and binge drinking: Assessing the moderating role of past behaviour within the theory of planned behaviour. *British Journal of Health Psychology, 11*(1), p. 60.

### $R$, $R^2$, $\Delta R^2$, and Adjusted $R^2$ in Multiple Regression

In multiple regression studies, the extent to which the regression analysis achieves its objective is usually quantified by means of $R$, $R^2$, or adjusted $R^2$. Sometimes two of these will be presented, and occasionally you will see all three reported for the same regression analysis. These elements of a multiple regression analysis are not superficial and optional add-ons; instead, they are as central to a regression analysis as the regression equation itself.

In bivariate regression, $r$ provides an indication of how well the regression equation works. It does that by quantifying the degree to which the predicted scores match up with the actual scores (on the dependent variable) for the group of individuals used to develop the regression equation. The $R$ of multiple regression can be interpreted in precisely the same way. **Multiple $R$** is what we would get if we computed Pearson's $r$ between $Y$ and $Y'$ scores for the individuals who provided scores on the independent and dependent variables.

Although the value of $R$ sometimes appears when the results of a multiple regression are reported, researchers are far more likely to report the value of $R^2$ or to report the percentage equivalent of $R^2$. By so doing, the success of the regression analysis is quantified by reporting the proportion or percentage of the variability in the dependent variable that has been accounted for or explained by the study's independent variables. Excerpt 16.19 illustrates the way researchers use $R^2$ in an explained variance manner.

### EXCERPT 16.19 • $R^2$ as an Index of Explained Variance

A multiple regression analysis was conducted to determine predictors of meeting length. The predictors were student age, student grade, and number of participants at the meeting. . . . The sample multiple correlation coefficient was .52, indicating that approximately 27% of the variance of length of meeting can be accounted for by the linear combination of these variables.

*Source:* Martin, J. E., Van Dycke, J. L., Greene, B. A., Gardner, J. E., Christensen, W. R., Woods, L. L., and Lovett, D. L. (2006). Direct observation of teacher-directed IEP meetings: Establishing the need for student IEP meeting instruction. *Exceptional Children, 72*(2), p. 195.

When a multiple regression analysis is conducted with the data from all independent variables considered simultaneously, only one $R^2$ can be computed. In stepwise and hierarchical regression, however, several $R^2$ values can be computed, one for each stage of the analysis wherein individual independent variables or sets of independent variables are added. These $R^2$ values will get larger at each stage, and the *increase* from stage to stage is referred to as $R^2$ **change.** Another label for the increment in $R^2$ that's observed as more and more independent variables are used as predictors is $\Delta R^2$, where the symbol $\Delta$ stands for the two-word phrase "change in."

Excerpt 16.20 illustrates nicely the concept of $\Delta R^2$. In the first step of the hierarchical multiple regression, three "control" variables were used to predict the dependent variable, student evaluation of the course. Those variables produced a very small $R^2$. Next, in the second step of the regression analysis, three additional independent variables entered the model and caused $R^2$ to change from .044 to .504. Thus, the increase in $R^2$ (i.e., $\Delta R^2$) was equal to .46. At the end of the second step, with the regression model using all six independent variables, 50.4 percent of the variability in the students' course evaluations was explained by the full set of independent variables.

Either in place of or in addition to $R^2$, something called **adjusted $R^2$** is often reported in conjunction with a multiple regression analysis. If reported, adjusted $R^2$ will take the form of a proportion or a percentage. It is interpreted just like $R^2$, because it indicates the degree to which variability in the dependent variable is explained by the set of independent variables included in the analysis. The conceptual difference between $R^2$ and adjusted $R^2$ is related to the fact that the former,

Research
Navigator.c⊕m

Adjusted $R^2$

## EXCERPT 16.20 • $\Delta R^2$ in Stepwise or Hierarchical Multiple Regression

We performed a hierarchical multiple regression analysis with student evaluations of course outcomes as the dependent variable. Variables entered the equation in two steps. First, the control variables of students' self-reported achievement (i.e., students reported their grade point average), dummy coded instructor, and student gender entered the equation. Results showed that the squared multiple correlation for this equation was [equal to] $R^2 = .044$. . . . Second, the predictor variables of course expectations, affective journal outcomes, and cognitive journal outcomes entered the equation. Results showed that the change in the squared multiple correlation for this equation was [equal to] $\Delta R^2 = .46$. . . . Overall, the [full] regression equation explained just over 50% of the variance. . . .

*Source:* Bolin, A. U., Khramtsova, I., and Saarnio, D. (2005). Using student journals to stimulate authentic learning: Balancing Bloom's cognitive and affective domains. *Teaching of Psychology, 32*(3), p. 157.

being based on sample data, always yields an overestimate of the corresponding population value of $R^2$.

Adjusted $R^2$ removes the bias associated with $R^2$ by reducing its value. Thus this adjustment anticipates the amount of so-called **shrinkage** that would be observed if the study were to be replicated with a much larger sample. As you would expect, the size of this adjustment is inversely related to study's sample size.[6]

When reporting the results of their multiple regression analyses, some researchers (who probably do not realize that $R^2$ provides an exaggerated index of predictive success) report just $R^2$. Of those who are aware of the positive bias associated with $R^2$, some will include only adjusted $R^2$ in their reports while others will include both $R^2$ and adjusted $R^2$. In Excerpt 16.21, we see an example of the latter situation.

## EXCERPT 16.21 • Adjusted $R^2$

A hierarchical regression model was used to explore the relationship of predictor variables to the criterion variable. . . . The contribution of age and education was significant, $R^2 = .19$, adjusted $R^2 = .18, p < .001$. ATG-S explained significant additional variance, 14%, in the second step, $R^2 = .33$, adjusted $R^2 = .32, p < .001$. In the final step, the block of GRCS-I variables accounted for 4% of additional variance ($R^2 = .38$, adjusted $R^2 = .35, p < .01$).

*Source:* Kassing, L. R., Beesley, D., and Frey, L. L. (2005). Gender role conflict, homophobia, age, and education as predictors of male rape myth acceptance. *Journal of Mental Health Counseling, 27*(4), p. 321.

---

[6]The size of the adjustment is also influenced by the number of independent variables. With more independent variables, the adjustment is larger.

## Inferential Tests in Multiple Regression

Researchers can apply several different kinds of inferential tests when they perform a multiple regression. The three most frequently seen tests focus on $\beta$, $R^2$, and $\Delta R^2$. Let's consider what each of these tests does and then we will look at an excerpt in which all three of these tests were used.

When the beta weight for a particular independent variable is tested, the null hypothesis says that the parameter value is equal to 0. If this were true, that particular independent variable would be contributing nothing to the predictive or explanatory objective of the multiple regression. Because of this, researchers frequently will test each of the betas in an effort to decide (1) which independent variables should be included in the regression equation that is in the process of being built or (2) which independent variables included in an already-developed regression equation turned out to be helpful. Beta weights are normally tested with two-tailed $t$-tests.[7]

When $R^2$ is tested, the null hypothesis says that none of the variance in the dependent variable is explained by the collection of independent variables. (This $H_0$, of course, has reference to the study's population, not its sample.) This null hypothesis normally is evaluated via an $F$-test. In most studies, the researcher will be hoping that this $H_0$ will be rejected.[8]

When $\Delta R^2$ is tested, the null hypothesis says that the new independent variable(s) added to the regression equation is totally worthless in helping to explain variability in the dependent variable. As with the null hypotheses associated with tests on beta weights and $R^2$, this particular $H_0$ has reference to the study's population, not its sample. A special $F$-test is used to evaluate this null hypothesis. This kind of test, of course, logically fits into the procedures of stepwise and hierarchical multiple regression; it would never be used within the context of a simultaneous multiple regression.[9]

Consider now Excerpt 16.22 which comes from a study involving a hierarchical multiple regression. Take the time to look at this excerpt closely. As you will see, it contains tests of beta weights, a test of $R^2$ at the first step of the analysis, a test of the incremental $R^2$ as the analysis moved from the first to the second step, and a test of $R^2$ for the full model as explicated in step 2.

Two additional features of Excerpt 16.22 are noteworthy. First, the size of the beta weights associated with the therapists' level and experience of self-awareness changed as the analysis moved from step 1 to step 2. (In step 1, therapist level of self-awareness was significant at $p \le .05$; in step 2, that same independent variable was significant at $p \le .01$.). Such a change in the assessed value of an independent

---

[7]The $df$ for this kind of $t$-test is equal to the sample size minus one more than the number of independent variables.

[8]The first $df$ for this kind of $F$-test is equal to the number of independent variables; the second $df$ value is equal to the sample size minus one more than the number of independent variables.

[9]The $df$ for this kind of $F$-test is equal to (a) the number of new independent variables and (b) the sample size minus one more than the total number of old and new independent variables.

**EXCERPT 16.22 • *Inferential Tests in Multiple Regression***

---

**TABLE 1**  *Hierarchical Multiple Regression Results for Clients' Perception of the Therapy Session Regressed onto Therapists' Level, Experience, and Management of In-Session Self-Awareness*

| Criterion variable: SIS Relationship Impact scores | B | SE B | β |
|---|---|---|---|
| Step 1: *df* = 2, 14 | | | |
|    Therapist level of self-awareness | 1.66 | 0.74 | 0.58* |
|    Therapist experience of self-awareness | −0.17 | 1.19 | −0.04 |
| Step 2: *df* = 3, 13 | | | |
|    Therapist level of self-awareness | 2.96 | 0.89 | 1.04** |
|    Therapist experience of self-awareness | −0.67 | 1.08 | −0.15 |
|    Therapist management strategies | −13.87 | 6.37 | −0.59* |

*Note:* $R^2 = .32$ for Step 1 ($p > .05$); $\Delta R^2 = .18$ for Step 2 ($p \leq .10$); $R^2 = .50$ for Step 2 ($p \leq .05$) for the full model. SIS = Session Impacts Scale.

*$p \leq .05$. **$p \leq .01$.

*Source:* Fauth, J., and Williams, E. N. (2005). The in-session self-awareness of therapist-trainees: Hindering or helpful? *Journal of Counseling Psychology, 52*(3), p. 445.

---

variable is not uncommon in stepwise and multiple regression. Hence, the hierarchical value of any independent variable is not absolute; rather, its usefulness depends upon the context (i.e., whether other independent variables are also involved in the multiple regression and, if there are other predictor variables, what kinds of relationships exist among the independent and dependent variables).

The second thing to notice about Excerpt 16.22 is the fact that the value of $R^2$ increased from step 1 to step 2, and it changed from being "$p > .05$" to being "$p \leq .05$." This shows that the independent variable that was added into the model at step 2 made a difference. Apart from just noting that the first $R^2$ was *not* significant whereas the second $R^2$ *was* significant, note that the estimated level of explained variance increased from 32 percent to 50 percent.

## *Logistic Regression*

**Research Navigator.com**

Logistic regression

The final kind of regression considered in this chapter is called logistic regression. Originally, only researchers from medical disciplines (especially epidemiology) used this form of regression. More recently, however, **logistic regression** has been discovered by those who conduct empirical investigations in other disciplines. Its popularity continues to grow at such a rate that it may soon overtake multiple regression and become the most frequently used regression tool of all.

Before considering how logistic regression differs from the forms of regression already considered, let's look at their similarities. First, logistic regression deals with relationships among variables (not mean differences), with one variable being the dependent (i.e., outcome or response) variable while the other(s) is/are the independent (predictor or explanatory) variable(s). Second, the independent variables can be continuous or categorical in nature. Third, the purpose of logistic regression can be either prediction or explanation. Fourth, tests of significance can be and usually are conducted, with these tests targeted either at each individual independent variable or at the combined effectiveness of the independent variables. Finally, logistic regression can be conducted in a simultaneous, stepwise, or hierarchical manner dependent on the timing of and reasons for independent variables entering the equation.

There are, of course, important differences between logistic regression, on the one hand, and either bivariate or multiple regression, on the other hand. These differences will be made clear in the next three sections. As you will see, logistic regression revolves around a core concept called the **odds ratio** that was not considered earlier in the chapter because it is not a feature of either bivariate or multiple regression. Before looking at this new concept, we need to focus our attention on the kinds of data that go into a logistic regression and also the general reasons for using this kind of statistical tool.

## Variables

As does any bivariate or multiple regression, logistic regression always involves two main kinds of variables. These are the study's *dependent* and *independent* variables. In the typical logistic regression (as in some applications of multiple regression), a subset of the independent variables is included for control purposes, with the label *control* (or *covariate*) designating any such variable. Data on these three variables constitute the only ingredients that go into the normal logistic regression, and the results of such analyses are inextricably tied, on a conceptual level, to these three kinds of variables. For these reasons, it is important for us to begin with a careful consideration of the logistic regression's constituent parts.

In any logistic regression, as in any bivariate or multiple regression, there is one and only one dependent variable. Here, however, the dependent variable is dichotomous (i.e., binary) in nature. Examples of such variables used in recent studies include whether or not a person survives open heart surgery, whether or not an elderly and ill married person considers his/her spouse to be the primary caregiver, whether or not a young child chronically suffers from nightly episodes of coughing, and whether or not an adolescent drinks at least eight ounces of milk a day. As illustrated by these examples, the dependent variable in a logistic regression can represent either a true dichotomy or an artificial dichotomy.

In addition to the dependent variable, at least one independent variable is involved in any logistic regression. Almost always, two or more such variables will be involved. As in multiple regression, these variables can be either quantitative or qualitative in nature. If of the former variety, scores in the independent variable are construed to represent points along a numerical continuum. With qualitative independent variables, however, scores carry no numerical meaning and only serve the purpose of indicating group membership. In any given logistic regression, the independent variables can be all quantitative, all qualitative, or some of each. Moreover, independent variables can be used individually and/or jointly as an interaction.

When using logistic regression, applied researchers normally collect data on several independent variables, not just one. In the study alluded to earlier in which the dependent variable dealt with nighttime coughing among preschool children, the independent variables dealt with the child's sex and birth weight, the possible presence of pets and dampness problems in the home, whether or not the parents smoked or had asthma, and whether or not the child attended a day care center. It is not unusual to see this many independent variables utilized within logistic regression studies.

As indicated earlier, a subset of the independent variables in a typical logistic regression are control variables. Such variables are included in a logistic regression so the researcher can assess the "pure" relationship between the remaining independent variable(s) and the dependent variable. In a very real sense, control variables are included because of suspected confounding that would muddy the water if the connection between the independent and dependent variables were examined directly.

In any given logistic regression wherein control is being exercised by means of the inclusion of covariate variables, it may be that only one such variable is involved, or that two or three are used, or that all but one of the independent variables are covariates. It all depends, of course, on the study's purpose and the researcher's ability to identify and measure potentially confounding variables. In the study concerned with preschoolers and chronic coughing at night, all but one of the independent variables were included for control purposes; by so doing, the researchers considered themselves better able to examine the direct influence of day care versus home care on respiratory symptoms.

In Excerpt 16.23, we see a case in which the three kinds of variables of a typical logistic regression are clearly identified. It is worth the time to read this excerpt closely with an eye toward noting the nature and number of these three kinds of variables.

As in all such logistic regressions, the study associated with Excerpt 16.23 had one dependent variable that was dichotomous in nature. That variable was whether children developed cavities in their teeth. In addition, this particular study involved five independent variables (dealing with socioeconomic characteristics of the children's

## EXCERPT 16.23 • *Dependent, Independent, and Control Variables*

To determine the independent impact of the socioeconomic variables on ECC [early childhood cavities], a multiple logistic regression model was built using all 5 socioeconomic variables and adjusting for age, family size, and oral health-related behavioral variables as possible confounders.

*Source:* Willems, S., Vanobbergen, J., Martens, L., and De Maeseneer, J. (2005). The independent impact of household- and neighborhood-based social determinants on early childhood cavities. *Family & Community Health, 28*(2), p. 173.

homes and neighborhood) along with several control variables. Although the term "control variable" does not appear in Excerpt 16.23, the terms "adjusting for" and "possible confounders" indicate that age, family size, and oral health-related behavioral variables were used as control variables.

Many logistic regression studies are like the one associated with Excerpt 16.23 in that they involve one dichotomous dependent variable, multiple independent variables, and multiple control variables. In some logistic regression studies, there will be multiple independent variables and a single control variable. Or, there might be a single independent variable combined with several control variables. It all depends on the goals of the investigation and the researcher's ability to collect data on independent and control variables that are logically related to the dependent variable.

### Objectives of a Logistic Regression

Earlier in this chapter, we pointed out that researchers use bivariate and multiple regression in order to achieve one of two main objectives: explanation or prediction. So it is with logistic regression. In many studies, the focus is on the noncontrol independent variables, with the goal being to identify the extent to which each one plays a role in explaining why people have the status they do on the dichotomous dependent variable. In other studies, the focus is primarily on the dependent variable and how to predict whether or not people will end up in one or the other of the two categories of that outcome variable.

Excerpt 16.24 illustrates the kind of logistic regression in which explanation is the goal. In this study, the researcher was interested in examining potential explanations as to why first-generation college students either do or don't complete their undergraduate programs. The focus in this study was not so much on the dichotomous dependent variable (completed or did not complete college) as it was on the independent variables that might explain why some first-generation students are successful in college while others aren't.

**EXCERPT 16.24 •** *Logistic Regression and Explanation*

The greatest benefits for explaining college success of first-generation students result from thorough examination of both precollege attributes of students and 'the
quality of their interactions with institutions of higher education. However, this
study will only investigate the effects of precollege attributes of students on their
attrition and degree completion behavior, mainly due to a lack of available time-
varying items in the study data, such as academic and social integration. . . . Since
logistic regression was identified as an appropriate statistical method for the analysis,
graduation status was coded as 1 in the dichotomous dependent variables.

*Source:* Ishitani, T. T. (2006). Studying attrition and degree completion behavior among
first-generation college students in the United States. *Journal of Higher Education, 77*(5),
pp. 865, 887.

In Excerpt 16.25, we see a case in which logistic regression was used for
predictive purposes. In the article associated with this excerpt, the researcher developed
an equation for predicting whether movies would or wouldn't win the Academy Award
for Best Picture. Near the end of the research report, the author cautioned that his prediction formula should not be used to make gambling bets. As he explained, betting on
the Academy Awards (even in Las Vegas) is illegal!

**EXCERPT 16.25 •** *Logistic Regression and Prediction*

The Academy Awards present a unique opportunity to explore voter preferences.
Every year the Academy of Motion Picture Arts and Sciences vote for the Best Picture of the Year. There are many influences to their decision. This study seeks to survey and weigh these influences. This paper analyzes the previous forty years of Best
Picture nominations for characterizations including personnel, genre, marketing and
records in other award competitions. Using a logistic regression model, each variable's effect on the odds of a given film winning the Best Picture Award is estimated.

*Source:* Kaplan, D. (2006). And the Oscar goes to . . .: A logistic regression model for predicting Academy Award results. *Journal of Applied Economics & Policy, 25*(1), p. 23.

## Odds, Odds Ratios, and Adjusted Odds Ratios

Because the concept of **odds** is so important to logistic regression, let's consider a
simple example that illustrates what this word does (and doesn't) mean. Suppose
you have a pair of dice that are known to be fair and not loaded. If you were to roll
these two little cubes and then look to see if you rolled a pair (two of the same number), the answer would be yes or no. Altogether, there are 36 combinations of how

the dice might end up, with six of these being pairs. On any roll, therefore, the probability of getting a pair is 6/36, or .167. (Naturally, the probability of not getting a pair would be .833.) Clearly, it's more likely that you'll fail than succeed in your effort to roll a pair. But we can be even more precise than that. We could say that the odds are 5-to-1 against you, meaning that you are five times more likely to roll a nonpair than a pair.

Most researchers utilize logistic regression so they can discuss the explanatory or predictive power of each independent variable using the concept of odds. They want to be able to say, for example, that people are twice as likely to end up one way on the dependent variable if they have a particular standing on the independent variable being considered. For example, in one recent study on the impact of child maltreatment on later delinquency, the researchers summarized their finding by saying that "youth maltreated during adolescence are about five times as likely to be arrested as are those never maltreated." In another study, the researchers found that "Snowboarders who wore protective wrist guards were half as likely to sustain wrist injuries as those who did not wear guards."

After performing a logistic regression, researchers will often cite the **odds ratio** for each independent variable, or at least for the independent variable(s) not being used for control purposes. The odds ratio is sometimes reported as **OR,** and it is analogous to $r^2$ in that it measures the strength of association between the independent variable and the study's dependent variable. However, the odds ratio is considered by many people to be a more user-friendly concept than the coefficient of determination. Because the odds ratio is so central to logistic regression, let's pause for a moment to consider what this index means.

Imagine that two very popular TV programs end up going head-to-head against each other in the same time slot on a particular evening. For the sake of our discussion, let's call these programs A and B. Also imagine that we conduct a survey of folks in the middle of this time slot in which we ask each person two questions: (1) What TV show are you now watching? and (2) Are you a male or a female? After eliminating people who either were not watching TV or were watching something other than program A or B, let's suppose we end up with data like that shown in Figure 16.2.

Research
Navigator.c⊛m
Odds ratio

|  |  | **TV Program Being Watched** | |
|---|---|---|---|
|  |  | Program A | Program B |
| **Gender** | Male | 200 | 100 |
|  | Female | 50 | 150 |

**FIGURE 16.2   *Hypothetical Data Showing Gender Preferences for Two TV Programs***

As you can see, both TV programs were equally popular among the 500 people involved in our study. Each was being watched by 250 of the folks we called. Let's now look at how each gender group spread itself out between the two programs. To do this, we'll arbitrarily select Program A and then calculate, first for males and then for females, the odds of watching Program A. For males, the odds of watching Program A are 200 ÷ 100 (or 2 to 1); for females, the odds of watching this same program are 50 ÷ 150 (or 1 to 3). If we now take these odds and divide the one for males by the one for females, we obtain the ratio of the odds for gender relative to Program A. This OR would be equal to (2 ÷ 1) ÷ (1 ÷ 3), or 6. This result tells us that among our sampled individuals, males are six times more likely to be watching Program A than women. Stated differently, gender (our independent variable) appears to be highly related to which program is watched (our dependent variable).

In our example involving gender and the two TV programs, the odds ratio was easy to compute because there were only two variables involved. As we have seen, however, logistic regression is typically used in situations where there are more than two independent variables. When multiple independent variables are involved, the procedures for computing the odds ratio become quite complex; however, the basic idea of the odds ratio stays the same.

Consider Excerpts 16.26 and 16.27. Notice that the phrases "an 85% reduction" and "a 66% reduction" appear in the first of these excerpts, whereas the phrase "1.3 times more likely" appears in the second excerpt. Most people can understand

### EXCERPTS 16.26–16.27 • *Odds Ratio and Adjusted Odds Ratio*

In comparing breastfeeding behaviors for immigrant versus nonimmigrant participants, we found that immigrants were significantly more likely to breastfeed than were nonimmigrants. Mothers born in the United States had an 85% reduction in the odds of breastfeeding (OR = 0.150, P < .01), and a 66% reduction in the odds of breastfeeding at 6 months (OR = 0.344, P < .01).

*Source:* Gibson-Davis, C. M., and Brooks-Gunn, J. (2006). Couples' immigration status and ethnicity as determinants of breastfeeding. *American Journal of Public Health, 96*(4), p. 643.

------

When adjusted for physician demographics and practice characteristics, specialty was still a strong predictor of program familiarity. Again, pulmonologists (adjusted odds ratio [OR] = 1.205), general/family practice physicians (OR = 1.000), and cardiologists (OR = 0.856) had the biggest rates of familiarity. . . . Increasing age was associated with lower odds of referral, and female physicians were 1.3 times more likely than male physicians to have referred patients to smoking cessation programs.

*Source:* Steinberg, M. B., Alvarez, M. S., Delnevo, C. D., Kaufman, I., and Cantor, J. C. (2006). Disparity of physicians' utilization of tobacco treatment services. *American Journal of Health Behavior, 30*(4), p. 381.

conclusions such as these even though they are unfamiliar with the statistical formulas needed to generate an odds ratio type of conclusion. In addition, I suspect you can see, without difficulty, that whether an odds ratio ends up being greater than 1 or less than 1 is quite arbitrary. It all depends on the way the sentence is structured. For example, the researchers who gave us Excerpt 16.27 would have presented an OR of .77 in the final sentence (and they would have said "about three-fourths as likely") if the position of the words "female" and "male" had been reversed.

When the odds ratio is computed for a variable *without* considering the other independent variables involved in the study, it can be conceptualized as having come from a bivariate analysis. Such an OR is said to be a crude or unadjusted odds ratio. If, as is usually the case, the OR for a particular variable is computed in such a way that it takes into consideration the other independent variable(s), then it is referred to as an **adjusted odds ratio.** By considering all independent variables jointly so as to assess their connections to the dependent variable, researchers often say that they are performing a multivariate analysis.

To see an example of an adjusted odds ratio, consider once again Excerpt 16.27. Notice that this excerpt begins with the words "when adjusted for physician demographics and practice characteristics." Because these variables were taken into account, all of the OR numbers in this excerpt (including 1.3) are adjusted odds ratios. The first number, 1.205, is clearly shown that way. The researchers expect us to apply the word "adjusted" to the other OR numbers they present.

### Tests of Significance

When using logistic regression, researchers usually conduct tests of significance. As in multiple regression, such tests can be focused on the odds ratios (which are like regression coefficients) associated with individual independent variables or on the full regression equation. Whereas tests on the full regression equation typically represent the most important test in multiple regression, tests on the odds ratios in logistic regression are considered to be the most critical tests the researcher can perform.

When the odds ratio or adjusted odds ratio associated with an independent variable is tested, the null hypothesis says that the population counterpart to the sample-based OR is equal to 1. If the null hypotheses were true (with OR = 1), it would mean that membership in the two different categories of the dependent variable is unrelated to the independent variable under consideration. For this null hypothesis to be rejected, the sample value of OR must deviate from 1 further than would be expected by chance.

Researchers typically use one of two approaches when they want to test an odds ratio or an adjusted odds ratio. One approach involves setting up a null hypothesis, selecting a level of significance, and then evaluating the $H_0$ either by comparing a test statistic against a critical value or by comparing the data-based $p$ against $\alpha$. In Excerpts 16.28 and 16.29, we see two examples in which this first approach was used.

Notice in Excerpt 16.28 that the researchers used the **Wald test** to see if the odds ratio was statistically significant. This test is highly analogous to the *t*-test in

## EXCERPTS 16.28–16.29 • *Testing an OR or an AOR for Significance*

Scores on the SST at recruitment were significant predictors of depression severity [mildly or severely depressed] at follow-up (Wald's $x^2(1) = 6.73, p < .01$), with an odds ratio of 0.69.

*Source:* Thomas, S. A., and Lincoln, N. B. (2006). Factors relating to depression after stroke. *British Journal of Clinical Psychology, 45*(1), p. 55.

---

Table 2 [not shown here] presents logistic regression results for bullies. As predicted, the friends of bullies reported more aggression, both in the entire sample (*AOR* [adjusted odds ratio] = 1.32, $p < .0001$) and in the subsample of females (*AOR* = 1.46, $p < .006$).

*Source:* Mouttapa, M., Valente, T., Gallaher, P., Rohrbach, L. A., and Unger, J. B. (2004). Social Network predictors of bullying and victimization. *Adolescence, 39*(154), p. 324.

multiple regression that is used to see if a beta weight is statistically significant. These two tests are only analogous, however, for they differ not only in terms of the null hypothesis but also in the kinds of calculated and critical values used to test the $H_0$. As illustrated in Excerpt 16.28, the Wald test is tied to a theoretical distribution symbolized by $x^2$ rather than *t*. (This is the chi-square distribution.) In Excerpt 16.29, the test used to test the adjusted odds ratios is not specified. The researchers probably used the Wald test, but they may have used an alternative test procedure.

The second way a researcher can test an odds ratio is through the use of a confidence interval. The CI rule of thumb for deciding whether to reject or retain the null hypothesis is the same as when CIs are used to test means, *r*s, the difference between means, or anything else. If the confidence interval overlaps the pinpoint number in the null hypothesis, the null hypothesis will be retained; otherwise, $H_0$ is rejected. Excerpt 16.30 illustrates how a CI can be used to test an odds ratio. Take

## EXCERPT 16.30 • *Testing an Odds Ratio via a Confidence Interval*

The use of spasm reduction interventions, however, was found to [significantly] decrease the likelihood of a successful outcome (OR = 0.77, 95% CI = 0.60–0.98). That is, the odds of achieving an increase of 14 points or greater in PCS-12 scores were reduced 23% in patients receiving spasm reduction interventions.

*Source:* Jewell, D. V., and Riddle, D. L. (2005). Interventions that increase or decrease the likelihood of a meaningful improvement in physical health in patients with sciatica. *Physical Therapy, 85*(11), p. 1146.

the time to look closely at this excerpt's CI, note its ends, and then recall that the pinpoint number in the null hypothesis being tested is 1.0. Can you see why the researchers' OR of .77 was considered to represent a significant reduction in the likelihood of success if patients were treated by spasm reduction intervention?

As indicated previously, it is possible in logistic regression to test whether the collection of independent and control variables do a greater-than-chance job of accounting for the status of people on the dependent variable. This test is typically made with a special form of the chi-square test. This test has the same symbol ($\chi^2$) as the test used to evaluate individual ORs or AORs; with this version, however, researchers usually talk about it in terms of it being a test of the **model**. In Excerpt 16.31, we see an example of this kind of test.

**EXCERPT 16.31 • *Testing the Full Logistic Regression Model***

In order to examine, more comprehensively, the effects of potential predictors, logistic regression was performed on the data. Age at onset, clinical severity of psoriasis, alexithymia, beliefs about time-line, consequences, and emotional causes were the predictor variables that were entered into the regression with adversarial growth dummy coded. . . . The regression model was significant ($-2 \log L = 55.63$, $\chi^2 = 25.83$, $p = .0001$).

*Source:* Knussen, C., Tolson, D., Swan, I. R. C., Stott, D. J., Brogan, C. A., and Sullivan, F. (2005). Adversarial growth in patients undergoing treatment for psoriasis: A prospective study of the ability of patients to construe benefits from negative events. *Psychology, Health & Medicine, 10*(1), p. 50.

## *Final Comments*

As we conclude this chapter, we need to consider five additional regression-related issues. These concerns deal with multicollinearity, control, practical significance, the inflated Type I error risk, and cause. If you will keep these issues in mind as you encounter research reports based on bivariate, multiple, and logistic regression, you will be in a far better position to both decipher and critique such reports.

Research
Navigator.c⊕m

Multicollinearity

In multiple and logistic regression, the independent and control variables should not be highly correlated with one another. If they are, a condition called **multicollinearity** is said to exist. Excerpts 16.32 and 16.33 illustrate the way dedicated researchers will demonstrate that they know about this potential problem and will examine their data to see whether their regressions would be "messed up" by an undesirable network of intercorrelations among their independent variables. In both of these excerpts, the technique of multiple regression was used. It should be noted, however, that multicollinearity can be a problem in logistic regression

## EXCERPTS 16.32–16.33 • *Multicollinearity*

Multicolinearity among the explanatory variables was assessed by calculating the tolerance level and bivariate correlations. A tolerance level of .40 or less was considered an indication of high multicolinearity. The tolerance level of each explanatory variable was greater than .50, and the bivariate correlation coefficients were less than .45, indicating that each explanatory variable contributed unique information.

*Source:* Greene, B. L., Haldeman, G. F., Kaminski, A., Neal, K., Sam Lim, S., and Conn, D. L. (2006). Factors affecting physical activity behavior in urban adults with arthritis who are predominantly African-American and female. *Physical Therapy, 86*(4), p. 514.

---

An interaction term was created as a product of SM and social leisure in order to test the hypothesis that the relationship of social leisure to life quality is moderated by level of SM. Aiken and West (1991) warned that statistical interactions, created as a product of two independent variables, can create problems of multicollinearity as the interaction term tends to be highly correlated to the variables used to create it. One method they offered to control for such problems is create "centered" variables in which the original variable is transformed into a deviation score from the variable mean. These deviation scores are then used in creation of the interaction term. The procedure outlined above was used in this study to minimize multicollinearity.

*Source:* Lee, Y., and McCormick, B. P. (2006). Examining the role of self-monitoring and social leisure in the life quality of individuals with spinal cord injury. *Journal of Leisure Research, 38*(1), pp. 10–11.

studies as well. Look for researchers to address this concern regardless of the type of regression they use.

In the discussions of both hierarchical multiple regression and logistic regression, we saw that researchers often incorporate control or covariate variables into their analyses. Try to remember that such **control** is very likely to be less than optimal. This is the case for three reasons. First, one or more important confounding variables might be overlooked. Second, potential confounding variables that *are* measured are likely to be measured with instruments possessing less than perfect reliability. Finally, recall that the analysis of covariance undercorrects when used with nonrandom groups that come from populations that differ on the covariate variable(s). Regression suffers from this same undesirable characteristic.

My next concern relates to *the distinction between statistical significance and practical significance.* We have considered this issue in connection with tests focused on means and *r*s, and it is just as relevant to the various inferential tests used by researchers within regression analyses. In Excerpt 16.34, we see a case in which a pair of researchers attended to the important distinction between useful and trivial findings. These researchers deserve high praise for realizing (and warning their

## EXCERPT 16.34 • *Practical versus Statistical Significance*

For the school counselors, only one significant variable entered the equation: the GRCS Restrictive Emotionality subscale score ($p < .0001$), with higher Restrictive Emotionality scores predicting fewer prestige choice preferences. Although this regression equation was statistically significant, $F(1, 98) = 15.98, p < .0001$, it accounted for only 14% of the variance in prestige choice score. A significant equation was also found for the engineers, $F(1, 98) = 5.15, p = .0075$, with two MRNS subscale scores being significant predictors. Both the Status ($p = .0102$) and Toughness ($p = .0174$) subscales predicted the prestige choice score. Again, although the model was statistically significant, these two variables combined accounted for less than 10% of the prestige score variance. Given the very low $R^2$ values, neither of these two prediction equations has much practical importance.

*Source:* Dodson, T. A., and Borders, L. D. (2006). Men in traditional and nontraditional careers: Gender role attitudes, gender role conflict, and job satisfaction. *Career Development Quarterly, 54*(4), p. 290.

readers) that inferential tests can yield results that are statistically significant without being important in a practical manner.

In many research reports, researchers make a big deal about a finding that seems small and of little importance. Perhaps such researchers are unaware of the important distinction between practical and statistical significance, or it may be that they know about this distinction but prefer not to mention it due to a realization that their statistically significant results do not matter very much. Either way, it is important that *you* keep this distinction in mind whenever you are on the receiving end of a research report.

Not too long ago, I came across an article (in a technical research journal) concerning youth and adolescents, their use of sunscreen and tanning beds, and their rate of sunburns. It turned out that there was a statistically significant connection between age (one of the predictor variables) and sunburning (one of the outcome variables). This finding was based on an adjusted odds ratio produced by a logistic regression. How large do you think this AOR was? Tucked away in one of the article's tables, I found it. The table contained this information: "adjusted OR = 1.09 (1.01–1.18)." In my opinion, this finding has questionable worth because the number 1.09 is so close to the null hypothesis value of 1.00. You have the right to make similar kinds of judgments when you read or listen to research reports.

As we have seen in the excerpts of previous chapters, competent researchers are sensitive to the inflated Type I error risk that occurs if a given level of significance, say .05, is used multiple times within the same study when different null hypotheses are tested. Give credit to researchers when they apply the Bonferroni adjustment procedure (or some other comparable strategy) within their regression studies. Excerpt 16.35 provides an example of this.

**EXCERPT 16.35 • *Bonferroni Adjustment Procedure***

To investigate our research questions, the data were analyzed using a series of hierarchical regression analyses. The independent variables included gender in the first step of each equation and universal-diverse orientation (MGUDS-S) and emotional intelligence (EIS) in the second step. The dependent variables were the four empathy subscales of the IRI: perspective taking, empathic concern, fantasy, and personal distress. A Bonferroni adjusted alpha level of .05/4 or .01 was used to test the significance of each regression analysis.

*Source:* Miville, M. L., Carlozzi, A. F., Gushue, G. V., Schara, S. L., and Ueda, M. (2006). Mental health counselor qualities for a diverse clientele: Linking empathy, universal-diverse orientation, and emotional intelligence. *Journal of Mental Health Counseling, 28*(2), p. 159.

As we turn to my last concern, recall the important point made in Chapter 3 that a bivariate correlation—even if found to be statistically significant with a large $r^2$ value—should not be automatically interpreted to mean that a **causal link** exists between the two variables on which data have been collected. The same point holds for bivariate, multiple, and logistic regression. Even when the results suggest strongly that the regression has achieved its predictive or explanatory objective, the analysis is correlational in nature. Even when multiple control variables are included in the model, a regression analysis is simply correlational in nature.

In Excerpt 16.36, we see a case in which a team of researchers provides their readers with a clear warning about cause-and-effect. In essence, that warning says *not* to think that the study's primary independent variable (mental health) had a causal influence on the study's dependent variable (physical health). I salute these researchers for providing this warning and for explaining, in the excerpt's final sentence, why it would be wrong to impute cause-and-effect into the study's findings.

**EXCERPT 16.36 • *Regression and Cause-and-Effect***

The goal of the current study was to compare the relationship between mental health problems and health status in a large sample of low-income children with and without serious emotional disorders (SED). . . . SED status contributed significantly to predictions of all three health-status indicators. . . . Neither this study [using hierarchical multiple regression] nor the research reviewed for it provides an explanation of the relationship between physical and mental health problems, of course; one might cause the other, or a third variable may influence both types of health problems.

*Source:* Combs-Orme, T., Helfinger, C. A., and Simpkins, C. G. (2002). Comorbidity of mental health problems and chronic health conditions in children. *Journal of Emotional and Behavioral Disorders, 10*(2), pp. 117, 121.

## Review Terms

| | |
|---|---|
| Adjusted odds ratio | Outcome variable |
| Adjusted $R^2$ | Prediction |
| Beta weight | Predictor variable |
| Bivariate regression | Regression coefficient |
| Criterion variable | Regression equation |
| Dependent variable | Regression line |
| Explanation | Response variable |
| Explanatory variable | Shrinkage |
| Hierarchical regression | Simultaneous multiple regression |
| Independent variable | Slope |
| Intercept | Standardized regression equation |
| Line of best fit | Stepwise multiple regression |
| Logistic regression | Unstandardized regression equation |
| Model | Wald test |
| Moderator variable | $R$ |
| Multicollinearity | $R^2$ |
| Multiple regression | $\Delta R^2$ |
| Odds ratio | |

## The Best Items in the Companion Website

1. An interactive online quiz (with immediate feedback provided) covering Chapter 16.
2. Ten misconceptions about the content of Chapter 16.
3. An interactive online resource entitled "Bivariate Regression."
4. An email message sent by the author to his students entitled "Logistic Regression."
5. Several e-articles illustrating the use of bivariate regression, multiple regression, and logistic regression.

To access chapter objectives, practice tests, weblinks, and flashcards, visit the companion website at www.ablongman.com/huck5e.

## Fun Exercises inside Research Navigator

1. **Do the same variables predict suicidal thoughts in college men and women?**

   In this study, 139 undergraduate females and 75 undergraduate males completed two personality inventories: the *Suicide Probability Scale* (which measures level of suicidal thinking) and the *MMPI-2* (which measures several kinds of psychopathology). Separately for the females and the males, the researchers performed a hierarchical multiple regression, using scores from the *SDS* as the dependent variable and scores from the various *MMPI-2* scales as the independent variables. In which group, males or females, do you think the *MMPI-2* scores better predicted suicidal thinking? Do you think the best predictors for males were also the best predictors for females? After you make your guess, refer to the PDF version of the research report in the Psychology database of ContentSelect and consult pages 600–604 (and Tables 5 and 6) to see if *your* predictions were correct!

B. A. Kopper, A. Osman, & F. X. Barrios. Assessment of suicidal ideation in young men and women: The incremental validity of the *MMPI-2* content scales. *Death Studies*. Located in the PSYCHOLOGY database of ContentSelect.

## 2. Are the predictors of adolescent violence different for boys versus girls?

In this study of adolescent violence, data on 2,643 high school seniors were analyzed by means of two logistic regressions, one for boys and one for girls. In each regression, the dependent variable was whether or not the adolescent had engaged in violent behavior during the previous 12-month period. In addition, the two regressions had the same independent variables (alcohol use, drug use, religious beliefs, grades, etc.) and the same demographic control variables (race and location of residence). Do you think these two logistic regressions produced the same results? In particular, do you think the independent variables of alcohol use, drug use, and grades showed up as predicting violent behavior for both gender groups? To see if your hunches are correct, refer to the PDF version of the research report in the Helping Professions database of ContentSelect and read (on page 14) the final two paragraphs of the "Results" section.

R. Bachman & R. Peralta. The relationship between drinking and violence in an adolescent population: Does gender matter? *Deviant Behavior*. Located in the HELPING PROFESSIONS database of ContentSelect.

**Review Questions and Answers begin on page 513.**

# C H A P T E R 17

# Inferences on Percentages, Proportions, and Frequencies

In your journey through the previous eight chapters, you have examined a variety of inferential techniques that are used when at least one of the researcher's variables is quantitative in nature. The bulk of Chapter 9, for example, dealt with inferences concerning Pearson's $r$, a bivariate measure of association designed for use with two quantitative variables. Beginning in Chapter 10, you saw how inferential techniques can be used to investigate one or more groups in terms of means (and variances), with the dependent variable in such situations obviously being quantitative in nature. In Chapter 16, we considered how inferential procedures can be used with regression techniques involving at least one quantitative variable.

In the present chapter, your journey takes a slight turn, for you will now look at an array of inferential techniques designed for the situation in which *none* of the researcher's variables is quantitative. In other words, the statistical techniques discussed in this chapter are used when all of a researcher's variables involve questions concerning membership in categories. For example, a researcher might wish to use sample data to help gain insights as to the prevalence of AIDS in the general population. Or, a pollster might be interested in using sample data to predict how each of three political candidates competing for the same office would fare "if the election were to be held today." In these two illustrations as well as in countless real studies, the study's data do not reflect *the extent* to which each subject possesses some characteristic of interest but instead reveal how each subject has been classified into one of the categories established by the researcher.

When a study's data speak to the issue of group membership, the researcher's statistical focus will be on frequencies, on percentages, or on proportions. For example, the hypothetical pollster referred to in the previous paragraph might summarize the study's data by reporting, "Of the 1,000 voters who were sampled,

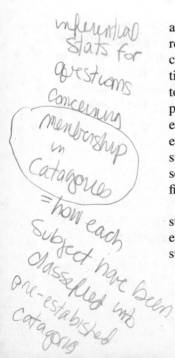

inferential stats for questions concerning membership in catagories = how each subject have been classified into pre-established catagories

443

428 stated that they would vote for candidate A, 381 stated that they would vote for candidate B, and 191 reported that they would vote for candidate C." Instead of providing us with **frequencies** (i.e., the number of people in each response category), the same data could be summarized through **percentages.** With this approach, the researcher would report that "candidates A, B, and C received 42.8 percent, 38.1 percent, and 19.1 percent of the votes, respectively." Or, the data could be converted into **proportions,** with the researcher asserting that "the proportionate popularity of candidates A, B, and C turned out to be .428, .381, and .191, respectively." The same information, of course, is communicated through each of these three ways of summarizing the data.

Regardless of whether the data concerning group membership are summarized through frequencies, percentages, or proportions, it can be said that the level of measurement used within this kind of study is nominal (rather than ordinal, interval, or ratio). As I pointed out in Chapter 3, a researcher's data *can* be nominal in nature. In focusing on inferential techniques appropriate for means, $r$, $R$, and $R^2$, we spent the last several chapters dealing with procedures that are useful when the researcher's data are interval or ratio in nature. In the present chapter, however, we restrict our consideration to statistical inferences appropriate for nominal data.

Although a multitude of inferential procedures have been developed for use with nominal-level data, we will consider here only six of these procedures that permit researchers to evaluate null hypotheses. These procedures are the sign test, the binomial test, Fisher's Exact Test, the chi-square test, McNemar's test, and Cochran's test. These are the most frequently used of the test procedures designed for nominal-level data, and a knowledge of these procedures will put you in a fairly good position to understand researchers' results when their data take the form of frequencies, percentages, or proportions.

I will also illustrate how $z$-tests can be used, in certain situations, to answer the same kinds of research questions as those posed by the six basic test procedures considered in this chapter. Moreover, I will show how the Bonferroni technique can be used with any of these test procedures to control against an inflated Type I error rate. The distinction between statistical significance and practical significance will also be considered. Finally, we will examine a few cases in which confidence intervals have been built around sample percentages or proportions.

## The Sign Test

Research
Navigator.c✺m
Sign test

Of all inferential tests, the **sign test** is perhaps the simplest and easiest to understand. It requires that the researcher do nothing more than classify each participant of the study into one of two categories. Each of the participants put into one of these categories receives a plus sign (i.e., a $+$); in contrast, a minus sign (i.e., a $-$) is given to each participant who falls into the other category. The hypothesis testing procedure is then used to evaluate the null hypothesis that says the full sample of participants comes from a population in which there are as many pluses as minuses. If the sample is quite lopsided with far more pluses than minuses (or far more minuses than pluses), the sign test's $H_0$ will be rejected. On the other hand, if the frequencies of pluses and minuses in the sample are equal or nearly equal, the null hypothesis of the sign test will be retained.

The sign test can be used in any of three situations. In one situation, there is a single group of people, with each person in the group evaluated as to some characteristic (e.g., handedness) and then given a + or a − depending on his or her status on that characteristic. In the second situation, there are two matched groups; here, the two members of each pair are compared, with a + given to one member of each dyad (and a − given to his or her mate) depending on which one has more of the characteristic being considered. In the third situation, a single group is measured twice, with a + or a − given to each person depending on whether his or her second score is larger or smaller than his or her first score.

Excerpt 17.1 illustrates the use of the sign test with a single group of individuals measured just once. As you can see, eight individuals were asked a question to which they could respond either "yes" or "no." Within the context of the sign test, the answers to the post-lunch nap question produced seven "+" signs and one "−" sign. The sign test concluded that this kind of split is quite unlikely if the sample came from a population in which there was a 50–50 split. Accordingly, the null hypothesis was rejected.

In Excerpt 17.2, we see a case in which the sign test was used with paired samples. In this case, the paired items were hospitals, not people. Within each pair,

### EXCERPTS 17.1–17.2 • *The Sign Test*

Seven of the eight subjects reported that it would be better to take the post-lunch nap . . . ($p < 0.016$ by one sample sign test).

*Source:* Takashashi, M., Nakata, A., Haratani, T., Ogawa, Y., and Arito, H. (2004). Post-lunch nap as a worksite intervention to promote alertness on the job. *Ergonomics, 47*(9), p. 1007.

Hospitals were matched by country, type of hospital (public, private or social security), and baseline caesarean section rate (15–20%, 21–35%, or >35%), and the paired units were randomly assigned to intervention or control. . . . The intervention consisted of the implementation of a policy of mandatory second opinion at the hospitals assigned to the intervention group. . . . Among the 17 pairs of hospitals, a reduced caesarean section rate was observed in 13 [of the intervention versus control hospitals] (sign test *p* value = 0.049).

*Source:* Althabe, F., Belizán, J. M., Villar, J., Alexander, S., Bergel, E., Ramos, S., Romero, M., Donner, A., Lindmark, G., Langer, A., Farnot, U., Cecatti, J. G., Carroli, G., and Kestler, E. (2004). *Lancet, 363*(9425), pp. 1934–1935.

one of the two hospitals received the intervention while the other hospital served as its control. At the time of data collection, the two hospitals within each pair were compared to see if the one that had received the intervention had a lower rate of C-section deliveries. Within each pair, the hospital with the lower C-section birth rate received a "+" sign (while the other hospital was given a "−" sign). Hospitals were randomly assigned to the experiment's two conditions. As you can see, the lopsided nature of the sample data—13 out of 17 "+" signs for the intervention hospitals—caused the sign test's null hypothesis to be rejected.

## The Binomial Test

The **binomial test** is similar to the sign test in that (1) the data are nominal in nature, (2) only two response categories are set up by the researcher, and (3) the response categories must be mutually exclusive. The binomial test is also like the sign test in that it can be used with a single group of people who are measured just once, with a single group of people who are measured twice (e.g., preintervention and post-intervention), or with two groups of people who are matched or are related in some logical fashion (e.g., husbands and wives). The binomial and sign tests are even further alike in that both procedures lead to a data-based *p*-level that comes from tentatively considering the null hypothesis to be true.

The only difference between the sign test and the binomial test concerns the flexibility of the null hypothesis. With the sign test, there is no flexibility. This is because the sign test's $H_0$ always says that the objects in the population are divided evenly into the two response categories. With the binomial test, on the other hand, researchers have the flexibility to set up $H_0$ with any proportionate split they wish to test.

In Excerpt 17.3, we see a case that shows the versatility of the binomial test. In the study associated with this excerpt, a group of people individually classified each of 68 competencies into one of three categories. After this had been done, the

*[handwritten margin note: Can set up split c proportion they wish to test]*

## EXCERPT 17.3 • *The Binomial Test*

Participants were asked to rate the 68 competencies identified in Stage 1 using a card-sort methodology. Competencies were initially sorted by participants according to their perceived importance in providing effective community support services using the categories of either "Absolutely Necessary," "Desirable" or "Not Necessary." . . . The first binomial test [identified] those competencies that were either Absolutely Necessary or Desirable, with a specified probability parameter of 0.66. The probability parameter was set based on the expectation that with three possible importance ratings there was a 66% chance of either of these two categories being chosen.

*Source:* Aubry, T. D. (2005). Identifying the core competencies of community support providers working with people with psychiatric disabilities. *Psychiatric Rehabilitation Journal, 28*(4), pp. 350–351.

researcher looked at the data connected to each competency and asked the simple question: How many times was the competency considered important (because it was thought to be "Absolutely Necessary" or "Desirable") versus the number of times that same competency was put into the "Not Necessary" category.

If there had been only two original categories in the card sort exercise ("Necessary" and "Not Necessary"), the data could have been analyzed with either a sign test or a binomial test (presuming that the null hypothesis would be analogous to a 50–50 split). However, the fact that there were three categories, with two of two them merged together, created a situation in which there was a two-thirds probability that a given competence would end up rated as important. The sign test cannot be used in situations like this, but the binomial test can be.

## Fisher's Exact Test

The sign test and the binomial test, as we have seen, can be used when the researcher has dichotomous data from either a single sample or from two related samples. However, researchers often conduct studies for the purpose of comparing two independent samples with respect to a dichotomous dependent variable. In such situations, **Fisher's Exact Test** often serves as the researcher's inferential tool.[1]

The null hypothesis of Fisher's Exact Test is highly analogous to the typical null hypothesis of an independent-samples $t$-test. With that kind of $t$-test, most researchers evaluate a null hypothesis that says $H_0: \mu_1 = \mu_2$ (or alternatively as $H_0: \mu_1 - \mu_2 = 0$). Using the symbols $P_1$ and $P_2$ to stand for the proportion of cases (in the first and second populations, respectively) that fall into one of the two dichotomous categories of the dependent variable, the null hypothesis of Fisher's Exact Test can be expressed as $H_0: P_1 = P_2$ (or alternatively as $H_0: P_1 - P_2 = 0$).

In Excerpt 17.4, we see an example of Fisher's Exact Test. As this excerpt makes clear, the raw data of Fisher's Exact Test are the $n$s (i.e., frequencies) of the

### EXCERPT 17.4 • *Fisher's Exact Test*

Occupational status was also related to the young people's VIQ scores (but no other outcomes) when young people were split into those scoring within 1 SD of the mean and those below this threshold (Fisher's exact $P < 0.05$). Only 3/12 (25%) children from 'professional' families showed VIQ scores below 1 SD from the mean, whilst 14/19 (74%) of children had low VIQ in families where the mother was a homemaker.

*Source:* Pratt, C., Botting, N., and Conti-Ramsden, G. (2006). The characteristics and concerns of mothers of adolescents with a history of SLI. *Child Language Teaching & Therapy*, 22(2), pp. 185–186.

[1] The word *exact* in the title of this test gives the impression that the Fisher test is superior to other test procedures. This is unfortunate, since many other tests (e.g., the sign test and the binomial test) possess just as much "exactness" as does Fisher's test.

two groups, not means. To get a feel for what was happening statistically, it's best to think in terms of percentages (especially when two groups have dissimilar $n$s, as is the case here). The researchers make it easy for us to do this, for they present each group's percentage. Fisher's Exact Test compared these two percentages and found them to differ more than could be expected by chance. Hence, the null hypothesis was rejected.

It should be noted that the null hypothesis of Fisher's Exact Test does *not* say that each of the study's two populations will be divided evenly into the two dichotomous categories. Rather, it simply says that the split in one population is the same as the split in the other population. Thus, if 3 of the 12 children in the first group had been below the cutoff along with 5 of the 19 from the second group, the two sample percentages would be 25 and 26, respectively. These two values, being quite similar, would not lead to a rejection of $H_0$.

*[handwritten margin note: Ho = proportions. the split in group 1 is the same split in group 2]*

If you will look again at Excerpt 17.4, you will see that the researchers said occupational status was *related* to the young people's VIQ scores. It is not unusual to see this term (or the term *association*) used to describe the goal or the results of a Fisher's Exact Test. This way of talking about Fisher's Exact Test is legitimate and should not throw you when you encounter it. If the two sample proportions turn out to be significantly different, then there is a nonzero relationship (in the sample data) between the dichotomous variable that "creates" the two comparison groups and the dichotomous dependent variable. Hence, the use of Fisher's Exact Test accomplishes the same basic goal as does a test of significance applied to a phi or tetrachoric correlation coefficient.[2]

## Chi-Square Tests: An Introduction

Research Navigator.com

Chi square

Although inferential tests of frequencies, percentages, or proportions are sometimes made using the sign test, the binomial test, or Fisher's Exact Test, the most frequently used statistical tool for making such tests is called **chi square.** As you will see, the chi-square procedure can be used, in certain circumstances, instead of the sign, binomial, or Fisher tests. In addition, the chi-square procedure can be used to answer research questions that cannot be answered by any of the inferential techniques covered thus far in this chapter. Because the chi-square test is so versatile and popular, it is important for any reader of the research literature to become thoroughly familiar with this inferential technique. For this reason, I feel obliged to consider the chi-square technique in a careful and unhurried fashion.

[2]Again we have a parallel between Fisher's Exact Test and the independent-samples $t$-test, since the $t$-test's comparison of the two sample means is mathematically equivalent to a test applied to the point-biserial correlation coefficient that assesses the relationship between the dichotomous grouping variable and the dependent variable.

## Different Chi-Square Tests

The term *chi-square test* technically describes any inferential test that involves a critical value being pulled from and/or a data-based *p*-value being tied to one of the many chi-square distributions. Each such distribution is like the normal and *t* distributions in that it (1) has one mode, (2) is asymptotic to the baseline, (3) comes from a mathematical formula, and (4) helps applied researchers decide whether to reject or fail to reject null hypotheses. Unlike the normal and *t* distributions (but like any *F* distribution), each chi-square distribution is positively skewed. There are many chi-square distributions simply because the degree of skewness tapers off as the number of degrees of freedom increases. In fact, the various chi-square distributions are distinguished from one another solely by the concept of degrees of freedom.

Certain of the inferential tests that are called chi square (because they utilize a chi-square distribution) have nothing to do with frequencies, proportions, or percentages. For example, a comparison of a single sample's variance against a hypothesized null value is conducted by means of a chi-square test. However, these kinds of chi-square tests are clearly in the minority. Without a doubt, most chi-square tests *do* involve the types of data being focused on throughout this chapter. In other words, it is a relatively safe bet that any chi-square test that you encounter will be dealing with nominal data.

Even when we restrict our consideration of chi square to those cases that involve nominal data, there still are different types of chi-square tests. One type is called a one-sample chi-square test (or a chi-square goodness-of-fit test), a second type is called an independent-samples chi-square test (or a chi-square test of homogeneity of proportions), and the third type is called a chi-square test of independence. We will consider each of these chi-square tests shortly, and then later in the chapter we will see how a chi-square test can also be used with related samples. Before we look at any of these chi-square tests, however, it is appropriate first to consider how to tell that a researcher is presenting results of a chi-square test.

## Chi-Square Notation and Language

Excerpts 17.5 through 17.8 illustrate the variation in how applied researchers refer to the chi-square tests used in their studies. Although the studies from which these excerpts were taken differ in the number of samples being compared and the number of nominal categories in the data, it should be noted that each of these studies had the same statistical focus as all of the other tests considered in this chapter: frequencies, proportions, or percentages.

Excerpt 17.5 is clear-cut since the authors used the phrase "chi-square tests." In Excerpt 17.6, we see the Greek symbol for chi square, $\chi^2$. Excerpt 17.7 contains a very slight variation of this test's name: *chi squared*.[3] Finally, in Excerpt 17.8, the phrase "Pearson chi square" is used.

---

[3]From a technical standpoint, the term *chi squared* is more accurate than *chi square*. However, most applied researchers use the latter label when referring to this inferential test.

### EXCERPTS 17.5–17.8 • *Different Ways of Referring to Chi Square*

Chi-square tests compared resuscitation wishes (verbal or written) with study group and patient location.

*Source:* Feder, S., Matheny, R. L., Loveless, R. S., and Rea, T. D. (2006). Withholding resuscitation: A new approach to prehospital end-of-life decisions. *Annals of Internal Medicine, 144*(9), p. 636.

---

There were no significant differences between males and females related to being laid off from a job ($\chi^2(1, N = 495) = 1.295, p > .05$).

*Source:* Madaus, J. W. (2006). Employment outcomes of university graduates with learning disabilities. *Learning Disability Quarterly, 29*(1), p. 28.

---

To assess whether there was a difference in helping between males and females, helping (help vs. no help) and gender were entered into a Chi-squared analysis.

*Source:* Karakashian, L. M., Walter, M. I., Christopher, A. N., and Lucas, T. (2006). Fear of negative evaluation affects helping behavior: The bystander effect revisited. *North American Journal of Psychology, 8*(1), p. 24.

---

The use of the Pearson chi-square analysis test was helpful in determining if there were any significant differences in demographics in relation to the perceptions and beliefs of respondents.

*Source:* Chandra, A., Smith, L. A., and Paul, D. P. (2006). What do consumers and healthcare providers in West Virginia think of long-term care? *Hospital Topics, 84*(3), p. 35.

The adjective *Pearson* is the technically correct way to indicate that the chi-square test has been applied to frequencies (rather than, for example, to variances). However, very few applied researchers use the phrase **Pearson chi square** (or the more formal label, *Pearson's approximation to chi square*). Accordingly, it's fairly safe to presume that any chi-square test you encounter is like those considered in this chapter, even though the word *Pearson* does not appear in the test's label. (Of course, this would not be a safe bet if the term *chi-square test* is used within a context in which it is clear that the test's statistical focus deals with something other than frequencies, proportions, or percentages.)

## Three Main Types of Chi-Square Tests

We now turn our attention to the three main types of chi-square tests used by applied researchers—the one-sample chi-square test, the independent-samples chi-square test, and the chi-square test of independence. Although applied researchers typically refer to all three using the same label (*chi-square test*), the null hypotheses of these tests differ. Accordingly, you need to know which kind of chi-square test has been used in order to understand what is meant by a statistically significant (or nonsignificant) finding.

## The One-Sample Chi-Square Test

With this kind of chi-square test, the various categories of the nominal variable of interest are first set up and considered. Second, a null hypothesis is formulated. The $H_0$ for the **one-sample chi-square test** is simply a specification of what percentage of the population being considered falls into each category. Next, the researchers determine what percentage of their sample falls into each of the established categories. Finally, the hypothesis testing procedure is used to determine whether the discrepancy between the set of sample percentages and those specified in $H_0$ is large enough to permit $H_0$ to be rejected.

Excerpt 17.9 provides us with an example of a one-sample chi-square test. The single sample was made up of 120 people who responded to a mailed questionnaire that contained 13 questions about online instruction. The question related to the material in Excerpt 17.9 asked how good the online instruction had been, and there were five possible answers: excellent, good, average, marginal, and poor. In essence, the null hypothesis in this study said that the five response options have equal "drawing power," and this $H_0$ would have been retained if the percentage of survey respondents choosing each response option had been about the same. However, the chi-square test showed that there was more variability among the percentages than would be expected by chance. Hence, the null hypothesis was rejected.

### EXCERPT 17.9 • *One-Sample Chi-Square Test*

The null hypothesis for one-way chi square states that the responses for each questionnaire item are even across response options and that any difference in the proportion of responses resulted from sampling error and is not meaningful. . . . The one-way chi square test confirms that these results are statistically significant ($\chi^2 = 80.03$, $df = 4$, $p \le .0001$). Thirty percent of the students indicated that online instruction offers an excellent academic experience. Forty-seven percent indicated that online instruction offers a good academic experience, 12 percent average, 7 percent marginal, and 3 percent, poor.

*Source:* Wyatt, G. (2005). Satisfaction, academic rigor and interaction: Perceptions of online instruction. *Education, 125*(3), pp. 463–464.

If you look again at Excerpt 17.9, you will see that the $\chi^2$'s *df* is not equal to one less than the number of people in the sample. Instead, it is equal to one less than the number of categories. This is the way the *df* for all one-sample chi-square tests are computed. That's because the sample percentages, across the various categories, must add up to 100. Because of this fact, you could figure out the final category's percentage once you have been given the percentages for all other categories. The final category's percentage, therefore, is not free to vary but rather has a value that's known as soon as the percentages for the other categories are recorded.

There's one additional thing you should know about the one-sample chi-square test. The null hypothesis is often set up in a "no difference" fashion. This kind of $H_0$ states that the population percentages are equal across the various categories. However, the null hypothesis can be set up such that these percentages are dissimilar. For example, in comparing the handedness of a group of college students, we might set up the $H_0$ with the right- and left-handed percentages equal to 90 and 10, respectively. These numbers come from census figures, and our little study would be asking the simple question, "Do the census figures seem to hold true for the population of college students associated with the sample used in our study?"

Because the one-sample chi-square test compares the set of observed sample percentages with the corresponding set of population percentages specified in $H_0$, this kind of chi-square analysis is often referred to as a **goodness-of-fit test.** If these two sets of percentages differ by an amount that can be attributable to sampling error, then there is said to be a good fit between the observed data and what would be expected if $H_0$ were true. In this situation, $H_0$ is retained. On the other hand, if sampling error cannot adequately explain the discrepancies between the observed and null percentages, then a bad fit is said to exist and $H_0$ is rejected. The researcher's level of significance, in conjunction with the data-based $p$-value, makes it easy to determine what action should be taken whenever this chi-square goodness-of-fit test is applied.

On occasion, researchers will use the chi-square goodness-of-fit test to see if it is reasonable to presume that the sample data have come from a normally distributed population. Of course, for researchers to have this concern, their response variable must be quantitative, not qualitative. If researchers have data that are interval or ratio in nature and if they want to apply this kind of a **test of normality,** the baseline beneath the theoretical normal distribution can be subdivided into segments, with each segment assigned a percentage to reflect the percentage of cases in a true normal distribution that would lie within that segment. These percentages are then put into $H_0$. Then, the sample is examined to determine what percentage of the observed cases fall within each of the predetermined segments, or categories. Finally, the chi-square goodness-of-fit test compares the observed and null percentages across the various categories to see whether sampling error can account for any discrepancies.[4]

---

[4]The Kolmogorov-Smirnov one-sample test is another goodness-of-fit procedure that can be used as a check on normality. It has several properties that make it superior to chi square in situations where concern rests with the distributional shape of a continuous variable.

## The Independent-Samples Chi-Square Test

Researchers frequently wish to compare two or more samples on a response variable that is categorical in nature. Since the response variable can be made up of two or more categories, we can set up four different kinds of situations to which the **independent-samples chi-square test** can be applied: (1) two samples compared on a dichotomous response variable, (2) more than two samples compared on a dichotomous response variable, (3) two samples compared on a response variable that has three or more categories, and (4) more than two samples compared on a response variable that has three or more categories. As you will see, considering these four situations one by one will allow you to generate some valuable insights about chi square and its relationship with other inferential tests we have covered.

When two independent samples are compared with respect to a dichotomous dependent variable, the chi-square test can be thought of as analogous to an independent-samples $t$-test. With the $t$-test, the null hypothesis usually tested is $H_0$: $\mu_1 = \mu_2$. With the chi-square test, the null hypothesis is $H_0$: $P_1 = P_2$; $P_1$ and $P_2$ stand for the percentage of cases (in the first and second populations) that fall into one of the two response categories. Thus the null hypothesis for this form of the chi-square test simply says that the two populations are identical in the percentage split between the two categories of the response variable.

In Excerpt 17.10, we see an example of this first kind of independent-samples chi-square test. The two groups were child care providers who either had or had not participated in a training session. The two categories of the response variable were set up to correspond with yes and no answers to the question, "Are you interested in serving children with disabilities?"

### EXCERPT 17.10 • *Two-Group Independent-Samples Chi-Square Test with a Dichotomous Response Variable*

A random survey of 41 child care providers was done. Of the 41 surveyed, 18 had participated in the training and 23 had not. Respondents were asked whether they were interested in serving children with disabilities. Among the providers who had participated in the training, 17 of 18 reported that they were interested with one responding that it was not. Among the providers who had not received the training, 12 reported that they were interested and 11 reported that they were not. Chi-square analysis of this distribution indicated a significant difference ($\chi^2[df = 1] = 8.21, p < .01$). The providers who had received the training were significantly more likely to report being interested in serving children with disabilities.

*Source:* Osborne, S., Garland, C., and Fisher, N. (2002). Caregiver training: Changing minds, opening doors to inclusion. *Infants and Young Children, 14*(3), p. 50.

*(handwritten margin note: looking @ percentage or proportion not raw data)*

To help you understand the chi-square test that was applied to the data of Excerpt 17.10, I have constructed a **contingency table**. In such a table, the data of a study are arranged in a 2 × 2 matrix for the purpose of showing how each group split itself up on the dichotomous response variable. Contingency tables are worth looking at (if they are provided in research reports) or creating (if they're not provided), because they make it easier to understand the chi-square null hypothesis and why the data led to the rejection or retention of $H_0$.

|  |  | **Would Serve Children with Disabilities** | |
|---|---|:---:|:---:|
|  |  | Yes | No |
| **Received Training** | Yes | 17 | 1 |
|  | No | 12 | 11 |

The null hypothesis associated with Excerpt 17.10 did *not* specify that each of the two populations—providers who went through training and those who didn't—had a 50–50 split between the two categories of the response variable (with half of each population saying "yes" in response to the question about serving disabled children). Instead, $H_0$ said that the two populations were identical to each other in the percentage (or proportion) of providers falling into each of the response categories. Thus, the null hypothesis of the study would not have been rejected if about the same percentage of the trained providers and untrained providers had said "yes," regardless of whether that percentage was close to 80, 33, 67, or any other value.

Since the null hypothesis deals with percentages (or proportions), it is often helpful to convert each of the cell frequencies of a contingency table into a percentage (or proportion). I have created such a table for Excerpt 17.10. As before, the rows and columns correspond to the groups and the response categories, respectively. Now, however, the cells on either row indicate the percentage split of that row's child care providers across the yes and no responses to the question. This contingency table shows why the chi-square null hypothesis was rejected, because the two samples clearly differed in their willingness to serve disabled children.

|  |  | **Would Serve Children with Disabilities** | |
|---|---|:---:|:---:|
|  |  | Yes | No |
| **Received Training** | Yes | 94.4% | 5.6% |
|  | No | 52.2% | 47.8% |

$x^2$ vs
Fishers

---

Fishers
= small
n

Earlier, I stated that a chi-square test that compares two groups on a dichotomous response variable is analogous to an independent *t*-test. This kind of chi square is even more similar to Fisher's Exact Test, since these two tests have the same null hypothesis and also utilize the same kind of data. Because of these similarities, you may have been wondering why some researchers choose to use a Fisher's Exact Test while others subject their data to an independent-samples chi-square test. Although I will address this question more fully later in the chapter, suffice it to say that Fisher's test works better when the researcher has a small number of subjects.

The second kind of independent-samples chi-square test to consider involves a comparison of three or more samples with respect to a dichotomous response variable. Excerpt 17.11 illustrates this second kind of chi-square test. In the study associated with this excerpt, the three comparison groups were called *music, nonmusic,* and *control.* If we were to create a contingency table to help us understand this chi-square test, our table would have three rows (one for each of the study's three experimental groups) and two columns (one for girls and the other for boys). Each of the six cells would then be filled with a frequency. Those *n*s would be 13 and 8 for the music group, 6 and 15 for the nonmusic group, and 6 and 14 for the control group. Converted into percentages, the girl and boy cells for each row of the contingency table would contain 62% and 38%, 29% and 71%, and 30% and 70%, respectively.

In Excerpt 17.11, look closely at the second sentence. Near the end of that sentence, 2 is positioned, by itself, inside the middle set of parentheses, just to the left of the number 6.16. This number was the chi square's *df.* In this or any other contingency table, the *df* for $\chi^2$ is determined by multiplying 1 less than the number of rows times 1 less than the number of columns. In this case, $df = (3 - 1)(2 - 1) = 2$.

### EXCERPT 17.11 • *Three-Group Independent-Samples Chi-Square Test with a Dichotomous Response Variable*

The final analysis consisted of data for 62 participants: 21 in the music condition, 21 in the nonmusic condition, and 20 in the control condition. . . . The groups were found to be significantly different in terms of the proportion of female to male participants (chi-square(2) = 6.16, $p < .05$). While the music group had more female participants than male (13 girls and 8 boys), both the nonmusic and control groups had fewer female participants than male (6 girls and 15 boys for nonmusic; 6 girls and 14 boys for control).

*Source:* Noguchi, L. K. (2006). The effect of music versus nonmusic on behavioral signs of distress and self-report of pain in pediatric injection patients. *Journal of Music Therapy, 43*(1), pp. 19, 24.

With three or more groups being compared, this second version of the independent-samples chi-square test is analogous to a one-way analysis of variance. Whereas a one-way ANOVA focuses on means, this kind of chi-square test focuses on proportions. Thus whereas the null hypothesis in a three-group one-way ANOVA would state $H_0: \mu_1 = \mu_2 = \mu_3$, the null hypothesis in a three-group chi-square of the kind being considered would state $H_0: P_1 = P_2 = P_3$, where $P$ stands for the percentage of cases in the population that fall into the first of the two available response categories (and where each subscript number designates a different population). The numerical value of the common $P$ in the chi-square null hypothesis is not specified by the researcher but instead is determined by the data and can be any value between 0 and 100.

Consider again Excerpt 17.11. The chi-square null hypothesis would have been retained if each of the three groups had contained about the same percentage of females, regardless of what that common percentage might have been. Thus, if the gender split in the first group had been reversed, the $\chi^2$ test would not have been significant. Or, if the gender split in each of the other two groups had been reversed, the null hypothesis would have been retained.[5]

The third kind of independent-samples chi-square test we need to consider involves two comparison groups and a response variable that has three or more categories. Excerpt 17.12 contains an example of this kind of chi-square test. Here, the two groups were made up of male and female college students. The three categories of the response variable were created to indicate whether these research participants were social drinkers, potential problem drinkers, or potential alcoholics. As you can see, these classifications were made on the basis of a questionnaire called the SMAST. Comparing the way the males versus the females were spread out across the three categories, the chi-square test yielded a statistically significant result.

### EXCERPT 17.12 • *Two-Group Independent-Samples Chi-Square Test with a Three-Category Response Variable*

SMAST total scores were used to place participants into one of three categories: Social Drinker (a score of 1 or below), Maybe Problem Drinker (a score of 2), and Possible Alcoholic (a score of 3 or above). Compared to women, men were classified as Social Drinkers (men, 48.82%; women, 62.80%) and Maybe Problem Drinkers (men, 23.62%; women, 25.12%) less often and Possible Alcoholic (men, 27.56%; women, 12.08%) more often, $\chi^2(2, N = 334) = 13.25, p = .001$.

*Source:* Shirachi, M., and Spirrison, C. L. (2006). Repressive coping style and substance use among college students. *North American Journal of Psychology, 8*(1), p. 106.

Although no frequencies or percentages appear in Excerpt 17.12, you still should be able to imagine or sketch out the contingency table for this particular chi-square test. Such a table would have two rows (for the two gender groups) and

[5]The actual result for either version of these two imaginary sets of results would be $\chi^2(2) = 0.5, p = .078$.

three columns (corresponding to the three kinds of drinkers). The *df* for this table would be equal to $(2 - 1)(3 - 1)$, and the resulting *df* appears immediately to the right of the chi-square symbol.

Whenever a chi-square test compares two groups on a response variable that has two or more categories, the null hypothesis states simply that the two populations are distributed in the same fashion across the various response categories. Thus the $H_0$ for the chi-square test in Excerpt 17.12 specified that the distribution of male college students in the three drinking categories is the same as the distribution of female college students. As with the other kinds of independent-samples chi-square tests being considered, the null percentages for the various categories of the response variable do not have to be specified by the researcher at the outset of the hypothesis testing procedure because $H_0$ simply says that "whatever is the case in the first population is also the case in the second population." This means, of course, that $H_0$ can be true even though the percentages vary in size across the response categories; however, the way they vary must be the same in each population if $H_0$ is true.

The fourth kind of independent-samples chi-square test involves three or more comparison groups and a response variable made up of three or more categories. An example of this kind of chi-square test appears in Excerpt 17.13.

### EXCERPT 17.13 • *An Independent-Samples Chi Square Involving Three Groups and a Three-Category Response Variable*

Participants were asked to give their program a preparation rating for both general instructional design tasks (competencies, use of ID models and learning theories, etc.), and for different aspects of workplace cultural preparation. Frequency data and $3 \times 3$ chi square analyses comparing program rating (excellent, fair, not adequate) to type of program (generalist, specific and other/combination programs), were calculated for both ratings questions. For preparation to practice *general instructional design tasks,* results of the chi-square were significantly different from what would be expected due to chance, $\chi^2(4, N = 86) = 22.51, p = .000$ [but results for] *workplace cultural preparation . . .* did not show a significant difference, $\chi^2(4, N = 86) = 1.317, p = .859$.

*Source:* Larson, M. B. (2005). Instructional design career environments: Survey of the alignment of preparation and practice. *TechTrends: Linking Research & Practice to Improve Learning, 49*(6), p. 27.

The null hypothesis in this fourth kind of independent-samples test is very much like the $H_0$ for a one-way ANOVA except that the one-way ANOVA focuses on means whereas the chi-square test focuses on proportions (or percentages). With the chi-square test, the null hypothesis simply says that the various populations are identical to one another in the way subjects are distributed across the various categories of the response variable. Hence, in the study associated with Excerpt 17.13, the null hypothesis was rejected in the first chi-square analysis because the 86 students from the three training programs (referred to as generalist, specific, and other/combination) were quite dissimilar in the way they distributed themselves across the three response categories (excellent, fair, not adequate). The second of the two chi-square analyses did not reveal this kind of difference for the students' responses to the question concerning workplace culture preparation.

### Chi Square as a Correlational Probe

In many studies, a researcher is interested in whether a nonchance relationship exists between two nominal variables. In such studies, a single sample of subjects is measured, with each subject classified into one of the available categories of the first variable and then classified once more into one of the categories of the second variable. After the data are arranged into a contingency table, a chi-square test can be used to determine whether a statistically significant relationship exists between the two variables.

In Excerpts 17.14 through 17.16, we see three terms used in conjunction with chi-square tests that let you know that the researchers were using chi square in a correlational manner. The first two of these terms—*association* and *relationship*—are not new; we saw them used in Chapter 3 while considering bivariate correlation. The third

### EXCERPTS 17.14–17.16 • *Terms Used When Chi Square Is Used as a Correlational Probe*

Chi square tests were used to evaluate the association between sociodemographic characteristics and correct interpretation (yes or no) of each of the eight PWLs [prescription warning labels].

*Source:* Michael, S. W., Davis, T. C., Tilson, H. H., Bass, P. F., and Parker, R. M. (2006). Misunderstanding of prescription drug warning labels among patients with low literacy. *American Journal of Health-System Pharmacy, 63*(1), p. 1050.

---

The relationship between maternal accuracy [high/medium or low] and child attributional style [unrealistically positive, rational/neutral, or negative] was found to be highly significant, $\chi^2(2, N = 354) = 23.90; p < .01$.

*Source:* Sharp, C., Fonagy, P., and Goodyer, I. M. (2006). Imagining your child's mind: Psychosocial adjustment and mothers' ability to predict their children's attributional response styles. *British Journal of Developmental Psychology, 24*(1), pp. 207–208.

---

A chi-square test of independence was calculated comparing the two categories. Alcohol Dependent (a total score of 8 or above) and Non-Alcohol Dependent (a total score less than 8) for gender and for repressor status.

*Source:* Shirachi, M., and Spirrison, C. L. (2006). Repressive coping style and substance use among college students. *American Journal of Psychology, 8*(1), p. 105.

term, however, is new. A chi-square **test of independence** is simply a test to see whether a relationship (or association) exists between the study's two variables.

When a chi-square test is used as a correlational probe, it does not produce an index that estimates the strength of the relationship between the two variables that label the contingency table's rows and columns. Instead, the chi-square test simply addresses the question, "In the population of interest, are the two variables related?" Focusing on the sample data, this question takes the form, "In the contingency table, is there a nonchance relationship between the two variables?"

To illustrate what I mean by "nonchance relationship," imagine that we go out and ask each of 100 college students to name a relative. (If anyone responds with a gender-free name like Pat, we would ask the respondent to indicate whether the relative is a male or a female.) We would also keep track of each respondent's gender. After collecting these two pieces of information from our 100th student, we might end up with sample data that look like this:

|  |  | **Gender of the Relative** | |
|---|---|---|---|
|  |  | *Male* | *Female* |
| **Gender of the Student** | *Male* | 30 | 20 |
|  | *Female* | 23 | 27 |

In the $2 \times 2$ contingency table for our hypothetical study, there is a relationship between the two variables—student's gender and relative's gender. More of the male students responded with the name of a male relative while more of the female students thought of a female relative. (Or, we could say that there was a tendency for male relatives to be thought of by male students while female relatives were thought of by female students.) But is this relationship something other than what would be expected by chance?

If there were *no* relationship in the population between the two variables in our gender study, the population frequencies in all four cells of the contingency table would be identical. But a sample extracted from that population would not likely mirror the population perfectly. Instead, sampling error would likely be in the sample data, thus causing the observed contingency table to have dissimilar cell frequencies. In other words, we would expect a relationship to pop up in the sample data even if there were no relationship in the population. Such a relationship, in the sample data, would be due entirely to chance. Although we should expect a "null population" (i.e., one in which there is no relationship between the two variables) to yield sample data in which a relationship *does* exist between the two variables, such a relationship ought to be small, or weak. It *is* possible for a null population to yield sample data suggesting a strong relationship between the two variables, but this is *not* very likely to happen. Stated differently, if researchers end up with a contingency table in which there is a meager relationship, they have only weak evidence for arguing that the two variables of interest are related in the population. If, in contrast, a pronounced relationship shows up in the contingency table built with the sample data, the researchers possess strong evidence for suggesting that a relationship does, in fact, exist in the population.

Returning to our little gender study, the chi-square test can be used to label the relationship that shows up in the sample data as being either meager or pronounced. Using the hypothesis testing procedure in which the level of significance is set equal to .05, the null hypothesis of no relationship in the population cannot be rejected. This means that the observed relationship in the contingency table could easily have come from a sample pulled from a population characterized by $H_0$. This means that the observed relationship is not of the nonchance variety.

In addition to using a chi-square test to see if a nonchance relationship exists in the sample data, researchers can convert their chi-square calculated value into an index that estimates the strength of the relationship that exists in the population. By making this conversion, the researcher obtains a numerical value that is analogous to the correlation coefficient generated by Pearson's or Spearman's technique. Several different conversion procedures have been developed.

The phi coefficient can be used to measure the strength of association in $2 \times 2$ contingency tables. I discussed this correlational procedure in Chapters 3 and 9 and pointed out in those discussions how phi is appropriate for the case of two dichotomous variables. Now, I can extend this discussion of phi by pointing out its connection to chi square. If a chi-square test has been applied to a $2 \times 2$ contingency table, the phi index of association can be obtained directly by putting the chi-square calculated value into this simple formula:

$$\text{phi} = \sqrt{\frac{\chi^2}{N}}$$

where $N$ stands for the total sample size. Researchers, of course, are the ones who use this formula in order to convert their chi-square calculated values into phi coefficients. As illustrated by Excerpt 17.17, you will not have to do this.

### EXCERPT 17.17 • *Chi Square and Phi*

We used a Chi-square test to examine differences in who started the meetings between the special education teachers and students in the control and intervention groups. The test indicated significant differences such that students who received the Self-Directed IEP intervention were much more likely to start the meeting compared to those in the control group $\chi^2(1, N = 221) = 70.94, p = .000$. The obtained Phi of .57 indicates a strong relationship between the Self-Directed IEP intervention and students starting the meeting (e.g., Cohen, 1988). (We used the following to determine the magnitude of the Phi effect size: .10 = small effect, .30 = moderate effect, .50 = large effect.)

*Source:* Martin, J. E., Van Dycke, J. L., Christensen, W. R., Greene, B. A., Gardner, J. E., and Lovett, D. L. (2006). Increasing student participation in IEP meetings: Establishing the self-directed IEP as an evidenced-based practice. *Exceptional Children, 72*(3), p. 307.

For contingency tables that have more than two rows or columns, researchers can convert their chi-square calculated value into a measure of association called the **contingency coefficient.** This index of relationship is symbolized by *C,* and the connection between *C* and chi square is made evident by the following formula for *C:*

$$C = \sqrt{\frac{\chi^2}{N + \chi^2}}$$

In Excerpt 17.18, we see an illustration of how the contingency coefficient can be computed following a chi-square test of independence.[6]

### EXCERPT 17.18 • *Chi Square and the Contingency Coefficient*

In the present sample, 33% of the women met lifetime criteria for MDD, and 8% met criteria for lifetime PTSD. The diagnoses were related to each other, $\chi^2(1) = 12.08, p < .001$ (contingency coefficient of .23).

*Source:* Green, B. L., Krupnick, J. L., Stockton, P., Goodman, L., Corcoran, C., and Petty, R. (2005). Effects of adolescent trauma exposure on risky behavior in college women. *Psychiatry: Interpersonal & Biological Processes, 68*(4), p. 371.

The formula for *C* shows that this index of association will turn out equal to zero when there is no relationship in the contingency table (since in that case, the calculated value of $\chi^2$ will itself turn out equal to zero) and that it will assume larger values for larger values of $\chi^2$. What this formula does not show is that this index usually cannot achieve a maximum value of 1.00 (as is the case with Pearson's *r,* Spearman's rho, and other correlation coefficients). This problem can be circumvented easily if the researcher computes **Cramer's measure of association** because Cramer's index is simply equal to the computed index of relationship divided by the maximum value that the index could assume, given the contingency table's dimensions and marginal totals.

In Excerpt 17.19, we see a case in which Cramer's measure of association, symbolized as *V,* was computed in conjunction with a 2 × 2 contingency table. Although the chi-square test was statistically significant (with *p* turning out to be very, very small), the researchers noted that the value of *V* was small. When this same thing happened after the researchers used $\chi^2$ and *V* to analyze the data from the same two groups of students on a different two-category variable, the researchers aptly stated that "the statistical significance we found was most probably due to the very large sample size." Did you note the *N* in Excerpt 17.19!

---

[6]A variation of *C* is called the *mean square contingency coefficient.* This index of relationship uses the same formula as that presented for phi.

## EXCERPT 17.19 • *Chi Square and Cramer's V*

> Also, a significant difference was found for the tests the students chose but with a small Cramer's V $[\chi^2(1, N = 25{,}989) = 45.5, p = .00,$ Cramer's $V = .04]$. Students who qualified for talent search via test scores were more likely to take the SAT (55.9%) than the ACT (44.1%), while students who qualified for the program via parent nomination were fairly evenly distributed across the two tests (SAT 47.9% vs. ACT 52.1%).
>
> *Source*: Lee, S., and Olszewski-Kubilius, P. (2006). Comparisons between Talent Search students qualifying via scores on standardized tests and via parent nomination. *Roeper Review, 28*(3), p. 160.

## Issues Related to Chi-Square Tests

Before we conclude our discussion of chi-square tests, a few related issues need to be addressed. Unless you are aware of the connection between these issues and the various chi-square tests we have covered, you will be unable to fully understand and critique research reports that contain the results of chi-square tests. Accordingly, it is important for you to be sensitive to the following issues.

### Post Hoc Tests

If an independent-samples chi-square test is used to compare two groups, interpretation of the results is straightforward regardless of what decision is made regarding the null hypothesis. If there are three or more comparison groups involved in the study, the results can be interpreted without difficulty so long as $H_0$ is not rejected. If, however, the independent-samples chi-square test leads to a rejection of $H_0$ when three or more groups are contrasted, the situation remains unclear.

When three or more samples are compared, a statistically significant outcome simply indicates that it is unlikely that all corresponding populations are distributed in the same way across the categories of the response variable. In other words, a rejection of $H_0$ suggests that at least two of the populations differ, but this outcome by itself does not provide any insight as to which specific populations differ from one another. To gain such insights, the researcher must conduct a post hoc investigation.

In Excerpt 17.20, we see a case where a post hoc investigation after an "omnibus" chi-square test yielded a statistically significant result. The original chi-square test involved a $3 \times 4$ arrangement of the data, involving three groups (lesbians, gay men, and bisexual men and women) and four categories of victimization (childhood sexual abuse, adult sexual abuse, nonvictims, and revictimized). After the omnibus $\chi^2$ turned out to be significant, the researchers probed their data with several different $2 \times 2$ chi-square analyses. In a very real sense, this post hoc investigation had the same goal as would a set of Tukey pairwise comparisons computed after a one-way ANOVA yields a significant $F$.

## EXCERPT 17.20 • *Post Hoc Investigation Following a Significant Chi-Square Test*

In contrast, a chi-square analysis found that sexual orientation and victimization categorization were related, $\chi^2(6, N = 307) = 15.94, p < .01$. Follow-up analyses were conducted by partitioning the $3 \times 4$ chi-square table into six orthogonal contrasts (i.e., six $2 \times 2$ tables). . . . Each $2 \times 2$ table represents an orthogonal contrast derived from the omnibus test that addresses a focused, precise question that cannot be answered with the results of an omnibus test. These analyses showed that gay men and bisexuals were more likely than lesbians to experience sexual revictimization, $\chi^2(1, N = 133) = 5.36, p < .02$.

*Source:* Heidt, J. M., Marx, B. P., and Gold, S. D. (2005). Sexual revictimization among sexual minorities: A preliminary study. *Journal of Traumatic Stress, 18*(5), p. 536.

Whenever two or more separate chi-square tests are performed within a post hoc investigation, with each incorporating the same level of significance as that used in the initial (omnibus) chi-square test, the chances of a Type I error being made somewhere in the post hoc analysis will exceed the nominal level of significance. This is not a problem in those situations where the researcher judges Type II errors to be more costly than Type I errors. Be that as it may, the scientific community seems to encourage researchers to guard against Type I errors.

In Excerpt 17.20, you saw a case in which a post hoc investigation, involving six pairwise comparisons (each performed as a $2 \times 2$ chi square), was conducted after an omnibus chi-square test yielded a significant result. In the research report that provided this excerpt, I could not find any indication that the researchers used the Bonferroni adjustment procedure (or some similar device) to protect against an inflated Type I error rate in their post hoc investigation. Perhaps they adjusted their alpha level but just did not report having done so. Or, perhaps they failed to lower $\alpha$ when they conducted their six post hoc chi-square tests.

### Small Amounts of Sample Data

To work properly, the chi-square tests discussed in this chapter necessitate sample sizes that are not too small. Actually, it is the **expected frequencies** that must be sufficiently large for the chi-square test to function as intended. An expected frequency exists for each category into which sample objects are classified, and each one is nothing more than the proportion of the sample data you would expect in the category if $H_0$ were true and if there were absolutely no sampling error. For example, if we were to perform a taste test in which each of 20 individuals is asked to sip four different beverages and then indicate which one is the best, the expected frequency for each of the four options would be equal to 5 (presuming that $H_0$ specifies equality among the four beverages). If this same study were to be conducted with 40 participants, each of the four expected values would be equal to 10.

If researchers have a small amount of sample data, the expected values associated with their chi-square test will also be small. If the expected values are too small, the chi-square test should not be used. Various rules of thumb have been offered over the years to help applied researchers know when they should refrain from using the chi-square test because of small expected values. The most conservative of these rules says that none of the expected frequencies should be smaller than 5; the most liberal rule stipulates that chi square can be used so long as the average expected frequency is at least 2.

In Excerpt 17.21 we see a case where a team of researchers compared a group of young children versus a group of monkeys in terms of their ability to perform a task. Because the sample sizes were small, some of the expected frequencies turned out to be problematic (because they were less than 5). For this reason, the researchers decided against using chi square to analyze their data and instead employed Fisher's Exact Test.

### EXCERPT 17.21 • *Use of Fisher's Exact Test Rather Than Chi Square Because of Small Expected Frequencies*

When comparing the degree of matching between the children and monkeys, some of the expected frequencies fell below 5, thereby precluding the use of chi-square. Therefore, two-tailed 2 × 2 Fisher's exact probability tests were used.

*Source:* Rigamonti, M. M., Custance, D. M., Previde, E. P., and Spiezio, C. (2005). Testing for localized stimulus enhancement and object movement reenactment in pig-tailed macaques (Macaca nemestrina) and young children (Homo sapiens). *Journal of Comparative Psychology, 119*(3), p. 262.

The option of turning to Fisher's Exact Test when the expected frequencies are too small is available in situations in which the sample data create a 2 × 2 contingency table. This option does not exist, however, if their researcher is using (1) a one-sample chi-square test with three or more categories or (2) chi square with a contingency table that has more than two rows and/or more than two columns. In these situations, the problem of small expected frequencies will be solved by the researcher's redefining of the response categories such that two or more of the original categories can be collapsed together. For example, if men and women are being compared regarding their responses to a five-option Likert-type question, the researcher might convert the five original categories into three new categories by (1) merging together the "strongly agree" and "agree" categories into a new single category called "favorable response," (2) leaving the "undecided" category unchanged, and (3) merging together the "disagree" and "strongly disagree" categories into a new single category called "unfavorable response." By so doing, the revised contingency table might not have any expected frequencies that are too small.

### Yates' Correction for Continuity

When applying a chi-square test to situations where $df = 1$, some researchers use a special formula that yields a slightly smaller calculated value than would be the case if the regular formula were employed. When this is done, it can be said that the data are being analyzed using a chi-square test that has been **corrected for discontinuity.** This special formula was developed by a famous statistician named **Yates,** and occasionally the chi-square test has Yates' name attached to it when the special formula is used. Excerpt 17.22 shows that Yates' correction is used in conjunction with chi-square analyses. It is not used with any of the other statistical procedures considered in this book.

### EXCERPT 17.22 • *Yates' Correction for Discontinuity*

Participant demographic characteristics (i.e., gender, race, lunch status, age) are presented in Table 1 [not shown here]. . . . Chi-square analyses with Yates correction on these nominal data showed no effects for treatment condition [experimental versus control]: Gender $(\chi^2(1) = 0.002, p = .966)$, Race $(\chi^2(3) = 0.88, p = .912)$, and Lunch Status $(\chi^2(1) = 0.127, p = .722)$.

*Source:* Nelson, J. R., Stage, S. A., and Epstein, M. H. (2005). Effects of a prereading intervention on the literacy and social skills of children. *Exceptional Children, 72*(1), p. 32.

Statistical authorities are not in agreement as to the need for using Yates' special formula. Some argue that it should *always* be used in situations where $df = 1$ because the regular formula leads to calculated values that are too large (and thus to an inflated probability of a Type I error). Other authorities take the position that the Yates adjustment causes the pendulum to swing too far in the opposite direction because Yates' correction makes the chi-square test overly conservative (thus increasing the chances of a Type II error). Ideally, researchers should clarify why the Yates formula either was or wasn't used on the basis of a judicious consideration of the different risks associated with a Type I or a Type II error. Realistically, however, you are most likely to see the Yates formula used only occasionally and, in those cases, used without any explanation as to why it was employed.

## McNemar's Chi-Square

Earlier in this chapter, we saw how a chi-square test can be used to compare two independent samples with respect to a dichotomous dependent variable. If the two samples involved in such a comparison are related rather than independent, chi square can still be used to test the **homogeneity of proportions** null hypothesis.

However, both the formula used by the researchers to analyze their data and the label attached to the test procedure are slightly different in this situation where two related samples are compared. Although there is no reason to concern ourselves here with the unique formula used when correlated data have been collected, it *is* important that you become familiar with the way researchers refer to this kind of test.

A chi-square analysis of related samples is usually referred to simply as *McNemar's test*. Sometimes, however, it is called McNemar's change test, McNemar's chi-square test, McNemar's test of correlated proportions, or McNemar's test for paired data. Occasionally, it is referred to symbolically as $Mc\chi^2$. Excerpts 17.23 and 17.24 illustrate the use of McNemar's test.

### EXCERPTS 17.23–17.24 • *McNemar's Chi-Square Test*

Between baseline and follow-up, significant reductions in illicit sources of income were reported, including: trading sex for drugs and/or money (100% vs. 71.0%, respectively, $p < 0.0005$); and selling drugs (35.0% vs. 10.5%, $p = 0.021$) . . . [with] $p$-values obtained using McNemar's Test for categorical data.

*Source:* Sherman, S. G., German, D., Cheng, Y., Marks, M., and Bailey-Kloche, M. (2006). The evaluation of the JEWEL project: An innovative economic enhancement and HIV prevention intervention study targeting drug using women involved in prostitution. *AIDS Care*, *18*(1), p. 6.

-------------------------------------------------------------------------------------

To obtain a control group of similar social background and expectations to the population of patients with congenitally malformed hearts, each adult with congenital heart disease was asked to give an identical questionnaire to a friend without congenital heart disease. . . . We used McNemar's test to compare matched pairs. . . . When compared to matched controls, adults with congenital heart disease were significantly more likely to be out of work, and also more likely to have been out of work for greater than 1 year.

*Source:* Crossland, D. S., Jackson, S. P., Lyall, R., Burn, J., and O'Sullivan, J. J. (2005). Employment and advice regarding careers for adults with congenital heart disease. *Cardiology in the Young*, *15*(4), pp. 392, 393.

**McNemar's chi-square test** is very much like a correlated-samples $t$-test in that two sets of data being compared can come either from a single group that is measured twice (e.g., in a pre/post sense) or from matched samples that are measured just once. Excerpt 17.23 obviously falls into the first of these categories because data from a single group are compared at two points in time, before and after an intervention. (This intervention involved trying to help a group of prostitutes who were drug addicts.) In Excerpt 17.24, we see a case where two comparison groups were first matched and then compared twice, first on whether or not the groups' members were employed, and then a second time on whether they had been out of work for more than a year. Because these comparison groups were matched, neither chi-square nor Fisher's

Exact Test could be used. Instead, McNemar's test was employed to make the desired comparisons.

Although the McNemar chi square is similar to a correlated $t$-test with respect to the kind of sample(s) involved in the comparison, the two tests differ dramatically in terms of the null hypothesis. With the $t$-test, the null hypothesis involves population means; in contrast, the null hypothesis of McNemar's chi-square test is concerned with population percentages. In other words, the null hypothesis of McNemar's test always takes the form $H_0: P_1 = P_2$ while the $t$-test's null hypothesis always involves the symbol $\mu$ (and it usually is set up to say $H_0: \mu_1 = \mu_2$).

## The Cochran Q Test

A test developed by Cochran is appropriate for the situation where the researcher wishes to compare three or more related samples with respect to a dichotomous dependent variable. This test is called the **Cochran Q test,** with the letter $Q$ simply being the arbitrary symbol used by Cochran to label the calculated value produced by putting the sample data into Cochran's formula. This test just as easily could have been called Cochran's chi-square test inasmuch as the calculated value is compared against a chi-square critical value to determine whether the null hypothesis should be rejected.

The Cochran Q test can be thought of as an "extension" of McNemar's chi-square test, since McNemar's test is restricted to the situation where just two correlated samples of data are compared whereas Cochran's test can be used when there are any number of such samples. Or, the Cochran Q test can be likened to the one-factor repeated-measures analysis of variance covered in Chapter 14; in each case, multiple related samples of data are compared. (That ANOVA is quite different from the Cochran test, however, because the null hypothesis in the former focuses on $\mu$s whereas Cochran's $H_0$ involves $P$s.)

In Excerpt 17.25, we see a case where Cochran's Q test was used. This excerpt comes from a study in which the researchers investigated the potential benefits of a treatment program designed for male alcoholics. One of the study's main dependent variables was aggression. The study's data were cast into a $2 \times 3$ contingency table, with each column corresponding to one of the three years of the study, and the two rows corresponding to the dichotomous response category (yes or no) that indicated whether or not a violent act had been committed. A regular chi-square test could not be used because the data in each column of this contingency table came from the same group.

In the study associated with Excerpt 17.25, the null hypothesis for Cochran's Q test could be stated as $H_0: P_{\text{Year Before}} = P_{\text{1st Year After}} = P_{\text{2nd Year After}}$, where each $P$ stands for the population percentage of individuals who committed a violent act. As you can see, the Cochran Q test led to a rejection of this null hypothesis. (In this excerpt, there are two numbers inside a set of parentheses next to the letter Q. The first of these numbers is the *df* associated with the Cochran test; the second number is the sample size.)

**EXCERPT 17.25 • *Cochran's Q Test***

First, we used omnibus tests to examine whether the extent of aggression differed across the three time periods (year before and 1st and 2nd year after BCT). Cochran's $Q(2, N = 243)$ showed that the three time periods differed significantly on each prevalence of aggression measure. . . . Next, to test whether aggression decreased from before to after BCT, we made a series of pairwise comparisons of baseline with each follow-up aggression score. . . . McNemar's test of change for [these comparisons] showed significant decreases in both the 1st year and the 2nd year after BCT, as compared with the year before BCT, for both alcoholic men and their female partners on all aggression measures studied.

*Source:* O'Farrell, T. J., Murphy, C. M., Stephan, S. H., Fals-Stewart, W., and Murphy, M. (2004). Partner violence before and after couples-based alcoholism treatment for male alcoholic patients: The role of treatment involvement and abstinence. *Journal of Consulting and Clinical Psychology, 72*(2), pp. 207–208.

When Cochran's test leads to a rejection of the omnibus null hypothesis, the researcher will probably conduct a post hoc investigation. Within this follow-up investigation, the researcher most likely will set up and test pairwise comparisons. Such post hoc tests can be made via McNemar's test, as illustrated in Excerpt 17.25. (In the post hoc investigation, note that separate McNemar tests compared baseline data with data collected at each of the two posttreatment points in time. Thus, this use of the McNemar test is similar to what a Dunnett's test does when it compares the mean of a control group against the mean of each other group. In the study connected with Excerpt 17.25, the "control" data came from the baseline point in time.)

## The Use of z-Tests When Dealing with Proportions

As you may recall from Chapter 10, researchers will sometimes use a z-test (rather than a t-test) when their studies are focused on either the mean of one group or the means of two comparison groups. It may come as a surprise that researchers will sometimes apply a z-test when dealing with dependent variables that are qualitative rather than quantitative in nature. Be that as it may, you are likely to come across cases where a z-test has been used by researchers when their data take the form of proportions, percentages, or frequencies.

If a researcher has a single group that is measured on a dichotomous dependent variable, the data can be analyzed by a one-sample chi-square test *or* by a z-test. The choice here is immaterial, since these two tests are mathematically equivalent and will always lead to the same data-based *p*-value. The same thing holds true for the case where a comparison is made between two unrelated samples. Such a comparison can be made with an independent-samples chi-square test or a z-test; the *p*-value of both tests will be the same.

Whereas the $z$-tests we have just discussed and the chi-square tests covered earlier (for the cases of a dichotomous dependent variable used with a single sample or two independent samples) are mathematically equivalent, there is another $z$-test that represents a **large sample approximation** to some of the tests examined in earlier sections of this chapter. To be more specific, researchers will sometimes use a $z$-test, if they have large samples, in places where you might expect them to use a sign test, a binomial test, or a McNemar test. In Excerpts 17.26 and 17.27, we see two examples of a $z$-test being used in connection with test procedures considered in this chapter. In the first of these excerpts, a large-sample approximation to the sign test was used. In Excerpt 17.27, a large-sample approximation to the binomial test was used.

**EXCERPTS 17.26–17.27 • *Use of z-Tests with Percentages (and Large Samples)***

The sign test confirms that the result is very highly significantly different (31 above, 3 below, and 0 ties, $Z = 4.63, p < .0005$) from the value that would be expected by chance.

*Source:* Moore, D., Cheng, Y., McGrath, P., and Powell, N. J. (2005). Collaborative virtual environment technology for people with autism. *Focus on Autism and Other Developmental Disabilities, 20*(4), p. 238.

A series of two-sample binomial tests showed that the observed rates of SLI in children with dyslexia based on estimated Full Scale IQ discrepancy plus low achievement were significantly higher than the base rate of the disorder in second and eighth grades ($zs = 2.0$ and $2.2, p < .05$).

*Source*: Catts, H. W., Adlof, S. M., Hogan, T. P., and Weismer, S. E. (2005). Are specific language impairment and dyslexia distinct disorders? *Journal of Speech, Language & Hearing Research, 48*(6), p. 1385.

## A Few Final Thoughts

As you have seen, a wide variety of test procedures have been designed for situations where the researcher's data take the form of frequencies, percentages, or proportions. Despite the differences among these tests (in terms of their names, the number of groups involved, and whether repeated measures are involved), there are many commonalities that cut across the tests we have considered. These commonalities exist because each of these tests involves the computation of a data-based $p$-value that is then used to evaluate a null hypothesis.

In using the procedures considered in this chapter within an applied research study, a researcher will follow the various steps of hypothesis testing. Accordingly, many of the "side issues" dealt with in Chapters 7 and 8 are relevant to the proper use of any and all of the tests we have just discussed. In an effort to help you keep these important concerns in the forefront of your consciousness as you read and evaluate research reports, I feel obliged to conclude this chapter by considering a few of these more generic concerns.

My first point is simply a reiteration that the data-based $p$-value is always computed on the basis of a tentative belief that the null hypothesis is true. Accordingly, the statistical results of a study are always tied to the null hypothesis. If the researcher's null hypothesis is silly or articulates something that no one would defend or expect to be true, then the rejection of $H_0$, regardless of how "impressive" the $p$-value, does not signify an important finding.

If you think that this first point is simply a "straw man" that has no connection to the real world of actual research, consider this *real* study that was conducted not too long ago. In this investigation, chi square compared three groups of teachers in terms of the types of instructional units they used. Two kinds of data were collected from the teachers: (1) their theoretical orientation regarding optimal teaching-learning practices and (2) what they actually did when teaching. The results indicated that skill-based instructional units tended to be used more by teachers who had a skill-based theoretical orientation, that rule-based instructional units were used more so by teachers who had a rule-based theoretical orientation, and that function-based instructional units were utilized to a greater extent by teachers who possessed a function-based theoretical orientation. Are you surprised that this study's data brought forth a rejection of the chi-square null hypothesis of no relationship between teachers' theoretical orientation and type of instructional unit used? Was a study needed to reach this finding?

The second point I wish to reiterate is that the chances of a Type I error increase above the researcher's nominal level of significance in the situation where multiple null hypotheses are evaluated. Although there are alternative ways of dealing with this potential problem, you are likely to see the Bonferroni technique employed most often to keep control over Type I errors. Excerpt 17.28 illustrates the use of this technique. As you can see, these researchers used both chi square and Fisher's Exact Test in their study. In this excerpt, note the phrase **comparison-wise Type I error rate.** This refers to the likelihood of falsely rejecting the null hypothesis whenever a single test is conducted. If the researchers had not used Bonferroni to adjust their level of significance when they conducted several tests, the comparison-wise Type I error rate would have been greatly inflated as compared with their nominal alpha level.

My third point concerns the distinction between statistical significance and practical significance. As I hope you recall from our earlier discussions, it is possible for $H_0$ to be rejected, with an "impressive" data-based $p$-value (e.g., $p < .0001$), even though the computed sample statistic does not appear to be very dissimilar from the value of the parameter expressed in $H_0$. I also hope you remember my earlier contention that conscientious researchers will either design their studies and/or conduct a more complete analysis of their data with an eye toward avoiding the potential error of figuratively making a mountain out of a molehill.

## EXCERPT 17.28 • *The Bonferroni Adjustment Procedure*

A survey covering issues dealing with the employment provisions of the ADA was conducted with private-sector employers. . . . The analyses presented in this article used primarily chi-square tests [and when] low expected cell counts were encountered, Fisher's exact test was used in place of the chi-square test. The $p < .05$ significance level was used throughout, applying Bonferroni's adjustment procedure for multiple statistical tests within issue categories where required to control for compounding comparison-wise Type I error rates.

*Source:* Bruyère, S. M., Erickson, W. A., and VanLooy, S. A. (2006). The impact of business size on employer ADA response. *Rehabilitation Counseling Bulletin*, *49*(4), pp. 197, 198.

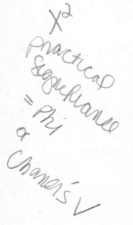

There are several ways researchers can demonstrate sensitivity to the distinction between practical significance and statistical significance. In our examination of *t*-tests, *F*-tests, and tests on correlation coefficients, we have seen that these options include (1) conducting, in the design phase of the investigation, a power analysis so as to determine the proper sample size; (2) calculating, after the data have been collected, an effect size estimate; and (3) computing, once again after the data have been gathered, a post hoc measure of power. These three options are as readily available to researchers who use the various test procedures covered in this chapter as they are to those who conduct *t*-tests, *F*-tests, or tests involving one or more correlation coefficients.

The main statistical technique discussed in this chapter was chi square. To judge whether a chi-square-based effect is small, medium, or large, researchers usually convert their computed value of $\chi^2$ into phi or Cramer's *V*. If you review Excerpts 17.17 and 17.19, you find examples where both phi and *V* were used by applied researchers to deal with the issue of practical significance. For ease of reference, Table 17.1 contains the standard criteria for judging these two estimates of effect size.

Before concluding this chapter, there is one more excerpt I'd like to share with you. In Excerpt 17.29, you will see the results of a post hoc power analysis conducted in conjunction with chi-square tests. On the one hand, I'd like to compliment these researchers for knowing about the concept of statistical power. On the other hand, doesn't the observed power estimate seem a wee bit on the small side of adequate?

**TABLE 17.1** *Effect Size Criteria for Use with Tests on Frequencies*

| *Effect Size Measure* | *Small* | *Medium* | *Large* |
|---|---|---|---|
| Cramer's *V* | .10 | .30 | .50 |
| Phi | .10 | .30 | .50 |

*Note:* These standards for judging relationship strength are quite general and should be changed to fit the unique goals of any given research investigation.

### EXCERPT 17.29 • *Chi Square and Power*

First, we tested whether participants in the two interventions differed in their five categories of vocational outcomes at three follow-up points in time: 9 months, 18 months, and 24 months after their baseline assessment. Table 3 [not shown here] provides the results of these chi-square analyses. . . . Given our failure to find differences between the experimental and control groups, we conducted post hoc power analyses to determine the power the study had to detect the observed difference between groups. For the first primary outcome (percentage employed in a competitive job at 9 months), the observed difference was 8.5% (PVR) vs. 4% (ESVR). With the available sample size, the power of this test was 7%. For the second primary outcome (percentage employed in a competitive, supported, or transitional job at 9 months), the observed difference was 11.9% (PVR) vs. 12% (ESVR). With the available sample size, the power of this test was 2%.

*Source:* Rogers, E. S., Anthony, W. A., Lyass, A., and Penk, W. E. (2006). A randomized clinical trial of vocational rehabilitation for people with psychiatric disabilities. *Rehabilitation Counseling Bulletin, 49*(3), pp. 148, 151–152.

---

## Review Terms

Binomial test
Chi square
Cochran Q test
Contingency coefficient
Contingency table
Cramer's measure of association
Expected frequency
Fisher's Exact Test
Frequencies
Goodness-of-fit test
Homogeneity of proportions
Independent-samples chi-square test

Large-sample approximation
McNemar's chi-square test
Observed frequency
One-sample chi-square test
Pearson chi square
Percentages
Proportions
Sign test
Test of independence
Test of normality
Yates' correction for discontinuity

---

## The Best Items in the Companion Website

1. An interactive online quiz (with immediate feedback provided) covering Chapter 17.
2. Ten misconceptions about the content of Chapter 17.
3. One of the best passages from Chapter 17: "Consider the Null Hypothesis before Looking at the *p*-Level."
4. Four interactive online resources.
5. The first of the two jokes, because it deals with one of the statistical tests covered in Chapter 17.

To access chapter objectives, practice tests, weblinks, and flashcards, visit the companion website at www.ablongman.com/huck5e.

Research
Navigator.c⊕m

## Fun Exercises inside Research Navigator

**1. If women could choose their first child's sex, would mothers want girls?**

In this study, 230 college men and 239 college women were asked, among other things, (1) whether they wanted their future first-born child to be a boy or a girl, and (2) whether they would determine (i.e., actively choose) that child's sex, if such were an option. Several chi-square tests were conducted in this study. One compared the stated preferences of the full groups of men and women, while another compared the stated preferences of just those individuals who said that they would determine their first-born's sex. What do you think these chi-square tests revealed? And do you think either group of women stated a preference for a girl? To find out what this study revealed, refer to the PDF version of the research report in the Psychology database of ContentSelect, look at Tables 1 and 2, and read the results on page 233.

D. Swetkis, F. D. Gilroy, & R. Steinbacher. Firstborn preference and attitudes toward using sex selection technology. *Journal of Genetic Psychology.* Located in the PSYCHOLOGY database of ContentSelect.

**2. Does psychotherapy help people get off antidepressant drugs?**

This study focused on individuals who had been on antidepressant drugs. One group was made up of 30 individuals who had been receiving psychotherapy for one year; the other group, matched to the first group (on the basis of age and sex), had not been in therapy. For the dependent variable, each person in each group was classified as either taking or not taking antidepressant drugs. The percentage still taking antidepressants was 47% (14 out of 30) in one group and 97% (29 out of 30) in the other group. A comparison of these two percentages, using McNemar's test for paired data, indicated a statistically significant difference (with $p < 0.001$). Which of the two groups—those in therapy or those not in therapy—do you think had all but one of its members still using antidepressant drugs at the point data were collected? Are you sure of your guess? To find out if you are right, refer to the PDF version of the research report in the Nursing, Health, and Medicine database of ContentSelect, go to page 630, and read the first two paragraphs in the section entitled "Antidepressant prescribing and patients in comparison group 1."

M. Ashworth, J. Wastie, F. Reid, & S. Clement. The effects of psychotherapeutic interventions upon psychotropic prescribing and consultation rates in one general practice. *Journal of Mental Health.* Located in the NURSING, HEALTH, AND MEDICINE database of ContentSelect.

## Review Questions and Answers begin on page 513.

# 18

# Statistical Tests on Ranks (Nonparametric Tests)

In the previous chapter, we examined a variety of test procedures designed for data that are qualitative, or nominal, in nature. Whether dealing with frequencies, percentages, or proportions, those tests involved response categories devoid of any quantitative meaning. For example, when a chi square test was used in Excerpt 17.11 to compare the gender composition of three groups involved in an experiment dealing with the pain and distress of pediatric injection patients, neither the grouping variable (made up of three conditions: music, nonmusic, and control) nor the response variable (gender of the group participants) involved categories that had any numerical meaning.

We now turn our attention to a group of test procedures that utilize the simplest kind of quantitative data: ranks. In a sense, we are returning to this topic (rather than starting from scratch), since in Chapter 9, I pointed out how researchers can set up and evaluate null hypotheses concerning Spearman's rho and Kendall's tau. As I hope you recall from Chapter 3, each of these correlational procedures involves an analysis of ranked data.

Within the context of this chapter, we consider five of the many test procedures that have been developed for use with ordinal data. These **nonparametric** procedures are the median test, the Mann-Whitney $U$ test, the Kruskal-Wallis one-way analysis of variance of ranks, the Wilcoxon matched-pairs signed-ranks test, and the Friedman two-way analysis of variance of ranks. Excerpts 18.1 through 18.5 show how researchers typically refer to these nonparametric test procedures.[1]

The five test procedures considered in this chapter are not the only ones that involve ranked data, but they are the ones used most frequently by applied

---

[1]The term *nonparametric* is simply a label for various test procedures that involve ranked data. In contrast, the term **parametric** is used to denote those tests (e.g., $t$ and $F$) that are built on a different statistical view of the data—and usually a more stringent set of assumptions regarding the population(s) associated with the study's sample(s).

**EXCERPTS 18.1–18.5 • *Five Test Procedures That Involve Ranked Data***

A two-sample median test was also conducted and the results were identical.

*Source:* Hyman, O. (2005). Religiosity and secondary traumatic stress in Israeli-Jewish body handlers. *Journal of Traumatic Stress, 18*(5), p. 493.

---

The two-tailed Mann–Whitney *U*-test was used to analyze differences between the nonparametric data of the groups in experiments 1 and 2.

*Source:* Verdaasdonk, E. G. G., Stassen, L. P. S., Monteny, L. J., and Dankelman, J. (2006). Validation of a new basic virtual reality simulator for training of basic endoscopic skills. *Surgical Endoscopy, 20*(3), p. 514.

---

We now examine horizontal equity from a nonparametric perspective. Specifically, we used the Kruskal–Wallis nonparametric test.

*Source:* Cornia, G. C., and Slade, B. A. (2006). Horizontal inequity in the property taxation of apartment, industrial, office, and retail properties. *National Tax Journal, 59*(1), p. 50.

---

Changes between evaluations were tested with the Wilcoxon signed-ranks test.

*Source:* Forsberg, A., Press, R., Einarsson, U., de Pedro-Cuesta, J., and Holmqvist, L. W. (2005). Disability and health-related quality of life in Guillain–Barré syndrome during the first two years after onset: A prospective study. *Clinical Rehabilitation, 19*(8), p. 903.

---

To give an overall impression of the variation among the different components, Friedman's two-way analysis of variance by ranks was used.

*Source:* Jackson, D. J. R., Carr, S. C., Edwards, M., Thorn, K., Allfree, N., Hooks, J., and Inkson, K. (2005). Exploring the dynamics of New Zealand's talent flow. *New Zealand Journal of Psychology, 34*(2), p. 114.

researchers. Because these five tests are used so often, we will examine each one separately in an effort to clarify the research "setting" for which each test is appropriate, the typical format used to report the test's results, and the proper meaning of a rejected null hypothesis. First, however, we need to consider the three ways in which a researcher can obtain the ranked data needed for any of the five tests.

## Obtaining Ranked Data

One obvious way for a researcher to obtain ranked data is to ask each research participant to rank a set of objects, statements, ideas, or other things. When this is done, numbers get attached to the things by the persons doing the ranking, with the numbers

1, 2, 3, and so on used to indicate an ordering from best to worst, most important to least important, strongest to weakest, and the like. The resulting numbers are **ranks.**[2]

In Excerpt 18.6, we see a case where ranks were used in a research study. In the study associated with this excerpt, the researchers wanted to see if a computer program could develop alterations of original line drawings that would be liked as much as the pictures humans create when they alter such pictures to make them "seem better." The data provided by the college students who evaluated the pictures were analyzed by two of the statistical procedures considered in this chapter, the Wilcoxon signed-ranks test and Friedman's two-way ANOVA for ranks.

**EXCERPT 18.6 • *Obtaining Ordinal Data by Having People Rank a Set of Things***

The participant sorted the 10 pictures from 1 (*like least*) to 10 (*like most*) and returned the packet with the sorted pictures. The participants sorted the pictures during the last 10 min of their class.

*Source:* Wolach, A. H., and McHale, M. A. (2005). Line spacing in Mondrian paintings and computer-generated modifications. *Journal of General Psychology, 132*(3), p. 286.

A second way for a researcher to obtain ranks is to observe or arrange the study's participants such that each one has an ordered position within the group. For example, we could go to the Boston Marathon, stand near the finish line and hold a list of all contestants' names, then record each person's standing (first, second, third, or whatever) as he or she completes the race. Or, we might go into a classroom, ask the students to line up by height, and then request that the students count off beginning at the tall end of the line.[3]

The third way for a researcher to obtain ranks involves a two-step process. First, each participant is independently measured on some variable of interest with a measuring instrument that yields a score indicative of that person's absolute standing with respect to the numerical continuum associated with the variable. Then, the scores from the group of participants are compared and converted into ranks to indicate each person's relative standing within the group.

In Excerpt 18.7, we see a case in which this two-step process was used. The data originally collected by the researchers were percentages. Each child's percentage score was determined by dividing the number of words read aloud by the

---

[2]Ranks are often confused with ratings. Ranks indicate an ordering of things, with each number generated by having a research participant make a *relative* comparison of the things being ranked. **Ratings,** on the other hand, indicate amount, and they are generated by having a research participant make an *independent* evaluation of each thing being rated (perhaps on a 0-to-100 scale).

[3]Although none of the tests discussed in this chapter could be applied to just the ranks obtained in our running or line-up-by-height examples, two of the tests could be used if we simply classified each subject into one of two or more subgroups (e.g., gender) in addition to noting his or her order on the running speed or height variable.

## EXCERPT 18.7 • *Converting Ratio-Level Data into Ranks*

Each month, a researcher visited the school and asked all 16 children to read passages from a standard English textbook into the Dragon STT program. From October, they [the researchers] took measurements of the students' reading, comparing the resultant text produced by Dragon with the correct text, and calculated the percentage of correctly identified words. . . . Analysis of the data was done at the end of the experiment. At this time, the children were ranked for each of the readings in each of the months in order of the percentage of words correctly identified by Dragon for each passage.

*Source:* Mitra, S., Tooley, J., Inamdar, P., and Dixond, P. (2003). Improving English pronunciation: An automated instructional approach. *Information Technologies & International Development, 1*(1), pp. 79, 80.

child into the number of words correctly identified by a computer program that could "listen" to the oral reading. As indicated in this excerpt, the 16 children were then ranked on the basis of the percentage scores. These ranks were then used in nonparametric statistical procedures to address the study's research questions.

## *Reasons for Converting Scores on a Continuous Variable into Ranks*

It may seem odd that researchers sometimes engage in the two-step, data-conversion process whereby scores on a variable of interest are converted into ranks. Since the original scores typically are interval or ratio in nature, whereas the ranks are ordinal, such a conversion might appear to be ill-advised in that it brings about a "loss of information." There are, however, three reasons why researchers might consider the benefits associated with the scores-to-ranks conversion to outweigh the loss-of-information liability.

One reason why researchers often change raw scores into ranks is that the test procedures developed for use with ranks involve fewer assumptions than do the test procedures developed for use with interval- or ratio-level data. For example, the assumptions of normality and homogeneity of variance that underlie $t$- and $F$-tests do not serve as the basis for some of the tests considered in this chapter. As Excerpts 18.8 and 18.9 make clear, researchers sometimes convert their raw scores into ranks because the original data involved nonnormality and/or heterogeneity of variance.

A second reason why researchers convert raw scores to ranks is related to the issue of sample size. As you will recall, $t$- and $F$-tests tend to be robust to violations of underlying assumptions when the samples being compared are the same size and large. When the $n$s differ or are small, however, nonnormality and/or heterogeneity of variance in the population(s) can cause the $t$- or $F$-test to function differently than

## EXCERPTS 18.8–18.9 • *Nonnormality and Heterogeneous Variances as Reasons for Converting Scores to Ranks*

Because there was evidence of non-normality of the distribution of home advantage values, nonparametric methods were employed in the analysis. Friedman's test was used to investigate differences between the three time periods.

*Source:* Wilkinson, T., and Pollard, R. (2006). A temporary decline in home advantage when moving to a new stadium. *Journal of Sport Behavior, 29*(2), p. 193.

-------------------------------------------------------------------------------

Nonparametric analyses were performed because of the heterogeneity of variance.

*Source:* Behne, T., Carpenter, M., Call, J., and Tomasello, M. (2005). Unwilling versus unable: Infants' understanding of intentional action. *Developmental Psychology, 41*(2), p. 334.

intended. For this reason, some researchers will turn to one of the five test procedures discussed in this chapter if they have small samples or if their *n*s differ. In Excerpt 18.10, we see a case where concerns about sample size prompted the researchers to use nonparametric tests.

## EXCERPT 18.10 • *Sample Size as a Reason for Converting Scores to Ranks*

In the case of nightmare frequency, we obtained small groups of subjects, and we decided to use for comparative analysis a nonparametric methodology (Mann–Whitney's *U* test), because, given Bryman and Cramer's (1990) indications, this is the most appropriate option when the sample size is less than 15.

*Source:* Miró, E., and Martínez, M. P. (2005). Affective and personality characteristics in function of nightmare prevalence, nightmare distress, and interference due to nightmares. *Dreaming, 15*(2), p. 95.

Regarding sample size, it is legitimate to ask the simple question, "When are samples so small that parametric tests should be avoided even if the *n*s are equal?" Unfortunately, there is no clear-cut answer to this question because different mathematical statisticians have responded to this query with conflicting responses. According to one statistician, researchers should use nonparametric tests if their sample size is 6 or less, even if all samples are the same size. According to a different statistician, parametric tests can be used with very small samples as long as the *n*s don't differ. I mention this controversy simply to alert you to the fact that some researchers use nonparametric tests because they have small sample sizes, even though the *n*s are equal.[4]

[4]The two statisticians referred to in this paragraph are Sidney Siegel and John Gaito.

The third reason for converting raw scores to ranks is related to the fact that raw scores sometimes appear to be more precise than they really are. In other words, a study's raw scores may provide only ordinal information about the study's subjects even though the scores are connected to a theoretical numerical continuum associated with the dependent variable. In such a case, it would be improper to treat the raw scores as if they indicate the absolute distance that separates any two participants that have different scores when in fact the raw scores only indicate, in a relative sense, which person has more of the measured characteristic than the other.

Consider, for example, the popular technique of having participants respond to a **Likert-type attitude inventory.** With this kind of measuring device, the respondent indicates a level of agreement or disagreement with each of several statements by selecting one of four or five options that typically include "strongly agree" and "strongly disagree" on the ends. In scoring a respondent's answer sheet, consecutive integers are typically assigned to the response options (e.g., 1, 2, 3, 4, 5) and then the respondent's total score is obtained by adding together the individual scores earned on each of the inventory's statements. In this fashion, two people in a study might end up with total scores of 32 and 29.

With Likert-type attitude inventories, the total scores derived from the participant responses are probably only ordinal in nature. For one thing, the arbitrary assignment of consecutive integers to the response options does not likely correspond to any participant's view of how the response options relate to another. Moreover, it is probably the case that certain of the inventory's statements are more highly connected than others to one's reason for holding a positive or negative attitude toward the topic being focused on—yet all statements are equal in their impact on a respondent's total score. For these reasons, it is not very plausible to presume that the resulting total scores possess the characteristic of equal intervals that is embodied in interval (and ratio) levels of measurement.

Excerpts 18.11 and 18.12 illustrate how a concern for level of measurement will sometimes prompt researchers to use nonparametric tests. The word *ordinal* that we see in the first of these excerpts may have been used because the data in that study were ranks. However, other kinds of data can be ordinal if the measurement scale lacks the quality of "equal intervals." (Rulers and thermometers yield numbers on a scale that has equal intervals because a difference of 2 inches or 10° means the same thing anywhere along the scale; in contrast, the numbers associated with most psychological inventories are not characterized by equal intervals.) In Excerpt 18.12, the researchers point out that each child's performance on each task yielded a score of 0, 1, or 2. These data were ordinal, for they divided the group of children into three ordered subgroups based on how they performed on each task.

Now that we have considered how and why a researcher might end up with ranked data, let us take a look at each of the five test procedures that deserve the label "popular nonparametric test." As noted earlier, these test procedures are the

**EXCERPTS 18.11–18.12 •** *Nonnormality and Heterogeneous Variances as Reasons for Converting Scores to Ranks*

Non-parametric statistics were employed as the data were ordinal.

*Source:* Thomas, S. A., and Lincoln, N. B. (2006). Factors relating to depression after stroke. *British Journal of Clinical Psychology, 45*(1), p. 52.

---

Children were asked to solve, for self and for other, two instances each of three types of pretence tasks. Because the range of success for each type of task was limited (0–2 correct), we used a non-parametric test to compare types.

*Source:* Mitchell, R. W., and Neal, M. (2005). Children's understanding of their own and others' mental states. Part A. Self-understanding precedes understanding of others in pretence. *British Journal of Developmental Psychology, 23*(2), p. 189.

median test, the Mann-Whitney $U$ test, the Kruskal-Wallis one-way ANOVA, the Wilcoxon matched-pairs signed-ranks test, and the Friedman two-way ANOVA. In looking at each of these test procedures, I want to focus our attention on the nature of the research setting for which the test is appropriate, the way in which the ranked data are used, the typical format for reporting results, and the meaning of a rejected null hypothesis.

## The Median Test

The **median test** is designed for use when a researcher wishes to compare two or more independent samples. If two such groups are compared, the median test is a nonparametric analog to the independent-samples $t$-test. With three or more groups, it is the nonparametric analog to a one-way ANOVA.

A researcher might select the median test in order to contrast two groups defined by a dichotomous characteristic (e.g., male versus female or experimental versus control) on a dependent variable of interest (e.g., throwing ability, level of conformity, or anything else the researcher wishes to measure). Or, the median test might be selected if the researcher wishes to compare three or more groups (that differ in some qualitative fashion) on a measured dependent variable. An example of this latter situation might involve comparing football players, basketball players, and baseball players in terms of their endurance while riding a stationary bicycle.

The null hypothesis of the two-group version of the median test can be stated as $H_0$: $M_1 = M_2$, where the letter $M$ stands for the median in the population and the numerical subscripts serve to identify the first and second populations. If three or more groups are compared using the median test, the null hypothesis takes the same form except that there would be additional $M$s involved in $H_0$. The alternative hypothesis says that the two $M$s differ (if just two groups are being compared) or that at least two of the $M$s differ (in the situation in which three or more groups are being contrasted).

To conduct a median test, the researcher follows a simple three-step procedure. First, the comparison groups are temporarily combined and a single median is determined for the entire set of scores. (This step necessitates that ranks be assigned either to all participants or at least to those who are positioned near the middle of the pack.) In the second step, the comparison groups are reconstituted so that a contingency table can be set up to indicate how many people in each comparison group lie above and below the "grand median" identified in the first step. This contingency table will have as many columns as there are comparison groups, but it will always have two rows (one labeled "above the median," the other labeled "below the median"). Finally, an independent-samples chi-square test is applied to the data in the contingency table to see if the samples differ (in the proportion of cases falling above the combined median) by more than what would be expected by chance alone, presuming that $H_0$ is true.

In Excerpt 18.13, we see a case where a median test was used in an experiment involving two groups. One group was in the "uncertain" condition; the other group was in the control condition. Near the end of this excerpt, you'll see the symbol for chi square. The symbol $\chi^2$ is there because the median test involved analyzing the study's data via a $2 \times 2$ contingency table.

**EXCERPT 18.13 • *The Median Test Used to Compare Two Groups***

People in the uncertain condition were significantly more likely to give a rating above the median than people in the certain condition, $\chi^2(1, N = 34) = 4.60, p = .03$.

*Source:* Wilson, T. D., Centerbar, D. B., Kermer, D. A., and Gilbert, D. T. (2005). The pleasures of uncertainty: Prolonging positive moods in ways people do not anticipate. *Journal of Personality and Social Psychology, 88*(1), p. 10.

In the study associated with Excerpt 18.13, perhaps the researchers set up the contingency table so that the columns corresponded with the groups (uncertain and control) and the rows corresponded to being above or below the grand median, with each person positioned in one of the four cells. If the two frequencies in each column had been about the same, the null hypothesis would have been retained. However, the actual frequencies in the contingency table produced a statistically significant value for chi square, with a greater-than-chance number of people from the uncertain group positioned above the grand median (and a greater-than-chance number of people from the control group below that median).

Excerpt 18.13 is instructive because the researchers use the phrase "the median." Note that this is singular, not plural. Many people mistakenly think that a median test involves a statistical comparison of two sample medians to see if they are far enough apart from each other to permit a rejection of $H_0$. However, there is only one median involved in a median test (the grand median based on the data from all groups), and the statistical question being asked is whether the comparison groups differ significantly in terms of the percentage of each group that lies above this single median. Given any set of scores, it would be possible to change a few scores and thereby change the group medians (making them closer together or further apart) *without* changing the median test's calculated value or *p*. To me, this constitutes proof that the median test is *not* focusing on the individual medians of the comparison groups.

In trying to interpret the results of the median test, one should recognize that the grand median computed from the sample data is unlikely to match the common median found in $H_0$. Because of this, the actual null hypothesis being tested is not that the populations being compared have the same median but rather that the various populations have the same proportion of scores above the value of the median of the combined *samples*. With larger samples, of course, there is likely to be a smaller discrepancy between the median value used to set up the contingency table and the common value of *M* hypothesized to exist in the populations. With small samples, however, it turns out that the median test (despite its name) is not really a test of equal population medians.

As mentioned earlier, the median test can compare two groups or more than two groups. In Excerpt 18.14, we see a case where the median test was used to compare three groups. These three groups were schizophrenic patients with delusions of influence, schizophrenic patients who did not have this kind of delusion, and "normal" controls. As you will see, the median test was used twice in this study,

**EXCERPT 18.14 • *The Median Test Used to Compare Three Groups***

Schizophrenic patients with delusions of influence gave globally more "yes" responses than noninfluenced schizophrenic patients and comparison subjects in both the trials with angular biases (median = 56.5 for influenced patients; median = 39.0 for noninfluenced patients; median = 33.0 for comparison subjects) and temporal biases (median = 53.5 for influenced patients; median = 49.5 for noninfluenced patients; median = 29.0 for comparison subjects). The median test for "yes" responses revealed that the differences between groups were significant both for the 84 trials with angular biases ($\chi^2 = 7.67$, $df = 2$, $p < 0.03$) and the 84 trials with temporal biases ($\chi^2 = 20.49$, $df = 2$, $p < 0.001$).

*Source:* Franck, N., Farrer, C., Georgieff, N., and Marie-Cardine, M. (2001). Defective recognition of one's own actions in patients with schizophrenia. *American Journal of Psychiatry, 158*(3), p. 456.

once on data dealing with angular biases and then a second time on data dealing with temporal biases. Within each of these two sets of data, the score for each individual was equal to the summed performance across 84 trials.

## The Mann-Whitney U Test[5]

**Research Navigator.c☗m**

Mann-Whitney *U* test

The **Mann-Whitney *U* test** is like the two-sample version of the median test in that both tests allow a researcher to compare two independent samples. Although these two procedures are similar in that they are both considered to be nonparametric tests, the Mann-Whitney *U* test is the more powerful of the two. In other words, if the two comparison groups truly do differ from each other, the Mann-Whitney *U* test (as compared to the median test) is less likely to produce a Type II error. This superiority of the Mann-Whitney test comes about because it utilizes more information from the subjects than does the median test.

When using the Mann-Whitney *U* test, the researcher examines the scores made available by measuring the research participants on the variable of interest. Initially, the two comparison groups are lumped together. This is done so that each person can be ranked to reflect his or her standing within the combined group. After the ranks have been assigned, the researcher reconstitutes the two comparison groups. The previously assigned ranks are then examined to see if the two groups are significantly different.

If the two samples being compared came from identical populations, then the **sum of ranks** in one group ought to be approximately equal to the sum of ranks in the other group. For example, if there were four people in each sample and if $H_0$ were true, we would not be surprised if the ranks in one group were 2, 4, 5, and 8 while the ranks in the other group were 1, 3, 6, and 7. Here, the sum of the ranks are 19 and 17, respectively. It *would* be surprising, however, to find (again assuming that $H_0$ is true) that the sum of the ranks are 10 and 26. Such an extreme outcome would occur if the ranks of 1, 2, 3, and 4 were located in one of the samples while the ranks of 5, 6, 7, and 8 were located in the other sample.

To perform a Mann-Whitney *U* test, the researcher computes a sum-of-ranks value for each sample and then inserts these two numerical values into a formula. It is not important for you to know what that formula looks like, but it *is* essential that you understand the simple logic of what is going on. The formula used to analyze the data will produce a calculated value called *U*. Based on the value of *U*, the researcher (or a computer) can then derive a *p*-value that indicates how likely it is, under $H_0$, to have two samples that differ as much or more than do the ones actually used in the study. Small values of *p*, of course, are interpreted to mean that $H_0$ is unlikely to be true.

---

[5]This test is also referred to as the Wilcoxon test, as the Wilcoxon rank-sum test, and as the Wilcoxon-Mann-Whitney test.

In Excerpt 18.15, we see a case in which the Mann-Whitney $U$ test was used three times to compare two groups, once on each of three dependent variables. As you can see, none of these tests yielded a significant result.

Although it is quite easy for a researcher to obtain a calculated value for $U$ from the sample data and to compare that data-based number against a tabled critical value, the task of interpreting a statistically significant result is a bit more difficult, for two reasons. First, the null hypothesis being tested deals not with the ranks used to compute the calculated value but rather with the continuous variable that lies behind or beneath the ranks. For example, if we used a Mann-Whitney $U$ test to compare a sample of men against a sample of women with respect to their order of finish after running a 10-kilometer race, the data collected might very well simply be ranks, with each person's rank indicating his or her place (among all contestants) on crossing the finish line. The null hypothesis, however, would deal with the continuous variable that lies beneath the ranks, which in our hypothetical study is running speed.

The second reason why statistically significant results from Mann-Whitney $U$ tests are difficult to interpret is related to the fact that the rejected null hypothesis says that the two populations have identical distributions. Consequently, rejection of $H_0$ could come about because the populations differ in terms of their central tendencies, their variabilities, and/or their distributional shapes. In practice, however, the Mann-Whitney test is far more sensitive to differences in central tendency, so a statistically significant result is almost certain to mean that the populations have different average scores. But even here, an element of ambiguity remains because the Mann-Whitney $U$ test could cause $H_0$ to be rejected because the two populations differ in terms of their means, or in terms of their medians, or in terms of their modes.

In the situation where the two populations have identical shapes and variances, the Mann-Whitney $U$ test focuses on means, and thus $H_0$: $\mu_1 = \mu_2$. However,

## EXCERPT 18.15 • *The Mann-Whitney U Test*

We also examined several continuous measures of employment success. Because the median value was zero for all these measures and the distributions highly skewed, we employed nonparametric Mann-Whitney $U$'s to examine differences by experimental condition. There were no significant differences between the experimental and control groups on any of the following outcomes: cumulative hours worked in any job ($U = 1429$, $p = 0.646$), total number of jobs held ($U = 1453$, $p = 0.757$), or cumulative dollars earned during the first 9 months of the study ($U = 1447$, $p = 0.713$).

*Source:* Rogers, E. S., Anthony, W. A., Lyass, A., and Penk, W. E. (2006). A randomized clinical trial of vocational rehabilitation for people with psychiatric disabilities. *Rehabilitation Counseling Bulletin, 49*(3), p. 149.

applied researchers rarely know anything about the populations involved in their studies. Therefore, most researchers who find that their Mann-Whitney $U$ test yields a statistically significant result legitimately can conclude only that the two populations probably differ with respect to their averages. Another way of drawing a proper conclusion from a Mann-Whitney $U$ test that causes $H_0$ to be rejected is to say that the scores in one of the populations tend to be larger than scores in the other population. This statement could only be made in a tentative fashion, however, since the statistically significant finding might well represent nothing more than a Type I error.

Take another look at Excerpt 18.15. Each of the three $U$ tests that was conducted produced a $p$-value that was nowhere near the researchers' level of significance (.05). Those $p$s turned out the way they did because the values for $U$ were so large. With the Mann-Whitney $U$ test, there is a direct relationship between $p$ and $U$. (With many other statistical tests, an inverse relationship exists between $p$ and the computed test statistic.)

## The Kruskal-Wallis H Test

Research Navigator.com

Kruskal-Wallis

In those situations in which a researcher wishes to use a nonparametric statistical test to compare two independent samples, the Mann-Whitney $U$ test is typically used to analyze the data. When researchers wish to compare three or more such groups, they more often than not utilize the Kruskal-Wallis $H$ test. Hence, the Kruskal-Wallis procedure can be thought of as an "extension" of the Mann-Whitney procedure in the same way that a one-way ANOVA is typically considered to be an extension of an independent-samples $t$-test.[6]

The fact that the Kruskal-Wallis test is like a one-way ANOVA shows through when one considers the mathematical derivation of the formula for computing the test's calculated value. On a far simpler level, the similarity between these two test procedures shows through when we consider their names. The parametric test we considered in Chapter 11 is called a one-way ANOVA whereas the nonparametric analog to which we now turn our attention is called the **Kruskal-Wallis one-way ANOVA of ranks.** Excerpts 18.16 and 18.17 show how the notion of an analysis of variance pops up in the way researchers describe the Kruskal-Wallis test.

The Kruskal-Wallis test works very much as the Mann-Whitney test does. First, the researcher temporarily combines the comparison groups into a single group. Next, the people in this one group are ranked on the basis of their performance on the dependent variable. Then, the single group is subdivided so as to reestablish the original comparison groups. Finally, each group's sum of ranks is entered into a formula that yields the calculated value. This calculated value, in the

---

[6]When just two groups are compared, the ANOVA $F$-test and the independent-samples $t$-test yield identical results. In a similar fashion, the Kruskal-Wallis and Mann-Whitney tests are mathematically equivalent when used to compare two groups.

### EXCERPTS 18.16–18.17 • *The Kruskal-Wallis Test Referred to as an Analysis of Variance*

To determine if there was any statistical difference between the students' drawings included in the study, a Kruskal-Wallis one-way ANOVA was conducted.

*Source:* Finson, K. D., Thomas, J., and Pedersen, J. (2006). Comparing science teaching styles to students' perceptions of scientists. *School Science and Mathematics, 106*(1), p. 12.

-------------------------------------------------------------------------------------------------------

The nonparametric Kruskal–Wallis (K–W) one-way analysis of variance (ANOVA) by ranks was used to examine group differences in the symptomatology of exercise dependence across at risk for exercise dependence, nondependent–symptomatic, and nondependent–asymptomatic exercisers with exercise behavior (LTEQ) and perfectionism (MPS).

*Source:* Downs, D. S., Hausenblas, H. A., and Nigg, C. R. (2004). Factorial validity and psychometric examination of the Exercise Dependence Scale-Revised. *Measurement in Physical Education & Exercise Science, 8*(4), p. 194.

Kruskal-Wallis test, is labeled $H$. When the data-based $H$ beats the critical value or when the $p$-value associated with $H$ turns out to be smaller than the level of significance, the null hypothesis is rejected.

In Excerpt 18.18, we see a case in which the Kruskal-Wallis test was used to compare three groups of children in terms of pain levels when those children received injections. There were two dependent variables: self-reported pain from the children and pain estimates from an observer. The three groups differed in terms of

### EXCERPT 18.18 • *Use of the Kruskal-Wallis Test*

Participants in the music condition tended to report less pain ($M = 2.67, SD = 2.79$) than participants in the nonmusic ($M = 4.00, SD = 2.55$) and control ($M = 3.53, SD = 2.76$) conditions. Similarly, experimenter ratings were lowest in the music condition ($M = 3.62, SD = 2.31$), followed by the nonmusic ($M = 3.86, SD = 1.68$) and control ($M = 4.53, SD = 2.09$) conditions. A Kruskal-Wallis test was used to examine if these differences were significant across the conditions. Neither the child ratings ($H(2) = 2.39, p > .05$) nor the experimenter ratings ($H(2) = 2.78, p > .05$) were found to be significantly different from each other.

*Source:* Noguchi, L. K. (2006). The effect of music versus nonmusic on behavioral signs of distress and self-report of pain in pediatric injection patients. *Journal of Music Therapy, 43*(1), pp. 26–27.

what the children were doing while the injection was taking place. One group listened to music, a second group listed to a story, and a third group did not listen to anything. Do the results shown in Excerpt 18.18 conform with your expectations?[7]

The Kruskal-Wallis $H$ test and the Mann-Whitney $U$ test are similar not only in how the subjects are ranked and in how the groups' sum-of-ranks values are used to obtain the test's calculated value but also in the null hypothesis being tested and what it means when $H_0$ is rejected. Technically speaking, the null hypothesis of the Kruskal-Wallis $H$ test is that the populations associated with the study's comparison groups are identical with respect to the distributions on the continuous variable that lies beneath the ranks used within the data analysis. Accordingly, a rejection of the $H_0$ could come about because the population distributions are not the same in central tendency, in variability, and/or in shape. In practice, however, the Kruskal-Wallis test focuses primarily on central tendency. In fact, two well-known statisticians—Leonard Marascuilo and Maryellen McSweeney—recently asserted that "the Kruskal-Wallis test is not too sensitive to differences in spread or form" and that "rejection of $H_0$ via the $H$ statistic is almost certain to be equivalent to differences in mean, median, center, or some other measure of shift."[8]

While the Mann-Whitney and Kruskal-Wallis tests are similar in many respects, they differ in the nature of the decision rule used to decide whether $H_0$ should be rejected. With the Mann-Whitney test, $H_0$ is rejected if the data-based $U$ turns out to be smaller than the critical value. In contrast, the Kruskal-Wallis $H_0$ is rejected when the researcher's calculated $H$ is larger than the critical value.[9] In Excerpt 18.18, therefore, it was the small values of $H$ that caused both test results to be nonsignificant.

Whenever the Kruskal-Wallis $H$ test leads to a rejection of $H_0$, there remains uncertainty as to which specific populations are likely to differ from one another. In other words, the Kruskal-Wallis procedure functions very much as an "omnibus" test. Consequently, when such a test leads to a rejection of $H_0$, the researcher will normally turn to a post hoc analysis so as to derive more specific conclusions from the data. Within such post hoc investigations, comparison groups are typically compared in a pairwise fashion.

The post hoc procedure used most frequently following a statistically significant $H$ test is the Mann-Whitney $U$ test. Excerpts 18.19 and 18.20 illustrate the use of the Mann-Whitney $U$ test in post hoc investigation following rejection of the Kruskal-Wallis null hypothesis. When used in this capacity, most researchers use the Bonferroni procedure for adjusting the level of significance of each post hoc comparison.

[7]In Excerpt 18.18, you can see that the researchers presented means and standard deviations for each of the three groups on each of the two dependent variables. In light of the fact that the group comparisons were made using a Kruskal-Wallis nonparametric test, I would have expected to see medians and IQR values rather than $M$s and $SD$s.

[8]L. A. Marascuilo and M. McSweeney. (1977). *Nonparametric and distribution-free methods for the social sciences.* Monterey, Calif.: Brooks/Cole, p. 305.

[9]If $U$ or $H$ turns out equal to the critical value, $H_0$ is rejected. Such an outcome, however, is quite unlikely.

**EXCERPTS 18.19–18.20 • *Use of the Mann-Whitney U Test within a Post Hoc Investigation***

We used the Kruskal-Wallis one-way analysis of variance for ranks to test for overall differences among the 3 age groups' values importance ratings. Where significant differences were found, 2-group comparisons were made with the Mann-Whitney $U$ test to determine which of the age groups differed.

*Source:* Nosse, L. J., and Sagiv, L. (2005). Theory-based study of the basic values of 565 physical therapists. *Physical Therapy, 85*(9), p. 842.

------------------------------------------------------------------------

Kruskal–Wallis tests examined omnibus differences among the four clusters, followed by post hoc Mann–Whitney $U$ tests, which compared each cluster with every other.

*Source:* Petry, N. M. (2005). Stages of change in treatment-seeking pathological gamblers. *Journal of Consulting and Clinical Psychology, 73*(2), p. 314.

## The Wilcoxon Matched-Pairs Signed-Ranks Test

Research
Navigator.c⊛m

Wilcoxon
matched-pairs
signed-ranks test

Researchers frequently wish to compare two related samples of data generated by measuring the same people twice (e.g., in a pre/post sense) or by measuring two groups of matched individuals just once. If the data are interval or ratio in nature and if the relevant underlying assumptions are met, the researcher will probably utilize a correlated *t*-test to compare the two samples. On occasion, however, that kind of parametric test cannot be used because the data are ordinal or because the *t*-test assumptions are untenable (or considered by the researcher to be a nuisance). In such situations, the two related samples are likely to be compared using the **Wilcoxon matched-pairs signed-ranks test.**

In conducting the **Wilcoxon test,** the researcher (or a computer) must do five things. First, each pair of scores is examined so as to obtain a *change* score (for the case where a single group of people has been measured twice) or a *difference* score (for the case where the members of two matched samples have been measured just once). These scores are then ranked, either from high to low or from low to high. The third step involves attaching a + or a − sign to each rank. (In the one-group-measured-twice situation, these signs will indicate whether a person's second score turned out to be higher or lower than the first score. In the two-samples-measured-once situation, these signs will indicate whether the people in one group earned higher or lower scores than their counterparts in the other group.) In the fourth step, the researcher simply looks to see which sign appears less frequently and then adds up the ranks that have that sign. Finally, the researcher labels the sum of the ranks that have the least frequent sign as *T*, considers *T* to be the calculated value, and compares *T* against a tabled critical value.

With computers readily available to do the computations, the researcher has a much easier task when conducting a Wilcoxon test. The raw data are simply entered into the computer and then, with a click of a button, the calculated value appears on the computer screen. The way many statistics programs are set up, this calculated value for the Wilcoxon test will be a $z$-score rather than a numerical value for $T$.

In Excerpt 18.21, we see a case in which the Wilcoxon matched-pairs signed-ranks test was used in a study dealing with the artistic drawing capability of sixth-grade school children. Both groups of children in this study received two 55-minute lessons from an artist, but not at the same time. A "cross-over" design was used, meaning that the children who initially served as the control group during the first week of the study received the art lessons during the following week. In a similar fashion, the experimental group was taught by the artist during the first week but not the second. A Wilcoxon test was used within each group of children to compare their drawing scores at the three points at which data were collected.

**EXCERPT 18.21 • *Wilcoxon's Matched-Pairs Signed-Ranks Test***

A Wilcoxon Matched Pairs Signed Ranks Test (Siegel, 1957) was carried out within the two groups across drawings (pretest to posttest-1 and follow up; pretest-1 to pretest-2 and pretest-2 to posttest for the control group). For the experimental group, there was a significant difference between the pre and posttest-1 scores ($Z = -4.042$; $p = .0001$). This difference was maintained for the pre to follow up ($Z = -4.3$; $p = .0001$). The comparison between posttest-1 and follow up was also significant ($Z = -2.188$; $p = .03$). For the control group, comparisons between pretest-1 and posttest-1 were not significant ($Z = .783$; $p = .4334$; NS). However, after training, the scores of the control group improved on the posttest-2. This difference was significant ($Z = -3.982$; $p = .0001$).

*Source:* Snow, C. S., and McLaughlin, T. F. (2005). Effects of teaching perspective in a structured and systematic way on still life drawing of elementary students: An empirical study. *Educational Research Quarterly, 28*(3), pp. 23–24.

When the Wilcoxon test leads to a numerical value for $T$, the researcher's conclusion either to reject or to retain $H_0$ is based on a decision rule like that used within the Mann-Whitney $U$ test. Simply stated, that decision rule gives the researcher permission to reject $H_0$ when the data-based value of $T$ is equal to or smaller than the tabled critical value. (This is because a direct relationship exists between $T$ and $p$.) On the other hand, if the Wilcoxon test's calculated value is $z$, the decision-rule is just the opposite. Here, it will be large values of $z$ that permit the null hypothesis to be rejected.

Although it is easy to conduct a Wilcoxon test, the task of interpreting the final result is more challenging. The null hypothesis says that the populations associated with the two sets of sample data are each symmetrical around the same common point. This translates into a statement that the population of change (or difference) scores is symmetrical around a median value of zero. Interpreting the outcome of a Wilcoxon matched-pairs signed-ranks test is problematic because the null hypothesis could be false because the population of change/difference scores is not symmetric, because the population median is not equal to zero, or because the population is not symmetrical around a median other than zero. Accordingly, if the Wilcoxon test leads to a statistically significant finding, neither you nor the researcher will know the precise reason why $H_0$ has been rejected.

There are two different ways to clarify the situation when one wants to interpret a significant finding from the Wilcoxon test. First, such a test can be interpreted to mean that the two populations, each associated with one of the samples of data used to compute the difference/change scores, are probably not identical to each other. That kind of interpretation is not too satisfying, since the two populations could differ in any number of ways. The second interpretation one can draw if the Wilcoxon test produces a small $p$-value is that the two populations probably have different medians. (This is synonymous to saying that the population of difference/change scores is probably not equal to zero.) This interpretation is legitimate, however, only in the situation where it is plausible to assume that both populations have the same shape.

## Friedman's Two-Way Analysis of Variance of Ranks

The Friedman test is like the Wilcoxon test in that both procedures were developed for use with related samples. The primary difference between the Wilcoxon and Friedman tests is that the former test can accommodate just two related samples whereas the Friedman test can be used with two or more such samples. Because of this, **Friedman's two-way analysis of variance of ranks** can be thought of as the nonparametric equivalent of the one-factor repeated-measures ANOVA that we considered in Chapter 14.[10]

To illustrate the kind of situation to which the Friedman test could be applied, suppose you and several other individuals are asked to independently evaluate the quality of the five movies nominated for this year's Best Picture award from the Academy of Motion Pictures. I might ask you and the other people in this study to rank the five movies on the basis of whatever criteria you typically use when evaluating movie quality. Or, I might ask you to rate each of the movies (possibly on a 0-to-100 scale), thus providing me with data that I could convert into ranks. One way or the other, I could end up with a set of five ranks from each person indicating his or her opinion of the five movies.

If the five movies being evaluated are equally good, we would expect the movies to be about the same in terms of the sum of the ranks assigned to them. In other words, movie A ought to receive some high ranks, some medium ranks, and some low ranks if it is truly no better or worse than the other movies up for the big award. That would also be the case for each of the other four movies. The Friedman

---

[10]Although the Friedman and Wilcoxon tests are similar in that they both were designed for use with correlated samples of data, the Friedman test actually is an extension of the sign test.

test treats the data in just this manner, because the main ingredient is the sum of ranks assigned to each movie.

Once the sum of ranks are computed for the various things being compared, they are inserted into a formula that yields the test's calculated value. I will not discuss here the details of that formula, or even present it. Instead, I want to focus on three aspects of what pops out of that formula. First, the calculated value is typically symbolized as $\chi^2_r$ (or sometimes simply as $\chi^2$). Second, large values of $\chi^2_r$ suggest that $H_0$ is not true. Third, the value of $\chi^2_r$ is referred to a null distribution of such values so as to determine the data-based $p$-value and/or to decide whether or not the null hypothesis should be rejected.

Excerpt 18.22 illustrates the use of the Friedman test. The study associated with this excerpt was concerned with art, just as Excerpt 18.21 was. Here, however, the study was focused on judging pictures rather than producing them. We considered this same study earlier in this chapter near the beginning of the section called "Obtaining Ranked Data." You might want to review that brief description of this investigation so you can better understand what is contained in Excerpt 18.22.

**EXCERPT 18.22 •** *Friedman's Two-Way Analysis of Variance of Ranks*

We used a Friedman two-way analysis of variance (ANOVA) by ranks to compare the rankings for the 10 pictures. Table 1 [not shown here] shows the medians (Mdns) and mean sums of ranks (MSR) for the 10 pictures (from the picture with the lowest MSR to the picture with the highest). The Friedman two-way ANOVA by ranks provided evidence for significant differences among the 10 rankings, $\chi^2(9) = 48.47, p < .05$.

*Source:* Wolach, A. H., and McHale, M. A. (2005). Line spacing in Mondrian paintings and computer-generated modifications. *Journal of General Psychology, 132*(3), p. 288.

If the Friedman test leads to a rejection of the null hypothesis when three or more things (such as movies in our hypothetical example) are compared, you are likely to see a post hoc follow-up test utilized to compare the things that have been ranked. Although many test procedures can be used within such a post hoc investigation, you will likely see the Wilcoxon matched-pairs signed-ranks test employed to make all possible pairwise comparisons. In using the Wilcoxon test in this fashion, the researcher should use the Bonferroni adjustment procedure to protect against an inflated Type I error rate.

## Large-Sample Versions of the Tests on Ranks

Near the end of Chapter 17, I pointed out how researchers will sometimes conduct a $z$-test when dealing with frequencies, percentages, or proportions. Whenever this occurs, researchers put their data into a special formula that yields a calculated value called *z*, and then the data-based *p*-value is determined by referring the calculated value to the normal distribution. Any *z*-test, therefore, can be conceptualized as a "normal curve test."

In certain situations, the *z*-test represents nothing more than an option available to the researcher, with the other option(s) being mathematically equivalent to the *z*-test. In other situations, however, the *z*-test represents a **large-sample approximation** to some other test. In Chapter 17, I pointed out how the sign, binomial, and McNemar procedures can be performed using a *z*-test if the sample sizes are large enough. The formula used to produce the *z* calculated value in these large-sample approximations varies across these test procedures, but that issue is of little concern to consumers of the research literature.

Inasmuch as tests on nominal data can be conducted using *z*-tests when the sample(s) are large, it should not be surprising that large-sample approximations exist for several of the test procedures considered in the present chapter. To be more specific, you are likely to encounter studies in which the calculated value produced by the Mann-Whitney *U* test is not *U*, studies in which the calculated value produced by the Kruskal-Wallis one-way analysis of variance of ranks is not *H*, and studies in which the calculated value produced by the Wilcoxon matched-pairs signed-ranks test is not *T*. Excerpts 18.23 through 18.25 illustrate such cases.

**EXCERPTS 18.23–18.25 • *Large-Sample Versions of the Mann-Whitney, Kruskal-Wallis, and Wilcoxon Tests***

ESM compliance did not differ significantly by gender, school type, or risk group: the median number of valid responses was 37 for HR and 38 for LR participants, Mann–Whitney *U* test, $Z = 0.99, p = .32$.

*Source:* Schneiders, J., Nicolson, N. A., Berkhof, J., Feron, F. J., van Os, J., and deVries, M. W. (2006). Mood reactivity to daily negative events in early adolescence: Relationship to risk for psychopathology. *Developmental Psychology, 42*(3), p. 547.

A Kruskal-[Wallis] H test indicated a significant relation between drawing level on how often children reportedly draw, $\chi^2(df = 3) = 10.06, p = .018$.

*Source:* Braswell, G. S., and Callanan, M. A. (2003). Learning to draw recognizable graphic representations during mother-child interactions. *Merrill-Palmer Quarterly, 49*(4), p. 487.

Only in Year 11 was there a significant difference between the examination grades predicted by the students and by their teacher (Wilcoxon matched-pairs signed-ranks test, $z = -5.251, p < .000$), with teachers predicting higher grades. . . .

*Source:* Graham, S. J. (2004). Giving up on modern foreign languages? Students' perceptions of learning French. *Modern Language Journal, 88*(2), p. 177.

In Excerpts 18.23 and 18.25, we see that the calculated value in the large-sample versions of the Mann-Whitney and Wilcoxon tests is a $z$-value. In contrast, the calculated value for the large-sample version of the Kruskal-Wallis test is a chi-square value. These excerpts thus illustrate nicely the fact that many of the so-called large-sample versions of nonparametric tests yield a $p$-value that is based on the normal distribution. Certain of these tests, however, are connected to the chi-square distribution.

The Friedman test procedure—like the Mann-Whitney, Kruskal-Wallis, and Wilcoxon procedures—can be conducted using a large sample approximation. Most researchers do this by comparing their calculated value for $\chi_r^2$ against a chi-square distribution in order to obtain a $p$-value. If you look again at Excerpt 18.22, you will see a case in which the Friedman test was conducted in this fashion.

It should be noted that the median test is inherently a large-sample test to begin with. That is the case because this test requires that the data be cast into a $2 \times 2$ contingency table from which a chi-square calculated value is then derived. Because this chi-square test requires sufficiently large expected cell frequencies, the only option to the regular, "large-sample" median test is Fisher's Exact Test. Fisher's test, used within this context, could be construed as the "small-sample" version of the median test.

Before concluding this discussion of the large-sample versions of the tests considered in this chapter, it seems appropriate to ask the simple question, "How large must the sample(s) be in order for these tests to function as well as their more exact, small-sample counterparts?" The answer to this question varies depending on the test being considered. The Mann-Whitney $z$-test, for example, works well if both $n$s are larger than 10 (or if one of the $n$s is larger than 20) while the Wilcoxon $z$-test performs adequately when its $n$ is greater than 25. The Kruskal-Wallis chi-square test works well when there are more than three comparison groups or when the $n$s are greater than 5. The Friedman chi-square test functions nicely when there are more than four things being ranked or more than 10 subjects doing the ranking.

Although not used very often, other large-sample procedures have been devised for use with the Mann-Whitney, Kruskal-Wallis, Wilcoxon, and Friedman tests. Some involve using the ranked data within complex formulas. Others involve using the ranked data within $t$- or $F$-tests. Still others involve the analysis of the study's data through two different formulas, the computation of an average calculated value, and then reference to a specially formed critical value. Although not now widely used, some of these alternative procedures may gain popularity among applied researchers in the coming years.

## Ties

Whenever researchers rank a set of scores, they may encounter the case of **tied observations.** For example, there are two sets of ties in this hypothetical set of 10 scores: 8, 0, 4, 3, 5, 4, 7, 1, 4, 5. Or, ties can occur when the original data take the form of ranks. Examples here would include the tenth and eleventh runners in a race crossing the finish line simultaneously, or a judge in a taste test indicating that two of several wines equally deserve the blue ribbon.

With the median test, tied scores do not create a problem. If the tied observations occur within the top half or the bottom half of the pooled group of scores, the ties can be disregarded since all of the scores are easily classified as being above or below the grand median. If the scores in the middle of the pooled data set are tied, the "above" and "below" categories can be defined by a numerical value that lies adjacent to the tied scores. For example, if the 10 scores in the preceding paragraph had come from two groups being compared using a median test, high scores could be defined as anything above 4 while low scores could be defined as less than or equal to 4. (Another way of handling ties at the grand median is simply to drop those scores from the analysis.)

If tied observations occur when the Mann-Whitney, Kruskal-Wallis, Wilcoxon, or Friedman tests are being used, researchers will typically do one of three things. First, they can apply mean ranks to the tied scores. (The procedure for computing mean ranks was described in Chapter 3 in the section dealing with Kendall's tau.) Second, they can drop the tied observations from the data set and subject the remaining, untied scores to the statistical test. Third, they can use a special version of the test procedure developed to handle tied observations.

In Excerpts 18.26 and 18.27, we see two cases in which the third of these three options was selected. In both of these cases, the phrase *corrected for ties* is an unambiguous signal that the tied scores were left in the data set and that a special formula was used to compute the calculated value.

### EXCERPTS 18.26–18.27 • *Using Special Formulas to Accommodate Tied Observations in the Data*

As shown by a two-tailed Mann-Whitney $U$-test, this sex difference was significant, $U = 16$, $z$(corrected for ties) $= 2.13$, $p = 0.033$.

*Source:* Hughes, R. N., and Kleindienst, H. F. (2004). Sex-related responsiveness to changes in tactile stimulation in hooded rats. *International Journal of Comparative Psychology, 17*(4), p. 345.

-----------------------------------------------------------------------------------------------

Using $\chi^2$ values derived from the Friedman test (corrected for ties, which occurred for about one-third of the comparisons), we found no differences in the rankings of success in the different tasks for any age group when interpreting self, or other.

*Source:* Mitchell, R. W., and Neal, M. (2005). Children's understanding of their own and others' mental states. Part A. Self-understanding precedes understanding of others in pretence. *British Journal of Developmental Psychology, 23*(2), p. 189.

Ties can also occur within the Friedman test. This could happen, for example, if a judge were to report that two of the things being judged were equally good. Such tied observations are not discarded from the data set, since that would necessitate tossing out all the data provided by that particular judge. Instead, the technique of assigning average ranks would be used, with the regular formula then employed to obtain the calculated value for the Friedman test.

## The Relative Power of Nonparametric Tests

It is widely believed that nonparametric procedures are inferior to parametric techniques because the former supposedly have lower power than the latter. This concern about power is appropriate, since any test having low power is likely to lead to a Type II error when $H_0$ is false. It is unfortunate, however, that nonparametric tests have come to be thought of as being less able to detect true differences between populations. I say this because nonparametric tests, in certain situations, are *more* powerful than their parametric counterparts.

If researchers have collected interval- or ratio-level data from two independent samples, they could compare the two groups by means of a parametric test (say an independent-samples *t*-test) or by means of a nonparametric test (say the Mann-Whitney *U* test). Similar statements could be made for the cases where data have been collected from three or more independent samples, from two correlated samples, or from a single sample that is measured in a repeated-measures sense. For these situations where data can be analyzed either with a parametric test or with a nonparametric test, it is possible to compare the power of one test procedure versus the power of a different test procedure. Such comparisons allow us to talk about a test's **relative power.**

If the assumptions of normality and homogeneity of variance are valid, then *t*- and *F*-tests will be more powerful than their nonparametric counterparts. On the other hand, if these assumptions are violated, nonparametric tests can, in certain circumstances, provide researchers with greater protection against Type II errors. As illustrated earlier in Excerpts 18.8 and 18.9, researchers often explain that they utilized a nonparametric test because their data sets were skewed and/or had nonequivalent variances. By deciding to use nonparametric procedures, these researchers may have increased the sensitivity of their tests over what would have been the case if they had used *t*- or *F*-tests.

The relative power of any nonparametric test as compared with its parametric counterpart varies depending on the distributional shape in the population(s) associated with the study. Because of this, I believe that applied researchers should explain why they decided to use whatever techniques they employed. The issue of relative power ought to be included in such explanations. Unfortunately, the typical applied research investigation suffers from inadequate power, and consequently it behooves the researcher to utilize the most powerful analytical technique available.

## *A Few Final Comments*

As we approach the end of this chapter, five final points need to be made. These points constitute my typical end-of-chapter warnings to those who come into contact with technical research reports. By remaining sensitive to these cautions, you will be more judicious in your review of research conclusions that are based on nonparametric statistical tests.

My first warning concerns the quality of the research question(s) associated with the study you find yourself examining. If the study focuses on a trivial topic, no statistical procedure has the ability to "turn a sow's ear into a silk purse." This is as true of nonparametric procedures as it is of the parametric techniques discussed earlier in the book. Accordingly, I once again urge you to refrain from using data-based $p$-levels as the criterion for assessing the worth of empirical investigations.

My second warning concerns the important assumptions of random samples and independence of observations. Each of the nonparametric tests considered in this chapter involves a null hypothesis concerned with one or more populations. The null hypothesis is evaluated with data that come from one or more samples that are assumed to be representative of the population(s). Thus the notion of randomness is just as essential to any nonparametric test as it is to any parametric procedure. Moreover, nonparametric tests, like their parametric counterparts, are based on an assumption of **independence.** Independence simply means that the data provided by any individual are not influenced by what happens to any other person in the study.[11]

My third warning concerns the term **distribution-free,** a label that is sometimes used instead of the term *nonparametric*. As a consequence of these terms being used as if they were synonyms, many applied researchers are under the impression that nonparametric tests work equally well no matter what the shape of the population distribution(s). This is not true for the two reasons discussed earlier. On the one hand, the power of each and every nonparametric test varies depending on the shape of the population distribution(s). On the other hand, the proper meaning of a rejected null hypothesis is frequently influenced by what is known about the distributional shape of the populations.

My next-to-last warning is really a reiteration of an important point made earlier in this book regarding overlapping distributions. If two groups of scores are compared and found to differ significantly from each other (even at impressive $p$-levels), it is exceedingly likely that the highest scores in the low group are higher than the lowest scores in the high group. When this is the case, as it almost always is, a researcher should not claim—or even suggest—that the individuals

---

[11]With the median, Mann-Whitney, and Kruskal-Wallis tests, independence is assumed to exist both within and between the comparison groups. With the Wilcoxon and Friedman tests, the correlated nature of the data causes the independence assumption to apply only in a between-subjects sense.

in the high group outperformed the individuals in the other group. What can be said is that people in the one group, on the average, did better. Those three little words *on the average* are essential to keep in mind when reading research reports.

To see clearly what I mean about "overlapping distributions," consider Excerpt 18.28.

### EXCERPT 18.28 • *Overlapping Distributions*

The 3 children who completed the original AB-X training successfully were older ($M$ = 5.6 yr, Range: 5.3–5.7) than the 7 children who failed this training ($M$ = 5.2 yr, Range: 4.9–5.5) (Mann-Whitney $U$ = 2, $p$ = 0.03).

*Source:* Carpentier, F., Smeets, P. M., and Barnes-Holmes, D. (2002). Establishing transfer of compound control in children: A stimulus control analysis. *Psychological Record, 52*(2), p. 154.

In this excerpt, the researchers report that they found a statistically significant difference (using the Mann-Whitney $U$ test) between the ages of the two groups of fifth graders. Because of this, they assert that the 3 children in the "success" group *were older* than the 7 children in the "failure" group. But is this really true? In other words, were all three of the "success" children older than all seven of the "failure" children?

By looking at the ranges provided in Excerpt 18.28, you can see the presence of overlapping distributions. The age range for the "success" group extends from 5.7 down to 5.3, while the age range for the "failure" group extends from 5.5 down to 4.9. As these ranges make clear, at least one of the seven children in the "failure" group was older than at least one of the three children in the "success" group.

I think Excerpt 18.28 provides a powerful example of why you need to be vigilant when reading or listening to research reports. Researchers frequently say that the members of one group outperformed the members of one or more comparison groups. When the researchers fail to include the three important words *on the average* when making such statements, you should mentally insert this phrase into the statement that summarizes the study's results. You can feel safe doing this, because nonoverlapping distributions are very, very rare.

My final warning concerns the fact that many nonparametric procedures have been developed besides the five focused on within the context of this chapter. Such tests fall into one of two categories. Some are simply alternatives to the ones I have discussed, and they utilize the same kind of data to assess the same null hypothesis. For example, the Quade test can be used instead of the Friedman test. The other kind of nonparametric test not considered here has a different purpose. The Jonckheere-Terpstra test, for instance, allows a researcher to evaluate a null hypothesis that says a set of populations is ordered in a particular way in terms of their average scores. I have not discussed such tests simply because they are used infrequently by applied researchers.

## Review Terms

Distribution-free
Friedman two-way analysis
   of variance of ranks
Independence
Kruskal-Wallis one-way analysis
   of variance of ranks
Large-sample approximation
Likert-type attitude inventories
Mann-Whitney $U$ test
Median test
Nonparametric test

Parametric test
Ranks
Ratings
Relative power
Sum of ranks
Tied observations
Wilcoxon-Mann-Whitney test
Wilcoxon matched-pairs
   signed-ranks test
Wilcoxon rank-sum test
Wilcoxon test

## The Best Items in the Companion Website

1. An interactive online quiz (with immediate feedback provided) covering Chapter 18.
2. Ten misconceptions about the content of Chapter 18.
3. One of the best passages from Chapter 18: "The Importance of the Research Question(s)."
4. The interactive online resource entitled "Wilcoxon's Matched-Pairs Signed-Ranks Test."
5. The website's final joke: "The Top 10 Reasons Why Statisticians Are Misunderstood."

To access chapter objectives, practice tests, weblinks, and flashcards, visit the companion website at www.ablongman.com/huck5e.

Research
Navigator.c⊛m

## Fun Exercises inside Research Navigator

**1. Do people with multiple sclerosis (MS) have high-level language problems?**

The data of this study came from three groups of elderly individuals who were given a newly developed test battery designed to assess high-level language skills. The test's tasks included (among other things) repeating long sentences, resolving ambiguities, making inferences, and understanding metaphors. The three comparison groups were (1) four MS individuals with self-reported language problems, (2) five MS individuals who said that they did not have language problems, and (3) nine individuals without MS who were matched with the MS participants in terms of age, gender, and educational level. The total scores earned on the test battery were first analyzed by a Kruskall-Wallis one-way ANOVA. Because that analysis yielded a significant *H*, the researchers then used the Mann-Whitney *U* test to make all possible pairwise comparisons within a post hoc investigation. What do you think the three Mann-Whitney tests revealed? To find out, first locate the PDF version of the research report in the Communication Sciences and Disorders database of ContentSelect and then read (on pages 339–340) the third paragraph of the study's "Results."

K. Laakso, K. Brunnegård, L. Hartelius, & E. Ahlsén. Assessing high-level language in individuals with multiple sclerosis: A pilot study. *Clinical Linguistics and Phonetics.* Located in the COMMUNICATION SCIENCES AND DISORDERS database of ContentSelect.

## 2. Acupuncture, massage, or both: which therapy best helps HIV patients?

In this study, three therapies for dealing with HIV-infected patients were compared: acupuncture, massage, and acupuncture plus massage. There were six groups of patients; three were "treatment" groups that received the different therapies, and each of those groups had its own set of "matched controls." Using data on blood cell counts as the dependent variable, the researchers evaluated each therapy group in two ways: (1) by comparing its blood counts pre-therapy versus post-therapy and (2) by comparing its post-therapy level against that of its control group. Wilcoxon's matched pairs signed-ranks test was used for each intragroup (i.e., pre-post) comparison. For the intergroup comparisons, the researchers used a nonparametric test that seems inappropriate based on the study's design. What test do you think they *should* have used? After coming up with an answer to that question, go to the PDF version of the research report in the Nursing, Health, and Medicine database of ContentSelect and read (on pages 745–746) the "Results" section of the research report.

M. Henrickson. Clinical outcomes and patient perceptions of acupuncture and/or massage therapies in HIV-infected individuals. AIDS Care. Located in the NURSING, HEALTH, AND MEDICINE database of ContentSelect.

**Review Questions and Answers begin on page 513.**

# 19

# The Quantitative Portion
# of Mixed Methods Studies

The previous 18 chapters of this book contain 506 excerpts taken from recently published journal articles. The vast majority of the studies that provided those excerpts were fully quantitative in nature. In such studies, only numerical data are collected, analyzed, and interpreted by the researcher(s) who conduct the investigations.

Recently, researchers in many disciplines have begun conducting empirical endeavors that are referred to as being **mixed methods** studies. In this kind of investigation, both quantitative and qualitative data are gathered, examined, and used as a basis for drawing conclusions. For example, a researcher might conduct a mixed methods study by sending a five-response Likert-type survey to 1,000 individuals and by conducting in-depth interviews with 15 individuals from the target population. Responses to the survey would be analyzed with statistical procedures, some descriptive and some inferential. Information from the interviews would be analyzed by having a group of research assistants examine (either independently or together) transcripts of what was said so as to identify, by consensus, "themes" that seem to characterize most or all of the interviewees.

In Excerpts 19.1 through 19.3, we see references to three different mixed methods studies conducted in different fields of inquiry. In the first of these excerpts, the researchers simply say that they used a mixed methods approach. In Excerpt 19.2, the researchers are a bit more informative by pointing out that both qualitative and quantitative methods were used in their investigation. In Excerpt 19.3, we see an example of how researchers sometimes specify the kinds of quantitative and qualitative procedures (here surveys and interviews) used in their mixed methods studies.

Just as there are many different kinds of studies that fall together under the quantitative umbrella, so too are there many different kinds of mixed methods studies. A wide variety of mixed methods studies exists partly because there are

## EXCERPTS 19.1–19.3 • *Mixed Methods Studies*

The purpose of this study is to develop a consumer typology based on analysis of consumer participation motivation data through a mixed-method approach.

*Source:* Rohm, A. J., Milne, G. R., and McDonald, M A. (2006). A mixed-method approach for developing market segmentation typologies in the sports industry. *Sport Marketing Quarterly, 15*(1), p. 30.

---

The major purposes of this study were to identify the most difficult times, unmet needs, and advice of caregivers during the first 2 years of caregiving; and to examine resource use and perceptions of resource importance. Qualitative and quantitative methods were used.

*Source:* King, R. B., and Semik, P. E. (2006). Stroke caregiving: Difficult times, resource use, and needs during the first 2 years. *Journal of Gerontological Nursing, 32*(4), p. 39.

---

Our research and evaluation program consists of a mixed methodological strategy, including survey and interview protocols.

*Source:* Barnett, M., Lord, C., Strauss, E., Rosca, C., Langford, H., Chavez, D., and Deni, L. (2006). Using the urban environment to engage youths in urban ecology field studies. *Journal of Environmental Education, 37*(2), p. 6.

many end-result possibilities if you blend together one of the many kinds of quantitative studies with one of the many kinds of qualitative study. However, mixed methods studies can and do differ from one another for other reasons. For example, in some studies there is a large quantitative component and a small qualitative component, while in other studies the scales are tipped in the opposite direction. Also, in some studies the qualitative portion of the study is executed first because its results are used to inform the design of the subsequent quantitative effort, whereas in other studies the order of the qualitative and quantitative efforts is reversed. Further still, mixed methods studies can differ in their purpose, with the terms "exploratory," "explanatory," and "triangulation" used by many authors to distinguish three different reasons for conducting such a study.

## *The Goals of This Chapter*

Before indicating what this chapter *is* intended to do, I want to clarify what is not intended. First of all, you will find no effort here to denigrate the potential worth of mixed methods studies (or studies that are totally qualitative in nature). Valuable insights can come from the "voices" of the individuals who serve as research participants, and certain studies are clearly limited if they fail to include a qualitative component. Second, no effort is made here to explain and show examples of different techniques for collecting, analyzing, and interpreting qualitative data. Other books accomplish that goal. Finally, this chapter will not deal with the proper ways to integrate the qualitative and quantitative components of a study into a single unified form that meets the criteria of a good mixed methods study. Again, other books should be consulted by the reader interested in that topic.

What, then, *are* the goals of this chapter? As you will see, I have two objectives for this final part of this book. First, I want to pose and then answer the simple question: How important is the quantitative portion of a mixed methods study? Second, I want you to see a variety of excerpts taken from mixed methods studies that illustrate the kind of care that ought to be devoted to the quantitative portion of any mixed methods study.

## *How Important Is the Quantitative Part of a Mixed Methods Study?*

When researchers draw conclusions from statistical analyses, the data should be of high quality, the quantitative techniques should be executed carefully, and the claims based on statistical results should be made cautiously in light of the inherent limitations of the data and procedures used to summarize the numerical information. This important point has been made repeatedly in earlier chapters of this book. It applies just as much to the quantitative portion of mixed methods studies as it does to investigations that are totally quantitative in nature.

If a study involves both quantitative and quantitative components, the statistical part should be done properly even if the qualitative part is larger ("big QUAL, little QUAN"), even if the quantitative part is auxiliary to the qualitative part, and even if the quantitative part comes first so as to inform the qualitative procedures. Stated differently, you should apply the same rigorous standards when examining the statistical portion of a mixed methods research report as you would to the entirety of a study that's solely quantitative in nature. The mixed nature of a mixed methods study usually gives you two different kinds of things to consider; however, the "whole" cannot be good unless both constituent parts are good.

## *Examples of Statistics in Mixed Methods Studies*

In this section, let's examine excerpts from 10 different studies, all taken from the reports of mixed methods investigation. Each excerpt focuses on the statistical findings, and I think you will discover that any of these excerpts could have been positioned earlier in this book. Collectively, these excerpts illustrate two points. First, researchers who conduct mixed methods studies use a wide array of quantitative techniques, many of which are just as advanced as those used in studies that are totally quantitative in nature. Second, well-trained mixed methods researchers are careful when dealing with the numerical data of their empirical investigations.

In Excerpt 19.4, we see an excerpt from an interesting study focused on gossip in the workplace. In this passage, we see descriptive statistics concerning how many gossip incidents were noted (in the diaries), how many people were gossiping on each occasion, how long the gossiping lasted, and the gender of those who gossiped. Look closely at the information provided on the amount of time per incident spent gossiping about work-related issues. By giving us the range (rather than just the mean and standard deviation), we can discern that the distribution of scores was positively skewed. As pointed out in Chapter 2, researchers should help us understand the distributional characteristics of the data they collect. More researchers should report the range, as was done in Excerpt 19.4.

## EXCERPT 19.4 • *Use of Descriptive Statistics in a Mixed Methods Study*

The overall research design combined qualitative and quantitative methods of data collection, analysis and inference. . . . Descriptive statistics showed that number of people (including the diary keeper) involved in an incident of gossip was typically small—on average 2.6 people ($SD = 0.5$). The amount of time spent gossiping about work related issues ranged from 1 to 2 minutes per incident for some, to 90 minutes on one occasion for one respondent. The number of incidents recorded per participant varied from 2 to 32 across the whole data set. The mean length of time per incident was 13.2 minutes ($SD = 5.7$), and the mean number of incidents recorded over a 10 day period was 13.7 ($SD = 7.6$). Women reported slightly more incidents (mean $= 14.1$) than men (mean $= 11.8$). . . .

*Source:* Waddington, K. (2005). Using diaries to explore the characteristics of work-related gossip: Methodological considerations from exploratory multimethod research. *Journal of Occupational and Organizational Psychology, 78*(2), pp. 222, 228.

Now consider Excerpt 19.5. This excerpt comes from a study that looked at the relationship between the organizational health of middle schools and the academic achievement of students. In part of the quantitative portion of this investigation, the research team computed Pearson *r*s. Lots of researchers collect data and compute *r*. However, most fail to exert the care demonstrated earlier in Excerpt 3.33 and here by the researchers associated with Excerpt 19.5. First, the researchers who did this mixed methods study demonstrated that they were aware of the fact that Pearson's *r* assumes a linear relationship between whatever *X* and *Y* variables are being correlated. More importantly, they inspected scatter diagrams before placing faith in the *r*s that came from an analysis of their data. In Chapters 3 and 9, I argued that this is an important thing for researchers to do when they deal with product-moment correlations.

The entirety of Chapter 4 was concerned with data quality. As I pointed out back then, fancy statistical procedures cannot magically undo the damage created in a study

**EXCERPT 19.5 •** *Checking on Linearity Before Computing r in a Mixed Methods Study*

This mixed-methods study focuses on three dimensions of organizational health (teacher affiliation, resource support, and academic emphasis) and their relationship to academic performance. . . . To ensure that the underlying relationships between the variables being studied were linear [before computing *r*], each of the relationships was graphed, and nonparametric correlations involving Spearman's rho were calculated. The results of the Spearman's rho were consistent with the Pearson correlations.

*Source:* Henderson, C. L., Buehler, A. E., Stein, W. L., Dalton, J. E., Robinson, T. R., and Anfara, V. A. (2005). Organizational health and student achievement in Tennessee middle level schools. *NASSP Bulletin, 89*, pp. 54, 60.

by low-quality data. With that in mind, take a look at Excerpt 19.6 that comes from a study focused on the possible effect of computers on high school students' sense of learning. Read the entire excerpt and be sure to note what is stated in the final sentence. The first four words of that sentence caught my eye and made me think that this mixed methods researcher followed an important piece of advice (first illustrated in Excerpt 4.19) about providing evidence of data quality. It would be nice if all researchers did this same thing. Unfortunately, many researchers collect data with a measuring instrument and do not check to see if the resulting data are reliable or valid.

In many mixed methods studies, sample-to-population inferences are made. In Chapter 5, we considered the notions of tangible and abstract populations, and we looked at various recommended sampling strategies available for use with

**EXCERPT 19.6 •** *Concern for Data Quality in a Mixed Methods Study*

The author used a mixed-method design to determine whether and how use of computers in the classroom affects sense of learning in a community among high school students. . . . I used the Sense of Classroom Community Index (SCCI) developed by Rovai, Lucking, and Cristol (2001) to evaluate the sense of classroom community and its component dimensions of spirit, trust, interaction and learning. . . . In describing the SCCI's reliability, Rovai and colleagues (2001) reported Cronbach's coefficient alpha as .96 for the overall SCCI score, .90 for the spirit subscore, .84 for the trust subscore, .84 for the interaction subscore, and .88 for the learning subscore. In the present study ($N = 181$), coefficients of internal consistency were .95 for the overall SCCI score, .86 for the spirit subscore, .80 for the trust subscore, .82 for the interaction subscore, and .87 for the learning subscore.

*Source:* Wighting, M. J. (2006). Effects of computer use on high school students' sense of community. *Journal of Educational Research, 99*(6), pp. 371, 373.

tangible populations. One kind of probability sample we considered (in Excerpts 5.5 and 5.6) is a stratified random sample. That kind of sample was used in the mixed methods study that provided Excerpt 19.7. The researchers who conducted this British investigation deserve high marks not only for using a recommended and respected sampling procedure but also for oversampling one strata so as to have sufficient data to accomplish their study's objectives.

### EXCERPT 19.7 • *Sampling in a Mixed Methods Study*

The research design adopts a mixed methods approach, including detailed statistical analyses of effectiveness and in-depth case studies of individual pre-school centres. . . . The sample was drawn from six English LAs [Local Authorities] in five regions, with children recruited from six main types of provision: nursery classes, playgroups, private day nurseries, LA day care nurseries, nursery schools and integrated (combined) centres. . . . Within each LA, centres of each type were selected by stratified random sampling and, due to the small size of some centres in the project (e.g. rural playgroups), more of these centres were recruited than originally proposed, bringing the sample total to 141 centres and over 3000 children.

*Source:* Sammons, P., Elliot, K., Sylva, K., Melhuish, E., Siraj-Blatchford, I., and Taggart, B. (2004). The impact of pre-school on young children's cognitive attainment at entry to reception. *British Educational Research Journal, 30*(5), pp. 692, 693, 694.

You may recall that we considered (in Chapter 5) the problems that might be caused by less than adequate response rates and by higher than desired levels of attrition and refusals to participate. Serious researchers are aware of the inferential dilemma these problems can create. Such researchers work hard to reduce the likelihood that these problems will occur (as illustrated in Excerpts 5.18–5.20), and they check to see if inferences are still legitimate even if not every invited person becomes and remains a participant (see Excerpts 5.21, 5.22, and 5.25). If you now look at Excerpt 19.8, you'll see why I was impressed with the team of researchers who conducted the study associated with this passage. I salute them for making the comparisons summarized in the excerpt's final sentence.

When researchers set up and test null hypotheses, the level of significance functions to hold down the probability of a Type I error. However, as we saw in Chapter 8, the level of significance underestimates the likelihood of this kind of inferential error when more than one null hypothesis is tested. As illustrated in Chapters 9 through 18, the Bonferroni adjustment procedure is frequently used to avoid the problem of an inflated Type I error rate. The Bonferroni procedure is just as useful in mixed methods studies as it is in studies that have no qualitative component. Excerpt 19.9 provides some evidence to back up this claim.

As indicated in several spots throughout earlier chapters of this book, there is an important distinction between statistical significance and practical significance.

### EXCERPT 19.8 • *Refusals to Participate in a Mixed Methods Study*

We used mixed methods to examine communication between physicians and primary family caregivers about incurable illness, life expectancy, and hospice. . . . A total of 391 caregivers were initially approached during the enrollment period by a hospice staff research liaison. Out of the 391 approached, 100 caregivers requested not to be contacted for the study, 28 could not be contacted because of missing or inaccurate telephone or address information, 6 of the caregivers were either too ill or cognitively impaired to participate as determined by the interviewer, and 51 of the caregivers were contacted but refused to participate. The 206 caregivers represented 78% of those contacted (206/263) and 53% of the original 391 caregivers originally sampled. There were no significant differences ($p > 0.10$) between caregiver participants and those who could not be contacted or did not participate in terms of gender, kinship relationship to the patient, or the number of days enrolled with hospice.

*Source:* Cherlin, E., Fried, T., Prigerson, H. G., Schulman-Green, D., Johnson-Hurzeler, R., and Bradley, E. H. (2005). Communication between physicians and family caregivers about care at the end of life: When do discussions occur and what is said? *Journal of Palliative Medicine, 8*(6), pp. 1177–1178.

### EXCERPT 19.9 • *Using Bonferroni in a Mixed Methods Study*

The present study was designed as a mixed-model research project wherein quantitative and qualitative data were collected simultaneously and analyzed in a complementary manner. . . . To examine the potential impact demographic characteristics may have had upon the variables of interest, a series of Bonferroni-adjusted t-tests (where $p = .002$) compared participants by school, by gender, and by grade on the SPCS, inverted SDO, perceived support for challenging racism, perceived support for challenging sexism, perceived support for challenging injustice, and total perceived support. Only one significant difference was detected, as young women perceived more support for challenging sexism than young men.

*Source:* Diemer, M. A., Kauffman, A., Koenig, N., Trahan, E., and Hsieh, C. (2006). Challenging racism, sexism, and social injustice: Support for urban adolescents' critical consciousness development. *Cultural Diversity & Ethnic Minority Psychology, 12*(3), pp. 448, 452.

Aware that a result can be statistically significant without being significant in a practical (or "clinical") sense, careful researchers have several options available to them. One is to estimate effect size. Can this be done in mixed methods studies? Of course. Should it be done? Yes! In Excerpt 19.10, we see an example where the strength of the association between the independent and dependent variables following a one-way ANOVA was estimated via the eta squared statistic.

Over the past three and half decades, I have been asked many, many questions about the proper design of quantitative studies. The single question that I've been

**EXCERPT 19.10 • *Estimated Effect Size in a Mixed Methods Study***

A one-way ANOVA for the effect of CP restriction on relational inferences indicated a significant main effect, $F(1, 69) = 44.21$, $MSE = 89.60$, $p < .01$. The restricted CP group described better relational inferences and more ideas in support of those inferences than the unrestricted group. The strength of the relationship between level of CP restriction and relational inferences was very strong, as assessed by eta squared, with level of restriction accounting for 39.0% of the variance in relational inferences.

*Source:* Igo, L. B., Bruning, R., and McCrudden, M. T. (2005). Exploring differences in students' copy-and-paste decision making and processing: A mixed-methods study. *Journal of Educational Psychology, 97*(1), pp. 103, 107.

asked most frequently typically is phrased like this: "How large should my sample size be if I plan to use the hypothesis testing procedure?" Although this question seems simple, several factors must be considered before a good answer can be provided. Some of these factors are connected to the one- versus two-tailed option, the selected level of significance, one's opinion as to what kinds of effect size should be considered trivial versus nontrivial, the degree of variability in the population(s), the kinds of statistical test being used, and the desired control over Type II error risk.

Careful researchers do not allow $n$ to be determined by convenience or luck. Instead, they do an a priori power analysis—with attention given to the factors cited in the previous paragraph—to determine how large their sample size should be. Earlier in this book, several excerpts pulled from quantitative studies illustrated this good technique of doing a power analysis so as to determine $n$. (You might wish to review Excerpts 8.11, 10.22, 11.23, and 15.24.) In Excerpt 19.11, we see an example of this kind of power analysis being done in a mixed methods study.

**EXCERPT 19.11 • *Determining the Sample Size in a Mixed Methods Study***

We undertook a concurrent mixed-methodological analysis [that] involved the use of qualitative and quantitative data analytic techniques in a complimentary manner. . . . Participants were 82 male juvenile offenders whom we drew randomly from the population of juveniles incarcerated at a correctional facility in a large southeastern U.S. state. The sample size of 82 was selected via an a priori power analysis because it provided acceptable statistical power (i.e., .80) for detecting a moderate correlation, $r = .30$, at the (two-tailed) .05 level of significance (Erdfelder, Faul, & Buchner, 1996). The 82 participants represented 15% of the offenders who were incarcerated at that facility.

*Source:* Daley, C. E., and Onwuegbuzie, A. J. (2004). Attributions toward violence of male juvenile delinquents: A concurrent mixed-methodological analysis. *Journal of Social Psychology, 144*(6), pp. 553, 557.

Throughout this book, I have pointed out that statistical techniques, both descriptive and inferential, carry with them important underlying assumptions. For example, Pearson's correlation assumes linearity, $t$-test and $F$-test comparisons of means assume equal variance in the populations, the analysis of covariance assumes equal within-group regression slopes, and ANOVAs involving repeated measures assume sphericity. If these or other important assumptions are violated, a statistical procedure will not function as intended.

Researchers should be alert to the assumptions of the statistical procedures they use. Important assumptions should be tested, and apparent violations of assumptions should bring about some form of compensatory action such as the application of a data transformation (as illustrated in Excerpt 10.28) or the use of an alternative test procedure (as illustrated in Excerpts 18.8 and 18.9). This should be done in mixed methods studies no less frequently than it should be done in quantitative-only investigations. Excerpt 19.12 shows how attention to statistical assumptions helps to increase the quality of a mixed methods study.

**EXCERPT 19.12 • *Concern for Statistical Assumptions in a Mixed Methods Study***

Because of the dearth of research examining well-being in Latino youth, the present mixed-methods study was conducted to expand researchers' understanding of the relationship between life satisfaction, acculturation, and perceived family support in Mexican American adolescents. . . . We conducted a hierarchical multiple regression of perceived family support and Mexican and Anglo acculturation orientations on life satisfaction. . . . Preliminary analyses included checking the data for outliers, normality, linearity, and homoscedasticity [and] the scatter plot of the studentized residuals against the predicted values of life satisfaction revealed no violations of assumptions of normality, linearity, and homoscedasticity.

*Source:* Edwards, L. M., and Lopez, S. J. (2006). Perceived family support, acculturation, and life satisfaction in Mexican American youth: A mixed-methods exploration. *Journal of Counseling Psychology, 53*(3), pp. 281, 283, 284.

When comparing sample means in a study that involves more than two comparison groups, researchers should tailor their statistical tests to their research questions. This often means that planned comparisons should be investigated. This requires a researcher to conduct statistical tests that are different from those dealt with by the omnibus $F$-tests associated with one-way, factorial, and repeated measures ANOVAs and ANCOVAs. Earlier, we saw planned comparisons used in Excerpts 12.21, 12.22, and 13.21.

In Excerpt 19.13, we see an example of planned comparisons being used in a mixed methods study. In this investigation, the researchers interviewed 79 Spanish-speaking adolescents who had been randomly selected from schools in Los Angeles. During each interview, the researchers noted (1) whether or not the adolescent

### EXCERPT 19.13 • *Testing Planned Comparisons in a Mixed Methods Study*

This study examines Latino/a adolescents' ethnic identities and academic achievement [using] open-ended interviews [and] various academic performance measurements to quantitatively explore relationships between ethnic identity and academic achievement. . . . [T]he adolescents were grouped into four groups according to presence of bicultural identity and use of cultural definition. Mean standardized percentile scores were tested for significant differences (analysis of variance) and the analysis revealed that the students who expressed a bicultural identity and used cultural definitions for ethnic labels significantly outperformed all other groups in middle school standardized reading ($p < .001$) and math ($p < .01$) test scores. . . .

*Source:* Zarate, M. E., Bhimji, F., and Reese, L. (2005). Ethnic identity and academic achievement among Latino/a adolescents. *Journal of Latinos & Education,* 4(2), pp. 95, 110.

expressed a bicultural identity and (2) whether or not cultural definitions were used to justify the chosen ethnic label. This information was used to place the research participants into the four cells of a 2 × 2 design, and then the students' achievement test scores were analyzed so as to make intergroup comparisons on two dependent variables, reading and math. Instead of using a regular two-way ANOVA, however, the researchers set up and tested a set of planned comparisons. First for reading and then for math, the researchers compared (via three pairwise contrasts) the mean score of those adolescents in one group—who expressed a bicultural identity and who used cultural/heritage terms to explain it—with the mean scores of the other three groups.

## Concluding Remarks

It should be noted that quantitative and qualitative research methodologies have evolved from highly different philosophical perspectives. Such differences bring about stark contrasts between the goals and methodologies of those who conduct "pure" qualitative investigations as compared with those who conduct "pure" quantitative studies. For example, research questions are usually stated at the beginning of quantitative studies; in contrast, a qualitative investigation may have the goal of illuminating (rather than answering) interesting questions. The notion of sample-to-population generalization that is positioned at the heart of quantitative studies involving statistical inference is of little concern to those who conduct qualitative studies in the tradition of existential phenomenology. The notion of a proper sample size is often dealt with via two altogether different approaches (statistical power and "saturation") depending on the kind of study being conducted.

As stated near the beginning of this chapter, I have no desire whatsoever to denigrate the work of those who use qualitative methodologies in their research investigations. Qualitative studies can provide insights that cannot be gained by even the best quantitative study. Moreover, qualitative studies have the potential, more than quantitative studies, to have a personal impact on the person who reads the research report. I have the highest regard for well-conceived and properly conducted qualitative studies, as indicated by my eagerness, a few years ago, to *lead* an effort to have a doctoral student's qualitative project receive the "Best Dissertation" award in a highly competitive national competition. It won!

Though not at all opposed to qualitative research, I nevertheless have concerns about the work of those who engage in mixed methods investigations. It's not that I think the qualitative component detracts from the quantitative part, and it's not that I think these two kinds of methodologies make for "strange bedfellows" in a single research report. Instead, my concern is with the quality and care exercised in the quantitative part of the mixed methods investigation.

The final 10 excerpts of this chapter were selected to illustrate good quantitative practice. Those who use statistical procedures on the numerical data of their studies should follow the examples provided in these excerpts. Such researchers should also follow the examples of good practice illustrated in the excerpts contained in Chapters 1 through 18. In reading or listening to the statistical portions of research reports, it is my firm belief that you should have the same standards for quality work irrespective of the presence or absence of a qualitative component.

## *Review Terms, Companion Website, and Fun Exercises*

At the end of each previous chapter, I have provided a set of review terms, a list of the five best items located in this book's companion website, and two fun exercises that involve Research Navigator. This final chapter has none of these three things.

What accounts for the absence here of the final three items that graced the last few pages of earlier chapters? As stated earlier, Chapter 19 is intended to show that careful mixed-methods researchers do things the same way, in the quantitative parts of their studies, as do researchers who collect only numerical information and who use only statistics to analyze their data. For this reason, the review terms for this chapter become the review terms of all previous chapters. For that same reason, this chapter's content is connected to (1) all previously shown lists of the best passages in the companion website and (2) the fun exercises in Researcher Navigator referred to at the end of Chapters 1 through 18.

I hope the important message of this final chapter is clear: To be in a position where you can competently evaluate others' mixed methods research reports, or for you to be in a position where you can conduct good studies of this type yourself, you must understand the material covered in earlier portions of this book.

To access chapter objectives, practice tests, weblinks, and flashcards, visit the companion website at www.ablongman.com/huck5e.

# Epilogue

The warnings sprinkled throughout this book were offered with two distinct groups of people in mind. The principal reason for raising these concerns is to help those who are on the *receiving* end of research claims. However, these same warnings should be considered by those who are *doing* research. If both parties are more careful in how they interact with research studies, fewer invalid claims will be made, encountered, and believed.

There are two final warnings. The first has to do with the frequently heard statement that begins with these three words, "Research indicates that. . . ." The second is concerned with the power of replication. All consumers of research, as well as all researchers, should firmly resolve to heed the important messages contained in this book's final two admonitions.

First, you must protect yourself against those who use research to intimidate others in discussions (and in arguments) over what is the best idea, the best practice, the best solution to a problem, or the best anything. Because most people (1) are unaware of the slew of problems that can cause an empirical investigation to yield untenable conclusions and (2) make the mistake of thinking that statistical analysis creates a direct pipeline to truth, they are easily bowled over when someone else claims to have research evidence on his or her side. Don't let this happen to you! When you encounter people who promote their points of view by alluding to research ("Well, research has shown that. . . ."), ask them politely to tell you more about the research project(s) to which they refer. Ask them if they have seen the actual research reports(s). Then pose a few exceedingly legitimate questions.

If the research data were collected via mailed questionnaires, what was the response rate? No matter how the data were collected, did the researchers present evidence as to the reliability and validity of the data they analyzed? Did they attend to the important assumptions associated with the statistical techniques they used? If they tested null hypotheses, did they acknowledge the possibility of inferential error when they rejected or failed to reject any given $H_0$? If their data analysis produced one or more results that were significant, did they distinguish between statistical and practical significance? If you ask questions such as these, you may find that the person who first made reference to what research has to say may well become a bit more modest when arguing his or her point of view. And never, ever forget that you not only have a *right* to ask these kinds of questions, you have an *obligation* to do so (presuming that you want to be a discerning recipient of the information that comes your way).

Second, be impressed with researchers who replicate their own investigations— and even more impressed when they encourage others to execute such replications. The logic behind this admonition is simple and shines through if we consider this little question: Who are you more willing to believe, someone who demonstrates something once or someone who demonstrates something twice? (Recall that a correlation matrix containing all bivariate *r*s among seven or more variables is more likely than not to be accompanied by the notation "$p < .05$" *even if all null hypotheses are true,* unless the level of significance is adjusted to compensate for the multiple tests being conducted. Similarly, the odds are greater than 50-50 that a five-way ANOVA or ANCOVA will produce a statistically significant result *simply by chance,* presuming that each *F*'s *p* is evaluated against an alpha criterion of .05.)

It is sad but true that most researchers do not take the time to replicate their findings before they race off to publish their results. It would be nice if there were a law stipulating that every researcher had to replicate his or her study before figuratively standing up on a soapbox and arguing passionately that something important has been discovered. No such law is likely to appear on the books in the near future. Hence, *you* must protect yourself from overzealous researchers who regard publication as more important than replication. Fortunately, there *are* more than a few researchers who delay making any claims until they have first checked to see if their findings are reproducible. Such researchers deserve your utmost respect. If their findings emanate from well designed studies that deal with important questions, their discoveries may bring forth improvements in your life and the lives of others.

# Review Questions

## CHAPTER 1

1. Where is the abstract usually found in a journal article? What type of information is normally contained in the abstract?
2. What information usually follows the review of literature?
3. If an author does a good job of writing the method section of the research report, what should a reader be able to do? *Replicate the study*
4. The author of this chapter's model article used the term *participants* to label the people from whom data were collected (see Excerpt 1.5). What is another word that authors sometimes use to label the data suppliers? *Subjects*
5. If a researcher compares the IQ scores of 100 boys with the IQ scores of 100 girls, what would this researcher's dependent variable be?
6. What are three ways authors present the results of their statistical analyses?
7. Will a nontechnical interpretation of the results usually be located in a research report's results section or in its discussion section?
8. What is the technical name for the bibliography that appears at the end of a research report? *References*
9. If a research report is published, should you assume that it is free of mistakes?
10. Look again at these four parts of the model article: the first sentence of the abstract (see Excerpt 1.1), the researcher's hypothesis (see Excerpt 1.4), the seventh and eighth sentences of the results section (see Excerpt 1.8), and the first sentence of the discussion section (see Excerpt 1.10). With respect to this study's purpose and findings, how many of these four sentences are consistent with one another?

## CHAPTER 2

1. What does each of the following symbols or abbreviations stand for: $N$, $M$, $s$, Mdn., $Q_3$, $SD$, $R$, $\sigma$, $Q_2$, $s^2$, $Q_1$, $\sigma^2$, $\mu$?
2. If a cumulative frequency distribution is created using the data of Excerpt 2.1, what would be the cumulative frequency for the TAS score of 4?

*Bar graph* →

3. Each of several people from your home town is asked to indicate his or her favorite radio station, and the data are summarized using a picture containing vertical columns to indicate how many people vote for each radio station. What is the name for this kind of picture technique for summarizing data?

4. True or False: In any set of data, the median is equal to the score value that lies halfway between the high and low scores.

5. Which one of these two terms means the same thing as negatively skewed?
   a. Skewed left
   b. Skewed right

6. If the variance of a set of scores is equal to 9, how large is the standard deviation for those scores?  *3*

7. If the standard deviation for a set of 30 scores is equal to 5, how large do you think the range is?

*Inter Quartile* →

8. What measure of variability is equal to the numerical distance between the 25th and 75th percentile points?

9. Which of the following three descriptive techniques would let you see each and every score in the researcher's data set?
   a. grouped frequency distribution
   b. stem-and-leaf display
   c. box-and-whisker

10. True or False: The distance between the high and low scores in a data set can be determined by doubling the value of the interquartile range.

## CHAPTER 3

1. Following are the quiz scores for five students in English (E) and History (H).

   Sam: E = 18, H = 4
   Sue: E = 16, H = 3
   Joy: E = 15, H = 3
   John: E = 13, H = 1
   Chris: E = 12, H = 0

   Within this same group of quiz-takers, what is the nature of the relationship between demonstrated knowledge of English and history?
   a. *high-high, low-low*
   b. *high-low, low-high*
   c. little systematic tendency one way or the other

2. If 20 individuals are measured in terms of two variables, how many dots will there be if a scatter diagram is built to show the relationship between the two variables?  *20*

3. Which of the following five correlation coefficients indicates the weakest relationship?

    **a.** $r = +.72$
    **b.** $r = +.41$
    **c.** $r = +.13$
    **d.** $r = -.33$
    **e.** $r = -.84$

4. In Excerpt 3.10, which two variables produced the lowest correlation?
    **a.** Injuries and Passive Leadership
    **b.** Safety Events and Transformational Leadership
    **c.** Safety Climate and Passive Leadership

5. What is the name of the correlational procedure used when interest lies in the relationship between two variables measured in such a way as to produce each of the following?
    **a.** two sets of raw scores *Pearsons r*
    **b.** two sets of ranks (with ties) *Kendalls*
    **c.** two sets of truly dichotomous scores *phi*
    **d.** one set of raw scores and one set of truly dichotomous scores *point biserd*

6. What does the letter $s$ stand for in the notation $r_s$? *Spearman*

7. If a researcher wanted to see if there is a relationship between people's favorite color (e.g., blue, red, yellow, orange) and their favorite TV network, what correlational procedure would you expect to see used?

8. True or False: If a bivariate correlation coefficient turns out to be closer to 1.00 than to 0.00, you should presume that a causal relationship exists between the two variables.

9. If a correlation coefficient is equal to .70, how large is the coefficient of determination? *0.49*

10. True or False: If a researcher has data on two variables, there will be a high correlation if the two means are close together (or a low correlation if the two means are far apart). *nothing to do ā means*

# CHAPTER 4

*consistancy*

1. The basic idea of reliability is captured nicely by what word?

2. What is the name of the reliability procedure that leads to a coefficient of stability? To a coefficient of equivalence? *test–retest; parallel forms*

$+ \; 1 \quad 0$

3. Regardless of which method is used to assess reliability, the reliability coefficient cannot be higher than __1__ or lower than __0__.

4. Why is the Cronbach alpha approach to assessing internal consistency more versatile than the Kuder-Richardson 20 approach?

5. True or False: If the slit-half and Kuder-Richardson 20 procedures are applied to the same set of test scores, both procedures will yield the same reliability estimate.

$f$

6. True or False: As reliability increases, so does the standard error of measurement.

7. What might cause the correlation coefficient used to assess concurrent or predictive validity to turn out *low* even though scores on the new test are *high* in accuracy?

8. Persuasive evidence for discriminant validity is provided by correlation coefficients that turn out close to

    **a.** +1.00
    **b.** 0.00
    **c.** −1.00

9. Should reliability and validity coefficients be interpreted as revealing something about the measuring instrument, or should such coefficients be interpreted as revealing something about the scores produced by using the measuring instrument? *the later*

10. True or False: If a researcher presents impressive evidence regarding the reliability of his or her data, it is safe to assume that the data are valid too. *f*

## CHAPTER 5

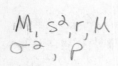

1. In which direction does statistical inference move: from the population to the sample or from the sample to the population?

2. What symbols are used to denote the sample mean, the sample variance, and the sample value of Pearson's correlation? What symbols are used to denote these statistical concepts in the population?

3. True or False: If the population is abstract (rather than tangible), it's impossible for there to be a sampling frame. *T*

4. In order for a sample to be a probability sample, what must you or someone else be able to do?

5. Which of the following eight kinds of samples are considered to be probability samples?

    cluster samples        simple random samples
    convenience samples    snowball samples
    purposive samples     stratified random samples
    quota samples        systematic samples

6. If you want to determine whether a researcher's sample is a random sample, which of these two questions should you ask?

    **a.** Precisely how well do the characteristics of the sample mirror the characteristics of the population?
    **b.** Precisely how was the sample selected from the population?

7. True or False: Studies having a response rate lower than 30 percent are not allowed to be published.

8. The best procedure for checking on a possible nonresponse bias involves doing what?

    **a.** Comparing demographic data of respondents and nonrespondents.

    **b.** Comparing survey responses of respondents and a sample of nonrespondents.

    **c.** Comparing survey responses of early versus late respondents.

9. If randomly selected individuals from a population are contacted and asked to participate in a study, and if those who respond negatively are replaced by randomly selected individuals who agree to participate, should the final sample be considered a random subset of the original population? *NO*

10. Put the words *tangible* and *abstract* into their appropriate places within this sentence: If a researcher's population is _____, the researcher ought to provide a detailed description of the sample, but if the researcher's population is _____, it is the population that ought to be described with as much detail as possible.

## CHAPTER 6

1. True or False: Sampling errors can be eliminated by selecting samples randomly from their appropriate populations.

2. If many, many samples of size *n* are drawn randomly from an infinitely big population, and if the data from each sample are summarized so as to produce the same statistic (e.g., *r*), what would the resulting set of sample statistics be called? *Sampling distribution*

3. The standard deviation of a sampling distribution is called the *standard error*.

4. True or False: You can have more faith in a researcher's sample data if the standard error is large (rather than small).

5. The two most popular levels of confidence associated with confidence intervals are *95* and *99*.

6. If the second confidence interval reported in Excerpt 6.6 had been a 99 percent CI, the lower end of the CI would have been:

    **a.** lower than 0.21

    **b.** higher than 0.21

    **c.** equal to 0.21

7. One type of estimation is called interval estimation; the other type is called *point* estimation.

8. True or False: When a researcher includes a reliability or validity coefficient in the research report, such a coefficient should be thought of as a point estimate.

9. Which type of interval is superior to the other, a confidence interval or a standard error interval?

10. Excerpt 6.6 contains two confidence intervals, each built around a Pearson's correlation coefficient. Does the sample value of *r* lie precisely in the middle of each CI?

## CHAPTER 7

1. How could the null hypothesis in Excerpt 7.2 be rewritten so as to make explicit a pinpoint numerical value?

2. Suppose a researcher takes a sample from a population, collects data, and then computes the correlation between scores on two variables. If the researcher wants to test whether the population correlation is different from 0, which of the following would represent the null hypothesis?
   a. $H_0: r = 0.00$
   b. $H_0: r \neq 0.00$
   c. $H_0: \rho = 0.00$
   d. $H_0: \rho \neq 0.00$

3. True or False: If the alternative hypothesis is set up in a nondirectional fashion, this decision will make the statistical test one-tailed (not two-tailed) in nature.

4. The null hypothesis is rejected if the sample data turn out to be _____ (consistent/inconsistent) with what one would expect if $H_0$ were true.

5. Which level of significance offers greater protection against Type I errors, .05 or .01?

6. Does the critical value typically appear in the research report?

7. If a researcher sets $\alpha = .05$ and then finds out (after analyzing the sample data) that $p = .03$, will the null hypothesis be rejected or not rejected?

8. If a researcher's data turn out such that $H_0$ cannot be rejected, is it appropriate for the researcher to conclude that $H_0$ most likely is true?

9. If a null hypothesis is rejected because the data are extremely improbable when compared against $H_0$ (with $p < .00000001$), for what reason might you legitimately dismiss the research study as being totally unimportant?

10. True or False: Even if the results of a study turn out to be statistically significant, it is possible that those results are fully insignificant in any practical sense.

## CHAPTER 8

1. Is it possible for a researcher to conduct a study wherein the result *is* significant in a statistical sense but *is not* significant in a practical sense?

2. What are the two popular strength-of-association indices that are similar to $r^2$?

3. Statistical power equals the probability of not making what kind of error?
   a. Type I
   b. Type II

4. What kind of relationship exists between statistical power and sample size?
   a. direct
   b. indirect
   c. power and sample size are unrelated

5. The statistical power of a study must lie somewhere between _____ and _____.

6. What are the numerical values for small, medium, and large effect sizes (as suggested by Cohen) when comparing two sample means?

7. If a study is conducted to test $H_0$: $\mu = 30$ and if the results yield a confidence interval around the sample mean that extends from 26.44 to 29.82, will $H_0$ be rejected?

8. When the Bonferroni adjustment procedure is used, what gets adjusted?
    a. $H_0$
    b. $H_a$
    c. $\alpha$
    d. $p$

$\varepsilon, P, S$

9. If a researcher wants to use the nine-step version of hypothesis testing instead of the six-step version, what three additional things must he or she do?

10. If the researcher's sample size is too _____, the results can yield statistical significance even in the absence of any practical significance. On the other hand, if the sample size is too _____, the results can yield a nonsignificant result even though the null hypothesis is incorrect by a large margin.
    a. small; large
    b. large; small

## CHAPTER 9

1. If a researcher reports that a sample correlation coefficient turned out to be statistically significant, which of the following most likely represents the researcher's unstated null hypothesis?
    a. $H_0$: $\rho = -1.00$
    b. $H_0$: $\rho = 0.00$
    c. $H_0$: $\rho = +1.00$

2. If a researcher reports that "$r(58) = -.61, p < .05$," how many pairs of scores were involved in the correlation?

3. When a researcher checks to see if a sample correlation coefficient is or isn't significant, the inferential test most likely will be conducted in a _____ (one-tailed/two-tailed) fashion.

4. Suppose a researcher has data on 5 variables, computes Pearson's $r$ between every pair of variables, and then displays the $r$s in a correlation matrix. Also suppose that an asterisk appears next to three of these $r$s, with a note beneath the table explaining that the asterisk means $p < .05$. Altogether, how many correlational null hypotheses were set up and tested on the basis of the sample data?

5. In the situation described in Question 4, how many of the $r$s would have turned out to be statistically significant if the Bonferroni technique had been applied?

6. Is it possible for a researcher to have a test-retest reliability coefficient of .25 that turns out to be statistically significant at $p < .001$?

7. A confidence interval built around a sample correlation coefficient will lead to a retention of the typical correlational null hypothesis if the CI overlaps which of the following numbers?
   a. $-1.0$
   b. $-.50$
   c. $0.00$
   d. $+.50$
   e. $+1.00$

8. Is it possible for $r^2$ to be low (i.e., close to zero) and yet have $p < .01$?

9. True or False: To the extent that the $p$-value associated with $r$ is small (e.g., $p < .01$, $p < .001$, or $p < .0001$), the researcher more confidently can argue that a cause-and-effect relationship exists between the two variables that were correlated.

10. Attenuation makes it _____ (more/less) likely that a true relationship will reveal itself through the sample data by means of a statistically significant correlation coefficient.

# CHAPTER 10

1. If 20 eighth-grade boys are compared against 25 eighth-grade girls, should these two comparison groups be thought of as correlated samples or as independent samples?

2. In the null hypothesis of an independent-samples $t$-test comparison of two group means, what kind of means are referred to?
   a. sample means
   b. population means

3. If the $df$ associated with a correlated-samples $t$-test is equal to 18, how many pairs of scores were involved in the analysis?

4. Based on the information contained in the following ANOVA summary table, the researcher's calculated value would be equal to what number?

| Source | df | SS | MS | F |
|--------|-----|-----|-----|-----|
| Between groups | 1 | 12 | | |
| Within groups | 18 | 54 | | |

5. If a researcher uses an independent-samples $t$-test to compare a sample of men with a sample of women on each of 5 dependent variables, and if the researcher uses the Bonferroni adjustment technique to protect against Type I errors, what will he/she adjust?
   a. each group's sample size
   b. each $t$-test's calculated value
   c. the degrees of freedom
   d. the level of significance

6. True or False: Whereas strength-of-association indices *can* be computed in studies concerned with the mean of a single sample, they *cannot* be computed in studies concerned with the means of two samples.

7. Suppose a researcher compares two groups and finds that $M_1 = 60$, $SD_1 = 10$, $M_2 = 55$, and $SD_2 = 10$. Based on this information, how large would the estimated effect size be? According to Cohen's criteria, would this effect size be considered small, medium, or large?

8. If a researcher uses sample data to test the homogeneity of variance assumption in a study involving two independent samples, what will the null hypothesis be? Will the researcher hope to reject or fail to reject this null hypothesis?

9. If the measuring instrument used to collect data has less than perfect reliability, the confidence interval built around a single sample mean or around the difference between two sample means will be _____ (wider/narrower) than would have been the case if the data had been perfectly reliable.

10. Suppose a one-way analysis of variance is used to compare the means of two samples. Also suppose that the results indicate that $SS_{Total} = 44$, $MS_{Error} = 4$, and $F = 3$. With these results, how large was the sample size, assuming both groups had the same $n$?

## CHAPTER 11

1. If a researcher uses a one-way ANOVA to compare four samples, and the statistical focus is on _____ (means/variances), there will be __*1*__ (how many) inferences, and the inference(s) will point toward the _____ (samples/populations).

2. In a one-way ANOVA involving five comparison groups, how many independent variables are there? How many factors?

3. If a one-way ANOVA is used to compare the heights of three groups of first-grade children (those with brown hair, those with black hair, and those with blond hair), what is the independent variable? What is the dependent variable?

4. For the situation described in Question 3, what would the null hypothesis look like?   $H_0: \mu^2 = 0$

5. Based on the information contained in the ANOVA summary table presented below, what is the numerical value for $SS_{Total}$?

| Source | df | SS | MS | F |
|---|---|---|---|---|
| Between groups | 4 | | | 3 |
| Within groups | | | 2 | |
| Total | 49 | | | |

6. Which of these two researchers would end up with a statistically significant finding after they each perform a one-way ANOVA?

   a. The *F*-value in Bob's ANOVA summary table is larger than the appropriate critical *F*-value.

    **b.** The *p*-value associated with Jane's calculated *F*-value is larger than the level of significance.

  **7.** Suppose a one-way ANOVA comparing three sample means (8.0, 11.0, and 19.0) yields a calculated *F*-value of 3.71. If everything about this study remained the same except that the largest mean changed from 19.0 to 17.0, the calculated value would get _____ (smaller/larger).

  **8.** Suppose a researcher wants to conduct 10 one-way ANOVAs, each on a separate dependent variable. Also suppose that the researcher wants to conduct these ANOVAs such that the probability of making at least one Type I error is equal to .05. To accomplish this objective, what alpha level should the researcher use in evaluating each of the *F*-tests?

  **9.** A one-way ANOVA is *not* robust to the equal variance assumption if the comparison groups are dissimilar in what way?

  **10.** Is it possible for a one-way ANOVA to yield a statistically significant but meaningless result?

## CHAPTER 12

  **1.** Which term more accurately describes Tukey's test: planned or post hoc?

  **2.** What are the differences among these three terms: post hoc comparison, follow-up comparison, a posteriori comparison?

  **3.** If a one-way ANOVA involves five groups, how many pairwise comparisons will there be if the statistically significant omnibus *F* is probed by a post hoc investigation that compares every mean with every other mean?

  **4.** Will a conservative test procedure or a liberal test procedure more likely yield statistically significant results?

  **5.** True or False: If three sample means are $M_1 = 60$, $M_2 = 55$, and $M_3 = 50$, it is impossible for the post hoc investigation to say $M_1 > M_2 < M_3$.

  **6.** Which kind of comparison is used more by applied researchers, pairwise comparisons or nonpairwise comparisons?

  **7.** True or False: When conducting post hoc investigations, some researchers use the Bonferroni technique in conjunction with *t*-tests as a way of dealing with the inflated Type I error problem.

  **8.** True or False: Whereas regular *t*-tests and the one-way ANOVA's omnibus *F*-test have no built-in control that addresses the difference between statistical significance and practical significance, planned and post hoc tests have been designed so that only meaningful differences can end up as statistically significant.

  **9.** If a researcher has more than two comparison groups in his or her study, it _____ (would/would not) be possible for him/her to perform a one-degree-of-freedom *F* test.

  **10.** True or False: In a study comparing four groups (A, B, C, and D), a comparison of A versus B is orthogonal to a comparison of C versus D.

# CHAPTER 13

1. If a researcher performs a univariate $3 \times 3$ ANOVA, how many independent variables are there? How many dependent variables?
2. How many cells are there in a $2 \times 4$ ANOVA? In a $3 \times 5$ ANOVA?
3. Suppose the factors of a $2 \times 2$ ANOVA are referred to as Factor A and Factor B. How will the research participants be put into the cells of this study if Factor A is assigned while Factor B is active?
4. How many research questions dealt with by a two-way ANOVA are concerned with main effects? How many are concerned with interactions?
5. Suppose a 2 (gender) $\times$ 3 (handedness) ANOVA is conducted, with the dependent variable being the number of nuts that can be attached to bolts within a 60-second time limit. Suppose that the mean scores for the six groups, each containing 10 participants, turn out as follows: right-handed males = 10.2, right-handed females = 8.8; left-handed males = 7.8, left-handed females = 9.8; ambidextrous males = 9.0, ambidextrous females = 8.4. Given these results, what are the main effect means for handedness equal to? How many scores is each of these means based on?
6. True or False: There is absolutely no interaction associated with the sample data presented in Question 5.
7. How many different mean squares serve as the denominator when the $F$-ratios are computed for the two main effects and the interaction?
8. True or False: You should not expect to see a post hoc test used to compare the main effect means of a $2 \times 2$ ANOVA, even if the $F$-ratios for both main effects turn out to be statistically significant.
9. How many simple main effects are there for Factor A in a $2 \times 3$ (A $\times$ B) ANOVA?
10. True or False: Whenever a two-way ANOVA is used, there is a built-in control mechanism that prevents results from being statistically significant unless they are also significant in a practical sense.

# CHAPTER 14

1. If you see the following factors referred to with these names, which one(s) should you guess probably involve repeated measures?
   a. treatment groups
   b. trial blocks
   c. time period
   d. response variables
2. How does the null hypothesis of a between-subjects one-way ANOVA differ from the null hypothesis of a within-subjects one-way ANOVA?
3. If a $2 \times 2$ ANOVA is conducted on the data supplied by 16 research participants, how many individual scores would be involved in the analysis if both

factors are between subjects in nature? What if both factors are within subjects in nature?

4. If the two treatments of a one-way repeated measures ANOVA are presented to 20 research participants in a counterbalanced order, how many different presentation orders will there be?

5. True or False: Since the sample means of a two-way repeated measures ANOVA are each based on the same number of scores, this kind of ANOVA is robust to the sphericity assumption.

6. If eight research participants are each measured across three levels of factor A and four levels of factor B, how many rows (including total) will there be in the ANOVA summary table? How many $df$ will there be for the total row?

7. How many null hypotheses are typically associated with a two-way mixed ANOVA? How many of them deal with main effects?

8. If each of 10 males and 10 females is measured on three occasions with the resulting data analyzed by a two-way mixed ANOVA, how many main effect means will there be for gender and how many scores will each of these sample means be based on?

9. Suppose the pretest, posttest, and follow-up scores from four small groups (with $n = 3$ in each case) are analyzed by means of a mixed ANOVA. How large would the interaction $F$ be if it turned out that $SS_{Groups} = 12$, $SS_{Total} = 104$, $MS_{Error(w)} = 2$, $F_{Groups} = 2$, and $F_{Time} = 5$?

10. True or False: One of the nice features of any repeated measures ANOVA is the fact that any statistically significant result is guaranteed to be significant in a practical sense as well.

# CHAPTER 15

1. ANCOVA was developed to help researchers decrease the probability that they will make a Type _____ (I/II) error when they test hypotheses.

2. What are the three kinds of variables involved in any ANCOVA study?

3. In ANCOVA studies, is it possible for something other than a pretest (or baseline measure) to serve as the covariate?

4. Suppose the pretest and posttest means for a study's experimental (E) and control (C) groups are as follows: $M_{E(pre)} = 20$, $M_{E(post)} = 50$, $M_{C(pre)} = 10$, $M_{C(post)} = 40$. If this study's data were to be analyzed by an analysis of covariance, the control group's adjusted posttest mean might turn out equal to which one of these possible values?

a. 5
b. 15
c. 25
d. 35
e. 45

5. For ANCOVA to achieve its objectives, there should be a _____ (strong/weak) correlation between each covariate variable and the dependent variable.

6. True or False: Like the analysis of variance, the analysis of covariance is robust to violations of its underlying assumptions so long as the sample sizes are equal.

7. One of ANCOVA's assumptions states that the _____ variable should not affect the _____ variable.

8. ANCOVA works best when the comparison groups _____ (are/are not) formed by random assignment.

9. In testing the assumption of equal regression slopes, does the typical researcher hope the assumption's null hypothesis will be rejected?

10. True or False: Because ANCOVA uses data on at least one covariate variable, results cannot turn out to be statistically significant without also being significant in a practical sense.

# CHAPTER 16

1. In a scatter diagram constructed in conjunction with a bivariate regression analysis, which of the two axes will be set up to coincide with the dependent variable?

2. In the equation $Y' = 2 + 4(X)$, what is the numerical value of the constant and what is the numerical value of the regression coefficient?

3. In bivariate regression, can the slope end up being negative? What about the $Y$-intercept? What about $r^2$?

4. True or False: In bivariate regression, a test of $H_0: \rho = 0$ is equivalent to a test that the $Y$-intercept is equal to 0.

5. In multiple regression, how many $X$ variables are there? How many $Y$ variables?

6. True or False: You will never see an adjusted $R^2$ reported among the results of a simultaneous multiple regression.

7. In stepwise and hierarchical multiple regression, do the beta weights for those independent variables entered during the first stage remain fixed as additional independent variables are allowed to enter the regression equation at a later stage?

8. In logistic regression, the dependent variable is _____ (dichotomous/ continuous) in nature.

9. An odds ratio of what size would indicate that a particular independent variable has no explanatory value?

10. In logistic regression, does the Wald test focus on individual ORs or does it focus on the full regression equation?

*[Handwritten in margin: Population]*

# CHAPTER 17

1. True or False: When the sign test is used, the null hypothesis says that the sample data will contain an equal number of observations in each of the two response categories, thus yielding as many pluses as minuses.

2. Which test is more flexible, the sign test or the binomial test?

3. What symbol stands for chi square?

4. Suppose a researcher uses a $2 \times 2$ chi square to see if males differ from females with regard to whether or not they received a speeding ticket during the past year. Of the 60 males in the study, 40 had received a ticket. The sample data would be in full agreement with the chi-square null hypothesis if _____ of the 90 females received a ticket.

5. How many degrees of freedom would there be for a chi-square comparison of freshmen, sophomores, juniors, and seniors regarding their answers to the question: "How would you describe the level of allegiance to your school?" (The response options are low, moderate, and high.)

6. Whose name is often associated with the special chi-square formula that carries the label "correction for continuity"?

7. McNemar's chi-square test is appropriate for _____ (two/more than two) groups of data, where the samples are _____ (independent/correlated), and where the response variable contains _____ (two/more than two) categories.

8. If a pair of researchers got ready to use a one-factor repeated measures ANOVA but then stopped after realizing that their data were dichotomous, what statistical test could they turn to in order to complete the data analysis?

9. True or False: Techniques for applying the concept of *statistical power* to tests dealing with frequencies, percentages, and proportions have not yet been developed.

10. Can confidence intervals be placed around sample percentages?

# CHAPTER 18

1. Why do researchers sometimes use nonparametric tests with data that are interval or ratio?

2. The median test is used with _____ (independent/correlated) samples.

3. If the median test is used to compare two samples, how many medians will the researcher need to compute based on the sample data?

4. A Mann-Whitney *U* test is designed for situations where there are _____ (how many) samples that _____ (do/don't) involve repeated measures.

5. Which of the test procedures discussed in this chapter is analogous to the correlated-samples *t*-test considered earlier in Chapter 10? Which one is analogous to the one-way ANOVA considered in Chapter 11?

6. Which of the nonparametric tests involves a calculated value that is sometimes symbolized as $\chi^2$?

7. True or False: The large-sample versions of the Mann-Whitney, Kruskal-Wallis, and Wilcoxon tests all involve a calculated value that is labeled $z$.

8. Are random samples important to nonparametric tests?

9. True or False: Because they deal with ranks, the tests considered in this chapter have lower power than their parametric counterparts.

10. The term *distribution free* _____ (should/should not) be used to describe the various nonparametric tests discussed in this chapter.

# CHAPTER 19

1. True or False. In Excerpt 19.4, the information on the average, *SD*, and range of the number of incidents per participant suggest that the distribution of these scores was negatively skewed.

2. In Excerpt 19.6, several numerical values appear in the third and fourth sentences. These numbers lie on a numerical continuum that extends from _____ to _____.

3. Was the population associated with the sample described in Excerpt 19.7 a tangible population or was it an abstract population?

4. True or False. Most likely, the statistical tests alluded to in the final sentence of Excerpt 19.8 were conducted in a one-tailed fashion.

5. How many dependent variables are mentioned in Excerpt 19.9?

6. Which of the three numbers contained in the first sentence of Excerpt 19.10 was the one-way ANOVA's calculated value?

7. What symbol denotes the strength-of-association measure used in Excerpt 19.10?

8. True or False. In Excerpt 19.11, the researchers obtained the *r* value of .30 by correlating data gathered from the study's 82 participants.

9. In the hierarchical multiple regression discussed in Excerpt 19.12, was life satisfaction the dependent variable or was it one of the independent variables?

10. Based on the information provided in the final sentence of Excerpt 19.13, what kind of inferential error may have been made, a Type I error *or* a Type II error?

# Answers to Review Questions

## CHAPTER 1

1. The abstract is usually found near the beginning of the article. It normally contains a condensed statement of the study's objective(s), participants, method, and results.
2. Statement of purpose
3. Replicate the investigation
4. Subjects
5. IQ (i.e., intelligence)
6. In paragraphs of text, in tables, and in figures
7. In the discussion section
8. References
9. No
10. All four

## CHAPTER 2

1. Size of the data set, mean, standard deviation, median, upper quartile point, standard deviation, range, standard deviation, middle quartile point (or median), variance, lower quartile point, variance, mean
2. 25
3. Bar graph
4. False
5. a
6. Three
7. 20
8. Interquartile range
9. b
10. False

## CHAPTER 3

1. a
2. 20
3. c
4. b
5. a. Pearson's $r$
   b. Kendall's tau
   c. phi
   d. point biserial
6. Spearman
7. Cramer's $V$
8. False
9. .49
10. False (Correlation says *nothing* about the two means!)

## CHAPTER 4

1. Consistency
2. Test-retest reliability; parallel-forms reliability (or alternate-forms reliability or equivalent-forms reliability)
3. 1.0; 0.0
4. Cronbach's alpha is not restricted to situations where the data are dichotomous
5. False
6. False
7. Poor measurement of the criterion variable
8. b
9. The score obtained by using the measuring instrument
10. False

528

# CHAPTER 5

1. From the sample to the population
2. $M, s^2, r, \mu, \sigma^2, \rho$
3. True
4. Assign a unique ID number to each member of the population
5. Cluster samples, simple random samples, stratified random samples, and systematic samples
6. b
7. False
8. b
9. No
10. Abstract; tangible

# CHAPTER 6

1. False
2. A sampling distribution
3. Standard error
4. False
5. 95 percent; 99 percent
6. a
7. Point
8. True
9. A confidence interval
10. No

# CHAPTER 7

1. $H_0: \mu_{10} - \mu_{11} = 0$
2. c
3. False
4. Inconsistent
5. .01
6. No
7. Rejected
8. No
9. A silly null hypothesis
10. True

# CHAPTER 8

1. Yes
2. Eta squared and omega squared
3. b
4. a

5. 0, 1.0
6. Small = .20, medium = .50, large = .80
7. $H_0$ would be rejected
8. c
9. Specify the effect size, specify the desired power, and determine (via formula, chart, or computer) the proper sample size.
10. b

# CHAPTER 9

1. b
2. 60
3. Two-tailed
4. 10
5. Most likely none of them
6. Yes
7. c
8. Yes, if the sample size is large enough
9. False
10. Less likely

# CHAPTER 10

1. Independent samples (because two groups with different $n$s cannot be correlated)
2. b
3. 19
4. Four
5. d
6. False
7. .50; medium
8. $H_0: \sigma_1^2 = \sigma_2^2$; not rejected
9. Wider
10. Five

# CHAPTER 11

1. Means; one; populations
2. One of each
3. hair color; height
4. $H_0: \mu_1 = \mu_2 = \mu_3$
5. 114
6. Bob
7. Smaller
8. .005
9. Group size
10. Yes

# CHAPTER 12

1. Neither. It depends on whether the researcher who uses the Tukey test first examines the ANOVA $F$ to see if it is okay to compare means using the Tukey test.
2. Nothing. They are synonyms.
3. 10
4. A liberal test procedure
5. True
6. Pairwise
7. True
8. False
9. Would
10. True

# CHAPTER 13

1. Two; 1
2. 8; 15
3. Participants will be randomly assigned to levels of Factor B from within each level of Factor A.
4. Two; 1
5. The main effect means would be equal to 9.5, 8.8, and 8.7 (for right-handed, left-handed, and ambidextrous individuals, respectively). Each would be based on 20 scores.
6. False
7. One
8. True
9. Three
10. False

# CHAPTER 14

1. b, c, d
2. They do not differ in any way.
3. 16; 64
4. Two
5. False
6. 8; 95
7. Three; two
8. 2; 30
9. Two
10. False

# CHAPTER 15

1. Type II error
2. Independent, dependent, and covariate (concomitant) variables

3. Yes
4. e
5. Strong
6. False
7. Independent; covariate
8. Are
9. No
10. False

# CHAPTER 16

1. The vertical axis (i.e., the ordinate)
2. The constant is 2; the regression coefficient is 4.
3. Yes; yes; no
4. False
5. At least two; just one
6. True
7. No
8. Dichotomous
9. 1.0
10. Individual ORs

# CHAPTER 17

1. False. (The null hypothesis is a statement about population parameters, not sample statistics.)
2. The binomial test
3. $\chi^2$
4. 60
5. Six
6. Yates
7. Two; correlated; two
8. Cochran's $Q$ test
9. False
10. Yes

# CHAPTER 18

1. Because researchers know or suspect that the normality and/or equal variance assumptions are untenable, especially in situations where the sample sizes are dissimilar.
2. Independent
3. One
4. Two; don't
5. The Wilcoxon matched-pairs signed-ranks test; the Kruskal-Wallis one-way ANOVA of ranks
6. Friedman's two-way analysis of variance of ranks

7. False (The Kruskal-Wallis test, when conducted with large samples, yields a calculated value symbolized as $\chi^2$.)
8. Yes
9. False
10. Should not

# CHAPTER 19

1. False
2. 0 to +1
3. It was tangible.

4. False
5. 6
6. 44.21
7. $\eta^2$
8. False. The value of .30 was *selected* by the researchers (before any data were collected) to be the effect size.
9. Life satisfaction was the dependent variable.
10. Type I error

# Credits

Excerpt 3.1    Clayton, D. M., and Stallings, A. M. (2000). Black women in Congress: Striking the balance. *Journal of Black Studies, 30*(4), pp. 593–594. Copyright 2000 by Sage Publications. Reprinted by permission from Sage Publications Inc.

Excerpt 3.7    Heppner, P. P., Heppner, M. J., Lee, D., Wang, Y., Park, H., and Wang, L. (2006). Development and validation of a collectivist coping styles inventory. *Journal of Counseling Psychology, 53*(1), p. 113. Published by the American Psychological Association. Reprinted with permission.

Excerpt 3.8    Swiatek, M. A. (2005). Gifted students' self-perceptions of ability in specific subject domains: Factor structure and relationship with above 3-level test scores. *Roeper Review, 27*(2), p. 106. Reprinted with permission.

Excerpt 3.9    Salgado, J. F., and Moscoso, S. (2003). Internet-based personality testing: Equivalence of measures and assessees' perceptions and reactions. *International Journal of Selection & Assessment, 11*(2/3), p. 199. Reprinted by permission of Blackwell Publishing.

Excerpt 3.10    Kelloway, E. K., Mullen, J., and Francis, L. (2006). Divergent effects of transformational and passive leadership on employee safety. *Journal of Occupational Health Psychology, 11*(1), Jan 2006, p. 82. Published by the American Psychological Association. Reprinted with permission.

Excerpt 3.21    Kunen, S., Niederhauser, R., Smoth, P. O., Morris, J. A., and Marx, B. D. (2005). Race disparities in psychiatric rates in emergency departments. *Journal of Consulting and Clinical Psychology, 73*(1), p. 121. Published by the American Psychological Association. Reprinted with permission.

Excerpt 6.2    Petry, N. M., and Steinberg, K. L. (2005). Childhood maltreatment in male and female treatment-seeking pathological gamblers. *Psychology of Addictive Behaviors, 19*(2), p. 228. Published by the American Psychological Association. Reprinted with permission.

Excerpt 6.3    Bushman, B. J., Bonacci, A. M., Pedersen, W. C., Vasquez, E. A., and Miller, N. (2005). Chewing on it can chew you up: Effects of rumination on triggered displaced aggression. *Journal of Personality and Social Psychology, 88*(6), p. 975. Published by the American Psychological Association. Reprinted with permission.

Excerpt 6.4    Reprinted by permission from "Effects of Prolonged Loud Reading on Normal Adolescent Male Voices" by L. N. Kelchner, M. M. Toner, and L. Lee. *Language, Speech, and Hearing Services in Schools, 37*(1), p. 101. Copyright 2006 by American Speech-Language-Hearing Association. All rights reserved.

Excerpt 6.8    Mitra, M., Wilber, N., Allen, D., and Walker, D. K. (2005). Prevalence and correlates of depression as a secondary condition among adults with disabilities. *American Journal of Orthopsychiatry, 75*(1), p. 81. Published by the American Psychological Association. Reprinted with permission.

Excerpt 6.9    Muller, M. J., Muller, K., and Fellgiebel, A. (2006). Detection of depression in acute schizophrenia: Sensitivity and specificity of 2 standard observer rating scales. *Canadian Journal of Psychiatry, 51*(6), p. 389. Reprinted with permission.

Excerpt 9.14    Newman, M. G., Holmes, M., Zuellig, A. R., Kachin, K. E., & Behar, E. (2006). The reliability and validity of the Panic Disorder Self-Report: A new diagnostic screening measure of panic disorder. *Psychological Assessment, 18*(1), p. 55. Published by the American Psychological Association. Reprinted with permission.

Excerpt 10.2    Heyman, G. D., and Legare, C. H. (2005). Children's evaluation of sources of information about traits. *Developmental Psychology, 41*(4), p. 638. Published by the American Psychological Association. Reprinted with permission.

Excerpt 10.10    Yoo, S. Y. (2005). The study of early childhood teachers' beliefs related to children's literacy at South Korea. *Reading Improvement, 42*(3), p. 141. Reprinted by permission.

Excerpt 10.14    Saxby, B. K., Harrington, F., McKeith, I. G., Wesnes, K., and Ford, G. A. (2003). Effects of hypertension on attention, memory, and executive function in older adults. *Health Psychology, 22*(6), p. 590. Published by the American Psychological Association. Reprinted with permission.

Excerpt 10.28  Coris, E. E., Walz, S. M., Duncanson, R., Ramirez, A. M., and Roetzheim, R. G. (2006). Heat Illness Symptom Index (HISI): A novel instrument for the assessment of heat illness in athletes. *Southern Medical Journal, 99*(4), pp. 343–344. Reprinted with permission from Lippincott Williams & Wilkins.

Excerpts 11.1 and 11.6  Kezim, B., Pariseau, S. E., and Quinn, F. (2005). Is grade inflation related to faculty status? *Journal of Education for Business, 80*(6), p. 360. Reprinted with permission of the Helen Dwight Reid Educational Foundation. Published by Heldref Publications, 1319 Eighteenth St., NW, Washington, DC 20036-1802. Copyright © 2005.

Excerpt 11.7  de la Fuente, M. J. (2006). Classroom L2 vocabulary acquisition: Investigating the role of pedagogical tasks and form-based instruction. *Language Teaching Research, 10*(3), p. 277. Reprinted with permission from Sage Publications.

Excerpt 11.10  Jennings, M., Werbel, J. D., and Power, M. L. (2003). The impact of benefits on graduating student willingness to accept job offers. *Journal of Business Communication, 40*(4), p. 297. Copyright 2003 by Sage Publications. Reprinted by permission from Sage Publications Inc.

Excerpt 11.11  Allan, E., and Madden, M. (2006). Chilly classrooms for female undergraduate students: A question of method? *Journal of Higher Education, 77*(4), p. 693. Reprinted with permission from The Ohio State University Press.

Excerpt 12.18  Newman, M. G., Holmes, M., Zuellig, A. R., Kachin, K. E., and Behar, E. (2006). The reliability and validity of the Panic Disorder Self-Report: A new diagnostic screening measure of panic disorder. *Psychological Assessment, 18*(1), p. 55. Published by the American Psychological Association. Reprinted with permission.

Excerpt 12.19  Miller, M. W., Greif, J. L., and Smith, A. A. (2003). Multidimensional Personality Questionnaire profiles of veterans with traumatic combat exposure: Externalizing and internalizing subtypes. *Psychological Assessment, 15*(2), p. 209. Published by the American Psychological Association. Reprinted with permission.

Excerpt 12.20  Houghton, R. J., Macken, W. J., and Jones, D. M. (2003). Attentional modulation of the visual motion aftereffect has a central cognitive locus: Evidence of interference by the postcategorical on the precategorical. *Journal of Experimental Psychology: Human Perception and Performance, 29*(4), p. 737. Published by the American Psychological Association. Reprinted with permission.

Excerpt 13.1  Wisman, A., and Goldenberg, J. (2005). From the grave to the cradle: Evidence that mortality salience engenders a desire for offspring. *Journal of Personality and Social Psychology, 89*(1), p. 52. Published by the American Psychological Association. Reprinted with permission.

Excerpts 13.10–13.11  Kisac, I. (2006). Stress symptoms of survivors of the Marmara region (Turkey) earthquakes: A follow-up study. *International Journal of Stress Management, 13*(1), p. 122–123. Published by the American Psychological Association. Reprinted with permission.

Excerpt 13.13  DeChurch, L. A., and Marks, M. A. (2006). Leadership in multiteam systems. *Journal of Applied Psychology, 91*(2), p. 321. Published by the American Psychological Association. Reprinted with permission.

Excerpt 13.16  Dunn, J. R., and Schweitzer, M. E. (2005). Feeling and believing: The influence of emotion on trust. *Journal of Personality and Social Psychology, 88*(5), p. 741. Published by the American Psychological Association. Reprinted with permission.

Excerpt 13.17  Mann, T., and Ward, A. (2004). To eat or not to eat: Implications of the attentional myopia model for restrained eaters. *Journal of Abnormal Psychology, 113*(1), p. 94. Published by the American Psychological Association. Reprinted with permission.

Excerpt 14.7  Stamps, A. E., III. Evaluating architectural design review. *Perceptual and Motor Skills,* 2000, 90, 265–271. © Perceptual and Motor Skills 2000. Reprinted with permission.

Excerpt 14.23  Kondo-Brown, K. (2006). How do English L1 learners of advanced Japanese infer unknown *Kanji* words in authentic texts? *Language Learning, 56*(1), p. 135. Reprinted with permission from Blackwell Publishing.

# Index